FEDERAL BUDGET POLICY IN THE 1980s

A Conference Sponsored by
the Changing Domestic Priorities Project
of The Urban Institute

FEDERAL BUDGET POLICY IN THE 1980s

Edited by
Gregory B. Mills and John L. Palmer

The Changing Domestic Priorities Series
John L. Palmer and Isabel V. Sawhill, Editors

 THE URBAN INSTITUTE PRESS · WASHINGTON, D.C.

Copyright © 1984
THE URBAN INSTITUTE
2100 M Street, N.W.
Washington, D.C. 20037

Library of Congress Cataloging in Publication Data
Main entry under title:

Federal budget policy in the 1980s.

   (The Changing domestic priorities series)
   1. Budget—United States—Addresses, essays, lectures. I. Mills, Gregory
B., II. Palmer, John Logan. III. Series.
HJ2051.F395 1984   353.0072′2   84-7227
ISBN 0-87766-336-X (paperback)
ISBN 0-87766-367-X (cloth)

Printed in the United States of America

THE CHANGING DOMESTIC PRIORITIES SERIES

Listed below are the titles available, or soon to be available, in the Changing Domestic Priorities Series

Books

THE REAGAN EXPERIMENT
  An Examination of Economic and Social Policies under the Reagan Administration (1982), John L. Palmer and Isabel V. Sawhill, editors
HOUSING ASSISTANCE FOR OLDER AMERICANS
  The Reagan Prescription (1982), James P. Zais, Raymond J. Struyk, and Thomas Thibodeau
MEDICAID IN THE REAGAN ERA
  Federal Policy and State Choices (1982), Randall R. Bovbjerg and John Holahan
WAGE INFLATION
  Prospects for Deceleration (1983), Wayne Vroman
OLDER AMERICANS IN THE REAGAN ERA
  Impacts of Federal Policy Changes (1983), James R. Storey
FEDERAL HOUSING POLICY AT PRESIDENT REAGAN'S MIDTERM
  (1983), Raymond J. Struyk, Neil Mayer, and John A. Tuccillo
STATE AND LOCAL FISCAL RELATIONS IN THE EARLY 1980s
  (1983), Steven D. Gold
THE DEFICIT DILEMMA
  Budget Policy in the Reagan Era (1983), Gregory B. Mills and John L. Palmer
HOUSING FINANCE
  A Changing System in the Reagan Era (1983), John A. Tuccillo with John L. Goodman, Jr.
PUBLIC OPINION DURING THE REAGAN ADMINISTRATION
  National Issues, Private Concerns (1983), John L. Goodman, Jr.
RELIEF OR REFORM?
  Reagan's Regulatory Dilemma (1984), George C. Eads and Michael Fix
THE REAGAN RECORD
  An Assessment of America's Changing Domestic Priorities (1984), John L. Palmer and Isabel V. Sawhill, editors (Ballinger Publishing Co.)

Conference Volumes

THE SOCIAL CONTRACT REVISITED
   Aims and Outcomes of President Reagan's Social Welfare Policy (1984), edited
   by D. Lee Bawden
NATURAL RESOURCES AND THE ENVIRONMENT
   The Reagan Approach (1984), edited by Paul R. Portney
FEDERAL BUDGET POLICY IN THE 1980s (1984), edited by
   Gregory B. Mills and John L. Palmer
THE REAGAN REGULATORY STRATEGY
   An Assessment (1984), edited by George C. Eads and Michael Fix
THE LEGACY OF REAGANOMICS
   Prospects for Long-term Growth (1984), edited by Charles R. Hulten and Isabel
   V. Sawhill
THE REAGAN PRESIDENCY AND THE GOVERNING OF AMERICA
   (1984), edited by Lester M. Salamon and Michael S. Lund

CONTENTS

Foreword   xi

Summary / *Gregory B. Mills*   xiii

PART 1
THE CONTEXT FOR BUDGET CHOICES

Introduction / *Alice M. Rivlin*   3

THE FEDERAL BUDGET IN FLUX / *Gregory B. Mills and John
L. Palmer*   9

HOW BAD ARE THE LARGE DEFICITS? / *Edward M. Gramlich*   43

    Comments / *Robert H. Haveman*   69
    William J. Beeman   74

PART 2
SPENDING AND TAX POLICIES

THE DEFENSE BUDGET / *Richard A. Stubbing*   81

    Comments / *Robert B. Pirie*   111
    Robert F. Hale   116

HEALTH CARE FINANCING AND PENSION PROGRAMS / *John
L. Palmer and Barbara Boyle Torrey*   121

    Comments / *Henry J. Aaron*   157
    Jack A. Meyer   162

FEDERAL AID TO STATE AND LOCAL GOVERNMENTS /
Helen F. Ladd   165

    Comments / *William G. Hamm*   203

TAX POLICY / *Joseph J. Minarik*   209

    Comments / *James M. Verdier*   243
                Richard A. Musgrave   248

PART 3
THE POLITICAL AND INSTITUTIONAL ENVIRONMENT

EXECUTIVE BUDGET MAKING / *Hugh Heclo*   255

    Comments / *Hale Champion*   292

EXECUTIVE AGENCY RETRENCHMENT / *Joseph S. Wholey*   295

    Comments / *Laurence E. Lynn, Jr.*   333
              Robert D. Behn   337

LEGISLATIVE POLITICS AND BUDGET OUTCOMES / *Kenneth
A. Shepsle and Barry R. Weingast*   343

    Comments / *John W. Ellwood*   368
              Charles L. Schultze   379

THE CONGRESSIONAL BUDGET PROCESS / *Robert D.
Reischauer*   385

    Comments / *Louis Fisher*   414
              Douglas J. Bennet   419

ISSUES IN BUDGET ACCOUNTING / *Robert W. Hartman*   423

    Comments / *Darwin G. Johnson*   448
              Michael J. Boskin   457

About the Authors   461

Participants in the Conference   467

FOREWORD

In late 1981 The Urban Institute initiated a three-year project—Changing Domestic Priorities—to examine the shifts in domestic policy occurring under the Reagan administration and the consequences of those shifts. This volume, a product of the Changing Domestic Priorities project, is one of six collections of analyses by leading scholars on subjects of considerable national interest in the 1980s. The other five volumes are focused upon social welfare, economic growth, governance, natural resources and the environment, and regulatory policy.

The past four years have witnessed an unprecedented role for the federal budget in the Reagan administration's pursuit of dramatic policy shifts. The enacted changes have led, among other things, to large and growing federal deficits.

Even without such projected deficits, there would be a continuing need to scrutinize budget policy choices and budget processes. The unsettling prospect of large future deficits, however, enlivens the public policy debate as budgetary concerns become increasingly dominant in the development of federal policy.

Among the issues expected to remain important throughout the 1980s are the following: How strong are the continuing upward pressures on federal spending? How have these pressures been altered by policy changes during the Reagan administration, and to what extent is spending growth now subject to policy control? What are the economic consequences of failure to reduce the projected federal deficits? What are the alternative strategies for spending restraint and increased revenue, and on what basis should policy choices be made if deficits are to be reduced? What are the implications of recent developments in the executive and congressional budget processes? What does recent experience suggest about reforming budget processes and budget accounting procedures to enable better fiscal control?

To address these issues, The Urban Institute sponsored a conference in September 1983. This volume includes the papers prepared for the conference, along with the comments of designated discussants.

The papers in part I of the volume examine the origins and implications of the current budget outlook. These first papers assess the major budget developments under President Reagan, the economic implications of projected deficits, and the basic budget tradeoffs confronting federal policymakers. Part II surveys the key programmatic issues raised by the widely shared view that policy measures to further restrain spending and raise revenue will be necessary. Separate papers are devoted to defense spending, health and pension programs, aid to state and local governments, and taxes. Part III addresses the political and institutional setting for budget choices, with attention to the executive and congressional budget processes and matters of budget accounting.

We believe this volume will be of considerable value to those who wish to understand the changes that have occurred in federal budget policy in the first half of the 1980s and the issues and choices they pose for the future.

The support of this effort by the Ford Foundation and the John D. and Catherine T. MacArthur Foundation is gratefully acknowledged.

John L. Palmer
Isabel V. Sawhill
Editors
Changing Domestic Priorities Series

SUMMARY

Gregory B. Mills

The federal budget has recently become the focus of unprecedented attention. Largely because of the general anxiety over the projected federal deficit, the policy choices facing the president and Congress are increasingly cast in terms of budget outcomes. This volume examines recent budget developments, budget issues on the federal policy agenda for the remainder of the 1980s, and the institutional setting in which budget policy choices are made. This summary briefly sketches the framework for the volume and summarizes each of the papers.

Part I sets the context for budget choices in the 1980s. In her introduction to the conference, Alice Rivlin focused immediately on the dominant budgetary concern—the federal deficit. She observed that in enacting President Reagan's program in 1981 Congress was insufficiently skeptical of the proposition that we could lower inflation, reduce taxes, and strengthen national defense without any sacrifice. Rivlin views the creation of such large federal deficits, with their upward pressures on interest rates and the dollar, as "just plain dumb," given the concern about U.S. productivity and industrial strength. The inability of the president and Congress to agree upon deficit reduction measures does not suggest failure of our established decision processes, says Rivlin, so much as it simply reflects a mismatch between public preferences for spending and taxes.

Spending cuts and tax increases will both be necessary, Rivlin says, and politics will require a "relatively simple plan that appears to spread the pain both widely and equitably." On the spending front, attention must focus on health and defense, where "there may be no better way to reduce spending increases . . . than to impose arbitrary rates of growth on overall spending and say to the practitioners, 'Do the best you can.'"

xiii

In the paper by Gregory Mills and John Palmer, the changes in the budget that have occurred under President Reagan and the prospects for future budgetary actions are analyzed. They believe the president has achieved his general tax and spending objectives, since defense outlays have been increased while tax burdens and domestic spending have been reduced substantially from the levels they would otherwise have attained. Because the economy failed to rebound immediately, however, the need for restraint in nondefense spending became even greater than the president had originally anticipated. What spending restraint the administration initially achieved was in politically vulnerable, low-income assistance and domestic discretionary programs that were not the principal sources of spending growth. As Congress increasingly resisted the administration's further proposed cuts in domestic programs and as the president resisted any compromise on his tax and defense policies, the projected budget outlook showed unprecedented deficits.

According to Mills and Palmer, politicians are tempted to rely on predicted strength in the economy as a way to avoid unpopular policy choices, but "present tax and spending policies embody so large a structural disparity between revenues and outlays that, even if one assumes that the economy could speedily achieve its high-employment potential, the deficit would remain above any peacetime precedent." The authors suggest that, in order to avoid serious risks to future economic performance, a combination of program spending cuts and tax increases amounting to at least $150 billion annually will be required by the end of the decade. Such a target would not be achieved even if Congress were to adopt the full measure of nondefense spending restraint proposed by President Reagan in addition to the tax increases and defense restraint supported by the Democratic leadership. Mills and Palmer believe that the prospects for restraining growth in either defense outlays or the domestic budget are so limited that two-thirds of the desired deficit reduction may have to come through higher revenues. Even larger tax increases would be essential if Congress is unwilling to seriously curb the growth in Medicare or Social Security spending or to drastically reduce other nondefense programs.

In the final paper of part I, Edward Gramlich discusses the threat that large federal deficits pose to the economy. He first establishes that the annual federal deficits projected for the late 1980s under current policy will exceed the annual deficits experienced in the 1970s by 2 to 3 percent of gross national product (GNP), depending on the adjustments made to standardize for unemployment and inflation. Gramlich argues that the principal reason for opposing these larger deficits is that they reduce the share of national output devoted to capital formation, not that they endanger short-term economic recovery. Indeed, he finds much of the current fear that deficits will abort the recovery to be based on reasoning that flies in the face of accepted economic wisdom. Gramlich concludes that the adverse effects of deficits through higher interest rates would not be large enough to offset the favorable effect of deficits on aggregate demand. He believes that deficits are a threat to short-term output only under extreme assumptions about future expected increases in inflation and interest rates.

Gramlich then argues that reducing the resources available for capital formation is a move in the wrong direction; the United States is already devoting too little to saving and investment. The natural implication of an even higher level of government ''dissaving'' through larger federal deficits is to enhance per capita consumption in the short term while adversely affecting the long-term standard of living. Gramlich's analysis suggests that larger deficits and diminished capital formation will indeed ultimately reduce per capita consumption, but this reduction may not occur until at least ten years after the onset of the larger deficits.

Although the fear that deficits threaten short-term economic recovery runs counter to accepted economic logic, the long-term threat that deficits pose to U.S. living standards is ample cause for concern. Whether or not the economic rationale is compelling, Congress will surely face a political imperative to lower the deficit. The papers in part II address the policy areas likely to receive greatest attention in the search for measures to reduce the deficit: the defense budget, health and pension programs, aid to state and local governments, and taxes.

In the paper on defense, Richard Stubbing examines both the increases in military spending initiated by President Reagan and the opportunities for future restraint in the defense budget. He first reviews the Reagan military buildup in the context of prior trends in defense spending. The prevailing view in the late 1970s was that U.S. strategic capabilities were insufficient to meet the Soviet threat. The Vietnam war had served to strengthen the nation's ground combat forces, but there had been no commensurate modernization of strategic weaponry. Little attention was given to further development of our strategic forces until, under the Carter administration, the United States and NATO allies agreed to make real increases in defense budgets of 3 percent annually. Then President Reagan initiated a pronounced acceleration of U.S. defense spending, with military appropriations to grow at a real rate of about 10 percent. Stubbing considers this buildup to have been rationalized by an exaggerated assessment of the Soviet threat. In his view, the purported Soviet advantage in military power was based on questionable estimating techniques applied by the Defense Department and Central Intelligence Agency.

Stubbing decries the 1981 Reagan defense initiative's magnitude and emphasis on technically sophisticated weapons systems. According to Stubbing, funds were committed without adequate planning for the respective roles to be played either by the separate armed services in military prepared-ness or by defense and foreign assistance in national security policy. Although Congress scaled back the administration's defense requests for FY 1983 and 1984, these cuts did not force termination of any ongoing weapons programs and "simply reflected congressional awareness that a sizable portion of 'cut insurance' can be skimmed off with no repercussions."

Stubbing believes that the current defense budget offers many oppor-tunities to improve operating efficiency. In the area of weapons procurement, he advocates greater competition in the selection of contractors, stronger cost-cutting incentives in contracts with weapons producers, and more rewards for defense contracting whistle-blowers who identify excessive costs. On the basic issues of defense planning, Stubbing argues that the missions of each military service must be more clearly distinguished to avoid redundant capabilities and that our military planners should shift their strategy of weapons acquisition toward systems that are less sophisticated and less costly, but more reliable. Stubbing concludes that the growth rate in defense spending can be restrained to the growth rate of GNP, and arguably even lower for FY 1985 and 1986, "with no ill effects on either strategic or conventional forces."

Although Stubbing's analysis suggests that some restraint can be imposed on defense spending, such savings will contribute only modestly to a reduction in the federal deficit. If policymakers seek significant spending restraint, they must also focus on the major sources of growth in domestic spending: health and retirement benefits. John Palmer and Barbara Torrey examine those ben-efits in their paper. Their analysis distinguishes the opportunities for short-term restraint (in the context of desired deficit reductions during the late 1980s) from the need for longer-term structural reforms.

The short-term assessment focuses on health care financing, in which federal outlays are rising rapidly despite a moderation in the growth of Med-icare and Medicaid beneficiary populations and recent legislation that limited Medicare reimbursements to hospitals, raised patient cost sharing for Medi-care, and reduced federal matching payments to the states for Medicaid. The projected growth in the health programs is attributable to further increases in the quantity of medical services provided per patient and continuing inflation in the price of such services. Palmer and Torrey believe these trends are encouraged by the weak cost-saving incentives that confront patients, hos-pitals, and physicians. To strengthen such incentives, especially in Medicare, the authors examine policy options such as higher out-of-pocket patient costs, less generous reimbursement to hospitals and physicians, and less favorable tax treatment of employer-paid health insurance.

Palmer and Torrey also observe that major reductions in benefits and/or increases in revenues will be needed to avert the extremely large Medicare trust fund deficits now expected in the early 1990s. In addition to the policies just mentioned, other means of improving the financial status of Medicare, which they discuss, include higher taxes on alcohol and tobacco, increased estate and payroll taxes, and some rise in the age of eligibility for Medicare. Although the authors concede that all the specific measures they discuss are politically unpopular, some might be phased in during the remainder of this decade and thus would serve to reduce the federal budget deficit in the late 1980s.

In their discussion of pension programs, Palmer and Torrey find that annual surpluses in the Social Security program substantially reduce the projected size of the overall deficit over the next two decades; the hard-fought 1983 bipartisan compromise on Social Security has thus taken the largest federal pension program off the legislative agenda. For the retirement programs in general, the only sensible short-term measures to reduce the deficit would be greater taxation of benefits or a reduction in the annual cost-of-living adjustments. Palmer and Torrey argue that although a major tightening of federal employee retirement systems is long overdue, any short-term savings would be small, since structural program changes would apply primarily to new retirees and new hires.

In the longer-term budgetary perspective, demographic changes will again place considerable upward pressure on pension and health spending early next century. Unless federal tax burdens increase substantially or other federal spending falls, retirement and health care outlays will again have to be greatly restrained. Palmer and Torrey believe the situation raises basic questions about the public provision of these benefits and about the distribution of the financial burden on society that is posed by an increasingly aged population.

The limited prospects for short-term restraint in the large health and pension trust fund programs probably imply continued austerity in other forms of federal spending, especially aid to state and local governments. Helen Ladd discusses the prospects for further restraint in this area, which has already been hard hit by cutbacks under the Reagan administration. Congress may nonetheless wish to further scrutinize such spending, since budget tightening in these programs could help reduce the deficit.

Ladd observes that federal aid to state and local governments encompasses both spending commitments and tax preferences. Indeed, the loss of federal revenues as a result of the favorable treatment of state and local taxes and the interest on municipal bonds is nearly one-half the size of the conventionally measured amount of federal outlays on direct grants-in-aid. Since recent legislation has restrained the growth in direct aid, especially Medicaid and Aid to Families with Dependent Children, "tax expenditures" are looming even larger as a form of federal support to states and localities.

The recent cuts in direct aid to state and local governments came largely in federal programs serving the low-income population and have not yet been offset by commensurate increases in state and local spending on the poor. These cuts have thus been borne, at least in the short run, by the recipient population, especially the working poor. Although states and localities are proceeding to raise their spending in such programs, these adjustments will clearly reflect the geographic disparity in fiscal conditions, a disparity related to wider economic circumstances beyond the control of individual states. Additional cuts in these programs may simply induce further responses at the state or local level that will make the geographic pattern of benefits and services even more arbitrary. Ladd concludes that "this seems a particularly inappropriate time to ask the states to provide more in income support programs."

States have had some success in containing Medicaid costs, however, and should be encouraged to continue their innovations in administering health care. In Medicaid "the central policy question is how to provide incentives for cost containment without imposing severe burdens on the poor or medically needy." In general, Ladd sees an increased need for grant restrictions that tie spending more closely to federally desired program outputs.

If policymakers seek to further restrain federal financial support for state and local governments, they should examine the federal tax provisions that effectively lower the taxpayer cost of state and local activities. Ladd discusses the deductibility of state and local taxes and the exclusion of interest on general and special purpose municipal bonds. She suggests that if the federal objective is to encourage particular forms of state or local spending, the tax subsidies should be more specifically targeted. If the federal interest is to generally enhance state and local fiscal capacity, revenue sharing may be more appropriate. The policy issue is not whether such subsidies can be simply reduced or eliminated, but whether they can be replaced by a mix of tax and spending policies that better serve federal, state, and local interests at lower federal cost.

A reexamination of the federal tax provisions favoring state and local governments is only part of a necessary review of the entire federal tax structure. The feasible options to reduce spending simply do not yield enough savings to close the projected federal deficit. In the final paper in part II, Joseph Minarik surveys recent developments in federal tax policy and considers alternative strategies for raising federal revenue.

Minarik describes the historical trends that brought the federal tax burden to a post-World War II high in 1981. The upward movement became pronounced in the late 1970s as rapid inflation drove individual taxpayers into higher brackets and as scheduled increases in payroll taxes came into effect. Although corporate taxes declined as a revenue source throughout the postwar period and state and local taxes subsided in the late 1970s, the upward forces on revenue were dominant. The resulting peacetime highs for the federal and total government tax burdens simply set the stage for the dramatic cuts in personal and corporate taxes initiated by President Reagan and enacted by Congress in 1981. Although Congress scaled back the corporate tax cuts in 1982 and raised payroll taxes in 1983, the share of GNP devoted to federal taxes is now projected to remain well below the 1981 level through the remainder of the decade.

Minarik considers a host of alternatives for boosting revenue by $50 billion to $100 billion above the annual levels projected by the end of the decade under current tax law. He argues that, in selecting from the available revenue-raising measures, policymakers should seek to distribute the financial sacrifice broadly and equitably and to maintain the economic incentives to work, save, and invest. Minarik then examines a range of options to raise personal tax rates, to broaden the tax base through "loophole closing" (i.e., limiting the favorable treatment of particular forms of individual or corporate income), to increase excise taxes on selected forms of consumption, to alter the individual income tax through wholesale broadening of the taxable income base and lowered tax rates, or to impose a new general consumption-based tax as a substitute for (or supplement to) the individual income tax.

Minarik believes that equity and efficiency are best served through continued reliance on income taxation, but with a much expanded tax base that would allow rates to be cut and still raise additional revenue. He concedes, however, that the political currents run against any ambitious attempt at base broadening. A major shift toward consumption as the tax base also presents both administrative and political problems. Beyond some strengthening of tax enforcement, Minarik sees the near-term search for revenue as focusing on modest loophole closing, selected excise tax increases, and some increase in individual income tax rates.

Part III turns from the substance of budget choices to the political and institutional context within which policy judgments are reached. Hugh Heclo examines the budget-making process in the executive branch, with particular attention to the strategy surrounding formulation of the president's budget proposals. He first describes how the Reagan administration elevated the budget as an instrument for presidential policy change. For many decades, the president's budget was viewed as simply a matter of descriptive fiscal accounting. Following World War II, the executive budget increasingly was used as a tool for countercyclical fiscal policy and domestic program initiatives. In Heclo's view, "Ronald Reagan's election in 1980 raised the political stakes of presidential budgeting to unprecedented levels." Budget reform became the very embodiment of President Reagan's political philosophy of a less intrusive federal government, albeit one with a strengthened commitment to national defense.

Heclo then describes how in 1981, in pursuing the president's ideological agenda, the Reagan White House transformed the normal executive budget-making routines. The need for a more centrally directed decision process was met through "top-down budgeting"; David Stockman served the critical role of "chief budget examiner," while cabinet appointees and the career staff of Stockman's Office of Management and Budget (OMB) had greatly diminished roles. By Heclo's assessment, the more centralized executive budget process succeeded in enacting the president's initial proposals because its energy was focused on establishing legislative advantage. In particular, OMB's prodigious capacity to collect and generate budget data was harnessed to support the decision needs of the Congress. Within OMB, a great premium was placed on quick response to Stockman's continuing demands for information specifically tailored to congressional decision making.

Heclo sees "good cause for worrying" about the long-term implications of the institutional stress that OMB has undergone in this period. Historically, the president's budget agency has prided itself on hard-headed policy analysis, not dogged political advocacy. Heclo argues that future administrations will not be well served by an OMB whose political responsiveness was bought at the expense of its capacity for knowledgeable program advice.

The next paper shifts perspective from the heights of the executive branch to the trenches of the operating federal agencies. Joseph Wholey uses case studies to assess the ways in which internal agency decision making responds to congressionally imposed spending restraint. He focuses on the decision criteria used in budget choices, on agency operations and program activities, and on agency funding and staffing in five agencies: the Food and Nutrition Service of the Department of Agriculture, the Employment and Training Administration of the Department of Labor, and three components of the Department of Health and Human Services—the Health Resources and Services Administration, the National Institute of Mental Health, and the Administration on Aging. The Reagan administration achieved substantial progress toward its retrenchment objectives in these agencies, whose budgets accounted for more than 40 percent of the spending restraint in human resources programs over the FY 1982–FY 1985 period.

From the agency perspective, the "top-down" approach of the Reagan administration resulted in a budget process that, in contrast to previous years, was far more an implementation process than a decision process. The development of the president's budget was dominated by the dictates of OMB and the White House rather than by agency assessments and requests. The result in the words of one of Wholey's interviewees was a "fast, efficient reduction of programs that do not agree with the (administration's) philosophy." Fast it clearly was, but how efficient? Here a more ambiguous picture emerges from the case studies.

Efficiency in this context can have two very different meanings. The first concerns the efficiency with which the cuts were achieved. Despite considerable turbulence in the agencies, or perhaps because of it, the process of retrenchment was less costly to the ongoing effectiveness of program operations than might have been expected, Wholey says. The reasons lie partly in the skill of political appointees in overcoming bureaucratic inertia and partly in "a substantial degree of resilience and significant capacity for constructive adaptation to change in agencies," as described by one of the discussants of Wholey's paper. Wholey suggests, however, that in several of the agencies "reductions in discretionary programs, grantee reporting, and federal monitoring and evaluation will limit agency ability to sense changing needs and to test responses to those needs."

The second aspect of efficiency concerns whether or not the less effective programs were the ones most deeply cut. Wholey argues that although the administration was not altogether discriminating in its budget proposals, Congress was much more so in its decisions. The end result according to Wholey was "sharp reductions . . . in ineffective and inappropriate programs" but not in programs with "demonstrated high performance." This conclusion was strongly challenged by both discussants who thought Wholey did not muster sufficient evidence to support it.

In contrast to Wholey's view that Congress exercised a strongly positive influence on recent budgetary outcomes, Kenneth Shepsle and Barry Weingast argue that Congress lies at the root of the fiscal problems prompting President Reagan's attack on domestic programs. Shepsle and Weingast examine the effect on congressional budget action of the political imperatives facing individual members of Congress. The authors' main hypothesis is that congressional incentives for reelection and the need for visible benefits to constituents create systematic biases in the provision of public goods. Such biases lead to excessive "budgetary growth, deficit financing, inexplicable programmatic forms, and attention to special interests."

Shepsle and Weingast elaborate on three principles to explain their views. The first is that federal activities with concentrated benefits but dispersed costs—such as military bases and waterway projects—tend to be adopted well beyond the level that can be justified on economic grounds. The second principle is that the need to gain majority support for new initiatives biases program design toward widely distributed benefits, even though efficient use of resources would require more concentrated targeting. Examples here are the model cities and economic development administration programs. The third principle is that any attempt at fiscal restraint will be met by political ingenuity to circumvent it. Here the authors cite the initial creation of entitlement programs, the exclusion of existing programs from the need for appropriations committee consent, and the ability of the authorizing subcommittees to block any program reforms.

Shepsle and Weingast believe that these biases, in conjunction with the decentralization of congressional decision making over the 1960s and 1970s, preclude effective control over the federal budget. The authors conclude that fiscal discipline will occur only if substantial changes occur in the incentives faced by individual members and in the institutional practices and power relationships of Congress. As with Wholey's paper, however, the authors' major theses are strongly challenged by their discussants, who believe that the first two principles, although important to understanding the dynamics of discretionary spending, are not particularly relevant to the entitlement programs that have been the major source of spending growth over the past two decades. Furthermore, they point to recent congressional use of the budget reconciliation process as evidence that the necessary tools exist for control over spending, if there is a will to use them.

This question of the prospects for deficit reduction under the current congressional budget process is discussed in the following paper by Robert Reischauer. He reviews the evolving congressional budget-making process and investigates the suitability of the established legislative procedures to deal with the emerging budget choices. Reischauer believes that the congressional process was instrumental in enabling President Reagan to enact his tax and spending proposals of 1981. Certainly other factors were critical to the president's early legislative success: the perception of the 1980 presidential election as a pro-Reagan mandate, rather than as a rejection of Jimmy Carter; newly gained Republican control of the Senate; David Stockman's mastery of budgetary detail; and the president's own active involvement in seeking congressional support. In addition, the established budget procedures allowed the president's program to be packaged effectively, as "the purity of the program's elements were preserved, the pleasure was integrated with the pain, and decisions were expedited to the point that the opposition had difficulty organizing."

Reischauer also observes that during the Reagan administration, the scope and enforcement of the congressional budget process continued to increase. As examples, Reischauer cites the multiyear focus of budget decisions, the use of reconciliation procedures to force committee action, and the imposition of limits on federal off-budget credit activity. Reischauer also notes that the process has imposed stricter discipline by elevating the annual first concurrent budget resolution to a more binding commitment on budget policy (the second concurrent resolution has virtually disappeared) and by introducing procedural devices to prevent committees from violating the terms of the budget resolution. Reischauer comments that political sensitivity about projected deficits has endowed Congress's adherence to the established procedures with a symbolic importance; no one wants to be accused of obstructing political compromise by failing to play by the rules.

Nonetheless, other recent developments—including the use of unrealistic economic assumptions and other accounting gimmickry—offer less promise for rational policymaking and maintenance of an organized decision process. The budget debate has become increasingly marked by gamesmanship between the executive and legislative branches, between the House and Senate, and between the party leaders within each legislative body. During the first three years of the Reagan administration, "players took positions not on policies they ultimately desired, but rather on ones that afforded a good bargaining situation." Heightened anxiety over the deficit has also meant that policies are now argued in terms of their budgetary impacts, not their programmatic merits. The ascendance of the Budget Committees and the use of reconciliation has come at the expense and indignation of the authorizing and appropriating committees, whose chairmen have sought to alter—if not undermine—the budget process. The Reagan administration itself, having so deftly exploited the congressional process at the outset, has subsequently encouraged its disregard.

This turbulence surrounding Congress and its budget process has led to recent reform proposals. Reischauer's assessment is that, although such reforms deserve serious consideration, they offer little promise in helping Congress to muster the necessary political courage to reduce the deficit. He believes that the current dilemma over budget policy is "the product of a rather peculiar confluence of recent events," and concludes that the large projected deficits would be better addressed through ad hoc mechanisms than through any fundamental realignment of power within Congress.

The policy debate provoked by large federal deficits has brought increasing attention to the accounting rules used in compiling the federal budget, as well as to the process by which budget decisions are made. As Robert Hartman candidly admits in his paper, such budgetary rules "have no peer in the roster of dull subjects.'' However, it is clearly appropriate to ask whether the budget characterizes federal activity in a way that encourages sound policy judgments.

Hartman first reviews the long-standing debate over proper budgetary treatment of such matters as Social Security, credit activities, tax expenditures, and capital outlays. He finds that current accounting practices often tend to obscure, more than illuminate, the relevant policy issues. The power of precedent makes it all the more important that budget rules not be allowed to serve as ''a smokescreen for obtaining a desired political outcome.'' For example, Hartman expresses some dismay over Congress's recent decision to remove Social Security from the regular federal budget beginning in 1993. He observes that ''its exclusion from the budget threatens to be imitated in scores of other programs, and that outcome would destroy the simplicity and controllability of the budget.''

Hartman then discusses a series of accounting issues that have recently emerged in the debate over budget policy. Some of these arise from the desire in Congress to initiate new spending programs while protecting existing ones in an era of fiscal restraint. Because of the need to contain the deficit, policymakers now favor schemes that push budget costs into the future. Hartman cites as examples the proposed Clinch River Breeder Reactor Project and the leasing of federal office space. The accounting of retirement benefits for federal military and civilian employees also raises thorny questions of timing. At present the budget entries for military and civilian retirement do not consistently treat the pension liabilities accruing to current workers.

The final issues Hartman addresses pertain to the adjustment for inflation of defense spending and interest on the public debt. Great attention is now given to the rate of real growth in defense appropriations as an indicator of budget policy. Hartman notes, however, that the inflation adjustment procedure can be quite arbitrary and misleading. In contrast, he questions the conventional practice of not correcting interest outlays to reflect the inflationary erosion of outstanding federal debt. The failure to do so gives a somewhat distorted sense of the degree of fiscal stimulus provided by any particular set of tax and spending policies. As a general proposition, Hartman finds an unavoidable tension between technical precision and simplicity in budget accounting, not to mention the difficulty of being consistent while providing the appropriate level of detail for policy decisions. He concludes that ''analysts and policymakers perhaps need to start and end with budget numbers, but good decisions make use of more information than can ever be crammed into one set of accounts.''

The issues raised by the authors and discussants of the papers in this volume are indeed complex and unsettling. In any era and at any level of government, fiscal prudence would seem to require a continuing reassessment of program commitments and funding arrangements. Such a reexamination now seems particularly warranted for federal policy, because the political and economic anxiety over the federal deficit will compel some policy response. Although deficit reduction may principally motivate forthcoming budgetary change, policymakers should not lose sight of the more basic objectives served by tax and spending policies and by the policymaking process itself. The papers in this volume are helpful in clarifying these budgetary objectives and the implications of recent developments and of possible future courses of action.

PART I
THE CONTEXT FOR BUDGET CHOICES

INTRODUCTION

Alice M. Rivlin

A good public policy conference has to have three ingredients:

1. An important subject—there is no point in arguing over something irrelevant to the nation's future;

2. Clear choices with distinct consequences—it is a waste of time to talk if nothing can be done or the options are murky;

3. Different points of view about which are the right choices and what consequences flow from each—indeed, it livens things up if there are differences over both substance and procedure, not to mention basic philosophical approaches.

This conference has all the essentials. It matters very much to our national security and the quality of our lives how we spend the 20 to 25 percent of everything we have that is devoted to the federal government, and it matters who contributes those resources. We have been through a major change of course in the past several years, both in budget policy and in our decision-making procedures. That change of course has brought us a new problem, a huge budget deficit that will persist even in an improving economy unless new policies are adopted. There are different ways of dealing with the deficit and strong views about the consequences and desirability of each. The challenge before this conference is to articulate the alternatives so that intelligent choices can be made, not only in resolving the current deficit dilemma, but in improving budget-making procedures in the future.

Although the dramatic budget decisions made in 1981 were the proximate cause of the current and prospective deficit, we have to go back another two decades to understand how we got here. In the 1960s and 1970s we asked the federal government to take on substantial new responsibilities in the domestic arena. Spending for nondefense programs rose from about 9 percent of the gross national product in 1961 to about 16 percent in 1976.[1] Most of the increase was for payments to individuals, especially Social Security and other pensions, and for health care for the aged, the disabled, and the impoverished. For a while we paid for these increases by shifting resources out of defense—outlays for defense declined from 9 percent of GNP in 1961 to 5.5 percent in 1976. But in the late 1970s we began the expensive process of modernizing our armed forces and reversed the decline in defense spending. We paid for these simultaneous increases in defense and domestic spending by allowing federal revenues as a percentage of GNP to creep up—mostly because the impact of inflation on a progressive income tax gave us unlegislated increases in effective tax rates. Then we ran out of patience with high taxes—which many economists said were creating a drag on the economy— and with inflation.

We elected a president who won at least in part because he articulated what a lot of people felt:

—That inflation must come down
—That taxes were too high
—That defense needed strengthening
—That some social programs were not working well

He promised to take action on all of these points, and to balance the budget as well.

Unfortunately, he created the impression that all these things could be done at once and without costs. He did not make clear that the monetary restraint he was advocating to cool inflation operates by slowing down the economy itself and that this economic slowdown in turn produces unemployment and budget deficits. He did not make clear that the social programs many people thought to be wasteful were not very expensive. Hence, cutting out "waste" would not nearly compensate for the proposed defense increases and tax cuts—even if the economy grew at a healthy rate. Compensating for the defense increase and the tax cut would take cuts in programs commanding a broad base of support. The president's program was enacted without too many hard questions being asked, because almost everyone wanted to believe it would work—that somehow we could cut inflation, strengthen defense, and lower taxes without giving up anything.

---

1. Gregory B. Mills and John L. Palmer, *The Deficit Dilemma: Budget Policy in the Reagan Era* (Washington, D.C.: The Urban Institute Press, 1983), p. 12.

So we ended up with a severe recession and a whopping deficit. The worrisome part is that the deficit will remain close to the $200 billion level even if the economy, which is now recovering smartly from the recession, continues to grow at a healthy pace. The pesky old rules of arithmetic still apply: cutting taxes without reducing spending produces a deficit.

At present there is no significant disagreement on the budget outlook. The analysis set forth in the Mills-Palmer paper is generally accepted. Some political rhetoric puts differential blame for producing the deficit on the tax cut, the defense increase, or the continued growth in entitlement programs, but everyone who has seriously examined the numbers knows that the blame belongs to "all of the above." The question for argument is not, How did we get here? It is, What do we do now?

The papers for this conference do reflect differences in the political-historical explanation of how we came to this pass, and the conclusions here could help us avoid similar difficulties in the future. Does the current deficit crisis reflect some basic flaw in our political system, or is it the result of an accidental, ideosyncratic combination of events? This is like the old argument about whether the outcome of a battle is determined by the basic strength and placement of the forces or by the single soldier who picks up the fallen flag, rallies his fellows, and turns the tide.

Shepsle and Weingast place the blame squarely on the system, specifically on the decentralization of power in Congress. In their view, the growth of government spending results from the fact that members of Congress want to get reelected and to do so must bring visible government spending programs to their districts. The decline of strong party leadership has left the field to subcommittee chairmen, each motivated to increase a particular kind of spending to enhance his personal power and reelectability. There is certainly some truth to this thesis, especially in defense, where the power of subcommittee chairmen and the geography of defense-related employment strongly affect budget outcomes. Domestic spending programs, however, have been moving rapidly in the direction exactly opposite to that predicted by the Shepsle-Weingast model. Traditional pork-barrel programs—water projects, rivers, and harbors—have been severely cut back, as have the categorical grants to state and local governments for health, education, and other purposes which were linked to subcommittee power. Instead, the growth in the domestic budget has been attributable to the impact of inflation, recession, and demography on the major entitlement programs, which provide no significant power for subcommittee chairmen and for which no logrolling is necessary because everyone is behind the same log.

The notion that basic flaws in our decision-making system have contributed to our present predicament is cogently argued by Stubbing with respect to defense. As described by Stubbing, defense spending decisions bear little relation to any assessment of threats to our security or plans to deal with them, are outside the discipline of OMB review, and are subject to few cost-reducing incentives within the Pentagon, Congress, or the wider military-industrial community.

Heclo's review of recent developments in executive budget making, which incidently confirms Stubbing's view of the apartness of defense, sees history in terms of individuals—in this case, Reagan and Stockman—rather than the impersonal decision-making system. It was Stockman who saw that Reagan's personal commitment to higher defense spending and lower taxes would lead to high deficits and who skillfully used the executive and, at least in 1981, the congressional budget decision process to push through substantial budget cuts. By 1983, however, Stockman's personal dynamism was not enough to overcome the fact that congressional budget priorities were simply not the same as the president's. Reischauer looks at the same events from the congressional side, confirming the personal impact of Reagan and Stockman in using the congressional budget process to make drastic budget alterations in 1981 and detailing the subsequent slide into deadlock over what to do about the deficit.

My own view is that the deficit dilemma arises not from any inherent failure of our decision processes to reflect what most of the public wants, but from the simple fact that most of us, including President Reagan, want more from our government that we want to pay for. There was a consensus in 1981 for strengthening defense, cutting taxes, and reducing waste in domestic programs, even for cutting back on some of them. It was the consensus that enabled the president and his able budget director to drive the budget through Congress in 1981, leaving subcommittee chairmen muttering about revenge. But the consensus did not extend to deeper cuts in broadly popular programs. The president and the public shared the hope that some economic miracle would make these choices unnecessary. It was a miscalculation born of reluctance to face the unpleasant.

So here we are with looming federal deficits. Do they matter? Yes, I believe they do, for reasons well articulated by Gramlich. In the short run, the deficits certainly contribute to sustaining the Keynesian consumer-led recovery that supply-side economics has brought us. But financing those deficits means using a big portion of our national savings for government operations rather than for investment. It will mean higher interest rates than we could have if we chose lower deficits or a less restrictive monetary policy. It will mean a high dollar and trouble for both our export industries and our import-competing industries. At best—if the Fed is clever, flexible, and lucky—we can have sustained growth with relatively low investment. With bad luck—or a high level of Fed concern about inflation—we could get rising interest rates and an economic slowdown.

For a nation worried about its productivity, its ability to modernize some basic industries, and its competitive position in world markets to be embarking on a deliberate policy of high structural deficits and high interest rates seems to me just plain dumb. It would be far more sensible to shift the mix of fiscal and monetary policy, to lower the deficits, to take the pressure off the Fed, and to get both interest rates and the value of the dollar down.

Moreover, it is important to act soon. Strong growth appears likely through 1984. If we wait too long to do something about the deficit, we may find the economy beginning to falter. Actions to raise taxes or cut spending will look far less appropriate then than they do right now.

Options for significant deficit reduction are limited. As the Ladd paper reminds us, grants to state and local governments have been substantially cut back. State-administered, means-tested entitlement programs have been tightened and are not growing much. Aid to state and local governments in the form of tax expenditures has grown rapidly but may be difficult to cut without damaging state and local finances. Although the structure of federal aid to states and localities needs to be reviewed, there is not much potential here for deficit relief.

Pension programs, as Palmer and Torrey point out, are not prime candidates for major reduction, partly because the biggest one, Social Security, has been so recently adjusted. The civilian and military retirement programs badly need structural reform, however, and a comprehensive plan calling for taxation of pension benefits or reductions in cost-of-living adjustments or both could help reduce the deficit if applied to all federal pensions including Social Security.

That leaves only two major growth areas, health and defense, which, indeed, seem to be growing for similar reasons. In both the defense and health care areas, technology is advancing extremely rapidly. The tools of the trade are becoming increasingly expensive and the practitioners—whether doctors or generals—naturally want the best possible tools. There may be no better way to reduce spending increases in these areas than to impose arbitrary rates of growth on overall spending and say to the practitioners, "Do the best you can." Prospective reimbursement of hospitals and fee schedules for health providers offer vehicles for this approach to health care costs. Congressional efforts to hold defense budget growth to 5 percent after inflation may foreshadow this approach to defense; and Stubbing suggests that a broader definition of our national security objectives (more focused on international stability and less on Soviet containment) could lead us to a defense budget growing at about the same rate as the GNP. In any case, it would be an advance to get Congress out of the business of choosing weapons systems and onto the questions of what is an appropriate, stable rate of growth.

If we cannot get within hailing distance of the Mills-Palmer goals of reducing the structural deficit to 1 percent of the GNP on the spending side alone—and I believe we cannot—then we have to turn to revenues. The options, both for adjusting current taxes and for restructuring the tax system, are well laid out by Minarik.

Getting the deficits down is going to take willingness to compromise on a relatively simple plan that appears to spread the pain both widely and equitably—some increase in taxes, some reduction in defense growth, some cuts in domestic spending. No changes in the budget process will make the decisions easier, although some may be in order. No changes in accounting methods or budget concepts will affect the deficit decisions either, although some sensible ones are offered by Hartman. The problem before us is not one of poor accounting or inappropriate decision processes. It's much simpler than that. We are spending more than we are taking in. We know what the problem is and what the options are. We simply have to screw up our courage and do what is necessary to resolve it.

THE FEDERAL BUDGET IN FLUX

Gregory B. Mills and John L. Palmer

President Reagan took office in 1981 with a pledge to reverse the major federal budgetary trends of the 1960s and 1970s. He proposed to cut taxes, accelerate the defense buildup, restrain domestic spending, and balance the federal budget. The president was remarkably successful at enacting his initial proposals. Consequently, the federal tax burden has been lowered by more than 2 percent of gross national product (GNP), and defense expenditures have greatly increased as a share of the federal budget at the expense of domestic spending. But total federal spending has continued to rise as a percentage of GNP. We now face annual deficits exceeding $300 billion by the end of the 1980s, threatening the prospects for economic growth and price stability.

To avoid such risks to the economy's future performance, the president and Congress must act to bring the deficit gradually down to a more reasonable level. An appropriate intermediate goal for the 1989 structural deficit would be about 2 percent of GNP, still above the level experienced during the 1960s and 1970s, but less than one-half the currently projected levels of between 5 and 6 percent. To attain such a target by the end of this decade would require tax increases and reductions in program spending that would amount annually to $150 billion by fiscal year (FY) 1989. Measured against this target, neither the president nor Congress has proposed sufficient action. If the prescribed deficit target is to be met, both the president and Congress must reconsider their positions on the three major fronts for deficit reduction:

The discussion in this chapter draws heavily on a longer treatment of the subject contained in Gregory B. Mills and John L. Palmer, *The Deficit Dilemma: Budget Policy in the Reagan Era* (Washington, D.C.: The Urban Institute Press, 1983).

tax increases, reductions in the planned defense buildup, and domestic spending restraint.

This paper examines the changing federal budget under President Reagan—how developments through the FY 1984 budget cycle have affected budget outcomes, and how the stage has been set for future budgetary choices. The first section considers President Reagan's initial budget plan against the historical backdrop. The second section discusses how congressional action on taxes and spending combined with changing economic conditions to alter the projected budget outlook that prevailed when President Reagan assumed office. The third section reviews the economic problems posed by large deficits. The final section examines the policy trade-offs that must be considered in reducing the deficit.

President Reagan's Budget Objectives

The budget reforms that Ronald Reagan proposed as a presidential candidate in 1980 and as president in 1981 included a major reduction in tax burdens, rapid growth in defense spending, and a balanced budget. These policies were a response to the widespread dissatisfaction with budgetary trends of the 1960s and 1970s—increasing federal tax burdens, no growth in inflation-adjusted defense spending, and rising federal deficits. The success of the president's plan depended critically upon considerable restraint in the growth of nondefense program spending and upon an immediate, strong, and sustained revival in economic growth. This section first describes the key elements of the administration's original budget. It then discusses the historical context for the proposed tax cuts, defense buildup, nondefense spending restraint, and consequent deficit reduction.

The President's Prescription for Revenues, Outlays, and the Deficit

Within a month of taking office, President Reagan presented a four-part program to reduce inflation and promote economic growth. He announced his "Program for Economic Recovery" before a joint session of Congress on February 18, 1981. The measures he proposed to combat a stagnating economy and rapid inflation included tax reductions, a slowdown in the growth of federal spending leading to a balanced budget, regulatory relief, and monetary restraint. Monetary restraint was expected to curb inflation; tax cuts, deregulation, and spending restraint were expected to encourage stronger and more sustained economic growth. The tax cuts were to play a central role, providing a supply-side boost to the economy by promoting savings, investment, work effort, and productivity. The result was predicted to be annual, real (inflation-adjusted) growth of GNP exceeding 4 percent during calendar years 1982 through 1986, with annual inflation dropping below 5 percent by 1986. (During the 1970s real GNP had grown at an annual rate of 3 percent, whereas the annual inflation rate had increased to above 9 percent by 1980.) In essence the president embraced a set of tax and defense policies that could be reconciled with his balanced-budget objective only through extremely optimistic economic projections and large reductions in domestic spending.

The Reagan administration's tax and spending proposals were submitted to Congress on March 10, 1981, as revisions to President Carter's budget proposals for FY 1982. The major provisions were as follows:

- A succession of three 10 percent reductions in personal income tax rates on July 1 of 1981, 1982, and 1983

- Accelerated depreciation provisions in the corporate income tax, shortening the depreciable lives of buildings, vehicles, and equipment

- A five-year path of national defense outlay increases reflecting annual real growth of about 9 percent

- A reduction in on- and off-budget nondefense program outlays of about $50 billion in 1982 and $100 billion annually by 1986, relative to baseline projections of pre-Reagan policies

- Additional unspecified spending reductions amounting annually to $30 billion in 1983 and more than $40 billion between 1984 and 1986, measured against baseline projections

The terms *baseline*, *baseline projection*, and *current policy projection* are used throughout this paper to refer to the expected path of federal revenues or outlays in the absence of policy changes. This path forms the standard by which to isolate the effect of the policy changes themselves, as distinct from economic conditions, demographic trends, or other factors influencing budgetary outcomes. An estimated reduction in outlays "relative to the baseline projection" is thus a reduction in the amount of expected growth in spending that would otherwise have occurred. The liability of such estimates is that they must rely on judgments about future circumstances that are subject to great uncertainty.

The budgetary shifts implied by the Reagan administration's economic forecast and the proposals just outlined were truly enormous by any historical standard. The expected economic recovery, along with the planned reductions in federal domestic spending, were to bring revenues into balance with total

TABLE 1

PRESIDENT REAGAN'S ORIGINAL BUDGET PROGRAM,
FY 1981–FY 1986

	1981	1982	1983	1984	1985	1986
	Percentage of GNP					
Revenues	21.1	20.4	19.7	19.3	19.3	19.5
Outlays (including off-budget)	23.9	22.3	20.6	19.5	19.4	19.1
National defense	5.7	5.9	6.3	6.4	6.9	7.1
Nondefense programs	15.9	14.3	12.5	11.4	11.0	10.6
Net interest	2.3	2.1	1.9	1.7	1.5	1.3
TOTAL DEFICIT (SURPLUS)	2.8	1.9	0.9	0.2	0.0	(0.4)

SOURCE: Office of Management and Budget, "Federal Government Finances," March 1981, pp. 6, 12, 77, 82, and 84.

NOTE: Based on the Reagan administration's economic forecast and technical assumptions. The unspecified outlay reductions included by the administration in the estimates for FY 1983–FY 1986 are assumed to come entirely from nondefense programs.

outlays by 1986, despite the large tax cuts and defense buildup (table 1). The administration indicated at the time that even further tax reductions would be sought, in line with the projected continued decline in outlays as a percentage of GNP.

In the presence of a rising GNP share devoted to national defense, the drop in total outlays relative to GNP implied a great reversal in the federal domestic commitment embodied in the policies President Reagan inherited. Adjusted for inflation, nondefense outlays were to fall at an annual rate of nearly 4 percent between 1981 and 1986, after having risen at an annual pace exceeding 6 percent during the previous twenty years. The president's projections for defense outlays, nondefense program spending, and interest outlays on the public debt for 1986 resembled the pattern of budget shares prevailing in 1971. This reversal in historical trends was embodied not only in the administration's original proposals, but also in its FY 1983 and 1984 budgets. The administration pinned its hopes for such spending restraint not only on its ability to reduce "fraud, abuse, and waste," but also on the spending discipline that presumably would be instilled in Congress through tax cuts and the need to reduce spending to avoid large deficits. Only with such presumed cuts in domestic programs and a forecast of very strong economic performance could the administration assert that large tax cuts, a defense buildup, and a diminishing deficit be achieved simultaneously.

The Administration's Tax Cuts as a Response to Rising Tax Burdens

The federal tax burden increased substantially between 1961 and 1981, most dramatically in the last five years of the period. (See the paper by Minarik in this volume for further discussion of the historical trend.) In contrast, state and local tax burdens rose through the mid-1970s but declined thereafter. The result was a steadily rising total tax burden since the late 1960s, with tax burdens for both federal and total revenues reaching peacetime highs in 1981 (table 2).

Federal receipts grew during the 1976–1981 period primarily because of inflation and the accompanying process known as bracket creep. During inflationary periods, personal and corporate incomes must rise simply to keep pace with price increases. However, these inflation-induced additions to income are taxed at progressively higher rates. Furthermore, the real value of exemptions, deductions, and credits that are fixed in dollar terms is eroded through price increases. As a result, taxes come to represent a higher fraction of income, even though before-tax purchasing power is unchanged. Nearly three-fourths of the rise in federal revenues during the 1976–1981 period could be attributed to these effects, as inflation proceeded at an annual rate exceeding 8 percent during the five-year period.[1]

The remaining rise in the tax burdens resulted from national economic growth and changes in tax policies. Because of the progressivity of tax rates,

TABLE 2

GOVERNMENT REVENUES,
FY 1961–FY 1981

	1961–1965	1966–1970	1971–1975	1976–1980	1981
	Percentage of GNP				
Federal	18.2	19.2	18.6	19.2	20.8
State and local	8.4	9.2	10.6	10.4	9.7
TOTAL	26.6	28.4	29.2	29.6	30.5

SOURCE: Office of Management and Budget, "Total Government Finances," February 1984.
NOTE: The multiyear entries are computed as the average of the corresponding five fiscal years.

---

1. The contribution of inflation to revenue growth was estimated from Frank de Leeuw and Thomas M. Holloway, "The High-Employment Budget: Revised Estimates and Automatic Inflation Effects," *Survey of Current Business*, April 1982, pp. 21–33.

real growth caused revenues to rise proportionately more than national income, thus pushing upward the ratio of tax receipts to GNP. Chief among the legislative changes were the increases in Social Security payroll taxes enacted in 1977 to stave off the impending insolvency of the system[2] and the enactment in 1979 of the windfall profits tax on income from domestically produced oil.

The Defense Buildup as a Move to Restore the Nation's Military Capabilities

The twenty-year period preceding the Reagan administration began and ended with defense outlays at virtually the same dollar level, after adjusting for inflation. The figures translated into a decline of more than one-third in the GNP share of defense outlays (table 3). (The Stubbing paper in this volume presents further information on defense outlays in the pre-Reagan years.) Accompanying this overall downward trend was a shift in the composition of defense spending. An increasing share of national defense outlays went

TABLE 3

FEDERAL OUTLAYS FOR NATIONAL DEFENSE AND NONDEFENSE PROGRAMS,
FY 1961–FY 1981

	1961	1966	1971	1976	1981
	Percentage of GNP				
National defense	9.7	8.0	7.6	5.5	5.5
Nondefense programs	8.1	9.3	11.3	15.5	15.6
Payments for individuals	5.5	5.2	8.0	11.2	11.5
Other grants to state and local governments	0.8	1.2	1.7	2.3	1.9
Other direct federal operations	1.8	2.9	1.6	2.0	2.3
TOTAL (excluding net interest)	17.8	17.3	18.9	21.0	21.1
Addendum: Total grants to state and local governments[a]	1.4	1.8	2.8	3.6	3.3

SOURCE: Office of Management and Budget, "Federal Government Finances," February 1984. Includes off-budget outlays.
   a. Includes the portion of "payments for individuals" that is administered through state and local governments (such as Medicaid and Aid to Families with Dependent Children), in addition to "other grants to state and local governments."

---

2. The taxable earnings base was nearly doubled, from $15,300 in 1976 to $29,700 in 1981, and the combined employee-employer payroll tax rate jumped from 11.7 to 13.3 percent.

for current operating expenses in defense-related activities, primarily the pay-roll for active personnel and the operation and maintenance cost of existing military facilities and equipment. The costs of retirement benefits for former military personnel also rose dramatically as a percentage of the defense budget. These changes meant a declining share of outlays for military investment—weapons procurement, research and development, and construction. Concern about the underfunding of defense was focused principally on this declining emphasis on the development of future military capabilities.

The downward trend in real defense spending was reversed during the late 1970s. In establishing U.S. commitments to the NATO alliance, President Carter pledged the country to 3 percent real defense growth, a trend that was achieved from 1979 to 1981. In fact, the FY 1981 budget authority enacted by Congress for Defense Department military activities represented a 12 percent real increase over the prior year; the investment component ex-perienced a 22 percent real increase.[3]

The Need for Nondefense Program Restraint

In marked contrast to national defense outlays, spending on nondefense programs rose dramatically as a percentage of GNP between 1961 and 1981 (see table 3), reflecting an annual real growth rate approaching 7 percent.[4] Although substantial growth occurred during this period in all three major components of nondefense program spending—payments for individuals, other grants to state and local governments, and other direct federal operations—the rapid growth in benefit payments to individuals was clearly dominant. (The paper by Palmer and Torrey in this volume discusses the role of health and pension programs in this upward trend.) Annual real growth in benefit payments averaged nearly 8 percent between 1961 and 1981. Outlays for

---

3. Congressional Budget Office (CBO), *Defense Spending and the Economy* (Washington, D.C.: U.S. Government Printing Office [GPO], 1983), p. 2. Congress does not directly control outlays but rather appropriates budget authority to federal agencies. This authority to make spending commitments does not result in outlays until the Treasury actually disburses funds, such as through payroll checks to federal employees or payments to federal contractors. In national defense spending, budget authority enacted in one year may not result in outlays until several years later, as in the case of long-term weapons procurement. A rising pattern of budget authority must eventually translate into higher outlays.

4. Estimates in this section exclude interest outlays necessary to finance the public debt but include the modest amount of off-budget program spending. Off-budget outlays are excluded from the federal budget by statutory provision but must be financed through tax revenues or government borrowing, as is the case with on-budget spending. The off-budget outlays are associated largely with the credit operations of the Federal Financing Bank, for such activities as rural electrification, agriculture credit insurance, rural farm housing, and foreign military sales.

benefit programs targeted on the low-income population grew faster than this average, and spending on social insurance and other non-means-tested benefit programs grew less rapidly.

Several interrelated factors promoted the rapid increase in real benefit payments through the early 1970s. New nationwide programs, such as Medicaid, Medicare, and Food Stamps, were introduced; the eligibility and benefit provisions of existing programs, such as Social Security and Aid to Families with Dependent Children (AFDC), were liberalized; economic and demographic shifts, such as the rapid growth in the aged and single-parent families, increased the numbers of eligible persons; the participation rate rose among the eligible population as the civil rights movement and War on Poverty increased public awareness of the benefits to which persons were entitled and reduced the stigma attached to receiving them; and more generous federal funding provisions were adopted under joint federal-state financing arrangements. Although these sources of real growth exerted little influence by the late 1970s, continuing medical cost inflation and the over-indexing of entitlements (especially in the face of the 1979 oil price shock) prevented any marked decline in benefit outlays as a percentage of GNP.[5]

These circumstances caused benefit payments to more than double as a percentage of GNP between 1961 and 1981, with virtually all this increase coming by the mid-1970s. Other grants to state and local governments also more than doubled as a percentage of GNP between 1961 and 1981. By the end of this period, however, such grant outlays were declining both as a percentage of GNP and in inflation-adjusted dollars, after having peaked in 1978. Other direct federal operations grew as a percentage of GNP between 1961 and 1966, declined in the following decade, and then stabilized between 2.0 and 2.5 percent of GNP in the late 1970s.

Reversing the Trend of Growing Deficits

The budget developments of the 1960s and 1970s led to an increasing disparity between the revenue yield of federal tax policies and the financing requirements of federal program activities. The growth in tax burdens was surpassed by the growth in total outlays, and annual federal deficits crept upward both in dollars and as a percentage of GNP (table 4). In part, this situation reflected the weakness of the economy. Higher unemployment not

---

5. Most programs were explicitly indexed to a measure of price change. Health care financing programs such as Medicare and Medicaid, though not explicitly indexed, experienced more rapid growth than the general rate of inflation because they reflected the even faster escalating costs of medical care through their cost reimbursement schedules.

TABLE 4

FEDERAL DEFICITS AND NET INTEREST OUTLAYS,
FY 1961–FY 1981

	1961–1965	1966–1970	1971–1975	1976–1980	1981
	Percentage of GNP				
Total deficit[a]	0.8	0.9	1.9	2.9	2.7
Net interest outlays[b]	1.3	1.4	1.5	1.8	2.4

SOURCE: Office of Management and Budget, ''Federal Government Finances,'' February 1984, pp. 5, 7, 72–73, and 91–93.

NOTE: The multiyear entries are computed as the average of the corresponding five fiscal years.

a. Includes off-budget outlays.

b. Interest payments on federal debt held by the public (including the Federal Reserve System) and interest paid on tax refunds, minus interest collected from federal agencies and the public.

only restrained the level of revenues by curbing the growth of taxable incomes, but also promoted a rise in outlays through greater demands for unemployment insurance and means-tested entitlements such as Food Stamps, AFDC, and Medicaid. Even when adjusted for changes in the unemployment rate, however, federal deficits exhibited a clearly upward trend as a percentage of GNP.

Inflation served to moderate the growth of the more recent deficits, as bracket creep tended to spur revenue growth faster than the outlay growth associated with the automatic indexing of income transfers and discretionary inflation adjustments in other programs. However, the higher interest rates that accompanied inflation led to a dramatic rise in the level of interest payments necessary to finance the accumulating federal debt. The credit markets exacted a heavy price each time the government sought either to refinance its existing debt, as outstanding securities matured, or to service the newly created debt caused by current deficits. Between 1961 and 1981, annual net interest outlays nearly doubled as a percentage of GNP.

The Budgetary Consequences of Policy Changes under President Reagan

The Reagan administration enjoyed considerable early success in gaining congressional enactment of its budget proposals, but the economy failed to respond to the policies as the administration predicted. Instead of experiencing an economic recovery that was to enable a balanced budget by 1984, the country entered a deep recession in July 1981. Although Congress made unprecedented spending reductions in nondefense programs, the budget outlook shifted toward enormous future deficits. The worsening state of the economy, in combination with tax cuts and increased defense outlays, resulted in a federal deficit that reached $128 billion in 1982 and $208 billion in 1983 and is projected under current policies to exceed $300 billion by 1989. The administration has attributed the deficit dilemma largely to unrestrained growth in entitlement programs, while others blame the tax cuts and defense buildup.

This section reviews the recent changes in federal tax and spending policies and their implications for projected deficits. The shifts in projected levels of revenues, outlays, and the deficit are first examined, with attention to the role of policy changes enacted in the separate areas of taxes, defense spending, and nondefense spending. The chapter ends with a discussion of competing explanations for the worsening budgetary outlook.

Budget Outcomes

During the past three years, the federal budget has departed dramatically from the broad outcomes sought by the Reagan administration. Largely because the economy failed to respond as the administration predicted, federal revenues and outlays moved onto increasingly divergent paths. Although the administration originally forecast that its policies would yield a surplus of 0.4 percent of GNP in 1986, current policies and projected economic conditions imply a 1986 deficit of $230 billion, or 5.4 percent of GNP (table 5). This projected doubling in the deficit as a percentage of GNP from 2.7 percent in 1981 can be attributed to a reduction in the federal tax burden by 2.1 percentage points of GNP and a rise in the outlay share of GNP by 0.6 percentage point. The projected fall in tax burdens exceeds that originally proposed by the administration, despite a tax increase in 1982 that offset one-third of the tax cut enacted in 1981. The projected outlay growth stands in marked contrast to the spending restraint embodied in the president's original program, whereby outlays were to fall as a percentage of GNP. By 1989, current policies will drive the deficit upward even further to an estimated $339 billion—6.3 percent of projected GNP. Even this may understate the long-term budgetary imbalance. If the president's requested defense buildup is also incorporated as current policy, the 1989 deficit would reach about $360 billion. Or, if there is a recession between now and 1989, the deficit would exceed $400 billion by the end of the decade.[6]

---

6. CBO's current budget projection under a "low-growth" economic forecast, which assumes a recession in 1986, yields a 1989 budget deficit of $390 billion. If off-budget outlays of $13 billion are included, the total deficit would thus exceed $400 billion. See Congressional Budget Office, *Baseline Budget Projections for Fiscal Years 1985–1989* (Washington, D.C.: GPO, 1984), p. 70.

TABLE 5

FEDERAL BUDGET TRENDS FOR SELECTED YEARS,
FY 1981–FY 1989

	Actual			*Projected*[a]		
	1981	*1982*	*1983*	*1984*	*1986*	*1989*
	Percentage of GNP					
Revenues	20.8	20.2	18.6	18.6	18.7	18.9
Outlays (including off-budget)	23.5	24.4	25.0	24.3	24.1	25.2
National defense	5.5	6.1	6.5	6.6	6.9	7.8
Nondefense programs	15.6	15.6	15.7	14.7	13.8	13.3
Net interest	2.4	2.8	2.8	3.0	3.4	4.1
TOTAL DEFICIT	2.7	4.2	6.4	5.7	5.4	6.3
			$ billions			
TOTAL DEFICIT	79	128	208	203	230	339

SOURCES: Congressional Budget Office, *Baseline Budget Projections for Fiscal Years 1985–1989* (Washington, D.C.: GPO, 1984); and Office of Management and Budget, "Federal Government Finances," February 1984.
   a.   Assumes continuation of all tax and spending policies enacted through 1983.

To what extent has the budgetary outlook been worsened by the weaker-than-expected economy of 1981 and 1982? Clearly a significant portion of the shift toward larger deficits stems from the poorer-than-anticipated economic performance. Virtually all the upward pressure on deficits posed by the disappointing performance of the economy was felt on the revenue side. The combination of unexpectedly poor economic growth and more moderate inflation translated into a lower path of nominal GNP, leading to less taxable income and thus lower revenues.

Further aggravating the long-term deficit outlook have been the changes in policy enacted thus far under President Reagan. The budgetary impact of these policy changes cannot be measured without first adopting some alternative set of tax and spending policies to serve as a standard of comparison. The counterfactual set of policies assumed here is as follows:

1. Inflation adjustments to the individual income tax to offset the bracket creep occurring from October 1981 onward (in order to hold personal tax burdens roughly constant over time), but no other changes in tax law

2. Annual real growth in defense outlays of 5 percent in 1982, 4 percent in 1983, and 3 percent thereafter

3. Full inflationary adjustment to spending in nearly all nondefense programs, thus maintaining the real value of goods, services, and benefits provided by virtually all programs

Measured against such a continuation of pre-Reagan policies, the changes in policy contribute $144 billion to annual deficits by 1989 (table 6). This is the net effect of both lower revenues and higher outlays than would have resulted under the assumed baseline policies. The drop in nondefense program outlays resulting from policy action thus far would eventually by exceeded by the combination of higher defense and interest outlays.

To the extent that neither spending growth nor the deficit has been restrained, the administration's broadest budget objectives have not been met. On more specific budget objectives, however, the president has achieved considerable success. Tax burdens have certainly been reduced, defense outlays increased, and nondefense program spending cut substantially from the levels that would otherwise have been attained. Indeed, the administration's

TABLE 6

INCREASE IN PROJECTED FEDERAL DEFICITS DUE TO POLICY
CHANGES ENACTED UNDER THE REAGAN ADMINISTRATION
FOR SELECTED YEARS, FY 1982–FY 1989

	1982	1983	1984	1986	1989
	\$ billions				
Revenues	32	57	65	86	98
Outlays	− 39	− 29	− 18	− 12	46
National defense	1	17	25	42	77
Nondefense programs	− 39	− 45	− 46	− 69	− 77
Net interest	− 1	− 1	3	15	46
TOTAL	− 7	28	47	74	144

SOURCES: Congressional Budget Office, *Baseline Budget Projections for Fiscal Years 1985–1989* (Washington, D.C.: GPO, 1984); CBO estimates of the revenue change necessary to offset bracket creep; and authors' calculations of net interest outlays as affected by shifts in revenues and program outlays.

NOTE: The assumptions regarding current policy include the continuation of all tax and spending policies enacted through 1983. The assumptions regarding the counterfactual baseline policies include annual real growth in defense outlays of 5 percent in 1982, 4 percent in 1983, and 3 percent thereafter; no change in corporate tax provisions and nondefense program policies as of January 1981, with full adjustment for inflation in nondefense programs; and tax reductions to offset bracket creep in the individual income tax.

success on taxes and defense heightened the need for nondefense spending restraint even beyond what the president originally proposed, especially in the absence of the predicted immediate resurgence of the economy. As the administration failed to achieve the necessary restraint on nondefense spending and resisted any compromise on its tax and defense policies, budget projections came to show a pattern of extremely large and growing deficits.

Changes in Revenues. To the extent that the deteriorating budget outlook for the 1980s can be attributed to legislation enacted thus far under President Reagan, the policy changes on the revenue side are responsible. The 1989 revenue loss associated with the recent tax changes is estimated under present economic assumptions to be $98 billion, as measured against the revenue yield anticipated under prior corporate tax laws and an indexed individual income tax. This shift of nearly 2 percent of projected GNP was largely the net result of a landmark piece of tax-cutting legislation, the Economic Recovery Tax Act of 1981 (ERTA), and a major revenue-raising measure enacted the following year, the Tax Equity and Fiscal Responsibility Act of 1982 (TEFRA). In addition, the gasoline excise tax was raised in the Surface Transportation Assistance Act of 1982, and higher revenues will result from the 1983 Social Security reforms. (The paper by Minarik in this volume describes the specific legislative changes.)

Changes in Defense Outlays. Congress accepted the president's proposed defense buildup without revision during 1981, placing defense outlays on a path of nearly 9 percent annual real growth between 1981 and 1986. In light of the worsening budget outlook in 1982, the administration adjusted downward its FY 1983 proposals to reflect a slightly lower growth trend.[7] Congress then adopted spending resolutions for FY 1983 and FY 1984 that further reduced the growth in defense outlays below the president's proposed trend. (See the Stubbing paper for more details.) Current policies would lead to defense outlays in 1989 that are $77 billion higher than those projected under the pre-Reagan policies. Under the currently enacted buildup, defense outlays would rise from 5.5 percent of GNP in 1981 to 7.8 percent in 1989. The more moderate, counterfactual growth path would have put defense outlays at 6.4 percent of GNP in 1989.

Changes in Nondefense Program Spending. Nondefense program spending is projected to rise from about $500 billion in 1983 to more than $700 billion in 1989 under current policies. Despite this continued growth, however, annual nondefense program outlays under current policies will be $77 billion lower by 1989 than they would have been if Congress had simply

---

7. Office of Management and Budget, "Federal Government Finances," March 1981 edition, p. 75, and February 1982 edition, p. 69.

continued the policies in place when President Reagan took office. This reduction amounts to a 10 percent drop from the pre-Reagan baseline estimate for that year. As a percentage of GNP, nondefense programs are now projected to fall from 15.6 percent in 1981 to 13.3 percent in 1989. As significant as this achievement is for President Reagan, it was less spending restraint than he sought (only one-half as much, by administration estimates) and far less than he needed to control the deficit in the face of the large tax cuts, the defense buildup, and the economy's performance.

Some categories of nondefense spending, of course, received proportionately greater reductions than others. The largest cuts have come in discretionary federal operations and grants to state and local governments. Under current policies, the projected 1989 funding for such activities will support services at only about three-fourths of their 1981 levels.

The spending category of benefit payments for individuals has received a proportionately smaller reduction than the other two categories just mentioned. Within the benefit payments area, programs providing assistance to the low-income population were cut proportionately far more than others. In social insurance and other non-means-tested benefit programs, there was some modest tightening of eligibility and benefit provisions, including less generous cost-of-living adjustments (COLAs). However, spending for these latter programs still will rise between 1981 and 1989, both in real dollars and as a percentage of GNP. This trend is due in large part to the aging of the population and the increased demands thus placed on health and pension programs, plus medical care cost increases that far exceed the general rate of inflation. Increases in these programs account for nearly all the projected growth in nondefense program spending over the period. (See the Palmer-Torrey paper for further discussion.)

Competing Explanations for the Rise in Projected Deficits

Views about the origins of the deficit problem depend on judgments as to the desirable level of tax burdens, defense capabilities, and the domestic commitments of the federal government. An examination of the Reagan administration's perspective and of competing interpretations of recent budget history illustrates the major points of contention in the present policy debate.

The administration asserts that, the unanticipated recession aside, the projected future deficits are due primarily to the unrestrained growth of nondefense program spending through policies adopted during the 1970s. This argument focuses particularly on entitlement benefits and the difficulty of reversing their upward momentum. Secondarily, the administration has charged that Congress enacted tax policies that reduce tax burdens beyond the level originally proposed by President Reagan. The administration rejects the claim that the defense buildup is excessive. Indeed, the president has continued to assert that such defense growth is essential to meet the Soviet threat and to ensure a strong American bargaining position in arms reduction talks. The principal opposing view is that the individual income tax cuts in ERTA and the planned defense buildup were excessive and should be scaled back substantially. There is merit to both arguments, as well as contrary evidence.

The revenue loss associated with the individual tax rate reductions and indexing provisions of ERTA does not appear excessive *if* the policy objective was to offset the effects of bracket creep since January 1979. That was the time at which taxpayers first became vulnerable to inflation following the most recent prior adjustment in personal tax rates. To offset the ensuing bracket creep under observed and projected inflation rates would have required individual tax cuts even greater than those granted by the rate reductions and indexing provisions of ERTA.[8] At the same time, because inflation then dropped below the rate projected before ERTA's enactment, the 1981 law now provides for a much larger real gain in personal disposable incomes than was originally expected.[9]

Before ERTA's enactment, concern was expressed about whether the American public would tolerate the rising tax share of GNP that was implied by pre-ERTA policy, or whether the economic incentives necessary for strong economic growth could be sustained in the absence of a large tax cut. The administration answered both questions in the negative. Critics of the administration's tax policy cite international comparisons to counter the proposition that a rising tax burden would inhibit economic growth; U.S. taxes are relatively low when compared with those of other industrialized nations that have experienced faster growth. The critics further contend that lower tax burdens were simply traded for higher interest rates. The 1981–1982 recession is thus attributed in part to the tax policy changes, as monetary tightening was deemed necessary through mid-1982 to contain inflation in the face of the expansionary, supply-side fiscal policy. The monetary restraint kept real interest rates high and thus adversely affected sectors such as housing, autos, consumer durables, and business investment. For this reason, many people judge the ERTA tax cuts to have been irresponsibly large.

The Reagan administration itself has joined in the criticism of ERTA. In early 1983, the administration faulted Congress for enacting provisions in

---

8. Congressional Budget Office, *Reducing the Deficit: Spending and Revenue Options* (Washington, D.C.: GPO, 1983) p. 238.

9. Committee on the Budget, House of Representatives, *First Concurrent Resolution on The Budget—Fiscal Year 1984* (Washington, D.C.: GPO, 1983), p. 80.

ERTA that "reduced the revenue claim on GNP in 1986–1988 by substantially more than was originally proposed."[10] Nevertheless, the White House vigorously supported ERTA, which, indeed, passed on the strength of the president's endorsement. Granted, ERTA provisions such as indexing and the easing of the marriage penalty had been absent from the administration's legislative proposals of early 1981. Ronald Reagan, however, had proposed indexing as an essential piece of his budget program during the 1980 presidential campaign and indicated after becoming president that the administration would propose both indexing and measures to address the marriage penalty in a subsequent tax package. If one includes these two provisions along with those formally proposed by the Reagan administration in February 1981, the total revenue loss by 1986 would have been virtually the same as that enacted in ERTA.

Whether the administration's planned defense buildup is excessive is a much more ambiguous proposition, given the difficulties in establishing the nature of the threat posed by our foreign adversaries and thus our increased vulnerability to aggressors under more moderate defense growth. The administration argues that its policies would simply restore the defense share of GNP by 1988 to 8 percent, still below the peacetime levels that prevailed during the late 1950s and early 1960s. Critics of the defense policy argue that defense needs simply do not require such a high level of spending, that such spending diverts resources from other problems and priorities, and that the speed of the buildup is so rapid as to prevent a rational procurement strategy and to create supply bottlenecks and inflationary pressures in some industrial sectors.

As mentioned earlier, the administration lays the blame for projected deficits primarily on continued growth in domestic spending. Projections of current policy show nondefense programs falling to 13.3 percent of GNP by 1989 from their 1981 level of 15.6 percent. This declining GNP share, in the presence of factors such as a growing elderly population that place upward pressures on spending, suggests that considerable spending restraint in domestic programs has in fact been exercised. The administration points out, however, that the projected GNP share of nondefense program spending still far exceeds that attained during the Great Society era of the late 1960s and the subsequent period leading up to the 1974–1975 recession. Also, the GNP share of its dominant component—benefit payments to individuals—is not projected to decline at all from its 1981 level of 11 percent.

---

10. Office of Management and Budget, *Budget of the United States Government, Fiscal Year 1984*, January 1983, pp. 3–19.

This argument belies the fact that the administration did not put forward a coherent strategy to address the future sources of growth in entitlement programs. President Reagan's FY 1982 budget revisions simply promised, but did not specify, future spending reductions. Under pressure from the Senate, the administration proposed a hastily formulated set of Social Security cuts in May 1981. After these were repudiated by both parties in Congress, the president proposed the creation of a national commission to make recommendations on Social Security financing. Although both Congress and the president were subsequently able to rally around the proposals of this commission and avert the impending trust fund shortfall, the enacted legislation did little to restrain the growth of Social Security benefits over the next several decades. The administration also failed initially to make appropriate proposals to restrain the Medicare program. Congress had to order it to submit legislation to contain Medicare hospital costs. The projected savings of the new legislation are modest relative to the expected growth of the Medicare program.

The president's efforts during 1981 and 1982 to restrain domestic spending were directed primarily at low-income assistance, grants to state and local governments, and discretionary federal operations. Such programs were politically vulnerable and have in fact been substantially reduced. However, it is the "middle-class entitlements," especially health care and pension benefits, that remain the principal sources of growth in domestic spending. In its first two years, the administration proposed little in well-designed structural reforms to achieve the long-term restraint in these areas needed to meet the administration's budgetary objectives.

How Serious Is the Deficit Problem?

Projected federal deficits are so large as to endanger the future health of the economy. The government's demands for available credit will probably discourage private investment and thus adversely affect long-term economic output. An intermediate program of tax increases and spending reductions, however, might also jeopardize the nation's economic health by curtailing personal consumption and business expenditures. Given these competing concerns, along with the role that value judgments must play and the controversy among experts over the precise economic consequences of deficits, there are no hard-and-fast rules as to what constitutes a desirable deficit trend. Budget choices should be based on a careful weighing of the risks of either persistently large deficits or the contractionary fiscal measures by which deficits might be reduced. The indisputable reality is that current policies will lead to unprecedented peacetime deficits, particularly when we abstract from the cyclical performance of the economy and consider only the structural deficit amount that would remain under high-employment conditions. Although reasonable people may disagree over the details, it is clearly desirable to phase in a set of substantial deficit reduction measures over the next several years.

This section of the paper discusses the extent to which past and projected deficits reflect a fundamental imbalance between tax and spending policies. Then we explore the reasons for concern over deficits and examine the desired degree of deficit reduction path.

Structural Deficits

Any discussion of the economic consequences of deficits must take account of the rise and fall in economic activity that occurs naturally in the course of the business cycle. Because of the sensitivity of both outlays and revenues to cyclical changes and inflationary trends, even a stable set of tax and spending policies would result in annual changes in the deficit. When economic activity falls off, revenues automatically decline and outlays automatically rise for certain benefit programs, such as unemployment compensation. (Currently, each percentage-point rise in the unemployment rate increases the annual deficit by more than $30 billion.)[11] Thus, deficits reflect, as well as influence, the level of economic activity.

We can adjust for these effects of the economy on the budget by computing the annual federal surplus or deficit that would result if the economy were operating at some standardized level. This approach allows us to isolate the extent to which budget deficits are a result of an underlying imbalance between tax and spending policies, independent of the state of the economy. Year-to-year changes in the standardized deficit measure also indicate the degree of economic stimulus inherent in fiscal policy. The standardized level usually adopted is that associated with high employment, now interpreted as an unemployment rate of about 6 percent. Deficit estimates that are derived using such high-employment assumptions are referred to as "structural deficits."

Over the past two decades, federal structural deficits have consistently ranged below 2 percent of the corresponding standardized GNP level.[12] The

---

11. Congressional Budget Office, *Baseline Budget Projections for Fiscal Years 1985–1989* (Washington, D.C.: GPO, 1984), p. 60.

12. Standardized GNP, when estimated under high-employment conditions, is commonly referred to as potential GNP. Consistent with CBO projections, potential real output is assumed here to grow enough to keep pace with productivity increases and growth in the labor force so as to maintain the unemployment rate at its high-employment level of 6 percent.

notable exception was 1968, when Vietnam war spending pushed the structural deficit to 4 percent of GNP. The highly stimulative fiscal policy reflected by this increased structural deficit during the Vietnam buildup is thought to be primarily responsible for the acceleration of inflation that began in the late 1960s.

In contrast to this historical pattern, the structural deficit is now projected to grow steadily from 3.4 percent of GNP in 1984 to 5.7 percent in 1989, assuming a continuation of current tax and spending policies (table 7). Such deficits would be unprecedented in peacetime. They not only begin at an historically high level but also grow as a percentage of GNP. Before the policy changes made in 1981, such baseline projections always showed movement toward budget surplus, largely because of the increase in revenues associated with bracket creep. However, the scheduled tax reductions enacted through ERTA (including the indexing provisions to be effective in 1985)

TABLE 7

THE STRUCTURAL COMPONENT OF PAST AND PROJECTED FEDERAL DEFICITS
FOR SELECTED YEARS, FY 1961–FY 1989

	Actual					Projected[a]		
	Average							
	1961–1970	1971–1980	1981	1982	1983	1984	1986	1989
	Percentage of GNP[b]							
Total deficit	0.9	2.4	2.7	4.2	6.4	5.9	5.0	5.2
Structural deficit	0.9	1.9	1.2	1.4	2.8	3.4	4.1	5.7
	$ billions							
Total deficit	—	—	79	128	208	203	230	339
Structural deficit	—	—	36	43	97	127	180	312
(Percentage of total)	—	—	(46)	(34)	(47)	(63)	(78)	(92)

SOURCES: Congressional Budget Office, *Baseline Budget Projections for Fiscal Years 1985–1989* (Washington, D.C.: GPO, 1984) and *The Economic Outlook* (Washington, D.C.: GPO, 1984); Office of Management and Budget, "Federal Government Finances," February 1984; and authors' calculations.

NOTE: All estimates include off-budget outlays, which are assumed not to be cyclically sensitive. Structural deficit projections are standardized at a 6 percent unemployment rate.

a. Assumes the continuation of all tax and spending policies enacted through 1983.

b. "Total deficit" estimates are expressed as a percentage of historical or predicted levels of *observed* GNP. "Structural deficit" estimates are expressed as a percentage of *potential* GNP. The reader is cautioned against any interpretation of the difference between the estimated percentages for any given year, because of their differing denominators.

serve to restrain projected revenue growth. In addition, the large increases in real defense spending and interest payments result in faster growth in outlays than has been the case in past budget projections.

It must be emphasized that this projected pattern of structural deficits cannot be significantly altered without changes in federal tax and spending policies. Since the measured structural deficit abstracts from the performance of the economy, the assumption of a stronger recovery from the 1981–1982 recession would have little effect on the projected structural deficit trend.

A stronger recovery might result in a slightly lower projected level of the structural deficit, for two reasons. First, interest outlays would be somewhat lower, since the cyclical component of the total deficit would decline more rapidly. (By convention, structural deficit estimates assume interest outlays to be based on the projected path of the *total* deficit through the preceding year.) Second, the higher rate of inflation that is likely to accompany a faster recovery would shift high-employment revenues upward by more than the upward shift in high-employment outlays, even with indexing in place after 1985. If annual real growth can be sustained at a rate that is 0.5 percentage point above the currently projected trend, the 1989 structural deficit would be reduced from its presently estimated level by about $25 billion, 0.5 percent of potential GNP.

Why Are Deficits Undesirable?

How concerned should we be about such large and growing deficits? Most economists would view as undesirable any large reduction in the deficits immediately confronting us. Through FY 1984, one-third or more of the deficit results from the recent recession. Some degree of fiscal stimulus is desirable to sustain the economic recovery. Unless large deficits prompt the Federal Reserve to significantly tighten monetary policy, the fiscal stimulus provided by such deficits will hasten the economy's return to full employment. However, the recovery will proceed in an unbalanced fashion. Private consumption and government purchases (especially defense) will grow, but the sectors more sensitive to interest rates and the value of the dollar will continue to weaken. High U.S. interest rates tend to support the exchange value of the U.S. dollar, as foreigners seek investments in this country. A strong dollar makes American-produced goods more expensive to foreigners and makes foreign products less expensive to Americans. Such conditions would continue to put at a disadvantage those U.S. companies that rely on export trade or face import competition. Most important, business investment in plants and equipment will suffer, resulting in a smaller capital stock than would otherwise be available to provide for subsequent economic output. (See the paper by Gramlich in this volume for further discussion of the economic consequences of large deficits.)

The adverse effect on private investment seems to be an inevitable consequence of current policies, given the scale of federal borrowing required by the projected budgetary imbalance. The amount of money available for public and private borrowing is determined primarily by the magnitude of net saving in the economy, which, during 1971–1980, averaged 8 percent of GNP (see table 8). Federal deficits absorbed less than one-third of this saving, with the rest available for other net investment (i.e., investment in excess of the amount required to offset capital depreciation). From 1981 to 1983, a lower saving rate and larger deficits led to a rising claim by the federal government on available domestic credit. By 1983 federal borrowing virtually equaled the total supply of domestic credit. Without the funds supplied by foreign sources, little net private investment could have been undertaken.

The Reagan administration had hoped simultaneously to reduce federal borrowing requirements (through a balanced budget) and increase the saving rate (through large business and personal tax cuts). There is little evidence to suggest a saving response. Furthermore, as table 8 demonstrates, the looming federal deficits threaten to reduce substantially the funds available for private investment, even if one projects a rising saving rate. Indeed, current tax and spending policies would leave nonfederal borrowers with domestically available credit that, as a share of GNP, is 3.7 percentage points less in 1989 than in the 1971–1980 decade (1.9 versus 5.6 percent). More than two-thirds of net savings was available to nonfederal borrowers during the 1971–1980 period; under projections of current policies, however, less than one-fourth of savings would be available for such borrowers in 1989. Net inflows of foreign credit might ease the conflict between federal and nonfederal borrowing demands, but a capital infusion sufficient to change this basic picture is highly unlikely. (Net foreign investment may reach 2 percent of GNP in 1984, but this level is unlikely to be sustained through the late 1980s.)

Whether the supply of savings will become a constraining factor depends on business investment plans. As long as capacity utilization is low, businesses have little incentive to increase their capital expenditures. As economic recovery proceeds and production increases, however, businesses will want to expand their capacity. The longer-term deficits are thus much more troublesome than those expected in the next year or so.

What Projected Deficit Path Should Be Sought?

If large deficits should be avoided as the economy nears full employment, but if total elimination of the deficit is neither politically possible nor

TABLE 8

FEDERAL DEFICITS AND NET SAVING FOR SELECTED YEARS, FY 1961–FY 1989

	Actual					Projected[a]		
	Average							
	1961–1970	1971–1980	1981	1982	1983	1984	1986	1989
	$ billions							
Total net domestic saving	56	135	200	206	219	276	346	442
Total federal deficit	6	42	79	128	208	203	230	339
Remaining amount available for other net investment[b]	50	93	121	78	11	73	116	103
	Percentage of GNP							
Total net domestic saving	7.8	8.0	6.9	6.7	6.8	7.7	8.1	8.2
Total federal deficit	0.9	2.4	2.7	4.2	6.4	5.7	5.4	6.3
Remaining amount available for other net investment[b]	6.9	5.6	4.2	2.5	0.4	2.0	2.7	1.9
	Percentage of Total Net Domestic Saving							
Total net domestic saving	100	100	100	100	100	100	100	100
Total federal deficit	11	31	41	60	95	74	66	77
Remaining amount available for other net investment[b]	89	69	59	40	5	26	34	23

SOURCES: Committee on the Budget, House of Representatives, unpublished tabulations; Congressional Budget Office, *Baseline Budget Projections for Fiscal Years 1985–1989* (Washington, D.C.: GPO, 1984); Office of Management and Budget, "Federal Government Finances," February 1984; and authors' calculations.

NOTE: All "total deficit" estimates include off-budget outlays. "Total net domestic saving" is the sum of personal saving, undistributed corporate profits (with inventory valuation and capital consumption adjustments), and state and local government surpluses.

a. Assumes the continuation of all tax and spending policies enacted through 1983.

b. The total amount of credit available for other net investment also includes net inflows of foreign credit, which are not incorporated in these estimates.

economically imperative, how much deficit reduction should be sought? What criteria can be evoked to guide future tax and spending policies?

As much as policymakers might desire a guideline that would yield a specific target level for future deficits, no standard exists. Nevertheless, the economic context of the present deficit dilemma does suggest something about the desired timing and magnitude of future fiscal actions. First, the economy is moving through a recovery from two back-to-back recessions that left real output no higher in 1982 than in 1979. The short-term impact of tax or spending measures—in conjunction with monetary policy—should not be so severe as to endanger this transition. But the structural deficits now projected for the late 1980s would almost certainly worsen the prospects for subsequent economic performance. A budget plan for the remainder of the late 1980s should thus reflect a progression in the impact of deficit reduction measures from a very mild impact in 1985 to increasingly more potent effects in subsequent years.

Although some delay in the impact of deficit reduction measures is thus desirable, the possible impact of inflationary expectations on long-term interest rates, and the importance of such rates in promoting housing construction and business investment, means that credible action should be taken now to allay the inflationary fears in the financial community. Such action might also enable the Federal Reserve to adopt a less restrictive monetary posture than it would otherwise pursue.

As indicated earlier, there is no clear-cut target for a deficit reduction plan commencing in 1985. Any number of alternative rules can be devised that would dictate a structural deficit ranging from zero to more than 2 percent of standardized GNP. In the presence of such uncertainty, a reasonable goal for current policy action would be to reduce the structural deficit to 2 percent of GNP by the end of the 1980s. Although this is an ambitious objective, it would still leave the structural deficit higher as a percentage of GNP than during either the 1960s or the 1970s. Both liberal and conservative observers have advocated such action, or more. Such a lowering of the total deficit would enable a decline in the stock of federal debt as a percentage of GNP, an indicator that has recently begun to rise.

Given that current policies imply a structural deficit of 5.7 percent of GNP by 1989, a deficit of 2 percent of GNP would require deficit reduction measures with 1989 impact amounting to 3.7 percent of potential GNP, or about $200 billion. Because of the savings in net interest outlays that would result from a progressive pattern of smaller deficits throughout the 1985–1989 period, the revenue increases and program spending reductions would have to sum to about $150 billion per year by 1989 (relative to the projections of current policy). This figure provides the basis for the discussion in the next section of alternative deficit reduction strategies.

Strategies to Reduce the Deficit

The choice of a target for the federal deficit requires a balancing of economic concerns, but the design of a deficit reduction scheme to meet such a prescribed target is primarily a political judgment. The appeal of any plan will depend on the importance assigned to limiting the growth of the tax burden, continuing a buildup of the nation's defense capabilities, and maintaining the current level of goods, services, and income support provided through federal domestic programs. The need for trade-offs among these objectives is the essence of the political problem that will continue to confront the president and Congress in seeking to control the deficit. Given the desired magnitude of deficit reduction, the competing alternatives can have dramatic implications for federal tax and spending policies.

The deficit reduction strategies thus far advanced by either President Reagan or the congressional leadership differ considerably with respect to the magnitude and timing of spending restraint and tax increases. The president has insisted that the deficit be reduced largely through further cuts in spending for nondefense programs. Congress has been more willing to consider major tax increases and a scale-back in the growth of the defense budget. However, even the most ambitious proposals fall short of the prescribed structural deficit target of 2 percent of GNP. To achieve this target would probably require further concessions on all three deficit reduction fronts: more defense restraint than the president has thus far been willing to accept; greater nondefense program reductions than Congress has thus far supported; and future tax increases beyond those proposed by either the president or Congress. Legislative compromises are thus necessary if projected deficits are to be substantially reduced, but the political incentives all discourage prompt action of sufficient magnitude. The risk in forestalling action is that the feasible policy options to reduce the deficits over the 1985–1989 period become increasingly limited.

This section first surveys the opportunities and constraints regarding measures to reduce outlays and increase revenues and then assesses the prospects and need for future legislative action.

Opportunities and Prospects for Deficit Reduction

Any plan to reduce the deficit must reckon with political realities and the inexorable dynamics of federal spending and taxes. Part II of this volume deals at length with these issues in the context of the major components of the federal budget: defense (chapter 4), health care financing and pension programs (chapter 5), aid to state and local governments (chapter 6), and taxes (chapter 7). More generally, what are the circumstances that now constrain budget choices? What are some of the specific trade-offs confronting policymakers who seek to control the deficit?

Restraining Nondefense Program Spending. Spending for non-defense programs stood at 15.6 percent of GNP when President Reagan took office and would have declined somewhat by 1989 had there been no changes in the policies he inherited. As a result of budget reductions to date, however, this spending is now projected to decline markedly to 13.3 percent of GNP by 1989. In his 1985 budget, the president proposed further reductions in nondefense program spending that would lower it to 12.4 percent of GNP by 1989.[13] Consistent with the pattern of prior reductions, the president is advocating proportionally much larger cuts in discretionary spending than in the entitlements and other mandatory spending. The largest reductions in discretionary spending would come in benefits and services—such as housing, education, social services, health, employment, and training—intended primarily for the low-income population. This category of programs is the same one that has been most severely cut thus far.

In contrast, the congressional budget resolution for 1984 prescribed no further overall domestic reductions. The resistance in Congress to further reductions in nondefense program spending indicates the political difficulties that lie ahead for any general deficit reduction scheme that attempts to rely substantially on this component of the budget. In particular there is a strong sentiment in Congress (and the general public) that programs serving the low-income population have already borne enough, if not too much, of the burden of spending restraint. Indeed, there is considerable support in Congress for selected *increases* in spending above current policy levels, especially in discretionary benefits and services to individuals—the very area in which the president desires to cut the most.

Projections of current policy illustrate the difficulty of reducing nondefense spending without acting significantly on entitlements and other mandatory spending that make up three-fourths of nondefense program outlays (see table 9). Social Security and Medicare alone constitute nearly one-half of nondefense program spending and, despite the recently enacted legislation reducing their outlay growth, are projected to account for nearly two-thirds of the growth in nondefense program spending over the next five years. Reducing the 1989 structural deficit to the desired level by relying substantially on restraint in nondefense spending, without making large further reductions in Social Security and Medicare, implies drastic reductions in other nondefense programs—well beyond what Congress and the public appear willing to support. The overall contribution of nondefense spending cuts will be marginal at best if limited to modest reductions in the other middle-class entitlement

---

13. Congressional Budget Office, *An Analysis of the President's Budgetary Proposals for Fiscal Year 1985* (Washington, D.C.: GPO, 1984), p. 9.

TABLE 9

PROJECTED GROWTH IN NONDEFENSE PROGRAM OUTLAYS, FY 1984–FY 1989

	Projected Outlays under Current Policy		
	1984	1989	Change
	$ billions		
Entitlements and other mandatory spending	400	570	170
Social Security	173	243	70
Medicare	64	120	56
Other social insurance[a]	80	93	13
Major means-tested programs[b]	61	81	20
Farm price supports	7	18	11
Other[c]	15	16	1
Discretionary spending	156	198	42
Benefits and services to individuals	50	63	13
Infrastructure, research and development	64	76	12
Assistance to business and commerce	8	10	2
Other[d]	34	50	16
Offsetting receipts	−46	−64	−18
Medicare premiums	−5	−8	−3
Other[e]	−41	−56	−15
Off-budget spending	13	13	0
Farm insurance	3	4	1
Other[f]	10	9	−1
TOTAL	523	717	194

SOURCES: Congressional Budget Office, *Baseline Budget Projections for Fiscal Years 1985–1989* (Washington, D.C.: GPO, 1984).

  a. Primarily Civil Service retirement, military retirement, railroad retirement, unemployment compensation, and veterans' benefits.

  b. Aid to Families with Dependent Children, child support enforcement, Food Stamps, Supplemental Security Income, veterans' pensions, Medicaid, guaranteed student loans, and child nutrition.

  c. The largest programs in this category are general revenue sharing and social services.

  d. Includes federal government operations and international assistance.

  e. Includes the rents and royalties from offshore oil operations, the proceeds from sale or lease of other mineral and timber resources, and the receipts from federal agencies of employer contributions for civil service retirement and health benefits.

  f. The largest programs in this category are the strategic petroleum reserve, the Postal Service, and federal credit funds to support rural electrification and foreign military sales.

and mandatory spending programs and the various discretionary programs not targeted on the low-income population. One important entitlement area in which restraint is needed is Medicare, but Congress is unlikely to act soon to avert the large deficits in this program projected for the early 1990s.

Scaling Back the Defense Buildup.   The opportunities to restrain defense outlays are severely limited in the short run by the magnitude of current spending that results from prior years' contracts and obligations. More than one-third of FY 1984's defense outlays flow from previously enacted budget authority. Under the president's FY 1985 budget, with its emphasis on weapons procurement and other long-term military commitments, defense spending would become even less subject to short-term restraint; by 1989, 41 percent of defense outlays would result from prior budget authority.[14]

Any discussion of defense restraint must therefore be cast in terms of a sustained, multiyear reduction in the rate of growth of budget authority enacted by Congress through its annual defense appropriations. The president's plan calls for real growth in defense budget authority at an annual rate of 8 to 10 percent during the 1984–1986 period, with growth diminishing substantially thereafter to less than 3 percent.[15] Current congressional policy now calls for 5 percent annual real growth. Each sustained percentage-point reduction in this growth rate results in annual outlay savings of only $1 billion in the first year, but $14 billion by the fifth year. The impact on the deficit of such congressional action thus comes with a considerable lag. Stated otherwise, any serious attempt to restrain outlays within the next five years must be initiated now. If the real growth in defense budget authority were sustained at 3 percent, rather than the 5 percent now assumed in projections of current policy, the 1989 savings in outlays would be $28 billion (or $41 billion when compared with the administration's request for 1989).

Excluding the costs of military retirement, the defense budget can be divided into military operations (the payroll for active duty civilian and military personnel, plus other operations and maintenance costs) and military investment (procurement of weaponry and equipment, construction of facilities, and research and development). Military operations now constitute one-half of defense outlays. This amount, along with the portion of procurement associated with spare parts, support equipment, and munitions, sustains the readiness of our defense forces. The remaining military investment outlays promote the modernization of our defense capabilities. It is the latter type of spending that is the principal source of growth in the administration's defense budget, projected to nearly double in real terms between 1981 and 1986.

---

14. Ibid., p. 54.
15. Ibid., p. 44. The eventual decline in growth under the president's request does not reflect a reduced commitment to the defense buildup as much as it reflects the practice of including only the budget authority associated with military purchases that can now be explicitly identified. As new weapons systems are developed, the future budget authority requested by the administration presumably would exceed the levels now cited in the president's plan.

It is also politically the most difficult to restrain, requiring that specific weapons purchases be stretched out, scaled back, or simply canceled.

The difficulty of exercising restraint on weapons procurement has led Congress in the past to seek savings through reduced funding for readiness needs. As a long-term strategy, however, this approach can only lead to weaker defense capabilities than could have been purchased otherwise. Personnel would be less well trained and equipped. The physical plant of ships, missiles, aircraft, armored vehicles, and other combat hardware, while perhaps reflecting state-of-the-art technology, would be less well maintained and thus less able to respond when needed.

Although a downward shift from 5 to 3 percent in defense budget growth may appear modest, it will be very difficult to achieve. Of the corresponding $28 billion in 1989 savings, $3 billion could be attained through a 4 percent limit on annual pay increases for defense personnel. It seems prudent to seek the remaining $25 billion primarily through restraint on weapons modernization, rather than a continued weakening of military readiness. Illustrative of the difficulty of achieving such a target, however, is the fact that the savings associated with scaling back or canceling eleven major weapons systems, including limiting the production schedule for the MX missile, would amount to less than $10 billion by 1989.[16] This illustration suggests the need for considerable restraint on both readiness and modernization spending, through purchases of fewer units and greater efficiency in the procurement process. It thus seems unlikely that Congress could achieve defense savings much in excess of those implied by the 3 percent growth trend.

Tax Increases. Even if Congress enacts further cuts in nondefense spending as large in their 1989 impact as those enacted thus far since 1981 ($77 billion), plus restrained annual defense growth of 3 percent (yielding $28 billion in savings), the reduction in 1989 program outlays would still only slightly exceed $100 billion. The political support necessary to achieve this large a reduction in public goods and services, let alone a greater one, is not now evident. Given this difficulty, a target structural deficit of 2 percent of GNP implies that 1989 revenues would have to be increased by at least $50 billion, and perhaps as much as $100 billion. The larger amount of tax increase would raise the 1989 federal tax burden to 20.7 percent of GNP, virtually the same as in 1981. The set of revenue measures to achieve such a tax boost would have to be selected with a host of considerations in mind, including distributional impacts and incentives to work, save, and invest. In

---

16. Congressional Budget Office, *Reducing the Deficit: Spending and Revenue Options* (Washington, D.C.: GPO, 1984), pp. 25–37.

addition, pragmatic political judgments may suggest that some alternatives are simply infeasible.

The potential need for such large future revenue increases has led to consideration of major structural reforms to the federal tax system that would broaden the tax base, relate tax liabilities more to consumption than to income or wealth, and simplify the schedule of tax rates. Such proposals include replacing the current individual income tax with a flat-rate income tax or a broad-based consumption tax, or imposing a new national sales tax (or value-added tax). Most flat-rate options would maintain some progressivity in individual tax rates but would enable lower marginal rates by repealing virtually all itemized deductions and exclusions. A consumption tax would make individual tax liabilities a function of personal expenditures, calculated as the difference between income and savings. Likewise, a value-added tax would discourage consumption and encourage savings, since the tax would be passed along to consumers through price increases.

Such wholesale tax reforms offer the prospect of higher revenues, improved economic incentives, and some simplification of the tax system, but they raise serious political, administrative, and distributional problems. With no apparent groundswell of public support or bipartisan backing to counter the expected opposition from a multitude of adversely affected groups, these reform strategies do not appear to offer significant potential for additional revenues within the five-year time frame discussed here.

If the necessary increases in revenue are not likely to come through sweeping tax changes, what revisions to the existing tax code might be enacted? It seems inevitable that a series of different revenue measures ultimately will be required, spreading the burden of additional taxes broadly across individuals and businesses. Such changes will most likely take the form of some increase in individual or corporate income tax rates, some broadening of the taxable base for both personal and business-related income, and some higher excise taxes, especially on energy. (See table 10 for some examples.) There is no politically feasible small set of tax increases that would yield a total annual revenue gain as large as $100 billion by 1989. For example, the tax measures that President Reagan conditionally supported in early 1983, a surtax of 5 percent on personal and corporate income tax liabilities in combination with a $5 per barrel oil excise tax, would yield about $50 billion in 1989. Thus an additional $50 billion would have to be raised through other means, such as a variety of base-broadening measures, each of which would face vigorous interest-group opposition.

There would be strong political resistance to near-term increases in Social Security taxes, because the recently enacted reforms included an acceleration of scheduled payroll tax increases in addition to other financing measures. The Medicare trust fund, however, will be bankrupt by the early 1990s if

TABLE 10

ILLUSTRATIVE INCREASES IN FY 1989 REVENUES

	Projected 1989 Revenues Under Current Policy	Estimated Increase in 1989 Revenues
	$ billions	
Individual Income Taxes	478	
Rate increases—		
Limit indexing adjustments[a]		24
Impose 10 percent surtax (on tax liability)		48
Repeal indexing		65
Base-broadening measures—		
Eliminate income averaging		7
Eliminate deductibility of state and local sales tax		8
Tax accrued interest on life insurance reserves		8
Tax some employer-paid health insurance[b]		8
Increase taxation of entitlement benefits[c]		11
Corporate Income Taxes	85	
Rate increases—		
Impose 10 percent surtax (on tax liability)		9
Repeal reduced rates on first $100,000		10
Base-broadening measures—		
Lengthen building depreciation period from 15 to 20 years		5
Require full basis adjustment for investment tax credit		6
Social Insurance Taxes	382	
Increase the Hospital Insurance payroll tax rate by 0.5 percentage point		22
Excise Taxes	33	
Double the excise taxes on alcohol and cigarettes		6
Impose an excise tax on domestic and imported oil ($2 per barrel)		9
Impose a broad-based tax on domestic energy (5 percent of value)		20

TABLE 10 (continued)

	Projected 1989 Revenues Under Current Policy	Estimated Increase in 1989 Revenues
Other Measures		
Eliminate tax-exempt revenue bonds		5
Restrict tax-motivated leasing by nonprofit institutions		5
Increase audit coverage and extend withholding[d]		11

SOURCES: Congressional Budget Office, *Reducing the Deficit: Spending and Revenue Options* (Washington, D.C.: GPO, 1984); and Congressional Budget Office, *An Analysis of the President's Budgetary Proposals for Fiscal Year 1985* (Washington, D.C.: GPO, 1984).

a. Limit adjustments to reflect increases in the consumer price index minus two percentage points.

b. Assumes taxation of monthly employer contributions exceeding $200 for family coverage and $80 for individual coverage. Estimated revenue gain includes $2 billion increase in payroll taxes.

c. Assumes taxation of 50 percent of Social Security benefits and Tier I Railroad Retirement benefits, and full taxation of unemployment and workers' compensation.

d. Estimated revenue gain is net of additional administrative outlays. Assumes increase in percentage of returns audited and extended withholding requirements for interest and dividends, royalties, and contractors.

steps are not taken to further restrain its growth in benefits and raise its revenues. Thus, it would be prudent for some portion of the tax increases between now and 1989 to be related to this program.

The particular selection of revenue-raising measures must strike a balance between policy objectives that often conflict, even in the context of particular proposals: surtaxes may be distributionally neutral, but they necessarily raise marginal tax rates and thus discourage work and saving; excise taxes on energy or other goods serve to encourage saving, but typically fall most heavily on the low-income population. While base-broadening proposals provoke strong interest-group opposition, they would not increase marginal tax rates and would remove the preferential treatment now accorded on questionable grounds to particular forms of economic activity. Just as direct outlay programs have been subject to close scrutiny in the search for spending restraint, so should the tax expenditures that we incur through such limitations to taxable income. These special subsidies are much less defensible in light of the compelling national interests at stake in the search for additional revenue.

A Concluding Assessment

Although few people would dispute that a phased reduction in the federal deficit would enhance the long-term prospects for the U.S. economy, there is no consensus about how to reduce the deficit. In seeking tax increases or spending cuts, politicians must ask voters to accept personal economic sacrifices when the presumed long-term gains for the national economy have uncertain consequences for any particular constituency. Without concerted bipartisan action between the president and Congress, any officials wishing to exercise fiscal statemanship must accept great risk to their own political future.

Under these circumstances, it is tempting for politicians to view the deficit as an issue that will go away under a strong economy. Unfortunately, any upward revisions in the strength of the anticipated recovery from the 1981–1982 recession will only slightly reduce the need for deliberate policy action. Present tax and spending policies embody so large a structural disparity between revenues and outlays that even if we assume that the economy could speedily achieve its high-employment potential, the deficit would remain well above any peacetime precedent.

Although economic concerns do not suggest the need for major immediate reductions in the projected deficit, the legislative measures necessary to achieve a progressive pattern of deficit reduction should be taken soon for several reasons. First, structural reforms to mandatory spending programs or the tax system usually must be phased in gradually in order to be politically acceptable and in order not to abruptly alter the economic conditions facing individuals and firms. This is especially true of base-broadening tax proposals, which provoke intense opposition from adversely affected interest groups. Second, defense spending has a built-in momentum through previous contractual commitments for weapons procurement. If future outlays are to be reduced, decisions must be made now about which weapons purchases should be stretched out or canceled. If these decisions are not made now and if Congress later seeks prompt reductions in defense outlays, the only recourse will be to weaken the readiness of our existing military forces through reductions in spending for operations and maintenance. Such trade-offs between military readiness and modernization tend to weaken defense capabilities more than an orderly scale-back in some combination of these expenditures. Finally, any limit to the inflationary adjustments in either entitlement or discretionary domestic spending programs will yield appreciable savings only if sustained over several years.

What do these observations on the timing of legislative action and budgetary impacts suggest about a particular five-year scheme of deficit reduction measures? In view of the fact that a prudent objective would be to enact explicit measures yielding at least $150 billion in deficit reduction by 1989, the political constraints and budgetary dynamics imply that a mix of measures to increase taxes and reduce spending will be necessary. The limited prospects for spending restraint mean that two-thirds or more of the $150 billion may have to come through higher revenues. The need to rely so heavily on tax increases is heightened if no significant further action is taken to restrain outlay growth in Social Security and Medicare. Any other strategy implies drastic reductions in other nondefense programs.

To outline a deficit reduction plan more specifically would require more detailed policy judgments, with the following considerations in mind.

- To the extent that tax increases are to occur, the equity and efficiency of our present tax system seem best preserved by relying as much as possible on base-broadening measures rather than tax rate increases.

- To the extent that defense outlays are to be restrained, it can be argued that our defense capabilities are best preserved through scaling back future weapons purchases rather than through reducing the commitment to current readiness.

- To the extent that the growth in domestic spending is cut, middle-class entitlements will need to be scrutinized.

Since tax increases and spending reductions impose collective sacrifices on the American public, with some groups inevitably being affected more adversely than others, the policy judgments are appropriately political ones. As the foregoing discussion suggests, the choices are indeed difficult and will sorely test the political courage of our elected officials. The abiding economic interests require that the president and members of Congress resist the temptation to take political advantage of people who step forward to support fiscally responsible, but politically unpopular, budgetary policies.

HOW BAD ARE THE LARGE DEFICITS?

Edward M. Gramlich

Perhaps the one thing that economists of all stripes can agree on is that the large "out-year" budget deficits now being forecast are alarming. These deficits have been blamed for high real interest rates, and they are said to impede economic recovery and reduce capital formation by crowding out investment. Fear of the deficits sometimes rises to such heights that apparently inconsistent actions are recommended. The president, for example, has been known to criticize people who do not want to cut government spending on grounds that their unwillingness to cooperate on this matter keeps deficits high and hurts the recovery, even though the spending cuts themselves would seem to hurt the recovery more. Democratic members of Congress have been known to propose tax increases in order to reduce deficits and stimulate the economy, even though tax increases themselves should hurt the economy.

When so many people are opposed to deficits, there must be some very good reasons, but these reasons are rarely stated explicitly. The usual statement— whether from liberals or conservatives, from people who support the administration or oppose it—is merely to invoke some platitude about how deficits hurt prospects for recovery. In this paper I try to go beyond the platitudes to ask the question of exactly why these out-year deficits seem to be so dangerous. Are there sound economic reasons for opposing these large deficits, or do they represent bandwagon hysteria? I find some good reasons for opposing the deficits, but the logical and empirical basis for opposition to the large deficits seems to differ from the more commonly heard arguments against the deficits.

The first section of the paper is basically factual. In it I assume that the path now being forecast for the current services budget, a path implying large out-year deficits, will come to pass—a debatable proposition because there is an outside chance that the administration and Congress may actually correct the deficits (although I make no pretense at political forecasting in the paper). I then ask how large these deficits really are when compared with those in the 1970s, with all numbers appropriately scaled by gross national product (GNP) and purged of cyclical effects. The latter adjustment focuses the discussion on what are now called the "structural" deficits; these deficits exist apart from cyclical swings in the budget resulting from its automatic stabilizers, and most economists feel these deficits more accurately reflect the impact of the budget on the economy. Even with all these, and other, adjustments, the conclusion of this section of the paper is that the deficits now being forecast for the latter part of the 1980s will indeed, if realized, represent a very sharp change from previous experience.

The next section of the paper analyzes the economic significance of these deficits. Because so many arguments have been made against the deficits, some discrimination is necessary. There are some convincing reasons and some not-so-convincing reasons for opposing deficits, and I try to sort them out. I believe there is one good reason for opposing federal deficits: higher deficits represent increased "dissaving" by the government. Unless offset by a corresponding increase in private saving, this increased governmental dissaving will lead to a large reduction in the share of total output devoted to capital formation in the United States in the long run. This impact of the deficits is analyzed later in the paper. A number of other reasons for opposing deficits have been advanced: Deficits may impede economic recovery, deficits may attract too much capital from abroad, and deficits may cause excessive money creation and inflation. I consider each of these reasons and discuss why each is either incorrect, is less convincing than the primary reason, or why it augments the primary reason.

The third section of the paper returns to what I consider to be the central reason for opposing deficits: in the long run they reduce the share of output devoted to capital formation. Before we can conclude that such a reduction is undesirable, we must obviously establish that the United States now devotes too few resources to capital formation. I give three ways of making a judgment about the extent of capital formation. The conclusion from all perspectives is that the United States appears to be undersaving to a significant degree: This conclusion implies that the large increase in dissaving indicated by the out-year budget deficits is, in the long run, a step in the wrong direction.

The final section of the paper inquires about the length of that run: Even if the out-year deficits reduce aggregate capital formation in some very long run, perhaps living standards will be higher for some medium horizon. I try to measure the length of this horizon with a simple simulation model, described in the appendix of the paper. This section contains the rather surprising finding that this horizon will be very long indeed.

How Large Are the Out-Year Deficits?

Recent forecasts suggest that the out-year budget deficits will approach $250 billion by 1988 under what is known as the current services budget, the budget that would obtain under currently enacted tax and expenditure laws. Of course, $250 billion is a large number, more than 1.25 times as large as the 1983 deficit of $195 billion, itself almost twice as high as the 1982 deficit, which in turn was almost twice as high as any other in the entire post-World War II period. The simple, uncorrected numbers are indeed striking.

But as almost everybody knows, one cannot make time series comparisons of budget deficits without making a set of adjustments to eliminate time-related distortions. (In constructing an adjusted time series, I have used budget data on a national income accounts basis, by calendar year, as is normal when making the relevant adjustments.) The first of such adjustments is to correct for rising prices, population, and per capita incomes by expressing all budget deficits and surpluses as a share of GNP. The second adjustment, a fixture in budget reports for almost twenty years now, is to eliminate cyclical movements in the budget by computing revenues and expenditures at a standard high-employment level of GNP. The latter adjustment produces a time series for a variable that used to be called the full-employment budget surplus or deficit and is now called the "structural" budget surplus or deficit. Why the name was changed is not obvious, but the series and its meaning remain the same. To make these calculations, one must choose an unemployment rate, and I have followed the Congressional Budget Office (CBO) in using an unemployment rate of 6 percent to estimate the annual structural deficit over the nineteen-year period from 1970 to 1988. As with the name of the series, this choice of unemployment rate has absolutely no normative or policy significance; it is only a way to standardize budget deficits.

The third adjustment is somewhat less standard, but seemingly noncontroversial. Inflation erodes the nominal value of the outstanding government debt and forces lenders to insist on higher nominal rates of interest to hold this debt. As nominal interest rates rise, nominal interest payments in the government's budget also rise, despite the fact that the difference between nominal and real interest payments is in no way an income gain or loss for the private sector (like everything else in the national income accounts budget), but simply an adjustment for the uncounted capital gains of the government on its outstanding debt. This difference between the nominal and the real level of interest payments should be deducted to put the deficit on a true inflation-accounted basis.[1]

---

1. A careful analysis of this question, including an attempt to adjust also for the capital gains and losses implicit in changes in real interest rates, is given by Robert Eisner and Paul J. Pieper, "A New View of the Federal Debt and Budget Deficits," *American Economic Review*, vol. 74 (March 1984), pp. 11–29.

The relevant deficit numbers, on a high-employment basis and as a share of potential GNP, are given in table 1. These deficits under the current services budget are shown with and without the nominal interest correction, so the importance of the correction can be assessed. Whatever adjustments are made, the forecast out-year deficits represent a sharp change from previous experience. Over the 1970–1981 period the high-employment deficit uncorrected for nominal interest averaged 1.1 percent of potential GNP: By 1987 it is forecast to be 4.0 percent of potential GNP, a difference of 2.9 percent of potential GNP. When corrected for nominal interest, both deficits are reduced, but the change between the 1970s and 1987 is still 2.2 percent. However we look at the numbers, the change is dramatic.

TABLE 1

STRUCTURAL BUDGET SURPLUS (+) OR DEFICIT (−), CALENDAR YEARS 1970–1987

Year	Uncorrected for Nominal Interest	Corrected for Nominal Interest
	Percentage of High-Employment GNP	
1970	−0.9	0.1
1971	−1.5	−0.1
1972	−1.5	−0.6
1973	−1.1	0.1
1974	−0.5	0.7
1975	−2.2	−1.0
1976	−1.4	−0.2
1977	−1.5	−0.2
1978	−1.2	0.3
1979	−0.5	1.1
1980	−1.1	0.5
1981	−0.3	1.2
1982	−1.3	0
1983	−1.9	−0.6
1984	−2.7	−1.6
1985	−3.1	−1.5
1986	−3.6	−1.9
1987	−4.0	−2.0
Average, 1970–1981	−1.1	0.2
Difference (between 1987 estimate and 1970–1981 average)	−2.9	−2.2

SOURCE:　Author's calculations based on published projections of the Congressional Budget Office.

NOTE:　All figures are by calendar year on a national income accounts basis. Data through 1982 are based on actual budget totals. Estimates for subsequent years are computed on a current services basis, reflecting federal policies in place as of January 1983.

At least three factual matters must be considered before completing the description of government fiscal policy implicit in these forecast structural deficits. The first is that since the federal government does not keep a capital budget, it is at least possible that these deficits are being used to finance increased public capital formation. If so, the rise in the deficit would have a much different interpretation: overall national capital formation rates would not be altered, but the share financed publicly would be. Whether this would be a desirable change or not turns out to be moot, because the anticipated rise in the structural deficits definitely does not reflect a rise in public capital formation. Under the most generous set of assumptions, the share of GNP devoted to federal government capital formation would show a rise of less than 0.4 percent between the 1970s and mid-1980s. Physical investment in defense is slated to rise, but that rise is offset by drops in the share of potential GNP devoted to federal civilian capital formation and grants to state and local governments for their capital formation. Even this defense investment, while it has the physical appearance of capital, may not be so in some underlying economic sense because its rate of technological obsolescence is high. Hence the public capital formation offset to the fall in the overall national capital formation share of GNP should eliminate at most one-fifth of the apparent change.

A second point is that even though I confine attention in this paper to the structural deficit forecast through 1987, there is a form of intertemporal multiplier operating here that makes the true long-term deficit prognosis even more alarming. Because interest payments on the accumulated stock of government debt are themselves one component of government spending, a high level of deficits incurred now builds in high future interest burdens and makes it harder for budget makers in the twenty-first century to control their deficits. Large deficits, once incurred, become increasingly difficult to eliminate.[2]

A final cautionary point is that this analysis concerns only the deficits in the national income accounts budget. The government conducts many other transactions with its citizens that raise or lower the consumption possibilities

---

2. To see how this works, let D refer to the outstanding stock of government debt, E to current (non-interest) expenditures, T to taxes, and r to the real interest rate on this (debt-ignoring inflation and money growth in this simple example). The government deficit, or change in the stock of public debt, dD, in any period is given by the identity

$$dD = E - T + rD.$$

Dividing through by D, we see that if E is equal to T, not far from being true in the federal budget for FY 1982, the rate of growth of the debt will equal just r, the real interest rate. Should r happen to exceed the real growth rate of the economy, a proposition for which there is some evidence (to be discussed below), this means that government consumption, the debt, and the deficit will all rise steadily as a share of GNP. The only way to stop the trend is to raise non-interest government saving (T − E) until the debt and deficit stop growing as a share of GNP.

of citizens living at different historical times. As one example, an unfunded Social Security system generates rises and falls in the implied rate of return realized on the pension contributions of participants of every age. Moreover, changes in pension tax rates, retirement ages, and the like can dwarf the long-term impacts of budget changes of the sort discussed here, even though these pension rules are nowhere reflected in the government's budget surplus.[3] My analysis will not get into a full-scale evaluation of all of the fiscal actions taken that have intergenerational implications, but it should be understood that focusing on just the budget deficits may give a misleading impression of the overall impact of present-day policies on future national consumption possibilities.

Why Are the Deficits So Bad?

There are any number of reasons for opposing deficits, not all of which are persuasive. In this section I try to separate the wheat from the chaff.

The most convincing reason for fearing deficits can be simply stated. Deficits represent governmental dissaving, and unless offset by increases in private saving or capital imports from abroad, deficits imply a lower proportion of output devoted to capital formation. This situation in turn implies reduced long-term growth in the supply of capital, and hence in future output and consumption levels. This is exactly the type of "supply side" effect economists worried about back in the nineteenth century.

With anything as complicated as fiscal policy, one cannot just leave things at this point. The first question that arises is whether these deficits will, in fact, be offset by private saving or capital imports. A second issue, deferred until the next section, is whether any resulting reductions in the overall share of output devoted to capital formation are desirable or undesirable.

There are three separate reasons for thinking that government dissaving will call forth at least some private saving. First, government dissaving raises the real interest rate; as a result, private households are encouraged to save more. There is little controversy about the qualitative reasoning but much controversy about how large the impact is. For now, I just leave it that in my own quantitative analysis of the impact of rising structural deficits later

---

3. An argument along these lines is made by Alan J. Auerbach and Laurence J. Kotlikoff, "Investment versus Savings Incentives: The Size of the Bang for the Buck and the Potential for Self-financing Business Tax Cuts," forthcoming in *The Economic Consequences of Government Deficits*, proceedings of a symposium at Washington University, October 1982.

in the paper, I have accounted for this interest rate offset, using mid-range estimates of its quantitative importance.

A second offset is more fundamental. Robert Barro has worked out the implications of a model under which far-sighted households are so bothered by the reduction in their children's living standards implied by today's deficits and drop in capital formation that they save more on their own to neutralize the government's action.[4] A number of questions can be raised about the plausibility of Barro's assumption: Are average households aware of the forecast level of deficits? Do households believe politicians will let the deficits happen? Can households compute their share of the government's implied future tax liabilities? Is it realistic to expect households to save for their grandchildren, particularly if they distrust the saving propensities of their children? The weight of the evidence seems to go against Barro's assumption, but should there be some truth to the argument, any positive or negative impacts of the change in deficit should be understood to overstate the true impact.[5]

A third offset is suggested by the new interest in open-economy macro models. A standard assumption in these models is that international capital movements are highly sensitive to real interest rate differentials in various countries. Were the United States to devote a lower share of its output to capital formation and drive up its own real interest rate, there would be some attraction of capital from abroad, the amount depending on the substitutability of international assets and the permanence depending on the dynamic assumptions (essentially whether the underlying model involves stocks or a steady flow of new savings to be invested or disinvested each year). But this "replacement" capital does not replace the national wealth not being generated, and does not forestall the drop in future national *income* and consumption levels.

Hence for larger deficits to have no long-term impact on U.S. welfare, the private saving offsets would have to fully counter the government's shift toward higher dissaving. Given the uncertainty of this offset, the adverse impact on long-term capital accumulation then appears to be one important and appropriate reason for opposing deficits.

A number of other reasons have also been suggested. By all odds the most widely debated involves the short-run impact of the deficits—do they

---

4. Robert J. Barro, "Are Government Bonds Net Wealth?" *Journal of Political Economy*, vol. 82 (November/December 1974), pp. 1095–1117.

5. See Martin S. Feldstein, "Government Deficits and Aggregate Demand," *Journal of Monetary Economics*, vol. 9 (January 1982), pp. 1–20, for a case against the Barro assumption. Some more recent contributions do question Feldstein's conclusions.

impede the economic recovery from the 1981–1982 recession? A typical statement is that there should be a recovery unless it is choked off by the high interest rates generated by expected future government borrowing. The implication is that measures to reduce expected future structural deficits will raise aggregate demand and boost the odds of a vigorous recovery.

This argument has several defects. The most basic is that the structural deficits envisaged here are expected to last for a long time, as much as a decade. Most economists now believe, most macroeconometric models predict, and most macro textbooks teach that over horizons this long, the natural stabilizing tendencies of the economy should assert themselves and the economy should move to a position of balance between aggregate demand and aggregate supply at high employment. If this is so, the level of deficits, and ultimately the question of how much the nation is saving and investing, are really concerns of long-term aggregate supply economics, as posed earlier. They are not concerns of short-term aggregate demand management involving the strength of the economic recovery for the next few quarters.

Some readers may be unpersuaded by this economist's dichotomy between short-term movements in aggregate demand and long-term movements in aggregate supply. But even if only the short-term movements in aggregate demand are considered, the argument is unconvincing precisely because there are so many conflicting political-macroeconomic theories of how the deficits will affect the level of aggregate demand.

To begin with what most observers still take as the basic case, consider the impact of structural deficits in the normal Keynesian type of analysis relied on by most macro textbooks. In this model it is certainly true that high real interest rates reduce demand and harm chances for a recovery, but the same cannot be said of deficits. The standard view is that structural deficits, or expansionary fiscal policies, raise *both* aggregate demand and real interest rates. One can hardly criticize the interest rate impact of deficits and forget about the income impact. And the analyst who operates under this standard view then must admit that if the structural deficits do anything to aggregate demand, they will raise it and *help* the recovery.

Obviously there are several reasons why this standard view may not be correct. A first is the monetarist argument that expansionary fiscal policy gets completely crowded out by the interest rate effect. The conditions for that view to be correct are quite stringent, but even if fulfilled, that view does not support the argument that deficits impede the recovery. It says only that structural deficits are irrelevant to the recovery, essentially the position I am arguing for different reasons. A second is the open-economy view discussed earlier—that high deficits raise interest rates and attract capital from abroad, thus raising the dollar and reducing net exports. The result is again that fiscal multipliers are weak and perhaps zero. If so, deficits are again irrelevant, not harmful, to the recovery.

There is only one way in which the out-year deficits could hurt the recovery, but it takes a strong set of assumptions to believe in it. The argument is that *expected* deficits generate expectations of interest rate increases, and these expectations drive up interest rates and lower capital investment now. The argument again seems to forget the income effect. If bond traders and capital investors expect interest rate increases, why do consumers and capital investors not expect income and sales increases due to planned expansionary fiscal policy? The only explanation for the apparent inconsistency would be that the forecasters envisage income changes to be completely crowded out by the interest rate increases within the relevant forecasting horizon. If this is what "the market" believes, everything does hold together, but I am not aware of any articulation of the underlying model or any supporting empirical evidence.

A different type of argument is that structural deficits are unwise precisely because they do attract capital from other countries, capital that is needed more abroad than here. As with the short-term argument, one cannot evaluate this claim without specifying a set of assumptions and an expected chain of events. The standard textbook view is based on what is known as the small-country assumption, that the United States capital market is too small to influence world real interest rates. If so, the U.S. deficits are simply not harmful to the rest of the world. The deficits imply that the U.S. capital market is willing to pay a higher rate of return on foreign savings than would otherwise be the case. Hence foreigners can raise their income and standard of living by investing here. That appears to be a clear net benefit to the rest of the world so long as the world real interest rate does not rise—that is, so long as foreign debtors are not made worse off by the U.S. capital imports.

But if, as seems likely, the high U.S. real interest rate does provide investment opportunities on a scale large enough to reduce the supply of world capital and pull up the world real interest rate, the situation becomes more complicated. Now the U.S. deficits crowd out world capital formation, and since world incomes are generally below U.S. incomes, that lost capital does have a high social value (higher than the crowded-out capital in the United States). In this case one should indeed oppose deficits more than in the closed-economy case. International crowding out adds to the seriousness of the problem.

A final argument that also may add to its seriousness involves the financing of these deficits. Government deficits do have to be financed, either by the Federal Reserve's creation of money or by the sale of government securities. If the deficits are financed by sale of securities, the arguments are the same as before: structural deficits will raise real interest rates, crowd out capital formation, and lower living standards in the long run. But if the deficits are financed by the creation of money, a new danger is added because the deficits might then generate higher rates of inflation. Fortunately, however, if the Federal Reserve does not want this added complication to occur, it has the legal authority to prevent it.

This journey through macroeconomics points up the fact that, in essence, deficits harm capital formation, which in turn harms output and in the long run, consumption. There may be complicating factors involving short-run dynamics, but these are as likely to be favorable as unfavorable. There will be complicating factors because capital markets are now sensitive to world interest rate differentials, if this world interest rate is influenced by U.S. deficits. There may also be complicating factors involving added money creation, although these can be prevented. Our fear of structural deficits should then be at least as great as our fear of them in a standard long-term closed-economy view of the world.

Is the United States Now Undersaving?

The first section of the paper established that the forecast current services deficits, if they come to pass, seem likely to reduce the share of aggregate output devoted to capital formation by two to three percentage points. The second section established that most fears about deficits do at bottom boil down to this implied, and feared, reduction in national capital formation. The next step is to ask whether this reduction in capital formation represents a step in the right or the wrong direction. Ultimately, the question becomes whether the United States is now under- or oversaving.

On a philosophical level, there is no good way to answer this question. The capital formation issue involves a trading of consumption possibilities between the present and the future, with most of the future people not yet born and hence not able to vote on an issue fundamental to their welfare. The only way the question could be phrased is in Rawlsian terms; that is, could society agree on intergenerationally neutral saving policies if the voting members in today's generation pretended that they operated under a Rawlsian "veil of ignorance" about when they would live, and hence acted "fairly" as regards intergenerational choices.[6]

When the saving issue is posed in such a manner, the optimal level of saving is that implied by the so-called Golden Rule of capital accumulation,

---

6. See John Rawls, *A Theory of Justice* (Cambridge: Harvard University Press, 1971).

generally associated with the writing of Edmund Phelps. This rule establishes the level of saving that will maximize the society's continued standard of living. Phelps and others have shown that there are two ways to determine whether a society is undersaving. If the society chooses a constant saving rate (any rate that steadily increases or decreases would end up at one or zero eventually), that saving rate should be such that the real interest rate (or marginal product of capital) should equal the long-term growth rate of real GNP (sometimes raised slightly to allow for rising living standards and time preference).[7] If the real interest rate exceeds this growth rate, a society is undersaving. Alternatively, the share of saving in net national product (NNP) should equal the percentage share of returns to capital in NNP (sometimes lowered slightly to allow for rising living standards and time preference). If the share of saving falls short of the share of returns to capital, a society is undersaving.

In the world of abstract models, these two conditions are identical.[8] But in the real world, where none of the relevant concepts can be precisely

---

7. The precise condition is that the real interest rate (or marginal product of capital) should equal $m + \alpha\gamma + \rho$, where m is the rate of growth of the labor force, γ is the rate of growth of labor-augmenting technical progress, $-\alpha$ is the elasticity of marginal utility with respect to per capita consumption growth, and ρ is the rate of time preference. In the United States, m has averaged about 2.3 percent for the past decade, γ is about 0.4 percent, α is often said to be about 1.5, and ρ should probably be assumed to be close to zero for long-term analysis. The right side then is only slightly in excess of the 2.5 percent rate of growth of real income assumed for most of the paper. In future calculations, I will make the simplifying assumption that the right-hand side is just equal to 2.5 percent, but it should be understood that if technological progress or positive time preference were taken into account, the case to be made for undersaving would not be so strong.

8. This proof goes as follows. If y equals the level of output (actually, net national product) per worker, k equals the capital stock per worker, n equals the fixed growth rate of the work force (adjusted for technological progress, as in note 7), and s equals the fixed aggregate saving share of y, the growth equilibrium solution for a closed economy is that

(1) $$sy = nk$$

or that the actual accumulation of capital is exactly sufficient to stabilize the capital-labor ratio in this economy. At this equilibrium solution, total output, capital, labor, and consumption all expand at rate n.

Suppose then that production in this economy can be represented by

(2) $$y = f(k).$$

Where $f'(k) = r > 0$ and $f''(k) < 0$. The Golden Rule solution comes simply from maximizing the level of per capita consumption in any generation, $y - nk$, with respect to the capital stock, or

(3) $$f'(k) = r = n$$

implying that the marginal product of capital equals the economy's growth rate. An economy that is undersaving in this sense will be characterized by $r > n$; one that is oversaving will have measured, it seems safer to make the test for undersaving with both standards. Indeed, because neither standard is completely reliable, I suggest a third way to making the test, more *ad hoc* than the other two: simply compare our rate of net capital formation with that of some other developed economies.

To begin with the interest rate test, table 2 presents four comparisons over the 1970–1982 period. The standard way to estimate the marginal product of capital is simply to assume that firms are buying real equipment until its marginal product equals the appropriate real interest rate. To measure the latter, I have first used the Aaa corporate rate, as if investment were relatively riskless, and subtracted from it a measure of expected inflation (the average rate over the previous three years). As an alternative, I recalculated using the Baa corporate rate, as if firms on average faced more risk. Both these measures show a sharp rise in the last two years, the conventional explanation for which is that bond markets are now anticipating the out-year deficits. Before this upward movement, the Aaa real interest rate averaged 2.1 percent, below the 2.7 percent rate of growth over the period. The Baa rate averaged 3.3 percent, above the growth rate. Using this conventional measure, it would be difficult to say whether the United States was under- or oversaving during the past decade. Perhaps the weak verdict would be in favor of undersaving because most firms probably borrow at the margin at the Baa rate.

But these conventional calculations make one important assumption. In equating the marginal product of capital to the real interest rate, they implicitly

---

$r < n$. From (3) we can establish that capital's share of output, a, is equal to rk/y. This expression can be used to replace r in (3), and equation (1) can be used to replace n, arriving at another way to put the Golden Rule condition

$$(4) \hspace{4cm} a = s^*$$

where s^* is now the Golden Rule saving rate. An economy that is undersaving is characterized by capital's share of output being larger than the share of output devoted to capital formation; an economy that is oversaving, by the reverse.

Were time preference or a greater rate of technological progress added, as in note 7, the appropriate Golden Rule r should be slightly greater than n and the appropriate savings rate s^* slightly less than a. As is argued in note 7, these adjustments are quite unlikely to be large enough to make a pragmatic difference.

The math becomes more complicated in the open-economy case, but the social value of increasing the domestic saving rate is not lessened. If international capital markets are perfect, the U. S. real interest rate is fixed at the world real rate, and the amount of capital located in this country is set by this condition. But the United States can still save more than is necessary to maintain this capital intensity, and accumulate claims on the rest of the world. If the nation were undersaving at the initial capital intensity in a closed economy, there would be an even greater incentive to increase the saving rate in an open economy because the foreign investments would pay a higher real rate of return.

The original citation for most of this is Edmund Phelps, "The Golden Rule of Accumulation: A Fable for Growthmen," *American Economic Review*, vol. 51 (September 1961), pp. 638–43.

TABLE 2

MEASURES OF THE MARGINAL PRODUCT OF CAPITAL, 1970–1982

	Real Interest Rate[a]		*Real Rate of Return*[b]	
	Aaa Corporate Bonds	*Baa Corporate Bonds*	*Producer's Equipment*	*Producer's Structures*
	Percentage Points			
1970	3.0	4.1	7.0	8.5
1971	2.3	3.5	7.0	8.5
1972	2.3	3.3	7.0	8.5
1973	2.4	3.2	7.0	8.5
1974	2.3	3.2	7.0	8.5
1975	0.9	2.5	6.7	8.8
1976	0.6	2.0	6.7	8.8
1977	1.2	2.2	6.7	8.8
1978	2.6	3.4	6.7	8.8
1979	2.3	3.4	6.7	8.8
1980	3.5	5.3	6.7	8.8
1981	5.1	6.9	3.5	6.4
1982	5.6	7.9	3.2	6.2
Average, 1970–1980	2.1	3.3	6.8	8.7
Average, 1981–1982	5.4	7.4	3.4	6.3

SOURCE: U.S. Council of Economic Advisers, *Economic Report of the President*, 1982 and 1983 issues; and Alan J. Auerbach and Dale W. Jorgenson, "Inflation-Proof Depreciation of Assets," *Harvard Business Review* (September/October 1980), pp. 113–18.

a. Using the average change in the GNP deflator over the previous three years as the measure of expected inflation.

b. Before-tax real rate of return necessary to earn an after-tax real rate of return of 4 percent.

assume that the tax treatment of physical investment is neutral, so that taxes can be ignored. But the tax treatment of physical investment clearly is not neutral. Until the recently passed Economic Recovery and Tax Act (ERTA), various nonneutralities penalized capital investment. (That is, the required before-tax rate of return exceeded the after-tax rate of return.)

Since ERTA's enactment, the tax system has subsidized investment in producer's equipment and penalized investment in producer's structures. Another way to measure the marginal product of capital, then, is to take the before-tax real rate of return, essentially the marginal product of capital, necessary to give some standard real after-tax return that could have been earned on equities. The two right-hand columns in table 2 present such numbers both for equipment and structures, using an after-tax real return of 4 percent.[9] These numbers average between 7 and 9 percent throughout the 1970s. When the interest rate standard is applied in this way, there is no doubt that the United States is undersaving.

The next approach for determining whether the United States is undersaving is to compare the share of NNP devoted to net investment with the share of capital earnings in NNP. The latter measure is not totally straightforward because one component of NNP, indirect business taxes, goes to neither capital nor labor and hence becomes difficult to allocate. The usual argument is that indirect taxes should be included in capital's share because output (NNP) and compensation of employees (labor's share) can be measured, whereas the remainder, capital's pre-tax share, can only be estimated residually. The shares of NNP reflecting this assumption (along with a column to show its importance) are given in table 3. Since both the shares of capital earnings and net capital formation have a cyclical component, the table gives

TABLE 3

SHARES OF NET CAPITAL FORMATION AND RETURNS TO CAPITAL IN
NET NATIONAL PRODUCT
HIGH-EMPLOYMENT YEARS, 1970–1979

| | Capital Formation | | | | Returns to Capital | |
	Producer's Investment	Net Exports	Government Investment	Total	Unadjusted	If Indirect Taxes Are Prorated
	Percentage of Net National Product					
1970	6.3	0.4	3.3	10.0	25.0	16.3
1971	7.2	0.2	3.1	10.5	26.4	17.2
1972	8.2	0.1	2.8	11.1	26.4	17.5
1973	9.2	1.4	2.7	13.3	26.0	17.6
1977	6.5	1.8	2.0	10.3	27.1	19.0
1978	7.3	1.9	2.1	11.3	26.9	19.4
1979	6.5	2.8	1.9	11.2	26.4	19.1
Average, 1970–1973	7.7	0.5	3.0	11.2	26.0	17.2
Average, 1977–1979	6.8	2.2	2.0	11.0	26.8	19.2

SOURCE: National income accounts.

9. Even this adjustment for taxes only considers the perfect certainty case. If there were investment uncertainty, the marginal product of capital would seem to be even higher.

numbers for only the high-employment years. The income share of 26 to 27 percent is significantly above the 11 percent share devoted to capital formation. Even then, the latter number is as high as it is only because of the inclusion of net exports and government capital formation in the total; the share devoted to producer's investment is very low. Method two then gives a much more definitive verdict on the side of undersaving.

The final approach for assessing the level of U.S. capital formation is not absolute but relative. Instead of closely examining our own economy, this approach is to compare U.S. saving propensities with those of our major international competitors—Canada, Japan, France, West Germany, Italy, and the United Kingdom. Since the international data are less complete, the comparisons cannot be so careful as those shown in table 3; there is not enough information to allocate proprietor's income or to include public capital in the definition of overall capital formation. Although the comparisons thus overstate the share of capital income and understate capital formation, as compared with table 3, they are standard across countries, and they do permit comparisons of saving policies in the United States with those of other countries.

Table 4 shows the (slightly overstated) returns to capital and the (slightly understated) level of new net capital formation, both as a percentage of NNP, for the United States and six other countries between 1970 and 1979. For many of the countries, something of a break occurs in 1975, so the table shows the averages separately before and after that date. Whatever set of numbers is used, however, it is clear that of the seven countries, the United States devotes the lowest share of NNP to private capital formation; in the 1975–1979 period, for example, our share was only 6.8 percent, against at least 9 percent for all other countries and 22.6 percent for Japan.[10]

There is one caveat with these international comparisons involving the definition of the capital stock, but the caveat does not appear to change the picture greatly in this case. All of these comparisons take a very physiocratic view of what constitutes capital formation. The public and private tangible capital stock is included, but the human capital stock and the stock of capital accumulated in the form of consumer durables are excluded. Would a broader definition of capital change the picture?

The answer is no. While undercounting the capital stock obviously understates the amount of investment, it also understates the returns from that

---

10. One potentially interesting phenomenon suggested by table 4 is that those countries with high s (net capital formation) values also tend to have high a (returns to capital) values, meaning that their saving deficiency by the Golden Rule standard (a − s) varies by less than their value of s varies. In the recent period, our deficiency measured this way is 23.5 percentage points, approximately the same as for six of the countries, and substantially larger than only the figure for Japan.

TABLE 4

INTERNATIONAL COMPARISON OF SHARES OF NET CAPITAL FORMATION AND RETURNS TO CAPITAL
CALENDAR YEARS 1970–1979

	Average, 1970–1974			Average, 1975–1979			Average, 1970–1979		
	Returns to Capital	Net Capital Formation	Diff-erence	Returns to Capital	Net Capital Formation	Diff-erence	Returns to Capital	Net Capital Formation	Diff-erence
				Percentage of Net National Product					
United States	30.9	9.0	21.9	30.3	6.8	23.5	30.6	7.9	22.7
Canada	38.2	15.2	23.0	36.7	13.0	23.7	37.5	14.1	23.4
Japan	45.6	29.2	16.4	37.7	22.6	15.1	41.6	25.9	15.7
France	44.4	18.0	26.4	38.7	13.2	25.5	41.6	15.6	26.0
West Germany	39.1	20.2	18.9	37.3	15.6	21.7	38.2	17.9	20.3
Italy	44.0	15.0	29.0	37.8	13.6	24.2	40.9	14.3	26.6
United Kingdom	33.0	10.0	23.0	30.4	9.0	21.4	31.7	9.5	22.2

SOURCE: UN Yearbook of National Accounts Statistics, 1980, vol. 2.

investment, and if the returns are greater than the net growth of this uncounted capital, the physiocratic test for undersaving does not make a qualitative error. Hence if by the interest rate comparison a country appears to be undersaving, the saving rate comparison will *understate* the degree of undersaving.[11] In the case at hand, possible mismeasurement of capital seems to play no role at all, except perhaps to understate the problem.

Hence, all three ways of evaluating U.S. saving rates suggest that the country is undersaving. The real marginal product of capital in the United States seems to be above its real output growth rate, particularly if the impact of nonneutral tax treatment up to 1981 is considered. The U.S. share of NNP devoted to net capital formation seems clearly below the share being returned as income to capitalists. Finally, the United States appears to reinvest a significantly smaller share of its NNP than do the six other developed economies with which our economy is most often compared.

For How Long Would the Large Out-Year Deficits Increase Consumption?

I have tried to show that the large out-year deficits now being forecast, if not offset by increases in private saving or capital imports, will lead to a large decline in the U.S. saving rate. I have also tried to show that this reduction in national saving is a movement in the wrong direction. If anything, the United States is already saving too little, both absolutely and relative to other similarly situated countries. This section combines both points and poses the question: If the large out-year deficits are interpreted as a type of national consumption binge, for how many years do they raise consumption above the path that would have been realized had the government deficits not increased?

The question is analyzed with the aid of a simple growth model, built along the lines first laid down by Robert Solow.[12] The model begins in hypothesized equilibrium with the share of NNP devoted to capital investment

---

11. To see this, suppose there were some undetermined type of capital, denoted (in per capita terms) by j, that was *not* considered to be capital in the NIA data. If households invest in j until its marginal return equals the marginal return on all other types of capital (an assumption that could be debated, but probably is safe in long-run analysis), the share of NNP returned to capitalists is then understated by rj/y. In equilibrium we can expect the net stock of this capital to grow at the same rate as that of all other capital, which means that additions to the stock as a share of NNP are understated by nj/y. Should $r > n$, exactly the interest rate comparison we have already used, the true a exceeds the true s by more than is apparent from the NIA.

12. Robert M. Solow, "A Contribution to the Theory of Economic Growth," *Quarterly Journal of Economics*, vol. 70 (February 1956), pp. 65–94.

equaling 11 percent (from table 3), and the growth rate of NNP set at 2.5 percent (close to the potential growth rate now adopted by most forecasters). The equilibrium real interest rate is derived to be 5.9 percent. Then, in year one, it is assumed that the share of NNP devoted to capital formation is reduced to 8.5 percent, an estimate of the reduction in the saving rate based on the numbers in table 1. A series of equations determines income, interest rates, consumption, and the new capital stock. This new capital stock produces a new income series, new consumption, and so forth. Consumption in this model first rises, as the saving rate is reduced, and then falls, as the lower saving reduces capital formation, output, and ultimately consumption. Running the simulation shows how long the consumption binge (deficit) path raises consumption.

Most of the model, described in detail in the appendix, consists of accounting or growth identities, but there are two key behavioral equations. The first is the production function, which determines how a fall in capital changes output and how the demand for capital responds to real interest rates. The second is the private saving function, which determines how a rise in real interest rates induces private saving and partly offsets the government dissaving.

Results for three different models are given in table 5. The first version, shown in section A of the table, uses a Cobb-Douglas production function with the distributive share of returns to capital in NNP equaling 26 percent, just the share derived in table 3. For the private saving function, I used the average of a value from Michael Boskin (who believes that private saving is highly sensitive to real interest rates) and of a value from Philip Howrey and Saul Hymans (who believe that private saving is quite unresponsive). The result is a mid-range estimate of this parameter.[13]

Much as expected, the capital-labor ratio declines gradually, gradually reducing per capita NNP and gradually raising real interest rates, thereby stimulating some private saving to counteract the government dissaving. Per capita consumption starts at a value of 0.89 (with initial NNP set at 1.0) rises for a while because of the consumption binge, and then gradually falls back down as NNP drops. In the long run consumption is lower, as is implied by

---

13. Michael J. Boskin, "Taxation, Saving, and the Rate of Interest," *Journal of Political Economy*, vol. 86 (April 1978), part 2, pp. S3–S27; and E. Philip Howrey and Saul H. Hymans, "The Measurement and Determination of Loanable Funds Saving," *Brookings Papers on Economic Activity*, no. 3 (1978), pp. 655–85. I should note that these papers address only the question of personal saving response to higher real interest rates. If responses from business saving or international capital inflows are greater than the household responses, the true parameter will be higher and, as stated earlier, the entire impact of structural deficits less.

TABLE 5

SIMULATION OF IMPACT OF OUT-YEAR BUDGET DEFICITS IN HIGH-EMPLOYMENT
ECONOMY

Time (Years after 1984)	Net National Product[a]	Saving Rate[b]	Consump- tion[c]	Capital Labor Ratio	Real Interest Rate	Change in Capital Stock
A. Elasticity of substitution = 1, no embodied technology						
0	1.000	0.110	0.890	4.400	0.059	0
5	0.994	0.085	0.909	4.302	0.060	−0.005
10	0.987	0.086	0.903	4.192	0.061	−0.005
15	0.981	0.086	0.897	4.095	0.062	−0.004
20	0.976	0.086	0.891	4.009	0.063	−0.004
25	0.971	0.087	0.887	3.932	0.064	−0.004
30	0.966	0.087	0.883	3.865	0.065	−0.003
B. Elasticity of substitution = 0.5, no embodied technology						
0	1.000	0.110	0.890	4.400	0.059	0
5	0.994	0.085	0.909	4.303	0.061	−0.005
10	0.987	0.086	0.902	4.195	0.063	−0.005
15	0.982	0.087	0.896	4.102	0.065	−0.004
20	0.976	0.088	0.890	4.022	0.067	−0.004
25	0.972	0.089	0.885	3.953	0.069	−0.003
30	0.976	0.089	0.881	3.893	0.071	−0.003
C. Elasticity of substitution = 1, embodied technology						
0	1.000	0.110	0.890	4.400	0.114	0
5	0.990	0.086	0.905	4.305	0.115	−0.005
10	0.977	0.086	0.893	4.197	0.116	−0.005
15	0.966	0.087	0.882	4.098	0.118	−0.005
20	0.955	0.087	0.871	4.006	0.119	−0.004
25	0.945	0.087	0.863	3.923	0.120	−0.004
30	0.936	0.087	0.854	3.847	0.121	−0.004

SOURCE: Author's calculations.

a. Per capita, expressed as a ratio of its initial equilibrium value (which is set arbitrarily at 1.0).

b. Expressed as a ratio of current-year NNP.

c. Per capita, expressed as a ratio of the initial equilibrium value of per capita NNP.

the fact that the economy is beginning in a position at which it saves too little. But it is surprising how long this run is. This is a simple model, to be sure, but parameters are set close to realistic values for the United States. And in this view, a consumption binge turns out to raise consumption for almost a quarter-century.[14] Not only that—while the numbers are not shown in the table, were I to compute a discounted value of lifetime consumption for average consumers of each age, that would rise for all age cohorts who die within fifty years of the policy change, for all positive discount rates.

The next question is whether changes in the behavioral parameters influence the results, particularly the length of time for which consumption is higher under the deficit scenario. The private saving response is already an average effect, so there is not much mileage in changing it. But there may be mileage in changing the production function. The Cobb-Douglas production function contains a restrictive assumption that the elasticity of substitution of factor demands with respect to changes in relative prices (such as the real interest rate) is unity. Most empirical studies find values somewhat below that, a consensus estimate being 0.75.[15] Were the elasticity lower, it would take more of a change in real interest rates to lower the capital-labor ratio a given amount; once that happened, however, NNP would decline more rapidly. To see how much this assumption matters, I redid the simulation with everything exactly the same except that the elasticity of substitution was set equal to 0.50, a bit below the consensus estimate. The results, shown in section B of table 5, are almost identical to those for the basic case in section A; the consumption binge raises consumption for twenty years. The conclusion is that over the realistic range, these surprising results are *not* due to my choice of an elasticity of substitution.

Another plausible modification in the production assumption is to alter not the elasticity of substitution, but the extent to which new capital formation is the vehicle by which new technology is adopted. The basic case in section A of table 5 assumes that the rate of technological progress is independent of the rate of capital investment. But if that is not the case, the reduction in capital formation generated by the higher deficits could lower the rate of tech-

---

14. For what it is worth, these results are by no means original. Twenty years ago, two articles first uncovered the result, generally arriving at much longer adjustment periods. See R. Sato, "Fiscal Policy in a Neoclassical Growth Model: An Analysis of Time Required for Equilibrating Adjustment," *Review of Economic Studies*, vol. 30 (February 1963), pp. 16–33; and K. Sato, "On the Adjustment Time in Neoclassical Growth Models," *Review of Economic Studies*, vol. 33 (July 1966), pp. 263–68. The matter was discussed in Edwin Burmeister and A. Rodney Dobell, *Mathematical Theories of Economic Growth* (New York: Macmillan, 1970), chapter 3. More recently, Alan J. Auerbach and Laurence J. Kotlikoff have done simulations with a twenty-year tax cut and found that consumption increases for about thirty years. See Auerbach and Kotlikoff "National Savings, Economic Welfare, and the Structure of Taxation," in Martin S. Feldstein, ed., *Behavioral Simulation Methods in Tax Policy Analysis*, (Chicago: University of Chicago Press, 1983).

15. See, for example, p. 514 of Daniel S. Hamermesh, "Econometric Studies of Labor Demand and their Application to Policy Analysis," *Journal of Human Resources*, vol. 11 (Fall 1976), pp. 507–25.

nological progress and lower consumption in the deficit scenario relative to the control case. I modified the production function in this way in section C of table 5, assuming that capital has twice the contribution to economic growth that would be suggested in the basic case. This number appears to be the upper bracket estimate among students of productivity as to the importance of capital investment. [16] When this change is made, as in section C, the deficit scenario raises consumption for only twelve years, roughly one-half the horizon in the basic case. This latter modification does change things substantially, but I intentionally used an extreme estimate of the impact of capital investment on economic growth, twelve years is still a long time, and the discounted value of lifetime consumption still rises for about half the adult population.

One other aspect of the final simulation is worth noting. Since capital investment is now the vehicle by which new technology is adopted, the marginal product of capital (equal to the real interest rate in the simulation) is almost twice as high as before. Because many other arguments about how simple growth models may not capture reality focus on this marginal product of capital, this third simulation can also serve to assess the impact of these changes. One of the arguments is that the model is too simple because it ignores uncertainty, which has the effect of deterring capital investment. If so, the marginal product of capital would have to be higher to compensate investors for their uncertainty, and section C would, at least in a crude sense, show how results would change in the presence of uncertainty.

Any number of other refinements could also be made, but most would not change the basic story that the consumption binge implicit in the forecast deficits raises consumption for a surprisingly long time. If, for example, the model were broadened to include short-term aggregate demand effects along with long-term aggregate supply effects, the standard view of macroeconomics described earlier would suggest that, if anything, high deficits would raise income and capital investment now, provide a consumption path even higher than that shown in table 5, and look relatively even more attractive than they do now. If time preference were added to the model (as in note 7), the consumption binge path that raises near-term consumption would look even more attractive.

---

16. This estimate resulted from combining output and capital growth slowdowns in the 1973–1978 period in the work of J. R. Norsworthy, Michael J. Harper, and Kent Kunze, "The Slowdown in Productivity Growth: Analysis of Some Contributing Factors," *Brookings Papers on Economic Activity*, no. 2 (1979), pp. 387–445. Discussants and Peter Clark (in the same issue) say why the Norsworthy, Harper, Kunze estimate may be extreme.

There are obvious reasons why the results of these simulations should not be taken too seriously. In any problem as complicated as this, many simplifications must be made and some of the real-world aspects of the problem will be lost. At the same time, the simulations do point up a real paradox in the evaluation of the out-year structural deficits. Viewed in straightforward terms under the most likely values of the critical parameters, the deficits imply a dominant consumption path for many, many years. One can modify these results by making complications in the model, but the basic results remain relatively unchanged. The clear lesson is that—if deficits are viewed in capital accumulation terms, using standard, accepted theoretical tools for analyzing that problem—analysts who oppose deficits must place great weight on consumption levels quite far in the future. If the analysts are not prepared to do that, the reasons for opposing deficits seem quite unconvincing.

Implications

There are four main implications of the paper. The first is the unsurprising one that even after many adjustments, the out-year deficits are indeed quite large. If no other budget changes are made, these deficits seem likely to reduce the share of output devoted to capital formation by two to three percentage points, amounting to one-sixth to one-fourth of the present eleven percentage-point share of output now devoted to capital formation even in good, high-employment, years.

The second lesson is that this drop in the share of output devoted to capital formation, if it does indeed come to pass, should be evaluated in terms of its long-run impact on interest rates, capital formation, and consumption levels in the future. Many other arguments about the strength of aggregate demand and the recovery, international capital flows, and inflation effects have been raised to complicate the evaluation of deficits: I argue that these issues, each reflecting serious problems, either are mistaken or simply embellish the basic problem.

The third lesson is that this reduction in the national saving rate is, if anything, a movement in the wrong direction. All ways of measuring national saving rates, absolute and comparative, suggest that the nation is already undersaving by a large amount, conceivably as much as 15 percent of potential output. But the fourth lesson is that even though a reduction in the national saving rate seems undesirable from a long-term perspective, that perspective must be a very long-term one indeed, from ten to twenty-five years if we just track annual consumption levels, and even longer if we track lifetime consumption levels. Deficits look undesirable only when thought about from a very long-term perspective, and we should probably begin thinking about (and worrying about) them from just such a standpoint. Any analysis of this problem that focuses only on the short term will completely miss the point.

The Simulation Model

The first version of the model assumes that the production elasticity of substitution equals 1 with no embodied technology. The basic behavioral equation determining total output (y) is then a Cobb-Douglas production function of the form:

A1) $y = bk^a$

where k is the capital stock, a is the capital earnings share of total output, and b is a scale parameter.

The second equation, for the marginal product of capital or real interest rate (r), comes from differentiating A1):

A2) $r = \partial y/\partial k = a\ y/k.$

The third equation determines the share of output devoted to capital formation as the sum of public saving (sg) and private saving (sp)

A3) $s = sg + sp = sg + sp' + zr$

where z refers to the impact of changes in the real interest rate on private saving.

The other three equations in the model are all national income or growth identities. Consumption per head is always equal to

A4) $c = y\ (1-s).$

The rate of growth of capital per head can be derived by noting that $dK = sY$, where upper-case letters refer to variables undeflated by the effective labor force. Dividing through by K, the rate of growth of the total capital stock is seen to equal sY/K or sy/k. But this rate of growth of the total stock is approximately equal to $n + dk/k$, which yields the growth identity

A5) $dk/k = sy/k - n$

with the new level of k then given by

A6) $k(+1) = k(1 + dk/k)$

where $k(+1)$ means the capital stock next year.

This model is solved by setting initial values, solving the six equations, getting a value for $k(+1)$, and redoing everything for the next year, and on out into the future. The model is assumed to start (in 1984) at the growth equilibrium position given by equation (1) of note 8, rewritten as

A7) $$n = sy/k.$$

n is set equal to 0.025, close to the growth rate achieved over the 1970s and a reasonable projection from now on. s is set equal to 0.11, from table 3. y is set initially at 1.0, with c then equalling 0.89 (from A4). The parameter a is set equal to 0.26 from table 3. The initial value of k is then found from A7) as 4.4. Substituting these values into A1) yields a value for b of 0.68, and inserting these values into A2) gives a value of r = 0.059. The average of the Hymans-Howrey and Boskin results for private saving suggests that a 10 percent rise in r (say from 0.06 to 0.066) will raise the private saving rate by 2 percent (from about 0.1 to 0.102), which yields a partial derivative z generously estimated at 0.4. Then, in year one, I reduced sg by 0.025 (from the discussion surrounding table 1) and ran the simulation, giving the results in section A of table 5.

The second version of the model assumes the elasticity of substitution is much lower than 1, equal to 0.5. I use a new form, a constant elasticity of substitution production function, to replace the Cobb-Douglas. This new form is written as

B1) $$y = \alpha[(1-\beta) + \beta k^{(\sigma-1)/\sigma}]^{\sigma/(\sigma-1)}$$

where σ is the elasticity of substitution, β is a distribution parameter, and α is a scale parameter. As before, the equation is in terms of the effective labor force (normalized at 1), with output also normalized at 1. Also, I fix r = 0.059 and k = 4.4 just as with the first version.

When σ = .5 we can rewrite B1) as

B2) $$y = \alpha/[(1-\beta)+\beta/k]$$

and differentiate to get

B3) $$r = .059 = \partial y/\partial k = .0516\ \alpha\beta[(1-\beta)+\beta/k]^{-2}.$$

Solving B2) and B3) together yields β = 0.607 and α = 0.531. A check on these values can be found by computing capital's share of total output

B4) $$\frac{\beta/k}{1-\beta+\beta/k}.$$

Inserting β = 0.607, we get just the 0.26 for capital's share that was derived back in table 3. Hence the low-elasticity version of the simulation uses B2) instead of A1), and B3) instead of A2), and redoes everything with the results given in section B of table 5.

For the third equation we go back to the first version, with an elasticity equal to 1 as in the Cobb-Douglas form. Everything is the same as before except that we measure a not by the share of capital in total output ($= 0.26$ from table 3), but by a growth analysis. Taking the logarithmic derivative of A1), it is apparent that

C1) $$\partial y/y = a\ \partial k/k.$$

Productivity studies place a as determined this way as ranging up to 0.5, almost twice as high as the estimate from distributive shares. I just use this value instead of 0.26. One byproduct of this new assumption is that the marginal product of capital from A2) now is also almost doubled—a higher capital intensity raises productivity growth and is thus worth more. Jogging the model in this way then might also conform to other theories suggesting that the marginal product of capital is higher than the real interest rate, such as if there is some kind of investment uncertainty that is now impeding capital investment. These results are in section C of table 5.

COMMENTS

Robert H. Haveman

Gramlich's story is a straightforward one. First, I will summarize it; then I will comment on it. The basic question is also the title: "How Bad Are the Large Deficits?" His answer is—not at all good; they reduce long-term capital formation. Still, because they induce increases in consumption for several years, they have some offsetting benefits. Here is his story.

Gramlich first establishes the "dramatic" magnitude of future projected structural deficits (appropriately scaled by potential GNP, purged of cyclical effects, and with interest payments adjusted for inflation) relative to those in the 1970s. These deficits, he concludes, represent dissaving that will *not* be offset by either increased public capital formation or increased private saving and capital formation (except that induced by endogenous changes in the interest rate). Moreover, the large deficit builds in a tendency for still larger deficits. These are the real reasons to oppose them; other common fears are quickly dismissed. In his view, these deficits will not choke off the recovery because a high-employment equilibrium will be attained even with their presence (changes in interest rates or fiscal policy or both will be offsets). Moreover, the foreign capital which higher interest rates attract should probably be invested in the United States if maximum wealth is what is desired. Finally, the potential monetary expansion is a problem of the deficit financing decision and not of the deficit itself.

Having then established his view of the only good reason for opposing out-year deficits, Gramlich is forced to ask the next questions: Has the nation been underinvesting? Is there a capital shortage? He answers yes on the basis of three pieces of information: (1) although the Golden Rule model indicates that the real interest rate should equal the long-term growth rate of GNP, the real before-tax rate appears to be above the long-term growth rate; (2) although the Golden Rule model indicates that saving and investment as a share of NNP (net national product) should equal the return to capital as a percentage of NNP, the return share has greatly exceeded the investment-saving share;

69

and (3) the United States devotes a smaller share of its NNP to private capital formation than do other developed countries.

Finally, employing simulations from a simple neoclassical growth model, Gramlich suggests that the deficits, regarded as dissaving and reduced capital formation, increase consumption for at least a decade and up to twenty-five years. He is left wondering what the long run really means.

Now for a few comments. The heart of the Gramlich argument appears to rest on two propositions:

1. The nation is now (and has been) underinvesting;

2. The out-year deficits will result in a dollar-for-dollar reduction in aggregate saving and capital formation (again, apart from changes in response to interest rate increases).

Consider, first, the undersaving-underinvesting argument. The case, I would suggest, is less clear-cut than Gramlich implies. The basic point is that the *savings and investment* concepts used in his paper are narrow ones— private income minus consumption, or net investment as recorded in the national accounts. A broader, more appropriate concept of saving or net investment would not necessarily yield this result. Were net investment defined to include investments in human resources, research and development, managerial infrastructure, and environmental and resources stocks, the evidence would be far less clear. Indeed, as a nation, we have rather consciously substituted human and environmental assets for investments in plant and equipment through health, education, welfare, and environmental investments and regulations. Gramlich's problem is that he reaches his undersaving conclusion on the basis of NIA (national income accounts)-measured values and returns, whereas it is the social counterparts of these variables that he requires.[1] Moreover, Gramlich's concept of net investment fails to reflect increments to the capital stock due to past increases in asset prices. Were the savings ratio in past years adjusted for these reinvested capital gains, the underinvesting case would be more difficult to sustain.

Such measurement problems directly undermine the empirical tests on which the underinvestment conclusion rests. Given distortions in the tax law

---

1. Indeed, Gramlich's point that including human capital in the Golden Rule calculations would not change the results would seem to be in error. Including human capital investment in the estimate of the share of NNP devoted to capital formation would increase that variable by more than inclusion of the imputed (low) return on human investment in the estimate of the return to aggregate human and nonhuman capital would increase that variable. As a result, the excess of the return to capital as a percentage of NNP over the share of investment in NNP would be narrowed. The same result would occur for his interest rate calculation.

and the uncertainty of investment, is it reasonable to take the rates on Aaa (or Baa) bonds as equal to the true marginal product of a correct concept of capital investment? And, is a comparison of the NIA measure of "profits" with the NIA measure of net investment (both as a share of NNP), a sufficent basis on which to conclude that aggregate national undersaving is large? Indeed, if true rates of return and income flows to capital were as high during the 1970s as he suggests, one would wonder why the expected investment has not occurred, especially in the face of substantial public encouragement to save in the form of lightly taxed capital gains, tax-deferred contributions to pension funds, the investment tax credit, and a series of accelerations of depreciation expenses for tax purposes. The Fed can't be blamed for everything!

Gramlich's second basic proposition—that out-year structural deficits will result in equivalent reductions in aggregate national capital formation— is also hard to swallow. That proposition rests on the assumption (implicit in Gramlich's simulations) that the public dissaving associated with the deficits will not be offset by increased public capital formation or private saving.

First, is the portion of public expenditures that is classified as net capital formation so slim as Gramlich implies? For example, is there no capital formation associated with the income transfers or health expenditures that the out-year deficits will finance? If, as seems likely, there is, the dollar-for-dollar equivalence of federal government dissaving and aggregate national dissaving assumed by Gramlich would be exaggerated.

Second, such dollar-for-dollar displacement will occur only under a particular macroeconomic regime. For example, if there is excess capacity in the out-years (as there is likely to be) and if there is some monetary accommodation (as there historically has been), the deficits will add to effective demand, thereby increasing aggregate output, consumption, saving, *and* net private investment. In this case, Gramlich's simulated reduction of NNP in the short run would appear exaggerated. And his estimates of the magnitude of the "consumption binge" and the length of its life would be wide of the mark.[2] In fact, private capital formation might well increase substantially because of the demand stimulus, thereby contributing to a reduction of whatever underinvesting exists. Moreover, what if the deficits are caused in part by increased tax-based incentives for private capital formation and saving, or

---

2. Gramlich's simulation, indeed, presumes the existence of full employment during the entire out-year deficit period. He defends this by saying that "over horizons this long, the natural stabilizing tendencies of the economy should assert themselves and the economy should move to a position of balance between aggregate demand and aggregate supply at high employment."

I find this defense unconvincing.

other supply-side inducements to output growth. Again, the assumption of *no* private sector offsets seems hardly reasonable.

Or consider another scenario. What if there is full employment in the out-years (as Gramlich assumes) but some monetary accommodation? In this case, the deficits will lead to price increases. The resulting fall in the real value of privately held public debt is likely to lead to reduced consumption and *increased saving*, ceteris paribus. This effect, emphasized recently by Robert Eisner, is another reason not to expect a zero private-sector offset to the increased public dissaving. Under this macroeconomic regime, Gramlich's simulation results again misstate the investment, income, and consumption impacts of the deficits.[3]

All this discussion, then, points up the macroeconomic regime that Gramlich implicitly assumes—future full employment with *no* monetary accommodation by the Fed.[4] Contrary to his assertion, it does make a difference how the deficit is financed; indeed, the deficit and its financing are a single package. The question then becomes, Is this scenario reasonable? I do not think so, at least for the next several years—all of which are out-years! The implication is that there will be some offsets to the public dissaving—and the question is how much.

These comments, however, should not be interpreted as implying that no problem of undersaving exists, or that the deficits will have no adverse impact on long-term capital formation. They may well, but the case is less strong than Gramlich implies. A more balanced view might run as follows:

> It is in the national interest to increase private net capital formation. The large projected out-year structural deficits may impede attainment of that objective. They do represent dissaving. Moreover, the increase in the real value of privately held public debt with which they are associated may increase private consumption and reduce private saving. In some ways, however, these same deficits may contribute to private net capital formation—in a period of less than full-employment, they will stimulate output and investment and saving. And, if some increase in prices results, saving may be further increased by the reduced consumption associated with the fall in the real value of the privately held public debt.

---

3. It would be interesting to calculate the discount rate at which the present value of consumption would be zero in Gramlich's simulation and in alternative simulations based on less extreme macroeconomic regimes. A comparison of this rate with estimated returns on appropriately defined capital formation might contribute to reconciling the conclusion of his third section (We are underinvesting, and that is bad) with that of his fourth section (But the increased consumption lasts for a long time, and that is good).

4. Although unstated, it is this implicit assumption that underlies Gramlich's assertion that foreign capital attracted here has no benefits ("There will be capital here, but no wealth"). With less than full employment, foreign investment in the United States will have employment and output effects, and thus positive impacts on investment *and* consumption.

In addition to this overall appraisal, one point (totally neglected by Gramlich) should be made: The sheer existence of $200 billion out-year structural deficits tends to undermine the credibility of government, in particular, the credibility of its commitment to restrain inflation. The impact of this loss of credibility on both short-term economic performance and long-term net capital formation could easily swamp any of the impacts discussed in the paper.

COMMENTS

William J. Beeman

Edward Gramlich has prepared a thoughtful paper dealing with the issue of the hour, "How Bad Are the Large Deficits?" Most of the popular debate on this issue deals only with the short-run economic effects of deficits. In contrast, Gramlich has provided a much-needed focus on long-run growth issues. Although the analysis reminded me how difficult it is to provide a convincing estimate of long-run policy effects, I nevertheless find myself in agreement with all but a few of the general conclusions put forth in this paper.

The Size of Deficits

The first section of the paper concludes that any way one looks at the numbers, projected deficits relative to GNP will be very large compared to previous experience, if budgetary action is not taken to reduce deficits. The conclusion appears correct to me; the estimates we have produced at the Congressional Budget Office (CBO) are of a similar order of magnitude.

In the analysis of the relative size of these deficits, I would have preferred a comparison of projected deficits with the post-World War II period rather than only with the 1970s, which was not a period of outstanding economic performance. Comparisons with the 1950s and the 1960s show an even sharper break with the past. I also find it somewhat curious that the high-employment budget is relied on so heavily to measure structural deficits. Originally, the high-employment budget deficit was intended to show the impact of discretionary fiscal policy on the economy. As such, emphasis was placed on changes in the high-employment budget deficit rather than its level, which most analysts did not take seriously, largely because of the difficulty of

---

Useful comments were provided by Christina Duckworth Romer, John Sturrock, and James Barth.

measuring potential GNP. But when it is used to measure the structural deficit—which I take to mean the persistent, noncyclical deficit—the levels become important. Given the infrequency of periods of full employment and the present dissatisfaction with the concept and measures of potential GNP used in the high-employment budget estimates, it may make more sense to standardize budget deficits at trend GNP or at the mid-expansion path recently developed by Frank de Leeuw and Thomas Holloway.[1]

These measures indicate that the structural deficit is an even worse problem than Gramlich's analysis suggests. The out-year deficits are very large and represent a sharp break with the past.

Are Deficits Bad?

The second section of the paper asks why budget deficits are bad. Gramlich concludes that the only sound argument against out-year budget deficits is that they lower the proportion of output devoted to capital formation. Most other economic arguments against out-year deficits such as excessive debt monetization are rejected. The arguments against deficits are not weighted against economic arguments favoring deficits (i.e., the supply-side argument against higher marginal tax rates and the Keynesian argument for short-run stimulus to reduce unemployment). The popular political argument for deficits—that large deficits will scare Congress into reducing spending—is not mentioned.

In regard to whether private-sector behavior will offset increased government dissaving, Gramlich considers only three issues: (1) the sensitivity of savings to interest rates; (2) the Barro equivalence theorem; and (3) the international mobility of capital. He apparently concludes that private savings are not likely to offset public dissaving. However, there are other, perhaps equally important, considerations. First, private savings are affected by the spending and tax changes causing the deficits. Not all deficits are the same. According to CBO estimates, about 22 percent of the 1986 deficit is caused by recent cuts in business taxes and tax incentives designed to encourage private savings. Although there is every reason to doubt the popular self-financing arguments of supply-siders, it seems reasonable to assume significant private savings resulting from these incentives.

Second, even if capital formation is reduced, it is important to know what capital spending is affected adversely. If the major impact is on housing

1. Frank de Leeuw and Thomas Holloway, "Measuring and Analyzing the Cyclically Adjusted Budget," Bureau of Economic Analysis (Draft) 1983.

rather than on nonresidential private capital, there may be little or no effect on long-run productivity. Recent tax changes have in fact made business investment more attractive than owner-occupied housing investment relative to the recent past. I mention these two considerations because I am not comfortable about the generalizations based on aggregate savings behavior.

I wish Gramlich had spent more time on the question of whether high future deficits can weaken the economy now. Any number of prominent economists and policy analysts now make the negative fiscal multiplier argument. This view is not restricted to people with a particular political leaning. I expect that Gramlich is correct in saying that negative fiscal multipliers, however temporary, require very special circumstances. Certainly, many of the popular arguments about deficits and expenditures are inconsistent. Nevertheless, the projection of large future deficits is currently the most credible explanation for what appears to be high real rates in long-term credit markets. Unfortunately, I have yet to see any detailed, formal analysis of this issue.

Another argument against large deficits that Gramlich seems to dismiss too easily is the risk that the large deficits will be monetized, leading to a resurgence of inflation. On this issue, Gramlich and I come to different conclusions. It is true that one cannot easily demonstrate from historical data that the Fed monetizes more debt when the deficits are large. But the Fed has not been faced with deficits of the magnitude now projected. This is a new regime. Elsewhere, Gramlich concedes that these deficits may place intense pressure on interest rates. I have heard members of Congress say that during the past several years the pressures to do something about high interest rates were much more intense than the pressures to do something about inflation; the White House staff apparently feels some of the same pressures. Politicians do not hesitate to express their feelings on this issue, and history clearly shows that despite its independence, the Fed responds to political pressure. As a practical matter, it is not sufficient to say that possible monetization is no argument against large deficits, but merely a question of how the deficits are financed.

By the way, the risk of excessive monetization of debt would be much greater, perhaps inevitable, in a situation of unstable deficits arising from very rapid growth in interest costs.

Is the United States Undersaving?

The third section of the paper asks whether the United States is undersaving. The author concludes, reasonably, I think, that the United States is undersaving. On a technical level, however, it is difficult to demonstrate undersaving. An exhaustive study of capital formation undertaken by the Fed staff and published in 1981 concludes, "There is little evidence to support the popular notion that the United States does not save enough."[2] They apparently found more problems with the composition of saving.

Gramlich's attempt to use the Golden Rule model to evaluate the question of undersaving appears to be a sound theoretical approach to the question, but it is hard to apply empirically because of the difficulty of defining and measuring capital and its return. Moreover, the Golden Rule is a very restrictive concept; it is doubtful that the relationship between the marginal product of capital and the growth rate of the economy is a reliable measure of the appropriateness of saving behavior in an economy as complex as that of the United States.

Gramlich's comparisons of U.S. and foreign saving behavior are more persuasive. It is not easy for economists to be critical of societal preferences, however, and apparently U.S. citizens prefer less saving.

How Long the Consumption Binge?

The last section of Gramlich's paper is an interesting attempt to answer the question of how long it will take for government dissaving to reduce standards of living (per capita consumption) by lessening capital formation. Using a golden-age growth model with alternative parameters, Gramlich concludes that we could enjoy a consumption binge for ten to twenty-five years before we would pay the price with a lower standard of living. Gramlich was surprised it took so long for deficits to affect standards of living, and he implies that we might seriously consider the merits of a consumption binge. I have three comments on this finding.

First, it is not surprising that it takes a long period for changes in savings to affect the standard of living. After all, the U.S. capital stock (fixed, private, and reproducible) is a very big number—something on the order of $2.5 trillion in 1972 dollars. In an average year, net investment adds about 3 percent to the capital stock. Thus, a reduction in savings of the magnitude assumed in the simulation would reduce the capital stock by about 0.5 percent in a given year. At that rate obviously it would take a number of years to significantly affect productivity.

---

2. "Public Policy and Capital Formation," Board of Governors of the Federal Reserve System, April 1983, p. 43.

Second, I am puzzled by the conclusion that "analysts who oppose deficits must place great weight on consumption levels quite far in the future," and the suggestion that perhaps we should consider a consumption binge. I doubt that this is a serious suggestion especially in view of the author's earlier conclusion that the United States is definitely undersaving. After all, I hope to be alive twenty years from now and my children will still be young. After such a consumption binge we would have three choices, all of them unpleasant.

1. A permanent reduction in our consumption path.

2. A further cut in consumption for a prolonged period to get back to the original consumption path.

3. Another increase in deficits (another consumption binge). Each time the deficit would have to be larger to get us above the original consumption path. Obviously the depletion of capital would be a prescription for poverty in America.

However, I must admit that we are not equipped to weigh the cost and benefits of a consumption binge to ourselves, our children, and future generations. History is replete with actions by various societies that improve the lot of future generations unknown. By some standards this action appears irrational. But I see no change in people's attitudes about the future, and (short of a greatly increased likelihood for nuclear war) I expect that our generation will continue to be concerned about the next.

My final comment about the growth model is simply to point out its limitations. Generally, I think an equilibrium growth model is a useful tool for analyzing the long-run effects of policies. But the full-employment assumption may lead to the wrong conclusion in a period of economic slack. Moreoever, a model with a financial sector is needed if we want to capture the full effects of deficits on the path of investment. Earlier in his paper, Gramlich agrees that deficits have a short-run effect on income and interest rates. The effects on output may be temporary, but the composition effects— the reduction in the stock of capital—may be permanent. If the financial link between deficits and investment is considered, the impact on investment and living standards may occur more quickly than indicated by the growth model. It is obvious, given our current situation, that short-run financial effects cannot be ignored.

PART 2

SPENDING AND TAX POLICIES

THE DEFENSE BUDGET

Richard A. Stubbing

We are all aware that the defense program is booming. Excluding inflation, the budget authority for defense in FY 1984 is 41 percent *above that* of 1980. The largest peacetime buildup in our nation's history is under way. The rhetoric supporting the buildup sounds persuasive:

- The Soviets are outspending and outproducing us militarily.

- In most areas, their forces are superior to those of the United States.

- Their aggressive behavior in recent years stems from this new-found military superiority.

- Our defense program buildup is a carefully honed response to these perceived threats in the context of defined national strategies and policies.

There is another side to this story that needs to be told. The realities shaping the defense program are far more mundane. Presidents arrive in office with widely varying perceptions of the Soviet threat and of the size and shape of the required U.S. response. Although new administrations often spend considerable energy defining national security needs and broad defense strategies, the real problem lies in relating specific defense funding levels and program actions to approved national defense strategies. The defense program is actually a composite of long-standing requests from the military services; almost all these requests have developed independently of shifts in defined national strategy. Congress, contractors, and lobbyists also shape the "national defense" program to satisfy their personal political and economic interests.

Decision making in defense matters is further complicated by the obscurity in which public discussion of the issues is often shrouded. Because much of the relevant information is classified—particularly information about the nature of the Soviet threat and our own military capabilities—most citizens feel ill-informed on defense matters and will defer to the president, top military leaders, or anyone perceived to possess the necessary competence on national security needs. Consequently, grass-roots support for the U.S. defense effort often rides a roller coaster of ill-founded perceptions and conflicting emotional responses. Within a span of two months in late 1979, for example, the takeover of the U.S. embassy in Iran and the Soviet Christmas Day invasion of Afghanistan, together with unsatisfactory U.S. responses in both cases, convinced many Americans that we were in deep trouble militarily. The Soviet "bear" was unleashed and the U.S. military could do nothing to contain it; even Third World nations such as Iran could thumb their noses at us with impunity. Our military forces were seen as inferior and in need of an infusion of funds to rebuild. In real military terms, however, could a U.S. defense program twice its size have prevented either of these actions? Probably not. But this perception of military inferiority and the national outpouring of emotions associated with the hostage taking contributed to President Carter's defeat and gave President Reagan the public support he needed to carry out his defense budget buildup.

This paper explores some of the irrationality embedded in defense decision making. To assess the impacts of the recent budget increases, the paper first examines defense budget trends over the past fifteen years. Next, to identify comparative strengths and weaknesses, the paper assesses the Soviet defense effort in terms of resources spent and military capability. To underline the need for and absence of explicit consideration of trade-offs between U.S. military spending and nondefense assistance programs, the paper then briefly surveys the broad range of U.S. foreign policy objectives and the types of programs that exist to serve these objectives. After examining some of the myths and realities of the defense budget process within the executive branch, the paper points out some of the inefficiencies inherent in the execution of the Defense Department budget that contribute to inflated budget totals. The paper concludes with some alternative proposals to redress the problems identified in earlier sections and produce a more coherent and efficient defense program.

The Defense Budget and Program: 1970–1984

The overall defense budget has grown from $75 billion in FY 1970 to $259 in FY 1984. Table 1 shows the total defense budget levels in current dollars and in constant 1984 dollars for key years from FY 1970 to FY 1984.

TABLE 1

DEFENSE PROGRAM IN CURRENT AND CONSTANT DOLLARS
FY 1970–FY 1984

	FY 1970	FY 1975	FY 1980	FY 1981	FY 1982	FY 1983	FY 1984
Current dollars (billions)	75.5	86.2	142.2	176.1	211.4	240.5	258.2
Constant 1984 dollars (billions)	214.5	167.4	183.5	204.4	229.2	249.2	258.2
Current real growth (percentage)	—	−22	+10	+11	+12	+9	5

SOURCE: Office of Defense Comptroller, National Defense Budget Estimates for FY 1984, March 1983, pp. 58–61 (1984 figures revised to reflect congressional action).

NOTE: Figures in this table and in the remainder of the discussion are in terms of total obligational authority (TOA) unless otherwise noted.

As a share of the gross national product (GNP), defense spending will grow from 5.3 percent in FY 1980 to about 6.7 percent in FY 1984. The Defense Department's share of budget authority within the total federal budget has grown from 21.5 percent in 1980 to 29 percent in 1984. Total resources allocated to defense have grown from $142 billion in 1980 to $258 billion in 1984—an 82 percent increase (41 percent, after inflation). If Congress had not cut President Reagan's 1984 defense budget from $274.1 billion to $258.2 billion, the defense budget would have grown by a whopping 49 percent in four years.[1]

As this rapid buildup has taken place over the past three years, defense suppliers have been premier performers in the national economy. The total impact of defense spending is impressive. In 1984, total employment in the United States will exceed 106 million; table 2 shows that more than 10 million persons (10 percent of the total employed) can attribute all or part of their annual personal income to the Defense Department. The political muscle emerging from this economic base is immense.

The Sun Belt, western, and several northeast states benefit greatly from defense spending, while federal domestic programs are spread more evenly across all the states. For example, a preponderance of defense bases and maintenance facilities (roughly 80 percent) employing several million military and civilian personnel and small contractors lies south of an east-west line drawn roughly across the middle of the country. Thus, the big increases in military pay between 1980 and 1982 (about 35 percent) and similar increases

---

1. *Budget of the United States*, 1970–1984.

TABLE 2

DEFENSE-RELATED EMPLOYMENT
FY 1984

Defense employees	
Active military personnel	2,160,000
Defense Department civilian personnel	1,070,000
Defense Department Paychecks to Civilian Workforce	
Paid reservists (excluding Defense Department civilians)	930,000
Military retirees (assumes 50 percent hold nondefense jobs)	720,000
Private Sector	
Jobs sustained by $170 billion in 1984 defense purchases (at $30,000 per job)	5,670,000
TOTAL	10,550,000

SOURCE: *Budget of the U.S. Government FY 1984*, plus author estimates.

in funds for equipment maintenance and base operations (30 to 40 percent beyond inflation in four years) primarily benefit communities in the southern half of our nation.

Defense procurement and research and development (R&D) contracts are the fastest growing portion of the budget (excluding inflation, they have almost doubled in only four years). Primary geographic beneficiaries are the West, Southwest, and Northeast states. More than 60 percent go to western and southern states; California alone receives more than 20 percent. The Midwest, however, receives a small proportion of the defense contracts. Areas with big defense suppliers were able to mitigate the economic doldrums of 1981 and 1982; regions without this infusion of funds bore the full brunt of the recession.

Trends in the Defense Budget Between 1970 and 1984

The resources allocated to defense in the past fifteen years can be considered in three time groupings—the Vietnam phasedown between 1970 and 1975, the post-Vietnam period between 1976 and 1980, and the defense buildup between 1981 to 1984.

The Vietnam Phasedown, 1970–1975. The 1970 budget reflected high-intensity Vietnam involvement. As our forces were removed from Vietnam, the extra defense costs attributed to the war shrank and the defense budget declined by 22 percent (after inflation). Army forces, which had mushroomed in the 1960s to meet the war needs, bore the brunt of the reductions. The Nixon administration's long-promised "Vietnam Peace Dividend"—a shift of resources away from defense and into domestic programs—was actually achieved with a strong assist from Congress, which was then in a mood to cut the defense budget. At the same time, Pentagon appeals to apply portions of the "peace dividend" to other unmet defense needs fell on deaf ears.

As an often unmentioned corollary to this phasedown, the U.S. military forces achieved by 1975 (far faster than planned) a modernization of its combat equipment. As older weapons were lost or used up in combat, they were replaced with the latest production models and, when the war ended, the production lines were still pouring out new equipment at high rates. At the close of hostilities, the army had a modern, vastly enlarged helicopter force and the latest models of ground combat equipment used in Vietnam, as well as ammunition and logistics support. The navy and air force, by 1975, had received large quantities of late-model fighter and attack aircraft as replacements for combat losses, as well as air-launched missiles and a complete pipeline of combat-related spare parts. In consequence, the services in fact had no urgent need for an across-the-board buildup in conventional force procurement programs (other than in selected areas, such as ships and tanks where rates of modernization did not accelerate during the war).

The Post-Vietnam Period, 1976–1980. Although our leaders during this period have often been condemned for inattention to defense, the total defense program actually grew at an average of 2 percent each year (after inflation). Force modernization programs and purchases of goods and services for our operational forces grew at 4 percent annually (beyond inflation), while military and civilian personnel levels declined by 6 percent. During this period, two major buildups in force structure began, as the army increased its combat divisions from thirteen to sixteen and the air force moved from twenty-two to twenty-six tactical airwings.

The 1981–1984 Defense Buildup. Excluding inflation, annual growth in defense spending averaged 10 percent for each of these four years. Unlike the emphasis on selective combat force increases in the prior five-year period, the current buildup is concentrated on new hardware. Each military service has embarked on a massive modernization of its combat equipment. The army is in the midst of a near-simultaneous replacement of all its combat equipment—including the M-1 tank, the Bradley armored fighting vehicle, several new helicopters, and air defense systems. (The army manpower level, in contrast, has not changed in ten years.)

The navy is on a shipbuilding boom, having added more than twenty new ships per year between 1981 and 1984 (in contrast to fifteen ships per year in the 1970s). The navy plans to increase this shipbuilding rate to twenty-five ships annually between 1985 and 1989. Two new aircraft carriers at $3.5 billion each were approved in 1983, but the first of these will not join the fleet until 1990. Each year three Aegis cruisers at $1 billion each will be purchased to help defend the carrier. The navy continues to purchase large numbers of F-14 and F-18 fighters with the same mission as the Aegis—to protect the carrier.

The air force has the highest modernization growth rate of the three military departments. This growth is attributable in large part to the B-1B and M-X, two expensive strategic programs that require $11.1 billion in 1984 alone and that will not be operational until the late 1980s. Modernization of the twenty-six wing tactical force continues with the purchase of the F-15 and F-16 fighter aircraft and the acquisition of highly accurate, precision-guided bombs and missiles.

Resource Trends by Function

For internal management and congressional appropriation purposes, the defense budget is grouped into six major functions: military personnel, operations and maintenance (O&M), procurement, R&D, retired pay, and military construction. Table 3 shows the FY 1970–FY 1984 funding trends for the four major budget categories.

Under the military personnel category come the funds to pay 2,130,000 active and 1,030,000 reserve personnel. Between 1975 and 1984 funding has doubled for this function, although total personnel has increased only by 1 percent annually since 1980. Military strength declined sharply from the swollen level exceeding 3 million in 1970 to 2.3 million in 1975, before

TABLE 3

FUNDING TRENDS BY DEFENSE FUNCTION FOR SELECTED YEARS, FY 1970–FY 1984
(In current dollars [billions])

	FY 1970	FY 1975	FY 1980	FY 1984
Military personnel	23.0	24.9	31.1	47.9
O&M	21.5	26.2	46.6	74.0
Procurement	19.2	17.3	35.3	94.1
R&D	7.4	8.6	13.5	29.6

SOURCE: *National Defense Budget Estimates for FY 1984*, pp. 58–61.

stabilizing at the current level.[2] Most of the increase in personnel costs is accounted for by pay increases exceeding 35 percent, plus expanded housing benefits between October 1980 and October 1982. With higher pay and a surge in national unemployment since 1980, the military has had no trouble meeting its recruiting needs over the past several years.

Under the operations and maintenance category come the funds to meet the annual operational needs of all the defense forces, providing them with fuel, travel, repairs, overhauls, supplies, and services. More than 1 million Defense Department civilians are paid from this account; in fact, civilian pay constituted about half the O&M funds in the 1970s. In the past five years civilian employment has remained stable while outside purchases of goods and services have grown by 50 percent (after inflation). Today, civilian pay claims only about one-third the O&M total, with outside purchases now consuming two-thirds.

Procurement, which provides funds to acquire military hardware, constitutes by far the fastest-growing category of defense expenditure, having increased by 86 percent (after inflation) between 1980 and 1984. Since procurement outlays tend to lag behind budget authority (TOA) by two to three years, the recent procurement budgets ensure continued growth in defense outlays for the next several years.

The growth in research and development expenditures in general is proportionate to growth in the defense budget. In fact, the overall level of the R&D program in the Defense Department is set by Congress and the department as a more or less constant percentage of the total defense budget. In the 1970s, this figure was 10 percent of the total defense budget; in the past five years, as procurement surged, the ratio fell to 9.5 percent.

Funding Patterns by Military Department. In peacetime the army, which is the most manpower-intensive military service, traditionally receives fewer resources than the navy or air force, which depend more on expensive capital investments in ships and aircraft. In wartime, the obverse holds and the army grows at a faster rate than its sister services. Table 4 shows the funding trends by military department since 1975.

The navy (including the Marine Corps) and air force are constantly jockeying for the largest share of the defense program. From the 1950s through 1971, the air force predominated due to its major investment in strategic bombers and missiles. In the 1970s investment in strategic programs diminished and from 1972 through 1983 the navy received the highest budget; in 1984 the air force, with its B-1B bomber and M-X missile programs, once again took the lead.

---

2. Ibid.

TABLE 4

DEFENSE PROGRAM BY MILITARY DEPARTMENT FOR SELECTED YEARS,
FY 1975–FY 1984
(Excludes Military Retirement and Defense Agencies)

	FY 1975	FY 1980	FY 1981	FY 1982	FY 1983	FY 1984
	(In $ billions)					
Program funding:						
Army	21.6	34.6	43.2	52.2	57.2	62.3
Navy	28.0	47.1	57.5	68.8	82.9[a]	81.9
Air Force	26.0	41.6	52.5	65.0	74.2	86.1
Cumulative growth (beyond inflation) since 1975 (percentage):						
Army		+11	+24	+39	+45	+53
Navy		+10	+21	+36	+57[a]	+49
Air Force		+5	+18	+36	+49	+67
(Defense department total)		(+10)	(+22)	(+37)	(+49)	(+56)

SOURCE: Office of Defense Controller, National Defense Budget Estimate for FY 1984, March
1983, p. 68 (1984 figures revised to reflect congressional action).
a. Includes two aircraft carriers.

The relatively even cumulative growth rate experienced by each of the
three military departments in peacetime is an interesting phenomenon. This
can be termed the "Rule of 3" principle under which the cumulative rate of
growth for each military department will be distributed in three equal shares.
Table 4 illustrates this Rule of 3 since 1975.

The rates of increase in the 1975–1980, 1975–1981, and 1975–1982
periods prove remarkably equal for each department. In fact, when inflation
is removed, the navy and air force increases between 1975 and 1982 are
exactly equal. This equality does not hold in every year: For example, in
1983 the unusual addition of two aircraft carriers swelled the navy budget;
in 1984 the demands of the B-1B and M-X caused the air force program to
grow more rapidly. Adding together the annual percentage growth by service
for each of the four years (1981–84) shows the army with total growth over
the 1975 base of 161 percent, the navy 163 percent and the air force 170
percent. This again demonstrates the Rule of 3 in action.[3]

3. George C. Wilson, "Reallocation: Pentagon Studies Shifting $10 Billion from Navy to
Army," *Washington Post*, August 9, 1983, p. 1.

Assessing the Soviet Threat

Concern about the Soviet threat is the primary impetus for augmenting our defense forces and budgets, yet evaluations of the Soviet military threat are necessarily highly subjective. We will never have certain knowledge of the Soviets' military capabilities or, more important, of their intentions regarding these capabilities. Given this uncertainty, the interpretation of the Soviet threat at any particular time will be greatly shaped by the views of a small number of people with responsibility for our national security: the president; his top advisers in the Defense Department, the Central Intelligence Agency (CIA), and the National Security Council; and the top White House staff. The judgment of these leaders will be colored by the latest Soviet behavior or misbehavior and by the political climate in the nation. People with an alarmist view of the Soviets and their intentions will tend to emphasize the more extreme, pessimistic view of the Soviet military threat, whereas those holding the opposite view will place the Soviet threat in a more optimistic light.

All these subjective factors should be kept in mind in weighing the Reagan administration's arguments in support of the current defense buildup. Essentially, these arguments have two themes: that the Soviet Union spends more on defense than the United States and that the Soviets have achieved equal or superior military capability in most areas. Purported Soviet advantages and strengths have been discussed at length, but Soviet weaknesses and U.S. and Allied strengths have received little attention. This section assesses the Soviet threat from a number of perspectives and concludes that the current administration overstates the size of the threat and understates U.S. (and Allied) military capabilities.

Who Spends More on Defense?

For years the public has been treated to dire reports on Soviet defense spending. The CIA tells us that the Soviet Union spends 12 percent to 14 percent of its GNP on defense while the United States spends only 5 percent to 6 percent. (We are not reminded that our GNP is almost twice the GNP of Russia.) We are told as well that in 1981 the Soviet Union spent $222 billion, 44 percent more than the United States, on defense. In the 1970s their spending has exceeded ours by more than $300 billion.[4]

---

4. CIA Research Paper, "Soviet and U.S. Defense Activities 1971–80: A Dollar Cost Comparison," January 1981.

More complete spending comparisons and a more balanced assessment of Soviet and U.S. strengths and weaknesses, however, present a different picture. What, in particular, is missing from comparisons like the one just mentioned is information on the relative contributions of U.S. and Soviet allies and the weaknesses inherent in the methodology of the comparisons.

Regarding the first topic, data from the prestigious International Institute for Strategic Studies (IISS) show that in 1982 the Soviets' Warsaw Pact allies spent between $20 billion and $25 billion on defense forces, compared with about five times that amount—more than $100 billion annually—for our NATO allies.[5] This more complete comparison reverses the Soviet-U.S. spending picture, since defense expenditures of the United States and its NATO allies exceeded the defense expenditures of the Soviet Union and its Warsaw Pact allies in the past decade by more than $300 billion. In Asia, the principal Soviet allies—North Korea and Vietnam—spend some $5 billion to $6 billion annually on defense, while the principal U.S. allies—Japan, South Korea, Australia, and New Zealand—spend close to $20 billion.

Furthermore, a major portion of the Soviet buildup has been aimed squarely at the People's Republic of China, a nation of 1 billion people (four times the Soviet population) that has been increasingly hostile to the Russians. Century-old border disputes between the two countries broke into open fighting in 1969, and since the 1970s China has improved long-dormant relations with the United States, Japan, and other Western nations. Americans can understand China's threat to Russia by considering the long, undefended border we share with Canada; a hostile nation with a military force of 4 million on our northern border would quite rapidly change our defense emphasis. The CIA has published estimates that 10 to 15 percent of Soviet defense spending is for units with a primary mission against China.[6]

On the subject of methodology, it should be noted that since 1975, some key assumptions about the patterns of Soviet defense spending have changed. The CIA estimate of Soviet military spending as a portion of Soviet GNP rose almost 50 percent in the mid-1970s, not because the CIA judged that the Soviets were increasing their capability, but because the agency concluded it had earlier misjudged Soviet production efficiency. Simply put, the revised estimate said the same Soviet military output required 50 percent more effort than the CIA had previously estimated. Also, published reports indicate a division of views within the intelligence community over more recent spending trends. Based on evidence of reduced production of Soviet military materiel

5. International Institute for Strategic Studies (IISS), *The Military Balance 1983–84* (London, September 1983), pp. 125–126.

6. Ibid.

than had been predicted, the CIA has sharply revised its estimate of Soviet defense spending in the past six years, setting the annual growth estimate at only about 2 percent in real terms.[7] This CIA analysis suggests that the Soviet Union's defense spending remains a constant proportion of its GNP. The official national intelligence estimate (a consensus of the entire U.S. intelligence community) agrees that Soviet production is slowing, but disagrees with the CIA conclusions; it argues that the Soviets are still increasing their defense spending by 3 to 4 percent each year and that the lower output is due to the production of more expensive weapons and to production inefficiencies. This disagreement has serious implications for the debate on the spending gap, because if the CIA conclusion is accepted, the 1981 estimate of Soviet defense spending would be reduced by 9 to 10 percent.

How Accurate Are Soviet Defense Spending Estimates?

Data on defense spending by the United States and its allies are available and accurate. Since comparable Soviet data are not available, the CIA attempts to approximate Soviet defense spending by determining the cost to equip, man, and operate the Russian military in the United States, using U.S. market prices and paying American wages. Although this method does provide a good indicator of the trend in Soviet spending over time, it ignores the relative efficiency with which the U.S. and Soviet economies turn materials and labor inputs into finished products. A Soviet factory producing artillery rounds, for example, may operate at 50 percent, 80 percent, or 110 percent of the efficiency of a comparable U.S. plant. We just do not know which is correct.

More particularly, the CIA overstates the Soviet military personnel costs by pricing this force of low-wage conscripts at pay rates received by members of the American volunteer army. Thus it happens that every pay raise for U.S. military personnel widens the U.S.-Soviet spending gap simply because the Soviet Union has nearly twice as many troops in uniform as the United States. Eliminating this misleading pricing formula would, by itself, cancel out one–third of the supposed 1981 U.S.–Soviet spending gap.

Also, estimating what Soviet equipment would cost if produced in the United States is an extremely chancy undertaking. U.S. contractors provide the CIA with initial estimates of these costs, but since final price tags on our own weapons systems often vary widely from contractor estimates, so much more should we expect estimates to miss the mark when applied to Soviet weapons about which we know little. Apart from the sheer difficulty of the

---

7. Richard Halloran, "CIA Analysis Now Said to Find U.S. Overstated Soviet Arms Rise," *New York Times*, March 3, 1983, p. 1.

task, self-interest argues for U.S. contractors to attribute advanced capabilities and high unit costs to Soviet systems, thereby widening the supposed spending gap and enhancing their prospects for more defense business. In fact, the capabilities of several emerging Soviet systems—most notably the MIG-25 Foxbat fighters and the T-80 tanks—have proved vastly overstated in the past. In recent years about half of the CIA estimated U.S.-Soviet spending gap has been in this area. Accepting the lower estimates of Soviet weapons spending offered by the CIA staff analysts (mentioned earlier) would halve this weapons investment gap.

Finally, the CIA readily admits that the area of the Soviet spending estimate in which it has the least confidence is R&D. Reliable data simply are not available. Nonetheless, the CIA identified one-quarter of the total U.S.-Soviet spending gap in this area, estimating Soviet R&D costs at roughly twice the U.S. level. Despite this estimate of relative Soviet extravagance, a 1983 Defense Department report assessing the relative technical skills of the two nations in twenty key areas found the United States superior in fifteen areas, the United States and Soviet Union equal in four areas, and the Soviets ahead in only one area. The overwhelming U.S. edge raises questions as to the level and effectiveness of Soviet R&D spending efforts.

Table 5 shows that recognizing the impact of NATO, Warsaw Pact, and Asian allies, deleting the Soviet spending directed toward China, correcting for the manpower pricing error, and using the slower investment spending estimate suggested by CIA staff analysts would transform an alleged 44 percent Soviet spending advantage in 1981 into a 16 to 41 percent edge for the United States and its allies.

Are the Soviets Ready to Fight?

There is substantial evidence that the Soviet Union's approach to manning and training its military forces—a very different approach from our own—produces serious problems that are reflected in actual performance. One problem results from the treatment of racial and cultural differences. As a result of falling birthrates in European Russia and much higher birthrates among Asian populations, the Soviet population is becoming increasingly Asian and non-Slavic. Cultural differences breed a large measure of distrust and tension between the two groups. Because the Soviet army draws conscripts from more than ninety racial and nationality groups in the Soviet Union, powerful ethnic and religious tensions have developed. In addition, soldiers from the large Moslem minorities of Central Asia are less educated than the Russian norm. Russian is a second language to as many as 20 to 30 percent of draftees today, and the proportion will increase in the future. As a result

TABLE 5

COMPARISON OF U.S.–SOVIET DEFENSE SPENDING IN FY 1981

	Spending Advantage			
	U.S.	U.S.S.R.	U.S.	U.S.S.R.
	(In $ billions)		(Percentage)	
Defense intelligence estimate (3%–4% average annual growth since 1976)	154	222		+44
CIA revised estimate (2% average annual growth since 1976)		−22		+27
Allies' defense spending				
Europe	100	30		
Asia	20	6		
Revised total	274	236	+16	
Adjustment for pay raise methodology error		−20		
Deletion of China-related Soviet spending (10%–15%)	___	−22		
	274	194	+41	

SOURCES: IISS, *The Military Balance 1983–1984;* CIA Research Paper, "Soviet and U.S. Defense Activities 1971–80;" *New York Times,* March 3, 1983, p. 1; and author estimates.

of these problems, the army assigns Central Asian soldiers to noncombat support units as much as possible. Western specialists report that 80 percent of the groups in support units come from the Asian minorities, while 80 percent of the combat troops are European Slavs.[8]

The Soviets emphasize set-piece, stereotyped, and repetitive combat unit training, discouraging individual initiative. U.S. unit training, in contrast, encourages individual initiative and emphasizes variation in scenarios. Soviet training prepares the ground forces well for handling armored offensive operations, but not for dealing with unforeseen difficulties such as defensive operations, prolonged combat in urban areas, and antiguerrilla warfare. Soviet naval units spend far less time at sea than U.S. units and Russian pilots fly half the hours of their American counterparts, with much emphasis on pre-planned maneuvers and ground control. Finally, the routine annual assignment of many Russian military personnel to the Soviet grain harvest is not enhancing the combat readiness of these forces.

---

8. For more detail, see Andrew Cockburn, *The Threat: Inside the Soviet Military Machine* (New York: Random House, 1983).

The Afghanistan conflict has revealed several things about Soviet combat capability. The performance of 100,000 Soviet troops there has been less than spectacular: Three years after the Soviet occupation, rebel forces effectively control most of the country outside the major cities. The U.S. State Department reports that the Red Army in Afghanistan has been riddled with problems of poor hygiene, alcoholism, and racial strife.

Can the United States and its Allies Deter, or, if Necessary, Defeat Potential Military Aggression?

This is the most important question we face today in defining our defense program. Where can we win? Where are we likely to lose in the tragic event of a military confrontation with the Soviets? Trends in recent years show the Soviet Union improving its military capability relative to the United States and NATO, primarily through higher production rates of new weapons. Experts disagree wildly in their predictions; the questions elude any clear answer. Nevertheless, a few general assessments can be made.

Strategic Forces. Despite the allegations of Soviet superiority, a decided U.S. edge in deliverable nuclear warheads balances Soviet advantages in throw weight and missile launchers. The 1983 Scowcroft Commission report concluded there was no near-term "window of vulnerability" affecting our strategic forces. The claims of "Minuteman vulnerability" may or may not be true (many technical difficulties exist), but there is no question that the survivable air and sea legs of the strategic triad leave us with a substantial nuclear deterrent. The fine points of arms control negotiations aside, there is equivalence in strategic force capability of the two superpowers and their allies today.

Naval Forces. The U.S. navy, with its great edge in carrier forces, has a capability that far exceeds that of the Soviet navy, which suffers from a lack of major surface ships, has limited access to the world oceans from its naval bases, and has great difficulty in resupplying its surface ships and submarines once they are at sea. The naval edge increases when the allies of the two powers are considered, since the Soviet allies have almost no naval capability. The greater naval capability of the United States and its allies must however, control long sea lanes and project power ashore—a far larger mission than the Soviet mission of simply challenging that control. Nonetheless, by using our superior antisubmarine technology and by blockading the Soviet Union's narrow passageways into the world oceans, it seems likely that we could defeat a Soviet attack submarine force and control the shipping lanes. It is highly unlikely, however, that the U.S. navy could project power against

the Soviet mainland in view of the Soviets' gigantic edge in firepower from
land-based aircraft and missiles operating from their home bases.

Ground Forces in a European War.   The Soviets derive their strongest
military advantage from armor, and a quantitative imbalance in Europe favors
the Soviet-Warsaw Pact forces. The U.S. and NATO forces, however, have
superior antitank missiles, mines, and tactical aircraft equipped to stop on-
coming Soviet tanks and would have the advantage of fighting from defensive
positions. Predictions about the outcome of a Soviet-Warsaw Pact conventional assault on Europe vary widely from ''the Soviets will march to the
English Channel in a week,'' to ''a battle of attrition will ensue after heavy
initial losses on both sides,'' to ''the war will quickly escalate to a nuclear
exchange which leaves both sides in virtual ruin.'' Overall, the chance of a
Soviet-Warsaw Pact assault seems remote. The September 1983 report by the
International Institute for Strategic Studies concluded that ''the [Warsaw] Pact
has superiority in some areas and NATO in others, and there is no fully
satisfactory way to compare these asymmetrical advantages. Tank superiority
can be negated by combinations of many different kinds of antitank systems. . . . The overall balance continues to be such as to make military
aggression a highly risky undertaking. . . . The consequences for an attacker
would be unpredictable, and the risks, particularly of nuclear escalation,
incalculable.''[9]

Mid-East Conflict.   The United States has a quantum advantage today
in airlift and sealift capabilities (192,000 marines, for example, compared
with 16,000 for the Soviet Union), but we face a severe geographic disadvantage. Despite our greater mobility, we need to enhance our lift capabilities
substantially to overcome this disadvantage. (Ironically, the record defense
budget increase since 1980 does not provide for a major lift enhancement
program.)

Tactical Air Forces.   U.S. aircraft remain about one generation ahead
of the Soviets in air combat and ground attack capability, but Soviet production
of new aircraft exceeds that of the United States. (The quality advantage of
U.S. equipment was clearly demonstrated in the 1982 Lebanon war where
the Israelis, using American-supplied military equipment, shot down more
than 100 Syrian aircraft—Soviet-supplied M-16s—without losing a single
aircraft themselves.) Warsaw Pact and NATO nations have roughly the same
number of available tactical aircraft, but with different mission emphases:
about two-thirds of the Warsaw Pact aircraft are oriented to the air superiority
mission while about two-thirds of the NATO aircraft are oriented to support

---

9. Ibid.

of ground forces against Soviet armor attacks. NATO pilots are better trained than their Soviet counterparts. In summary, the military forces of the United States and its allies provide a powerful capability against our potential adversaries. How can the higher defense spending by the United States and its NATO allies conform with the perceived relative improvement of the Soviet-Warsaw Pact military capability over the past decade?

One puzzling factor is the ability of the Soviet Union and its allies to outproduce the United States and NATO countries in military hardware. To some degree this situation reflects a conscious decision by our military services to emphasize high-cost weaponry, which limits our total output. The decision to rely on high technology rather than on high numbers of forces has been the declared policy of our military for decades, and thus a numerical imbalance in forces is to be expected. In recent years, critics have proposed requiring high quantities of lower-cost, simpler weapons to combat the existing numerical imbalance.

Another possibility is that the United States and its NATO allies are not spending their defense funds as effectively as the Soviets. This appears hard to believe since the Western nations are the most advanced industrial nations in the world, while the Soviet economy is reputedly replete with inefficiencies. When one considers the numerous wasteful practices inherent in the U.S. defense effort—the lack of competition in weapons programs, sizable cost overruns and "bail-outs" on many programs, sub-par weapons performance that generates unplanned orders for spare parts and system modifications, and the retention of a basing structure and an industrial contractor base far in excess of military needs—there may be cause for alarm. These factors tend to degrade sharply the value obtained from our military program. In this context, it seems that the Soviet program, with all its built-in weaknesses, generates more defense from fewer resources than the U.S.-NATO program.

The Contribution of Defense and Other Assistance Programs

In foreign policy, most presidents can agree on three broad objectives:

1. *National Security*: We must have the capability to deter or, if necessary, defeat a nuclear or conventional attack by the Soviet Union and its allies on the United States, our allies, and other nations important to our interests. The budgets for defense and for military and economic assistance programs serve this objective.

2. *International Economic Growth*: We aim to maintain a viable and stable international economic system with relatively open markets to advance U.S. economic interests through beneficial trade and investment policies. The budget allocations for U.S. trade policies, direct economic assistance programs, and support for international funding institutions serve this objective.

3. *Global Objectives*: Political stability, particularly in the Third World, tops the list. Through economic grant and loan programs, the United States leads in the pursuit of solutions to worldwide problems such as the need for food and shelter, protection of the environment, human rights, and nuclear nonproliferation.

Assessment of the appropriate contribution that various programs—defense, economic assistance, trade policy, and the like—could make to each of these objectives would take us far beyond the scope of this paper. Suffice it to note here that the Carter and Reagan administrations adopted drastically different approaches to foreign policy, yet under both administrations defense has received the lion's share (a very large lion) of federal funding in the area of national security and international affairs. Table 6 demonstrates how defense spending dominates this area.

The Carter administration initially placed high reliance on continuation of detente with the Soviet Union, on selected initiatives in economic assistance, and on pursuit of global objectives in human rights and nuclear non-

TABLE 6

RESOURCES ALLOCATED TO INTERNATIONAL SECURITY FUNCTIONS
BUDGET AUTHORITY OR EQUIVALENT, FY 1978–FY 1985
(In 1983 constant $)

	Average Carter Budget 1978–1981		*Average Reagan Budget 1982–1985*	
Defense	186		263	
International security assistance: includes foreign military sales and grants	5		5	
Subtotal	191	(92%)	268	(96%)
Economic assistance to other nations	8	(4%)	5	(2%)
Export-Import bank loans	6	(3%)	4	(1%)
Conduct of foreign affairs, international organizations, and foreign information and exchange	3	(1%)	3	(1%)
TOTAL	208	(100%)	280	(100%)

SOURCE: *Budget of the United States Government, FY 1978–1983.*

proliferation. Prospects for SALT II and detente looked bright until late 1979, when Senate opposition to ratification of the treaty and the Soviet invasion of Afghanistan (in December) severely strained U.S.-Soviet relations. These developments, together with the Iranian hostage situation, triggered a sizable U.S. defense buildup. Our allies, in response to an appeal by President Carter, promised to increase their defense spending, but almost all the nations found problems of greater urgency at home which kept them from fulfilling their commitment.

During the Carter administration, the average annual budget for defense and international affairs (in 1983 dollars) was $208 billion; annual real growth averaged $5 billion to $6 billion. Economic assistance, particularly multilateral funding and export-import loans, grew most rapidly. Defense spending grew at an annual rate of 2 percent in this period, although Carter did propose a larger defense buildup (5 percent annual growth) in each of his last two budgets. Overall, the Carter administration assigned to defense about 92 percent of its budget resources for foreign policy, with about 8 percent going to economic assistance programs.

The dominance of defense programs in the foreign policy arena increased during the Reagan administration. Containment of the Soviet Union became the overriding objective; global objectives such as human rights (Poland is an exception), nuclear nonproliferation, and programs to reduce worldwide hunger were noticeably downgraded. Economic aid is now closely linked with the East-West struggle, with bilateral aid (and the greater political leverage derived therefrom) replacing the (much more politically neutral) multilateral aid. Having noted the dominance of defense programs in the foreign policy arena, we should also at least note in passing the dubious fit between our defense programs and the one foreign policy objective—national security— these programs are intended to serve. Almost the entire defense budget (other than retired pay) seeks to deter the least probable events: Soviet attacks on the United States, its allies, or regions of critical importance to us. The low probability, of course, derives from the deterrent value of the enormous investment in military spending by the United States and its allies over the years. Former Secretary of Defense Harold Brown summed it up well:

> Neither strategic war nor conventional war between the Soviet Union and the industrialized democracies ranks as one of the more probable threats to security. However, the military balance and perceptions of it are a major factor in political behavior and, in periods of crisis, may well do so decisively.[10]

---

10. Harold Brown, "Letter from Brussels," *Arsenal*, November 1982.

But granted the importance of deterrence, what about the more immediately actionable threats to our security? Since 1945 there have been more
than 130 wars (three to four per year), nearly all of them fought in Third
World nations, and many more internal revolutions. Individual events in most
cases have had little impact on U.S. strategic or international interests, but
in recent years more and more conflicts have involved the major powers and
the use of surrogate forces (e.g., Cubans in Angola, Ethiopia, and Nicaragua)
that do have serious implications. The United States currently dedicates few
of its troops to non-Soviet conflicts, on the rationale that forces prepared to
stop Russian forces anywhere in the world can also be applied to Third World
contingencies, if needed. The lessons of Vietnam for us, and now Afghanistan,
for the Russians, suggest otherwise.

The Defense Budget Process

This section examines the myths and realities of the defense budgeting
process within the executive branch. Let us begin with the myths. According
to President Reagan, the defense budget is created this way:

> We start by considering what must be done to maintain peace and review all the possible
> threats against our security. Then a strategy for strengthening peace and defending against
> those threats must be agreed upon. And finally our defense establishment must be evaluated
> to see what is necessary to protect against any or all of the potential threats. The cost of
> achieving these ends is totaled up and the result is the budget for national defense.[11]

Regrettably, reality must intrude on this logical, albeit idealistic, view.
All presidents bring with them a sense of the national needs they wish to
address, but converting these needs into specific programs proves a major
stumbling block to all administrations. Broad foreign policy objectives can
also be outlined but, again, the specific programs and funding levels required
are incredibly difficult to define. Most ongoing federal programs—domestic
and defense—will continue because they serve some valuable purpose or at
least because they placate political interest groups; thus the range of possible
choices for a new administration is rapidly narrowed. Allocating funding
levels between defense and domestic program areas is seldom done from the
top down: the normal method is to continue most agencies at the level for
the prior year and then make marginal changes—up or down—as individual
circumstances dictate. Defense, for example, may receive a 3 percent or
5 percent increase without specific program emphasis, whereas NASA

---

11. Ronald Reagan, "Address to the Nation," March 23, 1983.

spending may decrease by 10 percent simply because costs drop as the space shuttle becomes operational.

How effective are the foreign policy budget instruments? What overall mix of defense and nondefense programs will best meet our foreign policy needs? These questions are never consciously addressed in developing the federal budget. Most experts shrug their shoulders and conclude there is no way to quantify the comparative benefits of different programs, and they are correct, to a point: there is no "scientific" way to relate budgetary inputs to foreign policy outputs. But the fact is that presidents, budget directors, and agency heads constantly make agency resource decisions on the implicit assumption (it is certainly never explicit) of some correlation with articulated foreign policy needs. Any more explicit weighing of alternatives, no matter how subjective, would be an improvement over the silence about trade-offs. Yet in my twenty years at OMB, not once was an explicit budgetary trade-off made among the three major foreign policy instruments—defense, military assistance, and economic assistance. Decisions were, and continue to be, made in a compartmentalized fashion on individual agency programs.

Presidents Kennedy, Nixon, Ford, and Carter all ordered major national security studies to identify defense capabilities needed to deter and, if necessary, defend successfully against a spectrum of possible military contingencies. Options considered included the "Fortress America" concept of strategic forces plus conventional forces to defend the U.S. mainland from attack; the "1½ War Strategy" to counter a full-scale Soviet attack in Europe plus one other non-Soviet conflict elsewhere in the world; and the "2½ War Strategy" to counter a Soviet attack in Europe, an attack from China, plus one other smaller conflict elsewhere. In each of these studies, defining the options proved relatively easy, but pricing each option extremely difficult. And no wonder. The force levels and types of military equipment required for any particular military contingency vary widely. Planners in the military services naturally prefer minimal risk and their estimates of requirements naturally are on the high side. Civilian analysts, in contrast, will accept a higher risk and, consequently, their estimates of requirements are far lower. The important point is that the range of cost estimates required to implement any single strategy far exceeds the range in costs among different strategies. Thus, for example, civilian analysts will state that for "x" level of defense funds over the next five years the United States can execute a "1½ War Strategy," while the military services will claim that the same strategy will cost $2X$. These pricing differences for a clearly defined strategy are so large that they overwhelm any attempt at objective selection from a broad range of strategies.

This point is critical to understanding the lack of correlation between an annual defense budget and our defense "needs." In blunt terms, the *equipment* portion of the defense budget could be 10 to 25 percent higher or lower in any single year or even over a period of years and the impact on our defense capability would be minimal. The rate of investment in new equipment for our strategic and general purpose forces is highly flexible; and there is also a long transition period between any shift in strategic emphasis at the top and its actual implementation within the military departments. Also, the requirements for new hardware are often loosely stated, the scheduled operational dates are arbitrary, and the costs inevitably understated. (The B-1 in the early 1970s, for example, was advertised at the then high cost of $30 million to $40 million each; ten years later the cost is ten times higher and no one blinks an eye.)

The current administration has been trying to convince the American people that there is a coherent military strategy behind the defense buildup. President Reagan has stated, "It isn't done by deciding to spend a certain number of dollars. Those loud voices that are occasionally heard charging that the government is trying to solve a security problem by throwing money at it are nothing more than noise based on ignorance."[12]

In fact, however, the March 1981 Reagan budget amendment—which provided for the largest peacetime increase in defense in history—was the product of an agreement between a few key Republican senators and the administration that the defense budget needed at least $30 billion in additional funds. This approach contrasted sharply with the approach taken in nondefense areas in which the entire gamut of domestic programs, as well as each foreign aid program, was subject to the line-item pruning of David Stockman, director of the Office of Management and Budget (OMB). (How the senators arrived at the magic number of $30 billion remains murky, but they obviously discounted the $20 billion real increase in the Carter 1981 and 1982 budgets.) This senatorial decision was communicated to Defense Secretary Caspar Weinberger, David Stockman, and the White House—and that was that. There was little Office of Secretary of Defense or OMB budget review; the task of adding the extra money was simply assigned to the three military departments, all of which had long-standing shopping lists. There was no balancing of individual department requests; potentially important national needs like sealift and airlift were not high on the navy and air force lists and consequently received short shrift. And thus we embarked on a massive defense buildup, committing the nation to a $50 billion real growth in the defense budget ($20 billion Carter plus $30 billion Reagan).

---

12. Ibid.

Congress has shown itself remarkably acquiescent in this shift of the federal budget effort toward defense and away from domestic programs. In contrast with the harsh congressional treatment of domestic programs, not *one* sizable ongoing defense program was terminated in 1981 (or, in fact, over the past three years). Given that the Defense Department generally expects Congress to make some cuts in the defense budget requests, the absence of such reductions is convincing testimony to the lack of scrutiny accorded to the Reagan defense budget. In the Vietnam war phasedown, major cuts in the defense request came as no surprise to the Pentagon leadership. Congressional reductions of 5 percent annually continued while Gerald Ford was president and then dropped to 2 percent under Jimmy Carter, whose defense budget requests were deemed austere. After the halcyon defense budget in 1982, when President Reagan's defense increases sailed through Congress almost untouched to the pleased surprise of the administration, the reductions of 7 percent and 6 percent in 1983 and 1984 simply reflected congressional awareness that a sizable portion of "cut insurance" can be skimmed off with no repercussions. Further testimony to the "robust" nature of the defense budget is the fact that, despite an FY 1983 cut of almost $10 billion in procurement alone, almost every major DoD hardware program continued at its planned production level prior to the congressional cut.

Defense Operating Efficiency

Developing and selling the annual budget has become a full-time job for many top Pentagon officials. The congressional defense debate each year focuses largely on the overall budget level and on a few large hardware programs that could marginally increase or decrease the total. As a consequence of this heavy focus on preparing and defending the budget total, budget execution often gets short shrift.

Knowledgeable critics argue that, while high-level managers fight the "battle of the budget" in Congress, back in the trenches vast portions of the defense budget are being spent on obsolete strategies, improper weapons choices, and poor business and management practices. The 1983 President's Private Sector Survey on Cost Control (the Grace Commission) identified more than $90 billion in potential savings in the defense budget over the next three years.[13] In mid-1983, Paul Thayer, then deputy defense secretary,

---

13. J. Peter Grace, "Testimony Before the House Budget Committee Hearings on Defense Spending Efficiency," October 4, 1983.

estimated that 10 to 30 percent of defense contract funds were being lost to ineffective management and poor workmanship.[14] If Thayer is right, then there may be as much as $50 billion in potential savings buried in the total 1984 defense purchases of $170 billion.

These criticisms suggest that the key question for defense in the next few years should not be "How much?" but rather, "How can the defense program be planned and executed more efficiently?" A top-to-bottom survey identifies six broad areas that generate problems today.

Changing Mission Needs.   The military services recognize their prime responsibility as being to deter, and, if necessary, defeat attacks from adversaries against us or our allies. Because this awesome task must always be carried out within financial constraints, the people entrusted with the task tend to be risk averse, preferring to rely heavily on the "tried and true" than to invest precious resources in experimental missions. In this century, major doctrinal changes have generally been initiated by mavericks in the military whose views run counter to their superiors. In the 1920s General Billy Mitchell was courtmartialed for his bold insistence on a role for military airpower. In the 1930s General Adna Chafee led the battle in the army to replace horse cavalry with armored tanks. The president of the Army War College dismissed his proposal as "visionary and crazy."[15] In the 1950s Admiral Hyman Rickover led the fight for nuclear submarines, achieving success only after Congress overrode the opposition of the entire naval leadership. Many knowledgeable defense experts argue that there are a number of modern equivalents to the 1930s horse cavalry (the navy's carrier task force and the air force's penetrating strategic bomber spring to mind as oft-cited examples) that ought to receive more serious scrutiny than military leaders are disposed to give them.

Overlapping Mission Responsibilities.   Combat mission responsibilities often cross military service lines, but, as has often been noted, the compartmentalized decision-making processes of each military service inhibit real cooperation. The three military departments—air force, army, and navy (which includes the marines)—tend to be strongly independent fiefdoms, each dedicated to attaining the complete capability needed for the accomplishment of its missions. The question of the extent to which the resulting capabilities encompass costly redundancies has been fought among the services, and between the services and civilian management, for years. Suffice it to say here that the question of redundancy has not been settled with regard to a number of modern military programs (such as the army and air force

---

14. Richard Halloran, "Pentagon Aide Says Shoddy Work Adds 10% to 30% to Military Costs," *New York Times*, June 2, 1983, p. 1.

15. *Congressional Record*, September 11, 1981, p. H6151.

programs for NATO air defense, the army and air force close air support programs, the navy and air force strategic missile programs) and that the elimination of any of these programs could save billions of dollars.

For example, when the air force was created in 1947, the army lost operational control of the close air support mission for army ground forces which the army viewed as vital. The army believes (with some justification) that the air force has not placed a high enough priority on this mission; consequently, the army has sought to create its own independent close air support capability. Because of a ruling prohibiting it from procuring fixed-wing aircraft, however, this army force is made up exclusively of helicopters—which are expensive and widely considered to be quite vulnerable under battlefield conditions. Today, the air force has just completed its planned acquisition of A-10 close air support planes (many of which have already been transferred from the active forces to the reserves) while the army continues its helicopter modernization plan at a cost of between $15 billion and $20 billion in the 1980s.

Weapons Requirements. The military services justify advanced-technology weapons to offset the Soviets' numerical edge in troops and weapons. And U.S. weapons, including aircraft, ships, tanks, and antitank systems, are all superior in performance to Soviet equivalents. The question remaining is the necessity for that last 10 percent of promised performance improvements in new systems—the so-called "gold plating"—which carries the risk of lower operational reliability and high cost. Many defense experts attribute the poor performance and cost record on new weapons in the past twenty years to this "gold plating" problem.[16] The incentives for gold plating derive from the military services' perception of the current force structure as fixed, a perception that motivates them to buy the very best that industry can provide in each new weapon program. As an air force general once told me bluntly, "We will be given only a fixed number of aircraft in the Tactical Air Command, and I am going to be damn sure that each one is equipped with the best that money can buy." Thus, while our military continues to buy the most sophisticated and theoretically capable systems possible, the key question too often ignored is whether the new weapons are worth the added cost and the risk of low reliability when simpler, less expensive weapons could be purchased with only marginal decreases in performance.

Source Selection. After a military service decides on requirements for a new weapon, a contractor team must be selected to do the work. A formal competition ensues among a few major defense firms for the contract to

---

16. For more detail on this issue, see James Fallows, *National Defense* (New York: Random House, 1981).

develop a new weapon. Officially, the criteria for determining the winner are the technical design and cost estimates in the contractors' proposals; but judging the technical merits of the proposals is difficult, because many of the technologies are unproven and costs are notoriously "soft." Thus it happens that informal factors—long-standing ties between a contractor and the services, for example—may translate into the opportunity to have a greater hand in the early development of the "requirements" for the new weapon, which confers a real competitive advantage. Also, because weapon competitions are normally limited to development and initial procurement, a large portion of the eventual program (twenty years or more) operates in a sole-source environment, without competitive pressure for cost control. And since the prices quoted in the initial competition can often be adjusted upward once a contract is won, contractors may quote unrealistically low prices initially in order to improve their chances of winning the competition. Finally, as was exhibited in the 1982 battle over the C-5B transport, political and economic factors can become important factors in contract awards.

Contract Execution for Major Systems.   Once a winning contractor team is selected, it can usually count on a continuing defense business for up to twenty years. As an extreme example, the B-52 has provided significant business volume to Boeing for more than thirty years.

Most of our major systems encounter adverse costs and performance and schedule problems during execution. How do contractors cope with these setbacks? The answers vary but ultimately the same answer emerges—charge them off to the U.S. government. The methods vary: Changes in weapon system design provide wide-ranging opportunities to recover any losses. Reallocation of corporate overhead is another favorite. Redefinition of inflation to justify an upward adjustment (but never downward) for individual contractors is another technique.

Thus, because a firm has little chance of losing money on its production contract and will probably be reimbursed for its growth in costs, the incentives to minimize costs are not strong. Later contracts for follow-on production, spare parts, and modifications then provide a steady business in a sole-source environment—a situation that works heavily to the contractors' advantage. The system in some cases actually rewards contractors for poor performance on their production contracts by granting increased spare parts and modification contracts to firms who produce trouble-plagued weapons.

The current purchasing strategy within the Defense Department protects firms in order to maintain the defense industrial base at the cost of higher unit prices for weapons. Several formal studies conclude, however, that there is an excess of aerospace industrial capacity among the prime contractors.

Expenses Outside the Major Weapons Areas.   Major weapons receive a disproportionate amount of time and attention. The 1984 defense
budget contains about $170 billion to purchase equipment and services from
the private sector. Major weapons constitute about one-third of this total, with
another one-third in smaller procurements and the remainder in support of
current operations and R&D. Also, almost $100 billion annually goes to pay
military and civilian personnel. These expenses outside the major weapons
area offer numerous opportunities to improve efficiency. Several examples
follow:

- Much of our current basing structure developed from World War II,
  when the nation had well over twelve million under arms, compared
  with two million today. If we could set aside political considerations
  and start all over to create a proper basing structure for today's U.S.
  forces, we could save between $4 billion and $5 billion annually in
  defense spending.

- The Davis-Bacon Act, written in 1934 to ensure fair wages for laborers
  working on government construction projects, requires these workers
  to be paid higher than the going market wages. Simply substituting
  the prevailing local wage rate in these contracts would save the government more than $1 billion annually.

- The General Services Administration (GSA) is the government's central purchaser of commonly used supplies. The Defense Department
  is the largest GSA customer, accounting for well over half of the
  annual GSA sales. Several years ago, a study of the GSA purchasing
  practices revealed that only one-third of the items acquired were
  bought through competitive bidding; as a result, the government pays
  premium prices for commonplace items at a cost of hundreds of
  millions each year.

- About half of the annual procurement budget buys a wide variety of
  support equipment for the combat forces—communication systems,
  vehicles, ammunition, modifications, and spares. The requirements,
  justification, timing of purchases, and degree of competition in all of
  these areas need much greater scrutiny and offer fertile fields for large
  savings.

Future Defense Planning Options

The foregoing sections identified serious flaws in the current process for
allocating resources to defense. Summarizing briefly, the official U.S.

estimates of the Soviet military threat are overstated. In allocating resources to achieve our foreign policy objectives, appropriate budgetary decisions and program trade-offs are not made between defense and foreign assistance programs. Although the precise military implications of any given defense budget elude even the most educated defense minds, the budget total has become a political symbol of overblown importance both at home and abroad. Meanwhile, actual execution of the defense program each year suffers greatly from the absence of incentives for efficiency among defense and contractor personnel. Rapid buildups in the defense program, such as in the past four years, foster this inefficiency.

Several broad guidelines can be suggested to improve future budgetary planning:

- Make a greater effort to recognize the different contributions of defense as well as foreign assistance programs in determining U.S. foreign policy needs. Defense forces and programs are geared to the most severe but least likely threats, whereas our military forces are of less value in the multitude of conflicts among small nations that are far more likely to occur. Foreign assistance programs, both economic and military, are potentially much more effective in preventing or helping to conclude such conflicts.

- Provide a more balanced assessment of the military threat posed by the Soviets. Recognizing Soviet military weaknesses as well as strengths, the greater contribution of U.S. allies, and the Soviets' problem with China will give a more realistic picture of threats posed.

- Within fiscal policy constraints, establish tight controls over the defense budget to encourage greater discipline in the selection and execution of the overall program. The large increases of the past four years have not carried with them any incentives—quite the contrary— to spend more wisely.

- Recognize that there is no "right" defense budget level in any given year or even over a series of years. To minimize "cut insurance" game playing, the president and key congressional leaders could try to reach agreement in advance on the total budget level to be presented to Congress.

With these guidelines in mind, we can identify two alternative defense planning options for the remainder of the 1980s.

1. Soviet containment is our overriding foreign policy objective. Acceptance of this objective implies that the U.S. military buildup must

continue rapidly to redress our inferior position; little can be expected
from our allies in the way of additional military contributions. Without a continued buildup there is little hope that successful strategic
or conventional arms control agreements can be achieved. If these
assumptions are accepted, the defense program should continue to
grow considerably faster than the nation's GNP, at annual rates of
7 to 10 percent above inflation ($20 billion to $30 billion annually)
for the remainder of this decade. The defense program should continue to emphasize weapons modernization, but should be coupled
with a program of improved incentives to achieve better program
performance. Economic assistance programs should grow no faster
than the overall rate of growth in GNP.

2. World stability and international economic growth are our major
foreign policy objectives. With these objectives, there is greater
potential for trade-offs between defense spending and foreign assistance. The Soviet military threat still appears serious, but U.S. and
Allied forces are viewed as having adequate military capabilities to
match the Soviets; and continued growth in military contributions
can be anticipated from three major European nations—West Germany, the United Kingdom, and France. Mutually satisfactory arms
control negotiations with the Soviets appear to be possible without
a continued rapid buildup. Economic assistance programs show promise
for curbing the numerous brushfires erupting each year in the developing nations.

If we accept the assumptions in the second option, the defense program
could be set at a level no higher than the nation's GNP growth; in fact, slower
growth in the next two years would be preferable to provide the Defense
Department with some breathing space to absorb the 41 percent increased
activity since 1980 and to improve management efficiency. For planning
purposes, defense real growth could be half the GNP growth rate for 1985
and 1986, increasing to the full rate of GNP growth for the remainder of the
decade, with no ill effects on either strategic or conventional forces. In addition, up to 1 percent of the Defense budget (between $1 billion and
$3 billion annually) in 1985 and 1986 could be set aside for an expanded
program of economic assistance to developing nations considered vital to our
national interests. This expanded program would thereby increase far faster
than the rate of GNP growth, since (for example) a $1 billion increase in
each of two years would produce a 40 percent increase in the current level
of economic assistance.

To complement these broad policy changes, improved efficiency in our defense program is, as had been often noted in this paper, sorely needed. Two broad themes consistently emerge in explanations of defense management problems. The first relates to the poor incentives operating on military and industry personnel. Competition is not seriously demanded across the spectrum of defense purchases; tough actions against contractors or base realignments are not rewarded; program managers, with their short time horizons, see "success" as keeping their programs funded and avoiding publicity, not as challenging the status quo. Incentives for industry are even worse: "Low ball" contract bids, poor performance, and large cost overruns are regarded as acceptable practices because the government in fact routinely accepts them. As one industry official described the situation, "It's not the type of ballgame we would choose to play, but it's the only ballgame in town."[17]

The other cross-cutting theme in defense is an aversion to change. The military problems faced in the next twenty years will require creative options in force planning and some realignment of priorities. New ideas inevitably challenge powerful entrenched interests inside and outside the Pentagon, making reform extremely difficult. Consider, for example, the numerous proposals over the years to reorganize the Joint Chiefs of Staff. After thirty-five years of experience with the current organization, many experts have concluded that the current system is of little value in providing independent military advice to civilian leaders; yet despite increasing pressure for change, opposition from the services—particularly the navy—has successfully stymied reform.

Here are five examples of reforms that can reap large benefits:

1. Reexamining the fundamentals that underlie the highest priorities in each of the departments. Candidates should include the future requirement for air force penetrating strategic bombers, for large naval aircraft carriers, and for army tactical doctrines in the defense of Europe.

2. Reassessing the roles and missions assigned to each service with a view toward reducing the overlap between services. Specific mission areas should include close air support, air defense, and strategic forces.

3. Choosing more new weapons that emphasize low cost and high reliability. The military services should be encouraged to consider

---

17. In Ronald Fox, *Arming America: How the U.S. Buys Weapons* (Cambridge, Mass: Harvard University Press, 1974), p. 297.

trade-offs between force size and quality improvements. Larger quantities of less-expensive equipment could be more attractive than smaller quantities of sophisticated weaponry. More and tougher testing should be required of all new equipment before it is introduced into the force.

4. Reforming the acquisition process for major weapons systems. The current process provides little incentive for firms to minimize their costs and to assure high performance because the government usually picks up the tab for failure. Greater competition in all aspects of defense purchases, recognition of past performance in the award of new contracts, and willingness to allow some shrinkage in the number of dedicated prime contractors are initial steps that promise a high payoff. Defense managers need greater rewards for good performance (in particular, for tackling contractors that perform inadequately).

5. Focusing greater attention on the many opportunities for increased efficiency in the "soft underbelly" areas of defense, which include the thousands of small contracts, the facilities structure, and the codified subsidies built into business practices. Billions in subsidies are paid out annually in these areas. Congressional leaders need to work more closely with the Defense Department and the White House in demanding reforms in these areas, which—because of their political sensitivity—are probably susceptible only to a joint executive-legislative reform.

COMMENTS

Robert B. Pirie

There is a lot to like in this paper. It is at least aimed at the right target, which is to develop a sense of how well our defense programs do or do not support our main national objectives, and to suggest some innovative ways to support those objectives better. And Stubbing comes up with a fairly clear solution, which is that we are really not badly off in the defense area and can afford some budget restraint in the next few years.

Do we believe the answer? Has Stubbing offered enough evidence to support his claims? Is his analysis persuasive to wider audiences who are not specialists and who may have sincere concerns over the state of our national defenses?

Here I have reservations about the paper. I believe Stubbing has slighted some of the main areas of interest in deciding how much is enough, while giving undue emphasis to secondary issues. The fundamental question here is not whether our defense budget process is ineffective, or whether the Armed Services Committees are enlightened, or whether defense spending corrupts the economy. It is instead whether our military forces can do what we call upon them to do. That boils down to deterring Soviet attacks on ourselves and our allies, and being able to terminate hostilities rapidly and under favorable conditions if deterrence fails. Also there is an important corollary, which is that real or perceived disparities in the military balance should not be such as to afford political leverage to the Soviets or to tempt them to what we regard as antisocial international behavior.

The evidence that bears on these issues includes the relative size of the forces on both sides, their organization, readiness, and capability, and the like. The paper deals with some of these matters, but in what seems to me to be a highly superficial way. The question of relative capabilities is dealt with in a section of just over four pages. One should be skeptical about the misleading precision of many estimates of the military balance, but one cannot escape the need to do some fairly serious analysis of the balance. And one has to go beyond first-order effects. It is perfectly true, for example, that the

Soviet navy would not stand a chance against ours in a major fleet engagement on the high seas. But that is not what they intend to do with their navy, at least at present, nor is it a reasonable test of the kind and amount of capabilities that best equip our own navy to support the national strategy. It is also true that there is rough parity of military manpower between NATO and the Warsaw Pact in Europe. For example, NATO ground forces number 2,720,000 and Warsaw Pact number 2,618,000. However, of the NATO total, 931,000 are in Southern Europe, away from the critical central region, and 350,000 must come from the United States by air and sea at some stage in the war's development. Finally, it may be true that the United States has 9,300 deliverable strategic warheads and the Soviets have 7,300, but those figures are not determining the administration's strategic programs. The determining factors are the obsolescence of much of our force, the large throw-weight disparity in favor of the Soviets, and a perceived Soviet advantage in prompt, hard-target kill capability.

Now, I am not suggesting that Stubbing must solve all these weighty issues before we can sign up with his assessment of the balance. But I do think that it is necessary to acknowledge that such questions exist, and that people take them seriously in their own assessments.

Where are we really with respect to the threat and the military balance? I think it is fair to say, and the paper indeed acknowledges, that Soviet military capabilities have improved substantially in relation to NATO's in the past decade. That is reason for concern, not panic. We would not wish to see a similar relative change at the end of the next decade, because at some point, not well defined, the concern about overwhelming military force providing political leverage becomes important.

Assessments of key elements of the military balance do not support the notion that the Soviets have preemptive military options. In the central strategic forces, we continue to maintain a secure second-strike capability despite increasingly vulnerable land-based missile systems. The administration's strategic buildup seems motivated primarily by what began as a sensible idea but has now been taken to extreme conclusions. That is, it was quite reasonable to ask how we might respond to some Soviet attack short of a full countervalue strike. But this has now degenerated into a pursuit of large-scale, prompt, hard-target kill capability that promises to give us the worst of all worlds. Such a capability will be vulnerable, thus usable only in a preemptive mode, and inviting preemption. The next logical step of strategic defense makes matters even worse, since it compounds the uncertainties in estimating the balance, pulls the teeth of our allies' independent deterrent forces, and creates strong incentives to break out into further deployments of MIRVED (multiple independently targetable reentry vehicle) missiles. To maintain the deterrent, the aging parts of our strategic forces should be modernized, but the large buildup being pursued by the administration seems misguided and excessive.

The military balance in Europe is a subject that can be depended on to provoke lively discussion and a wide range of predicted outcomes. The Soviets will walk to the channel in a week, over the bodies of refugees and soldiers whose efforts to flee or fight condemn each other to futility. Or, a war of attrition will ensue, in which anything moving on the battlefield larger than a rat will be instantly obliterated by an intelligent projectile. Or, the Soviet armies, hampered by tenuous lines of communications and betrayed by their reluctant East European allies, run out of supplies and can be destroyed piecemeal. We can find examples in history of military events as improbable as any of these, but several observations seem appropriate:

1. Conventional calculations of the outcome of combat, the familiar 1:1, 2:1, 3:1 ratios, are bound to be misleading in a context as rich and complex as war in Central Europe.

2. It is hard to think of a favorable outcome of a European war, from the Soviet point of view, that could not be better achieved, at less risk, in some other way.

3. Given the uncertainty, it is quite difficult to see what more POMCUS (prepositioned overseas material configured in unit sets) or more divisions or tactical airwings on U.S. soil would add to our conventional deterrent that offsets the costs they would entail in resources and readiness.

The Soviet navy has attracted much attention recently; in the past two decades it has made progress comparable to that of the Soviets' strategic rocket forces. Even so, however, it remains true that where the Soviets cannot go by marching or cover with aircraft based in the Soviet Union, they cannot maintain a military presence if we choose to evict them. Future Soviet aircraft carriers will change this situation slowly, if at all. The major challenge from the Soviet navy will remain their submarines. Many analysts see an emerging tendency in Soviet military thinking toward the possibility of a prolonged, perhaps indefinite, conventional phase in a world war if one should break out. In such a war, maintenance of the sea lines of communication and maintenance of access to raw materials could be at least as important as the entering military balance on the ground. It is important to maintain our navy, which supports such capabilities, because a navy that did not would leave our deployed forces as hostages, and because the deterrent effect of the means and will to prevail in a protracted war is an important, if underrated, component of our conventional deterrent. But there are no compelling arguments to the effect that the knee in the curve of the navy's effectiveness occurs between fourteen and sixteen carrier battle groups. And the resources devoted to protecting the carriers in high-threat environments, now including the bulk of the navy's shipbuilding program, seem disproportionate to either putative effects on the outcome of the war, or equivalent protection to be offered through other means, such as land-based aviation.

There are other important military balances, and other missions that require resources. On the whole I am persuaded that a period of modest but steady real growth in defense is the best policy. The paper suggests this also, linking defense growth to growth in the GNP. I lean to the 5 percent per year endorsed by the Budget Committees. Such growth should permit us to modernize our strategic forces, complete the equipment of the sixteen-division army, and maintain adequate lift and support to enable us to deal, along with our rapidly deployable forces, with contingencies outside Europe not involving the Soviets. It would permit maintaining naval and tactical air forces with modern equipment of about the size we now have, but would probably not allow much force expansion. Analysis of the merits of such expansion are not found in the paper, but strike me as directly relevant to the choice between the administration's program and the alternatives we are discussing.

Also relevant to that choice, and not mentioned in the paper, are some fairly serious structural problems in the administration's defense program that may make restraint more difficult in the future. The very large surge in procurement obligational authority in the 1983 and 1984 defense budgets particularly will tend to make outlays difficult to reduce in the next five years. The nonprocurement accounts will have to be raided to support investment outlays. And at the end of the cycle there will be much new equipment to be supported with spare parts, ammunition, training, and so on. Smoothing out this pernicious ratchet effect will not be easy, because, as the paper points out, almost all the major actors—the services, Congress, industry—have incentives to keep it going, or at least to avoid the pain of slowing down. But it must be smoothed out if we are to avoid having hollow armed forces. Part of the answer is avoidance of boom-and-bust defense budgets that redouble incentives to make hay while the sun shines. And part of the answer is attention to, and better analyses of, the effects of such unbalanced programs.

There is much irrelevant material in the paper that can be jettisoned; for example, the discussion on cost comparisons could be reduced to about two paragraphs. The comparisons are mildly interesting indicators of relative efforts and trends, but tell us nothing about the capabilities created; for that, we need to do analyses of the sort I suggested earlier. The critique of cost comparisons is longer than the subject deserves and technically wrong in places, and the counter-comparison is strained and highly arguable. Also, the paper throughout would be improved by moderation of its polemical tone.

In summary, then, I think Stubbing's paper is aimed at the right target, and that he courageously presses through to a conclusion that merits serious attention. But I also think that its substantive analysis is inadequate to support the major message, it contains excessive extraneous detail, and it has too rhetorical a tone.

COMMENTS

Robert F. Hale

I found Richard Stubbing's paper on the defense program an interesting discussion, made more vivid by the author's many years of access to the inner workings of the debates over defense. I also agree with some of the major points in the paper. I was, however, distracted from those major points by the paper's lack of evenhandedness. Most of all, I was disappointed that it did not provide a more thorough and creative discussion of the prospects for improving the U.S. defense program.

Many Major Points Seem Reasonable

I agreed with some of the paper's major points. Stubbing argues, and I agree, that this administration tends to concentrate only on Soviet strengths. Indeed, during testimony before the Senate Armed Services Committee early this year, the secretary of defense and the chairman of the Joint Chiefs of Staff spent several hours recounting Soviet strengths. When asked to indicate some of their weaknesses, the chairman said that—although the services constantly sought such weaknesses—he could not discuss them in an open forum.[1]

Yet, as this paper notes, there are weaknesses in the Soviet military. The quality of Soviet military training and the cohesiveness of their units are questionable. So too is the reliability of their allies.

Stubbing also makes some good points about the way U.S. budgets are developed. Some parts of the budget, like research and development, do seem to retain a constant share. Such strategies are probably a way of dealing with great uncertainty.

---

1. Hearings before the Committee on Armed Services of the U.S. Senate, 98:1, February 1, 1983, p. 35.

Finally, the paper makes some valid and important points about what motivates various actors in the defense budget debate. Congress, heavily pressured by lobby groups from corporate America and elsewhere, clearly does not cancel major systems once they are in production. Nor, I suspect, do most staff members in the administration, though their votes are less public. Also, the military chain of command—with clear ranks and subordination— does not foster innovative strategies for warfare or alternative weapons plans.

Paper Tends to Overstatement

There were many other nuggets of wisdom that rang true to me in this paper. Unfortunately, I found that I was distracted from them because the paper lacked evenhandedness. Like so many critiques of defense planning, this one tends to overstatement. Let me illustrate my concern with several examples.

Stubbing argues that estimates of Soviet defense spending, which this administration uses to defend its budget increases, are highly uncertain. By implication, Soviet estimates should be used with care—if at all—in the debate. But the paper then proceeds to use these estimates to argue for less defense spending, after making a series of questionable adjustments. For example, the paper discounts 10–15 percent of Soviet spending altogether because it is related to China. Surely the weapons and forces bought with this 10–15 percent could be used against the United States and our allies. Why shouldn't they count, just as U.S. forces aimed at non-Soviet contingencies count in our spending? Also, the paper argues that it is wrong to evaluate Soviet manpower costs at U.S. pay rates. The paper, however, uses Soviet and U.S. estimates to compare defense capability. Do the Soviets have less capability just because they choose to pay part of their defense costs by conscripting their young men at low wages?

Nor was the paper evenhanded or thorough in its treatment of Congress and defense spending. As the paper asserts, the Armed Services Committees historically have been, and still are, the advocates of defense. The paper might note, however, that some less prodefense members (Senator Edward Kennedy, Representatives Les Aspin and Ronald Dellums) are joining or assuming leadership roles on these committees; thus, the committees are changing in important ways. Moreover, the paper's own numbers belie the simplistic arguments about "cut insurance" that is put in for Congress to remove. There is, of course, gaming in the administration's defense budget, as in other budgets. But the administration must be mighty good guessers if they can select a level of cut insurance that corresponds with widely varying reductions by Congress over the past few decades. Indeed, Congress added to the defense budget during nine of the years since 1950 (but only in one year of the past ten).

More fundamentally, the paper ignores the key role that I believe Congress plays in defense policy. Congress provides a way for public opinion to influence defense planning. For example, it allows the public—through its elected representatives—to make clear its reluctance to increase the number of troops in Lebanon under current circumstances. It allows that same public to pressure the administration to be more forthcoming on arms control. I think it naive to assume that these pressures do not influence policy, but they never show up in the budget or in this paper's analysis of Congress.

Need for Better Discussion of Prospects for Defense

Along with evenhandedness, a better discussion of the prospects for defense policy would be helpful. As it is, the paper contains twenty-six interesting pages on what influences defense budgets but only four pages on what they are likely to be and how to design them more effectively.

Stubbing's discussion of defense spending options illustrates my point. The paper's first option calls for increases in real budget authority of 7 percent to 10 percent a year throughout this decade, more than what even the administration proposes. The second option lacks numbers but would probably call for increases of 1 percent to 2 percent a year for the next few years and about 3 percent to 4 percent a year thereafter. Interestingly, Congress is heading toward a compromise right in the middle of this range. In its latest long-term plan, Congress called for real increases of 5 percent a year for defense budget authority in 1984 to 1986. Clearly, this option—perhaps the most likely one to emerge from the political process if President Reagan is reelected—deserves mention.

Moreover, Stubbing does not treat one of the major factors leading Congress to its decision. If large deficits are to be reduced, federal spending will have to be cut. Congress understands, I believe, that slowing the rate of growth in defense spending will not solve the deficit problem. Indeed, 5 percent growth in defense budget authority will reduce outlays in 1986 by about $25 billion below the administration's planned level; this would scarcely dent the expected deficit of more than $200 billion. Nonetheless, Congress also understands that a slowdown in the rate of growth in defense spending will have to be part of any compromise package that reduces the deficit by large amounts.

Many factors drive the administration and Congress in their decisions on defense: U.S. foreign policy goals, perceptions of the Soviet threat, the state of the economy, and domestic policy. The paper provides a discussion of three of these four factors, although the discussion of the Soviet threat would benefit from a more neutral discussion that mentioned the many assessments of force balance that have been made. The paper should also include some mention of the effects of large federal deficits on future defense spending. How should new ideas be implemented?

Stubbing concludes with some intriguing ideas about how to get more out of the U.S. defense budget, regardless of its level. The author's experience and analysis would be helpful in determining how to implement these ideas. The paper argues, for example, that we need to allow defense managers to keep some of the savings they create by better management and use them on projects which they deem important but which are not funded. I could not agree more. Without such a program, there is little or no incentive for middle managers to take risks and do business differently. Yet these middle managers are the ones who know how real efficiencies can be achieved. But we have tried such schemes in the past with mixed success. Which have been the winners? Can these winners be implemented on a grander scale?

The paper also suggests that tight fiscal constraints on defense spending provide an incentive to select the most important and cost-effective weapons. The likely slowdown in the rate of growth in defense spending will probably create this discipline in the next few years. But I believe that any suggestions for major change in defense programs must ultimately come from—or at least be embraced by—the services; otherwise the changes will not be implemented effectively. How can we encourage the services to make changes? Would a national commission help if it were charged with evaluating the many ideas for new ways to enhance our defense? Would it help if civilian leaders acknowledge that new weapons inevitably carry some risk—risk that perhaps should be offset by continued purchase of proven weapons systems?

Finally, the paper suggests that we are spending too little on military and economic assistance and that more spending could help prevent or contain brushfire wars. I find this an intriguing notion. But how much more might be appropriate? Is there any historical evidence that higher military and economic assistance contained brushfire wars, or at least brought them to a conclusion more to our liking?

Reviewing this paper reminded me again how much easier it is to be a critic than a creator. As the biggest single employer and business in the country, with one-quarter of the entire federal budget, the defense program presents an awesome challenge to any author. I found this paper a good review of some of the problems. I could only urge that it concentrate more on the solutions.

HEALTH CARE FINANCING AND PENSION PROGRAMS

John L. Palmer and Barbara Boyle Torrey

Mounting concern about the large structural deficits in the federal budget in the late 1980s will inevitably lead analysts and politicans to focus on pension and health care financing programs, which together make up the largest and, until the recent defense buildup, fastest-growing component of the federal budget. Because these programs account for nearly three-quarters of all non-defense spending (and even more of its projected growth), any further efforts at curbing domestic outlays will have to address health and pension financing problems—or face the prospect of a drastic curtailment of other federal domestic activities. And because these programs were cut by only one-fifth as much (proportionally) as other domestic programs over the past three years, it will surely be argued that they are, in some sense, ripe for plucking. The largest federal pension program, Social Security, has already precipitated a fiscal crisis on its own—a crisis that would have occurred independent of the federal deficit problem. The largest federal health care financing program, Medicare, can shortly be expected to do the same. For all these reasons, we consider some change in budget policy toward these programs not only inevitable, but desirable. The question remains: What sort of change?

This paper argues that any change must be predicated on a fundamental rethinking of federal policy concerning the aged (the chief beneficiaries of the pension and health programs). That is, we must not allow current concern for the structural deficit to obscure the longer-term issue of fiscal disequilibrium within the programs, caused by changing population demographics and disproportionate inflation of health care costs. These phenomena have serious

---

NOTE: Whenever a budget year is mentioned through 1988 it is the federal fiscal year that begins in October and ends in September. All years after 1988 in this paper refer to calendar years.

121

disproportionate inflation of health care costs. These phenomena have serious implications for our societal commitment to care for the aged. And no budgetary quick-fix is going to be able to adequately address the implications. Finally, in preparing ourselves to resist the temptation of a quick-fix, we must bear in mind the high political costs of reaching any consensus in these emotionally charged areas. The recent Social Security Amendments, for example, required intensive bipartisan negotiations and should not, therefore, be lightly tampered with. The political atmosphere surrounding health care financing is equally charged, and the programmatic and institutional issues are far more complex.

With these concerns in mind, we first project the long-term trends of health and pension outlays under current policies and then examine the broad issues for federal budget policy suggested by these trends. In the second and third sections of the paper we provide more information about the programs themselves and analyze the budget policy options for each—health care financing and pension programs, respectively—in light of the broad budget issues outlined in the first section. We devote the bulk of our attention to the health programs, particularly Medicare, because health policy raises the most immediately compelling issues.

The Budgetary Implications and Issues Posed by Current Policies

The projections of current budget policies presented in this section are intended to provide a context for future budget decisions, not to forecast future budget outcomes. Changes in policies will undoubtedly occur and, even apart from such changes, the projections are subject to considerable uncertainty since they embody assumptions about future economic and demographic trends. Nevertheless, they do provide a useful basis for understanding the fiscal implications of present policies and for considering future options.

Trends in Outlays

Several measures of trends in federal outlays are displayed in table 1, with more detail provided on individual health and pension programs in appendix tables A.1 and A.2. The data for the 1980s are based on the standard Congressional Budget Office (CBO) current policy projections, while the longer-term data for health and pension outlays and the gross national product (GNP) are based on the most recent actuarial reports of the Social Security, Medicare, and other retirement plans. Here the trends are projected under two sets of economic and demographic assumptions. In addition, the sixth column of table 1 shows how the GNP share of total federal outlays adjusts to the changes in health and pension programs, holding the 1988 GNP share of defense, net interest, and other nondefense program outlays constant. In contrast, the final column shows what could happen to the relative share of other nondefense programs if the overall budget is assumed to be constrained to 24 percent of GNP—approximately the 23.9 percent projected for 1988.

Two trends are particularly notable under the immediate or ''best guess'' economic and demographic assumptions in table 1. First, the combined health care financing and pension outlays stay relatively flat as a percentage of GNP through the 1980s and 1990s. However, beginning in the next century, their combined percentage gradually increases as the decline in pension outlays moderates and health care financing expenditures rise more rapidly. The increase then accelerates as the post-World War II baby-boom cohorts begin to retire.

Second, if total budget, defense, and interest outlays are assumed to remain at their 1988 shares of GNP in subsequent years, the share of total budget outlays devoted to pension and health care financing programs would increase rapidly after the turn of the century, and other nondefense programs eventually would be squeezed out of the budget. Alternatively, if all other components are assumed to retain their 1988 share of GNP and overall federal outlays are not constrained, the rise in pension and health outlays will lead to continuous increases in total budget outlays as a percentage of GNP beginning early in the next century.

The foregoing observations focus on the combined trend of health care financing and pension outlays. But as a comparison of the first two columns in table 1 shows, the behavior over time of the two components differs markedly. The projected rapid growth in the aged population, particularly throughout this decade and again in the second and third decades of the next century (see table 2), places upward pressure on both series as a percentage of GNP. However, factors specific to the retirement programs—particularly Social Security—more than offset the adverse influence of demographic forces until the explosion in the aged population in the next century.[1]

In marked contrast, health care financing outlays, led by the Medicare program, are projected to increase substantially as a percentage of GNP for the foreseeable future for two reasons: First, the upward pressure on costs in

---

1. The major factors are the Social Security benefit reductions enacted in the past three years and the slower-than-GNP rise in the initial real benefit levels of successive cohorts of new retirees due to the lack of growth of their real earnings level in the 1970s and early 1980s. This lack of growth depresses the earnings histories on which benefit calculations are based.

TABLE 1

LONG-TERM FEDERAL OUTLAY TRENDS UNDER CURRENT POLICIES AS A PERCENTAGE OF GNP

	Pension Programs[a]	Health Care Financing Programs[b]	Total Pension and Health Care Financing Programs	Other Nondefense Programs[c]	Defense and Net Interest[c]	Total Budget	Other Nondefense Programs Assuming Total Budget is 24 Percent of GNP From 1990 on
1965	4.1	0.3	4.4	5.3	8.3	18.0	NA
1970	4.7	1.4	6.1	4.8	9.3	20.2	NA
1975	6.4	2.0	8.4	7.1	7.0	22.5	NA
1980	6.5	2.3	8.8	6.4	7.8	23.0	NA
1982	7.1	2.7	9.7	6.4	8.5	24.6	NA
1984	7.0	2.8	9.8	5.9	8.9	24.6	NA
1986	6.6	3.0	9.6	4.7	9.4	23.7	NA
1988	6.4	3.2	9.6	4.5	9.8	23.9	NA
Intermediate Economic and Demographic Assumptions[d]							
1990	6.6	3.1	9.7	4.5	9.8	24.0	4.5
1995	6.2	3.7	9.9	4.5	9.8	24.2	4.3
2000	5.8	4.0	9.8	4.5	9.8	24.1	4.4
2005	5.6	4.4	10.0	4.5	9.8	24.3	4.2
2010	6.0	4.7	10.7	4.5	9.8	25.0	3.5
2015	6.0	5.0	11.0	4.5	9.8	25.3	3.2
2020	6.5	5.4	11.9	4.5	9.8	26.2	2.3
2025	7.0	5.9	12.9	4.5	9.8	27.2	1.3
2030	7.1	6.4	13.5	4.5	9.8	27.8	0.7
2035	7.1	7.0	14.1	4.5	9.8	28.4	0.1
2040	7.0	7.5	14.5	4.5	9.8	28.8	—

Pessimistic Economic and
Demographic Assumptions[e]

1990	6.5	3.6	10.1	4.5	9.8	24.4	4.1
1995	6.5	4.3	10.8	4.5	9.8	25.1	3.4
2000	6.1	5.1	11.2	4.5	9.3	25.5	3.0
2005	6.0	5.9	11.9	4.5	9.3	26.2	2.3

SOURCE: For years 1965–1982: Federal Government Finances; 1983 Budget Data, February 1983; for years 1984–1988: CBO baseline estimate made in August 1983, revised to include congressional action on defense in FY 1984; these estimates are consistent with estimates in chapter 2; 1990–2040: The Social Security and Health Insurance Trustees Report, May 1983; actuarial reports of other federal retirement systems; and authors' own estimates.

a. See appendix table A.2 for included programs.

b. See appendix table A.1 for included programs.

c. Assumed constant from 1988 on.

d. The intermediate alternative assumes that the average increase will ultimately be 2.6 percent for real GNP, 4.0 percent for the Consumer Price Index (CPI), and 5.5 percent for average wages. This alternative also assumes that mortality improvements will be at one-half the historical rate. Health financing outlays increase at an ultimate average annual rate of 9 percent a year. The discontinuity in the estimates of pension and health programs as a percentage of GNP between 1988 and 1990 is due to the Social Security trustees' assuming that OASDI will grow at a faster rate than the CBO in the later 1980s and the Health Insurance trustees' assuming that Medicare will grow at a slower rate than CBO assumed.

e. The pessimistic alternative assumes that the average annual increase ultimately will be 2.1 percent for GNP, 5.0 percent for CPI, and 6.0 percent for average wages. This alternative also assumes that mortality improvements will continue at the historical rate. Health financing outlays increase at an ultimate average annual rate of 14 percent a year.

TABLE 2

THE ABSOLUTE AND RELATIVE SIZES OF THE AGED POPULATION

	Number of Aged (in millions)	Percentage Increase in the Number of Aged Over Past Decade	Aged as a Percentage of Population	Aged as a Percentage of Working-Age Population[a]	Aged and Children as a Percentage of Working-Age Population[b]	As a Percentage of Total Aged, Persons Aged	
						65–75	75 +
	(1)	(2)	(3)	(4)	(5)	(6)	(7)
1960	17.1	34.7	9.1	17.4	91.5	65.5	34.5
1970	20.7	20.6	9.7	18.4	90.1	60.6	39.4
1980	26.3	27.3	11.1	19.6	75.8	59.9	40.1
1990	32.7	24.1	12.6	21.6	71.0	56.7	43.3
2000	36.3	11.3	13.1	22.2	69.3	50.3	49.7
2010	40.7	12.0	13.9	23.0	66.2	51.7	48.3
2020	53.2	30.8	17.3	30.1	74.5	58.0	42.0
2030	66.2	24.4	20.8	38.3	84.1	52.9	47.1
2040	69.0	4.2	21.2	39.1	84.4	43.8	56.2

SOURCE: The 1983 Annual Report of the Board of Trustees of the Federal Old-Age and Survivors Insurance and Disability Insurance Trust Funds.

NOTE: The aged include the total population eligible for Social Security and Medicare benefits who are sixty-five years old or older. Historically this number has been about 800,000 higher than the Census count of the United States aged population (age sixty-five and over) because it includes people who live overseas.

a. Population aged sixty-five and over as a percentage of population between the ages of twenty and sixty-four.

b. Population aged sixty-five and over plus population under age twenty as a percentage of the population between the ages of twenty and sixty-four.

the health programs from the aging of the population is exacerbated by the growing share within the aged population of the very old, who average much higher medical expenses than do people aged sixty-four to seventy-five. More important, however, are increases in general health care costs per capita that are assumed to continuously exceed the growth rate of GNP.

To show the sensitivity of the outlay projections to economic and demographic trends, table 1 also shows a partial series of long-term estimates based on the more pessimistic actuarial assumptions. Not surprisingly, they show health care financing and pension outlays placing much greater upward pressure on the budget as a percentage of GNP than do the intermediate assumptions. For example, when total federal outlays are unconstrained, they rise above 26 percent of GNP within twenty years under constant policies and the pessimistic assumptions instead of remaining about 24 percent.

In the past, the actuaries' pessimistic assumptions have proven more accurate than the intermediate ones in predicting GNP shares under constant policies. Although the intermediate projections contain reasonable assumptions about long-term trends for the general economy, they also reflect some slowdown in improvements in the historical mortality rate and in health care cost inflation for which there is not yet any strong evidence. If either of these changes does not materialize, the intermediate projections shown in table 1 will understate the future costs of health and pension programs.[2]

Although the figures in table 1 give a good picture of expected growth of pension and health programs, they do not precisely characterize the contributions these programs will make to future structural deficits—which is, after all, the subject of immediate concern. To measure the contribution of these programs to the deficits, we compared the projected changes in program outlays with the appropriate revenue base. Not all revenues will grow at the same rate as the GNP. With the personal income tax indexed to inflation, as it will be in the future, general revenues, in fact, are likely to grow at approximately the same rate as the GNP. Thus, growth in those programs— or program components—financed from general revenues can be directly

---

2. The intermediate projections assume that improvements in mortality will occur at half the rate of improvement since 1900. If improvements continue at the same pace as in the last ten years, the life expectancy of people sixty-five and over could increase three years by the year 2000. This would be consistent with recent improvements and closer to the life expectancy improvements assumed in the pessimistic assumptions (2.8 years) than the intermediate assumptions (1.4 years). In both sets of assumptions, the difference in life expectancy between men and women would continue to grow.

Under the intermediate economic assumptions the average annual percentage increase in real GNP is 2.6 percent, average wages is 5.5 percent, and consumer price index is 4.0 percent. Under the pessimistic assumptions the respective growth rates are 2.1 percent, 6.0 percent, and 5.0 percent.

the GNP will necessitate an increase in taxes, a cut in the programs, or an increase in the structural deficit.

On the other hand revenues for the Social Security program (Old-Age, Survivors, and Disability Insurance—OASDI) and the Hospital Insurance component of Medicare (HI) come from earmarked payroll taxes, which are scheduled to rise somewhat as a percentage of GNP. In addition, approximately 25 percent of the cost of the Supplemental Medical Insurance component of Medicare (SMI) is financed by the premiums of beneficiaries. Thus, for the purpose of assessing the change in the net fiscal burden that will result from future growth in these programs, we should look at the difference between the scheduled payroll taxes and premiums and projected program costs.

Projected changes in the net fiscal burden for both types of programs—those financed from general revenues and those financed by earmarked revenues—are shown in table 3. Surprisingly, under the intermediate assumptions, this measure of the fiscal burden declines substantially from its 1982 level until 1988, even though program outlays do not decline as a percentage of GNP. This decline is attributable to the 1983 Social Security Amendments, which will yield annual surpluses in the OASDI trust funds that more than offset the added net fiscal burden generated by the Medicare program. These programs will thus help reduce the overall federal deficit as a percentage of GNP under current policies. Beginning in the next century, however, the net fiscal burden from these programs will begin to grow, and they will add to whatever structural deficits exist in the overall federal budget.

The projections for HI and SMI in table 3 also illustrate the rapidly deteriorating financial status of the Medicare program. Until recently, the HI trust fund had run such large surpluses that OASDI was able to borrow from it to meet benefit obligations until Congress acted in the spring of 1983 to shore up Social Security financing. Now, however, the HI trust fund is projected to run into deficit. Annual HI expenditures will soon exceed, by ever increasing amounts, the payroll tax revenues earmarked for the trust fund to finance them. Alternative estimates differ as to the precise timing and magnitude of the deficits, all the estimates agree that HI will accumulate total trust fund deficits in the hundreds of billions of dollars in the 1990s under current policies (see table A.3). In order to achieve actuarial balance in the HI trust funds over the next twenty-five years under the intermediate assumptions, outlays would have to be reduced 30 percent or income increased 43 percent.[3] These HI trust fund deficits also measure only part of the

---

3. *1983 Annual Report of the Board of Trustees of the Federal Health Insurance Fund*, May 1983, p. 49.

TABLE 3

CHANGES IN THE NET FISCAL BURDEN OF PENSION AND HEALTH CARE FINANCING
PROGRAMS AS A PERCENTAGE OF GNP

	Trust Fund Programs, Projected Costs Minus Earmarked Revenues			Other Programs, Projected Costs		
	$OASDI^a$	HI	SMI^b	Health	$Pensions^c$	Total
1982	0.4	−0.1	0.4	1.0	2.0	3.7
1984	d	d	0.5	1.0	2.0	3.5
1986	−0.1	d	0.5	1.0	1.8	3.2
1988	−0.4	0.1	0.6	1.0	1.7	3.0
Intermediate Assumptions						
1990	−0.5	0.2	0.6	1.0	1.7	3.0
1995	−0.8	0.5	0.7	1.0	1.6	3.0
2000	−1.0	0.7	0.8	1.0	1.5	3.0
2005	−1.1	1.0	0.9	1.0	1.4	3.2
2010	−0.9	1.1	1.0	1.0	1.3	3.5
2015	−0.4	1.4	1.0	1.0	1.2	4.2
2020	0.1	1.7	1.2	1.0	1.3	5.3
Pessimistic Assumptions						
1990	−0.4	0.4	0.6	1.0	1.7	3.3
1995	−0.3	0.9	0.8	1.0	1.7	4.1
2000	−0.5	1.4	1.0	1.0	1.5	4.4
2005	−0.5	2.0	1.3	1.0	1.5	5.3

a.   The revenues include the income tax on Social Security benefits, which is earmarked for the OASDI trust fund.

b.   Estimates assume that SMI premiums continue at their present level of 25 percent of total costs. Under current law, however, the indexing of the premium lapses in 1985, which would decrease this percentage. Therefore, this assumption may underestimate the future fiscal burden of SMI.

c.   The civil service and railroad retirement trust funds are partially funded from sources other than general revenues that are not reflected in these numbers. Inclusion of these funding sources would reduce the projected fiscal burden of these programs only very slightly, and would not change the basic trends at all.

d.   Less than 0.05 percent.

contribution of Medicare to future federal deficits, since they do not include the effects of the even faster-growing SMI component.

As might be expected, the changes in the fiscal burden as measured in table 3, and in the financial status of the Medicare program, are more severe under pessimistic economic and demographic assumptions. Under current policies, health care financing and pension programs would increase the overall structural deficit two percentage points of GNP between 1990 and 2005. And both the timing and magnitude of Medicare's financial problems would be more acute.

Broad Budget Issues

Immediate concern about structural deficits may lead to further changes in health care financing and pension programs in the 1980s. But, as we hope is apparent from the preceding discussion of outlay trends, policy changes motivated solely by concern for the deficit would be ill-conceived. We need, rather, to come to terms with some of the larger issues caused by the projected growth of these programs. In particular, we need to address the overriding questions of how much of our national pension and health care needs should be met through collective (i.e., public) arrangements and what particular form these arrangements should take. Although we cannot answer these questions within the scope of this paper, we can suggest three broad considerations that bear on them and should guide our present focus on budgetary policy in the pension and health care area. These issues involve the adjustment of the budget to the aging of the population, the long-term controllability of outlays, and the distribution of the growing fiscal burden implicit in current federal health care and pension programs.

Adjustment of the Budget to the Aging of the Population. Much of the increased pension and health care financing costs of the federal government over the past fifteen years results from the simple fact of growth in the aged population. The increase in the number of aged people in the past decade contributed to an increase in federal expenditures exceeding 1 percent of GNP (holding policies constant). Under current policies, this experience will be replicated in this decade.[4] The budget produced by current policy—projected to exceed 24 percent of GNP, would be under 22 percent of GNP were it not for the aging of the population since 1970. Thus, a substantial part of the projected structural deficit can be blamed on our failure to accommodate the fiscal pressures already created by the growth in the aged population.

Insofar as the large portion of past and present federal budgets devoted to the aged reflects a public consensus that this populuation group deserves more communal support than other groups, we should be in some measure prepared to accept the idea that budgetary allotment for the aged will increase as our society ages. That is, we should not regard the budgetary trends already discussed in entirely the same light as we might regard similiar trends in other federal programs. The trends do not necessarily constitute evidence of gross inefficiency, uncontrolled expenditures, or any of the other arguments that have been advanced for curbing domestic programs. To some extent, the

---

4. Barbara Boyle Torrey and Douglas Norwood, "Death and Taxes: The Fiscal Implication of American Mortality," paper presented at the American Association for the Advancement of Science, May 1983.

trends are simply a result of a phenomenon quite outside the government's control: more people are growing old.

The first question to be asked, then, is not how to cut programs for the aged to reduce the structural deficit, but, rather, whether or to what extent programs for the aged should be sacrificed to some more or less arbitrary notion of the appropriate overall size of the federal budget. Restricting the size of the federal budget to 20 percent of GNP has been an informal goal of recent administrations. The Reagan administration explicitly reset this goal at 19 percent, and recent tax changes have stabilized revenues at about this level. But even if we accept the idea (and some of us don't) that under normal circumstances the federal budget should be some set percentage of GNP, we should still question the wisdom of holding to that percentage come hell or high water. Many people would argue that, in times of war, natural disaster, or other circumstances beyond the reach of domestic policy, we should increase the federal budget relative to our nation's output, rather than abandon social principles to which we have a long-established allegiance. Our point is simply that, before embarking on any examination of options for curtailing outlays for the aged, we need to evaluate the possibility that growth in outlays in this area may be more socially—and consequently, politically—desirable than elsewhere.

Controllability of Future Growth in Outlays. Assuming that we can agree on an acceptable level of growth in outlays, we need to determine whether or how outlays could actually be controlled to stay within this level. Largely because of the recent changes in Social Security, the future growth in federal pension outlays in relationship to GNP is relatively predictable and controlled. The new Social Security provision limiting cost-of-living adjustments (COLAs) to the rate of increase of covered wages will prevent episodes of stagflation (low economic growth coupled with high inflation) from driving up outlays faster than GNP, as they did in the past.

As table 1 showed, overall pension outlays should grow more slowly than GNP for the next twenty years. After that, the renewed rapid increase in the aged population will cause outlays to rise more rapidly than GNP. As we discuss later, most of the steps necessary to adjust to this rise have already been taken in the Social Security program—at least if intermediate assumptions prove a reasonable guide to the future. No further near-term actions in the program are warranted by the currently projected long-run trends. There is, however, a need for long-run reforms in the much smaller military and civil service retirement programs that are not evident in the pension projections (dominated as they are by Social Security).

Health care presents a radically different picture. Here, rapidly rising costs will continue to cause growth in outlays that is neither controlled nor predictable.

No appropriate long-term policy adjustments have yet been made to the inevitable increase in the aged population. And, despite some gratifying improvements in the health and longevity of the aged population, continued increases in age-adjusted per capita health care costs well in excess of GNP growth cannot be sustained indefinitely. Later we discuss the dilemma of whether the growth of Medicare outlays can be controlled by program reforms without unduly undermining other policy objectives or whether broader reforms affecting the entire health sector will be required. But for the present, let us merely caution against the obvious temptation to use the large surpluses in the OASDI trust funds that will accumulate over the next several decades to finance the deficits in Medicare. This politically appealing solution would obscure the real problem of uncontrolled growth in the health sector and the severe fiscal disequilibrium of the health programs, not to mention the fact that it would imperil Social Security surpluses needed to finance retirement costs in the next century.

Distribution of the Added Fiscal Burden. Finally, even if we settle the issues of acceptable levels of growth and appropriate measures for controlling costs within these levels, we must confront the question of how the increased costs and decreased benefits should be shared among different segments of the population. Traditionally in our society, as in most others, the nonaged generation has been largely responsible for the support of the aged. At no time in our history, however, has an aged or retired population been as large relative to the working population as it is today. The Social Security and Medicare programs have helped to spread the burden of cross-generational support beyond the family unit throughout the working population at large. But how the added future economic burden of the aged should be shared across generations has now become a major issue confronting society.

In the past, the working people have borne a high proportion of the costs of their parents primarily because the aged were poorer than their children. In large part because of our generous public policies toward the aged, however, the aged population group now enjoys, on average, an economic status similar to that of the working people and might be expected to do even better in the future.[5] Although the aged depend more on assets, have less income, and enjoy a less equal income distribution than the working population,[6] the aged receive greater tax benfits and have lower consumption needs. As a consequence the effective income level of the average aged person is now on a par with that of younger people. Therefore the aged as a group can more easily absorb some of

5. Michael D. Hurd, John B. Shoven, "The Economic Status of the Elderly," *The American Economic Association Papers and Proceedings*, vol. 72, no. 2, May 1982.

6. Sheldon Danziger, Jacques van der Gaag, Eugene Smolensky, Michael K. Taussing, "Income Transfers and the Economic Status of the Elderly," presented at the Conference on Research in Income and Wealth, National Bureau of Economic Research, May 14–15, 1982.

the added fiscal burden they will impose in the future. Greater use of income testing of benefits for the aged can help protect the most vulnerable among the aged and result in a more equitable sharing of any financial burden.

In essence, the 1983 Social Security Amendments reflect congressional decisions about how the added fiscal burden of pension costs should be shared. These amendments acknowledged the growing cost of providing retirement income for present and future generations of aged, the added fiscal burden implicit in a continuation of prior policies, and the measures that society was willing to take to distribute that burden (see table 4). In the short run, the

TABLE 4

SHORT- AND LONG-TERM DEFICIT REDUCTION EFFECTS OF MAJOR PROVISIONS OF THE 1983 SOCIAL SECURITY AMENDMENTS

	Total 1983–1989 (In $ billions)	*75-Year Change (as a Percentage of Payroll)[a]*
Additional Burden on the Retired Population		
Delay cost-of-living adjustment for 6 months	39.4	0.30
Increase the retirement age to 67 beginning in 2000	—	0.71
Tax 50% of benefits if adjusted gross income is $25,000 or more for single, and $32,000 or more for joint, returns	26.6	0.61
Additional Burden on the Working Population		
Accelerate previously scheduled tax rate increases	39.4	0.03
Make the self-employment OASDI tax rate comparable to the combined employer-employee rate	18.5	0.19
Extend coverage to all new federal employees and nonprofit institutions; prohibit state and local terminators	25.0	0.44
Other	17.3	−0.18
Total, Deficit Effect	166.2	2.1

SOURCE: Social Security Bulletin, July 1983, vol. 46, no. 7, pp. 42 and 44.

a. Based on intermediate assumptions. In the absence of these changes, the average cost ratio of the program over the next seventy-five years was projected to be 14.4 percent of payroll and the average tax rate 12.3 percent, with a resulting actuarial deficit of 2.1 percent. As a result of the changes, average costs and tax rates are projected to be brought into balance at 12.9 percent of payroll.

amendments placed a burden on beneficiaries amounting to a little less than half the total deficit reduction measures, with increased payroll taxes accounting for the rest. And the total burden was roughly equally divided among the general working population, special groups within the working population, general recipients, and high-income recipients. But, in the longer run, most of the burden of closing the fiscal gap will be borne by the retired rather than the working-age population through an increase in the age of eligibility for full benefits and the partial taxation of benefits. The aged who are less well-off will be less affected than others, since the taxation of benefits is an implicit form of income testing the benefit reduction.[7]

As recently as a few years ago, such reductions in Social Security benefits were politically unimaginable; but the combination of fiscal exigencies, the current resistance to further tax increases and, perhaps, a growing awareness of the greatly improved economic status of the aged have made the reductions possible. Dealing with emerging problems of the health care financing programs will require another major renegotiation of the social contract between the generations, and the same factors are likely to be important.

Health Care Financing Programs

Of the four major health care financing programs (which together provide major health financing support for a quarter of the population), the most significant is Medicare, which is an entirely federal program serving the aged and severely disabled. Like Social Security, its Hospital Insurance component (HI) is financed through payroll taxes and a trust fund. Supplemental Medical Insurance (SMI), which covers other medical services associated with acute care, such as physician charges, is financed through a combination of participant premiums and general revenues. Both components involve beneficiary cost sharing in the form of deductibles and copayments.

The Medicaid program is administered by states under broad federal guidelines, with government at both levels paying the costs from general revenues. Medicaid finances the acute and chronic care needs of the populations receiving Aid to Families with Dependent Children (AFDC) and Supplemental Security Income (SSI) and, in some states, broader categories of the low-income medically needy. The other two relatively small programs included in our data provide health care to veterans and military personnel.

---

7. Greater use of IRAs and other tax subsidized forms of private savings could soften the effective reduction in net federal benefits to both early retirees and the higher-income aged inherent in these amendments.

This section provides more detailed background on the past and projected growth of these programs and recent policy changes. We then consider the options for dealing with the issues the programs raise for federal budget policy.

Background

Before 1966 the federal government provided 11 percent of the total payments for personal health costs, primarily through veterans, military, and poverty programs. The introduction of Medicare and Medicaid in the late 1960s, however, tripled the federal share in less than fifteen years; at the same time, personal health costs increased their share of GNP from just over 5 percent to nearly 9 percent. By far the most significant increase in federal health care responsibility has been for the aged: federal outlays for this group have increased from about 15 percent of the aged's total personal health costs in 1965 to 54 percent currently.

Increases in personal health care costs can be caused by three factors: (1) increases in the population; (2) increases in the units of health care service used per person, which we term utilization in this paper; and (3) increases in the cost per unit of care.[8] Increases in utilization can be further divided into increases in per capita visits or patient days and increases in the intensity of services (such as nursing hours and diagnostic and therapeutic procedures) per visit or patient day. And increases in unit costs can be attributed to general inflation, as well as to the rate of price increases for medical care (for a fixed set of goods and services) in excess of this general rate. General inflation and rapid growth in the beneficiary populations have played the major roles in the growth of federal health care financing outlays over the past fifteen years[9]. But other factors have produced continuous growth in utilization of health care services and, therefore, in the amount of real resources flowing into the health sector relative to the rest of the economy. This flow of real resources in turn has contributed to price inflation for medical care in excess of the general rate of inflation, resulting in a crisis for private as well as public health care financing.

---

8. $(\text{Total costs} = \text{persons} \times \dfrac{\text{units}}{\text{person}} \times \dfrac{\text{costs}}{\text{unit}})$.

9. Between 1971 and 1981, community hospital inpatient care costs increased at an average annual rate of growth of 15.2 percent. Fifty-two percent of the growth was due to the general inflation in the economy and 7 percent to the general increase in the population. Increases in intensity of services per admission accounted for half of the growth unexplained by these general economic and demographic conditions. The increases in the prices of goods and services that hospitals purchase in excess of increases in the CPI accounted for 29 percent of the remaining growth, and 21 percent was due to growth in the rate of admissions per capita. Medicare HI

Among the many influences that have been cited for their contribution to the problem, the most important is the failure of insurers to constrain payments in the absence of consumer sensitivity to price[10]. As more consumer costs are financed by third parties, providers and consumers alike appear increasingly to treat medical care as a free service at the time of decision making. There is no question that third-party payments play a significant and beneficial role in increasing access to quality care; but in divorcing utilization and price from ability to pay at the individual level—and, to a lesser extent, at the aggregate level—third-party payments remove natural constraints on demand. Third-party reimbursement systems also typically incorporate incentives to increase costs. Retrospective cost-based reimbursement for hospitals and fee-for-service reimbursement for physicians reward providers who supply greater, and more costly, services.

The undesirable impact of third-party payments on medical costs has been augmented in the past fifteen years, as the third-party share of total personal health care expenditures has risen from less than one-half to more than two-thirds. Federal policy has encouraged this expansion through the creation of Medicare and Medicaid and through the provision of open-ended tax subsidies for employer-financed private health insurance. Current tax policies also provide

---

outlays grew at an annual rate 2 percent faster than overall hospital care expenditures over this same period. The eligible Medicare population for HI grew 38 percent between 1971 and 1981 and the number who actually received benefits increased 61 percent, whereas the general population grew only 8 percent. Also, the rate of admissions per beneficiary increased at an average of 2.6 percent annually (from 1972 to 1982), whereas the admission incidence for all private hospitals increased at a rate of only 1.4 percent (from 1970 to 1980). SMI outlays expanded at an annual rate of about 18 percent from 1970 to 1981. Increases in utilization and costs per unit of care played similar roles in this expansion as for HI, but SMI had a larger increase in its beneficiary population.

Unlike the Medicare program, which has had steady increases in the number of its beneficiaries, the number of Medicaid beneficiaries leveled off in 1974 and has stayed relatively flat since then, after doubling in the preceding six years. From 1968 to 1974, Medicaid outlays grew at an annual rate of nearly 20 percent; more than half this growth was attributable to increases in the recipient population. A little more than one-quarter was due to price increases in medical care and less than 10 percent was due to increases in utilization. For the rest of the decade, Medicaid costs grew at an annual rate of about 15 percent. About two-thirds of this growth was the result of medical care price increases; the contribution of the growth in the recipient population was quite small. Increases in utilization, however, became more important, accounting for more than 25 percent of the outlay increases in the more recent past.

Mark Freeland, Carol Ellen Schendler, "National Health Expenditure Growth in the 1980's: An Aging Population, New Technologies, and Increasing Competition," *Health Care Financing Review*, March 1983, vol. 4, no. 3, p. 19; *1983 Annual Report of the Board of Trustees of the Federal Hospital Insurance Trust Fund*, p. 65.

10. Other factors are low increases in productivity in the health care sector, physician-induced demand for their services as the number of doctors per capita increases, and greater demand due to the more rapid diffusion of information on new techniques, procedures, and supplies and increases in consumer incomes.

an incentive to shift employee compensation from cash to health insurance, since the latter is not included in taxable income. As a result, employer-based health insurance coverage has greatly expanded, and relatively comprehensive coverage, which requires very little employee cost sharing, is not uncommon.

Thus, federal policies have contributed both explicitly (through Medicare and Medicaid) and implicitly (through fostering third-party payments) to the remarkable growth in federal health-related outlays that have been noted. This growth in outlays is projected to moderate from an annual rate of nearly 18 percent between 1970 and 1981, to just under 11 percent between 1982 and 1988 (see table 5), principally as a result of the assumed reduction in the general rate of inflation. Regardless of this moderation in growth, however, federal health care financing outlays are still projected to increase indefinitely as a percentage of the nondefense program budget, the total budget, and GNP. Both the Medicare and Medicaid programs are expected to continue to grow faster than the economy—despite the facts that (1) no growth is expected in the number of Medicaid beneficiaries, (2) growth in the number of Medicare

TABLE 5

HEALTH CARE FINANCING OUTLAYS

	CBO Baseline						
	Actual					Estimates	
	1965	1970	1975	1980	1982	1984	1988
	(In $ billions)						
Medicare							
HI	—	5.0	10.6	24.3	34.9	43.4	69.1
SMI	—	2.2	4.2	10.7	15.6	21.1	37.3
Medicaid	0.3	2.7	6.8	14.0	17.4	21.2	31.3
VA Medical	1.3	1.8	4.6	6.5	7.5	7.9	8.7
Military Medical	0.5	1.5	2.8	3.9	5.2	6.5	9.1
Total	2.1	13.2	29.0	59.4	80.6	100.1	155.5
Health Care Financing Outlays—							
—As a percentage of total budget	1.8	6.8	8.7	10.0	10.8	11.5	13.1
—As a percentage of nondefense program budget[a]	3.3	12.3	12.5	14.2	16.3	18.0	22.3
—As a percentage of GNP	0.3	1.4	2.0	2.3	2.7	2.8	3.2

SOURCES: Office of Management and Budget, "Federal Government Finances," February 1983; and Congressional Budget Office projections published in August 1983.
a. Includes military medical and retirement outlays.

beneficiaries is expected to be considerably less rapid than in the past decade, and (3) a number of recent policy changes are expected to slow cost increases, particularly those attributable to increased utilization. Since options to control health care costs are a major concern of this paper, we need to look briefly at what has recently been done before moving on to examine the prospects.

In brief, the reforms enacted between 1981 and 1983 to deal with Medicare and Medicaid financing problems are estimated to reduce overall federal outlays for these programs 5.5 percent below the levels previously estimated for the 1982–1985 period; the reduction in Medicaid is expected to be slightly more than this overall percentage and the reduction in Medicare is expected to be slightly less.[11] In particular:

- Congress fundamentally changed the HI reimbursement system. Initially, hospital charges per admission have been restricted to hospital market-basket inflation (the increase in the price of inputs to hospitals) plus 1 percent. Over a period of three years, this approach will be superseded by a system of prospective reimbursement, which bases hospital charges per admission on the hospital industry's average costs for treatment of an illness defined by diagnostic-related groupings.

- Congress established a target rate of Medicaid increases, with reductions in federal matching payments to penalize states with excessive increases. (These provisions are currently scheduled to expire after 1984.) For the first time states have been penalized for excessive error rates in Medicaid. Congress also gave the states more discretion in (among other things) developing alternatives to current reimbursement systems.

- Congress raised the copayments for SMI premiums and deductibles in HI and SMI.

Between 1982 and 1985, 45 percent of the estimated deficit reduction from reforms in Medicare is attributable to lower reimbursement to providers, 33 percent to increased HI payroll taxes (as a result of coverage of federal employees), and 22 percent to increased cost sharing by beneficiaries.

Issues and Options in the Control of Outlay Growth

As we argued earlier, the major question for health care budget policy is how to control growth of all programs outlays and how to restore financial

---

11. "Major Legislative Changes in Human Resources Programs Since January 1981," staff memorandum, Congressional Budget Office, August 1983.

equilibrium to the Medicare program without unduly compromising other policy objectives.[12] Any attempt to seek an answer to this question in Medicare and Medicaid themselves is doomed to some frustration, since both programs finance services purchased from the private sector with little restriction on beneficiaries' choice of provider. Consequently, the programs cannot be readily insulated from general inflation in health care costs. And, because the programs finance only about half of total private hospital costs and about a third of private physician costs, there is limited potential for changes in program policies to effect larger changes in the national health care system.[13] Thus, in the following discussion, we consider not only program-specific changes, but also more far-reaching changes in national health care policy. Also, because Congress has repeatedly shown itself (despite the proposals by Presidents Nixon and Carter) ill-disposed toward federalization of Medicaid and well-disposed toward reliance upon the states to control health care financing costs for the low-income population, we will confine our discussion to the Medicare program—for which the federal responsibility and the need for substantial further actions in the 1980s are clear. Accordingly, the discussion that follows examines two basic program changes to reduce the growth in outlays—increased beneficiary cost sharing and tightened provider reimbursement—as well as two broad federal health policy options—increased competition and federal regulation of the overall health care sector.

Increased Beneficiary Cost Sharing. Both portions of Medicare require beneficiaries to share some of the costs of covered services. Hospitalized beneficiaries must pay a deductible amount in each benefit period but are not liable for additional cost sharing until they have been confined more than sixty days. Enrollees under SMI pay premiums and 20 percent of each covered service once a relatively small deductible has been met.

---

12. No explicit attention is given here to either veterans or military health programs. The single most important change that could be made to the veterans medical programs would be to place requirements in addition to age on access to full (free) VA medical care. Currently any veteran who is sixty-five years or older is automatically defined as disabled and, therefore, eligible. The cost of medical care for aged veterans who do not have service-connected disabilities is estimated at $1.5 billion in 1982. If such steps were taken, much of the medical costs would be transferred to Medicare or Medicaid, so that the net deficit reduction is likely to be small. But the present overlapping medical coverage for aged veterans does not make the best use of the VA's limited resources.

13. Medicare pays 45 percent of private hospital bills and 25 percent of physician costs. Thus its leverage over the hospital system is probably higher than over physician reimbursement. The number of physicians is also growing much faster than their potential Medicare patients. If physicians can continue to increase demand by increasing the intensity of services they provide per patient, as the evidence suggests they have done in the recent past, federal leverage will be reduced. However, if the large increase in the number of physicians introduces much greater competition among them for a limited demand, Medicare's effective leverage may increase.

Beneficiaries could pay a greater share of the costs of Medicare-covered services through higher premiums, deductible amounts, or copayments (a share of the cost of each unit of care received). Such changes could generate large federal savings, but they would do so by substantially increasing out-of-pocket costs for the aged and disabled. Although beneficiaries have not been subject to major increases in cost sharing to date, they already pay about one-fourth of the rapidly rising costs of Medicare-covered services, and even more for other health services not covered by Medicare.

Choosing among strategies for beneficiaries' paying a greater share of costs often involves important trade-offs. The broadest measures—instituting a premium in HI and raising the premiums in SMI—would affect all beneficiaries by a small amount. Any resulting financial hardship could be ameliorated by income-testing the premiums. The disadvantages of such an approach are that it would be administratively complex and could undermine the philosophical view of HI as an earned right (because it is financed from payroll taxes). This latter issue would pose less of a problem for SMI because it is financed from general revenues. Income testing would also, of course, reduce the overall cost savings from such premiums.

Although options tying increased beneficiary cost sharing to the utilization of medical care services, such as copayments, might result in somewhat more prudent use of health care services, this approach would concentrate the additional liability on the small percentage of beneficiaries who already have the highest out-of-pocket expenses. (For example, only about 25 percent of enrollees are actually hospitalized each year.) Such persons might be protected from financial hardship by relating the copayments to income or placing upper limits on the total financial liability of any one beneficiary, but these measures have some of the same problems that have already been cited. The existence of so-called "Medigap" insurance plans, which pay for most services that Medicare does not, considerably complicates the cost-sharing issue. The three-quarters of the aged and disabled protected by these plans or by Medicaid would not, in fact, experience increased costs tied directly to their utilization, so the efficiencies to be derived from cost sharing would be limited.

The administration has proposed several changes to expand beneficiary cost sharing under Medicare (and a minor change for Medicaid), including an increase in the SMI premium and a expansion of HI payments, combined with a cap on total out-of-pocket liability for hospital bills. The associated savings are shown in table 6, along with other variations in increased cost sharing developed by the Congressional Budget Office.

Tighter Provider Reimbursement. The new prospective hospital reimbursement system is designed to control Medicare costs related to

TABLE 6

EFFECTS OF HEALTH CARE FINANCING OPTIONS ON 1988 BUDGET DEFICIT
(In $ billions)

Program	Administration Proposals	CBO Cost Estimates
Medicare—Health Insurance (HI)		
Increase HI Coinsurance		
Provide catastrophic coverage and deliver coinsurance of 8% of deductible for days 2 through 15 and 5% for days 16 through 60	−1.5	—
Require HI coinsurance of 10% of deductible from day 2 to day 30	—	−2.8
Require HI coinsurance of 10% of deductible for each day beginning on day 2		
With no limits	—	−3.9
With $1,500 limit for people with incomes below $20,000; rising thereafter to $3,000	—	−0.3
With $2,000 limit for people with incomes below $20,000; rising thereafter to $4,000	—	−1.3
Introduce HI Premiums ($10/month)	—	−4.8
Medicare—Supplementary Medical Insurance (SMI)		
Increase SMI Premium		
Gradually increase to recover 35% of annual costs	−2.6	—
Immediate increase to recover 35% of annual costs	—	−3.7
Increase SMI Deductible		
Adjust by Medicare economic index	−0.3	—
Increase to $100 and then index to per capita SMI reimbursements	—	−1.1
Freeze SMI Physicians' Reimbursement for One Year	−1.4	—
Increase SMI Coinsurance to 25% of All Covered Services	—	−1.9
Medicaid		
Increase Management Incentives Plus Beneficiary Copayment	−0.8	—
Extend Cuts in Matching Grants	—	−1.0
Private Health Insurance		
Limit Employer-Provided Health Insurance Tax Benefit	−8.0	—
Tax Medigap Policies	—	−5.5

SOURCES: Administration Proposals: Office of Management and Budget, back-up table for the 1984 budget. Some of these proposals were not resubmitted in the 1985 budget. CBO Cost Estimates: "Changing the Structure of Medicare Benefits: Issues and Options," Congressional Budget Office Study, March 1983, and "Reducing the Deficit: Spending and Revenue Options," Congressional Budget Office Study, February 1983.

NOTE: Both the original CBO and administration estimates for 1988 assumed that proposals would be enacted by 1984. Since no proposals were enacted by the end of 1983, both the effective dates and deficit reduction effects are assumed to slip a year. Therefore this table shows the original 1987 deficit reduction estimates as the present estimates for 1988.

increased utilization, although the system addresses only the service intensity component, not admission rates. A critical question is how successful this new prospective reimbursement system will be in reducing the growth of HI outlays. And, if the system does restrain federally financed hospital costs but not privately financed ones, will it precipitate a two-class system of care, with Medicare patients shunted to the back wards of private hospitals?

The current reimbursement for hospitals limits increased costs for service intensity to 1 percent per year. Beyond 1985 the secretary of Health and Human Services has discretion in determining the stringency of reimbursement under the new system. Current Medicare cost projections assume reimbursement based on an increase of service intensity of 1 percent a year indefinitely. By 1985, reimbursements are projected to be about 9 percent below the level they would have been if they had continued to be based on actual costs. Continued successive tightening of reimbursements according to this formula should restrain the growth of Medicare outlays. But it will also place increasing pressure on hospitals to reduce the quality of care of Medicare patients relative to others and to pass on to private payers whatever actual cost increases Medicare will not cover. Thus, the gamble is that these new tighter limits on Medicare reimbursement will dramatically improve the efficiency with which hospitals provide health care to all patients. Otherwise, taxpayers will simply pay the costs through higher private health insurance premiums rather than payroll taxes, or Medicare patients' access to quality care will be reduced, or both.[14]

None of the recent policy changes in Medicare addresses the even more rapid growth of SMI outlays, which is due mainly to increased use of physician services and the outpatient diagnostic and therapeutic procedures that physicians prescribe. Thus, another compelling question for Medicare is how to limit reimbursement to physicians in such a way as to reduce the incentives to increase the intensity of services per patient. Reimbursement of physicians under SMI is now limited to "reasonable" charges, which may not exceed the lowest of physicians' actual charges, their customary charges for service, or the applicable prevailing charges in the locality. Since 1976, annual increases in prevailing charges have been limited by an economic index designed

---

14. In the past it would have been much easier for hospitals to shift the costs in excess of HI payments of treating Medicare patients equivalently to privately financed patients onto private health insurers, since the latter provided little resistance to such practices. However, rapidly escalating hospital costs and private health insurance premiums have raised the consciousness of private payers (employers, insurance companies, and consumers) who are beginning to pressure hospitals to adopt practices to restrain their cost increases.

to cut growth in physician reimbursements. By 1981, reimbursable charges averaged 32 percent lower than actual submitted charges.

One way to cut federal costs further would be to apply more stringent limits to the growth of "reasonable" charges. For example, the administration has proposed freezing all physician reimbursement rates for one year. Alternatively, there could be more basic changes in the structure of reimbursements for particular services or types of physicians. For example, the growth in fees for surgery could be limited for several years. Many people contend that our medical care system overemphasizes surgery and other acute procedures relative to primary care; changing relative reimbursements might influence this mix of medical services. But, as long as physicians are permitted to charge patients in excess of what Medicare will reimburse, budget savings from reduced reimbursements might be achieved mostly at the expense of higher costs for beneficiaries. (Hospitals are not permitted to bill patients for costs in excess of the HI payment limits.) To avoid this problem, limits on growth in physician fees could be combined with a change in rules concerning assignment of fees. Physicians practicing in hospitals, for example, might be reimbursed under the new HI prospective reimbursement system. (About half of all SMI physician reimbursements are for inpatient services.) Although these options could limit the additional charges that would be passed on to beneficiaries, they could also result in some physicians' refusal to participate in Medicare, thereby limiting beneficiaries' access to care. Also, these options are unlikely to have a major impact on the increasing utilization of physicians' outpatient services.

The various program changes in Medicare that have been discussed, and the steps that states are taking to control Medicaid costs could significantly reduce the growth in future outlays, but many of the changes will be extremely unpopular politically because they add substantially to the financial burden of the vulnerable poor, aged, and disabled. Furthermore, the effects of these changes on the utilization rates and, more important, on the entire health care system are highly uncertain. If the changes do not improve efficiency in health care delivery and reduce overall utilization, general taxpayers may not be better off and program beneficiaries could be far worse off. For these reasons, as well as because of the general concern about rising medical care costs, we foresee the necessity for federal policy changes that would affect the private health care sector in general. The next sections sketch two broad possibilities.

Increased Competition. The competitive approach to controlling health care costs involves increasing economic incentives for more judicious use of medical services. According to the advocates of this approach, its most important component is a change in the tax treatment of employer-based private health insurance.[15] A limitation of this subsidy, estimated to result in a revenue loss of $21.3 billion in 1984, should increase the use of cost-sharing provisions in insurance policies and spur experimentation with other forms of containing costs. It would also substantially and directly reduce the budget deficit by raising revenues. The administration has proposed an approach to such a limitation that would yield $8 billion in increased annual revenues by 1988. (A similar, less significant measure would be to tax Medigap premiums in order to discourage their first-dollar coverage and encourage more prudent utilization by the aged and disabled.)

Increased Regulation.   One variant of the competitive approach, which would actually be a major step toward regulation, would entail providing tax benefits only to health plans that paid the HI and SMI reimbursement rates or used an index based on these rates. This action would be similar to the tax treatment of private pensions, in which the tax benefits provided for employer contributions are contingent on the plans' fulfillment of a number of specific criteria about the size and allocation of benefits. The incentives of the tax system would be used to support what the federal health care financing program reforms might not be able to do on their own. The result would be better integration of federal health policy with the incentive structure in the private sector.

The regulatory approach that has been most frequently discussed is the extension of the new Medicare prospective reimbursement system for hospitals to all payers, which would encourage overall cost reductions by preventing hospitals from shifting costs. A few states now have such hospital cost control programs and have apparently succeeded in slowing the growth of health care costs. Physician fees could also be limited by fee schedules applying to all payers. Although these measures run counter to the prevailing sentiment in this country about government regulation of the private sector and have many problems associated with them,[16] many other Western countries have been forced to turn to them to deal with similar problems of rapidly rising health care costs.

Additional Measures to Reduce Deficits and Distribute the Fiscal Burden.   For most changes made to Social Security, given overall economic and demographic assumptions, analysts can predict the magnitude and distribution of future outlay consequences with reasonable accuracy. But the

15. Jack A. Meyer, ed., *Market Reforms in Health Care Current Issues, New Directions, Strategic Decisions* (Washington, D.C.: American Enterprise Institute, 1983).

16. Judith Feder, John Holahan, Randall Bovbjerg, and Jack Hadley, "Health," in John L. Palmer and Isabel V. Sawhill, eds., *The Reagan Experiment* (Washington, D.C.: The Urban Institute, 1982).

consequences of the changes we have discussed for Medicare are much less clear. Beneficiaries obviously will bear the burden of increased cost sharing, although their relatives (particularly their children) may eventually assume some of that burden. The ultimate impact of more restrictive provider reimbursement, however, is highly uncertain. Such steps could result in varying degrees of reduced benefits (less care, but not necessarily lowered health status), higher health care costs for private payers, lower provider incomes, or increased efficiencies in the provision of health care services. The outcomes will depend on the response to the changes by a wide range of participants in the health care system. Similarly, the effects of some forms of beneficiary cost sharing, tighter provider reimbursement, and broader competitive and regulatory approaches on utilization and health care cost inflation—and therefore on program outlays—are unpredictable.

Most of the measures to control increases in Medicare outlays discussed earlier are politically unpopular, although the intense fiscal pressures undoubtedly will facilitate difficult political compromises as they did for Social Security. The deficit problem for Medicare, however, is so large that additional measures with more predictable budgetary consequences will have to be considered. Here we suggest four.

Two of the measures would increase revenues in a way that would spread the burden across both the working and beneficiary populations. The first would be to increase alcohol and tobacco taxes substantially and use the new receipts for federal medical costs. Neither tax had been increased for thirty years until 1983, when taxes on cigarettes were doubled. If rates on both cigarettes and alcohol were tripled, however, these taxes would simply be restored to approximately the same effective levels as in 1952. This step would yield revenues of approximately $10 billion annually by 1988.

Second, a final Medicare contribution could be made from a deceased beneficiary's estate when appropriate—giving new meaning to the concept of "pay as you go" financing. For example, contributions could be for benefits that were used in excess of the present value of the decedent's past HI contributions and limited to only a proportion of the total estate. Most beneficiaries receive ten to twelve times more benefits than their past contributions would have afforded. Contributing 25 percent of the beneficiaries' estates to Medicare to pay for these benefits would provide roughly $10 billion to $20 billion annually by 1988. There are, of course, substantial problems with such a proposal. However, to the extent that providing an inheritance yields psychic income and receiving it provides real income, a Medicare estate tax would affect both generations without unduly burdening either.

A third measure would be an increase in the age of eligibility for Medicare to parallel the increase in the retirement age for Social Security (now scheduled to be phased in starting in 2000). This change would ease the added fiscal pressures caused by the extraordinary increase in the aged population early next century. However, unlike Social Security, under which reduced benefits will be available for early retirement, Medicare benefits are not graduated. Thus, to avoid undesirable hardship, other adjustments also would have to be made.

Finally, of course, the HI payroll tax and other more general taxes can be raised at any time to help meet the projected costs of HI and SMI under any expected outlay regime. Although such tax increases are currently out of favor, they may have to be considered if attempts to restrain inflation in health care costs are inadequate and society does not want to impose the full added fiscal burden on beneficiaries.

Pension Programs

Social Security (OASDI), the behemoth of the pension programs, accounts for more than two-thirds of total federal pension outlays. It provides wage-related pensions to retirees, their spouses and survivors, and the severely disabled. The benefits are financed from trust funds, most of the revenues for which come from payroll taxes. Other major federal pension programs include federal civilian and military retirement, railroad retirement, and veterans compensation. In addition, there are two means-tested programs— Supplemental Security Income (SSI) for the aged and disabled populations and veterans pensions.[17] Although most of the data reported in this paper include outlays for disabled populations, we focused on retirement outlays, since these constitute the vast bulk of the benefits.

The organization of this section is parallel to that of the previous one on health care financing programs. We first present some background on the past and projected growth in pension programs and the recent policy changes. Then we discuss options for further policy changes in the 1980s in light of the issues we have identified.

---

17. These seven programs represent the vast majority of federal retirement beneficiaries and outlays, although the federal government in fact administers nine other federal employee retirement programs on-budget and thirty-two off-budget. However, these additional programs are of such slight fiscal importance that their omission does not significantly change either past or future fiscal trends.

Background

Ever since the advent of the Social Security system in the late 1930s, the federal government has provided most of the retirement benefits in the United States. This share has declined only modestly, from 86 percent in 1960 to 78 percent in 1980, as the enormous rate of growth in private retirement benefits over the past two decades has been nearly matched by that of Social Security and other federal pensions. Between 1965 and 1981, federal outlays for pension programs increased more than sevenfold, accounting for more than half of the increase in the federal budget as a percentage of GNP and increasing from 23 percent to 29 percent of total federal spending.

Inflation, of course, was a major factor in these escalating program costs. Virtually all these programs had automatic cost-of-living adjustments (COLAs) by the early 1970s, as well as a prior legislative history of ad hoc benefit increases intended to compensate for inflation. In addition, the number of beneficiaries of the major retirement programs increased by more than one-third between 1970 and 1981.[18] And real benefit levels per recipient grew at an annual rate of 3.3 percent, reflecting both legislated benefit increases in excess of inflation and large cohorts of new retirees with successively higher real wage histories.

In contrast, the annual real growth rate of federal retirement programs for the remainder of this decade is projected under current policies to be less than half that of the prior decade. Annual growth in number of beneficiaries is expected to decline by a third, reflecting a modest slowdown in the rate of growth of the aged population, and real benefit increases per recipient are expected to decline by two-thirds. As a result, total federal spending for pensions should decline gradually as a percentage of GNP throughout the remainder of the 1980s. The current share of the budget devoted to these programs is also projected to decline slightly under current policies, but the share of the domestic budget these programs represent will increase slightly because they still will grow faster than the other domestic programs, excluding health care (see table 7).

The large projected decline in real benefit increase per recipient is due to three factors: First, no liberalizations in real benefit levels are assumed. Second, the increases in initial real benefits for new pensioners are expected to be smaller than those in previous decades because initial benefit levels are

---

18. The largest increases in beneficiaries were for the civil service and military retirement systems (86 percent and 70 percent, respectively) as a large number of people who had entered government service during and after World War II retired. Beneficiaries for veterans pensions actually declined as the number of poor, aged veterans was reduced by the substantial increases in Social Security benefits.

TABLE 7

FEDERAL PENSION OUTLAYS

	Actual					CBO Baseline Estimates	
	1965	1970	1975	1980	1982	1984	1988
	(In $ billions)						
Social Security	17.0	29.7	63.6	117.1	154.1	177.5	227.8
Federal Employee Retirement	1.5	2.7	7.0	14.7	19.4	23.0	30.4
Military Retirement	1.4	2.8	6.2	11.9	14.9	16.7	20.9
Railroad Retirement	1.1	1.6	3.0	4.7	5.7	7.8	8.4
Supplementary Security Income	2.1	3.0	4.8	6.4	7.7	8.0	10.0
Veterans Compensation and Pensions	4.2	5.5	7.9	11.7	13.2	13.9	14.8
Total	27.3	45.3	92.5	166.5	215.0	246.9	312.3
Federal Pension Outlays—							
—As a percentage of total budget	23.1	23.2	28.4	28.2	28.8	28.2	26.3
—As a percentage of nondefense program budget[a]	42.5	42.3	40.6	39.8	43.5	44.2	44.9
—As a percentage of GNP	4.1	4.7	6.4	6.5	7.1	7.0	6.4

SOURCES: Office of Management and Budget, ''Federal Government Finances,'' February 1983;
Congressional Budget Office Projections published in August 1983.
a. Including military retirement and medical outlays.

based on past wage histories, and per capita real wage growth has been much lower since 1970 than in the preceding decades. Third, the reforms in the first three years of the Reagan administration will reduce outlays in federal pension programs over the 1982–1985 period by 2.5 percent below their prior policy levels, and by a much larger amount in the long run once the Social Security retirement age is increased.[19]

The 1983 Social Security Amendments, discussed earlier, were the most dramatic of these reforms,[20] and they have important implications for civil service retirement. The coverage of federal workers under Social Security beginning in 1984 will require a redesign of the civil service retirement system

19. ''Major Legislative Changes in Human Resources Programs Since January 1981.''
20. This legislation was in addition to the roughly 2 percent outlay cut resulting from legislative changes in 1981 and 1982 that were targeted on small, specific groups of beneficiaries, most notably postsecondary students.

for new employees, which could have significant effects on its long-term outlays.

Several other legislative changes are expected to reduce spending in the civil service and military retirement programs by about 3 percent annually by 1985. Annual COLAs were substituted for the previously semiannual ones, and COLAs for retirees under age 62 were restricted to one-half of the Consumer Price Index (CPI), starting in 1983. This latter provision, however, is scheduled to terminate after 1985.

Unlike other pension programs, veterans compensation and pension programs were relatively unaffected by the budget reductions between 1981 and 1983, and both real expenditures and the number of beneficiaries are expected to decline in the remainder of the 1980s. Veterans' compensation benefits increased substantially in real terms in the 1970s, because coverage was extended to new groups and because benefit levels for certain disability ratings were increased. Even without further liberalizations, however, the average veterans' compensation benefit is likely to increase slightly in the 1980s as the World War II veterans die, since Vietnam veterans receive higher disability ratings and, therefore, benefits. Conversely, real outlays for income-tested veterans' pensions will decline because of rising real Social Security benefits. Since 70 percent of all veterans' pension beneficiaries currently also receive Social Security, increases in Social Security benefits reduce both the number of veterans beneficiaries and their average benefit.

The railroad retirement system has been in the midst of an acute fiscal crisis, because declining employment has led to more than twice the number of retirees as workers. Bipartisan reforms enacted in August 1983 require retirees to bear 24 percent of the costs of reducing the shortfall between receipts and benefits, largely by taxing their benefits and delaying COLAs. Current rail employees would bear 11 percent and rail management 21 percent of the costs through increased contributions, and the general taxpayer will bear 44 percent by continuing the windfall payments established in 1974 and by general fund borrowing. These changes will reduce the deficit by an estimated $2.6 billion between 1983 and 1988 and make the rail industry pension fund solvent through the end of the decade.[21]

As a result of reforms in the past two years, benefits under SSI actually increased over previous policy estimates. This increase was due to the exclusion of an additional $30 of Social Security benefits from the calculation of the SSI benefit.

---

21. Testimony of David Stockman, director, Office of Management and Budget, before the Senate Finance Committee on Railroad Retirement and Railroad Unemployment Insurance, August 2, 1983.

Issues and Options

Although the long-term growth of federal pension programs relative to GNP is now reasonably controlled and predictable as a result of the Social Security Amendments, several programs still need major reforms to make them more equitable and efficient. These reforms are likely to create budgetary savings, but not in time to have much effect on the structural deficits of the late 1980s. For pension programs to contribute significantly to the efforts to reduce deficits in this decade, a number of steps—such as COLA restrictions—would have to be taken that are not necessarily related either to long-term needs or to otherwise desirable program reforms. This section provides a brief catalogue of some of the most likely candidates to reduce the deficits, with an indication of whether they make long-term sense.

The 1983 Social Security Amendments were intended to restore fiscal health to Social Security in both the short and long run; and thus, they have seemingly bought Social Security an immunity from further deficit reduction measures as long as its trust funds remain adequate to cover projected expenses. As we have already noted, however, in the face of persistent, large, structural deficits for the overall budget, this immunity may be called into question. If it is, there are only three reasonable options for savings: further reductions in COLAs, greater taxation of benefits, and increases in payroll tax rates. (Most other possible changes to Social Security would affect only new retirees and therefore be of little help with the current deficit problem.) The first two measures would affect only beneficiaries, whereas an increase in the payroll tax rate would affect all workers. A reduction in COLAs would spread the burden in small doses over a large number of beneficiaries, while low-income recipients could be sheltered from net benefit reductions by appropriate adjustments in the SSI program.

Increased taxation of benefits would be accomplished by lowering, or eliminating, the income limits above which benefits are currently included in taxable income. The 1983 Social Security Amendments made half of Social Security benefits taxable for individuals with adjusted gross incomes above $25,000 and joint filers above $32,000. An additional $2 billion a year could be raised by 1988 if these limits were lowered to the level of the limits now applicable to unemployment insurance ($12,000/$18,000) and if the other federal pension programs not now taxed were subjected to the same treatment. This measure would place Social Security more on a par with private pensions and would concentrate the burden on higher-income recipients, but the measure leaves a lot to be desired as a near-term deficit reduction measure. Unless the income limits were lowered considerably, the amounts of revenues generated in the 1980s would be quite small. But even a modest lowering of the limits will—over the long term—greatly reduce the effective benefit levels of future retirees, who will already be bearing the brunt of the long-term savings under the recent amendments. And any lowering of the limits will produce large increases in the trust fund balances that are not needed under current economic and demographic assumptions. (Of course, the additional revenues need not be earmarked for the OASDI trust funds.)

COLA reductions, however, would affect only current recipients and yield substantial short-term savings with modest long-run effects. The Social Security Amendments delayed the 1983 COLA adjustment for six months, producing a real decrease of about 2 percent in the value of the benefits for current recipients.[22] But since they, and the recipients of other federal pension programs, have been treated quite generously compared with beneficiaries of other federal programs, further reductions in COLAs in all non-means-tested pension programs deserve serious consideration. For each one-percentage-point annual reduction in the COLAs effective in 1985 (for all non-means-tested pension programs), the federal deficit would be lowered $9 billion annually by 1988.

Other deficit reduction measures that might be considered would be more specific to individual programs. A recent accounting change has been made in the military retirement program to show the long-term actuarial costs of the system, raising once again the issue of whether employee contributions should be required in this system as they are in other federal employee systems. A 5 percent employee contribution would amount to an estimated $1.5 billion increase in revenues by 1988. Another change would be to extend the current temporary provision reducing the COLAs for early retirees in both the military and civil service retirement systems. Although the short-term savings would not be large—only $1.1 billion in 1988—the provision would have the desirable effect of gradually scaling back the overly generous benefit levels for early retirees.

The measures just described would tinker with the civil service and military retirement systems and yield minor immediate savings consistent with longer-term objectives. Both these systems, however, are sorely in need of major structural reform. They share several common undesirable characteristics, including poor fiscal accountability, poor integration with other pensions, excessively generous benefits relative to private pensions (especially for early retirees), and several perverse incentives for federal employees' career decision making. A number of studies have documented these problems and proposed solutions. The recent extension of Social Security coverage to

---

22. The delay in the cost-of-living adjustment does not affect new retirees' benefits.

civil servants is now forcing the redesign of their retirement system, and similar action is overdue on military retirement. In both cases the structural reforms should be developed by considering the ideal configuration of a total compensation package, including pay as well as pension and health benefits. Although the desirable reforms should reduce the long-term growth rate of military and civil service pensions, the reforms are unlikely to substantially affect budget deficits in the 1980s, because the reforms presumably would affect only relatively new employees.[23]

Despite the railroad retirement system's very recent changes, more reforms in this relatively small program will be needed in the 1980s to keep its trust fund solvent in the 1990s. But veterans' compensation and pensions are declining in real terms, partly because of the Pension Reform Act of 1978, and thus are shrinking targets for further reductions, except through the COLA and taxation changes already discussed.

Conclusions

In conclusion, we offer several observations on the general directions for federal budget policy concerning pension and health care financing programs in the remainder of the 1980s.

As a result of the recent Social Security Amendments, the projected federal outlays for pensions are reasonably predictable and controlled as a percentage of GNP, with the programs actually contributing to reductions in the structural deficit over the next fifteen years. However, if pension programs are targeted for further short-term deficit reduction measures, an across-the-board scaling back of COLAs (excluding means-tested programs) is the measure that promises to yield the most substantial short-run savings in a sensible fashion.

It will be tempting to use the large surpluses in the Social Security trust funds that will soon result from the recent amendments and from the temporary slowdown in the growth of the aged population to fund the emerging Medicare trust fund deficits. However, this action would be an abdication of federal responsibility to control health care costs. Moreover, these Social Security surpluses are needed to reduce projected federal borrowing needs and to increase both the private and public economic base that will be necessary to support the rapidly growing aged population in the twenty-first century.

---

23. Robert Hartman, *Pay and Pensions for Federal Workers* (Washington, D.C.: The Brookings Institution, 1983).

Large increases in aged beneficiaries of federal programs have contributed substantially to current structural deficits and will do so again in the next century. Federal policymakers need to find ways to adjust these pressures. To reduce or restrain total outlays to some arbitrary percentage of GNP, without accommodating any demographic-driven fiscal pressures, will require either very large reductions in the relative benefits provided the old people of the future or the gradual elimination of most other federal domestic activities. Neither extreme is desirable. Nevertheless, the greatly improved economic status of the aged does suggest that they can be asked to bear a larger share of the fiscal burden imposed by the rapid growth of this group relative to the total population.

Finally, it is evident that continuing, escalating health care costs pose a serious threat to our ability to meet other social needs and must be brought under better control. The priority attached to health care access, the complexity of the problem and the magnitude of Medicare's financial disequilibrium indicate that the process of addressing this issue will be difficult and prolonged—essentially involving another major negotiation of the social contract for the aged. A wide range of options, including ones beyond those now receiving serious attention, will have to be considered. Some of the options will reduce the structural deficits projected for the overall federal budget, but more importantly they should also help control future health care costs.

TABLE A.1

CURRENT POLICY PROJECTIONS OF FEDERAL HEALTH CARE FINANCING OUTLAYS AS
A PERCENTAGE OF GNP

	Medicare[a]	Medicaid[d]	Veterans and Military Medical[d]	Total
1982	1.7	0.6	0.4	2.7
1984	1.8	0.6	0.4	2.8
1986	2.0	0.6	0.4	3.0
1988	2.2	0.6	0.4	3.2
Intermediate Economic and Demographic Assumptions[b]				
1990	2.1	0.6	0.4	3.1
1995	2.7	0.6	0.4	3.7
2000	3.0	0.6	0.4	4.0
2005	3.4	0.6	0.4	4.4
2010	3.6	0.6	0.4	4.6
2015	4.0	0.6	0.4	5.0
2020	4.4	0.6	0.4	5.4
2025	4.9	0.6	0.4	5.9
2030	5.4	0.6	0.4	6.4
2035	5.9	0.6	0.4	6.9
2040	6.6	0.6	0.4	7.6
Pessimistic Economic and Demographic Assumptions[c]				
1990	2.6	0.6	0.4	3.6
1995	3.4	0.6	0.4	4.4
2000	4.1	0.6	0.4	5.1
2005	5.0	0.6	0.4	6.0

SOURCE: 1982 to 1988 estimates are from Congressional Budget Office projections published
in August 1983. HI estimates are from the "1983 Hospital Insurance Board of Trustees
Report."

a.   SMI (outlay) estimates assume that SMI is 54 percent of HI outlays, the proportion CBO
estimates SMI will be in 1988. This proportion has steadily increased over the past ten years.
If the increase continues, these estimates would understate the SMI costs.

b.   Assumptions are the same as those used in the II-B projections of the Social Security
actuaries in the 1983 Trustees Report.

c.   Assumptions are the same as those used in the Series III projections of the Social Security
actuaries in the 1983 Trustees Report.

d.   Medicaid, military, and veterans medical programs are projected to increase at the same
rate as GNP after 1988. To the extent that these programs are affected by the price increases in
the private health sector and the aging of the population, this assumption will understate their
future costs. However, since there is more discretionary control on these programs than on
Medicare, their cost increases may be insulated to some extent from trends in the private sector.

TABLE A.2

CURRENT POLICY PROJECTIONS OF FEDERAL PENSION OUTLAYS AS A PERCENTAGE
OF GNP

	OASDI	Civil Service, Military, and Rail Retirement[c]	Veterans Compensation and Pensions and SSI[d]	Total
1982	5.1	1.3	0.7	7.1
1984	5.0	1.3	0.7	7.0
1986	4.8	1.3	0.5	6.6
1988	4.7	1.2	0.5	6.4
Intermediate Economic and Demographic Assumptions[a]				
1990	4.9	1.2	0.5	6.6
1995	4.6	1.2	0.4	6.2
2000	4.3	1.1	0.4	5.8
2005	4.2	1.0	0.4	5.6
2010	4.3	1.0	0.3	5.6
2015	4.7	1.0	0.3	6.0
2020	5.2	1.0	0.3	6.5
2025	5.6	1.0	0.3	6.9
2030	5.9	1.0	0.2	7.1
2035	5.9	1.0	0.2	7.1
2040	5.9	1.0	0.2	7.1
Pessimistic Economic and Demographic Assumptions[b]				
1990	4.9	1.2	0.5	6.6
1995	5.0	1.2	0.5	6.7
2000	4.8	1.1	0.4	6.3
2005	4.7	1.1	0.4	6.2
2010	4.9	1.0	0.4	6.3
2015	5.4	1.0	0.3	6.7
2020	6.1	1.0	0.3	7.4
2025	6.8	0.8	0.3	7.9
2030	7.3	0.8	0.3	8.4
2035	7.7	0.8	0.3	8.8
2040	7.9	0.8	0.3	9.0

SOURCE: The estimates for 1982 to 1988 are from Congressional Budget Office projections published in August 1983. Trustees Report on Social Security, Social Security Administration, May 1983; Formal Actuarial reports of federal retirement program actuaries in compliance with P.L. 94-494; and authors' estimates of veterans compensation, pensions, and SSI projections.

a.   Assumptions are the same as those used in the II-B projections of the Social Security actuaries in the 1983 Trustees Report.

b.   Assumptions are the same as those used in the Series III projections of the Social Security actuaries in the 1983 Trustees Report.

c.   Estimates were made by program actuaries in the fall of 1982. The same estimates were used for the intermediate and pessimistic assumptions.

d.   Programs were assumed to remain constant in real terms.

TABLE A.3

RECENT ESTIMATES OF HI TRUST FUND ANNUAL DEFICITS
(In $ billions)

	CBO[a]	Social Security Intermediate Assumptions[b]	Social Security Pessimistic Assumptions[b]
1984		−0.5	−2.3
1985		−1.0	−3.6
1986	−0.6	1.5	−3.7
1987	−4.0	0.8	4.5
1988	−8.2	3.5	−13.9
1989	−12.8	−8.4	−13.9
1990	−18.3	−12.6	
1991	−24.9		
1992	−32.5		
1993	−41.3		
1994	−51.4		
1995	−63.2	−38.4	
2000		−76.6	
2005		−137.8	

NOTE: The numbers in the table reflect the differences between the expected annual revenues and expenditures and, thus, the change in the status of the balances in the HI trust fund for each year.

a.   "Changing the Structure of Medicare Benefits," CBO Study, March 1983. Assumes hospital payment rates consistent with the new prospective reimbursement system.

b.   1983 Annual Report of the Board of Trustees of the Federal Hospital Insurance Trust Fund, June 24, 1983. Assumes that the new prospective reimbursement system for HI has the same fiscal impact as the policies currently in place.

COMMENTS

Henry J. Aaron

In a brief introduction, Palmer and Torrey sketch the problems they are going to address and state a recurring theme. If federal expenditures on pensions and health are to be reduced more than they have been already, what changes would be consistent with long-term goals for structural reform? They do not take a position on whether such cuts are desirable but make clear their conviction that long-run structural reforms, especially of the health programs, are both necessary and desirable.

The first part of the paper examines budgetary implications of current policies. This section presents estimates of the ratio of the sum of projected health and pension outlays to GNP, the total budget, and nondefense spending.

The story is quite simple: health and pension outlays are big, and, although pension outlays will not again reach the share of GNP they did in 1982 until 2030, outlays for health care programs are zooming. As a result, the total will surpass 1984 levels before 1995 and keep on growing. Palmer and Torrey show that the aged population is rising as a fraction of the total, but that the dependency ratio—the ratio of children plus the elderly to active workers—has fallen sharply since 1960, will keep dropping to 2010, and will not again reach 1970 levels until after 2040, if ever.

Palmer and Torrey introduce a special definition of the concept of fiscal burden, which they define as the excess of projected outlays under current law over projected earmarked taxes, divided by gross national product (see table 3). Despite the large deficits projected for HI and SMI, the large surpluses projected for OASDI will enable health and pension programs to actually produce a fiscal burden in each year until 2015 less onerous than the burden they produced in 1982, according to the intermediate assumptions of the Social Security actuaries. Under the pessimistic assumptions, the balance swings by 1995.

A section entitled "Broad Budget Issues" points out that in addition to short-term fiscal issues posed by the structural deficit, there are several longer-

157

term issues that might appear to make an examination of health and pension programs desirable.

The first is the aging of the population. But, as Palmer and Torrey point out, this trend really has nothing to do with the current deficit, and insofar as it suggests changes in health and pension programs, it would do so even if we had a structural surplus as large as the deficit we now face.

The second long-term issue is the controllability of future outlays. Palmer and Torrey state that recent legislation has made pension growth more predictable but that health outlays are neither controlled nor predictable. I believe they exaggerate the difference. The 1983 change in the cost-of-living adjustments for cash benefits did reduce the sensitivity of real benefit obligations to stagflation, but substantial differences continue to separate the costs and rates of trust-fund accumulation under the alternative actuarial projections. Furthermore, recent amendments to the Medicare program have produced short-term changes in outlays at least as significant as those enacted in the cash benefits programs.

The third long-term issue that implies the need for a close look at pensions and health programs is how the increased burden of an aging population should be distributed. Pointing out that the aged are now about as well off, on average, as are people under age sixty-five, Palmer and Torrey suggest that if government services are to be cut, benefits for the aged should get a close look.

The next main section examines health care financing programs in more detail. In examining the forces causing rapid growth of health expenditures, public and private, Palmer and Torrey point to, the absence of any effective budget constraint on the key actors who decide on health care. Third-party payments insulate patients at the time care is demanded, and retrospective cost-based reimbursements insulate providers or actually reward them for rising medical costs. Palmer and Torrey point out that small changes in the last two years have somewhat reduced prospective growth of federal spending on health care, but the data presented in table 5 make clear that federal spending on health care is projected to continue growing rapidly.

Palmer and Torrey then turn to options for cutting the growth of federal spending on health care. These include direct expenditure controls; increases in the cost to patients at the time care is demanded; cuts in benefits by increasing the age of eligibility for Medicare; tightened reimbursement of providers; increased regulation; and, although they do not put it that way, increased taxes. In the last category falls the proposal to charge a premium for part A hospital benefits that would yield $4.8 billion per year according to table 6; or increases in alcohol and tobacco taxes and estate taxes to defray costs of Medicare, both of which are mentioned in the text. These measures may be good or bad ideas, but they are questions of tax policy. They are related to Medicare not because they will have any influence on medical decisons, but because some public relations link may be drawn between them and Medicare.

The final major section is devoted to pensions where with little zest Palmer and Torrey mention a number of ways by which pension benefits might be reduced, mostly by curtailing COLAs. They seem not to have their hearts in this section, because, I suspect, they doubt that Congress will have the stomach to make further cuts in Social Security or railroad retirement (on both of which Congress has legislated recently) or any cuts in veterans' benefits, unless members feel threatened with tortures even more exquisite than the political pain they would endure if they voted for such cuts. They endorse certain long-run structural changes, but point out that the savings the changes would generate will come too late to do much about the current deficit.

This paper is ostensibly about federal budget policy for the 1980s, a time when closing the intolerably large deficits created in the past three years will be the central problem. The options to modify pensions would help deal with this problem; Palmer and Torrey do not relate these options to any changes in structure desired over the long run. This approach can be justified on the ground that structural changes, such as a change in the benefit formula for new retirees, would have little immediate budgetary effect. In addition, Congress solved the long-term financing problem in 1983.

Palmer and Torrey take a rather different tack on health. In this case they suggest that each of the proposed short-term changes be evaluated on the basis of how much it promotes or retards desired long-term structural reform.

If structural changes in the financing of health care are indicated, they should be pursued, but if no structural changes in pensions are indicated, why cut pensions now? The answer presumably is the current deficit. But this line of argument seems suspect, given our budget history. We started with no structural deficit three years ago. We have cut nondefense spending, including health and pensions, which would have tended to create a structural surplus. But we had cut taxes and increased defense spending so much that we now face deficits unprecedented in peacetime. Further cuts in health and pensions made sense, it would appear, only if these programs are bad buys. They have not created the deficit, nor as Palmer and Torrey point out, will they be adding to it for the next quarter-century. Yet they are being scrutinized for cuts.

This approach makes sense only if health or pension programs are too large irrespective of the deficit. The right questions, therefore, concern how much we should be spending on pensions for the elderly, survivors and the disabled, and on health, and how much of these outlays the federal government should be responsible for. Then we should set taxes to cover the bill in a fiscally responsible way. Let me start with pensions.

The American population is getting older. Even if birthrates increase more than anyone anticipates, the proportion of the population that is over age sixty-five will grow. Unless we feel it desirable to encourage people to work longer than they are expected to do under current incentives, the fraction of the adult population that is nonproductive will increase. If the consumption level of this group relative to active workers does not decrease below current levels, it follows that an increasing proportion of the current production of active workers must be diverted to the pensioners. We might conclude that the ratio of consumption of the elderly to that of active workers is too high and that steps should be taken to decrease that ratio, or that people should work longer. And a debate on these issues is worth having.

If we don't decide to cause the relative consumption of the elderly to decline, the only generic policy question concerns how much of current production we wish to save in order to expand future productive capacity in anticipation of the increased relative burden that retirees will place on future workers. If we were to conclude that the consumption of the elderly is not excessive relative to that of active workers, then, in the absence of any indication that public policy is tending to upset this relationship, nothing should be done to alter the average contribution of federal policy to pension income of the elderly. We might, to be sure, disapprove of the structure—try to cut veterans' pensions and increase SSI, for example.

A somewhat different story can be told with respect to health care. In this case, the evidence is strong that there are serious problems with the financing of health care and the reimbursement of providers. A powerful case can be made that we are making expenditures at the margin—and perhaps well inside the margin—that yield benefits worth less than they cost. This problem is not confined to federal programs, although, as of now, federal programs are definitely part of the problem. Palmer and Torrey clearly state that many of their proposed changes in Medicare would do little to solve these problems and would serve primarily to shift costs from the general taxpayer to affected patients or to other persons through increased health insurance costs. But the point, once again, is that these are problems of how to finance health care and that the budget issues arise because the federal government pays for a large part of health care, not because there happens to be a deficit. The problems would be no less serious if the federal budget were in surplus.

We all understand as well, I think, that deficits are an important political and economic fact. In today's political climate the deficit has an importance greater than, and perhaps largely unrelated to, the distortions it causes in the allocation of resources between consumption and investment, and between import and export industries. But I think that this paper would better help us to think about the deficit if it did more to clarify the reasons why the federal government has a role in health and pension policy and examined existing programs from the standpoint of whether they are doing an adequate job and could do it more efficiently. Going back to Musgrave's three-way division of the responsibilities of the fisc, I think that this paper should have made clear that however much the stabilization branch has botched its job, that is no excuse for the allocation branch to abandon the principles upon which decisions concerning public spending should be made.

COMMENTS

Jack A. Meyer

The paper by John Palmer and Barbara Torrey is an excellent, balanced treatment of a complex subject. I have no major problems or objections to record. Instead, I will register some minor misgivings and suggest a few ways in which I believe the analysis could be strengthened.

The paper leaves me with this message: Social Security is now on solid, long-term financing ground, but federal health programs and other federal retirement programs are not, and it would be imprudent to mortgage our future by using near-term surpluses in OASDI to forestall trouble in Medicare. The authors argue sensibly that short-term financial viability in either the federal health or retirement program areas should *not* exempt these areas from making a contribution to the reduction in structural deficits. They convincingly contend that our valid concern with structural deficits should not deflect us from designing longer-term program reforms that reflect more fundamental concerns.

My concern with the way Palmer and Torrey develop this valid conceptual framework is twofold. First, while they differentiate policy options involving tax increases from those involving benefit changes, there could be more discussion of the advantages and disadvantages of differing mixes of these two categories of options. Second, they stress the need for more basic, long-range approaches to program reform, but I find no concept of the principles that should guide such long-range policy development in this paper.

Palmer and Torrey's brief reminder of the mix of tax and benefit changes in the recent Social Security compromise highlights the need to assess this issue as we move into other major program reform areas such as Medicare or civil service retirement. The authors note that a little less than half of the short-term burden of the 1983 Social Security Amendments was placed on beneficiaries, with greater reliance placed on increased payroll taxes.

I think that it would be useful to stress the implications for the payroll tax rate (and, in a derivative sense, for employment and output) of a policy mix that is heavily skewed toward an increase in the HI portion of payroll taxes. Palmer and Torrey mention this option only briefly, noting that it is out of favor politically now. But the policy mix in the Social Security Amendments should remind us that when last-minute compromises are patched together, tax hikes are likely to play a substantial role. We need further debates on the efficiency and fairness effects associated with alternative mixes, and an analysis of the trade-offs between these effects. A package combining a high tax increase with a low benefit cut, for example, would be more "fair" to the elderly (at the expense of fairness to the working population), but would impose some degree of adverse employment effects on the economy. Although I do not want to overestimate these efficiency effects, it would be useful to illustrate how high the tax rate would be if little or no change is made in the Medicare benefit stream.

With regard to the need for more guiding principles for change, I believe that Palmer and Torrey's analysis would benefit from placing greater emphasis on the relatively small savings likely to emerge, at least in the near term, from either the competitive reforms or the regulatory options outlined in their paper. Their four categories of options entitled increased beneficiary cost sharing, tighter provider reimbursement, increased competition, and increased regulation seem somewhat overlapping (e.g., tighter reimbursement involves greater regulation of providers, while greater cost sharing is one aspect of, though by no means all there is to, greater competition). More important, all these options, even taken together, are unlikely to make more than a minor fill in the projected funding shortfall in the HI trust fund. DRGs, TEFRA formulas, all-payers regulation, and greater cost sharing under Parts A or B of Medicare may each save some money, but I believe that even their most enthusiastic champions would concede (and Palmer and Torrey's table 6 illustrates) that the likely savings are a few drops in the HI bucket, where shortfalls of hundreds of billions are expected in the next decade.

What this analysis tells me is that Palmer and Torrey should give somewhat greater attention to their options involving increases in alcohol and tobacco taxes, payroll taxes, and beneficiary cost sharing, and a minor change in the age of eligibility keyed to corresponding OASDI changes now scheduled for the early part of the next century. Palmer and Torrey have mentioned these options too briefly, or seem to have brushed some of them aside.

One implication of my remarks is that although there is little to choose between market-oriented and regulatory policies from the point of view of bailing out the HI trust fund (as both are inadequate), there is much to choose between them on the basis of the kind of guiding principles and philosophical framework that we want to shape our long-term policy framework.

My own view is that a market-incentives approach, fostering pluralistic, decentralized decision making about health care utilization and prices, will lead to better outcomes than more government formulas and limits. I think that the government's role in subsidizing care for people who cannot afford it should be shored up (and incidentally, executed more equitably than at present), while the government's role in setting allowable increases in fees, charges, capital expansion, and utilization should be scaled back.

I would not, of course, attempt to foist this preference on Palmer and Torrey. Rather, I suggest that analysts of these questions make these kinds of distinctions and state their own preferences.

I believe that Palmer and Torrey were too quick to dismiss the option of greater beneficiary cost sharing. In part, this occurred because they brushed aside the one variant of this option that I believe is fair and viable—an increase in cost sharing that is limited to households that are not poor. Palmer and Torrey seemed to stack the deck against cost-sharing that is income-related, listing three disadvantages but neglecting the clear advantages of this feature of the cost sharing approach.

They contend that relating cost sharing to beneficiaries' resources would be "administratively cumbersome and expensive" and would "greatly reduce the cost savings." Although a finely graduated scale for cost sharing might be administratively complex, it would be possible to use a less sophisticated "poor, nonpoor" split (with perhaps a limited phase-in range to avoid large notch problems) that would probably yield *net* benefits to society, even when reasonable administrative costs are taken into account. Moreover, I believe that Martin Feldstein has argued convincingly (in the different, but analogous case of slowing the growth in Social Security benefits) that exempting the poor elderly from a new bite on benefits not only is fair, but also represents only a relatively small drain on the expected savings in outlays.

Finally, I would like to urge that further consideration be given to some specific policy steps designed to bring a greater measure of cost control to the area of civil service pay and benefits. In particular, suggestions would be welcome for improving the flawed system of comparability used to set wage and salary scales for federal civilian white-collar workers, as well as for bringing federal retirement benefits more in line with typical private-sector practices.

FEDERAL AID TO STATE AND LOCAL GOVERNMENTS

Helen F. Ladd

Federal aid to state and local governments covers a wide range of program areas and takes a number of different forms. It includes grants for income supplements and social services on the one hand and grants for capital facilities on the other. It includes lump-sum revenue sharing, block grants, and narrowly defined categorical grants, some of which have local matching requirements and some of which do not. It includes program commitments that are open-ended and, hence, uncontrollable from the perspective of the federal budget, and others that are limited by annual appropriation. It also includes indirect aid through tax expenditures, such as tax deductibility of state and local taxes and exemption from taxation of the interest on municipal bonds. The only elements common to all forms of federal aid to state and local governments are (1) full or partial financing from the federal government and (2) program control, at least in part, at the state or local level.

One approach to the analysis of federal aid views state and local governments as the primary actors, with the federal government stepping in to correct market failures (such as spillovers across jurisdictions) and to equalize resources across jurisdictions. An alternative approach views state and local governments as agents of the federal government. According to this view, some programs are essentially federal programs, which, for a number of reasons, the federal government has chosen to implement through state and local governments. Although one approach is sometimes more appropriate than the other in the context of a particular program, both approaches should be kept in mind throughout this paper.

The author is grateful to Andrew Nelson for his attention to detail and his insights as a research assistant for this project.

165

In discussions of federal intergovernmental aid, attention typically focuses on grants-in-aid. These grants grew dramatically during the 1960s and 1970s, rising from 7.6 percent of federal expenditures in fiscal year (FY) 1960 to 17.4 percent in FY 1978. In recent years, however, a dramatic reversal has occurred. Not only has growth been reduced, but grants have actually been declining in inflation-adjusted terms, and this trend is likely to continue.

In a few programs, such as Medicaid, controlling expenditure growth is still an issue. In general, however, the federal budgetary issues surrounding intergovernmental grants currently have little to do with limiting expenditure growth. Instead, a major question is the appropriateness of transferring some fiscal responsibilities from the federal government to state and local governments. For example, what are the implications of giving states more responsibility for Medicaid, income support, or social service programs? How are states likely to respond, and which level of government should assist poor people? A second policy issue concerns the more effective structuring of a declining pot of aid. For example, should state and local governments be given more flexibility in the use of federal aid, as the Reagan administration advocates, or should current targeting and program restrictions be maintained and perhaps increased?

Aid given in the form of tax expenditures has received much less attention than have grants. Nonetheless, the federal revenue loss associated with the treatment of state and local taxes and interest on state and local bonds was almost one-half of total grants-in-aid in 1982 and has since been growing much more rapidly than have grants. These tax expenditures may be a suitable target for federal budgetary reductions, especially given the projections of large federal deficits and the continuing need for federal budgetary restraint.

This paper begins by discussing the past and projected trends in intergovernmental aid, including grants-in-aid and tax expenditures. It then focuses on the two largest intergovernmental grant programs, Aid to Families with Dependent Children (AFDC) and Medicaid, considering both the effects of recent federal policy changes and the question of the appropriate federal role in income support. The next section concentrates on the design of grants-in-aid for state and local governments, while the following sections discuss the two categories of tax expenditures. The paper has a brief concluding section.

Trends and Outlook

Table 1 describes trends in federal aid to state and local governments since 1960. In addition to intergovernmental grants, the table includes tax

TABLE 1

AID TO STATE AND LOCAL GOVERNMENTS FOR SELECTED YEARS
(FY 1960–FY 1982)

	1960	1970	1978	1982	*Percentage Change, 1978–1982*
	Billions of current dollars				
Grants-in-aid	7.0	24.0	77.9	88.2	13.2
To governments	4.5	15.0	51.9	47.5	−8.5
To individuals	2.5	9.0	26.0	40.7	56.5
Tax expenditures	NA	10.8	19.3	41.1	113.0
Interest exclusion	NA	2.3	6.1	10.6	73.8
Tax deductibility	NA	8.5	13.2	30.5	131.0
Total	NA	34.8	97.2	129.3	33.0
	Billions of constant (1972) dollars				
Grants-in-aid	10.8	27.0	49.5	40.5	−18.2
To governments	7.4	17.2	32.0	20.9	−34.7
To individuals	3.4	9.8	17.5	19.6	12.0
Tax expenditures	NA	12.3	12.1	18.2	50.4
Interest exclusion	NA	2.6	3.8	4.7	23.7
Tax deductibility	NA	9.7	8.3	13.5	62.7
Total	NA	39.3	61.6	58.7	−4.7
Grants-in-aid as a percentage of					
—total federal budget	7.6	12.3	17.4	12.1	−30.5
—domestic federal budget[a]	19.6	25.1	26.3	19.8	−24.7
—state and local revenues	11.6	16.0	21.0	18.7	−11.0

SOURCES: U.S. Office of Management and Budget, *1984 Budget Data, Federal Grants-In-Aid to State and Local Governments*, March 1983; Congressional Budget Office, *Tax Expenditures: Current Issues and Five-Year Budget Projections for Fiscal Years, 1982–1986*, September 1981, tables 1 and 7; and Congressional Budget Office, *Tax Expenditures: Budget Control Options and Five-Year Budget Projections for Fiscal Years 1983–1987*, table A-1.

NA = not available.

a. Excludes defense, international affairs, and net interest.

expenditures—aid delivered through the revenue side of the federal budget in the form of special tax provisions.

Following the practice of the Office of Management and Budget, intergovernmental grants are divided into two categories: grants to governments and grants-in-aid to individuals. Although all intergovernmental aid ultimately benefits individuals, this separation emphasizes the fact that some aid is for programs providing cash or in-kind benefits to identifiable individuals or households. The aid-to-individuals category includes Medicaid, AFDC, subsidized housing, child nutrition, and low-income energy assistance. The grants-to-governments category includes narrowly defined categorical programs, block grants for broadly defined purposes such as community development, and general revenue sharing which provides essentially unrestricted grants to more than 38,000 local governments.

FY 1978 is a key year in the history of intergovernmental aid. After nearly two decades of rapid growth, federal aid peaked in FY 1978 in real terms, as a fraction of the federal budget and as a fraction of state and local government revenues. The first three columns of table 1 show this dramatic growth since FY 1960. Grants increased almost fivefold in constant dollars. In FY 1978 more than one in five dollars spent by the federal government on domestic programs took the form of grants to state and local governments. A similar proportion of revenue available to state and local governments was financed by federal taxpayers.

The tide turned in FY 1979. The inflation-adjusted value of federal grants started to decline and by FY 1982 had fallen 18.2 percent. Similarly, grants began to fall as a share of the federal budget and as a fraction of state and local revenues. In FY 1982, grants accounted for 19.8 percent of the domestic budget, the same share as in the early 1960s. As will be discussed, much of this recent decrease in intergovernmental aid reflects President Reagan's attempts to reduce the size of government and to reduce the federal involvement in state and local affairs. However, this trend antedates the Reagan administration, and hence did not result solely from the policies of a single administration.

With respect to tax expenditures, the relevant provisions are the exclusion of interest on state and local bonds from the federal income tax and deductibility of state and local taxes from the federal income tax. Both provisions serve to reduce federal tax revenues. These forgone revenues constitute intergovernmental aid in that they subsidize particular activities; state and local capital spending is financed through bonds, while state and local general-purpose spending is financed by deductible taxes. Unlike direct federal aid, however, the costs to the federal government of these tax expenditure programs exceed the direct benefits as perceived by state and local public officials. Indeed, in the case of tax deductibility, all the benefits initially accrue to itemizing taxpayers. Since our focus here is on the federal budget, we account for these programs in terms of their full costs. In later sections, we return to the impact of such programs on state and local spending.

By FY 1978, tax expenditures accounted for about one-fifth of total federal aid to state and local governments. California's passage (in June 1978) of Proposition 13, a measure to roll back local property taxes, resulted in lower local tax payments and higher federal tax payments, because California taxpayers had smaller amounts to deduct for purposes of federal income taxation. Despite similar tax restraint in state and local governments throughout the country in subsequent years, however, the value of these deductions continued to grow in real terms between 1978 and 1982. This growth resulted in part from inflation-induced increases in state and local tax collections and in federal marginal tax rates. The central point here is that the value of these tax expenditures is largely outside the control of the federal government; tax deductibility acts like an open-ended matching grant to people and firms in their capacity as payers of state and local taxes.

FY 1978 also marks the acceleration of growth in tax expenditures related to special-purpose debt. Beginning in the mid-1970s, new forms of tax-exempt municipal bonds were developed to finance nontraditional activities such as pollution control and industrial development by private firms. The cost to the federal treasury of special-purpose debt doubled in FY 1979; the cost doubled again in FY 1981 with the introduction of additional uses for tax-exempt bonds. At the same time, tax expenditures associated with the tax exemption of general-purpose state and local debt showed little growth.

Between FY 1978 and FY 1982, the four components of federal aid to state and local governments grew at very different rates. The final column of table 1 shows that grants to governments, which are the most visible and the most susceptible to cuts, fell during the period by 35 percent in inflation-adjusted dollars, reflecting annual reductions that ranged from 5 percent in FY 1979 to 18 percent in FY 1982. In contrast, inflation-adjusted aid to individuals, the bulk of which is distributed through entitlement programs, grew by 12 percent during the period. The rate of growth is well below that of the previous four years, however, and federal expenditures on these programs actually declined in real terms during FY 1982 as a consequence of policy changes in AFDC and Medicaid. Thus, although these programs continued to grow in real terms between FY 1978 and FY 1982, the evidence suggests a leveling off of the rapid rates of growth of earlier years.

There is no evidence of a leveling off in the tax expenditure categories, however. Between FY 1978 and FY 1982, the inflation-adjusted federal revenue loss from the interest exclusion increased by 24 percent, while the loss from tax deductibility of state and local taxes increased by almost three times as much. Moreover, these growth rates far exceeded those of the previous four years. Thus, during the FY 1978 to FY 1982 period, a major shift occurred in the way the federal government gives aid to state and local governments: In FY 1978, only one out of five aid dollars was given in the form of tax expenditures; by FY 1982, almost one of three dollars was given in this form.

What is the Outlook for Federal Intergovernmental Aid?

Despite President Reagan's FY 1982 proposals for sweeping change in the division of responsibilities among levels of governments, no major changes in the relationship between federal and subnational governments are expected during the next few years. The president sought to transfer fiscal responsibility for the federally financed Food Stamp program and the jointly financed AFDC program to the states, in return for federal takeover of the jointly financed Medicaid program. In addition, he planned to phase out many federal intergovernmental aid programs by placing them in a trust fund that would have expired in 1991. The president had called for the initial consolidation of programs into block grants with few strings. By strengthening the role of the states in program design and administration, these block grants were to facilitate eventual state takeover of a wide range of programs.[1]

Starting in FY 1984, the effects of this shift would have been substantial. Federal grants would have decreased from their nominal dollar peak of $94.8 billion in FY 1981 to $53.5 billion in FY 1988 and, with the phase-out of the trust fund in FY 1991, would have reduced the federal fiscal involvement with state and local governments to a level not seen since the 1930s.[2]

Although the president's call for less federal involvement struck a responsive chord among public officials who were concerned about excessive federal interference, the president's vision of the new federalism went nowhere. State and local officials were reluctant to support the program, both because of their own fiscal pressures and because of concerns about reversing the recent trend of a larger federal role in income support programs. Nor was Congress supportive; its willingness in FY 1981 to support the consolidation of small grants into block grants seems to reflect the desire to cushion the impact of necessary and inevitable cuts in aid programs more than a commitment to the president's vision. Had this not been the case, Congress would have gone further in setting up block grants and eliminating federal strings

---

1. These proposals have been widely discussed and evaluated. See, for example, Edward Gramlich and Deborah S. Laren, "Reagan's Proposals for a New Federalism," in *Setting National Priorities, The 1983 Budget* (Washington, D.C.: The Brookings Institution, 1982); Helen F. Ladd, "Financing Public Services in the Federal System," *Federalism: Making the System Work, Alternatives for the 1980s*, No. 6 (Washington, D.C.: Center for National Policy, 1982); and George Peterson, "The State and Local Sector," in John L. Palmer and Isabel V. Sawhill, eds., *The Reagan Experiment* (Washington, D.C.: The Urban Institute Press, 1982), pp. 157–218.

2. Estimate of impact in 1988 based on Robert W. Rafuse, "The Outlook for State-Local Finance under the New Federalism," in New York State Legislative Commission on State-Local Relations, *Summary of Proceedings from the Conference on New York's Fiscal System: Reviewing the Blueprint, Strengthening the Partnership*, April 1982, p. 123. See also Peterson, "The State and Local Sector," p. 168.

in response to the administration's FY 1981 proposals. Instead, it gave the president only part of what he asked for and retained a number of restrictions and limitations.

In 1983, President Reagan substantially modified his federalism proposal and called for the creation of four ''megablocks'' that would have consolidated more categorical programs into blocks and would have regrouped and consolidated most of the 1981 block grants into larger blocks. The four megablocks included a block grant for states that combined twenty-two health, social services, education, and community development programs; a block grant for local governments that combined the entitlement portion of the Community Development Block Grant and General Revenue Sharing programs; a transportation block grant that consolidated six highway programs; and a block grant to states for rural housing programs. These, like his 1981 block grant proposals, were designed to facilitate eventual state takeover of responsibilities in these program areas. So far, however, there has been little legislative action, and it appears that these proposals, like the more sweeping 1982 reform proposal, will never get off the shelf.[3]

Instead, the more likely outcome is one of limited growth in federal aid, with probable declines in real terms in many program areas. Table 2 shows predicted grant outlays for FY 1983 to FY 1988 under two scenarios. The first shows the federal budgetary costs that would be incurred in future years if FY 1983 federal grant policies were maintained in real terms.[4] The other set shows projected grant outlays under President Reagan's FY 1984 budget proposals (excluding the megablock proposals). Under the Reagan proposals, total grant outlays would grow annually at 3 to 4 percent in contrast to the 5 or 6 percent required to maintain current policies. One component, aid to individuals, is projected to grow at about 6 percent per year. The other component, aid to governments, would be funded approximately at the FY 1983 nominal level, implying a substantial decline in real terms. Within this category, some programs are projected to grow, while others will decline even in current dollars. The Surface Transportation Act of 1982, which boosted funding for transportation aid, shows that under certain circumstances particular intergovernmental aid programs can still successfully compete with other federal programs for scarce dollars. Supporters effectively appealed to concerns both about the nation's deteriorating infrastructure and recession-

---

3. For a discussion of the status of the megablock proposal, see Susan Szaniszlo, ''Latest in the New Federalism: The Megablocks . . . One Giant Step,'' working draft for the Advisory Commission on Intergovernmental Relations, Washington, D.C., 1983.

4. Most programs are simply adjusted upward for inflation, or, in the case of entitlement programs, also adjusted for changes in the number of eligible recipients. General revenue sharing is an exception because it has a multiyear appropriation.

TABLE 2

OUTLOOK FOR FEDERAL GRANTS
(FY 1983–FY 1988)

	Current Policy Baseline Estimates		President Reagan's FY 1984 Budget	
	$ Billions	*Percentage Change*	*$ Billions*	*Percentage Change*
Total grants				
1983	94.0	6.6	93.6	6.1
1984	100.3	6.7	96.4	3.0
1985	106.2	5.9	100.0	3.7
1986	111.7	5.2	103.5	3.5
1987	117.5	5.2	106.9	3.3
1988	123.6	5.2	110.4	3.3
Aid to individuals				
1983	43.3	6.4	42.8	5.2
1984	46.1	6.5	44.5	4.0
1985	50.1	8.7	47.9	7.6
1986	53.1	6.0	50.7	5.8
1987	56.8	7.0	53.7	5.9
1988	60.6	6.7	57.0	6.1
Aid to governments				
1983	50.7	6.7	50.8	6.9
1984	54.2	6.9	51.9	2.2
1985	56.1	3.5	52.1	0.4
1986	58.5	4.3	52.7	1.2
1987	60.8	3.9	53.1	0.8
1988	63.0	3.6	53.4	0.6

SOURCE: Congressional Budget Office, *Multiyear Projections System: Grants in Revised Baseline* (run date: May 23, 1983) and *Multiyear Projections System: Grants in President's January Budget Reestimated* (run date: August 4, 1983).

induced unemployment. By contrast, however, it also illustrates the absence of widespread support for growth in other intergovernmental aid programs.

The mix of intergovernmental aid programs is projected to continue to shift toward those given through the tax side of the federal budget. A comparison of tables 2 and 3 shows that the federal revenue losses from the two tax-expenditure categories are likely to grow substantially faster than intergovernmental grants. The 1983 decrease in federal revenue losses from the deductibility of state and local taxes reflects a combination of recession-induced declines in tax revenues in the state-local sector and reduced federal tax rates. The decrease is only temporary, however. Now that states throughout the country are raising tax rates, federal revenue losses are projected to

TABLE 3

OUTLOOK FOR TAX EXPENDITURES
(FY 1983–FY 1988)

	Deductibility of State and Local Taxes					
	Total		*Property Taxes*		*Other*	
	$ Billions	*Percentage Change*	*$ Billions*	*Percentage Change*	*$ Billions*	*Percentage Change*
1983	28.9	− 5.3	8.8	− 12.9	20.1	− 1.5
1984	31.3	8.3	9.5	8.0	21.8	8.5
1985	37.1	18.5	10.5	10.5	26.6	22.0
1986	41.7	12.3	11.7	11.4	30.0	12.8
1987	47.3	13.4	13.2	12.8	34.1	13.7
1988	54.0	14.2	15.0	13.6	39.0	14.4

	Exclusion of Interest On State and Local Debt					
	Total		*General-Purpose Debt*		*Special-Purpose Debt*	
	$ Billions	*Percentage Change*	*$ Billions*	*Percentage Change*	*$ Billions*	*Percentage Change*
1983	18.5	a	10.4	a	8.1	a
1984	21.3	15.1	11.7	12.5	9.6	18.3
1985	23.9	12.2	13.0	11.1	10.9	13.7
1986	26.8	12.1	14.2	9.2	12.4	13.3
1987	29.2	9.0	15.5	9.2	13.7	10.4
1988	31.8	8.9	16.9	9.0	14.9	8.9

SOURCE: Calculated from *Estimates of Federal Tax Expenditures for Fiscal Years 1983–1988.*
Prepared by the Joint Committee on Taxation, March 7, 1983 (Washington, D.C.:
U.S. Government Printing Office, 1983).

   a.   The reported estimates imply that the one-year percentage changes between FY 1982 and
FY 1983 are about 70 percent. These are potentially misleading since the 1982 estimates appear
to be underestimates of the true figures. At the same time, however, they correctly capture the
dramatic recent growth in these tax-expenditure categories.

return to their rapid upward trend. Federal revenue losses from the interest
exclusion are also likely to continue their recent growth.

Grants-In-Aid to Individuals

   AFDC and Medicaid are the two largest programs in the category of
federal grants-in-aid for individuals. Both are entitlement programs financed
by open-ended matching grants to state governments, and both are targeted
to needy individuals or households.

From a budgetary perspective, entitlement programs are always problematic. Once eligibility standards and benefit levels are set, the budgetary commitment is open-ended. One might expect federal budgetary problems to be even worse for entitlement programs such as AFDC and Medicaid, which the federal government supports by providing open-ended matching grants to subnational governments. Subject to loose federal guidelines, the states have the power to set both eligibility standards and benefit levels for the AFDC program and can choose whether to provide optional services in the Medicaid program. Moreover, in both programs the states presumably have less incentive to control spending than they would if they were paying for the full costs, a concern particularly relevant for Medicaid because of soaring medical care costs. Thus, the federal government's open-ended commitment varies both with the number of eligible participants, as is true for all entitlement programs, and with decisions by units of government outside its control. Dramatic annual increases in Medicaid spending that averaged 15 percent during the 1970s illustrate the potential magnitude of the federal budgetary problem.

But recent experience shows that federal spending on such programs need not grow inexorably. Recent changes in federal eligibility requirements and regulations in the AFDC program, for example, have reduced both federal and state-local spending on this program, and severe fiscal pressures at the state level have interacted with federal program changes to curb the growth rate of Medicaid spending.

Controllability of federal expenditures, however, is not the only policy goal. If it were, a simple solution to the federal budget problem would be to turn programs over to the states. Also important is the question of the appropriate federal role in income-assistance programs. Thus we begin by describing the recent federal budgetary experience with AFDC and Medicaid. We then address the nature of the federal interest in such programs and the implications for program design and the federal budget.

Aid to Families with Dependent Children

Table 4 shows the growth in federal aid for AFDC from FY 1960 to FY 1982. The program has shown little growth in inflation-adjusted terms since the mid-1960s and has substantially declined as a percentage of total grants-in-aid and as a percentage of the federal domestic budget.

The 1981 Omnibus Budget Reconciliation Act made a number of changes in the operation of the program. The most important changes affected the working poor by reducing the amount of income that states may disregard in determining eligibility for the program and by setting an income ceiling of 150 percent of the state-determined standard of need. The Reagan adminis-

TABLE 4

AID TO FAMILIES WITH DEPENDENT CHILDREN
SELECTED YEARS
(FY 1960–FY 1982)

	Billions of Current Dollars	*Billions of Constant (1972) Dollars*[a]	*AFDC Outlays as a Percentage of—*	
			—Total Grants	*—Domestic Budget*[b]
1960	2.1	2.9	30.0	5.9
1965	2.8	3.6	25.7	5.1
1970	4.1	4.5	17.1	4.3
1975	5.1	4.1	10.2	2.5
1978	6.6	4.4	8.5	2.2
1979	6.6	4.1	8.0	2.1
1980	7.3	4.1	8.0	2.0
1981	8.5	4.4	9.0	2.1
1982	7.9	3.8	9.0	1.8

SOURCES: AFDC and total grant data: Office of Management and Budget, *1984 Budget Data, Federal Grants-In-Aid to State and Local Governments*, March 1983. Domestic budget data: 1960–1979 from 1980 *Supplement to Economic Indicators*, Office of Federal Statistical Policy and Standards, Department of Commerce, 1980, p. 121; 1980–81 from *Economic Report of the President 1982* (Washington, D.C.: U.S. Government Printing Office, 1982), p. A-7; 1982 from Office of Management and Budget, *Special Analyses, Budget of the United States Government, Fiscal Year 1984*, p. 317.
   a.   Deflated by implicit price deflator for personal consumption expenditures, converted by the author from calendar year to fiscal basis.
   b.   Excludes defense, international affairs, and net interest.

tration estimates that, nationwide, the changes made about 10 percent of the existing caseload ineligible and reduced benefits for another 7 percent.[5] The effect was dramatic in some states; Massachusetts, for example, reduced its caseload by 21 percent in less than a year, the largest drop in the state's history. Overall, the legislative changes reduced federal outlays on AFDC by 9.9 percent in FY 1982 and are projected to reduce them by 12.7 percent between that year and FY 1985.[6]

   These changes in AFDC should be viewed largely as a reflection of the Reagan administration's philosophy about the appropriate role of income support programs. In contrast to previous administrations, the current

---

   5. Cited in Richard P. Nathan and Fred C. Doolittle, *The Consequences of Cuts: The Effects of the Reagan Domestic Program on State and Local Governments* (Princeton, N.J.: Princeton University Press, 1983), p. 28.
   6. These estimates of changes in federal outlays represent the effects of the legislative changes alone as reported in Congressional Budget Office, ''Major Legislative Changes in Human Resources Programs Since January 1981,'' staff memorandum, August 1983.

administration believes that income support programs should be used only for temporary relief, not for long-term assistance to the working poor. Consistent with this philosophy, similar changes were made in the eligibility requirements for the Food Stamp program. In the case of that program, however, eligibility requirements and benefit levels were fully under federal control. In the case of AFDC, the effect of the federal changes depended on the response of the states.

Most of the federal changes in the AFDC program appear to have been ratified by the states. That is, the states typically made few changes at the state level that would offset the federal changes. In the most comprehensive study to date of the state responses to the federal changes, Nathan and Doolittle report that none of the states in their fourteen-state sample set up new state-funded general relief programs, and that at least one state, New York, limited the number of former AFDC recipients who would be eligible for its existing state-financed general relief program.[7] Several states raised their standard of need to get around part of the 150 percent income limitation, but other states changed the AFDC program in ways that compounded the federal cuts. According to Nathan and Doolittle, most states ended up spending less of their own funds on AFDC or substitute programs in FY 1982 than they would have spent without the 1981 omnibus budget act. The clear implication is that, in the short run at least, the changes in AFDC relieved pressures on both federal and state budgets. The bulk of the burden was thus borne by the working poor.

The future response of state governments is less clear. Stringent voter-initiated tax limitation measures and recession-induced revenue losses may have kept many states from expanding their own programs for the working poor to offset the federal cuts. When some of these pressures moderate, states may be more willing to offset some of the federal cuts. The states are not likely to offset the cuts completely, however, since any state spending on these groups will have to be fully financed by state taxes. Thus, the states will no longer have the price incentive associated with an open-ended matching grant to provide income assistance to the groups cut from the AFDC program.

Thus the short-term policy question is whether it was fair to make low-income people bear the brunt of reductions in federal spending. Because it is likely that local political pressures will eventually force the states to restore some of the cuts, thereby reducing somewhat the burden of the federal cuts on the working poor, an additional longer-run policy question emerges: What is the appropriate division of fiscal responsibilities for income support

---

7. Nathan and Doolittle, *The Consequences of Cuts: The Effects of the Reagan Domestic Program on State and Local Governments*, chapter 3.

programs among levels of government in our federal system? We return to this question later.

Medicaid

Medicaid is a huge program that expanded dramatically during the 1970s. Between FY 1968 and FY 1975, total Medicaid spending grew at a 19.5 percent annual rate, fueled largely by 9 percent average annual increases in recipients and 7 percent average annual increases in medical costs. By FY 1982, expenditures by all three levels of government totaled $29.8 billion; the federal contribution of $17.4 billion accounted for about 20 percent of total federal grants-in-aid to state and local governments.

Table 5 shows the growth in total Medicaid spending between FY 1975 and FY 1982. In contrast to the pre-1975 period, growth since 1975 does not reflect a rising number of recipients. Instead it reflects rising medical costs

TABLE 5

MEDICAID PAYMENTS ADJUSTED FOR CHANGE IN RECIPIENTS AND PRICES
(FY 1975–FY 1982)

	Total Provider Payments, $ Billions	Recipients, $ Millions	Payments per Recipient, in Current $	Medical Care Price Index[a] (1967 = 100)	Payments per Recipient, in Constant (1967) $
1975	12.1	20.7	587	165.2	355
1976	14.0	23.2	605	181.1	334
1977	16.2	21.2	762	198.4	384
1978	17.9	20.7	864	215.0	402
1979	20.4	20.1	1014	234.5	433
1980	23.2	20.3	1143	262.0	436
1981	27.1	20.5	1321	288.1	459
1982	29.8	20.4	1463	318.8	459
Average Annual Compound Rate of Growth (Percentage)					
1975–1980	13.8	−0.4	14.3	9.7	4.2
1980–1981	16.8	1.0	15.6	10.0	5.2
1981–1982	9.9	−0.8	10.7	10.7	0.0

SOURCE: Unpublished data provided by John Holahan of The Urban Institute. The entries for 1975 to 1979 are comparable (but not identical) to those reported by Randall R. Bovbjerg and John Holahan, *Medicaid in the Reagan Era* (Washington, D.C.: The Urban Institute Press, 1982), table 5.
  a. Medical care component of the consumer price index.

and, until 1982, rising inflation-adjusted payments per recipient.[8] Between FY 1979 and FY 1981, federal outlays for Medicaid grew at an annual rate of 16.2 percent.

From the perspective of the federal budget, two major problems arise.[9] First, because the federal contribution takes the form of an open-ended grant with a relatively high federal share, the states have no incentive to restructure their Medicaid programs to reduce Medicaid spending. To the contrary, they have an incentive to include as much spending as possible in the Medicaid budget to secure the maximum amount of federal aid for spending that might otherwise have to be financed fully at the state level. Some of the fastest-growing items of Medicaid directly reflect these incentives. Many states, for example, have upgraded their state-operated facilities for the mentally retarded to meet Medicaid standards specifically to obtain federal matching funds for patients eligible for Medicaid. Moreover, while states have made some cuts in eligibility standards in recent years in response to fiscal pressures, they have made no major cuts, such as eliminating the programs for the noninstitutionalized medically needy. To do so might simply shift the full costs onto state and local taxpayers.

Rising medical costs are the second major problem. Here, however, the interests of the federal and state governments coincide. By controlling costs per unit of service, the states reduce their own spending as well as that of the federal government. Recent fiscal pressures at the state level have provided strong incentives for the states to control costs, and many have developed innovative means of doing so. Until recently, however, federal rules and regulations under the Medicaid program have severely limited the states' freedom to pursue cost-containment strategies.

In FY 1981, President Reagan tried to deal with these federal budgetary problems by proposing a 5 percent cap on the growth of federal Medicaid spending, to be combined with greater flexibility for cost containment at the state level. Given that expenditures were likely to have grown much faster than 5 percent, the cap would have made the states pay 100 percent of the marginal Medicaid dollar. The states protested that this was an unfair way to achieve federal cost control, since it would have shifted the entire burden of controlling Medicaid spending onto the states. The increased flexibility, they argued, would be insufficient to control costs over which they had little control. As a result, the president's proposal was rejected.

---

8. The 144 percent increase in total Medicaid spending between FY 1975 and FY 1982 is still substantially below the 241 percent growth in Medicare spending during this same period.

9. This discussion draws heavily on Randall R. Bovbjerg and John Holahan, *Medicaid in the Reagan Era* (Washington, D.C.: The Urban Institute Press, 1983).

The actual changes in the Medicaid program enacted in the 1981 omnibus budget act were much more modest. First, instead of eliminating the open-ended feature of federal aid, federal matching rates were reduced by 3 percent in FY 1982, with reductions of 4 and 4.5 percent scheduled for FY 1983 and FY 1984. Thus, after the FY 1982 cut the minimum matching rate of 50 percent becomes 48.5 percent. Second, states were given incentives to economize; a number of waiver and offset options allow states that economize to recover some of the lost federal aid. Third, states were given more flexibility to make many kinds of selective efficiencies. One of the most important changes permits states to change the way they pay for hospital costs. The states no longer have to pay hospitals their "reasonable costs," which are virtually equivalent to actual spending. States can now set prospective rates below the actual spending by individual hospitals, as long as reasonable access to medical care is maintained and the special needs of hospitals that serve disproportionate numbers of poor people are recognized. Although the actual limit on state authority awaits court action, many states have already acted to control hospital costs in new and innovative ways.

Between FY 1981 and FY 1982, federal Medicaid spending declined by 6.5 percent in inflation-adjusted dollars, despite rising unemployment. Drawing on comparisons with the uncontrolled growth of the federal Medicare program, some observers have interpreted this experience as evidence that with responsibility at the state level, spending on health care programs can be controlled. This is true. Stringent fiscal pressures combined with the flexibility to change programs certainly will lead to less spending.[10] The effects vary across states, however, and raise questions about the appropriate division of responsibilities among levels of government.

Appropriate Federal Role

One cannot discuss policy options related to the current aid programs without first inquiring about the nature of the federal interest in these programs. In the absence of a federal interest, the appropriate approach is to turn over full responsibility to the states, as proposed by President Reagan for the AFDC program in his 1982 federalism initiative. On the other hand, a strong federal interest in the level and distribution of payments may suggest the need for an increased federal role.

A strong federal interest in income redistribution programs can be justified on two grounds. First, as economists often point out, financing at the

---

10. The AFDC changes enacted in the 1981 omnibus budget act also served to restrain Medicaid spending through the eligibility linkage between the two programs.

state level may lead to inappropriately low spending levels. This outcome will occur if state policymakers are constrained by the fear that high-income taxpayers or firms will leave the jurisdiction to avoid paying for high benefit levels or that potential beneficiaries will enter the jurisdiction in search of higher welfare payments. A logical extension of the migration argument is that the potential for income redistribution within jurisdictions would be severely limited because some jurisdictions would end up as havens for the wealthy and others for the poor. The strongest empirical support for this argument comes from several recent statistical studies of the location decisions of potential beneficiaries. By showing that potential AFDC beneficiaries are more likely to choose states with high welfare benefits and are less likely to leave such states, these studies lend credence to the argument that migration may distort the local decision-making process.[11] At the same time, we note that empirical support is at best limited for the hypothesis that taxpayers avoid states with high poverty-related taxes or expenditures.

A second argument for a strong federal interest turns on the nature of the spatial dimension to concern about poverty and specifically the extent to which taxpayer voters in a particular state value expenditures made on behalf of poor people living in other states.[12] If people care only about the poor people in their own state and, in addition, if attitudes toward the poor vary across states (as they clearly do in the United States), decentralized financing of income support programs could be justified on public choice grounds: decentralization would help assure that public assistance payments correspond to the variation in voter preferences across states. To the extent that assistance to the poor is motivated by altruism, however, it seems highly plausible that taxpayers would want to assist the poor everywhere: Television and other forms of the media, for example, assure that taxpayers are as familiar with the plight of the distant poor as with the plight of the nearby poor. In this case, poverty becomes a national concern that requires a national solution. In particular, national minimum standards for assistance payments would be required to assure beneficiaries a minimum level of benefits regardless of where they live or the generosity of other state residents. Moreover, full

11. See, for example, Rebecca M. Blank, "Welfare, Wages and Migration: An Analysis of Locational Choice by Female-Headed Households," mimeo, September 1983. See also Lawrence Southwick, Jr., "Public Welfare Programs and Recipient Migration," *Growth and Change*, vol. 12, no. 4 (October 1981), pp. 22–32; Edward M. Gramlich, "An Econometric Examination of the New Federalism," *Brookings Papers on Economic Activity*, vol. 2, 1982, pp. 327–370; and Edward M. Gramlich and Deborah S. Laren, "Migration and Income Redistribution Responsibilities," mimeo, March 1983.

12. For a more complete discussion of this argument, see Helen F. Ladd and Fred C. Doolittle, "Which Level of Government Should Assist Poor People?" *National Tax Journal*, vol. 35, no. 3 (September 1982), pp. 323–336.

federal financing of the minimum benefits would be called for, since generally accepted notions of tax equity imply that the financing burdens of any national program should be distributed among taxpayers in line with their ability to pay and independent of the state in which they live. Without federal financing, some taxpayers could avoid their fair share of the financing burden simply by avoiding states with above-average concentrations of poor people.

Thus, a strong federal interest in the AFDC and Medicaid programs seems clear on the grounds that poverty is a national concern and that beneficiaries are potentially mobile. Open-ended federal grants are not the most appropriate federal tool, however. If one ignores cost-containment considerations, a strong case can be made for the federal government to take full fiscal responsibility for nationally uniform minimum benefit levels that rise appropriately with inflation over time. If the states were permitted to supplement the federal minimum, additional equalizing federal aid might be appropriate. Such aid should be closed-ended, however, on the grounds that beyond a certain point additional expenditures in one state yield no additional benefits to out-of-state residents. The closed-ended feature of the aid would help to minimize the adverse impacts of state decisions on the federal budget. Although this policy may be conceptually appealing, it has one serious drawback; it would probably impose an unacceptably large federal fiscal burden under current budgetary conditions.

In addition, it might be argued that increased federal responsibility is inappropriate in the case of Medicaid because the federal government would be unable to contain costs per unit, as is evident from its experience with Medicare. Severe fiscal pressures, of the type now faced by the states, and the ability to innovate appear to be necessary to control costs. The policy trade-off is clear. Increased state fiscal responsibility is likely to mean more interstate variation in financing burdens and benefits. At the same time, greater state responsibility may lead to more benefits per dollar spent as a result of innovative state programs and, almost by definition, will result in a smaller federal burden. Thus, the central policy question is how to provide incentives for cost containment without imposing severe burdens on the poor or medically needy in poor or ungenerous states.

Grants-In-Aid to State and Local Governments

The federal government provides grants to state and local governments for a wide range of programs and in a variety of forms. Table 6 summarizes the composition of grants in FY 1982, ignoring the $40.7 billion classified

TABLE 6

COMPOSITION OF GRANTS TO GOVERNMENTS, BY MAJOR FUNCTIONS AND LARGEST
PROGRAMS WITHIN FUNCTIONS (FY 1982)

	$ Billions	Percentage of Total
Education, Training, Employment, and Social Services	16.6	35
Compensatory Education	2.9	
Social Services Block Grant (Title II)	2.6	
Comprehensive Employment and Training Act	1.8	
Transportation	12.2	26
Federal-Aid Highways	7.6	
Urban Mass Transit	3.8	
Community and Regional Development	5.4	11
Community Development Block Grants (entitlement grant)	2.7	
Community Development Block Grants (small cities)	0.8	
Natural Resources and Environment	4.9	10
Wastewater Treatment	3.8	
Other Program Grants	2.1	4
General-Purpose Fiscal Assistance	6.3	13
General Revenue Sharing	4.9	
Total	47.5	100

SOURCE: OMB, *Special Analyses, Budget of the United States Government, Fiscal Year 1984*, tables H-2 and H-11.
NOTE: Items in the percentage column do not total 100 percent because of rounding.

as grants-in-aid for individuals. Of the total, 35 percent support education, training, employment, and social service programs. Broad-purpose grants distributed by formula, such as the social services block grant and aid for compensatory education, account for about one-half of this human service aid; a multitude of narrow-purpose grants account for the rest.

A detailed examination of the policy issues associated with each of these program areas is outside the scope of this paper.[13] Instead, this discussion focuses on some of the broader issues that arise either because of the recent cuts or because of the prediction that budgetary pressures at the federal level

13. For a thorough, up-to-date discussion by program area, see Congressional Budget Office, *The Federal Government in a Federal System: Current Intergovernmental Programs and Options for Change* (Washington, D.C.: Government Printing Office, 1983).

will continue to limit the growth of grants to state and local governments. The section begins with a description of the magnitude and nature of the recent changes. It then looks at the response of state and local governments. Finally, it draws on the lessons from the recent period and existing literature to determine whether the structure of intergovernmental grants should be modified.

Magnitude and Nature of Recent Changes. Intergovernmental grants were hard hit by the budget cuts incorporated in the 1981 omnibus budget act. Compared with what would have been had there been no policy change, FY 1982 budget authority for grants was cut by 38 percent and budget outlays by 18 percent.[14] These cuts are large both absolutely and relative to other cuts. Although spending on grant programs represented less than 10 percent of spending on all programs that were cut, they absorbed 29 percent of all reductions in budget authority and 20 percent of all reductions in budget outlays.

At the same time that Congress reduced the funds available to subnational governments, it also gave state governments more discretion over the use of grant money. It accomplished this by consolidating over seventy narrow-purpose categorical grants primarily for health and social services into nine block grants (seven of which were new), by substituting state governments in a number of cases for local governments as the funding recipients, by reducing regulatory and reporting requirements, and by allowing states in some cases to transfer funds from one block grant to another up to a specified ceiling. Although administration spokesmen initially argued that the increase in flexibility and reduction in administrative burdens would fully compensate state and local governments for funding reductions and thereby would forestall service cuts, the administration soon backed off and emphasized instead that such changes would cushion funding cuts that were necessary because of the overall budget situation.[15]

The State Response. States apparently replaced only a small percentage of the FY 1982 federal cutbacks in human service programs. This conclusion is based on two recent studies, one by The Urban Institute based on a sample of twenty-five states and one by Nathan and Doolittle of Princeton

---

14. From John William Ellwood, ed., *Reductions in U.S. Domestic Spending* (New Brunswick, NJ: Transaction Books, 1982), table 1.11. The magnitude of the cuts depends crucially on the assumed baseline. See Ellwood, chapter 4, for further discussion and estimates based on a current law baseline as well as the current policy baseline. The current policy baseline assumes that programs will be held constant in real terms.

15. See quotation from OMB Deputy Director Edwin L. Harper, cited in Peterson, "The State and Local Sector," p. 171.

University based on a sample of fourteen states.[16] Although the studies differ in some of the details and in their conclusions about what happened in particular states, they agree on the basic conclusion.[17] According to The Urban Institute study, thirteen of twenty-five sample states replaced none of the federal cuts associated with the formation of five new human service block grants. Replacement of the funds lost by the formation of the social services block grant was most common, but only eight of the twenty-five states replaced any of these cuts, and the replacement rates were generally low.

A similar picture emerges from the Nathan-Doolittle study; replacement of funds lost through grant consolidation was generally low, with four out of fourteen states replacing some of the cuts in one or more of the health block grants. In addition, the Nathan-Doolittle study reports that state and local governments made no attempt to replace public service jobs lost through the elimination of the Comprehensive Employment and Training Act (CETA) public service jobs program and that only a few tried to offset some of the cuts in the CETA training programs. Thus, in the short run, service recipients, rather than state and local taxpayers, bore the brunt of the cutbacks in these federal programs.

A different picture emerges with respect to capital grants. First, federal funding for capital spending was more stable than that for human service spending. This was true because (1) cuts in capital programs were generally smaller than those for human services; (2) cuts in one major area of capital spending, transportation, were offset the next year by increased spending financed by a five-cent per gallon increase in the gasoline tax; and (3) some cuts, such as the reduction in the federal matching rate for wastewater treatment programs, had a delayed implementation date. Second, many states responded much more actively to actual or anticipated cuts in federal capital aid then they did to cuts in social programs. A number of states increased state commitments for capital projects, increased state aid for local projects, or developed plans for state infrastructure banks. As Nathan and Doolittle note, some of the actions may have the paradoxical effect of increasing state spending to make up for anticipated federal cuts that never actually materialize.[18]

One interpretation of the short-run state-local response to the federal cutbacks is based on the view that many federal grant programs, especially

---

16. Results from The Urban Institute survey are reported in Peterson, "The State and Local Sector." The Nathan-Doolittle results are in Nathan and Doolittle, *The Consequences of Cuts.*

17. The studies differ, for example, in their findings for Massachusetts. The Urban Institute study shows no replacement in Massachusetts, while the Nathan-Doolittle study shows more replacement in Massachusetts than in most other states.

18. Nathan and Doolittle, *The Consequences of Cuts*, p. 64.

those in the human services area, are really national programs which the federal government has chosen to implement through state and local governments. In other words, in spending these grant funds for, say, CETA public service jobs, state and local governments have simply been acting as administrative agents of the federal government, rather than trying to achieve their own program goals. Support for this view comes in part from institutional arrangements at the state level; in many cases, federal grant funds are segregated from own-source revenues and not subject to annual budgetary appropriation. According to this view, cutbacks in federal grants would not put direct pressure on state and local budgets and hence would exert little immediate pressure for replacement. Only in the longer run, after the effects are perceived by local provider and recipient groups, would pressures emerge for additional state spending to replace the lost federal funding.

This model appears to explain the short-run state and local response to spending cuts reasonably well. In many human service programs, for example, provider and constituency groups are only now beginning to feel the full effects of the federal cutbacks, as service cutbacks were delayed by the use of carryover funds and by federal provisions that delayed the effective date of some of the cuts. Until that pressure is brought to bear at the state level, states have little incentive to replace federal dollars. Consistent with this view, ongoing research at The Urban Institute shows that many states are now beginning to replace significant portions of the cuts in the social services and maternal and child health block grants, program areas in which states have had direct involvement in the past. Researchers continue to find little or no replacement of cuts in the other block grants, however.[19]

An alternative and equally powerful explanation for the behavior of state and local governments in 1982 focuses on the severe fiscal pressures under which they have been operating for the past few years. Faced with the combined effects of the taxpayer revolt, which has rolled back taxes in some states and limited the growth of taxes in many others, and a recession that was much more severe than anticipated and that created serious revenue shortfalls throughout the country, state and local governments were simply not in a position to offset the cutbacks in federal aid. The importance of budgetary distress is evident from the differential response across states. States facing severe fiscal pressures, such as Michigan, Minnesota, and Ohio, committed themselves to no replacement spending in 1982 or 1983. Meanwhile, four states (out of a sample of twenty-five, that were in a relatively strong

---

19. Based on discussions with Eugene Durman about work in progress with Barbara Davis on ''Block Grants and the New Federalism,'' The Urban Institute, Washington, D.C.

fiscal position engaged in substantial replacement, despite the fact that some of them had historically low levels of human service spending.[20]

Both explanations for the short-run response are helpful in understanding the longer-run implications for the change in federal policy. Tight budgetary conditions are likely to prevail at the state and local levels for several years. State and local officials throughout the country have been coping with the recession-induced revenue shortfalls by drawing down fiscal reserves and engaging in a variety of creative stopgap measures that pushed obligations into the future. This means that even as the recovery occurs and revenues expand, state and local governments will face continued budgetary pressures as they try both to maintain services and to restore their depleted balances. As a result the states, especially those that were hardest hit by the recession, will have limited ability to respond to local political pressures to offset the effects of the federal cutbacks.

To the extent that political pressures eventually restore cuts in some states but not in others, the result will be a less even distribution of services and tax burdens across states than was true previously. Some people might argue that this outcome is preferred, given the different attitudes toward health and social services across states. A pattern of replacement that varies with the short-run fiscal condition of particular states is hard to defend, however, especially since variations in fiscal conditions are so dependent on the national economy, over which the states have little control. In addition, many of these human service programs have a strong redistributive goal and serve as substitutes or complements for direct cash payments for poor people. Hence the arguments made earlier for a strong federal role in income support programs apply to social services and other programs for the needy as well. Consequently, to the extent that the federal cutbacks increase the geographic variation in services available to poor people and in the tax burdens needed to finance those services, horizontal equity—that is, fair treatment of people in similar situations—is adversely affected.

Grant Design

Recent cuts in federal grants and the projected outlook for continued declines in inflation-adjusted aid focus attention on the question of grant design. With fewer funds to grant, should the federal government loosen or

---

20. Peterson, "The State and Local Sector," pp. 182–183. A third potential explanation for the states' response is that the "Reagan Revolution" was more the result than the cause of a changing national consensus on the proper role of government. That is, the antiwelfare sentiment had been growing even before Reagan was elected, so it is not surprising that state and local governments went along with most of the cuts in social welfare programs.

tighten targeting and other restrictions that limit the flexibility of state and local governments?

On the one hand, it can be argued that restrictions and limitations on federal grants should be reduced to encourage the most effective use of the smaller pot of aid. The argument here is that the federal government can no longer afford to impose targeting, matching requirements, and other restrictions that in the past have led to inefficiencies in production and have distorted the behavior of state and local governments. Instead, federal officials should recognize that state and local governments are in a much better position than the federal government to respond to variations in local conditions and service needs and should consequently give them more freedom to decide how to spend the federal aid.

Early experience with the recently formed block grants supports the proposition that state priorities differ from federal priorities. A number of states have already taken advantage of the opportunity to shift funds from the low-income energy assistance block grant for use in other programs. In administering the Community Development Block Grant program for small cities, some states have begun to emphasize economic development and public works projects over the housing rehabilitation projects favored by the Department of Housing and Urban Development. Initial evidence from Massachusetts, North Dakota, and California also suggests that states may favor using Community Services Block Grant money to finance direct service provision, rather than to support the community organizing and advocacy activities favored by the federal government.[21] At the same time, there is no evidence yet of a wholesale shift in priorities. This situation results from institutional realities, however, more than from a consistency between federal and state priorities. States, for example, have been constrained in their allocation decisions by the need to cushion the impact in spending cuts. In addition, Congress refused to go along with the wholesale removal of restrictions advocated by the president for the block grants. Under the Alcohol, Drug Abuse, and Mental Health block grant, for example, Congress mandated that states continue to give money to all community mental health centers that had received operating grants in 1981. Similarly, under the Community Services block grant, Congress earmarked 90 percent of the funds for existing community action agencies.

Given the different priorities of the federal and state governments, it is no doubt true that more flexibility is preferable to less flexibility from the perspective of a recipient jurisdiction, provided that the design change does

---

21. Based on Nathan and Doolittle, *The Consequences of Cuts*, chapter 3.

not alter the distribution of grants across jurisdictions.[22] When one takes the perspective of the federal government, however, more flexibility is not necessarily preferred to less. The justification for giving aid in the first place typically reflects the failure of state and local governments to account for spillovers from one jurisdiction to another or to provide a minimum of public services to all citizens. Although the weight attached to various federal goals will, and should, vary over time with changes in the national political climate, achievement of legitimate federal goals may specifically require interference with the decisions of state and local governments. Similarly, for the range of aid programs that are appropriately viewed as federal programs that the federal government has chosen to implement through state and local governments, the need for spending restrictions should be obvious.

Furthermore, in an era of scarce resources, a strong case can be made for the federal government to pay more attention to the cost-effectiveness with which it meets its policy objectives. Cost-effectiveness often calls for matching grants, for restrictions on the recipients of federally supported programs, or for process requirements. In addition, a cost-effective aid program will often require that aid be carefully targeted to either those jurisdictions that would not have undertaken the activity without federal aid or those that have the greatest need.

At the same time, certain types of restrictions and limitations do not promote the cost-effective achievement of federal goals. Detailed restrictions on program inputs, for example, can lead to inefficient provision of public services by distorting production decisions at the local level and failing to exploit the fact that local decision makers are far better equipped than federal policymakers to decide how to repair local highways or house the needy. The challenge here is for federal policymakers to define aid programs in terms of program outputs, such as improving the education of disadvantaged children or promoting community development, rather than inputs, such as the type of buses that must be bought or the size of classrooms. This task is not easy, both because program outputs are conceptually difficult to measure and because the task requires a clear notion of program goals.

---

22. The National Governors' Association and the National Conference of State Legislators explicitly acknowledged the value of flexibility in the debate over the FY 1982 aid cuts by their willingness to trade block grant consolidations and regulatory relief for 10 percent funding cuts. The provision about maintaining the distribution of funds across jurisdictions plays an important role in a more recent recommendation of the National Association of State Budget Officers. As part of their proposal that the Governors Association support a large new revenue-sharing program to replace twenty-two existing health, social services, education, and community development programs, the state budget officers recommended that the funds be allocated among states in line with distribution formulas in effect in 1984. See "Proposal on Improving the Federal-State Partnership," The National Association of State Budget Officers, April 12, 1983.

In general, the consolidation of narrowly defined categorical programs into larger block grants oriented toward broader purposes probably represents a step in the direction of more cost-effective aid. The removal of matching requirements, of targeting provisions, and of auditing requirements, however, works against the achievement of federal goals in most cases. In the absence of federal strings, federal aid designated for one purpose becomes fully fungible and equivalent to unconditional grants. That is, federal aid becomes substitutable with own-source revenues and may be diverted to other uses including local tax reduction. Unconditional grants are appropriate only if the federal goal is equalization of fiscal resources in relation to overall service needs, with no reference to programmatic goals. Only in this case would the federal government not care whether the recipient jurisdictions spent the money or returned it to taxpayers in the form of tax reductions; in either case, the aid would reduce fiscal pressures in fiscally stressed jurisdictions. If fiscal equalization is the goal, however, cost-effective use of federal grants requires that they be much more targeted to needy jurisdictions than they currently are.[23]

Federal Aid to Cities

A central feature of the growth in federal aid during the 1960s and 1970s was the development of a direct federal-local partnership. With programs such as General Revenue Sharing, the Comprehensive Employment and Training Act, the Community Development Block Grant program, urban mass transit aid, and a variety of countercyclical assistance programs, direct aid to local governments grew from 2.6 percent of the general own-source revenues of local governments in 1960 to almost 18 percent in 1978. By the late 1970s, direct federal aid accounted for more than 28 percent of the own-source revenues of large cities and exceeded 15 percent in cities such as Boston, St. Louis, New Orleans, and Los Angeles. In addition, local governments receive additional federal aid indirectly in the form of federal grants to the states which by law are passed through to local governments. This pass-through aid is substantial; in 1977, it was estimated to be about three-quarters the size of direct federal aid to local governments.[24] Although aid to large cities was cut back some with the elimination of countercyclical aid programs in the late 1970s, many cities are still heavily dependent on federal aid.

---

23. Unconditional grants can also be used, as in the Reagan approach, as a bridge to facilitate the eventual state takeover of program responsibilities previously financed by the federal government.

24. Advisory Commission on Intergovernmental Relations, *Recent Trends in Federal and State Aid to Local Governments*, M-118 (Washington, D.C., July 1980), table 10.

A current issue of grant policy is whether the federal government should continue to give money directly to local governments or whether it should place more emphasis on aid to states. By designating state governments as the recipients of the new block grants set up in 1981, the Reagan administration expressed its philosophy that state governments are often in a better position than the federal government to deal with the fiscal problems of cities and other local governments. Of the seventy-seven grants that were consolidated into block grants in 1981, forty-seven formerly delivered federal funds directly to localities.

Although Congress mitigated the short-run impacts of this reorientation to some extent by pass-through requirements and earmarking funds to previous recipients, there is already some evidence that the effect will be a redistribution of aid away from larger cities to rural areas and smaller communities. This is particularly true in the education block grant that consolidated twenty-nine small programs into one block grant. Funds that were formerly distributed for special purposes such as school desegregation, for example, will now be distributed by formulas that tend to spread the funds out evenly among jurisdictions. The ultimate effects on local government tax and spending policies of shifting federal aid to states are hard to predict, since they depend on a complex set of behavioral responses by both state and local governments. A recent econometric study that uses historical data to model the complex interactions among levels of governments for education spending suggests that the impact of reorienting education funds to states and removing restrictions would be substantial and, in particular, would lead to less spending for education.[25] The basic question, however, is which allocation of resources is more desirable, the one formerly determined by the federal government or the one that eventually will be determined by the state governments. There seems to be no simple answer to this question.

How the federal government ought to relate to local governments is especially pertinent for the nation's fiscally distressed cities. Their previous dependence on federal aid makes them particularly vulnerable to a weakening of the federal-local partnership. A recent Joint Economic Committee study of the effects of federal aid reductions on large cities highlights this point. The report concludes that cities with high unemployment and declining populations are experiencing the largest cutbacks and that "a disproportionate number of the cities most in need of assistance . . . are losing the largest

25. Steven G. Craig and Robert P. Inman, "Federal Aid and Public Education: An Empirical Look at the New Fiscal Federalism," *The Review of Economics and Statistics*, vol. 64, no. 4 (November 1982), pp. 541–552.

share of federal funds."[26] Thus, even if strengthening the federal-state partnership is a desirable long-run goal, special care needs to be taken to avoid
the short-run disruptive effects on large cities.

In considering the longer-run role of the federal government vis-à-vis
large cities, two facts should be noted. First, 1980 data show that 17.2 percent
of the population in central cities were poor compared with 8.2 percent in
the suburbs. If one accepts the notion that the federal government, rather than
the states, should take primary financial responsibility for poor people, part
of the solution to the fiscal problems of central cities must come from the
federal government, either as direct cash payments to poor people or as
intergovernmental grants to cities to assure minimum levels of essential services or to provide social services for the poor. A second fact is that some
of the fiscal problems of cities arise from an inappropriate division of financing
and spending responsibilities among levels of government within states. Thus,
for example, urban transit financing burdens in some areas fall most heavily
on central city taxpayers despite the fact that benefits from transit services
accrue to the entire region. In addition, local governments share the burden
of financing welfare payments in some states. Because these fiscal arrangements vary across states, however, state governments are in a better position
than the federal government to deal with their consequences. Thus, some of
the fiscal pressures of large cities can most effectively be relieved by state
actions, such as state assumption of certain spending or financing responsibilities, new regional taxes for mass transit systems, state aid programs to
offset benefit spillovers, and state revenue-sharing programs.

Deductibility of State and Local Taxes

Under the current tax code, federal taxpayers may deduct state and local
income, sales, and property taxes for purposes of federal income taxation.
(Prior to 1978, they could also deduct state gasoline excise taxes.) Tax expenditures in this category refer to federal revenue losses from personal taxes
only; state and local tax payments made by firms are treated as a cost of
doing business and consequently are viewed as legitimate deductions, not
counted as tax expenditures. In the case of the federal tax exemption of
municipal bond interest, tax expenditures include the tax savings not only of

---

26. U.S. Congress, Joint Economic Committee, "Emergency Interim Survey: Fiscal Condition of 48 Large Cities," Joint Committee Reprint 97/1, January 14, 1982 (Washington, D.C.:
Government Printing Office), page xi.

individuals under the personal income tax but also of corporations under the corporate income tax. Proposals to limit these types of tax expenditures are being discussed in a variety of contexts, including revenue raising, broadening the tax base for equity reasons, and flat-rate tax proposals. The focus here is on how such proposals are likely to affect state and local governments.

Comparability to Direct Federal Aid

A recent proposal to finance an increase in general revenue sharing with revenue raised by limiting the deductibility of state and local taxes highlights the similarities between direct intergovernmental aid and indirect aid in the form of tax expenditures.[27] At the same time, however, the superficial differences between these two forms of federal aid make it worthwhile to focus briefly on their comparability.

Unlike direct intergovernmental aid programs, tax deductibility initially had little to do with the desire to aid state and local governments. Instead, it was justified on grounds of tax equity. It seemed inappropriate for the federal government to tax income used to pay state and local taxes that represented nondiscretionary spending over which individual taxpayers had little control. In addition, there was concern about confiscatory income taxation. When maximum federal marginal income tax rates were 90 percent, the possibility arose that combined federal and state income tax rates would exceed 100 percent. Now that maximum marginal rates are down to 50 percent, this latter concern is less relevant. The former issue is still alive, although the distinction between discretionary and nondiscretionary payments is often unclear.[28] Regardless of original intent, the point is that tax deductibility provides an incentive for state and local governments to spend more than they otherwise would; consequently tax deductibility can be evaluated as if it were a direct intergovernmental subsidy program. Note, however, that if tax deductibility is deemed appropriate using the criterion of a comprehensive income tax base, any proposal to limit deductibility would have to be evaluated in terms of the loss in tax equity, as well as in terms of its effects on state and local governments.

---

27. This proposal and a variety of other proposals to limit the deductibility of state and local taxes are discussed and evaluated in Nonna A. Noto and Dennis Zimmerman, *Limiting State-Local Tax Deductibility in Exchange for Increased General Revenue Sharing: An Analysis of the Economic Effects*, a report by the Congressional Research Service of the Library of Congress for the Senate Committee on Governmental Affairs, Subcommittee on Intergovernmental Relations, August 1983.

28. For further discussion, see Richard A. Musgrave and Peggy B. Musgrave, *Public Finance in Theory and Practice* (New York: McGraw-Hill Book Company, 1980), p. 359.

It might still be argued that tax deductibility is fundamentally different from a direct aid program in that it provides benefits to taxpayers rather than governments. Its only impact on governments is indirect and dependent on state and local taxpayers being more willing to support state and local public services when the taxes to pay for those services are deductible than when they are not. One might be tempted to argue that tax deductibility is comparable to many other provisions of the federal tax code. Any provision that reduces federal taxes makes people feel wealthier and therefore may increase their willingness to support higher levels of state and local public services. But there is an important distinction; in the case of deductibility of state and local taxes, the amount of federal revenue loss depends directly on the collective choices made at the state and local levels about how much to raise in taxes for public services. In this sense, the tax expenditure is equivalent to a federal subsidy to one particular public-sector activity, levying taxes for state and local public-sector spending.

Moreover, aid in this form is not so different from more direct forms of intergovernmental aid as it may at first appear. Consider a federally funded public jobs program like CETA that operates through local governments to provide jobs for low-income people. If all the money is used for the designated purpose, the direct beneficiaries are the job recipients and the only impact on state and local governments is indirect. State and local governments benefit only if they otherwise would have provided jobs to these people and now provide fewer as a result of the federal program, or if they can manipulate the program to substitute the new employees for workers they otherwise would have hired for public-sector jobs. In this case, like the case of tax deductibility, the effect of the federal aid program on the ability of state and local governments to finance their own programs is indirect and dependent on a variety of behavioral responses.[29]

Impact of Proposed Changes on State and Local Governments

A number of recent proposals would limit the deductibility of state and local taxes. In light of the severe fiscal pressures on the federal government, limiting this tax expenditure seems like an easy way to raise more federal revenue without adverse distributional implications. Since itemizers are concentrated in the higher-income classes, the bulk of the additional revenue

---

29. With respect to this point, economists might also refer to the attempt by Wallace Oates to demonstrate the equivalence of general revenue sharing aid and federal tax reductions to taxpayer voters in the recipient jurisdiction. See Wallace Oates, *Fiscal Federalism* (New York: Harcourt, Brace, Jovanovich, Inc., 1972), pp. 105–118.

would come from high-income rather than low-income taxpayers. Two policy questions arise: First, what effect would eliminating tax deductibility have on the operation of state and local governments? Second, how does this federal policy option compare with alternative cuts in federal aid that might be contemplated, given current pressures on the federal budget?

Eliminating tax deductibility would raise the price of local public spending to all taxpayers who itemize deductions on their federal income tax returns. With deductibility, the price to a taxpayer of one dollar of additional local spending depends on the taxpayer's marginal tax rate under the federal income tax. For example, the price of one dollar of local spending to someone in a 20 percent tax bracket is eighty cents, since the dollar in local taxes saves the taxpayer twenty cents in federal taxes. If the deductibility of state and local taxes were eliminated, the price to this taxpayer would rise to one dollar, or by 25 percent.

In general, if the price of a good rises, people will demand less of the good, depending on their responsiveness to price. A change in the price of local public spending for itemizers, however, need not lead to a change in the collective demand for public services. The outcome hinges on the role of itemizers in the collective choice process. For example, the impact on public spending would be minimal if only a small portion of the voters in each state or local jurisdiction were taxpayers who itemized their deductions. In this case, local decisions about public spending levels would effectively be made by nonitemizing taxpayers, a group unaffected by the federal policy change. The result would be little or no change in public spending and higher taxes for all itemizers.

If, conversely, itemizing taxpayers play a large role in the collective choice process, eliminating deductibility could have a large adverse impact on the willingness of taxpayers to support state and local spending. This is the more likely outcome. Although itemized returns accounted for only 30 percent of the tax returns nationwide in 1980, the proportion of voters who itemize is substantially higher than 30 percent.[30] This follows in part from the observation that in 1980 the proportion of itemized returns exceeded 50 percent for taxpayers with adjusted gross income between $20,000 and $25,000 and rose steadily to 99 percent in the highest income categories. The larger the fraction of all voters that have income in these above-average income categories, the larger is the fraction of voters who itemize. In addition, above-

---

30. The 1980 percentage of itemized returns and the disaggregated data in the following sentences come from Noto and Zimmerman, *Limiting State-Local Tax Deductibility in Exchange for Increased General Revenue Sharing: An Analysis of the Economic Effects*, tables A.1 and A.2.

average proportions of joint returns in the higher-income classes point to the same conclusion.

Survey information from Massachusetts provides the most direct evidence that more than one-half the voters in many jurisdictions are itemizers. A statewide sample of 1,114 voters indicated that 56 percent of Massachusetts household heads who voted in 1980 lived in households that itemize deductions on their federal tax return. Moreover, within the fifty-eight cities and towns represented in the sample, itemizers accounted for more than 50 percent of the voters in all but sixteen, the exceptions being some of the larger cities such as Boston with heterogeneous and generally low-income populations and some of the smaller rural communities.[31]

Since the average itemizer has a marginal tax rate of 32 percent, eliminating deductibility would raise the price of state and local spending by about 47 percent (from sixty-eight cents to one dollar). Using a mid-range estimate of the responsiveness of demand to price changes, such an increase would reduce the demand for state and local public spending by about 14 percent, a relatively large percentage drop.[32] This does not mean that state and local spending would immediately fall by this much. Instead, it indicates the magnitude of the pressure for spending reduction at the state and local levels and represents the potential long-run impact of the change. The fact that the proportion of itemizers varies from one jurisdiction to another suggests that the pressures for spending reduction would vary across jurisdictions, with the largest pressures coming in the middle- and upper-income suburbs.

Despite these potentially large contractionary pressures on state and local governments, eliminating deductibility may still be preferred to other cuts in federal aid that might be contemplated. First, eliminating deductibility is likely to be more politically acceptable to state and local officials than cuts in revenue sharing or block grant funds because deductibility affects state and local governments only indirectly; individual taxpayers rather than governments would be the immediate losers. Second, the elimination of deductibility would probably have a smaller impact on public spending in poor than in wealthier jurisdictions. Third, unlike other federal aid programs, federal aid to state

---

31. The Massachusetts survey is described in Helen F. Ladd and Julie Boatright Wilson, "Proposition 2-1/2: Explaining the Vote," *Research in Urban Economics*, forthcoming. A short description is also available in Helen F. Ladd and Julie Boatright Wilson, "Why Voters Support Tax Limitations: Evidence from Massachusetts' Proposition 2-1/2," *National Tax Journal*, vol. 35, no. 2 (June 1982), pp. 121–148.

32. Empirical studies of local public spending suggest that -0.3 is a reasonable estimate of the relevant price elasticity of demand, although estimates in the literature range from -0.1 to -0.7. Most of the relevant studies are surveyed by Robert D. Inman, "Fiscal Performance of Local Governments," in Peter Mieszkowski and Mahlon Straszheim, eds., *Current Issues in Urban Economics* (Baltimore: The Johns Hopkins University Press, 1979).

and local governments in the form of tax deductibility serves no clear federal policy goal. To the contrary, deductibility distorts state and local decisions by reducing the price to local taxpayers below the full cost of providing public services. A possible counterargument that this federal price subsidy serves to offset the positive spillovers from state and local public-sector spending is not compelling. To accept the counterargument, one would have to believe that such spillovers are positive in jurisdictions with large proportions of itemizing taxpayers and zero elsewhere. In fact, the reverse is more likely to be true; that is, positive spillovers from public-sector spending are more likely in low-income or heterogeneous cities than in the higher-income communities where itemizing is more common.

Full elimination of deductibility would, however, be subject to the criticism that the federal government is simply balancing the federal budget on the backs of state and local governments. Less than full elimination, or limitation combined with new general-purpose aid to state and local governments, could significantly reduce some of the contractionary pressures on state and local governments. If the deductibility provision were maintained but changed to disallow the deductibility of tax payments below some floor (either in terms of absolute dollars or as a percentage of adjusted gross income), the price incentive for additional spending at the state and local levels would not be affected; the only pressure for lower spending would come through an income effect. Since their federal taxes would rise, taxpayers would feel poorer and might be less willing to support state and local spending. Moreover, if this change were combined with partial replacement of funds in the form of additional revenue sharing, state and local budgets in the aggregate might actually increase at the same time that the federal budgetary situation improved.[33]

Thus, as in most policy areas, the specifics of the actual proposal greatly affect the outcome. One fact seems relatively clear, however. Any change in the deductibility of state and local taxes should apply to all state and local taxes. Otherwise, state and local governments would have an incentive to alter their revenue structures in favor of the tax or taxes that were not affected. (The federal tax code already biases local revenue decisions away from user charges by treating taxes and charges differently. Indeed, this existing bias provides a rationale for reducing or eliminating the deductibility of taxes.) Thus proposals such as that to eliminate the deductibility of sales taxes alone seem patently undesirable on the grounds that they would needlessly distort decisions about the composition of revenues at the state and local levels.

---

33. For simulations of the effects of various policy packages, see Noto and Zimmerman, *Limiting State-Local Tax Deductibility*, section VI.

Tax Exemption of Interest on Municipal Bonds

Tax exemption of interest on municipal bonds provides a subsidy for the types of spending eligible to be financed through the municipal bond market, including capital spending on a range of activities traditionally undertaken by state and local governments, such as sewer and water systems, public buildings, streets and highways, and parks. In addition, within the past ten or fifteen years, spending financed through the municipal bond market has come to include spending for activities not traditionally within the purview of state and local governments: building power plants, providing mortgages for owner-occupied housing, financing private development, and providing student loans. These two sets of activities correspond to the two categories used earlier to document the trends in this form of federal tax expenditure: Tax expenditures for general-purpose debt correspond to spending on traditional activities, while tax expenditures for special-purpose debt correspond to spending on the other activities. The two components of this tax-expenditure category raise very different policy issues for the federal budget, so we discuss them separately in the following sections.

General-Purpose Bonds

Federal tax exemption of interest in general-purpose state and local bonds acts like an open-ended matching grant to state and local governments, with the cost to the federal treasury dependent on the capital spending decisions of state and local governments. Thus, in an important sense, federal spending (in the form of lower federal revenues) is outside the control of the federal government. Despite this open-ended commitment, however, controllability is not now the central issue for federal budgeters. Even with the benefit of the federal subsidy that reduces the interest rate at which they can borrow, state and local governments currently have to pay relatively high rates of interest, which in turn impose substantial pressures on their operating budgets. This fiscal pressure, combined with a variety of debt limitations, keeps state and local governments from expanding their general-purpose borrowing at excessive rates. (As is noted below, the situation differs for special-purpose debt.)

Instead, the main issue is one of efficiency in the use of scarce federal resources. When the federal government gives aid through tax expenditures, only a portion of the federal revenue loss benefits state and local governments in the form of lower borrowing costs; the rest accrues to investors with relatively high marginal tax rates. This situation occurs because the interest rate on municipal bonds adjusts to make the marginal investor in municipal bonds indifferent between taxable and tax-exempt bonds. This market interest rate determines the amount that state and local governments have to pay, despite the fact that nonmarginal investors—those in higher tax brackets— would have been willing to lend money at a lower tax-exempt rate. In the past, supply-and-demand conditions in the municipal bond market typically led to a 30 to 35 percent differential in interest rates, implying that the marginal investor was in a 30 to 35 percent tax bracket. With the introduction of a wide variety of alternative tax-exempt investment options and an increased supply of municipal bonds for nontraditional purposes, market conditions are now quite different, and the interest rate differential has fallen to about 20 percent. This narrowing of the differential between tax-exempt and taxable interest rates tends to make the interest subsidy even less efficient. The closer the two rates are, the smaller is the proportion of the federal revenue loss that is reflected in lower interest costs for state and local governments (ignoring any possible effect in the other direction resulting from lower marginal tax rates).

This tax expenditure also causes another type of inefficiency, since it applies only to capital spending projects financed by bonds. Thus, the tax exemption distorts the capital financing decisions of local governments by lowering the costs of borrowing while not lowering the costs of capital projects financed from current revenues.

From the perspective of the federal government, the obvious solution to the first problem is to replace the tax exemption of municipal bond interest with direct subsidies to state and local governments. The inefficiency of the current approach means that existing benefits to state and local governments could be achieved at substantially lower cost to the federal government. Tying the subsidies to capital spending rather than to interest payments would solve the second problem as well. Experience with taxable-bond option proposals suggests, however, that this solution is not likely to be adopted. State and local governments legitimately fear that direct subsidies may bring with them additional strings and that the subsidies would be less permanent than the current indirect aid. Recent cutbacks in some federal grant programs for capital spending and fears of cutbacks in others serve only to exacerbate the concerns of state and local officials about having aid be subject to the vagaries of the annual appropriation process.

Special-Purpose Tax-Exempt Debt

The major budgetary issue related to the exemption of special-purpose debt is one of controllability. As shown in table 7, federal revenue losses increased from $200 million in FY 1975 to $4.8 billion in FY 1982. Moreover,

TABLE 7

SPECIAL-PURPOSE BONDS ANNUAL REVENUE LOSS AND VOLUME OF NEW ISSUES
(FY 1975–FY 1982)

	Annual Revenue Loss		*Volume of New Issues*	
	$ Billions	*Percentage Change*	*$ Billions*	*Percentage Change*
1975	0.2	—	6.8	—
1976	0.4	100	9.0	32
1977	0.5	25	14.3	59
1978	0.7	40	16.7	17
1979	1.4	100	25.3	51
1980	1.9	36	29.3	16
1981	3.9	105	27.9	−5
1982	4.0	23	42.8	53

SOURCES: Annual revenue losses: Congressional Budget Office, *Tax Expenditures: Current Issues and Five-Year Budget Projections for Fiscal Years, 1982–1986*, September 1981, tables 1 and 7; and Congressional Budget Office, *Tax Expenditures: Budget Control Options and Five-Year Budget Projections For Fiscal Years 1983–1987*, table A-1. Volume of new issues: table 1 of statement by Alice M. Rivlin, Director, Congressional Budget Office, before the Committee on Ways and Means, U.S. House of Representatives, June 15, 1983.

they would have grown even faster had Congress not imposed a number of restrictions on the use of special-purpose bonds during this period. The federal revenue loss represents the effects of tax exemption on the total volume of special-purpose bonds outstanding in any single year, which in turn is ultimately determined by the annual volume of new issues. The right-hand panel of table 7 shows the dramatic growth in new issues between FY 1975 and FY 1982. In FY 1977, 1979, and 1982, new issues increased by more than 50 percent over the previous year. The FY 1982 growth reflects a 157 percent increase over FY 1981 in housing bonds, an 89 percent increase in private hospital bonds, and a 40 percent increase in pollution control bonds. Small-issue industrial revenue bonds, the largest single category of special-purpose bonds, grew the least according to the estimated figures, but it appears that the FY 1982 estimate for this category may understate the true figure.[34] By FY 1982, special-purpose tax-exempt issues accounted for nearly one-half of the total long-term tax-exempt issues in the municipal bond market.

The federal budgetary problem is one of incentives. State and local governments have little incentive to limit their use of special-purpose bonds. Unlike general-purpose bonds, the debt service on these bonds typically does

---

34. This is the judgment of Alice Rivlin in her statement before the Committee on Ways and Means, U.S. House of Representatives, June 15, 1983.

not come out of local tax revenues. In most cases, the bonds are for essentially private or quasi-public purposes and the private beneficiary, which may be a private firm, power company, homeowner, or private hospital, pays the debt service. The advantage to the beneficiary is the lower cost of tax-exempt borrowing and, in some cases, the availability of funds that would not otherwise be available. The public benefits accruing to the local community need not be large to justify the undertaking, because federal, rather than local, taxpayers bear the cost of the interest subsidy. Thus, in the absence of specific federal limitations on the uses to which special-purpose bonds can be put or on the volume that can be issued by each state or jurisdiction, the federal budgetary commitment can grow almost without limit.

Another controllability issue relates to the multiyear nature of the federal commitment.[35] Whenever a state or local government issues a tax-exempt bond, the federal government sustains revenue losses for as long as the debt is outstanding. But since the federal commitment is in the form of a tax expenditure rather than a direct expenditure, the multiyear commitment is not recorded in any budget document. Thus, for example, Congress has recently considered a repeal of the "sunset" legislation for single-family mortgage revenue bonds. If the sunset legislation is repealed, new issues of mortgage revenue bonds in the fiscal years 1984 through 1988 are projected to reduce federal revenues by $2.8 billion. In fact, however, these new issues commit the federal government to a $24 billion loss of revenues over the life of the bonds, or a $12 billion loss in present value terms (that is, accounting for the fact that dollars in the future are worth less than dollars in the present). Thus, the tendency to focus narrowly on annual revenue losses in the discussion of special-purpose debt may impose large burdens on future federal budgets.

Each of the specific types of special-purpose debt raises issues about the desirability of the particular subsidy and about the efficiency with which the subsidy achieves federal goals. In some cases, the tax exemption might serve federal goals reasonably well, provided there are sufficient restrictions to limit the federal commitment. In other cases, however, the subsidy may be obsolete or could be provided more effectively and more cheaply through the expenditure side of the federal budget. In any case, the current pressures on the municipal bond market, combined with the generally acknowledged need for state and local governments to invest heavily in traditional areas of capital spending during the next several years, suggest that this may be an appropriate time for federal policymakers to bite the bullet and drastically limit the use

---

35. This discussion of the multiyear accounting problem relies heavily on ibid.

of special-purpose debt. Removing this large source of competition for limited investment dollars in the tax-exempt market would reduce tax-exempt interest rates and ease the capital financing problems of state and local governments throughout the country.

Conclusion

The past few years have seen some dramatic changes in federal aid to state and local governments. Although some of the FY 1981 cuts in grants were later partially restored, the fact remains that federal aid to state and local governments is now declining in inflation-adjusted terms and is likely to continue to decline in the future. An unintended consequence of the cutbacks in federal grants is a shift in the mix of intergovernmental assistance away from aid given through the expenditure side of the budget toward aid given through the tax side of the budget in the form of tax expenditures.

Part of the decline in grants was accomplished by federal policy changes in AFDC and Medicaid, policy changes that focus attention on the question of which level of government should assist poor people. Because state governments did not offset much of the federal cuts, the short-run impact of the federal changes was on the working poor. In the longer run, states are likely to pick up some of the federal reductions, but the extent to which this happens will vary across states. Unfortunately, some of the resulting geographic disparities are likely to reflect differences in state budgetary conditions, which in turn reflect economic conditions largely beyond the control of individual states. Thus, this seems a particularly inappropriate time to ask the states to provide more in income-support programs. Moreover, a strong case can be made for more, rather than less, federal responsibility for income-support programs. In the case of Medicaid, the states' relative success in controlling Medicaid costs poses the challenge of how to provide incentives for cost containment without imposing severe burdens on medically needy people in poor or ungenerous states.

The continuing decline in grants focuses attention on the appropriate grant structure. Despite pleas from state and local governments for more flexibility in the use of grant funds, certain restrictions and requirements are required to achieve federal goals. Moreover, limited federal resources may require more targeting of aid to needy jurisdictions.

Proposals to limit the federal deductibility of state and local taxes are worth pursuing, especially if they are designed to limit the adverse impact on state and local governments. Since itemizers appear to be well represented among voters in many state and local jurisdictions, complete elimination of state and local tax deductibility could significantly reduce the willingness of taxpayers to support state and local spending. Finally, federal aid for state and local capital spending provided through the interest exclusion on state and local debt raises fundamental questions about the efficiency of the subsidy mechanism and the budgetary implications of the growth in special-purpose debt.

COMMENTS

William G. Hamm

In her paper, Helen Ladd makes two important contributions to the debate over federal-state fiscal relations in the 1980s. First, she demonstrates the weaknesses involved in using grant-in-aid outlays as *the* measure of federal assistance to states and local governments. Second, she highlights a number of important issues associated with current trends in federal aid and gives us an analytical framework for thinking about these issues.

In my commentary, I suggest that the way Ladd tallies up federal assistance to state and local governments is also flawed, particularly with regard to the treatment of tax expenditures. Before doing so, however, I have some brief comments on the portion of her paper that deals with grants-in-aid.

Federal Grants-in-Aid

Flexibility in the Use of Federal Grants

To me, the most surprising aspect of Ladd's paper was the case she makes for *greater* restrictions, limitations, and targeting in connection with federal grants-in-aid. This, of course, runs contrary to what has become an article of faith with most state and local officials: the need for fewer restrictions on and greater flexibility in the use of federal funds.

In making the case for more, rather than fewer, strings, Ladd is not defending the multitude of procedural and input-oriented requirements that so often are designed in or added on to federal grant programs. Rather, she is criticizing the inefficiency with which federal aid is distributed and brought to bear on problems having a national significance.

Looked at in these terms, her point is well taken, and not necessarily inconsistent with the desire of state and local officials for more flexibility. In fact, the interests of officials at all three levels of government can be served if the federal government seeks to target federal grants more effectively, while leaving state and local governments more discretion to design specific remedies for problems having a clear federal interest.

For this to happen, however, the federal government—primarily Congress—needs to better define its objectives and ignore those that are not uniquely federal in nature but are shared with the states. Were it to do so, I am confident we could have far fewer than 543 separate federal grant-in-aid programs, and the states' responsibilities in the grant-in-aid system would be considerably easier to carry out.

Aid to Cities

A second issue stemming from recent developments on the grant-in-aid front, and addressed by Ladd in her paper, involves the nature of the fiscal relationship between the federal government and large cities: Should the federal government provide aid directly to these cities or work through the state?

I found Ladd's treatment of this issue incomplete. Specifically, the paper implies that the federal government has more leverage in urban areas than it actually has—at least in a state like California. In recent years, states have become a more important factor shaping the fiscal context in which cities operate. As a consequence, they are now better equipped to intercept federal aid provided directly to large cities and reallocate it among suburban and rural areas. Whether they do so depends on the political structure of the individual states and how states perceive the problems of the cities relative to the problems facing other areas.

Where state legislatures share the federal government's concern for the plight of large cities, they will be responsive to the cities' needs in allocating funds at the state level, be they state or federal funds. Where legislatures attach less importance to city problems than does the federal government, they can counter an increase in direct federal aid with a reduction in state aid, offsetting some—perhaps most—of the intended benefit to the cities.

This does not mean that the federal government is without leverage in changing the relative fiscal position of cities. It means only that federal officials must be mindful of the "leakages" in the federal aid system—particularly when they seek to intervene in states where fiscal power is centralized.

Federal Aid Provided Through the Tax System

As I have already indicated, the primary innovation contained in Ladd's paper is the broader definition of federal aid used in assessing the federal government's contribution to the fiscal well-being of states and local governments. Specifically, Ladd recognizes not only aid provided through the expenditure side of the budget, which is what most of us use to measure intergovernmental assistance, but also aid provided through the revenue side of the budget in the form of tax expenditures. According to Ladd, the forms of primary aid in this latter category are: the exclusion from taxable income of interest received on state and local debt, and the deductibility of state and local tax payments from income on the federal tax return.

Exclusion of Interest Earned on Municipal Debt

Clearly, the tax treatment of interest earned on state and local government-issued paper is every bit as much a subsidy to the issuers as a direct federal grant. In fact, many economists have suggested replacing the tax-exempt borrowing privilege with such a grant. Thus, there can be no question that this tax expenditure belongs on the list of federal aid to states and local governments.

Whether it is proper to add the revenue "lost" by the federal government as a result of this tax expenditure to the amount spent by the federal government through the grant-in-aid system in order to arrive at an estimate of total federal aid is another matter. When the focus is on the *costs* incurred by the federal government in assisting state and local governments, the two may be added together. If, instead, the focus is on *benefits* received, the revenue loss associated with the exclusion of interest must be reduced in order to reflect the subsidy received by taxpayers rather than by the debt-issuing governments. All federal subsidy programs—even general revenue sharing—involve some leakages of this type, but the leakages tend to be smaller where aid is provided to the recipient directly, rather than indirectly through the tax system.

Deductibility of State and Local Taxes

I have much more difficulty accepting Ladd's inclusion of federal revenue losses resulting from tax deductibility in her tally of federal aid to state and local governments. In my view:

- The analytical basis for treating tax deductibility as a subsidy to state and local governments is weak;

- The long-term effects of ending deductibility are likely to be far less important than what Ladd maintains; and

- The policy implications that Ladd draws from her discussion of deductibility may point state and local governments in a direction away from their own best interests.

Should Tax Deductibility be Viewed as a Subsidy?   Ladd stated her rationale for including in her tally of federal aid to state and local governments the federal revenue losses associated with deductibility in this way: "Tax deductibility provides an incentive for state and local governments to spend more than they otherwise would and consequently can be evaluated as if it were a direct intergovernmental subsidy program."

I believe it is dangerous to lump together tax deductibility and direct grants. In the first place, an incentive to spend is not at all comparable to a direct subsidy, or else Section 504 of the 1973 Rehabilitation Act and other federal mandates can also be evaluated as if they were subsidies. Few state and local officials would go along with this, and for good reason.

More importantly, revenue losses from tax deductibility do not belong on the list of federal aid to state and local governments because these governments receive *none* of the forgone revenues. The entire financial benefit from this tax expenditure accrues to the taxpayers who itemize deductions on their federal income tax form. The direct benefits accruing to state and local governments from tax deductibility are political, rather than financial: an environment that is more conducive to gaining the public's acceptance of higher taxes. Granted, the money used to pay these higher taxes may be the same money "saved" as a result of tax deductibility. But the transfer of funds does not occur automatically and may not occur at all unless tax *policy* at the state or local level changes.

In any event, the political "benefits" from tax deductibility do *not* constitute a subsidy in the same way that direct grants or tax-exempt borrowing privileges do.

The Value of Deductibility.   What about the value of tax deductibility to state and local governments and the long-term effects of ending it? Ladd's paper suggests that however one defines the nature of the benefits from tax deductibility, the value of these benefits to state and local governments is substantial.

In theory, the tax treatment of state and local tax payments does affect the public's willingness to support the cost of state and local government services. As Ladd demonstrates, tax deductibility keeps the price to taxpayers of state and local services below the cost to the state of providing them, making these services relatively more attractive than other goods and services available to the taxpayers. Consequently, other things being equal, eliminating tax deductibility would tend to shift taxpayer demand toward these other goods and services (the "price effect").

Whether the theory is worth mentioning in this context, however, depends on the price elasticity of demand for state and local services when the price change occurs as a result of a change to federal tax laws. In her paper, Ladd uses a price elasticity of −0.3, based on a survey paper by Robert Inman. This paper is not discussed in the text; it is merely cited in a footnote.

When a −0.3 elasticity is combined with estimates of the average itemizer's marginal tax rate (32 percent), Ladd finds a strong relationship between tax deductibility and the demand for government services. In fact, she concludes that "eliminating tax deductibility . . . would reduce the demand for public services in many jurisdictions by about fourteen percent."

Given the way taxing and spending decisions are made at the state and local levels, this estimate strikes me as being well in excess of what the true relationship is. In the first place, public services do not carry price tags in the conventional sense. As a result, there is an exceedingly weak link between price and demand in the public sector. Much of the demand for public services comes from groups whose members see *no* direct relationship between their success in lobbying for more governmental services and the amount they will have to pay as taxpayers. Individually, they are usually right.

In fact, the weak linkage between price and quantity demanded in the public sector lies at the very heart of this volume. The primary cause of the current "budget crisis" is that what we as a nation are willing to pay for governmental services bears little relationship to the amount of services we expect from the federal government.

Second, the mechanism through which a change in tax deductibility would have to influence the demand for services is too complex to allow for a significant price elasticity of demand. Elimination of tax deductibility would increase a taxpayer's *federal* tax liability. For there to be a price effect (in addition to an income effect), taxpayers would have to recognize (or behave as if they recognized) the connection between this increase and the implicit price of police protection, welfare programs, and education. Clearly, some will; in my judgment, however, most will not.

Finally, I see no empirical evidence that the price elasticity of demand for governmental services is particularly strong. For example, it is not apparent that federal bracket creep during the later 1970s and early 1980s *increased* the demand for public services at the state and local level relative to the demand for other goods and services, as Ladd's paper implies would happen. In fact, it was during this very period that the so-called taxpayers' revolt reached its zenith.

Policy Implications.   Let me now turn to the policy conclusion that Ladd draws from her analysis of tax deductibility. She implies that because outright elimination of deductibility might have "unacceptably large adverse effects on state and local governments," this policy option should be dismissed or at least substantially altered before it is implemented.

As I indicated earlier, Ladd has not made a convincing empirical case that the effects of ending tax deductibility on state and local governments would be "large." Even if the effects were large, however, they could only be termed "adverse" if the result were a level of public services below the optimal level. Nothing in the paper, however, demonstrates that this would be the result. In fact, one could make the opposite case: Since eliminating deductibility would cause the price system to work better by equating the "price" of public services with the "cost" of delivering these services, the result might be a level of services closer to the optimum. From this perspective, the option of eliminating tax deductibility seems to deserve a more favorable appraisal than Ladd gives it.

But I have a more practical reason for suggesting that the elimination of tax deductibility is an appealing option—even from the perspective of state and local governments. In assessing this option, one simply cannot assume that other things will be equal. As Mills and Palmer make clear in *The Deficit Dilemma*, major changes in both federal spending and federal taxing are inevitable if the federal deficit as a percentage of GNP is to be reduced. Clearly, state and local governments cannot expect to emerge unscathed from this painful exercise. Thus, from the standpoint of state and local governments, the issue is not so much whether tax deductibility is desirable, but whether it is more desirable than the other types of federal aid on Ladd's list.

Speaking for myself, the answer to this question would seem to be no. The amount of aid Ladd attributes to tax deductibility—$30.5 billion in 1982—is roughly equal to the amount of aid provided through (1) general revenue sharing; (2) *all* broad-based grants in the areas of community development, employment, and training, social services, and low-income home energy assistance; and (3) all federal transportation programs, combined. The $30.5 billion in grants represent money in the bank to state and local governments. The $30.5 billion in forgone federal revenues as a result of tax deductibility represent, from the state and local perspective, something else—I'm not quite sure what.

With this in mind, I think the states would be well advised to trade tax deductibility for additional grant money on, say, a two-for-one basis. Doing so would reduce the federal deficit, improve the condition of state and local government budgets, shift more of the burden associated with reducing the deficit to high-bracket taxpayers, and, arguably, improve the workings of the price system.

TAX POLICY

Joseph J. Minarik

By now, there is almost unanimous agreement that the federal budget will be in substantial deficit for the foreseeable future, notwithstanding the prospect of sustained recovery from our recent deep recession, unless government policies change. This paper explains the recent changes in the federal tax system and discusses several tax increase options designed to narrow the budget gap. The search for more revenue can open the entire federal tax system to wholesome scrutiny. The effects of the tax system on overall economic efficiency, through reduced incentives for productive activity and distortions of resource allocation, are now widely discussed. And at the same time, as opinion polls show, the public increasingly believes that the federal tax system is unfair. So even people who want only an alternative way to collect the current level of revenues may welcome an airing of tax policy issues.

The first section of this paper shows how economic and tax policy developments led to the watershed legislation of 1981 and 1982, while the second section explains those major tax bills. Section three explores the current policy dilemma and potential strategies for dealing with it, and a closing section weighs the merits of the available options.

The Federal Tax System Since World War II

At the end of World War II, the United States inherited its first peacetime mass tax system. The pressures of war finance had required new levels of government revenues, and so federal tax collections, which had grown from only 3.8 percent of the gross national product (GNP) in 1929 and 5.5 percent in 1939, leaped to 19.5 percent in 1946. Federal tax receipts as a percentage of GNP since 1946 have changed little, at least in relation to the leap in the World War II years (see table 1); the peak tax share of GNP in 1981 exceeded the 1946 figure by less than two percentage points.

Total federal tax revenues have by no means been a constant share of GNP, however. For one thing, two of the most important federal taxes—the individual and the corporate income taxes—are highly sensitive to the state of the economy. The individual income tax is the highest yielding of all federal taxes, supplying at least 40 percent of total revenues in every year since 1950. Individual income tax liabilities increase more than in proportion when income increases, either from real growth or inflation, because the additional income is taxed in each taxpayer's highest marginal rate bracket. And in a recession, individual income tax revenues fall more than in proportion to the decline in incomes. The substantial increases in such revenues in the late 1960s and 1970s and the equally sharp declines in the early 1960s and mid-1970s demonstrated the sensitivity of income tax revenues to the state of the economy (see table 2). Magnifying this sensitivity has been the frequent use of the income tax as a countercyclical economic policy tool; taxes have been cut in economic downturns (when revenues are already reduced) to add purchasing power in the private sector, and taxes have been raised at times of excessively fast growth. The discretionary tax cuts of 1964 and 1974–1975 and the Vietnam war surtax of 1968–1970 are examples.

The corporate income tax is also highly sensitive to economic conditions. Corporate net income is a residual—gross revenues less a number of costs that are generally fixed in the short run. When business turns down, the bills still have to be paid, so most of the reduction in sales is compensated for from profits. When business rebounds, profits jump sharply. Corporate tax liabilities move with the economy just as sharply as profits do, as the jump with economic recovery in 1977 and the drop with the recession in 1983 exemplify.

The federal tax take has changed for more than cyclical reasons, however; there have been structural changes in the tax system as well. Corporate income tax revenues, beyond fluctuating with the economy, have tended to drop because of the discretionary tax cuts targeted on investment and capital formation—particularly accelerated depreciation and investment tax credit. Revenues have declined still further because rapid inflation has encouraged firms to finance their investment through debt rather than equity. Inflation depreciates the value of outstanding debt principal, thus benefiting debtor corporations; the interest outlays to service this inflation-motivated debt are tax deductible, thus reducing corporate tax liabilities.

While the trend in corporate tax liabilities has been downward, Social Security payroll tax liabilities have been zooming up. Increasing real benefits,

TABLE 1

FEDERAL REVENUES AND STATE AND LOCAL TAX REVENUES,
FISCAL YEARS 1946–1982

	Federal Revenues	*State and Local Tax Revenues[a]*	*Total*
		Percentage of GNP	
1946	19.5	5.2[b]	24.7
1947	17.3	5.4	22.7
1948	17.0	5.6	22.6
1949	15.1	5.8	20.9
1950	14.9	6.3	21.2
1951	16.5	6.0	22.5
1952	19.5	6.0	25.5
1953	19.3	6.1	25.4
1954	19.1	6.4	25.6
1955	17.2	6.6	23.8
1956	18.1	6.8	24.9
1957	18.4	7.1	25.5
1958	18.0	7.3	25.3
1959	16.7	7.4	24.1
1960	18.6	7.8	26.4
1961	18.5	8.2	26.8
1962	18.2	8.3	26.4
1963	18.4	8.4	26.8
1964	18.2	8.5	26.7
1965	17.7	8.6	26.3
1966	18.1	8.5	26.6
1967	19.2	8.7	27.9
1968	18.4	9.2	27.6
1969	20.5	9.4	29.9
1970	19.9	10.0	29.9
1971	18.1	10.2	28.3
1972	18.4	11.1	29.5
1973	18.4	10.7	29.1
1974	19.1	10.5	29.6
1975	18.9	10.6	29.5
1976	18.2	10.7	28.9
1977	19.1	10.8	29.9
1978	19.1	10.6	29.7
1979	19.7	10.0	29.6
1980	20.1	9.9	30.0
1981	20.9	9.7	30.6
1982	20.4	9.9	30.3

SOURCE: Office of Management and Budget, "Total Government Finances." February 1984, p. 2.

NOTE: Percentage shares for individual years may not add to totals because of rounding.

a. State and local tax revenues equal state and local receipts less grants-in-aid from the federal government.

b. Author's estimate.

TABLE 2

Federal Government Revenues by Source,
Fiscal Years 1946–1986

	Individual Income Tax	Corporate Income Tax	Social Insurance Taxes	Excise Taxes	Estate and Gift Tax	All Other Receipts	Total
			Percentage of Total Receipts				
1946	41.0	31.1	7.8	16.9	1.7	1.4	100.0
1947	46.7	22.4	8.7	18.7	2.0	1.5	100.0
1948	46.2	23.2	9.5	17.6	2.1	1.4	100.0
1949	39.4	28.4	9.7	19.0	2.0	1.5	100.0
1950	39.9	26.5	11.1	19.1	1.8	1.7	100.0
1951	41.8	27.3	11.1	16.7	1.4	1.7	100.0
1952	42.2	32.1	9.8	13.4	1.2	1.4	100.0
1953	42.8	30.5	9.8	14.2	1.3	1.4	100.0
1954	42.4	30.3	10.3	14.3	1.3	1.4	100.0
1955	43.9	27.3	12.0	13.9	1.4	1.4	100.0
1956	43.2	28.0	12.5	13.3	1.6	1.4	100.0
1957	44.5	26.5	12.5	13.2	1.7	1.6	100.0
1958	43.6	25.2	14.1	13.4	1.7	2.0	100.0
1959	46.4	21.8	14.8	13.3	1.7	1.9	100.0
1960	44.0	23.2	15.9	12.6	1.7	2.5	100.0
1961	43.8	22.2	17.4	12.6	2.0	2.0	100.0
1962	45.7	20.6	17.1	12.6	2.0	2.0	100.0
1963	44.7	20.3	18.6	12.4	2.0	2.1	100.0
1964	43.2	20.9	19.5	12.2	2.1	2.1	100.0
1965	41.8	21.8	19.1	12.5	2.3	2.6	100.0
1966	42.4	23.0	19.5	10.0	2.3	2.8	100.0
1967	41.3	22.8	22.0	9.2	2.0	2.7	100.0
1968	44.9	18.7	22.2	9.2	2.0	3.0	100.0
1969	46.7	19.6	20.9	8.1	1.9	2.8	100.0
1970	46.9	17.0	23.0	8.1	1.9	3.0	100.0
1971	46.1	14.3	25.3	8.9	2.0	3.4	100.0
1972	45.7	15.5	25.4	7.5	2.6	3.3	100.0
1973	44.7	15.7	27.3	7.0	2.1	3.1	100.0
1974	45.2	14.7	28.5	6.4	1.9	3.3	100.0
1975	43.9	14.6	30.3	5.9	1.7	3.7	100.0
1976	44.2	13.9	30.5	5.7	1.7	4.1	100.0
1977	44.3	15.4	29.9	4.9	2.1	3.3	100.0
1978	45.3	15.0	30.3	4.6	1.3	3.5	100.0
1979	47.0	14.2	30.0	4.0	1.2	3.6	100.0
1980	47.2	12.5	30.5	4.7	1.2	3.9	100.0
1981	47.7	10.2	30.5	6.8	1.1	3.6	100.0
1982	48.2	8.0	32.6	5.9	1.3	4.0	100.0
1983[a]	48.0	6.0	35.2	5.8	1.0	4.0	100.0
1984[b]	44.1	9.0	36.5	5.6	0.9	3.9	100.0
1985[b]	44.2	9.3	37.1	5.1	0.8	3.6	100.0
1986[b]	44.4	9.8	37.6	4.2	0.6	3.3	100.0

Source: Office of Management and Budget; 1983–1986 estimates and projections, Congressional Budget Office.
Note: Percentage shares for individual years may not add to 100 percent because of rounding.
a.   Estimate.
b.   Projections, assuming no change in current law.

unfavorable demographics, above-average inflation in medical care costs, a stagnant economy, and a period of overcompensating indexing for inflation have combined to swell the system's revenue needs. The decline of the corporate tax was more than offset by the increase in the payroll tax share of total revenues, which more than tripled between 1946 and 1981.

By the early 1980s, the cyclical fluctuations in the economy and changes in the tax system combined to drive federal tax revenues to a post-World War II peak. While Social Security payroll tax revenues continued to climb, rapid inflation pushed individual income taxpayers into higher tax brackets. In fiscal 1981 federal taxes hit 20.9 percent of GNP, well above the highest peacetime value then on record. At the same time, taxpayers were hard-hit by state and local taxes, which had more than doubled as a share of GNP since 1946. Despite some relief as a result of a tax-cutting drive in the late 1970s, state and local taxes had retreated little from their record levels of 1976 and 1977. The federal revenue peak in fiscal 1981 coincided with a record tax take of 30.6 percent for the entire government sector.

It is not surprising that this confluence of factors and the highest total tax take in postwar history led to irresistible pressure for tax cuts.

Tax Policy Changes between 1981 and 1983 and the New Outlook for Revenues

The Economic Recovery Tax Act of 1981 (ERTA) was the response to the cyclical peak in federal tax revenues reached in that year. ERTA was an especially far-reaching piece of tax legislation, with provisions affecting individual and corporate income taxes, the estate and gift tax, and other taxes.

ERTA aimed to increase economic efficiency and incentives, much as the Kennedy-Johnson tax cuts of 1962 and 1964 had done. Like those tax bills, the "supply side" emphasis of ERTA was embodied primarily in cuts in individual income tax rates and more favorable tax treatment of fixed investment for business.

Also like the legislation of the early 1960s, ERTA was universally recognized to cause a substantial loss of revenue, abstracting from any possible changes in taxpayer behavior. The most hotly debated issue was whether taxpayer behavior would change under the influence of the act, and if so, to what degree.

The supply-side case for ERTA never really came to trial. The economy fell into a deep recession in mid-1981, and substantial unemployment and idle capacity turned the work and investment incentives into moot issues.

As the economy languished in the recession of 1982, the new risk was the federal deficit. ERTA had drastically reduced federal revenues; congressional estimates at the time of enactment showed the six-year revenue loss at $700 billion (see table 3). Enacted spending cuts were far short of this magnitude. With the economy operating well below the capacity expected just a year or two before, an extraordinary deficit loomed. The deficit forecast was all the more disturbing because it showed a continuing budget gap even as the economy grew toward full utilization over several years. The tax cuts were simply too large, given the amount of spending reductions that were forthcoming, to yield budget deficits anywhere near the historical range even with rapid economic growth.

The will of Congress was galvanized by the danger that these continuing deficits would collide with business and consumer credit demands as the economy grew, driving up interest rates and choking off the recovery. In response to the mandate of the budget resolution for FY 1983, Congress passed the Tax Equity and Fiscal Responsibility Act of 1982 (TEFRA). Like ERTA, TEFRA was a broad-ranging piece of legislation. Unlike ERTA, TEFRA was intended to increase tax burdens.

ERTA had emphasized the reduction of tax rates and the increase in economic incentives. TEFRA trod lightly over or avoided the incentive issues, achieving its revenue gain through structural changes relating to leakages in the tax base (see table 4). Because these changes offset only a small part of the revenues lost as a result of ERTA, TEFRA's net effect in company with ERTA should not be exaggerated. With respect to both incentives and fiscal policy, TEFRA was only a retreat, not a change of direction.

Provisions Primarily Affecting Individual Taxpayers

The individual income tax provisions of ERTA received the most public attention because they represented a significant departure from the provisions of previous legislation.

Rate Reductions. ERTA reduced marginal tax rates under the individual income tax by a total of approximately 23 percent over three years. Tax rates for calendar year 1982 were cut about 10 percent below those under prior law; rates for 1983 were cut about 19 percent; and in 1984 and later years, rates would be the full 23 percent lower. (Of course, most taxpayers actually felt the reductions in tax rates through changes in withholding on wages and salaries, which took effect on October 1, 1981, July 1, 1982, and

TABLE 3

ESTIMATED REVENUE EFFECTS OF SELECTED PROVISIONS OF THE ECONOMIC
RECOVERY TAX ACT OF 1981, FISCAL YEARS 1982–1986

Provision	1982	1983	1984	1985	1986
	Billions of Dollars				
Individual income tax provisions					
Rate cuts	− 25.8	− 65.7	− 104.5	− 122.7	− 143.8
Deduction for two-earner couples	− 0.4	− 4.4	− 9.1	− 11.0	− 12.6
Indexing	—	—	—	− 12.9	− 35.8
Other	− 0.9	− 2.8	− 5.3	− 7.3	− 12.5
Total	− 27.1	− 72.9	− 118.9	− 153.9	− 204.7
1983 Reestimate[a]	− 28.9	− 68.0	− 105.2	− 126.5	− 155.3
Business incentive provisions					
Accelerated cost recovery	− 9.6	− 16.8	− 26.3	− 37.3	− 52.8
R & D Credit	− 0.4	− 0.7	− 0.9	− 0.8	− 0.5
Other	− 0.7	− 1.2	− 1.2	− 1.3	− 1.4
Total	− 10.7	− 18.7	− 28.4	39.4	− 54.7
1983 Reestimate[a]	− 9.2	− 17.2	− 25.7	− 34.5	− 42.5
Estate and gift tax provisions					
Unified credit	[b]	− 1.1	− 2.0	− 2.8	− 3.8
Reduction in rates	[b]	− 0.2	− 0.4	− 0.6	− 0.9
Other	− 0.2	− 0.8	− 0.8	− 0.8	− 0.9
Total	− 0.2	− 2.1	− 3.2	− 4.2	− 5.6
All other	0.3	1.0	0.5	− 1.7	− 2.7
TOTAL	− 37.7	− 92.7	− 150.0	− 199.2	− 267.7
1983 REESTIMATE[a]	− 38.4	− 87.8	− 134.8	− 166.6	− 205.2

SOURCE: Joint Committee on Taxation, *General Explanation of the Economic Recovery Tax Act of 1981*, table V-3, pp. 382–391; Congressional Budget Office, *Reducing the Deficit: Spending and Revenue Options*, table X-2, p. 230.

NOTE: Revenue effects shown were estimated at time of passage of legislation. Estimates at time of this writing, if available, would differ because of changes in actual and forecast economic conditions. Columns may not add to totals because of rounding.

a. The 1983 reestimates account for changes in economic assumptions. The reestimates do not allow allocation of miscellaneous provisions to estate and gift tax category. Only Accelerated Cost Recovery System (ACRS) revenue losses applicable to corporations are included in the business category, which is therefore a slight underestimate.

July 1, 1983. Withholding affects only wage and salary income, however, and does not determine total tax liabilities. The withholding changes are thus irrelevant to the incentive aspects of the tax cut.)

Effective January 1, 1982, all tax rates that would have exceeded 50 percent, given the 10 percent rate reduction then in effect, were

TABLE 4

ESTIMATED REVENUE EFFECTS OF SELECTED PROVISIONS OF THE TAX EQUITY AND
FISCAL RESPONSIBILITY ACT OF 1982, FISCAL YEARS 1983–1987

Provision	1983	1984	1985	1986	1987
	Billions of Dollars				
Individual income tax provisions					
Alternative minimum tax	[a]	0.7	0.7	0.7	0.7
Medical expense deduction	0.3	1.8	1.7	1.8	1.9
Casualty loss deduction	—	0.7	0.7	0.8	0.9
Total	0.3	3.1	3.1	3.3	3.6
1983 Reestimate[b]	4.9	12.7	12.5	14.8	17.8
Provisions primarily affecting business					
Tax preferences	0.5	0.9	0.9	0.9	1.0
ITC basis adjustment	0.4	1.4	2.7	4.1	5.6
Repeal 1985 and 1986 accelerations of cost recovery	—	—	1.5	9.9	18.4
Leasing	1.0	2.6	4.3	5.5	7.0
Other	3.5	8.4	7.1	7.6	8.1
Total	5.4	13.3	16.5	28.0	40.1
1983 Reestimate[b]	7.4	16.3	19.2	26.2	31.6
Compliance provisions					
Withholding on interest and dividends[c]	1.3	5.2	4.0	4.6	5.2
Other	2.0	3.6	4.7	5.6	6.0
Total	3.4	8.9	8.7	10.2	11.2
Additional IRS enforcement	2.1	2.4	2.4	1.3	0.6
Other	4.0	6.0	7.3	6.9	6.9
TOTAL	18.0	37.7	42.7	51.8	63.9
1983 REESTIMATE	17.9	37.7	41.7	46.9	54.2

SOURCE: Joint Committee on Taxation, *General Explanation of the Revenue Provision of the Tax Equity and Fiscal Responsibility Act of 1982*, table V-3, pp. 457–459. Congressional Budget Office, *Reducing the Deficit: Spending and Revenue Options*, table X-2, p. 230.

NOTE: Revenue effects shown were estimated at the time of passage of legislation. Estimates at time of this writing, if available, would differ because of changes in actual and forecast economic conditions. Items may not add to totals because of rounding.

a. Less than $50 million.

b. The 1983 reestimates account for changes in economic assumptions. Reestimates do not allow allocation among all categories. Individual income tax category includes compliance and enforcement revenue gains. Business category includes only revenue changes attributable to corporations, and is therefore a slight underestimate.

c. Repealed before taking effect.

immediately reduced to 50 percent. This reduction in the highest tax rates carried with it an equivalent reduction in the maximum tax rate on capital gains, from 28 percent (that is, the 40 percent of long-term gains subject to tax times the 70 percent maximum statutory rate) to 20 percent (40 percent times the new 50 percent top statutory rate). In fact, through a special legal provision, the capital gains rate reduction was even further accelerated, applying to all asset transactions after June 9, 1981. So two of the major incentive provisions of ERTA, reductions in the highest capital gains tax rate and in the highest tax rate on other forms of income from capital, took effect on June 9, 1981, and January 1, 1982, respectively, earlier than many people perceived.

Indexing of Tax Rates. ERTA provided that tax rate brackets, personal exemptions, and zero bracket amounts be indexed for inflation beginning in 1985. The purpose of indexation is to prevent bracket creep—inflation combining with the progressive income tax—from increasing real tax liabilities.

Social Security Amendments of 1983. These provisions were enacted to shore up the system against expected short-term and long-term trust fund deficits. The legislation did increase revenues, but its near-term budgetary implications were limited for two reasons. First, some of the revenue gain for the Social Security trust funds was implicitly achieved through transfers of general revenues that would have been collected in any event; and second, some of the balance of the revenue pickup came through accelerated increases in tax rates that were already scheduled for later years, thus adding to revenues temporarily rather than permanently. All in all, the legislation will raise a significant amount of revenue over the seventy-five-year planning period commonly used for Social Security, but its effect on the more immediate budget projection period is far more limited.

Surface Transportation Assistance Act of 1982. This bill raised the federal gasoline excise tax from 4 to 9 cents per gallon. Although it increased federal revenues by about $5 billion per year, this increase had no net budgetary impact, because the additional revenues were dedicated to transportation improvements.

Provisions Primarily Affecting Business

While ERTA's business tax provisions received less public attention, at least at first, they were if anything a more radical departure from prior law than the provisions affecting individuals. The departure proved so great that TEFRA staged a significant retreat the next year.

Accelerated Cost Recovery. Through its new Accelerated Cost Recovery System (ACRS), ERTA provided businesses with a substantially more prior law's complex asset depreciation range system, assets had been categorized according to their expected useful lives. ACRS divided equipment into only three categories, with virtually all equipment assigned a useful life of five years; very short-lived equipment (including vehicles) is assigned a three-year life, and some public utility property a ten-year life. Over these lifetimes ERTA prescribed a declining-balance cost recovery allowance of 150 percent, with acceleration to 175 percent in 1985 and 200 percent in later years. Buildings were assigned useful lives of fifteen years and 175 percent declining-balance allowances.

ACRS also allowed a 6 percent credit for investments in equipment in the three-year-life class and a full 10 percent credit for investments in longer-lived equipment. This was substantially more generous than prior law, which gave a 3⅓ percent credit for three- and four-year assets, a 6⅔ percent credit for five- and six- year assets, and the full 10 percent credit only for seven-year and still longer-lived assets. Under these terms, ACRS substantially liberalized capital cost recovery. ERTA left some potential tax policy problems, however. Cost recovery was not uniform from one type of asset to another.[1] Such a distortive government policy makes businesses reject investment options that provide more value in the marketplace in favor of other options that provide less value. The result was a reduction of total output. Furthermore, the schedule of future accelerations of capital cost recovery, to a declining-balance of 175 percent, and ultimately to a declining-balance of 200 percent in 1986 and thereafter, was an incentive to postpone investment and thereby take advantage of the more generous provisions in the future.

Finally, the new fifteen-year depreciable life for buildings was a substantial acceleration from prior depreciation and could easily lead to overinvestment in apartment and office buildings. Industry reports indicate that investments in tax shelters in 1983 could increase by as much as 50 percent over 1982, and the greatly liberalized cost recovery provisions for buildings could be a major reason.[2] Despite these apparent flaws, ACRS did reduce the tax burden on business capital investment in general, potentially increasing such investment.

TEFRA sought to tie up some of the loose ends in ERTA with respect to capital cost recovery. The largest single step was unquestionably the repeal of the scheduled 1985 and 1986 accelerations of capital cost recovery allow-

---

1. Jane G. Gravelle, "Effects of the 1981 Depreciation Revisions on the Taxation of Income from Business Capital," *National Tax Journal*, vol. 35, March 1982, pp. 1–20.
2. "Real-Estate Tax Shelters Booming, But Critics Move to Trim Benefits," *Wall Street Journal*, July 5, 1983, p. 25.

ances for equipment, making the current 150 percent declining-balance system permanent. This slowdown of future cost recovery allowances unquestionably made investment somewhat less attractive, but it also eliminated the incentive to defer investment until the more favorable rules took effect. Furthermore, it made the tax system more neutral among investors and reduced (but did not eliminate) the opportunities for outright tax sheltering.

Also in TEFRA, Congress established a basis adjustment for the investment tax credit. In so doing, it eliminated a double benefit in which firms were allowed to depreciate the portion of an investment that was, in effect, paid for by the federal government through the investment tax credit. Congress determined that a basis adjustment for one-half of the amount of the tax credit, rather than the full credit, would provide sufficient additional revenue and bring effective tax rates on equipment investments to an acceptable level (taking into account TEFRA's other changes in ACRS). Although the one-half basis adjustment might well satisfy those criteria, it left tax policy in a highly unstable position. Tax policy theorists will probably criticize the one-half basis adjustment because only a full-basis adjustment accurately accounts for the government's contribution to the purchase of an asset through the investment tax credit. Advocates of capital formation will argue that the one-half basis adjustment reduces the investment tax credit's incentive for investment. No one will defend the one-half basis adjustment on principle. Thus, the investment tax credit and its basis adjustment will probably be debated further whenever tax policy issues come to the fore.

Leasing. As has already been noted, ACRS substantially liberalized cost recovery and investment tax credits. In fact, the liberalization was so great that many firms could not take full advantage of it. This situation would especially afflict not only new firms, which make large ''set-up'' investments and are thus unprofitable in their early years, but also older, recently unprofitable firms with large net operating losses that make them nontaxable. In contrast, a large, highly profitable firm might find that the ACRS deductions and credits from a particular new investment would wipe out its tax liability on the income generated by that investment, sheltering income from other sources besides. This divergence in the cost of capital investments could force disadvantaged firms to forgo profitable investments, while strong firms consolidated their hold on markets. Even worse, profitable firms could buy firms in related or unrelated lines of business with large reserves of net operating losses, simply to use up the tax benefits.

To release these pressures of built-up unusable tax deductions and credits, ERTA eliminated or eased the prior law's restrictions against leasing as a means of transferring tax benefits.[3] Under the new "safe harbor" leasing, a profitable firm could nominally buy an asset, claim the tax benefit, and lease it back to the actual user at a favorable rate. The result was a much simpler transfer of tax benefits, and probably a greater share of those benefits for the equipment user, than in the leasing practiced under pre-ERTA law. In the first months after the passage of ERTA, the leasing market was highly active, aided at least in part by a retroactivity provision allowing the leasing of equipment purchased as early as January 1, 1981—well before the enactment of ERTA.

In response to a public outcry over conspicuous use of the safe harbor leasing provision and in search of revenue, TEFRA repealed this liberalized means of transferring tax benefits. In its place Congress established a new mechanism known as "finance" leasing, which was more liberal than pre-ERTA leasing but more restrictive than safe harbor leasing. TEFRA cut back on the worst of the dangers of unusable tax benefits by reducing the deductions and credits under ACRS, as already described. The potential imbalances that motivated safe harbor leasing remain, though to a reduced degree, and the issue could easily arise again through new legislative proposals or economic or legal pressures in mergers, antitrust actions, or other areas.[4]

Corporate Tax Preferences. TEFRA provides for a 15 percent cutback in a list of tax preferences. The cutback applies only to corporations; small-business (Subchapter S) corporations are not affected. The existing corporate minimum tax is adjusted to prevent interactions with the new provisions. The cutback works by reducing each deduction by 15 percent.

Other Provisions

There were many ERTA provisions beyond those specifically discussed in this paper. Most notable were a tax exclusion for two-earner couples, to encourage labor supply; an expansion of the individual retirement account

---

3. Among the relevant requirements were (1) the leased equipment must have been usable by firms other than the actual user (thus, highly specialized equipment could not be leased); (2) the owner must have maintained at least a 20 percent interest in the equipment; (3) the owner must have shown a profit from the lease without reference to the tax benefits; (4) the user of the equipment could not have a right in the lease to purchase the equipment at the end of the lease term at less than its fair market value; and (5) the user must not have had an investment in the lease and could not lend any of the purchase price of the asset to the owner.

4. Indeed, a proposal that firms be enabled to borrow against unused investment tax credits (H.R. 3434, the Work Opportunities and Renewed Competition Act of 1983) has already been cosponsored by Representatives James R. Jones and Barber B. Conable, Jr. Furthermore, perhaps because of heightened awareness of the potential of leasing after ERTA, a rash of leasing by nonprofit institutions and governments has broken out.

(IRA) provisions, and a net interest exclusion to encourage savings effective for taxable years beginning in 1985; a tax credit for increases in research and development activities; a reduction in corporate tax rates applying to the first $50,000 of profits; and substantial reductions in the estate and gift tax.[5]

TEFRA was projected to raise substantial revenues from a number of provisions designed to improve taxpayer compliance. One of those provisions—withholding of tax on interest and dividend income by banks and other financial institutions—was subsequently repealed on the grounds that it would pose an administrative and financial burden on interest and dividend payers and recipients, and that it would discourage saving. Federal excise taxes on air travel, telephone services, and cigarettes were temporarily increased. Taxation of unemployment insurance benefits under the individual income tax was made more stringent.[6] The alternative minimum tax for individuals was strengthened, and the system for itemizing deductions for medical expenses and casualty losses was simplified and rules tightened.

Revenue Implications

As has already been noted, ERTA indisputably caused substantial revenue losses abstracting from any changes it induced in economic behavior. Cuts in individual income tax rates accounted for well over one-half of the projected six-year loss of $700 billion in revenues; ACRS and related provisions accounted for another $100 + billion (see table 3). Advocates of ERTA had claimed that it would stimulate enough additional work, saving, and investment to yield more revenue than the static estimates, but the 1981 recession eliminated that possibility for virtually the entire forecast period. Real incomes and inflation declined enough to reduce the ERTA revenue losses significantly below the original estimates, as table 3 shows.

The business tax provisions of TEFRA provided for almost one-half of the bill's revenue pickup through FY 1985 and more than one-half thereafter (see table 4). The compliance provisions, including the since-repealed withholding on interest and dividends, were the second-largest contributor. TEFRA proved to be a retreat rather than a reversal in the drive toward greater economic incentives. The individual income tax provisions of TEFRA had extremely small revenue implications and did not touch the ERTA tax rate

---

5. These and all other provisions of ERTA are described in Joint Committee on Taxation, *General Explanation of the Economic Recovery Tax Act of 1981* (Washington, D.C.: Government Printing Office, 1981).

6. These and all other provisions of TEFRA are described in more detail in Joint Committee on Taxation, *General Explanation of the Revenue Provisions of the Tax Equity and Fiscal Responsibility Act of 1982* (Washington, D.C.: Government Printing Office, 1982).

reductions. The compliance provisions were nearly as modest in terms of expected revenue pickup and can be identified with economic incentives only through tortuous and questionable logic. In the business provisions the picture is much more mixed; TEFRA provided for less than one-half of the original projected revenue loss in ERTA to be recaptured between 1984 and 1986, but more than one-half in later years.[7] TEFRA did raise revenue, but the deficit problem and the need for additional revenue remain.

Revenue Strategies to Deal with the Deficit

In TEFRA, Congress acknowledged that tax increases are needed to move the budget toward balance. Congress acted, but from today's perspective it did not move far enough. As noted earlier in this volume, the current policy budget deficit will still exceed $200 billion, 5 percent of GNP, by FY 1988. Even with substantial spending cuts, between $50 billion and $100 billion per year in revenues over and above TEFRA would be needed by FY 1988 to cut the structural deficit to manageable proportions.

The Problem

Raising so much additional revenue is a daunting challenge; to add some perspective, TEFRA will raise just about $50 billion in 1988 under current economic assumptions. So the difficulty of this task should be obvious— considering that TEFRA itself came under such heavy criticism, including the subsequent repeal of one of its most important provisions. And as logic suggests that TEFRA included the most palatable revenue options, we can only expect that the remaining alternatives will be even harder to swallow.

Before going into specifics, we must discuss principles. Economic recovery has apparently taken hold, but a large and immediate tax increase could reduce demand and slow or even stop real growth. Tax increases ideally should be relatively small in the initial years and should grow as the economy moves toward full employment. A tax increase that is properly timed to shrink federal credit demands as private demands for investment financing grow could keep credit needs and available funds in balance, facilitating capital formation and long-term growth.

But a tax increase that grows over time may lack credibility. A pledge to raise $50 billion in 1988 could be greeted with the same lack of respect

---

7. There is some inconsistency between the economic forecasts underlying the revenue loss estimates of the two laws.

as a resolution to quit smoking at the same date. Unless deficit reduction policies are considered reliable, they will not calm the credit markets. The contingency tax plan proposed in the administration's FY 1984 budget, consisting of a 5 percent income tax surcharge and a $5 per barrel excise tax on oil to take effect in 1986, is a case in point. The new taxes were made contingent on several factors, including congressional compliance with other administration proposals, the rate of growth of the economy, and the level of the deficit. Although an administration proposal for a tax increase might have been expected to impress the credit markets, the many contingencies apparently convinced most observers that the proposal was not serious, and so its effect has been nil.

The prescribed tax increase, then, must equal or perhaps double the revenue yield of TEFRA in a credible form. Political and economic criteria for such a revenue initiative are numerous and often conflicting. A few large revenue-raising provisions might be enacted more easily than many smaller items, but raising tens of billions of dollars at a single stroke is not easy. Some promising initiatives simply will not yield that much revenue; others would involve serious costs if stretched that far, either in perceived fairness (such as a national sales tax or value-added tax) or in economic efficiency and incentives (such as increases in income tax rates). Thus, no one or two provisions will fill the revenue gap. In all likelihood, only a package at least as complex as TEFRA will do.

Any such package must balance competing economic objectives. Collecting more revenues can mean heavier burdens on the taxpayers who must struggle to bear them, along with stifled incentives for all. Thus, sparing low- and moderate-income taxpayers would seem to require making the individual income tax more progressive; such measures would maintain consumer demand as the economy climbs toward full employment. But if substantial revenues were drained from the people who do most of the saving in our economy in a way that also dampened their incentive to save, the investment needed for growth of output and productivity would not be forthcoming. So just as consumption and investment must be balanced over the course of the recovery, tax fairness and efficiency must be balanced in any revenue-raising legislation.

Strategies to Deal with It

Several revenue strategies could reduce the budget deficit, some to a larger extent than others. Each strategy has its own advantages and disadvantages, and it appears likely that several of the strategies must be pursued together to raise sufficient revenue.

Some approaches would build on existing taxes; examples are increases in individual income tax or excise tax rates. Other approaches would involve entirely new taxes, such as taxes on energy or on consumption in general. New taxes tend to involve greater uncertainty and costs of transition, including long start-up periods, but existing taxes have some well-known flaws. Choosing among these strategies ultimately requires balancing conflicting values.

The strategies discussed in this section include increasing the rates under the current individual income tax, either directly or by repealing indexing; eliminating income tax preferences, either selectively or almost completely to create a new broad-based income tax; broadening the base of the corporate tax; taxing consumption; taxing energy; and increasing existing excise taxes.

Increasing Tax Rates.   One strategy would be to run ERTA in reverse, taking back some of the revenue that ERTA lost. The most obvious target for a weary revenue hunter is surely ERTA's reductions of marginal tax rates under the individual income tax. The rate reductions were the largest single revenue item in ERTA, and TEFRA left them untouched. As an example of this strategy, the administration's 5 percent surtax (part of the contingency tax proposals), in effect a rate increase, was estimated by the Congressional Budget Office (CBO) to raise $20 billion per year by FY 1988. The revenue potential of this strategy is obviously substantial.

Nonetheless, the revenue hunter can approach this enticing target only with trepidation. Marginal rate reductions are an imposing adversary, not just because people viscerally favor them, but also on the merits. Between the tax cuts of 1964 and 1981, substantial inflation made the federal income tax more progressive, because taxable incomes of middle- and upper-income households were disproportionately pushed into higher tax brackets. Changes in the tax law returned almost all the resulting revenue increase to the taxpayers, but in ways (increased exemptions and zero bracket amounts, per capita tax credits) that gave disproportionate relief to low-income taxpayers. As a result, the income tax became still more progressive (see table 5). Thus, it can be argued that by 1981 the income tax had become *too* progressive by historical standards, and such complaints cannot be dismissed out of hand.[8]

Beyond these issues is the problem of implementation. ERTA broke a psychological barrier when it reduced the maximum tax rate on any form of income from 70 percent to 50 percent. With this reduction, the federal

---

8. In fact, the situation is even more complex. While the federal individual income tax was becoming more progressive, regressive taxes such as the payroll tax and state sales taxes were growing in their share of total revenues, leaving the progressivity of the overall tax system little changed. It is highly debatable whether the individual income tax should compensate for shifts in the progressivity of other taxes, including state and local taxes.

TABLE 5

AVERAGE AND MARGINAL INDIVIDUAL INCOME TAX RATES AT MULTIPLES OF
MEDIAN INCOME, SELECTED YEARS

Year	25 Percent of Median Income	50 Percent of Median Income	Median Income	Twice the Median Income	Five Times the Median Income	Ten Times the Median Income
			Average Rates			
1965	0	2.8	7.4	12.2	20.5	36.5
1978	−7.3	3.4	11.6	17.3	30.9	41.0
1981	−8.4	5.7	13.3	18.5	31.7	40.6
			Marginal Rates			
1965	0.0	14.0	17.0	22.0	39.0	55.0
1978	10.0	16.0	22.0	36.0	55.0	66.0
1981	12.5	18.0	24.0	43.0	59.0	68.0

SOURCE: Computed by author.
NOTE: Computed for families of four with typical standard or itemized deductions for the particular income level in the particular year. The median income is for tax-filing families: In 1965, that figure was $7,500; in 1978, $18,500; and in 1981, $23,700. The 50 percent maximum rate on income from labor is assumed not to apply. The 1981 tax rates do not include the influence of ERTA.

government moved from the role of senior partner to equal partner in many investments and enterprises. Should that step be reversed? While an increase of a small number of percentage points might be expected to have only modest effects from a strictly dispassionate viewpoint, it could have powerful symbolic connotations.

Further questions arise. Under pre-ERTA law, the maximum marginal tax rate on income from labor was limited to approximately 50 percent by the maximum tax provision of the Tax Reform Act of 1969.[9] If the top rate were increased from 50 percent to perhaps 52 or 55 percent (the administration's contingency tax would make it 52.5 percent), would we accept an increase in the tax rate on labor incomes? Or would we reintroduce the complicated tax forms that the maximum tax provision required to reduce the highest tax rate on labor income by just two or five percentage points? Thus, the apparently simple decision about the top tax rate is seen upon examination to be rather involved.

---

9. Emil M. Sunley, Jr., "The Maximum Tax on Earned Income," *National Tax Journal*, vol. 27, December 1974, pp. 543–52, explains how the marginal tax rate could be higher than 50 percent in some cases.

Suppose it is decided to raise marginal tax rates but to leave the highest rate at the landmark 50 percent level. Then a whole new set of problems arises, most of them related to perceptions of fairness. If the tax rates below the top bracket are increased to 50 percent or less, but the top rate remains at 50 percent, the amount of the tax increase in dollars reaches a plateau at the bottom of the highest tax bracket and does not further increase no matter how much income increases. This is precisely the problem that arose in, and drew considerable criticism to, the proposal to cap the July 1983 tax cut at $700.

Table 6 illustrates this problem, using the July 1983 tax cap as an example. Because tax rates below the top bracket are increased, the impact is first felt (though in very small dollar amounts) at comparatively modest income levels. The tax increase reaches a peak at what might be called the upper-middle income level, when the tax rate hits 50 percent. The tax increase in dollars then remains constant as income increases (because the 50 percent top rate does not increase), which means that, in percentage terms, the tax increase falls. Critics of such an increase in tax rates argue that the burden on middle- and upper-middle income taxpayers, in comparison with the small percentage increase for the highest-income taxpayers, is unfair.

A final issue also relates to fairness. A major complaint about the existing income tax is that some taxpayers can avoid paying tax, but a rate increase would hit only the people who already pay taxes. As Senator Robert Dole said in dismissing a 10 percent surtax as part of TEFRA, "Ten percent of nothing is nothing."

So recapturing the revenue cost of the ERTA tax rate cuts is not a simple matter. The magnitude of the incentive benefits of the rate cuts is debatable, but their existence is not. The symbolic 50 percent top bracket rate poses problems of complexity and perceived unfairness whether it is pierced or not. Increases in marginal tax rates should not be ruled out if the need for additional revenue is pressing, but policymakers should understand the problems associated with their choices.

Repealing Indexation.   Like increases in marginal tax rates, the repeal of indexing has a certain appeal as a revenue-raising step. It would raise no revenues until FY 1985, so there would be no fiscal drag on the recovery while it is still getting off the ground. However, the drag comes on strong in later years, with a likely revenue pickup of $65 billion in FY 1989. The repeal of indexation would spread the tax increase over all taxpayers, making the burden on any one fairly modest. The burden would nevertheless increase with income, up to a dollar ceiling. Repeal of indexing also would raise a substantial amount of revenue in a single policy step, making the political

TABLE 6

COMPARISON OF FEDERAL INDIVIDUAL INCOME TAX BURDENS UNDER 1984 LAW AND $700 CAP (RATE INCREASE) PROPOSAL

Income	Single Taxpayers				Joint Returns, Two Dependents			
	Present Law Tax	Proposed Tax	Change (Dollars)	Change (Percentage)	Present Law Tax	Proposed Tax	Change (Dollars)	Change (Percentage)
30,000	4,385	4,385	0	0	3,003	3,003	0	0
35,000	5,540	5,540	0	0	3,903	3,903	0	0
40,000	6,827	6,959	132	1.9	4,874	4,874	0	0
45,000	8,210	8,496	286	3.5	5,952	5,952	0	0
50,000	9,673	10,113	440	4.5	7,165	7,273	108	1.5
55,000	11,222	11,838	616	5.5	8,436	8,698	262	3.1
65,000	14,456	15,457	1,001	6.9	11,159	11,729	570	5.1
75,000	17,915	19,188	1,273	7.1	14,085	14,963	878	6.2
85,000	21,611	23,038	1,427	6.6	17,205	18,391	1,186	6.9
95,000	25,307	26,888	1,581	6.2	20,439	21,933	1,494	7.3
100,000	27,155	28,813	1,658	6.1	22,056	23,704	1,648	7.5
200,000	65,585	67,313	1,728	2.6	58,190	61,836	3,646	6.3
300,000	104,085	105,813	1,728	1.7	96,600	100,336	3,736	3.9
500,000	181,085	182,813	1,728	1.0	173,600	177,336	3,736	2.2
1,000,000	373,585	375,313	1,728	0.5	366,100	369,836	3,736	1.0

SOURCE: Joint Committee on Taxation.

NOTE: Assumes itemized deductions are 23 percent of adjusted gross income. Computed without reference to tax tables.

process somewhat more manageable. And an unindexed progressive income tax is a built-in stabilizer against too-rapid economic growth and inflation.

As with tax rate increases, however, the repeal of indexing has drawbacks. The perception that the government profits from inflation would be troublesome, as would increases in individual taxpayers' real tax burdens because of inflation. It can be argued that repeal of indexation is an underhanded way to increase revenues and expand the federal government. And indexing certainly could not be defended as a deficit solution over the long term; continuously increasing revenues through bracket creep could soon force compensating rate cuts. Without indexation, Congress has traditionally cut taxes periodically in response to inflation. In all likelihood such discretionary tax cuts would continue if indexing were repealed.

Another problem with the repeal of indexing is the possible perception of unfairness. Changes in tax liabilities at different income levels with and without indexation can be interpreted in several different ways. Under likely rates of inflation, repeal of indexation would increase low-income taxpayers' liabilities most when measured in percentage terms, although the increase would be very slight in dollar terms (see table 7). This result might suggest that repeal of indexation would be unfair. But in dollar terms repeal of indexing most increases upper-income taxpayers' liabilities, and in percentage terms, most reduces middle-income taxpayers' disposable income. Thus, who would

TABLE 7

THREE MEASURES OF THE TAX INCREASE FOR TYPICAL FOUR-PERSON FAMILIES IN
1985 DUE TO REPEAL OF INDEXATION

1983 Income (Dollars)	1985 Income (Dollars)	1985 Tax with Indexation (Dollars)	1985 Tax without Indexation (Dollars)	Tax Increase (Dollars)	Tax Increase (Percentage)	Decrease in After-Tax Income (Percentage)
5,000	5,496	0	0	0	0	0
10,000	10,993	365	410	45	12.3	0.4
15,000	16,489	1,079	1,117	38	3.5	0.2
20,000	21,986	1,748	1,800	52	3.0	0.3
30,000	32,979	3,404	3,513	109	3.3	0.4
50,000	54,965	8,148	8,427	279	3.4	0.6
100,000	109,930	24,751	25,267	516	2.1	0.6
500,000	549,648	191,765	192,715	950	0.5	0.3

SOURCE: Congressional Budget Office.
NOTE: Assumes all income is from wages and salaries earned by one spouse; deductions are
            the greater of the zero bracket amount or 23 percent of income; and income increases
            equal the rate of inflation. Earned income tax credit is omitted. Inflation projections
            are from the CBO economic projections.

be the primary victims of repeal of indexation is essentially a matter of interpretation. What is certain is that, confronted with the prospect, almost everybody would complain. Low-income taxpayers have suffered considerably from the absence of indexing since 1978; the personal exemption and zero bracket amounts have been substantially eroded. But future indexing is not a remedy for past bracket creep; it merely keeps the process from going further. A discretionary increase in the personal exemption and zero bracket amounts is the proper, belated, remedy for the inflation of the early 1980s.

So, like marginal tax rate increases, repeal of indexation has potential to reduce the deficit and has obvious real or perceived drawbacks as tax or distributional policy. As with just about every other option in this imperfect world, we must weigh the benefits against the costs and compare the alternatives. There are several options other than outright repeal of indexation; among them are postponement of the effective date of indexation, indexation for only part of inflation (such as indexation for inflation in excess of 2 percent or for one-half of actual inflation), or indexation of only the personal exemption and zero bracket amounts (to protect low-income taxpayers, but make others bear some of the costs of inflation).

Repealing Selected Individual Income Tax Preferences.   Another approach to increasing individual income tax revenues is to broaden the tax base, rather than increasing tax rates. TEFRA trimmed a small number of tax preferences in what came to be known as a "cats and dogs" approach. The stray animals caught by TEFRA were probably the slowest; although the next roundup will be more difficult, there are many more strays around. If only a small number of preferences are to be repealed, then each candidate can be considered on its own merits. In contrast, repealing most or all preferences would change the basic character of the income tax and raise an entirely different set of tax policy questions. That option will be discussed later.

The preferential income tax provisions discussed in this section include savings incentives, wage supplements, and miscellaneous individual provisions. Repeal of any of these preferences would have both a strong economic rationale and significant revenue implications. A longer list could be made under less stringent restrictions.[10] (Revenue effects are shown in table 8.)

The individual retirement account (IRA) provision included in ERTA has some definite weaknesses as a savings incentive. Because the maximum

---

10. For longer lists of options and more detailed discussion, see Congressional Budget Office *Reducing the Deficit: Spending and Revenue Options* (Washington, D.C.: Government Printing Office, 1983), and Joint Committee on Taxation, *Description of Possible Options to Increase Revenues* (Washington, D.C.: Government Printing Office, 1982).

TABLE 8

REVENUE EFFECTS OF TAX INCREASE OPTIONS,
FISCAL YEARS 1985–1988

	1985	1986	1987	1988	1989
	Billions of Dollars				
Reduce R&D credit to 10 percent	0.3	0.4	a	a	a
Repeal percentage depletion for oil and gas	0.6	1.4	1.2	1.3	1.3
Repeal expensing of intangible drilling costs	3.1	5.4	5.1	5.0	4.9
Repeal capital gains treatment of timber	0.3	0.7	0.8	0.8	0.8
Eliminate tax exemption for pollution control bonds	a	0.1	0.3	0.4	0.5
Limit nonbusiness, noninvestment interest deductions to $10,000	0.3	2.0	2.2	2.4	2.6
Lengthen the building depreciation period to 20 years	0.3	1.3	2.5	3.6	4.9
Tax accrued interest on life insurance reserves	2.1	5.7	6.2	6.8	7.5
Repeal the net interest exclusion	1.0	2.9	3.1	3.4	3.6
Eliminate tax exemption for small-issue industrial revenue bonds	0.1	0.6	0.9	1.0	1.1
Require full-basis adjustment for the investment tax credit	0.4	1.5	2.8	4.1	5.5
Tax employer-paid health insurance premiums over $80 per month ($200 for families)	1.8	3.5	4.7	6.1	7.8
Eliminate tax exemption for private hospital bonds	0.1	0.3	0.6	1.0	1.4
Eliminate deductibility of state and local sales taxes	0.8	5.6	6.3	7.2	8.1
Increase IRS audit coverage	0.8	1.7	3.0	4.7	6.7

SOURCE: Congressional Budget Office.
  NOTE: Assumes January 1, 1984, starting date for all changes.
  a. Less than $50 million.

tax-deductible contribution for each worker is limited to $2,000 under most circumstances, the IRA provides no marginal incentive, only a windfall, to taxpayers who would save more than $2,000 even without the subsidy. The value of the deduction is greatest for those who need it least—taxpayers with the most income and therefore the highest tax rates. Finally, the deduction can be claimed by taxpayers who do no new saving at all, but rather borrow money (or withdraw it from prior savings) and deposit it in an IRA. The net interest exclusion to take effect in 1985 under ERTA avoids this last tax-gaming flaw, but has all the other failings of the IRA. Repealing the net interest exclusion and the broadened IRA would save about $6 billion per year.

Among other savings incentives, the exclusion from tax of interest earned on life insurance reserves provides a questionable subsidy to this form of saving relative to others. Repeal of this exclusion would raise revenues by more than $5 billion per year. Perhaps even more suspect, the deductibility of interest on consumer loans (credit card balances, auto loans, etc.) acts as a negative savings incentive: it encourages and subsidizes borrowing. Repeal of these deductions would make saving more attractive and encourage capital formation, while raising significant amounts of revenue. Even limiting annual interest deductions (including the deduction on mortgages) to $10,000 plus the amount of investment income would raise about $2 billion per year.

Employees may receive income in several noncash forms free of tax. Employer contributions toward life and health insurance premiums and pensions are the largest of these wage supplements, but others include legal insurance, employer discounts, and subsidized meals and parking. This tax exemption encourages compensation in these forms, which narrows the tax base and forces tax rates up. This exemption also favors taxpayers who receive income in these forms over those who do not. The exemption for health insurance premiums encourages the purchase of first-dollar coverage that may add to inflation in health care costs in the long run. Taxing only employer-paid health insurance premiums over $200 per month ($80 per month for single people) would raise almost $8 billion by FY 1989.

Among the remaining major tax preferences, the itemized deduction for state and local sales taxes has questionable merit. It is a highly inaccurate compensation for such expenses, which are generally small and uniformly spread across most of the population in any event. Eliminating this deduction would increase revenues by almost $5 billion per year. (See the paper by Ladd in this volume for further discussion of this option.)

Repealing or restricting preferential tax provisions like these would require some taxpayers to make painful adjustments. But raising any taxes would cause some pain, and targeting on tax preferences has the virtue in placing the burden where there was once an extraordinary benefit. Another targeted step to effectively broaden the tax base would be to increase IRS audit coverage to see that taxable incomes are accurately reported and that taxes due are actually paid. Almost $7 billion per year could be raised by 1989, net of additional outlays, if the number of returns audited were increased from 1.3 percent to 1.9 percent of the total.

Repealing Business Tax Preferences. Another strategy would be to broaden the base of the corporate income tax. Such a step would be controversial because increases in corporate taxes would tend to reduce investment. But again, raising taxes requires imposing burdens somewhere in the economy, and the business sector was treated relatively generously in ERTA, even after TEFRA. Further, such changes could make the taxation of business income more neutral and improve the allocation of investment. This strategy could include retrenchments of cost recovery under the Accelerated Cost Recovery System (ACRS) and repeal of various tax preferences for corporations.

TEFRA has already reclaimed some of the revenues lost through ACRS in ERTA, but there may be a case for still further paring back the ACRS tax cuts. The basis adjustment for one-half of the investment tax credit under TEFRA is unjustifiable on tax policy grounds. A basis adjustment would eliminate the double benefit of the investment tax credit and cost recovery deductions and would thus take some of the shine off many tax shelter schemes that are based partly on the investment tax credit.

Tax shelter concerns also arise in the depreciation of buildings. Some economists believe that the nation is overinvesting in residential and office buildings; as evidence they cite the boom in tax shelter investments that are made through real estate. The rapid growth of sale-leaseback arrangements involving governments and other nonprofit entities is cited as evidence of possible excessive depreciation of buildings (and some equipment). Building depreciation could be trimmed either by increasing the assumed useful life of fifteen years, or by slowing the 175 percent declining-balance rate of cost recovery, or by a combination of these. Legislation has already been introduced to cut back on sale-leasebacks by nontaxable institutions through targeted denial of ACRS benefits.

A final potential area for increasing tax revenues is ACRS itself. As was noted earlier, ACRS tends to favor some investments over others, distorting economic decisions and reducing output. It is possible to improve the system so that it distorts less and is simpler. At the cost of somewhat reduced investment incentives, revised depreciation rules could also raise revenue. (Of course, if investment were allocated more efficiently, the economy need not be worse off.) Legislation has been introduced to streamline ACRS and make it more efficient; it would raise no revenue, however.[11]

Simple tightening of the ITC and cost recovery provisions of ERTA would obviously reduce incentives for investment to some degree. In a period when capital formation is badly needed, this consideration should not be ignored. Yet it must be weighed against the need for revenue and the efficiency

---

11. S. 1758, the Accounting Cost Recovery Simplification Act of 1983, introduced by Senator Lloyd Bentsen.

gains that could be reaped through greater tax neutrality and reduced tax sheltering. Carefully planned corporate tax increases as part of a deficit reduction program could leave both the tax system and the economy better off.

Turning to other corporate tax preferences, ERTA's tax credit for increases in qualifying research and development (R&D) expenditures (effective only through calendar 1985) is complex and arguably inefficient. "Qualifying expenditures" can be difficult to interpret, and restricting the credit to increases in research and development expenditures eliminates the incentive to continue programs in progress. The credit also may be used as a tax shelter. Despite the benefits of additional R&D expenditures, it may be better to allow firms to undertake projects on their own initiative, rather than attempting to influence their judgments through tax incentives.

The selective tax benefits for oil production—the expensing of intangible drilling costs and the use of percentage depletion—were originally intended to maintain a sound domestic industry in the face of cheap imports. That situation no longer obtains. Moreover, these provisions can distort the operation of the market by attracting capital from other activities into petroleum production, by changing the way individual firms explore for and extract oil, and (because percentage depletion is now available only to independent firms) by altering the allocation of resources among firms. Finally, these provisions are used in arranging tax shelters. Repeal of these tax preferences would surely be controversial at a time when the domestic industry is in some distress. However, the problems of the oil industry may be caused not by the tax system, but rather by fluctuations in the world market, conservation, and the slow domestic and world economy. Another consideration is that ACRS treatment of comparable investments is almost as generous as the expensing of intangible drilling costs.

Income from cutting timber is now treated as long-term capital gain and thus receives the 60 percent capital gains exclusion, even though timber is produced for sale in the same way as any other product. Repeal of capital gains treatment of timber would increase tax revenues and reduce distortions in the allocation of capital. Administrative complexities would result, however, and tightening of this provision would hit the timber industry after it had suffered disproportionately through the recent recession. Again, in assessing this decline, policymakers must weigh carefully the role of tax factors as opposed to market forces.

Use of tax-exempt state and municipal securities to finance private-purpose activities has been growing rapidly. (Examples include small-issue industrial revenue bonds, private hospital bonds, and mortgage subsidy bonds. See the accompanying paper by Ladd for further discussion.) Such financing can crowd the market for state and local securities and convey competitive advantage to private users. Cutback or repeal of these financing opportunities would help public-purpose state and local financing and reduce the deficit. (Mortgage subsidy bonds were scheduled to expire December 31, 1983, although legislation has been introduced to renew them.)

Revising the Income Tax. An alternative strategy is to repeal most or all individual and corporate tax preferences, rather than a selected few. The tax base would be so broadened that tax rates could be reduced in partial compensation, still leaving an increase in revenue.

Repealing income tax preferences is seldom easy, as has been noted, so the wholesale broadening of the income tax base might be judged extremely difficult. In this case, however, the whole could be less than the sum of its parts. Repealing one tax preference appears to single out its beneficiaries, and the gains for other taxpayers and the budget deficit tend to be relatively small. A wholesale approach that touches most or all preferences could appear fairer, and everyone can benefit at least to some degree from a general rate reduction.

Proposals for a "flat-rate tax" gained great prominence in 1982, and many bills were submitted in Congress. Although some bills were quite general, those that proposed a single rate structure were criticized as sharply redistributing the tax burden from upper-income taxpayers to middle- and lower-income taxpayers. Perhaps for this reason, there are fewer genuine flat-rate proposals in the current Congress. With a broadened base and graduated rates, however, such redistribution can be avoided, and some proposals have followed that line. Maximum tax rates of 28 to 30 percent, in contrast to the current law's 50 percent, have been proposed to Congress.[12] Substantially reducing marginal income tax rates would increase capital formation and the incentive to work. And if the tax base had fewer (or no) preferential provisions, the allocation of resources would be more efficient. If the tax stayed within the conceptual confines of the current law, the transition could be much simpler than any transition to a new and different tax.

The individual and corporate income taxes together yield more than one-half of total federal revenues. These taxes are thus not only likely sources of

---

12. A broad-based income tax that merely equaled the revenue yield of the current law in one year might raise more revenue later. In recent years, untaxed noncash employer compensation (described earlier) has grown faster than the economy as a whole, moving an increasing share of national income outside the tax base. Taxing such compensation, and any other growing tax-preferred income source or deduction, would thus increase the expected rate of growth of the tax base, apart from raising the level of revenue. If noncash forms of compensation are made taxable, they surely will become less attractive to employees, who may ask to be compensated in cash instead. Even with this change in behavior, however, the currently untaxed noncash compensation will be moved into the tax base, raising its growth rate over time.

further revenues but also essential elements in the current revenue system. By all accounts, however, the public at large highly distrusts the income tax; because these taxes rely heavily on voluntary taxpayer compliance, some remedy is essential. The perceived unfairness, complexity, economic distortions, and inefficiency of the current tax system can all be traced to the array of special tax preferences that narrow the tax base and force the imposition of high marginal rates. Eliminating or cutting back tax preferences is always painful, because individual taxpayers are reluctant to yield the particular preferences from which they benefit, and there is no excess revenue for a general tax cut to ease the transition. But barring an end run around the income taxes through an entirely new tax, some restructuring may be unavoidable.

Taxing Consumption. Another strategy to narrow the deficit would be a broad-based tax on consumption, either in place of or in addition to the income tax. There are basically two ways to tax consumption: through a value-added tax or a personal expenditure tax. The value-added tax (VAT) is intended to shift the burden of taxation away from income and toward consumption. A VAT would be the economic (though not the administrative) equivalent of a national sales tax and thus would fall directly on consumers.

A VAT could be added to our current tax system to yield whatever additional revenues were desired to narrow the deficit, thereby shifting the relative balance of federal taxation away from income and toward consumption. A VAT with a higher rate could substitute in full or in part for the existing income tax, increasing the shift toward taxing consumption.

The revenue potential of the VAT is considerable. The tax base theoretically would be all of personal consumption; at 1983 levels of roughly $2.2 trillion, a 10 percent VAT would raise $220 billion, or more than enough to wipe out the deficit. In practice, however, some classes of expenditures almost certainly would be excluded from the tax, for administrative or hardship reasons (although such exclusions would make the tax less neutral). Food, housing, and medical care taken together constituted about $900 billion of total consumption in 1983; so the revenue of a 10 percent VAT excluding those items would be cut to $130 billion. Of course, draining that much purchasing power from the economy would significantly alter the federal government's fiscal policy stance and would require some compensating adjustments. A VAT could completely replace the corporate income tax, which will yield about $60 billion in FY 1984, or it could significantly reduce the individual income tax, which will yield about $300 billion in FY 1984.

The objective of such a shift of taxation from income to consumption is to increase capital formation. If saving is tax deductible, it will tend to increase, and consumption will tend to fall. More output will thus be channeled into investment; the capital stock will grow and output will increase in the future. The degree to which capital formation increases, of course, depends on the responsiveness of savings and consumption to these tax rates. The evidence suggests that this responsiveness is small.[13] Furthermore, there is the problem of stimulating more investment when demand is reduced for the consumer goods that this investment would produce.

The VAT is sometimes criticized for its treatment of taxpayers at different income levels. The VAT allows no exemption or deduction. Each taxpayer, regardless of means, pays tax on the first dollar of consumption of taxable goods. As a result, the tax would bear more heavily on people with the lowest incomes than does the income tax, which exempts the poorest outright and has rates that are graduated by income. The VAT would also be regressive over the entire income range, because low-income taxpayers spend a larger fraction of their incomes than do taxpayers with higher incomes. Low-income households could be provided relief through a refundable income tax credit, but such a mechanism would be extremely complex. To claim the credit, many persons now exempt from filing returns would have to file, adding a heavy administrative burden on the IRS.

A VAT as an additional tax would add substantially to the workloads of business and the federal government. Retail firms in states with sales taxes are prepared generally to deal with the kind of accounting a VAT requires, so there is a strong argument on administrative grounds for a national sales tax rather than a VAT. Even so, where state sales tax bases differ from the federal, confusion would result. For the federal government, either tax would be an entirely new and heavy burden. The United Kingdom has found that the collection cost per dollar of revenue for its VAT is as great as for its income taxes.[14]

Similarly, exempting certain kinds of products to reduce the burden of the tax has administrative consequences. Presumably, if food were to be exempted from the VAT, food producers should be exempted from the VAT on the food containers they purchase. But the manufacturer of the food containers might also make containers for nonfood products. That manufacturer would have to keep separate records for food and nonfood container sales,

---

13. Assuming a 30 percent increase in the real after-tax rate of return because of the changeover to consumption taxation, and further assuming a 0.2 percent elasticity of savings to that rate of return, personal savings would increase by 6 percent. At 1982 levels, the savings would mean an increase from $125.4 billion to $132.9 billion. However, that $7.5 billion increase would add only 1.4 percent to the actual $521.6 billion of total private savings.

14. Richard Hemming and John A. Kay, "The United Kingdom," in Henry J. Aaron, ed., *The Value-Added Tax: Lessons from Europe* (Washington, D.C.: The Brookings Institution, 1981), pp. 75–89.

and the IRS would have to verify them. Similarly, we might not want the American Cancer Society to pay VAT on a typewriter, but we would want to collect from American Motors. Some nations with VATs have gone so far as to charge different rates on different kinds of commodities. For all the reasons suggested here, such differentiation adds tremendous complexity.

Both the administrative load and the perceived fairness of a VAT would depend heavily on the features of the tax. The reporting and collection burdens of any VAT are the same regardless of the tax rate charged, so it might not be worth imposing at any rate less than about 10 percent. The higher the rate, however, the greater the burden on low-income taxpayers, and the greater the likelihood that a complex and cumbersome refund scheme will be deemed necessary. In addition, imposition of a VAT or national sales tax would cause a one-time increase in inflation, and the higher the tax rate, the greater the inflation.

In the final analysis, however, the key points about the VAT are what it would do to the economy and who would have to pay. Collecting additional revenue through a VAT instead of a tax on income might result in greater capital formation, but the extent of the beneficial effect is uncertain, and the best evidence suggests that it would be quite small. The VAT would least affect people with the greatest ability to pay, and would most heavily affect people who need to spend all their modest incomes to maintain an adequate standard of living. Compensating for the effects on low-income taxpayers might require complicated programs. The weighing of benefits and costs depends on each person's perception of the need for capital formation and concern about the distributional consequences.

Unlike the value-added tax, which is collected by sellers on each transaction, the expenditure tax (or consumption tax) is collected from individuals or families on an annual basis, like our current income tax. But like the VAT, the expenditure tax moves the basis of taxation from income to consumption.

Most simply put, the expenditure tax is like our income tax, but with two changes: Any income that is saved would be tax deductible, whereas any money that is borrowed, or any prior saving that is spent, would be taxable. In practice, taxpayers would report their income on annual tax returns, just as they do now, but they would add to income all money borrowed and all withdrawals from savings, and would deduct from income all deposits in savings. The result, called taxable receipts, would be the basis for computing the expenditure tax liability. The expenditure tax so computed would replace the current income tax, in whole or in part.

The main reason for choosing an expenditure tax rather than a VAT would be the ability to control the distribution of the burden. An expenditure tax could include substantial personal exemptions or some form of standard deduction to make low-income persons nontaxable. To increase the liability more rapidly as expenditure increased, the expenditure tax could have graduated rates.

The objective of the expenditure tax, like the VAT, is greater capital formation. With savings tax deductible, taxpayers might save more and consume less. That action would lead to more investment and a larger capital stock. As with the VAT, the size of the beneficial effect is unknown but likely to be small. The definition of savings for tax purposes is likely to be contentious. Speculative purchases of precious metals and collectibles could be defined as savings but would not advance capital formation. However, the expenditure tax would surely be a more efficient savings incentive than provisions like the IRA under our current income tax. Because savings would be deductible without limit, taxpayers would always have a marginal incentive to save. Furthermore, because borrowed money would be taxable, the expenditure tax could not be gamed by the borrowing-and-lending schemes that are used on the IRA provision.

The impact of an expenditure tax on different taxpayers is hard to assess. Theoretically, the tax rate schedule could be chosen to duplicate the current distribution of taxes by income group, but the data needed to determine such a tax rate schedule do not exist. Because the tax base of the expenditure tax is smaller than that of the income tax by the amount of savings, the expenditure tax rates must be higher. (Some people assert that the many "loopholes" that exist under the income tax would be repealed under an expenditure tax, but there is no way to know if that would occur.) What evidence there is suggests that people with higher incomes save greater proportions of their income, so the tax rate schedule will have to be steeper as well. Those higher rates will discourage extra work for purposes of consumption.

Perhaps the greatest distinction among taxpayers would be based on wealth. People who had already accumulated wealth could reinvest and accumulate the proceeds without tax. The taxation of gifts and bequests therefore would be crucial; unless such transfers were treated as taxable receipts to the donor or the recipient, wealth could pass from generation to generation while bearing little tax. Some economists have argued for a strengthened gift and estate tax or even a periodic wealth tax to supplement an expenditure tax. Others have argued that either practice would be inconsistent with the purpose of greater capital formation.

Another question about the burden of the expenditure tax relates to the timing of payment. People tend to borrow in the early years of forming a household, save over the more prosperous middle age, and spend their savings in retirement. The expenditure tax would increase the tax burden in youth, in old age, and in years of below-average income due to illness or unemployment, while it would decrease the tax burden in the peak earning years.

Patterns of wealth-holding and timing raise an important administrative question as well. To simplify, if people work today and retire on their earnings tomorrow, they pay tax today under the income tax but tomorrow under the expenditure tax. It follows that people who save in taxable forms under an income tax and retire at the time of transition to an expenditure tax could be badly hurt by double taxation; they would pay income tax when their income was earned and expenditure tax when it was spent. These people would need some form of basis adjustment so that their consumption out of fully taxed income would not be taxed again. At the same time, people who retire on untaxed income (such as withdrawals from IRAs, benefits from qualified pensions, and unrealized capital gains) should be taxed on their expenditures. Distinguishing between taxed and untaxed wealth at the time of transition to an expenditure tax could be a major administrative problem. To prevent concealment of wealth, balance sheets would be needed at the time of transition; this could be a major burden for the taxpayer and the IRS. In addition, a large-scale education program would be needed to acquaint taxpayers with the concepts involved in the expenditure tax.

In sum, the case for the expenditure tax is much like the case for the VAT. Capital formation might increase under the expenditure tax, but the available evidence cannot suggest the size of that effect with any certainty. The effects on taxpayers at different levels of income or consumption could raise perceptions of unfairness, and the changeover to an entirely new tax system cannot be easy. And so, again, the conclusion depends on the individual observer's subjective weighing of the pluses and minuses of the alternatives.

Increasing Existing Excise Taxes. Yet another deficit-narrowing strategy would be to increase existing federal excise taxes. Although excise taxes are currently a small part of the federal revenue system and could not reduce the deficit sufficiently without other action, these taxes could play a significant role in a larger package.

TEFRA increased several excise taxes, but it passed over the excise taxes on alcoholic beverages. These taxes have not been increased since the early 1950s, and because they are defined as a certain number of dollars for a particular volume of beverage, they have been substantially eroded by inflation. The federal excise tax is only about 3.4 cents on a 750-ml bottle of wine, 12 cents on a six-pack of beer, and $1.68 on a fifth of 80-proof liquor. Obviously there is room for an increase. Furthermore, alcohol consumption imposes many public costs and a higher excise tax may be seen to compensate for those costs. There might be less resistance on fairness grounds to increased excise taxes on alcoholic beverages than to a more general consumption tax. However, the beverage and restaurant industries opposed increases in these taxes during deliberations on TEFRA, and their continued opposition can be expected. Doubling excise taxes on alcohol would raise about $4 billion per year.

TEFRA temporarily increased excise taxes on cigarettes and airline and telephone services. The telephone tax was increased from 1 to 3 percent, and its scheduled expiration was postponed from the end of 1984 to the end of 1985. The cigarette tax, which had not been increased since 1951, was doubled through October 1, 1985. Both tax increases raised revenue, but the cigarette tax increase was also motivated by the public costs of smoking. The air passenger ticket tax was increased from 5 to 8 percent; the air freight waybill tax was reimposed (having expired in 1980) at 5 percent; and the international departure ticket tax was reimposed (also having expired in 1980) at $3. These increases are to expire in 1985 and 1987 (air transportation only). Extending these tax increases would narrow the deficits projected for fiscal 1985 and beyond by more than $4 billion per year.

Imposing an Excise Tax on Energy.   A final strategy for reducing the deficit would be to impose an excise tax on energy. Among the best news for the economy in recent years has been the softening of oil prices. To some people, taxing energy in this period of relief has all the appeal of shooting oneself in the foot. To others, however, the weakness of oil prices today simply portends renewed tightness tomorrow, and the growing complacency, as evidenced in the greater demand for large automobiles, is extremely disturbing.

People who believe that oil prices will rebound find some appeal in an oil import fee. A fee of $4 per barrel would leave prices below their recent peak. In fact, given the softness of the market, foreign producers might have to cut their prices and thereby absorb part of the tax. Such a fee would encourage domestic conservation and the production of coal and gas as well as oil. If the international market should later tighten, the fee could be reduced or eliminated to cushion the blow to consumers and the economy.

The oil import fee does have some drawbacks: (1) Beyond raising energy prices and thereby boosting inflation, it would initially burden disproportionately the areas of the country (primarily the Northeast) that burn imported oil. In the longer run, however, energy prices should equalize around the country. (2) A more general energy tax, on either all oil or all energy, could have a more uniform burden initially; but a general oil tax would not have the same incentive effect on domestic production as the oil import fee, and the general energy tax would not even encourage production of domestic coal and natural gas. Furthermore, the oil import fee would be simpler to administer. The revenue gain from an oil import fee would be between $1.5 billion and $2.0 billion per year for every $1 per barrel.

Sorting Out the Options

As the editors of this volume have indicated, additional revenues of $50 billion to $100 billion per year by 1988 seem essential to hold the deficit to manageable proportions. The foregoing discussion suggests that only a substantial undoing of ERTA will hit the upper end of that range in one easy stroke, and that option would be costly in political and economic policy terms.

Some smaller steps can probably be taken first. The excise taxes were called on early for contributions in TEFRA, and they will probably be called on again. Extension of the cigarette, telephone, and air travel taxes imposes no new pain, and so is a live option. The alcohol taxes escaped in TEFRA but might be caught in a more careful policy search this time. Then, despite the pain, some energy tax could emerge; the political costs of dependence on foreign oil could impel action. Despite the interest and dividend withholding debacle, further steps on compliance could be implemented. Together these steps would raise between $20 billion and $25 billion per year by 1988.

At this point, distinct alternative pathways begin to emerge. The simplest way to complete a deficit reduction package would be to raise tax rates by a small amount. Either a belated rollback of the third year of the ERTA tax cuts or a repeal of indexation would raise about $40 billion in 1988, and the president's proposed 5 percent surtax (part of the contingency tax package in the FY 1984 budget) would yield about $20 billion. Because Congress has already rejected a $700 cap on the third-year tax cut worth less than $10 billion, action on this front would require a change of heart. On the merits, a tax rate increase is not the best solution, but inaction may prove to be worse.

A second path involves a limited closing of loopholes, à la TEFRA. The options described in this paper show that closing more loopholes causes more pain, but the perceived unfairness and economic distortions associated with tax preferences also cause problems. At current tax rates, the options described here could raise more than $30 billion. Fiscal policy and economic efficiency would benefit, but the burden of narrowing the deficit would rest heavily on the taxpayers whose preferences were chosen for the sacrificial altar.

A third path, more radical than the first two, is the wholesale repeal of income tax preferences, coupled with a lower rate schedule as partial compensation. Under this option everyone's ox is gored and everyone gets the benefit, either psychological or financial, of sharply reduced marginal tax rates. (As already noted, a 30 percent maximum rate with deficit reduction is feasible.) Perceived fairness and economic efficiency could substantially improve; however, it would be difficult for policymakers to reach a collective decision to forgo the many tax preferences now in the law, and for the users of those preferences (potentially including the homeowner deductions) to endure a possibly painful transition.

A fourth option is the value-added tax or a national sales tax to supplement the excise taxes discussed earlier. This approach might be characterized as more adventurous than the more broadly based income tax because it requires the establishment of an entirely new tax (even though the sales tax has been a fixture at the state level for many years). Especially if the national sales tax is chosen, this approach can boast relative simplicity for individual tax-payers, but it would add substantially to the workloads of businesses and the federal government. The one-time inflationary shock upon enactment would be a serious cost. Another disadvantage would be the burden on taxpayers with modest incomes; for political reasons, a complicated refund mechanism might be necessary.

The final option would be a personal consumption tax to back up the excise taxes. This option is clearly the farthest from the terra firma of our current tax system, involving as it does an entirely new tax in use nowhere else in the world. The personal consumption tax has distinct theoretical advantages, but the uncertainty about its practical operation and the certainty of transition problems make it a questionable choice.

Beyond a rerun of the short list of cats and dogs from TEFRA, the simplest and probably least controversial revenue-raising strategy would be increases in the income tax rates, or a cutback or repeal of indexation. Compared with no action at all such an approach might be welcome for fiscal policy, but from the tax policy perspective it would be a disappointment. A better, more politically ambitious, approach would be a restaging of TEFRA, with a new cast of preferential tax provisions cleared from the tax code. Better still would be a complete restructuring of the income tax law, reducing distortions and perhaps even reducing marginal tax rates. This course would answer long-term and widely held concerns about the fairness and complexity of the tax code. Clearly, however, under the pressures of time and politics that the deficit dilemma imposes, restructuring the law would be a giant step indeed.

COMMENTS

James M. Verdier

Joseph Minarik's paper is a thorough, balanced summary of how the United States finds itself some $100 billion to $200 billion short of the revenue needed to meet current spending commitments. Assuming that about half the action needed to reduce currently projected deficits will come on the spending side, Minarik's paper sets out a number of options for raising revenues by about $50 billion to $100 billion a year in the mid- to late-1980s.

The Analyst's Dilemma

In preparing options of this sort, the analyst always faces a dilemma. The community of academic, think-tank, and government tax experts always has a wider range of options on its collective plate than politicians have on theirs. Partly the matter is one of timing: politicians generally have little interest in issues that are unlikely to make it onto the government's agenda within a year or two. In addition, politicians tend to take political and administrative obstacles to change more seriously than outside experts do. The analyst preparing a list of options for politicians must therefore decide how much of the politician's point of view to adopt. How long a perspective should the analyst take, and how seriously should political and institutional obstacles to change be taken?

There is no simple answer. At a minimum, the analyst should learn enough about the politician's perspective to realize that these problems exist. With that grounding in reality, the analyst can then be a bit more venturesome than the politician. An option that politicians have ruled out in the past because of political opposition or difficulties of implementation may take on new life because of changed economic, political, or administrative conditions. The sharp cutback of the oil depletion allowance enacted in 1975 after decades

243

of futile assaults is one example; withholding on interest and dividends was almost another one.

Applying the politician's perspective to specific options is very much an art, one at which politicians are generally much better than analysts. When laying out options, therefore, analysts should err on the side of inclusiveness, but not by so much that their credibility is impaired.

The Need for Greater Stability

As a way of bringing to bear some of that politician's perspective, we might consider adding one more criterion to the usual tax policy standards of efficiency, simplicity, and fairness: stability.

Since 1969, Congress has passed a major tax bill about every two years. Hence the tax code is continually in flux, the Internal Revenue Service is almost hopelessly behind in getting out interpretive regulations, taxpayers and their advisers are unable to tell from one year to the next what they can and cannot do, and politicians are continually plagued by interest groups and constituents who want their taxes lowered and by tax and budget experts who want taxes increased. Some respite from this continual jerking around of the tax system and those it affects would, I suspect, be welcome in many quarters.

Before that respite can come, however, there is still that matter of $100- to $200-billion-a-year deficits. Politicians must go at least once more into the revenue breach. If stability is an important criterion, however, they should make an effort to do it right this time. By "doing it right" I mean putting together a revenue package that will put the tax system on a stable long-term path, one that will produce enough revenues to finance spending commitments without requiring the president and Congress to continually come back for more.

Preparing for a 1985 Tax Package

What, then, does this imply about the timing of action on the budget, and about the options Minarik's paper gives us?

With respect to timing, I reluctantly conclude that it means no serious action on taxes until after the 1984 election. Some "quick fix" solutions may be possible before then—scaling back the scheduled 1985 indexing of the individual income tax, for example, or a large tax on energy—but nothing that people are likely to be satisfied with for the longer term.

The reason for this likely delay is twofold. In terms of politics, it is hard to see a consensus forming in the next year that would produce any stable agreement on a long-term tax increase. President Reagan opposes major tax increases in principle and the Democrats hope to get a president and a tax policy more to their liking after the 1984 election, so no one has any incentive to put lasting tax increases in place.

In terms of the substance of tax policy, the range of options discussed in Minarik's paper suggests that tax policy experts are also some distance from a stable consensus. Should individuals be taxed on the basis of income or consumption? Should there be a corporate income tax at all? Should we institute a value-added tax? If so, should it be an additional tax, or a substitute for some existing tax? Should we have an energy tax, and if so, what should it look like? Should we view it as a permanent revenue raiser, or as just a temporary corrective for imperfections in energy markets?

Evaluating Major Revenue Options

I suspect that differences on substance among tax policy experts might well narrow, and our advice to politicians be made much more useful, if we took seriously the criterion of stability. If I am right about the timing of tax action, there is likely to be a window of opportunity in 1985 for major tax action. What kind of options can we suggest for 1985 that would raise $50 billion to $100 billion a year, and not require continual tinkering thereafter? Applying the standard of stability to Minarik's list of revenue-raising options suggests, to me at least, the following tentative conclusions:

First, we should put aside any full-blown consumption tax for the foreseeable future. The charm and beauty such a tax has for economists are largely lost on politicians and their constituents, and the transition problems involved in implementing it would require at least a decade of complex adjustments and readjustments.

Second, value-added taxes should be put aside because of the difficulties in implementing a new tax from scratch, and because contests over exemptions would consume the lives of tax writers and administrators for years to come.

Third, new taxes on energy represent only a short-term expedient to correct imbalances in energy supply and demand that are best left to the marketplace over the longer term. These taxes should not be viewed as a long-term source of revenue. In addition, wrangling over the structure of the taxes, and thus over which sections of the country and which industries should bear the burden, could bog politicians down for months and years. If a bill should actually be enacted, fights over interpretation and administration could occupy courts and administrators for still more years.

Fourth, small-scale tinkering and base-broadening of the type seen in the Tax Equity and Fiscal Responsibility Act of 1982 are not likely to do the trick. It is like the pudding Winston Churchill complained of: it has no theme. Something more than selective "ad hocery" is needed.

In political terms, the theme should be approximate equality of sacrifice. There should be a long list of options that make as many people mad as possible, just like the list the staff of the National Commission on Social Security Reform put together in late 1982. With that kind of list, and with a given revenue goal, skillful politicians can put together a package that spreads the burden evenly.

Applying the Criterion of Stability

In putting together the initial "big list" from which politicians can choose, tax experts who take seriously the criterion of stability should focus on two major types of revenue raisers:

First, provisions that will deal with major sources of disequilibrium in the current income tax. This disequilibrium may be due to large current or prospective revenue losses, serious equity or efficiency distortions, or both. Examples include the exemption from tax of fringe benefits (including those for pensions and health), large and uneven incentives for business capital investment, the growing use of private-purpose tax-exempt bonds, the deductibility of interest when investment income is taxed lightly or not at all, the uneven effect of inflation on the measurement of income, and the erosion of taxpayer compliance. Since these are problems the president and Congress will have to deal with in any event during the 1980s, the criterion of stability suggests they be dealt with as part of any large package that may emerge in 1985.

Second, provisions on which there is general agreement among tax economists of both the income and consumption tax persuasions. There is a good deal of overlap with the first category here. Most tax experts, I expect, would agree with greater taxation of fringe benefits, limits on the deductibility of consumer interest and private-purpose tax-exempt bonds, and improved compliance measures. Other areas where economists are likely to agree were suggested at a conference in May 1983, by Henry Aaron: limits on the deductibility of state and local taxes, repeal of charitable deductions for nonitemizers, limits on the deductibility of business entertainment deductions, and inclusion of more transfer payments in the tax base.

Beyond these revenue-increasing options, the criterion of stability also suggests that indexing of the individual income tax be preserved in some form. Without indexing, major tax legislation is continually forced onto the congressional agenda as inflation pushes up tax burdens and builds up pressure for tax "cuts." The experience of the last decade suggests, at least to me, that Congress finds it harder to adhere to good tax principles when it is cutting taxes than when it is raising them. The difference shows up most strikingly in the case of special interest "base narrowing" provisions. People can think up all sorts of reasons to enact tax cuts of this kind—some good and some not so good—but there are hardly any reasons other than good tax policy for eliminating them. Keeping indexation in place would minimize the opportunities for special interest tax cuts and tax expenditures, and keep the pressure on for the kind of base broadening that generally leads to greater equity and efficiency in the tax system.

Politicians and their constituents will probably like few of the revenue-raising proposals required by the approach I am suggesting, but that is part of my point. The tax experts' "big list" should have something that hurts everyone. The politicians' "short list" will then look good by comparison.

COMMENTS

Richard A. Musgrave

Joseph Minarik has offered a fine survey of past events and the current tax situation to which they have led, but he was careful to withhold judgment on what has been done and what to do about it. This is regrettable since, as we know, he has distinctive and constructive views to offer. I shall compensate and give a rather more positive set of comments.

I begin with a few remarks on the tax policy of recent years, as summarized at the beginning of Minarik's paper. First, with regard to the macro aspects, if we take the Fed's tight money stance as given, the tax cut of 1981 was surely a fortunate event. While proposed for the wrong reasons (substantial supply-side effects could not possibly have materialized in the short run, and they did not), the cuts expanded consumer demand in textbook (Keynesian) fashion and thus prevented an even deeper downturn. It is unfair, however, to take monetary policy as fixed. With a smaller tax cut and a tighter fiscal position, money would have been easier. The net restriction might have been the same, with its dramatic gain in checking inflation and its heavy cost in creating unemployment. But the changed fiscal monetary mix would have left the economy in a better position for recovery; and it would have avoided the future dilemma that has been created by enshrining the deep tax cuts as a permanent device. The administration's purpose, I take it, was to install permanent tax reduction as a lever to force future expenditure cuts, thus serving its long-term objective of reducing the size of the public sector. Whatever the merits of that objective, it is evident that the desired symmetry in expenditure and tax cut has not materialized. Instead, the budget has been left with the prospect of an unsustainable deficit, a problem not only for the future but also a detriment to current recovery.

Turning to structural changes, it has been noted many times that the income tax cut of 1981 was highly favorable to taxpayers in the upper-income brackets. While the tax cut more than offset previous bracket creep for high-income taxpayers, failure to raise the zero bracket amount and to inflation-adjust the earned income credit deprived people with low incomes of a similar benefit. Some structural improvements were made, such as the implementation of the second-earner credit and the tightening of the minimum tax, but other provisions added to the list of tax preferences. The one major improvement, as I see it, was the indexing of the income tax, to begin in 1985. This change will be timed inconveniently, as a matter of macro policy, and will require further increases in rates; but it is nevertheless a basic improvement. When policy requires an increase in the tax-to-GNP ratio, this should be implemented by explicit legislation, not by hidden bracket creep. The disfavor into which the income tax has fallen is substantially due to just this effect. Correction for bracket creep, therefore, is a move to be supported, not opposed, by people who wish to strengthen the income tax as the mainstay of the federal tax system. It is ironic, to say the least, that this one good part of the 1981 legislation is the most likely part to be dropped.

Whatever the merits of the 1981 income tax cut as a temporary or permanent change, little good can be said for the 1981 corporation tax reform. Although a change in depreciation rules was needed to account for inflation, the legislation of that year was ill designed. The compounding of acceleration and investment credit led to wide differentials and drastic negative rates of tax. Although the 1982 corrections improved the situation, we still lack a neutral and inflation-proof set of depreciation rules. Moreover, the drastic reduction of the effective rate of corporation tax is incompatible with continued deductibility of interest.

Turning now to the future, it is evident that the cuts of 1981 have reduced the potential of the revenue system to much below the level of revenue that will be needed to sustain outlays at even a high level of economic activity. Using Minarik's figures and taking 1988 as the target year, it appears that the deficit will run at 5 percent of high-employment GNP. Such a level of deficit is unacceptable unless (1) the economy should remain severely stagnant or (2) the current lopsided fiscal-monetary mix (with its detrimental effect on growth) is continued in future years. Barring these situations, tax policy must prepare to provide for a substantial increase in revenue. Some people have suggested a reduction in the deficit to 1 percent of GNP as a sensible target. With tax revenues equal to 20 percent of GNP, a 20 percent increase in revenues would be needed to cut the deficit to that level. This required increase, it should be noted, falls short of the revenue loss caused by the 1981–1982 legislation. In the absence of the latter, the 1 percent deficit target would leave a permissible tax cut of about 7 percent. But the beans have been spilled and tax policy must address the question of how to achieve the required increase—meaning from $150 billion to $200 billion of additional revenue at 1988 levels. This order of magnitude is too large to be dealt with by piecemeal adjustments in excise or energy taxes. The administration's standby plan for a "down payment" in 1984 points in the right direction, but the amounts involved are inadequate. It seems evident that the gap cannot be closed without a substantial increase in income tax or the creation of some federal consumption tax.

Going along the income tax route, it should be quite possible, from the economist's point of view, to obtain at least half of what is needed by curtailing preferences, including those listed in Minarik's paper. Argued about at length over the past four decades, this approach remains the choice of my generation of tax reformers. In addition, a small, say 10 percent, increase in rates would be needed. I am worried, however, that this approach may defeat current proposals for income tax reform. As offered by the Bradley-Gebhard plan, and distinct from the Hall-Rabushka version, the reform would have the merit of leaving the vertical distribution of tax liabilities unchanged, and would permit rate cuts and reduce horizontal distortions and inequities through broadening of the tax base.

Turning to the consumption route, the choice would be between the traditional "in rem" approach and the newer idea of a personalized expenditure tax. As a firm believer in personalized taxation, I much prefer the latter, but I cannot see it as a major source of additional revenue in the near future. As a complex new device, the expenditure tax would have to be introduced gradually, beginning, I suggest, as a supplement to the higher-bracket income tax. As a rapid source of substantially increased revenue, an in rem consumption tax offers a more realistic approach.

Such a tax can take the form of a value-added or a retail sales tax. They have a similar impact on consumption and both invade a territory traditionally reserved for the states, but there are good reasons for preferring the retail tax. It is more easily understood as a tax that falls on consumption, and the additional administrative apparatus would be less, especially if coordinated with state taxes. The European setting in which the value-added tax was introduced as a replacement for the turnover tax does not apply here, nor is there a U.S. case for the value-added approach (applicable in developing countries) on grounds that a retail tax cannot be administered. If a broad-based federal consumption tax were to be introduced, so it is argued, a substantial rate of, say 8 percent, might be used to make it "worthwhile." As this rate might yield more revenue than is needed, so the argument continues, the income tax could be further reduced. I disagree with this proposition. For one thing, the rate should not be set higher than needed. For another, use of surplus revenue for income tax reduction would further reduce the upper-range progressivity of the income tax. Any excess revenue generated should be used to relieve the payroll tax.

Even though I prefer the additional revenue to be drawn from the income tax, introduction of a sales tax is to be preferred to no additional revenue. Moreover, if the emphasis on the taxation of consumption is to increase, a broad-based consumption tax is to be preferred to a dismantling of the income tax by stressing its "consumption base." The current trend toward "going easy" on saving and on capital income leads to a tax on consumption from wage income only, which is unacceptable. This, I think, is the most important point to keep in mind in the current debate.

Let me conclude with a few words on the connection between tax and budget policy, a topic which Minarik's paper did not deal with, but which is pertinent to this conference. As Wicksell pointed out nearly a century ago, the purpose of taxation is not simply to obtain revenue but also to be an instrument in expenditure choice. Thus tax and expenditure decisions should be linked, and the linkage should pertain not only to how much is to be spent in the aggregate but also to what is to be spent in particular, and how it is to be paid for. Our fiscal system, as it stands, provides only a weak link between taxation and the overall size of the budget, and practically none between the particulars of tax and expenditure selection. Fundamental budget reform sooner or later will require that such a linkage be established.

To mention a rather outrageous idea, consider for instance a division of the tax system into a defense tax, a tax for nondefense services, and a tax for redistributive programs. Consider the implications that such a division would have for fiscal politics. I realize that these thoughts run counter to the traditional approach (which, alas, I have shared and in which I have considerable vested interest) of looking at the tax system as a whole, independent of expenditures. It also runs counter to the valid macro-policy requirements of viewing the demand impact of taxes and expenditures in the aggregate. Yet we may well have gone too far in allowing for these aspects while disregarding the role of taxation in budget determination. The tax-expenditure linkage has been stressed in some recent literature on public choice but, I believe, in a largely one-sided way. The problem as I see it is not to establish tax barriers to reduce and limit the size of the public sector, but to create an efficient system of budget determination that reflects voters' preferences and leaves open whatever the resulting budget size may be.

PART 3

THE POLITICAL AND INSTITUTIONAL ENVIRONMENT

EXECUTIVE BUDGET MAKING

Hugh Heclo

During the past three years, presidential budgeting—usually a one-day story in January each year—has repeatedly captured the headlines. What once had seemed an anesthetizing subject is now portrayed as a matter of high drama. Consider some recent headlines: "Red Ink Blues," "Reagan's Aides Pull Together in Tight Fiscal Harness," "Administration Slips and Stumbles," "Reagan Regains Dominant Role on Budget," "Budget Agreement Called Vital," "Budget Talks Collapse," "Stockman Still Cooking the Numbers." Budgeting has become good press.

This paper tries to look behind the headlines to some of the underlying trends in the process by which an executive budget is prepared and presented for decision. Its intended focus is on the central processes of budgetary strategy in and near the White House. But one of the important themes to emerge is how difficult it has become to separate executive decisions on the budget from calculations about Congress. The intended time frame is the Reagan administration, but to appreciate the changes that have occurred, it is also necessary to understand something about the traditions of the process and of the president's budget agency. My attention will be mainly on domestic spending, leaving defense issues and tax policies to other chapters in this volume.

Budgets are complicated documents and the processes by which they are created are even more complex than the budget books. The following discussion begins by briefly describing the way in which the functions associated with the once-simple idea of an executive budget have expanded over the

The author wishes to thank the Woodrow Wilson Center of the Smithsonian Institution for research facilities provided during the summer of 1983.

years and the especially high political stakes that became attached to the Reagan budget process.

The second section of the paper traces what I regard as the two major changes in the recent budget process as seen from a central executive perspective. It is, of course, always tempting to exaggerate the importance of recent developments and to underestimate the continuities. What the Reagan administration has basically done is to give much greater impetus to two trends that were already underway: an intensified centralization and a broader congressional orientation in executive budgeting.

The third section moves from the process to the structure responsible for preparing the executive budget, the Office of Management and Budget (OMB). The dominance of OMB Director David Stockman has brought new energy but also exacerbated old problems in an agency that is at once politically powerful and institutionally disoriented.

The final section of the paper considers the lasting impact of the Reagan administration on the way in which the executive and legislative branches deal with budget policy. The resulting verdict is mixed, too mixed to be expressed in any simple headline. But whatever one might say about the policies, it is reasonable to ask if our vital institutional relationships are not in worse shape today than they were in 1980.

The Stakes

The modern period of executive budgeting began with the Budget and Accounting Act of 1921. Since that time, when federal spending was barely $3 billion, the underlying intent of the executive budget process has remained the same: to arrive at a single, coordinated budget proposal for the executive branch as a whole. The 1921 act placed this coordinating responsibility on the president and his budget staff.[1] This action has had the natural effect of increasing the apparent power of the president. But it should never be forgotten that Congress agreed to increase the president's budgetary responsibilities as a means of helping the legislature do its work. Having a single executive budget, rather than hundreds of separate, uncoordinated bureau budgets submitted directly to Congress, allowed Congress to deliberate on finances in a much more orderly way. This should alert us to an important preliminary fact: Any executive budget process that strikes members of Congress as more of a hindrance than a help in their jobs is likely to be disregarded.

---

1. The Bureau of the Budget was organizationally lodged in the Treasury Department until 1939, when it was moved into the newly created Executive Office of the President. In 1970 the bureau was renamed the Office of Management and Budget.

Over the years the functions associated with the unified executive budget have varied and increased. Basically, the changes in budgeting have reflected changes in the larger political context. During the 1920s executive budgeting served as a means for exercising strict control over the costs of government; this in turn reflected the fact that there was little political interest in initiating expensive domestic or defense programs. In the 1930s and 1940s, the executive budget became less a control and more an accounting device for tallying the costs of coping with the Depression and World War II. Under President Eisenhower in the 1950s the budget again became a strong instrument of control. In this case it was used by a fiscally conservative president with long military experience both to reduce the growth rate in domestic spending and to contain the size of the defense establishment. Under the Kennedy and Johnson administrations in the 1960s, new attention was given to the executive budget as an instrument for managing countercyclical fiscal policy as well as for planning new domestic spending programs. While "setting national priorities" through budgets became a common theme in the growing community of policy analysts, defense spending for Vietnam escalated largely outside the normal budget process.[2] During the 1970s, the executive budget increasingly became a method of accounting for spending decisions taken outside the routine of the annual budget cycle. By the end of the 1970s, most of the increases in the presidential budget were not stimulated by White House initiatives or new agency spending requests. Rather the growth was due mainly to previously enacted entitlements and to automatic spending increases triggered by high inflation and high unemployment.

Stylized as the preceding account is, it does serve to indicate how greatly the stakes of executive budgeting expanded between 1921 and 1981. Instead of one function supplanting another, a complex accretion of tasks has been assigned to the president's budget. First is the traditional function of paying for the cost of running the government machinery itself; financing the salaries and expenses of federal operations is obviously a necessary and important function, but it has become only a small portion of total spending. Second, the budget has come to be viewed as an expression of national priorities. At the global level this refers to the split between civilian and military spending, but the budget numbers are also used to symbolize how much or how little we are doing for education, small businesses, environmental protection, and a host of other worthy causes. Third, the president's budget is widely expected to serve as an instrument of fiscal policy, stimulating the economy during periods of slack resource use and restraining it during periods of overheating.

---

2. Mark S. Kamlet and David C. Mowery, "Bureaucrats, the President, and the Growth of Government, 1955–1972," September 1982, mimeographed.

By the 1980s economists themselves were divided over how much to count on federal budgets for this purpose. Meanwhile financial markets were increasingly sensitive to the implications of budget deficits for interest rates and economic instability. Finally, and whatever one might think about national priorities, the federal budget process by 1981 had also become a device for regularly distributing income to large numbers of Americans. At the end of the 1970s, 42 percent of American households received some form of government cash benefit; this group overlapped in part with the one-third of households that received in-kind benefits for health care, food, education, and the like.[3] Some professors of social policy called this the secondary, nonmarket distribution of income. As a young congressman in the late 1970s, David Stockman called it a coast-to-coast soupline.

By 1981, therefore, high stakes surrounded the executive budget as a device for paying for government operations, setting national priorities, managing the economy, and distributing income. In addition, complex tensions developed among these four functions. Countercyclical economic management and priority setting imply flexibility and short-term adaptability to changing circumstances. Maintaining the government machinery and distributing income encourage attention to routine stability and predictability in government spending. Economic management and priority setting call for a general, macroscopic view of the budget. The distribution of funds among government bureaus and private groups favors a distributive, microscopic view of budgeting as to who gets what.

While these tensions may or may not be regarded as insurmountable, they certainly added to the complexity of any presidential agenda expressed through the budget process. By 1980 there was a widespread perception that the budget was being driven more by economic events and uncontrollable entitlement programs than by any presidential actions. In January 1980 President Carter proposed a FY 1981 budget that financial markets feared would stimulate ever-mounting inflation. Within two months Carter proposed a second budget projecting lower deficits of $15.6 billion. Congress responded with a budget predicting a $27.4 billion deficit. And the economy actually delivered a deficit of $57.9 billion in FY 1981. To miss targets on this scale did not build confidence either among financial circles or the general public. President Carter's last budget, submitted in January 1981, described long-term trends in a way that seemed scripted as an audience warm-up for the Reagan administration:

---

3. Robert J. Lampman, "Secondary Consumer-Income: Interfamily Transfer Flows, 1950–78," 1983, table 3.3, mimeographed.

Although growth in the [social] programs for which spending is relatively uncontrollable may have been desirable during the past three decades,[4] we have reached a point where uncontrollable spending threatens the effectiveness of the budget as an instrument of discretionary national economic policy.[5]

Ronald Reagan's election in 1980 raised the political stakes of presidential budgeting to unprecedented levels. To the new president and many of his supporters, budget policy represented more than a set of spending priorities or an economic management strategy. It expressed a political philosophy—one that had remained unchanged for at least fifteen years.[6] Well before the advent of stagflation in the 1970s, Ronald Reagan had argued that big government in Washington was crippling the economic prosperity that could be produced by free markets. Well before the passage of landmark civil rights, consumer, environmental, and health care legislation in the 1960s and 1970s, Reagan had argued that federal intervention was undermining individual liberties and local government responsibilities. And well before the post-Vietnam hostility to military spending, Ronald Reagan had argued that the national security effort was too timid. These three arguments were the pillars of the Reagan political philosophy, and in 1980 the man, the message, and the times seemed to come together. Outgoing President Carter's valedictory budget for FY 1981, with its warnings about the economic perils of social entitlements and its hefty 5 percent real increase for defense spending, indicated how far prevailing opinion and Reagan's basic stump speech had come into alignment.

Inevitably the executive budget was the central instrument for executing the Reagan philosophy. The new president's simple message to his budget makers was, in effect, to cut civilian spending, reduce taxes as well as other market intrusions, and increase military spending. The who, what, and how of doing these things were left to others to work out. No one in 1980 could predict what would happen when the predetermined simplicity of the Reagan agenda ran up against the accumulated complexity of executive budgeting. What was clear was that budgeting traditions in the executive branch were likely to become more unsettled.

---

4. Spending on social entitlements rose from 27 percent of the budget in FY 1967 to 48 percent in FY 1981; during the same period, this spending as a proportion of the gross national product doubled, increasing from 5.5 percent to 11 percent.

5. Office of Management and Budget, *Budget of the United States Government, Fiscal Year 1982* (Washington, D.C.: Government Printing Office, 1981), p. 38.

6. Excerpts dating back to 1964 can be found in the *National Journal*, August 29, 1981, p. 1533.

The Process

During Ronald Reagan's long campaign for the presidency, the candidate and his closest advisers were not burdened by substantial knowledge about the federal budget process or its contents. As a Republican spokesman in the 1978 congressional campaigns, Reagan had agreed with the Republican National Committee's endorsement of the Kemp-Roth bill (proposing 10 percent across-the-board cuts in federal income tax rates for three successive years) on the condition that there would be offsetting but unspecified spending cuts. Candidate Reagan's September 9, 1980, speech on economic policy represented the most advanced stage of thinking on the subject in the Reagan headquarters. In this speech the candidate called for a 2 percent cut in the FY 1981 budget, rising progressively to a promised 7 percent cut in what would otherwise have been spent in FY 1985 (with a suggestion that a 10 percent cut in FY 1984 was possible). The overall objective was a balanced budget in FY 1983, with even a hoped-for surplus of $23 billion in that year. The entire amount of these cuts was to be achieved by "a comprehensive assault on waste and inefficiency" in federal spending.[7] In fact there was no evidence available that an efficiency campaign could produce anything like these projected savings. Nor was it likely that the budget could be reduced by 2 percent in a fiscal year that would be one-third over by the time the new president was inaugurated.

Given his announced positions, President-elect Reagan had four basic options during the transition. The first, and softest option, was simply to continue the publicity themes of the campaign: cutting taxes, increasing military spending, and trying somehow to wring savings out of the fat in the federal administration. Because such savings were unpredictable and could take years to materialize, the implication was a larger near-term deficit. Furthermore, and this was probably the consideration that loomed largest at the time, quick and highly visible spending cuts would be necessary to gain congressional support for the tax cuts to which the president was committed. A second option was to delay or reduce the proposed tax cuts, while a third was to delay or reduce defense increases. President-elect Reagan was unmovable on both counts. A fourth option was to risk political unpopularity by immediately mounting a major attack on domestic spending, a choice that in any event corresponded with the administration's longer-term goals. By early December 1980 the president's newly designated budget director, David Stockman, was vigorously pursuing the fourth option. It was a course that

---

7. "Ronald Reagan's Strategy for Economic Growth and Stability in the 1980s," fact sheet issued by the Reagan-Bush Committee, Sepember 9, 1980.

would vastly accelerate changes that had already been underway in the traditional processes and institutions of executive budgeting.

To appreciate these changes, we should recall the customary postwar routine. The normal pattern found a new president arriving in office inclined to downplay campaign promises, appointing an OMB director who gradually became familiar with the budget process, assembling spending proposals from the new agency heads, and working out a compromise budget proposal that the spending agencies then defended before the committees and subcommittees of Congress.

The Reagan presidency broke with these traditions in most respects. First, Ronald Reagan had an unquestioning commitment to execute the promises derived from his long-term political philosophy. This confidence was only reinforced by the surprising scale of the 1980 victory and the fateful brush with assassination a few months later. Second, the new president had the good fortune, whether by design or accident, to appoint as his budget director a rare person who could translate the president's simple aims into the complexity of budgeting, both in general strategy and line-item detail. Convinced that they knew what to do, neither the president nor his budget director hesitated to tackle what other politicians and bureaucrats had regarded as impossible. Finally, the Reagan White House tried to dominate the budget process vis-à-vis both agencies and Congress as never before.

To be sure there were precedents. As economic conditions deteriorated and undermined budget plans throughout the 1970s, an increasing number of stopgap measures and mid-course corrections (supplemental appropriations, continuing resolutions, debt ceiling extensions) were necessary; these tended to require centralized executive responses that could only come from the presidency and not individual spending departments. Likewise, after 1974 the congressional budget reform act[8] had provided new opportunities for presidential budget spokesmen to become involved with the new, more centralized legislative devices (budget committees in each house, omnibus budget resolutions, functional spending categories, and reporting requirements) that cut across and aggregated agency-level spending decisions. During its desperate try at a second budget in February–March 1980, the Carter administration and senior OMB officials had struck a new note in centralizing budget negotiations with Congress and making early use of the reconciliation process in each house to advance the administration's negotiated agreement. Still, the precedents pale in comparison with what happened after 1980. The Reagan White House and David Stockman showed how much further the trends could be carried when pursued with greater determination and political skill.

---

8. Congressional Budget Impoundment and Control Act, PL. 93-344.

The major changes in the executive process can be discussed under two headings: top-down budgeting and budgeting for legislative advantage.

Top-Down Budgeting. Despite the new administration's talk of "cabinet government," the commitment to balancing the budget and curtailing civilian spending necessarily implied a major centralization of the budget process. Only by this means could discipline be established over the multitude of piecemeal bargains between agencies and congressional committees and over the long-term legislative commitments that produced inertial growth in total spending. The real question was how such centralization could be achieved and sustained amid the centrifugal forces of Washington.

The new pattern began to emerge early. By Christmas 1980 the initiative for federal budget policy had passed decisively to OMB director-designate David Stockman and away from the free-floating advisory groups that had surrounded Reagan the candidate. From that time onward, decision making on the president's domestic budget was dominated by Stockman and a small circle of senior White House advisers that eventually became known as the Legislative Strategy Group. Defense spending, on the other hand, followed its own track between the president and secretary of defense (and important Republicans in Congress) with only periodic and largely unsuccessful interventions by Stockman throughout 1981.

The dominance of David Stockman, and by extension of OMB, first found expression in his twenty-three-page memorandum presented to Reagan in November and leaked to the press in December entitled "Avoiding a GOP Economic Dunkirk."[9] (Born in the 1940s, Stockman's generation had apparently forgotten that Dunkirk was not a military disaster, but a brilliant rescue operation.) The details of this memo were less influential than its general message: Budget policy, it argued, should be seen as part of a co-ordinated response to an economic crisis. Without major reductions in budget outlays and authority for fiscal years 1981 and 1982, not only would deficits mount and credit markets panic, but the very capacity of the Reagan coalition to govern would be undermined by a civil war between "supply side" tax cutters and orthodox Republican budget balancers. The memo demonstrated Stockman's ability to range from the details of the budget to general political strategy. In addition, the memo brought into the White House inner circle a way of thinking about budget policy as a means of political management in the executive branch and Congress.

With the president-elect's blessing in late November, Stockman began masterminding a frontal attack on domestic spending well before his confir-

---

9. The memo bore the signatures of David Stockman and Congressman Jack Kemp of New York. Excerpts appeared in *The New York Times*, December 14, 1980.

mation hearings had begun. In fact he was in a position to move farther and faster than any budget director in living memory. One advantage was that most subcabinet positions were filled late, leaving cabinet officers under-staffed to meet the new budget director's onslaught. Moreover, those ap-pointees who were selected had already been required to affirm their support for the president's goal of cutting back on the domestic role of the federal government. As a result, it was difficult for any presidential appointees, some of whom were labeled "trained seals" by the White House staff, to fight vigorously for their agencies' budgets against OMB demands.[10] Another ad-vantage was that by early December, director-designate Stockman was re-ceiving discreet help from certain OMB staff who were well-stocked with budget-cutting ideas. OMB staff warnings about the momentum of federal entitlements and outlays had gone largely unheeded by political executives in the administrations of the 1970s, so OMB bureaucrats had an abundance of proposals to take off the shelf for the new budget director. Yet another asset for Stockman was the fact that the president and his closest advisers were willing to delegate vast amounts of discretion to Stockman in framing domestic budget policy. A budget review group of senior presidential aides provided strong backing for Stockman as cabinet officers came in individually to face a united White House front and Stockman's unequaled grasp of their agencies' budget numbers.

One of the most important factors that accounted for Stockman's dom-inance of domestic budget making was Stockman himself. Bright and hard-working (eighteen-hour days at least six days a week were the norm), David Stockman as a freshman congressman in 1976 had devoted himself to learning the intricacies of the federal budget in the way other young people work at mastering videogames. In 1979–1980 he and Democratic Congressman Phil Gramm of Texas had done what no other congressmen had ever done before: Using information generated by the congressional budget process, Stockman prepared a complete, detailed federal budget as a substitute for President Carter's FY 1981 proposal. Many of these same cuts now reappeared in the new OMB director's black notebooks of Reagan administration spending reductions.

By all accounts Stockman's abilities as a budget director were outstand-ing. His knowledge of the technical detail (not to mention the accounting gimmicks) behind the budget numbers astounded seasoned OMB staffers.

---

10. The willingness of the new secretary of state, Alexander Haig, to publicly fight with Stockman on foreign aid budget cuts won the budget battle for the secretary, but added to the White House perception of his not being a loyal team player. This perception and its consequences for Haig were not lost on other cabinet officers.

Stories circulated of the director's catching flaws in complex tables that had escaped the notice of full-time professionals in the OMB examining divisions. Charts that would fail to make the desired impact in White House presentations (e.g., on the proportion of cuts falling on discretionary versus nondiscretionary spending) were redrawn at the director's desk. At the same time, Stockman was intrigued by the strategies and gamesmanship necessary to enact a budget in the aggregate and in its component parts. This sense of the larger picture made the OMB director a welcome member of the inner circle of White House advisers, none of whom had any interest in budget technicalities. In short, David Stockman was justifiably impressed by his own abilities as a grand strategist and a budget examiner of detailed numbers.

While publicly portrayed as a Reagan ideologue, Stockman in fact was open to new information and demonstrated a healthy respect for budgetary facts of life. It became clear almost immediately that to cut FY 1981 spending by the promised 2 percent would be impossible and that the goal of a balanced budget would have to be moved back from FY 1983 to FY 1984.[11] At the same time, Stockman assured the Senate Budget Committee in his January confirmation hearings that the president's proposed 30 percent tax cut would be largely offset by spending reductions. The president's original tax proposal called for a revenue loss of approximately $300 billion in the three fiscal years 1982 through 1984. During the frantic weeks before the February 18 announcement of the Reagan economic program, OMB officials worked desperately, and departmental officials largely acquiesced, as Stockman sought to find the needed spending cuts to project over the three years.

In the end, the president unveiled his economic "recovery" program (the term "crisis" used in the Dunkirk memo was dropped for fear of upsetting financial markets) and asked for $197 billion in spending reductions for the fiscal 1982–1984 period. The cuts in the current services budget for on- and off-budget civilian outlays for FY 1982 would total about $50 billion when compared with the costs of existing policy. Projecting these changes and adding in unspecified spending reductions of $30 billion for 1983 and more than $40 billion annually for the fiscal 1984–1986 period still left a gap of approximately $100 billion, if the budget was to be balanced in FY 1984 against a $300 billion loss in tax revenues. Closing this gap, on paper at least, depended on heroic assumptions about how much and how quickly the American economy would respond to the Reagan economic program. To simplify a great deal of wrangling that occurred within the administration between the

---

11. In the president's budget presentation of February 18, 1981, federal spending for FY 1981 was proposed to be cut by $4.4 billion, or by well under 1 percent.

utopian and the merely optimistic points of view, the issue boiled down to positing rates of economic growth and inflation that would be sufficient to balance the FY 1984 budget as promised.

The supply-side economists in the administration who championed the tax cuts were accommodated in the forecast with a projection of rapid growth in the real GNP (5.2 percent during calendar 1982 and 4.9 percent in 1983, compared with the outgoing Carter administration's forecast of 3.5 percent and 3.7 percent when measured from fourth quarter to fourth quarter.) Monetarists in the Reagan administration who were intent on controlling the money supply were accommodated with a projected sharp decline in inflation rates (7.2 percent for calendar 1982 and 6 percent in 1983, compared with the Carter forecast of 9.6 percent for 1982). These economic assumptions allowed the Reagan administration to show on paper a balanced budget by FY 1984. The numbers were at first greeted with confusion and then increasingly ridiculed as inconceivable outcomes of the prescribed monetary tightening and fiscal stimulus. By the time the administration produced its required mid-term economic assessment in July 1981—and reaffirmed its original forecasts—few experienced observers took the figures as more than wishful thinking. But by then the original economic forecasts had sufficed to carry the momentum of the president's economic recovery program in Congress.

The highly centralized executive budget process of the first months of the Reagan administration set the pattern for subsequent periods. To be sure, some slippage occurred as agency executives became more experienced in defending their budgets and as Congress eventually proved reluctant to follow the president's budgetary lead. After a string of glowing successes on domestic spending cuts and tax reductions in 1981, the White House found it increasingly difficult in 1982 and 1983 to dominate the agenda with its budget proposals. Indeed what had been a president-led national budget process in the first year had become virtually a president-less and stalemated process by 1984. As in earlier periods in the twentieth century, this situation had less to do with what the president and his budget managers intended than with a changing political climate. In this case an unexpectedly severe recession intervened in 1982 and the mid-term congressional elections of that year failed to confirm the presumed Reagan mandate.

Still, what matters for present purposes is the fact that the tendency within the bureaucracy throughout the last three years has been to invert the usual executive budget process. That traditional process produced a presidential budget by filtering agency spending requests up toward the budget director and president through a series of discussions, hearings, and reviews.

The budget season would normally unfold with a spring preview in which OMB examiners received agency spending requests and sought, with mixed success, to establish agency planning ceilings under general guidance from the OMB director. In the fall review, OMB examiners would develop revised planning figures following the receipt of new agency bids and any new guidelines from the director or president. OMB hearings with agency representatives would culminate in a "director's review," in which the director would meet with OMB program division staff to evaluate the difference between the agencies' requests and the planning ceilings. The director's decisions, along with any appeals by the agencies, would then go to the president for final action.

Top-down budgeting of the Reagan-Stockman era has overlaid and supplemented this traditional process rather than replaced it. The basic decisions affecting multiagency budget categories flow downward from the director and his negotiations with the White House and agency appointees. These are intended to set the framework within which the traditional process of examining agency budgets occurs. In the FY 1984 budget process, for example, a three-year freeze on discretionary spending programs was the basic top-down policy, but within that framework the familiar bottom-up process carried a host of pluses and minuses in individual budget decisions. Alongside the traditional (but increasingly automated) task of producing a physical budget document each January, budget planning and decision making has tended to become a continuous process powered by the director's interests and the political/strategic calculations of the moment. The usual spring previews, in which examining divisions displayed their ideas about the agency budgets before the director, have all but disappeared. For example, the spring (1983) preview of the FY 1985 budget was devoted to an evaluation of what lessons for controlling spending could be learned from the prior two years. Simultaneously, the attention of the director and his close aides was taken up with tracking and fighting for the administration's position on FY 1983 supplemental spending bills and the FY 1984 budget then pending before Congress.

Many of the details of the Stockman system of budget management have fluctuated with the issues and political pressures at the time, but a few generalizations seem valid. First, from the beginning, the OMB director's central idea was to deal with the total budget, thus forcing political decisions on all the components driving total spending. (Again a caveat must be entered for defense.) Seen from this perspective, the traditional executive budget process was largely a successive winnowing of discretionary programs at the margins. Stockman sought to put onto the budget bargaining table all parts of the budget, including entitlements and cost-of-living adjustments that previous administrations had labeled uncontrollable. The commitment to limiting the resources devoted to domestic government in the aggregate was a strong centralizing force in the budget process, as well as in the Reagan administration generally.

Second, the top-down approach was reinforced by Stockman's need to constantly readdress the deficit problem. By spring of 1981 it was becoming clear in the director's meetings with OMB staff that the optimistic assumptions of the economic forecast had only temporarily papered over a large structural deficit in the Reagan program. Again and again after that, the budget director had to return to the White House to report that deficit forecasts were worse than expected. The president repeatedly rejected Stockman's attempts to make major inroads in the large defense increases, leaving Stockman to look for still more cuts in domestic spending. In the beginning of the administration, the targets of opportunity had been obvious enough: excessively generous student loans, free school lunches for families that could afford to pay, and so on. Each new round of searching for spending cuts forced OMB to push beyond the areas of obvious waste and into the heart of domestic programs. None of these efforts involved decisions that were likely to emerge from the normal budget routine of processing agency requests. Hence top-down budgeting from OMB was strengthened.

To have concentrated on comparing the merits and demerits of individual spending programs and their priorities with those of other programs would have been a time-consuming, intellectually exhausting, and politically divisive task. Hence a third major aspect of budget management under Stockman was an attempt to move the debate from program particulars to general politico-economic justifications. Cuts in social spending were justified on economic policy grounds, not in terms of the social policy consequences for beneficiaries of funding a given activity at level A rather than level B. On some issues the resulting controversy was dramatic, as in the cases of the heavy-handed cutoff of disability benefits and a trimmed-down school lunch program supposedly redeemed by the nutritional value of catsup. But in general domestic budget cutting was successfully subsumed in an argument—as with the original Reagan speeches and the Dunkirk memo—that a smaller civilian government would produce a healthier economy.

General economic and philosophical arguments alone would have been inadequate tools for driving budget decisions. Hence a fourth element in the Stockman system was needed: extensive reliance on very broad spending categories to make major budget decisions. For the first time, an administration was attempting to fight with, in effect, a single strategy in domestic government. That strategy was to cut back wherever politically possible, and it was constantly reenergized by defining the budget position in terms of ever-worsening deficits. And yet the traditional budget categories of individual programs and complex accounts were almost by definition a means of fragmenting any single strategy. Indeed, normal budget routines paid little attention to the three-quarters of the federal budget that was customarily labelled "uncontrollable," mainly due to entitlement legislation. Of course much of the hand-to-hand fighting to maintain the president's budget with the agencies and Congress took place at the level of individual spending agencies and accounts. But the guiding choices that were made by the White House and that forced these struggles to occur were made in terms of other, more aggregated budget categories. Since the 1974 congressional budget reform act, most of these categories had been used in OMB and on Capitol Hill to display information. Now they were used in Stockman's office and in his consultations with senior presidential staff and Ronald Reagan to make decisions. Because the small number of decision categories cut across or subsumed most spending agency budgets, their use presumed and reenforced top-down executive budgeting.

Thus from August and well into the autumn of 1981, the budget director repeatedly returned to the White House with news of deepening deficits. The decisions to be made were framed not in terms of departments and their budgets but in terms of Stockman's categories, which bore the marks of his experience with the congressional budget process. One started with a statement of the existing status of expenditures compared with revenues and, assuming existing policy remained the same, extrapolated the aggregate figures into the future along several different lines of assumptions (e.g., administration versus Congressional Budget Office estimates, varying forecasts of economic growth, and so on). Then decision makers were presented with alternative changes in a small number of categories—domestic discretionary spending, entitlements, defense, cost-of-living adjustments, revenue enhancements, and so on—to see what the effects of various combinations of changes in the numbers filling the categories would be on projected deficits. That autumn of 1981, the president stood firm against any major changes in defense spending or tax reductions and endorsed a 12 percent cut across the board in all discretionary civilian spending for FY 1982.

As 1982 unfolded it became difficult to argue, and to maintain political support for the idea that every domestic program (regardless of intervening events or political sensitivities) was of equal value at the margins and thus should be indiscriminately subject to a common 12 percent spending cut. In subsequent months some flexibility was allowed within the categorical totals, but the categories within which budget decisions continued to be made remained Stockman's.

Negotiations with Congress carried through the same themes. In March and April of 1982 the so-called Gang of Seventeen[12] administration and congressional leaders sought to negotiate a scale-back of defense increases and tax reductions. The political posturing on both sides was monumental, but everyone negotiated from Stockman's worksheets listing a baseline budget deficit projected for the fiscal 1983–1985 period, and then eleven of Stockman's spending categories followed by a category for offsetting receipts and general revenues, followed by a bottom-line figure of remaining deficits for the three years. These budget categories subsumed a multitude of intricate programmatic choices under aggregate numbers for (1) defense and international, (2) all federal cost-of-living adjustments, (3) government pay, retirement, and Social Security, (4) medical entitlements, (5) other entitlements, (6) other mandatory programs, and (7) four other discretionary programs.

Although negotiations in the Gang of Seventeen eventually broke down, the important fact was that almost everyone was willing to consider budgetary policy within the intellectual framework of Stockman's categories. As Richard Bolling, the chief Democratic negotiator, belatedly complained, "The papers were always their papers, the figures were always their figures. I kept saying that I had to have a whole package and look at the detail. I was looking for the smaller pieces that would tell me who was going to get screwed on health care, food stamps, and all the rest."[13] In a sense, David Stockman drove the executive budget process from the top downward through his aggregated spending categories, just as these functions drove the real-world budget numbers of total spending.

The major disjuncture in top-down budget management lay in the one category that Stockman typically put at the top of his worksheets: defense. Here too the experiences in the first months of the Reagan administration set a pattern that was very difficult to alter. During this period extremely far-reaching spending commitments were allowed to develop with only the most cursory scrutiny from top decision makers in OMB and the White House. If published accounts are to be believed,[14] the gap between budgetary scrutiny

---

12. In addition to senior White House aides such as James Baker, the group included Ernest Hollings and Russell Long representing the Senate Democratic minority, Jim Jones, Dan Rostenkowski, and Richard Bolling (Democratic chairmen of the House Budget, Ways and Means, and Rules Committees), as well as the House and Senate Republican leaders. Speaker Tip O'Neill remained outside the group in order to maintain his bargaining parity with President Reagan.

13. Quoted in Laurence I. Barrett, *Gambling with History* (New York: Doubleday, 1983), p. 358.

14. Published news accounts are contained in Steven R. Weisman, *The New York Times Magazine*, October 24, 1982, p. 26ff.; and Sidney Blumenthal, *The Boston Globe Magazine*, May 2, 1982, p. 10ff.

and defense spending aspirations was so great that the Pentagon largely defined its own preferred rate of spending increase. During the 1980 presidential campaign, Reagan's issue papers had called for a 5 percent real increase in defense spending for coming years, but when the final Carter budget for FY 1982 called for this same 5 percent increase, the Reagan camp upped the ante to a promised 7 percent real increase in defense spending.

During the spring of 1981, as Stockman and senior White House aides concentrated on domestic spending cuts and the tax reduction fight in Congress, defense officials were allowed to write into the new president's March budget submission a 7 percent real increase on top of an upward recalculation of the value of Carter's proposed 5 percent increase. Reportedly, Stockman and White House aides took the numbers as little more than a hastily contrived opening bid for a more fully worked out defense program. The secretary of defense and the Pentagon, on the other hand, took the percentages as a firm commitment and sought with considerable success to persuade the president— and not much persuasion was needed—that backing down from the spending projections would be backing down on national security in the eyes of the Soviets. The drift into uncharted levels of defense spending reached almost comic proportions in September 1981 when, after admonitions to Stockman and Defense Secretary Caspar Weinberger to work things out, the president along with top advisers Edwin Meese and James Baker reached a ''command decision'' that managed to add up the wrong column of numbers, thereby giving Weinberger more than even he had expected.[15]

During late 1981 and throughout 1982, the president did reluctantly indicate his willingness to accept more modest defense spending increases when compared with his original March 1981 budget proposals. Most of these were grudging, ad hoc accommodations taken in the cause of finding some common ground with Congress in order to cope with the seemingly inexorable rise in projected deficits. But the ad hoc nature of these positions simply illustrate the fact that the defense budget was never effectively included within the regime of top-down budget management that characterized and has constrained the myriad purposes of civilian spending. Budget policy, understood as an executive-branch-wide view of national resources was and has remained bifurcated, with defense as the favored exception.

At first glance, top-down budgeting would seem to be a perfect recipe for closed, authoritarian management. That this has not happened is due to the second major feature of the recent executive budget process, namely that it has been designed for negotiation with Congress.

---

15. Barrett, *Gambling with History*, pp. 178–179.

Budgeting for Legislative Advantage. To speak of the budget as a subject for bargaining sounds like a truism. Certainly all presidential budgets have been subject to tortuous negotiations with Congress. The difference in the past three years is that the Reagan budget process has been much more self-consciously crafted to obtain bargaining advantages with Congress. The traditional presidential budget emerged from an executive-oriented process; it was a mechanism to produce a proposal describing the financial resources needed in the executive branch. Developments since 1980 have not wholly abandoned that approach. But President Reagan's budget policy has been crafted with an eye to its strategic bearing on Congress at least as much, if not more, than its effects within the executive branch.

This political peripheral vision, if I may call it that, has been the saving grace of top-down budgeting in the sense of forestalling a rigid, authoritarian mindset. Compared with their recent predecessors, the Reagan budget makers have been crisp and clear about their policy preferences on many issues both large and small. But the ideology has generally been handled in a nonideological manner. The Reagan budget process came to be managed by persons who understood, accepted, and indeed enjoyed the legislative politics and gamesmanship of budgeting.

Not since the beginning of the New Deal and the ill-fated tenure of Lewis Douglas had there been a budget director with any significant experience in Congress. David Stockman not only came from Congress, but he thoroughly understood the arcane world of congressional budgeting. At the same time there quickly evolved in the White House a senior group that busied itself with not only the tactics of lobbying, but also the strategic planning to deal with the budget and other issues in Congress. This group, centered in James Baker's office, started operating as early as February 1981 when it became clear that OMB, the Treasury Department, and the White House legislative liaison office were previewing uncoordinated versions of what would be the Reagan economic recovery program. Since the budget was to be the centerpiece of this program and since Stockman knew both the budget and the Congress, the OMB director quickly became a key member of the White House strategy group.

What all this meant was that the numbers in the president's budget came to depend not simply on what the executive branch needed but also on what numbers and tactics would move congressional outcomes in the desired direction. Thus the bold domestic spending cuts proposed in the first Reagan budget were regarded as a necessary step in gaining congressional support for the subsequent Kemp-Roth tax reductions. These major tax reductions would in turn constrict the flow of federal revenues and increase pressure for further domestic budget cuts. Similarly, although the proposed domestic policy cuts were unpopular with many groups, this opposition could be partially offset by taking the pledge not to touch the "social safety net" programs for the truly needy. Stockman was later reported as calling the safety net pledge a "political gimmick."[16] Certainly it was a budgeting gambit publicized by the White House without any serious analysis of what, in a complex industrial society, might actually constitute a social safety net. Likewise OMB's retrospective evaluations in the 1983 spring preview period pointed out some of the lessons learned on how to divide and encourage social policy beneficiaries to fight against one another in the Congressional jungle.

Prior to 1980 OMB had made sporadic attempts to move more aggressively into the legislative budget process. In the Ford administration budget chief James Lynn had explored ways of paying more attention to how the spending agencies presented and defended the presidential budget on Capitol Hill. These ideas did not get very far, apart from the brief appearance of a new advocacy document to accompany the formal budget trying to focus congressional and public attention on the president's issues.[17] With the arrival of David Stockman and the Reagan administration, the tradition of giving the agencies the main responsibility for defending the president's budget in congressional committees and subcommittees was transformed. Not merely was a new and more sophisticated advocacy document published by OMB.[18] It now became Stockman's mission to take the lead in making the administration's case on Capitol Hill wherever and whenever budgetary decisions were being made.

The aim of the executive budget strategies remained fixed: to gain whatever bargaining leverage could be had over congressional budget decisions. The means employed were constantly changing, first, because the political context within Congress was always in motion as the perception of a Reagan mandate eroded after 1981 and second, because economic realities and worries in financial markets about the deficit were continually upsetting budget plans and their attendant bargains. The result was a constant jujitsu-like maneuvering by the executive with few reliable institutional relationships from one budget engagement to the next. In essence, Stockman and the White House strategists sought to use Congress's ponderous budget procedures against itself, wherever they could find a handhold. At times this meant packaging and repacking omnibus budgets to exploit the budget process managed by congressional

---

16. Ibid., p. 145.

17. Office of Management and Budget, "Seventy Issues for FY 1977" (Washington, D.C.: Government Printing Office), January 21, 1976.

18. Executive Office of the President, Office of Management and Budget, *Major Themes and Additional Budget Details, Fiscal Year 1983* (Washington, D.C.: Government Printing Office, 1982).

budget committees. At other times it meant bypassing if not subverting the budget committees' process with particularized budget deals for annually funded items before appropriations subcommittees or multiyear spending plans before authorization committees. And at still other times calculations of political advantage saw the president withdrawing to let the congressional budget effort stall and fall of its own weight.

In 1981, the Stockman and White House approach was to use the 1974 congressional budget reforms to advance the administration's policies. The first step was to take the first congressional budget resolution seriously as a constraint on subsequent legislative decisions. To do that meant, in turn, taking the reconciliation process seriously. And from that flowed a need to develop statements of what the president's desired budgetary outcome was before each congressional committee and subcommittee. Not to do so simply left the president's case invisible at the level of real congressional decision making on the federal budget.

As is widely known, that approach succeeded brilliantly in the first year of the administration, but results in 1982 and 1983 were much more mixed. In 1982, the president proposed a budget extending major cuts in domestic programs, continued rapid increases in defense spending, and no new taxes. OMB's deficit projections were widely regarded as being unrealistically low and, as in 1981, politically motivated to gain bargaining advantages against Congress. This rather ideologically pure budget was pronounced dead on arrival in Congress, but after repeated efforts the Democratic-controlled House was unable to agree on any alternative budget. In the Senate, the Republican leadership crafted a scaled-back version of the original Reagan proposals and eventually won presidential support for a substantial tax increase to moderate the more realistic Congressional Budget Office projections of federal deficits. It was not a bad bargain for the president. He was allowed to appear first as a man of resolute principle and then as a reasonable negotiator who would compromise. In return for allowing Congress to take public responsibility for a tax increase, the president still obtained a major military spending increase along with further restraint in the growth of domestic spending.

To use the president's budget as a bargaining tool in 1983 was more difficult because of the changing political and economic climate noted earlier. The president's budget proposal sought to appear more accommodating from the outset, given a congressional atmosphere in which Democrats were buoyed by the mid-term House elections and Republicans were increasingly sensitive to complaints about the unfair effects of already enacted domestic spending cuts during a recession. The president's original 1983 proposal would have trimmed currently planned defense spending increases as well as nondefense spending; it also contemplated a "contingency" tax increase that would come into effect in FY 1986 if the deficit picture had not improved. This time, however, the resurgent and more disciplined Democrats in the House were able to produce an alternative in the first budget resolution, and there was almost no constituency in the Senate for major cuts in domestic programs. Spurred by the prospects of deficits exceeding $200 billion into the foreseeable future, the Senate and House finally agreed to a budget resolution that set spending and revenue targets for the fiscal 1984–1986 period. As table 1 indicates, the congressional action substantially rejected the president's budgetary priorities. Although the administration and Congress each managed to arrive at projections that would lower the projected deficit from $207 billion

TABLE 1

COMPARISON OF MAJOR CHANGES IN BUDGET OUTLAYS PROPOSED BY THE
PRESIDENT AND CONGRESS, FY 1984–1986
(In $ billions)

Budget Category	1984	1985	1986	Three-year Total
Spending changes				
National defense				
President's budget[a]	0	2.7	10.7	13.4
Congressional resolution	−2.1	−12.4	−15.0	−29.5
Nondefense spending				
President's budget	−12.3	−22.8	−33.3	−68.4
Congressional resolution[b]	9.5	3.4	−6.5	6.4
Total outlays				
President's budget	−12.3	−20.1	−22.6	−55.0
Congressional resolution[b]	7.4	−9.0	−21.5	−23.1
Revenue changes				
President's budget	3.1	5.8	46.7	55.6
Congressional resolution	12.0	15.0	46.0	73.0
Deficit changes				
President's budget	−15.3	−26.0	−69.4	−110.7
Congressional resolution	−4.6	−24.1	−67.6	−96.3

SOURCE: Congressional Budget Office, *The Economic and Budget Outlook: An Update* (Washington, D.C.: Government Printing Office, August 1983), table 28, p. 100.

a. Budget changes are calculated from a base defined in terms of the cost of existing policies at the time of the adoption of the first congressional budget resolution for 1984, which is June 1983.

b. Figures include nearly $20 billion of spending increases between FY 1983 and FY 1986 allocated to a reserve fund for domestic programs that will be released upon enactment of authorizing legislation.

in 1983 to approximately $145 billion in 1986, they did so in substantially different ways.

In 1983 and early 1984 the presidency largely withdrew from a general congressional budget process that it could no longer dominate. This in turn made it extremely difficult for Congress to use its budget committees and omnibus budget resolutions to arrive at a total package for dealing with the deficit problem. As the 1984 election approached the basic fear was that without a joint stand between the president and congressional leaders, any unpopular combination of spending cuts and tax increases could be too easily attacked and turned into votes by political opponents. "You first, Alphonso" became the theme at both ends of Pennsylvania Avenue.

The dramatic confrontations between the president and Congress on budgetary aggregates made the headlines after 1980. Less visible has been the way in which the executive budget has also been contested in the trench warfare of the congressional committee system. In the Stockman era, executive budgeting as a process has become heavily conditioned by an endless series of engagements between the OMB director and individual committees and subcommittees. At a technical level this attempt at selling the president's program has meant a willingness to translate the president's budget from the traditional executive branch accounting conventions into the various accounting systems by which Congress makes its budget decisions in committees. At an operational level, this involvement has meant a continuous OMB presence on Capitol Hill to trace and keep score of each congressional budget transaction, from subcommittees on up. At a political level executive budgeting has become an interactive process continually reshaped as the OMB director and his personal legislative liaison staff intervene and bargain about evolving budget decisions on the Hill. Thus, for example, if a subcommittee has approved authorizing legislation without due regard for budget outlays, the OMB can be expected to raise the issue with the parent committee through the director's testimony, a new position paper, talking points passed to friendly committee members or staffers, or some other device. As Stockman negotiates the point with legislators, requests filter back to OMB staff for budget recalculations based on alternative technical or political assumptions.

The general point of all this activity has been to present and negotiate the president's—rather than the agencies'—desired budget before every relevant committee and subcommittee of Congress. But executive budgeting for legislative advantages has been in the form of capitalizing on short-term opportunities at the expense of building longer-term institutional relationships. The president's stunning budget victories in the spring and summer of 1981 were achieved not just by negotiating but by virtually expropriating Congress's budget resolution and reconciliation process. Chastened by this experience, many legislators on appropriation and authorization committees came to associate the budget committees and their process with a loss of legislative control. Economic miscalculations about the deficit and nervous financial markets forced the White House to continually return to Congress for midcourse corrections to the budget. As the president found it increasingly difficult to muster the political support to make his budget prevail through any omnibus resolution and reconciliation process, the administration put more of its effort into fighting for restraint in the appropriation and authorization committees and subcommittees. These serial negotiations often had the effect in turn of undercutting the budget committees and their more comprehensive process. In 1981 David Stockman had been the prime mover in a national budget process of epic scale. But in 1984 he was mainly in the role of chief damage control officer fighting a defensive, rearguard action throughout the congressional committee system.

Has all of this made a difference in budgetary outcomes? No one can say because in political management there is no "current services baseline" against which one can measure what the effects would have been without Stockman's and OMB's involvement. Moreover, the experiences at OMB's political levels derived from trying to sell the president's budget on the Hill inevitably feed back into the same budget managers' thinking on strategy and tactics for preparing their next round of proposals. Whatever the effect on the numbers, it does seem clear that the top-down and legislative orientation of the last three years has produced new uncertainties as to just how participants in the processes of executive budgeting are expected to behave. In another volume in this series, Alan Schick has persuasively argued that upsetting established budgetary routine and practice has been essential to any presidential effort to redirect national budget policy. But it is one thing to replace old routines and institutional relationships with new ones. It is quite another thing to tear down old routines without putting any reliable, widely accepted structures of practice in their place. So far it is more the tearing down than the building up of budget institutions that has taken place as central executives have improvised to pursue their policy objectives. Any assessment of this legacy also depends on appreciating the impact of recent changes on the president's budget agency itself, the Office of Management and Budget.

The Institution

Among long-time Washington officials, the Office of Management and Budget (and its forebear, the Bureau of the Budget) has commonly been regarded as a special place. There is, of course, its reputation for power. Sitting astride the budget process, OMB is in a position to influence the supply of life-giving financial resources to the spending agencies, and it simultaneously commands one of the few action-forcing processes that must command presidential attention. No president can escape the requirement of presenting an annual budget, and hence no president can avoid relying heavily on the one agency designed to help him with that task. In addition, the president's budget agency was for a long time regarded as one of the few places to find in-depth knowledge of government programs without the accompanying parochialism of a spending agency's perspective. There obviously always was the bias of an organization interested in controlling the budget, but still, in a world populated by claimants for spending, OMB's willingness to examine all the facts could pass for a kind of objectivity.

And yet there has been more to the feeling of specialness. There are probably a few organizations in Washington that can boast such loyally attended meetings of agency alumni, some of whom date back to the Roosevelt era. In his first talk to assembled OMB staff, David Stockman said he had always hoped to work at OMB someday; it was a place of the best and the brightest, but to become the agency's director was more than he could have hoped for. These and similar feelings reflect the fact that for two generations, dating back to the time when FDR appointed a full-time replacement for Lewis Douglas in the form of Michigan's Republican budget director Harold Smith, the permanent career staff had sought to inculcate a special ethos in the agency. It was not a place to be just another bureaucrat. It was a place to work for the presidency broadly understood. The career officials who managed the Bureau of the Budget from the late 1930s into the late 1960s wanted their agency to be a place where very bright, young people would want to be. The bureau would be staffed by people who had general ability and a capacity to master detail and yet who did not want to be lawyers or academics, people who sought a career in public service but did not want to be politicians. The residue of respect still felt for the budget agency is a mark of how well these institution builders succeeded.

During the 1970s criticisms of the "politicization" of OMB began to circulate. No one seemed quite sure what that term meant. On the one hand there was the obvious addition of first one layer and then two layers of political appointees between the director and the career program divisions. On the other hand no one suggested, even in the worst days of the Nixon White House, that the career staff of OMB engaged in any misconduct of a partisan political nature. Perhaps the most balanced way of putting the issue is to say that the career structure and traditions of the budget agency found it hard to adjust to the changing stakes of presidential budgeting. As we have seen, these stakes carried heavy political overtones. The old traditions of the budget agency ran counter to the higher political profile required to deal with a burgeoning White House staff interested in policy development, with a myriad of interest groups mobilized by the distributive functions of the budget, and with a more internally fragmented Congress that legitimately believed it too had a role in setting national priorities, managing countercyclical fiscal policy, and distributing income. None of the doubts about OMB's role helped the morale of career staff in the 1970s. The gloom deepened in the Carter administration with the widely perceived personal weaknesses of Carter's budget directors (Bert Lance and James McIntyre) and the palpable fact that the White House domestic affairs staff carried more weight with the president than did his budget agency.

Not surprisingly, the Stockman era has brought a surge of energy and self-confidence to OMB. Once again the agency is at the center of things. Stories of inhuman working hours circulate and are reveled in. Rarely if ever has the power of OMB been so great compared with that of domestic government agencies. After years of drought, OMB staff are awash in the influence that comes from having a director who, even after a disastrously candid interview in the *Atlantic Monthly*,[19] can intellectually dominate any discussion of budget policy in the White House, with the agencies, or in negotiations with Congress. On top of all this is the fact that their political leaders' agenda corresponds with the natural instincts of the organization to cut budgets.

The legislative orientation of presidential budgeting not only has given OMB a greater presence on the Hill but also has added to its power in dealing with the rest of the executive branch. No executive agency other than OMB has realistically been able to represent the administration in dealing with the consolidated spending accounts and reconciliation bills that cut across many agencies in the congressional budget process. Likewise, because of their heavy involvement with not only budget committees but appropriation and authorizing committees and subcommittees as well, David Stockman and his closest aides have tended to know the intricacies and negotiating possibilities in Congress at least as well as any head of a spending department. Of course this does not mean that OMB has always prevailed either within the bureaucracy or on Capitol Hill. It does mean that the president's budget and OMB have not been passive onlookers amid the scores of traditional alliances between spending agencies and congressional committees.

But the glory days have not come without a price. The fact that OMB (or those parts of the organization of interest to Stockman) has been an exciting place to be during the last three years should not be allowed to obscure the strains on the institution. In view of the administration's preoccupation with

---

19. William Greider, "The Education of David Stockman," *The Atlantic Monthly*, December 1981, pp. 27–54.

winning policy objectives rather than building or maintaining government institutions, it is particularly important to take note of these strains.

Top-down budget management has affected developments inside OMB no less than spending agencies and members of Congress who are on the receiving end of the executive budget process. In the pre-Stockman era the normal working assumption was that OMB staff had ideas and arguments worth listening to. Even if not always accurate, it was an assumption that added to an aura of high-level professionalism among career staff. More than that, the expectation that important policy choices would evolve from the suggestions of the permanent staff provided an incentive and rationale to build a stock of substantive knowledge that could be called upon to generate ideas. To a young budget examiner just joining OMB, the traditional ethos of the organization went something like this: "The president's budget is a statement of value about every program the federal government runs; you are joining an organization that has to be able to respond competently to any issue—and they vary from president to president—that may arise. That means knowing something of the history, the law, the happenings in the agency, and the academic studies, so that when called upon you can judge the worth of a program. You are joining the only staff able to give presidents a judgment on the worth of programs independent of the agency's view. You have to be knowledgeable enough to pull together what we can know about the programs in your area."

Operations in the past three years have rendered much of that ethos irrelevant. Top-down budgeting developed precisely because the political leadership in the White House and OMB believed that they already knew what to do. This was true not simply in general terms. The self-confidence and budgetary brilliance of Stockman produced a never-ending stream of ideas about what to cut and how to cut. From the beginning, OMB staff have been used and used heavily by the director, but they have been used largely in the way that a project director uses research assistants. Staff are used to provide backup information for the director's ideas, to chase down details, to work up new materials in some prescribed way, and to follow directions rather than to be consulted.

David Stockman has in fact run OMB much like a congressional office rather than an executive institution. The leader is surrounded by a small circle of close personal assistants (mainly carryovers from his days on the Hill). It is here that ideas and strategies are developed and the negotiations with outsiders occur. The remainder of the organization is called upon for quick responses to help the front office do what it has decided to do. Business is conducted on a transaction-by-transaction basis. Each transaction (a new briefing to the White House, a development on the Hill, an idea for recalculating an agency's budget) brings with it a new request for information, moving restlessly through the organization in search of fast answers. Few of the people who supply such information know how it is to be used or what it all means. Staff are judged on the basis of how well and how quickly they can meet the demands of the front office. The organization becomes driven by the director's transactions, by the nonstop need for new numbers and by the sense that the front office will tell one what to do. That, with some exaggeration, is the ethos generated by the excitement of the past three years.

Of course there is a great deal of variation in any organization as complex as OMB. Persons in some divisions have been brought into intimate consultations in the director's office. This is particularly true in the areas in which the largest dollar amounts are to be saved and where staff have the competence to stand up intellectually in debates with the director. I suspect that few persons in the budget agency would contend that Stockman and his personal staff have consciously sought to suppress creative thinking from below. But the fact remains that the consultations and debates occurring are largely derivative from Stockman's interests and ideas at the moment. Some research assistants are simply more important and useful than others.

As much as he respects and admires its reputation, there is little evidence that David Stockman thinks about OMB institutionally. He and his aides draw on OMB staff much as a congressman's office goes to an agency to get information. As one division director who consults closely with Stockman put it:

> He bangs on you for information on the day that he needs it. He doesn't think about how to strengthen the agency's general ability to provide what is wanted. He gets what he wants when he wants it and wherever he can. He doesn't say to himself, ''I'd better get an organization and process in motion to be able to supply what is needed.''[20]

The danger to OMB as an institution is that the "topside" demand for quick answers, without allowing career staff enough access to understand the context of these demands, may indeed encourage agency personnel to become like a congressional staff. This means encouraging the creation of an OMB that knows more about how to get informants to supply substance than knowing the substance of programs themselves. The difference between the traditional Bureau of the Budget/OMB ethos and congressional staff work is in fact the basic difference between an institution and a mere organization. An institution contains enduring capacities of its own regardless of the personal interests of the participants of the moment. Many congressional offices are

---

20. Interview with the author, Washington, D.C., June 28, 1983.

effective organizations for their individual representatives; none has ever been accused of being an institution.

At first glance there would appear to be an important exception to what has just been said. In the past three years David Stockman has presided over the creation of a new piece of machinery to help him cope with the second major feature of the recent budget process identified earlier, the legislative orientation of executive budgeting. The Central Budget Management System (CBMS) is a computerized operation that tracks and keeps score of budgetary decision making in Congress, projects the budget implications of alternative decisions along a variety of dimensions, and is increasingly used to keep score of all OMB decision making as the budget season progresses. Prior to the Reagan era there had been several internal OMB reports foreshadowing the need for such an intelligence system, but it was never developed until Stockman and his aides insisted. CBMS was fashioned out of volunteers from the program division staffs and gave some relief to the overworked Budget Review Division (BRD), the OMB unit responsible for pulling together the final budget document. CBMS has in fact been quickly grafted onto the budget agency precisely because Stockman could not obtain the urgent services he needed from established institutional routines. To understand why, we need to return to the crucial first year of the Reagan administration.

The OMB that Stockman inherited in 1981 was historically built around the task of preparing an executive branch budget and then presenting it to Congress for further action. The OMB that Stockman needed was one that could help the president's budget preferences prevail through a labyrinth of congressional negotiations and decision making. There are a host of detailed ways in which Congress pulls a budget apart in order to deal with it, and until 1981 all of this was foreign territory to almost every careerist at OMB. As Stockman struggled to shepherd the president's first budget through a House vote on the first budget resolution and then through the reconciliation process, the director and his personal aides demanded new information, backup data, and spending projections based on alternative assumptions from the budget agency daily and hourly. To have any chance of being effective on the Hill, Stockman had to speak in the language of the congressional budget process. This meant arguing the president's budget desires in terms of the way congressional committees kept accounts and not the way OMB kept executive agency numbers. It meant understanding the congressional rules by which the totals in the budget resolution were allocated and scored against individual appropriation or authorization committees and subcommittees.

Requests for budget updates and alternative projections poured forth from Stockman and his aides in terms that seemed to make no sense. An emergency staff was thrown together and kept in almost constant session to backstop the director as he fought on a hundred fronts to put teeth into the reconciliation process during the spring of 1981 (and the "rec room" entered OMB lore). As the director pressed for more cuts, and Congress was pushing up against its fall 1981 deadline for action on FY 1982 appropriations, Stockman was still plagued by billion-dollar differences in the ways OMB and congressional analysts prepared budget estimates. The spectacle of the OMB director sitting before congressional committees using his own hand calculator to arrive at budget estimates suggested that something might be wrong. What was wrong was that the president's budget agency had no way of keeping track of overall budget numbers as Congress made hour-to-hour changes in specific programs and policies.

By mid-1982 Stockman's CBMS mechanism was functioning, and by the end of the year most of the bugs in the CBMS computer system had been removed for tracking congressional spending decisions and keeping score of OMB's ever-changing budget numbers. CBMS is more than a sophisticated technology for gathering and analyzing information about the total budget process. It also represents an important organizational adaptation to the new demands imposed by the Reagan-Stockman budget strategy. And like all changes, it brings organizational strains. The changes of the past three years have (1) increased the "topside" reporting requirements and demands for budget numbers from the already hard-pressed program divisions; (2) forced changes in some of the traditional procedures of the Budget Review Division; and (3) pushed OMB into much more intimate contact with the highly political world of congressional accounting and negotiations. For the first time a half-dozen OMB "bill trackers" from BRD are systematically engaged in the routine, grinding work of attending all congressional meetings and hearings to report on the progress of spending legislation, cultivating minority and majority committee staffs to try to keep on top of developments. A newly created legislative liaison staff under the OMB director concentrates on the political nuances of developments in Congress.

Amid all this activity, CBMS remains not only a formal part of BRD but also David Stockman's personal vehicle for budget intelligence. Since mid-1982, CBMS has allowed him almost instantaneously to break down the president's budget into comparisons with previous congressional budget resolutions, or with the final Carter budget, or with the costs of existing policy under a variety of assumptions. And for each of these or any other breakdowns that the director might invent, CBMS allows Stockman to have a day-to-day account of the spending implications of decisions made in all parts of Congress. As OMB's own internal budget process moves into high gear in the fall of the year, CBMS also allows Stockman to keep daily or weekly track of budget decisions being made at all levels—from examiner to White House—

in terms of budget authority, outlays, or whatever category he chooses. This in turn becomes a guide for managing approaches to the White House strategy group as well as monitoring internal OMB operations. As the tracking numbers unfold, there may be an issue that needs to be brought to the White House for guidance. Or it may be that the data buried in the large books of CBMS tables look odd in terms of what Stockman thought would happen. The OMB staffer responsible for that program may then be called directly to see what is happening. "It is as if," said one OMB official, "Stockman has a rudder in his head showing him the general and the detailed shape of the budget he wants."[21]

There seems little room to doubt that the budget agency has become more personalized in the past three years. Personalization has been the effect of top-down budgeting in which the real executive budget emerges as a rolling game plan from the director's office, in consultation with the White House strategy circle. Personalization has also been the effect of the legislative orientation that came naturally to Stockman and for which new services inside OMB had to be tailored. People in the organization who meet the director's immediate needs are involved and stimulated; the rest may go to seed. And even people who are stimulated are stimulated in terms of the director's needs of the moment and not in terms of a more general institutional need to be knowledgeable.

The pressures of the Stockman era have exacerbated a preexisting identity problem among OMB's career staff: What is it to be a good OMB staff person? Some staff objected to having to work on the more or less blatant advocacy contained in the *Major Themes* volume initiated by Stockman. This volume was a more polished and aggressive version of advocacy documents produced for OMB's political leadership in the Ford administration (*Seventy Issues* dealt with the FY 1977 budget proposal and *Issues '78* with the FY 1978 budget) and in the Carter administration (*Major Accomplishments* dealt with the FY 1981 budget proposal). OMB staff who found this work objectionable maintained that their job should have been to lay out all the arguments and not just selected pros and cons. Other OMB staff believed that their job was to do what they were told and even—if told to do so by their immediate political superior—to send forward to the president information that they knew to be heavily slanted. Some staffers willingly did the work on *Major Themes* but kept careful notes in the files to be able to distinguish for a new administration the information they provided from the political rhetoric they did not.

---

21. Interview with the author, Washington, D.C., July 19, 1983.

Similarly, Stockman's heavy demands for various and constantly updated budget numbers intensified a long-standing difference in perspective between the OMB program divisions that do the day-to-day work of examining agency budgets and the Budget Review Division that produces the general budget document. By tradition, examiners chided BRD staff for being accountants and number crunchers who did not understand the programmatic content of budgets. BRD loyalists could respond that examiners never understood the professional skills and general viewpoint needed to produce a coherent budget document. The Reagan-Stockman era produced immense pressures on both groups, but it was generally BRD that was advantaged. Strains on the distinctive skills in the examining divisions had been growing for years. As one former official recalled:

> When I began my career with the Bureau [in the early 1960s], summers were slow. Even a senior examiner had no difficulty finding the time to get out in the field, read the basic laws and regulations, and "kick around the department" to find out what was going on. Enactment of the Congressional Budget and Impoundment Control Act of 1974 was the first massive assault on the time available to learn and thoroughly analyze programs. By the mid-1970s a lot of this free time had been soaked up by drills, reporting requirements, and the like.[22]

The Stockman regime vastly increased the demand for short-order budget data without explaining how the information was to be used. Time for learning about and seriously analyzing programs became in even shorter supply.

By the same token, the priorities of Stockman and the Reagan strategists in the White House tended to work in BRD's favor. The greater interest in budget numbers than program analysis, along with the desire to deal with the budget as a whole and control general budget categories, played to BRD's strong suit. So too did the administration's desire to use three- to five-year budget projections to make its case for the eventual success of Reaganomics. Since the early 1970s BRD had developed a capacity to make such projections in the face of criticisms that no politician would ever look beyond the next budget year. As Stockman made greater use of such aggregated numbers, the BRD found for the first time in years that it, rather than the examining divisions, was becoming the first choice of many of the brightest staffers joining OMB.

Tensions between the examining divisions and BRD have grown. Neither has it helped that the management staff of OMB, a separate, non-budgetary side of the organization that Stockman has left to go its own way under different political leadership, has been allowed to make increasing time demands on budget examiners to produce estimated cost savings and other data

---

22. Interview with the author, Washington, D.C., September 29, 1983.

relevant to federal management improvement schemes, schemes that budget staff typically regard as political window dressing for the Reagan administration. During FY 1981–1982 a revolt of sorts occurred as the program division directors challenged the amount and type of information required from them in preparing the budget document, arguing that it was distracting staff from dealing with the programmatic and policy aspects of the budget. Leaders of the BRD replied that much of the information was required on behalf of the director and that in any event the U.S. budget is a financial document whose accounting conventions have to be protected. In the end a decision had to be made at the political level of OMB, and some of the BRD's reporting requirements were eliminated or simplified.

The BRD-program division fight was arcane and highly technical, but it symbolized the program division's frustration—a perception that its personnel were becoming glorified "bean counters." However, the most noteworthy point is that such issues touching on the career identities within OMB have to be resolved by temporary political personnel. Before the 1970s, the budget agency would have had a senior career official somewhere close to the director and potentially capable of dealing with such problems of institutional self-definition. Most of the time this person would have been a career deputy director of the agency or some other officer with institutionwide responsibilities. The centralized budgeting of the Stockman regime simply reinforced the tendency of recent years to clearly separate politically appointed and career staffs and to supplant career officials from any major role in the running of the budget agency as a whole.

Seemingly small details are important in an institution's identity. In the early 1960s the budget agency's career staff and its two to three political appointees lived cheek-by-jowl in the Old Executive Office Building beside the White House. Construction of a new executive office building in the Johnson administration facilitated the process of setting apart the career staff from hourly and daily involvement at the highest agency levels. During the 1970s the Old Executive Office Building filled up with the expanding White House staff and newly created layers of political appointees to OMB. In 1973 a Congress suspicious of OMB's power in the Nixon administration required Senate confirmation of OMB's director and deputy director. By the mid-1970s the only OMB career official remaining with an office in the old building was (and is) the director of BRD. During the Carter administration, advisers with little prior experience in presidential staffing produced a reorganization that meant that OMB lost control of its own library and personnel administration to a new central Executive Office of Administration, again headed by a temporary appointee. In the Stockman years, the director's top-down approach and reliance on personal aides largely completed the process by which the identity of OMB as a whole was put in the hands of people without any enduring career commitment to the organization. "We are," said one permanent division head, "becoming just another agency."

Should anyone care? On the one hand, a case can be made that OMB has simply done what a government agency should always do: It has become adaptable and has adjusted to the changing needs of the times. To expect a presidential staff to have an institutional character or will of its own is to court the danger of bureaucratic power, ingrown perspectives, and unresponsiveness.

I believe there is a good cause for worrying. What presidents as a group need (though not what they always want) is more than simple responsiveness; it is knowledgeable responsiveness. In a political world with a surfeit of advocacy and salesmanship, the islands of more or less objective analysis are fragile and require nurturing. In recent years OMB has been more exploited than nurtured. There have been fewer incentives to think about accumulating experience or to prepare for contingencies beyond the tenure of a sitting administration or the political appointees of the day.

If the argument of this volume is correct and we are in for a period of continuing deficits and expenditure restraint, then at a minimum we need an OMB with the analytic capacity to help identify which programs are expendable and which programs can make the strongest case for scarce resources. The knowledge necessary to justify such advice should be broader and deeper than that acquired simply by serving the informational needs and bargaining tactics of the political leaders of the moment. But the point goes deeper. Perhaps the future will not turn on the deficit issue. We have a right to expect that OMB should be prepared to deal with a political agenda that is less preoccupied with budget cutting and more concerned with programmatic results. The test of a staff serving the presidency as an ongoing institution is not its responsiveness to one set of demands, but its ability to respond to one set of demands without diminishing its capacity to respond to the next. It is in this sense that the institutional ethos of OMB remains relevant for the years ahead—not to look back nostalgically to a golden age that never existed but to stay prepared for a constantly changing future.

The Legacy

It has been impossible to discuss recent trends in executive budgeting without paying heavy attention to the role of a personality like David Stockman and the particular agenda of the Reagan administration. The natural question to ask is what will have proved to be the enduring changes once this cast of characters has left the stage.

Other chapters in this volume provide judgments of the Reagan legacy based on the budget numbers. To me at least, these numbers indicate that despite the immense exertions in the executive budget process, the long-run result will have proved to be a tidying up, not a major transformation, of the American welfare state. Those social programs and provisions that have withstood the Reagan-Stockman onslaught are now part of the political firmament and ready to be built upon. Moreover, it is far from clear that executive budgeting has come to grips with the major driving forces of federal spending: social entitlements, Medicare, and defense.

Of course the argument can always be made that in the absence of the administration's efforts, the momentum of federal domestic spending would have been much greater and the defense commitment much smaller. To make the case appears to be part of the purpose behind Stockman's requests inside OMB for repeated updates of what would have been the costs of existing policy at the time Carter left office. The problem is that no one can ever know how "existing policy" might have changed if Reagan had not taken office. The games that can be played with various baseline projections are probably less important than the impact of recent developments on the way our political institutions arrive or fail to arrive at budgetary decisions. These unquantified features may be the truly lasting impact of the Reagan-Stockman era.

If the preceding account in this paper has merit, a number of conclusions about this kind of legacy seem plausible. By way of summary I will try to outline these points under the three categories used earlier: the stakes, the process, and the institution of executive budgeting.

The Stakes. 1. If nothing else, the Reagan-Stockman regime has forced the political system to think about the major forces driving the federal budget. The notion of uncontrollables, especially as regards entitlement spending, has become a less neglected feature of the national budget debate. No budget process can inject courage or otherwise force politicians to make difficult decisions. What budgeting can do and has done is to reveal the financial consequences of political decisions taken and avoided. That is no small accomplishment.

2. The problem of projected deficits has not only haunted the Reagan administration and Congress. It has served to illuminate the stakes of monetary authorities in conjunction with financial markets as a third player in the national budget process. Without the bad news periodically turned in by financial markets, it is unlikely that politicians at either end of the Avenue would have felt sufficiently pressured to constantly return to readdress the budget problem.

3. And yet this third player can be only reactive, vetoing the good news that Congress and the White House want to tell about their budget projections. Thus the partisan stakes have grown too with no accepted mechanism for resolving them. The president's opposition to major tax increases or defense reductions and Congress's increasing reluctance to impose further domestic spending cuts have produced a general stalemate. Deficits have reached proportions that four years ago would have been politically unthinkable. The initial Reagan-Stockman strategy had been to use deficit fears to squeeze out more domestic spending cuts. Financial markets have eagerly registered the fears, but the political effect has been to develop a kind of scar tissue against the deficit numbers. Executive budget strategy has inadvertently encouraged such a political calculus. Congressmen in individual spending committees bargaining with OMB can see that no particular action on their part will make a noticeable impact on the aggregate deficit; it is at least as easy to blame deficits on the miscalculations in the original 1981 Reagan program which was hastily enacted by Congress; and White House maneuvering clearly suggests that congressional action against the deficits may well be disavowed and used for partisan purposes by the president or his backers. That the administration has proposed vastly unbalanced budgets while the president has urged a constitutional amendment to prohibit such proposals has only added to the aura of unproductive partisanship. When the preacher is caught sinning, why should the parishioners repent?

4. In using the executive budget to exert leverage on Congress, the Reagan administration has raised the symbolic stakes of budget projections in a way that is not likely to soon disappear. Little of what the administration promised could be accomplished in the near term. However, extending the time horizon of the president's budget proposals and economic projections could help the White House make its case by showing unspecified savings, declining deficits, and other results in the future. Executive budgeting under Reagan gave a new political importance to the multiyear budget projections that had been routinely printed and forgotten since the 1974 congressional budget reform (projections that are three years ahead in the congressional budget resolution and five years ahead for the baseline costs of existing policies). In response, Congress has also found the out-year projections a politically comfortable place to argue about who is tougher on defense or more opposed to higher taxes. The politics of projective budgeting, combined with the fact that debates on congressional budget resolutions are merely about guidelines and not real spending decisions, has greatly enlarged the scope for budget negotiations that are richer in symbolism than in substance.

5. Because it had a largely negative domestic agenda (the things it wanted government to stop doing), the Reagan administration tended to reduce the

role of the federal budget as an instrument of more positive policy development. The type of information created in the budget debates of the last three years has been primarily in the form of pricing alternative savings packages. Stocks of information allowing a more complete evaluation of programs and their effectiveness have not been replenished because this type of information has not usually been sought by executive or congressional budget managers. This analytic shortage will be felt whenever future political priorities shift from cost-control exercises to more in-depth program analysis and an active domestic agenda.

The Process. 6. Few observers are convinced that the budget process in the Reagan administration came to effective grips with the defense establishment. Widely circulated stories of the OMB director's generally unsuccessful campaigns against the defense budget in the past three years have only added to that feeling. It seems likely that important counter-pressures have now been set in motion which will eventually produce proposals for less favored treatment of the Pentagon at the hands of OMB.

7. Top-down budgeting probably reached its apogee in the first year of the Reagan administration. To repeat that performance will be difficult because few administrations are likely to impose the same degree of ideological unity on agency heads, nor are they likely to find another David Stockman as budget director. Still, the Reagan administration has shown what can be done, and future administrations may be emboldened to try again. If so, one can expect that there will be in Washington some lore about how the Reagan system worked, with some former participants available to give advice or lend a hand.

8. The Reagan-Stockman era has shown how important it is to think about the federal budget process as a whole and not simply as two separate executive and congressional budget processes. Each half reverberates on the other. In theory the budget "integrators" of each branch—president and OMB in the executive; congressional leadership, budget committees, and CBO in the legislature—share a common interest. It is to see that individual budget decisions are related to each other and to available resources as a whole. But it is only an abstract interest. Handled carefully, top-down integration in the executive branch may strengthen the forces of integration in Congress. Handled carelessly and for short-term bargaining advantages, centralized budgeting in the executive branch may eventually increase the strains on the already weak forces of integration in Congress, as spending agencies excluded from serious consideration by the presidency shop for ways around the centralized procedures of the congressional budget process. Similarly, to use or bypass the legislature's budget resolution and reconciliation process for strictly momentary tactical advantages has the effect of weakening budget committees

to the benefit of uncoordinated appropriation and authorization committees. There *is* a joint long-term interest between the presidency and Congress in having a reliable and coordinated federal budget process. The Reagan experience has shown that, unfortunately, there are few incentives for individual politicians to build and sustain the institutional relationships to realize that interest.

9. Probably the most enduring change in executive budgeting is the congressional orientation it received during the Reagan years. No president or budget director is likely to want to go back to the days when the president's proposal was largely left to the tender mercies of spending agencies and the committee system. After Stockman's tenure there will be in place a working system that allows the president's senior staff to make the president's case in all the congressional forums where the real budget decisions are made. It will be a very peculiar president who does not want to make that case (though peculiarity has obviously been no bar to the office).

The Institution.　10. One part of Reagan-Stockman legacy will be an energetic, animated budget agency. OMB has enjoyed presidential confidence, and its writ has run far in the executive branch. That power must decline as top-down budgeting inevitably erodes, but after a barren period in the Carter administration, a politically stronger and more visible OMB is certainly in place today.

11. It follows from what has been said earlier that the scope of OMB's involvement, once enlarged to the enactment of the president's budget in Congress, is unlikely to diminish. Unless a future director wants to withdraw from defending the president's budget or to rely solely on the numbers Congress provides, some version of the Central Budget Management System and congressional liaison office is likely to remain in existence. That form will obviously have to accommodate budget directors who do not have Stockman's ability to absorb massive amounts of complex information and to relate to Capitol Hill.

12. The experience of the last three years leaves more open than ever the question of what kind of organization the Office of Management and Budget is to be. Externally, OMB must always be seen as being close to the president. But it is unlikely to sustain constructive alliances with budget integrators in Congress if it is seen as no more than the president's salesman. Today it is more the Congressional Budget Office than OMB which is seen as a more or less objective purveyor of non-partisan numbers and analyses. Internally, OMB's identity problem is at least as serious though rarely spoken about. Certainly any prolonged use of OMB staff as research assistants will tend to produce an organization that can provide little more than research assistance. The problem with Stockman's way of doing business is not its

intent but its effect. It does not simply deplete the stock of independent ideas from below; it undercuts any incentive to replenish the stock. The attenuated two-way communication between the larger political layers and career staff has the same effect of undermining institutional capacities. As career officials are less expected to understand the uses to which their information is put in the front office, so they become less able, and ultimately less interested, in understanding the larger picture. In this sense OMB's political power may have increased while its institutional strength has eroded.

COMMENTS

Hale Champion

Hugh Heclo's paper "Executive Budget Making" is a useful and perceptive look at the changing behavior in the Office of Management and Budget in the Reagan administration as OMB responded both to changes in budget process in the Congress and to the new policies and resulting budget environment of the administration.

What happened in what Heclo calls the "top-down approach" in OMB under David Stockman, as contrasted with the traditional bottom-up method, almost excluded cabinet departments and agencies from the formulation of the budget. As Heclo notes, the Department of Defense was a notable exception, but one that was a special case, not one that invalidated the general perception that OMB dominated the process to an unprecedented extent at the expense of the departments. Even agency feedback to White House budget determinations was severely limited. That was true not only in the executive budget process, but to a surprising extent in the subsequent congressional negotiation.

Thus, the first institutional victims of the changed process, whether for good or ill, were the domestic cabinet departments and agencies. Not surprisingly, the process losers were the substantive losers. They lost money, which was intended. They also lost budget consideration of program effectiveness, which may or may not have been intended, depending on the program involved. Cost control was elevated over program effectiveness, sometimes even without consideration of easily available knowledge of the best ways to cut costs without undue harm to program effectiveness. The early Social Security fiasco was a case in point; the attack on the disability rolls was another that is still causing trouble. And, of course, there were the lesser, symbolic "catsup for lunch" problems.

What happened in the executive budget process under Reagan lends new force to Nelson Polsby's recent truth-in-jest that there are now four branches in the federal government—executive, legislative, judicial, and presidential.

292

If the presidential and congressional branches can establish better working processes at the macrolevels of size and allocation in the fiscal policy debate, this subordination of the executive branch (defined as nonpresidential) might be beneficial. But more departmental feedback still would be desirable, and so would delegation of many microdeterminations hastily made in the macrobudget process without sufficient information to make them either effective or efficient.

The major reservation I have concerning the Heclo paper has to do with the importance of Stockman. Heclo suggests that Stockman's personal capacities and orientation were critical to Reagan's 1981 success. They were very important, especially in the creation of OMB capacity to keep track of the congressional process and interact with it, and in Stockman's function as a remarkably adept and perceptive scorekeeper.

I believe, however, that the White House legislative strategy group, of which Stockman was an important member, was even more essential. That group could deal with Congress across a much wider range of issues than budget items alone; the Stockman and OMB efforts were secondary. I think their efforts also had a limited impact on the president, who was rightly understood not to be ready to bend to a lot of conventional political and budgetary wisdom, and who has proved willing—if painted into a corner—to walk right over his own wet paint on occasion. The handling of defense spending and the mounting overall deficits were cases in point.

The White House coordination of the budget-making processes in OMB and Congress the first time around, informed, except in defense, by Stockman, was a remarkable feat. That coordination, paralleling the rapid increase in House and Senate Budget Committee authority, seem to move us a step closer to many much-needed reforms in the executive budget-making process by aligning that process much more closely with the congressional one. The executive budget failure the second time around was a political breakdown, not a failure of process.

Perhaps Stockman's almost exclusive attention to working out the budget with the White House and Congress in the Reagan administration is the final evidence required that OMB cannot also deal with the critical and still growing management problems in the federal government. Stockman did not use much management information in formulating the budget, certainly not having the time and probably not having either the personal or institutional competence in OMB to do so.

Both the president's Private Sector Survey on Cost Control (generally known as the Grace Commission, after its chairman, Peter Grace) and a National Academy of Public Administration panel on management issues already have concluded, with sadness and some reluctance in the case of the academy, that some new institution is needed if management reforms in personnel, procurement, information systems, and the like are going to be undertaken urgently and continued effectively through more than one administration. OMB just cannot handle them, given the increased demands for urgent attention that the new relationship with the congressional budget process requires. Creation of a separate overhead management unit would let OMB again become the Bureau of the Budget and the appropriate presidential parallel to—and match for—the Congressional Budget Office.

Reagan actually campaigned on an assumption that most domestic budgetary savings could come from management reforms to eliminate "fraud, waste, and abuse" rather than from reduction or elimination of programs, but Stockman paid little attention to the campaign oratory. Given the fact that management reforms require long lead time and, in some cases, substantial new front-end investment in people and in data-processing hardware and software, Stockman had little choice. Others in OMB and the White House, including the Grace Commission, did get a management reform effort under way, at least the commission produced a report and got some publicity for reform—but few reforms have resulted, except for the so-called Carlucci procurement initiatives in the Defense Department.

With respect to Heclo's other observations on OMB institutional legacies, I share his concern about turning career inhabitants of OMB into searchers for politically useful numbers and advocates with little concern for either the institution's or their own long-term credibility. They need to have continuity and credibility as even-handed enforcers of standards and as historians.

The appropriate behavior for careerists throughout the government is to be responsive to the administration within reasonable norms of preserving individual and institutional capacity to function usefully and credibly over the longer term. The Stockman regime has shown insufficient sensitivity to this careerist problem, with OMB having done some advocacy with numbers that damaged its analytic credibility, particularly with respect to the safety net.

Heclo notes appropriately that OMB was also a big institutional loser in dealing with the Defense Department, not being able to define the terms or the magnitudes of the growth numbers in the defense debate, even for the president. That inability was basically Stockman's fault, not the institution's. He didn't get to the problem early enough, and I suspect it will take more time than is generally recognized to repair both the budgetary and the institutional damage to OMB because of the "out-year" commitments fastened into place while Stockman and the legislative strategy group were busy on the domestic scene.

EXECUTIVE AGENCY RETRENCHMENT

Joseph S. Wholey

In its first three years, the Reagan administration made major changes in the federal government's domestic programs. With the help of administration appointees in federal agencies, the Office of Management and Budget (OMB) and the White House took control of the federal budget process, broke or seriously dented many "iron triangles," and achieved dramatic changes in federal programs—including many changes that had been sought by prior administrations. Between January 1981 and July 1983, Congress agreed to reduce human resources spending between fiscal year (FY) 1982 and FY 1985 by approximately $110 billion (7 percent) below the projected expenditures under the laws in effect at the beginning of 1981 (see table 1).

How was the budget environment for federal agencies changed by the pressures for cutbacks in nondefense programs? Did the pressures for cutbacks lead to different decision criteria? What happened to agency funding and staffing? What happened to programs that had demonstrated high performance? What were the effects on agency operations and program activities? In this paper we examine budget making and operations in five federal agencies that experienced important changes in budgets, staffing, and program direction between 1981 and 1983.

In the first three years of the Reagan administration, the federal agency budget-making environment changed from one open to exploration of budget

Robert Behn, Laurence Lynn, other conference participants, Frederick Thayer, and my colleagues on the study team provided valuable criticism at several stages in the analysis. James Bell, William Holland, Alfred Schwartz, John Waller, and Jane Wholey conducted interviews, gathered useful documentation on the five agencies, and made helpful comments on earlier versions of this paper.

TABLE 1

OUTLAY CHANGES FOR SELECTED HUMAN RESOURCES PROGRAMS:
FY 1982–FY 1985

| Programs | Changes in Total Outlays, FY 1982– FY 1985, Resulting from Legislative Actions Between January 1981 and July 1983 | |
	In $ Billions	As a Percentage of Program Outlays
Retirement and Disability	−25.8	−3
Other Income Security	−27.1	−10
Unemployment Insurance	−7.8	−7
Food Stamps	−7.0	−13
Child Nutrition	−5.2	−28
WIC (and Commodity Supplemental Feeding Program)	+0.2	+4
Health	−18.5	−5
Health Services Programs	−1.4	−22
Educational and Social Services	−13.7	−20
Employment and Training	−25.0	−60
General Employment and Training	−7.4	−35
Job Corps	−0.1	−6
Public Service Employment	−16.9	−99
Total	−110.1	−7

SOURCE: Adapted from "Major Legislative Changes in Human Resources Programs Since January 1981: Staff Memorandum," Report prepared for Speaker Thomas P. O'Neill (Washington, D.C.: Congressional Budget Office, August 1983).

alternatives to one in which policymakers and staff focused their energies on achieving specific reductions in spending, staffing, and federal leadership of state and local program activities. OMB made most budget decisions before receiving agency inputs. Agency budgets were driven by both the administration's retrenchment objectives and traditional budget criteria like reduction of ineffective and inappropriate program activities. Even in this "top-down" budgeting environment, agencies made a number of successful appeals from initial OMB decisions. In implementing administration budget decisions, moreover, agency policymakers often moved beyond the administration's original budget proposals.

In 1981 and 1982, Congress, strongly influenced by the administration's constant pressures to reduce domestic spending, accepted budget changes of unprecedented scope. In each of the agencies examined, the administration achieved substantial progress toward most of its retrenchment objectives.

Ineffective and inappropriate programs were sharply cut back. A number of the administration's proposed block grants were enacted. When programs had demonstrated high performance, however (for example, the WIC—Women, Infants, and Children—nutrition program and the Job Corps), Congress resisted administration pressures.

Although administration and congressional decisions often disrupted and delayed agency operations between 1981 and 1983, most agencies survived and functioned reasonably well. And although staffs and programs were reduced in every agency examined, the agencies achieved a number of changes designed to strengthen agency and program performance. In three of the five agencies, however, reductions in discretionary programs, grantee reporting, and federal monitoring and evaluation will limit agency ability to sense changing needs and to test responses to those needs.

On balance, the picture of conditions at the agency level that emerges is more encouraging than might have been expected. Further research is needed to compare this perspective with those that could be obtained from states, local governments, and clients.

Research Approach

My colleagues and I examined impacts on five agencies selected to represent the major human resources functions:

1. The Food and Nutrition Service (FNS) of the U.S. Department of Agriculture, which is responsible for federal support for income security programs including the Food Stamp program, child nutrition programs, the food distribution program, and the Special Supplemental Food Program for Women, Infants, and Children (WIC).

2. The Employment and Training Administration (ETA) of the Department of Labor, which is responsible for federal support for the Job Corps and other employment and training programs, unemployment insurance, and state employment services.

3. The Health Resources and Services Administration (HRSA) of the Department of Health and Human Services (HHS), which is responsible for federal support for maternal and child health care, community health centers, the Indian Health Service, health professions education, health planning, the medical facilities guarantee and loan fund, and the health maintenance organization (HMO) loan and loan guarantee fund.

4. The National Institute of Mental Health (NIMH), also of HHS, which provides federal support for research, training, and other activities related to the promotion of mental health, prevention and treatment of mental illness, and rehabilitation of affected individuals.

5. The Administration on Aging (AoA), also of HHS, which is responsible for federal support for social services, nutrition services, training, research, discretionary programs, advocacy on behalf of the elderly, and related activities designed to meet the needs of elderly people.

These five agencies account for $45 billion of the $110 billion projected to be cut from human resources programs between FY 1982 and FY 1985 (see table 1). Some programs in the agencies sustained severe cuts (for example, public service employment, child nutrition, and health services programs), whereas other programs suffered less or even made modest gains between FY 1981 and FY 1983 (for example, the WIC nutrition program, the Job Corps, and social and nutrition services for elderly people).

We collected information on these agencies by reviewing budget documents and other reports available outside the agencies; by interviewing more than sixty agency respondents at policy, management, and staff levels; and by reviewing documents provided by the respondents. Our primary data source was a series of interviews with fifty-six career staff members, eight political appointees, and four other persons knowledgeable about agency activities (see table 2.) Respondents were asked to discuss (1) problems and constraints their agency faced; (2) responses by the agency and other major factors; (3) changes in decision makers and criteria; (4) changes in the budget process and outcomes; (5) changes in staff performance and morale; and (6) changes in agency efficiency, effectiveness, and responsiveness (see the discussion guide in exhibit 1). Respondents were assured anonymity.

Changes in the Budget-Making Environment and Decision Criteria for Budget Requests

Once in office, the Reagan administration moved quickly to change the direction of the federal government. Within four weeks of Inauguration Day, the administration introduced a "program for economic recovery" that included $35 billion in reductions from the expenditure levels in the FY 1982 budget that the Carter administration had just proposed. Seven weeks after Inauguration Day, the new administration produced a revised FY 1982 budget that included another $14 billion in proposed expenditure reductions. The

TABLE 2

RESPONDENTS FOR FIVE FEDERAL AGENCIES

| | Agencies[a] | | | | | |
	FNS	ETA	HRSA	NIMH	AoA	Total
Career						
Department level						
Staff organizations	1	4[b]	4	0	2	11
Operating Division level						
Line management			1	0	0	1
Staff organizations			0	0	2	2
Agency level						
Line management	0	0	2	1	1	4
Staff organizations	2	4	4	1	4	15
Institute level						
Line management				1		1
Staff organizations				3		3
Program level						
Management	0	2	3	3	3	11
Staff	0	0	3[c]	3	2	8
Total Career	3	10	17	12	14	56
Noncareer						
Department level						
Line management	1	0	0	0	0	1
Staff organizations	0	0	1	0	1	2
Operating Division level						
Line management			0	0	1	1
Staff organizations			0	0	1	1
Agency level						
Line management	0	2	0	0	0	2
Staff organizations	1	0	0	0	0	1
Total Noncareer	2	2	1	0	3	8
Other	2	0	0	1	1	4
Total	7	12[b]	18[c]	13	18	68

a. FNS = Food and Nutrition Service, U.S. Department of Agriculture; ETA = Employment and Training Administration, Department of Labor; HRSA = Health Resources and Services Administration, Department of Health and Human Services; NIMH = National Institute of Mental Health, Department of Health and Human Services; AoA = Administration on Aging, Department of Health and Human Services.

b. One of the respondents was a recently retired career senior executive.

c. One of the respondents was a former HRSA staff member who had been RIFfed.

revised FY 1982 budget included rescissions from FY 1981 appropriations consistent with the program changes proposed for FY 1982.

This section examines changes in the budget-making environment for human resources agencies, in the relationships between federal agencies and OMB, and in the decision criteria used in preparing budget requests.

EXHIBIT 1
DISCUSSION GUIDE

BUDGET DEVELOPMENT AND PROGRAM OPERATIONS, FY 1981–FY 1983:
AREAS FOR DISCUSSION

1. Developing the FY 1982, 1983, and 1984 Budgets:
   a. What problems and constraints did the agency face?
   b. How did the agency and other major actors respond to the problems and con-
      straints? Were there changes in decision makers or in decision criteria in com-
      parison with earlier years?
   c. What were the most important outcomes of the budget development process?
      What happened to funding for agency programs and staff activities? To what
      extent did the budget development process tend to promote agency economy,
      efficiency, or effectiveness?
   d. Were there uncertainties or changes in the agency's budget or authorized staffing
      level during the fiscal year?

2. Program Operations and Staff Activities in FY 1981, 1982, and 1983:
   a. What other problems or constraints did the agency face? Were there actual or
      threatened hiring freezes or RIFs? What happened to FTP and FTE staffing
      levels between January 1981 and September 1983?
   b. How did the agency and other major actors respond to the problems and con-
      straints? Were there changes in planning time horizons, decision criteria, or
      types of program or staff activities in comparison with earlier years? Were there
      changes in staff performance or morale?
   c. What were the most important outcomes in terms of program and staff services?
      To what extent were there changes in agency efficiency, effectiveness, or
      responsiveness?

"Top-Down" Budgeting for Retrenchment

In working on the FY 1982 and 1983 budgets during the calendar year
1981, the executive branch shifted to a "top-down" budgeting process. The
White House and OMB agreed on broad budget objectives; the White House
then delegated most budget decisions to OMB. OMB asked the agencies to
prepare budgets in accord with detailed guidance that translated administration
objectives into specific changes to be made in program expenditures and
staffing levels. Although agencies could and did successfully appeal some
budget decisions, the administration's budgets were very close to the original
OMB decisions. Severe time constraints, the administration's delay in filling
subcabinet positions, and the ideology of political appointees made it difficult
for agencies to do other than accede to OMB budget guidance for FY 1982
and 1983. In preparation of the FY 1984 and 1985 budgets, in contrast, there
was much more interaction between the agencies and OMB.

Staff members in the Department of Agriculture reported, for example, that the department's participation in the FY 1982 budget process was extremely limited: the major budget reductions that OMB proposed were "final"; there was no opportunity for a full budget process in the time available. Staff members were not asked for substantive options or for strategy suggestions. For subsequent fiscal years, normal timing, phasing, and interaction occurred. Political appointees were then on board at the Department of Agriculture, and they participated in development of the budget.

Staff members in the Department of Labor reported that in 1981 and 1982 the primary decisions on Employment and Training Administration budgets and on the Job Training Partnership Act were made with little input from department or ETA staff. OMB, the White House, and Congress debated the major policy changes and made the major decisions. Administration advocates had been placed in policy positions in the department and in ETA, so there was little resistance to OMB's proposed budget cuts. Policy analysis and program evaluation were not used to any extent. Decision papers exploring budget alternatives were not requested from the department's budget staff or from ETA. One budget staff member in the Department of Labor commented, "It has been a masterful performance of taking charge and cutting out things you don't like. Masterful! . . . They did this without a lot of paper. There was little guidance; mainly numbers from the secretary or OMB to be met." A former Department of Labor career executive called it "Fast, efficient reduction of programs that do not agree with the philosophy."

In contrast, the secretary of Health and Human Services (Richard Schweiker) and the Public Health Service (PHS) were closely involved in the development of the Reagan administration's FY 1982 budget. HHS budget staff spent a good deal of the available time trying to specify the staffing needed to operated agency programs. Because time was so limited (HHS had only five days to respond to OMB with appeals), the secretary and PHS had to focus their attention on specific problem areas. The secretary intervened particularly on biomedical research, his main concern in PHS. He also helped salvage funding for health professions education from OMB's attempts to eliminate it. As one Health Resources and Services Administration manager commented,

> Secretary Schweiker made a direct appeal to OMB. . . . The secretary's involvement helped to shape Bureau of Health Professions priorities: focus on more targeted needs/activities; no more general support; emphasis on primary care, the appropriate distribution of health professionals, and disadvantaged assistance. . . . The FY 1983 and 1984 budget cycles were much more tranquil because the secretary's compromise agreement of a $120 million funding base was in force. As part of the fiscal year 1982 cycle, we got a fix on the health professions budget through FY 1986.

Most of the Reagan administration's FY 1982 budget for HRSA programs mirrored OMB's budget guidance to the department. As one PHS manager commented, "In a few weeks during the FY 1982 cycle, many of the PHS programs were reconfigured. Whether one agrees or disagrees, the amount of change that occurred in a very short period was significant."

Budget Objectives and Decision Criteria

OMB budget proposals reflected five administration objectives:

1. Reduce federal spending.

2. Reduce or eliminate program activities judged to be ineffective or inappropriate; target available resources on people most in need.

3. Combine categorical programs into block grants to the states; reduce funding and federal staffing for the combined programs.

4. Reduce agency staffing, and agency salaries and expenses (S&E) accounts.

5. Reduce federal regulations, reporting requirements, and programmatic leadership.

OMB's FY 1982 budget guidance contained brief explanations of the amounts of dollars and staff identified in the document. For health resources and health services programs, for example, the following criteria were to be used in developing the budget for FY 1982 to FY 1984:

● Stop providing direct health services, except in areas where such services are not provided by others.

● De-emphasize categorical discretionary grants.

● Shift program responsibilities to the states.

● Reduce regulation of states and other organizations funded by agency programs.

● Reduce the number of federal employees.

● Reduce support for institutions, such as capitation grants.

● Wherever possible, target expenditures more narrowly.

● Do not use substantial amounts of federal money for health planning, health maintenance organizations, or health care for merchant seamen.

OMB specified dollar amounts and staffing down to the bureau level.

Four of the agencies were under heavy pressure to reduce spending, reduce staffing, and reduce the federal role (see table 3). The Administration on Aging (AoA), which enjoyed broad political support, was not under pressure to include its programs in the proposed social services block grant, and the proposed cuts in AoA programs were less deep than the cuts proposed in the other four agencies.

Agency budgets were driven both by administration objectives and by traditional budget criteria. Except where the administration's ideology dictated proposed program and staffing reductions, decision criteria were extensions of those traditionally used (see table 3). Many of the proposed reductions were in programs known to be weak or inappropriate and already on a downward trend, including public service employment, health professions education, and health planning. As one HRSA staff member commented, "It's important to note that reductions in many areas were sought by prior administrations. There is general evidence that we've completed the job of establishing the capacity to educate health professionals and completed the job of filling most major gaps in unmet need for health professions graduates."

Given the pressures to reduce spending and reduce federal staff activities in nondefense areas, OMB proposed specific reductions in four types of program activities:

- Program activities considered inappropriate because they were in conflict with the ideology of the administration (for example, provision of food stamps to strikers or to middle-income people, social research, and health planning)

- Programs that were to be replaced by broad-purpose block grants to the states (for example, maternal and child health programs; primary health care programs; and programs to provide alcohol, drug abuse, and mental health services)

- Programs that had long been considered inappropriate federal activities (for example, Public Health Service hospitals and programs for training health professionals where supplies were already adequate)

- Programs generally considered inefficient or ineffective (for example, Public Service Employment and Trade Adjustment Assistance).

In the Alcohol, Drug Abuse, and Mental Health Administration (ADAMHA), for example, the White House decided to propose an alcohol, drug abuse, mental health (ADAMH) block grant, with reduced funding for the service programs included in the block grant. As in prior administrations,

TABLE 3

ADMINISTRATION OBJECTIVES AND PROPOSALS

Agency/Program	Administration Objectives[a]					Proposed Changes and Decision Criteria
	01	02	03	04	05	
Food and Nutrition Service	X	X	Y	Y	Y	Save money.
Food Stamp Program	X	X				Tighten eligibility; delay cost-of-living increases.
Child Nutrition	X	X				Tighten eligibility; require greater cost-sharing by participants above the poverty line.
WIC Nutrition Program	X		X	X	X	Include in maternal and child health block grant.
Employment and Training Administration	X	X	X	X	X	Reduce expenditures and reduce or eliminate activities considered ineffective or inappropriate.
General Employment and Training	X	X	X		X	Eliminate public service employment; eliminate stipends for trainees.
Job Corps	X					Substantially reduce.
Public Service Employment	X	X		X		Eliminate inefficient program.[b]
Unemployment Insurance	X	X				Tighten eligibility.
Trade Adjustment Assistance	X	X				Eliminate inefficient program.[b]
Health Resources and Services Administration	X	X	X	X	X	Consolidate programs into block grants and eliminate programs considered inappropriate.
PHS Hospitals	X	X		X		Eliminate inappropriate program.[b]
Community Health Centers	X		X	X	X	Include in primary care block grant.
Maternal and Child Health	X		X	X	X	Include in MCH block.
Family Planning	X		X	X	X	Include in MCH block.
Indian Health Service	X					Finance more IHS operations by collecting third party reimbursements; restrain spending.

TABLE 3 (continued)

Agency/Program	Administration Objectives[a]					Proposed Changes and Decision Criteria
	01	*02*	*03*	*04*	*05*	
Health Professions Education	X	X		X		Eliminate unneeded programs; reduce support for institutions.[b]
Health Planning	X	X		X	X	Eliminate program that conflicts with administration ideology.
HMO Development	X	X		X		Eliminate program that conflicts with administration ideology.
National Institute of Mental Health	X	X	X	X	X	Consolidate service programs into block grants; eliminate unneeded and inappropriate programs.
Services	X		X	X	X	Include in alcohol, drug abuse, mental health block grant.
Community Support Program	X		X			Let the states fund through the ADAMH block.
Research	X	X				Eliminate social research.
Training	X	X				Eliminate unneeded clinical training.[b]
Administration on Aging	Y	Y		Y	Y	Restrain spending; give states greater flexibility.
Social Services and Nutrition	Y				Y	Maintain services with same or reduced federal funding; consolidate appropriations for nutrition and social services.
Training, Research, Discretionary	X	X				Reduce programs considered ineffective.

a. 01 = Reduce federal spending.
    02 = Reduce or eliminate program activities judged to be ineffective or inappropriate; target available resources on those most in need.
    03 = Combine categorical programs into block grants to the states; reduce funding and federal staffing for the combined programs.
    04 = Reduce agency staffing—and salaries and expenses (S&E) accounts.
    05 = Reduce federal regulations, reporting requirements, and programmatic leadership.
    X = Major impact on agency/program budget.
    Y = Some impact on agency/program budget.
b. Reduction had been sought by prior administrations.

OMB also proposed to cut NIMH support for clinical training, on the ground that there already were sufficient supplies of (and training opportunities for) psychiatrists, psychologists, psychiatric nurses, and psychiatric social workers. Finally, in 1981 OMB proposed deep cuts in NIMH research, on the ground that it was "soft" social science research. Educating the new HHS team on the types of research that were actually being funded, ADAMHA successfully appealed a portion of the proposed cuts in NIMH research. As one ADAMHA manager stated,

> The preconception in the NIMH context was that most of the research we did here was "soft," that it was "social research": even if you got good reports, there was not very much that the government could do about the problems. That was a very small part of [the NIMH research program]. So we had to . . . go through sort of an educational process and establish the kinds of good stuff that we were doing. . . . We turned out to be, to my knowledge, the only PHS agency to appeal its budget mark, both in the decisions of '81 and '82, to the new secretary. . . . We thought we were being treated disparately to the NIH [National Institutes of Health] funding situation. . . . We talked about cutting that part of the research we call "social research," where there wasn't a direct link between the research and a mental disease. That was a definitional process. We'd started looking at that prior to the change in administration, so we were in fairly good shape to make some intelligent paring backs. The magic number [was] 15 percent. We cut back 15 percent that represented social research activities, and that was a compromise that everyone could feel comfortable with.

For FY 1981 and 1982, OMB and HHS agreed to cut the "15 percent" of NIMH research that was social research not directly related to mental illness, and agreed not make the remaining cuts in NIMH research that OMB had originally directed. (The administration later proposed 10 to 15 percent increases in NIMH research funding for FY 1983 and 1984.)

Agency Budget Making in the New Budget Environment

In the early 1980s, budget making in human resources agencies changed from the exploration of budget alternatives to implementation of administration decisions to reduce program funding, agency staffing, and federal program leadership. One HRSA staff member commented:

> The current budget development process is qualitatively different from the preceding administration's. There is no serious effort to determine what resources programs need for purposes beyond bare minimum maintenance. There is little or no room for alternative plans outside those established in the fiscal year 1982 budget cycle. There is little sympathy for maintaining the program supports—like travel—needed to keep programs working well. In most programs, the budgets are trimmed by eliminating "nonessentials" like staff development. The problem with this approach is that many "nonessentials" are critical to the long-term success of the program. How can IHS [Indian Health Service] offer quality care if its employees can't be trained in the latest procedures?

Some agency policymakers used the pressures for retrenchment to move beyond the changes that OMB had proposed. In February 1981, for example, OMB proposed broad cuts in the NIMH budget and staffing, based on the proposed movement to block grants. NIMH leaders then cut many activities related to services, preferring to emphasize basic research. As one NIMH manager commented, "This level used block grant implementation to cut programs they really didn't support anyway. . . . Here you have two things working: administration and institute."

In ETA, the assistant secretary for employment and training proposed and got OMB and congressional approval for a 90 percent reduction in federal discretionary funds for employment and training programs. The assistant secretary saw the discretionary programs as creating unnecessary problems (often involving funding for special interests). The secretary and the assistant secretary also viewed ETA administrative costs and staff size as larger than necessary and thus required successive reductions in ETA salaries and expenses and staff. They tended to favor across-the-board object-class cuts in spending for travel, equipment, and consultants. Workload comparisons and space-to-staff ratios were calculated and used in decisions on the ETA S&E budget. Expenditures for capital improvements were minimized.

As already mentioned, the administration's proposed cuts in Administration on Aging (AoA) programs were less severe than the cuts proposed in other human resources agencies. OMB imposed overall budget "marks" reducing proposed AoA expenditures by 10 to 12 percent, with little opportunity for input on different budget or program levels. (From AoA's point of view, the lack of dialogue was not all bad: An early determination of the budget mark meant that less staff time had to be used in exploring the implications of budget alternatives.) AoA discretionary funds were cut because the administration believed that AoA R&D projects had relatively little value and because AoA needed to achieve some savings in each year's budget request. One AoA manager acknowledged, "Frankly, I don't think we could show we had managed the [R&D projects] very well. The administration came in believing our R&D grants were pretty worthless." The same AoA manager reported:

> We did recommend a cut in the nutrition program on the assumption that we would be able to reduce the federal dollar level while maintaining the same level of services. To make that possible, we decided on several management initiatives. They [the administration] went along with us in spite of reluctance on ASMB's [the Assistant Secretary for Management and Budget] and OMB's part. As a result, we came in under OMB's original budget mark.

In each of the agencies examined, the budget process was more an implementation process than a decision process. In implementing administration budget guidance, however, agency policymakers often moved beyond the administration's original budget proposals.

Budget Outcomes

This section examines changes in program budgets and agency staffing achieved through executive branch and congressional actions between January 1981 and December 1983.

In 1981 and 1982, Congress agreed to budget reductions of unprecedented scope. In each of the agencies examined, the administration achieved substantial progress toward most of its retrenchment objectives. When programs had demonstrated high performance, however, Congress resisted administration pressures and less "progress" was achieved.

In 1983, Congress resisted further cuts in most programs and expanded some.

Congressional Decision Making

Congress was strongly influenced by the administration's constant pressures to reduce spending in domestic programs: proposed rescissions for FY 1981, a revised budget for FY 1982, actual and threatened vetoes of appropriations that exceeded administration proposals for further reductions for FY 1983 and 1984. Faced not only with administration pressures for retrenchment but also with a deepening recession that increased the numbers in need and reduced state tax revenues, Congress had difficulty making budget and appropriations decisions.

In the Omnibus Budget Reconciliation Act of 1981 and the series of four continuing resolutions that financed the Departments of Labor and Health and Human Services in FY 1982, Congress agreed to substantial reductions in food and nutrition programs, employment and training programs, health resources and services programs, and mental health programs (see tables 4 through 7). Faced with actual and threatened vetoes, Congress made across-the-board cuts in FY 1982 appropriations for the Departments of Labor and of Health and Human Services. Congress restored some of these cuts later in the fiscal year.

By FY 1983, Congress was less inclined to agree to further program reductions. In the Jobs Bill of 1983 (P.L.98-8), Congress increased funding for several human resources programs including the WIC nutrition program, the maternal and child health block grant, the community health centers/

primary care block grant, and the alcohol, drug abuse, and mental health block grant.

Progress Toward Administration Objectives

By the end of FY 1982, the administration had achieved substantial progress toward most of its budget objectives in each of the agencies

TABLE 4

TRENDS IN FEDERAL SUPPORT FOR NUTRITION PROGRAMS

	Total Obligations ($ Millions)				Percentage
	1980 Actual	1981 Actual	1982 Actual	1983 Actual	Change, FY 1983 vs. FY 1980
Child Nutrition Programs	3,208	3,477	2,884	3,295	+3
Food Donations Program	107	129	121	156	+46
Food Program Administration	84	85	87	82	−2
Food Stamp Program	9,147	11,303	11,059[a]	11,838	+29
Nutrition Assistance for Puerto Rico				825	
Special Milk Program	156	120	20	19	−88
Special Supplemental Food Program (WIC and CSFP)	796	973	929	1,218	+53

SOURCE: *Budget of the United States Government*, Fiscal Years 1982, 1983, 1984, and 1985.
  a. Includes $206 million in Nutrition Assistance for Puerto Rico.

TABLE 5

TRENDS IN FEDERAL SUPPORT FOR SELECTED EMPLOYMENT AND TRAINING ADMINISTRATION PROGRAMS

	Total Obligations ($ Millions)				Percentage
	1980 Actual	1981 Actual	1982 Actual	1983 Actual	Change, FY 1983 vs. FY 1980
Empl. & Tr. Assistance	6,611	6,470	3,739	4,005	−39
CETA/Block Grant	3,342	3,692	2,108	2,179	−35
Title IID Employment	(1,502)	(1,308)	(0)	(0)	−100
Job Corps	401	573	583	617	+54
ETA Program Administration	122	131	120	122	+0
Public Service Employment	1,660	750	0	0	−100
State Unempl. Ins. and Emp. Service Ops.	1,874	2,102	2,166	2,468	+32
Trade Adjustment Assistance	1,664	1,481	84	0	−100

SOURCE: *Budget of the United States Government*, Fiscal Years 1982, 1983, 1984, and 1985; *Employment and Training Report of the President*, Fiscal Years 1980 and 1981.

TABLE 6

TRENDS IN FEDERAL SUPPORT FOR SELECTED HEALTH RESOURCES AND
HEALTH SERVICES PROGRAMS

	Total Obligations ($ Millions)				Percentage Change, FY 1983 vs. FY 1980
	1980 Actual	1981 Actual	1982 Actual	1983 Actual	
Health Care Delivery and Assistance					− 18
PHS Hospitals and Clinics	168	130	140	—	− 100
Community Health Centers/ Primary Care Block Grant	260	338	281	295	+ 13
Jobs Bill of 1983				+ 65	
Primary Care Res. & Demo.	8	11	2	—	− 100
Maternal and Child Health/ MCH Block Grant	404	432	374	373	− 8
Jobs Bill of 1983				+ 105	
Family Planning	147	182	124	124	− 16
National Health Service Corps	78	92	88	88	+ 13
NHSC Scholarships	80	63	43	16	− 80
Indian Health Service					+ 28
Services: Direct Program	549	590	616	679	+ 24
Services: Reimbursable Program	5	15	22	32	+ 540
Health Professions					− 53
Institutional Assistance	83	16	8	8	− 90
Student Assistance	108	91	—	—	− 100
Nurse Training	106	80	51	48	− 55
Primary Care	64	65	51	54	− 16
Assistance to Disadvantaged	19	20	17	17	− 11
Health Maintenance Organizations and Resources Development					− 42
Health Planning	167	126	57	58	− 65
HMO Development	21	25	4	—	− 100

SOURCE: *Budget of the United States Government*, Fiscal Years 1982, 1983, 1984, and 1985;
          HRSA budget memoranda.

examined. Expenditures had been reduced either in absolute terms (see tables
4 through 8) or in comparison with the expenditures that would have occurred
under the laws in effect at the beginning of 1981 (see tables 1 and 9). (The
recession resulted in increased expenditures for the Food Stamp program and
for unemployment insurance benefit payments in FY 1982 and 1983, even

though Congress had agreed to tighten eligibility requirements for both these programs.)

A number of programs and subprograms were eliminated in FY 1981 and 1982; for example, Public Service Employment, the Public Health Service

TABLE 7

TRENDS IN FEDERAL SUPPORT FOR ALCOHOL, DRUG ABUSE, AND MENTAL HEALTH PROGRAMS

	Total Obligations ($ Millions)				Percentage
	1980 Actual	1981 Actual	1982 Actual	1983 Actual	Change, FY 1983 vs. FY 1980
Alcohol Abuse Services	133	110			
Drug Abuse Services	198	210			
Mental Health Services	294	272			
Alcohol, Drug Abuse, Mental Health Block Grant			428	438	− 30
Jobs Bill of 1983				+ 30	
Mental Health Research	144	140	138	152	+ 6
Community Support Program	(8)	(7)	(6)	6	− 25
Mental Health Training:					
Clinical Training	72	62	42	21	− 71
Research Training	18	19	15	15	− 17
NIMH Program Support	35	38	28	33	− 6

SOURCE: *Budget of the United States Government*, Fiscal Years 1982, 1983, 1984, and 1985; NIMH Funding History.

TABLE 8

TRENDS IN FEDERAL SUPPORT FOR ADMINISTRATION ON AGING PROGRAMS

	Total Obligations ($ Millions)				Percentage
	1980 Actual	1981 Actual	1982 Actual	1983 Actual	Change, FY 1983 vs. FY 1980
Federal Council on Aging	0.4	0.4	0.1	0.2	− 50
Grants to Indian Tribes	6	6	6	6	+ 0
National Clearinghouse	1	2	1	—	− 100
Nutrition	317	348	585[a]	381	+ 20
Social Services and Centers	245	251		241	− 2
State Agency Activities	22	24	22	22	+ 0
Training, Research, Discretionary	55	39	22	22	− 60

SOURCE: *Budget of the United States Government*, Fiscal Years 1982, 1983, 1984, and 1985.

TABLE 9

PROGRESS TOWARD ADMINISTRATION OBJECTIVES

Agency/Program	Administration Objectives[a]					Major Changes, FY 1982–1985, Resulting from Legislative Actions between January 1981 and July 1983[b]	
	01	02	03	04	05	Percentage Change	
Food and Nutrition Service	X	X		Y	Y		
Food Stamp Program	X	X				−13	Eligibility tightened; cost-of-living increases delayed.[c]
Child Nutrition	X	X				−28	Eligibility tightened; federal subsidies reduced.[c]
WIC Nutrition Program						+4	Funding reduced for FY 1982, subsequently increased.
Employment and Training Administration	X	X	X	X	X		
General Employment and Training	X	X	X		X	−35	Discretionary programs sharply reduced; public service employment eliminated; trainee stipends eliminated.
Job Corps	Y					−6	No major changes.
Public Service Employment	X	X		X		−99	Program eliminated.
Unemployment Insurance	Y	X				−7	Eligibility tightened; federal UI taxes increased.[c]
Trade Adjustment Assistance	X	X					Program sharply reduced.
Health Resources and Services Administration	X	X	Y	X	Y		
Health Services	X	X	Y	X	Y	−22	Block grants approved in limited form; funding reduced for FY 1982, subsequently increased.
PHS Hospitals	X	X		X			Program eliminated.
Community Health Centers	Y		Y				Primary care block grant approved as an option; funding reduced for FY 1982, subsequently increased.
Maternal and Child Health	Y		Y		Y		Block grant approved, but without related programs; funding reduced for FY 1982, subsequently increased.

TABLE 9 (continued)

Agency/Program	Administration Objectives[a]					Major Changes, FY 1982–1985, Resulting from Legislative Actions between January 1981 and July 1983[b]
	01	*02*	*03*	*04*	*05*	*Percentage Change*
Family Planning	X					
Indian Health Service	Y		Y			Reliance on third-party payers increased.
Health Professions Education	X	X	X			Funding reduced for lower-priority training.
Health Planning	X	X		X	X	Program funded at reduced level but not reauthorized.
HMO Development	X	X				Program eliminated.
National Institute of Mental Health	X	X	X	X	X	
Services	X		X	X	X	Block grant approved with restrictions.
Community Support Program						Program maintained.
Research	Y	X				Social research eliminated.
Training	X	X				Clinical training sharply reduced.
Administration on Aging	Y	Y		X	Y	
Social Services and Nutrition	Y				Y	Consolidated appropriation not approved; states allowed to reallocate up to 20% of funds between allotments.
Training, Research, Discretionary	X	X				Funding sharply reduced.

a. 01 = Reduce federal spending.
    02 = Reduce or eliminate program activities judged to be ineffective or inappropriate; target available resources on those most in need.
    03 = Combine categorical programs into block grants to the states; reduce funding and federal staffing for the combined programs.
    04 = Reduce agency staffing—and salaries and expenses (S&E) accounts.
    05 = Reduce federal regulations, reporting requirements, and programmatic leadership.
    X = Major impact on agency/program budget.
    Y = Some impact on agency/program budget.
b. Percentage changes are Congressional Budget Office projections of reductions from FY 1982 through FY 1985 made by comparing CBO August 1983 projections with the program expenditures that would have occurred under the laws in effect at the beginning of 1981. See Congressional Budget Office, "Major Legislative Changes in Human Resources Programs Since January 1981: Staff Memorandum" (Washington, D.C.: August 1983).
c. The recession increased the numbers entitled to benefits and therefore increased expenditures.

hospitals, health professions student assistance, Health Maintenance Organization development, and mental health "social research" unrelated to mental illness. By the end of 1982, the administration had also achieved substantial reductions in projected expenditures for the Food Stamp program (levels of support were reduced and eligibility was restricted to families with incomes no more than 130 percent of the poverty level unless the families had elderly or disabled members); child nutrition programs (federal support was sharply reduced for full-price and reduced-price meals); unemployment insurance; trade adjustment assistance (benefits now are payable only after recipients have exhausted their unemployment benefits); employment and training programs (trainee stipends were eliminated and allowable grantee overhead costs were reduced under the Job Training Partnership Act, and discretionary programs were sharply reduced); National Health Service Corps scholarships; programs for the training of health and mental health professionals (most of the remaining funds have been targeted on meeting needs for specialized training); the national health planning program; and Administration on Aging training, research, and discretionary programs (see tables 4 through 9). In all these programs, the sharpest reductions came in FY 1982.

In every agency, program activities considered ineffective or inappropriate, either entire programs or portions of programs, were eliminated or suffered sharp reductions. As noted above, previous administrations had sought reductions in several of these programs.

Block grants were enacted for job training (replacing the programs funded under the Comprehensive Employment and Training Act), for three groups of programs that had been administered by the Health Services Administration, and for alcohol, drug abuse, and mental health services. Many of the administration's proposed block grants, however, were rejected or were enacted in forms that maintained more federal control than the administration desired. The maternal and child health block grant contains a 15 percent set-aside for discretionary grants by the federal government for programs of regional or national significance—and is therefore very similar to the "categorical" program that it replaced. The ADAMH block grant contained requirements that specific portions of appropriations be spent on specific types of services and that the states continue to provide some funds to each of the community mental health centers that had been funded by the National Institute of Mental Health. (In successive years the legislation did allow the states to shift 5 percent, then 10 percent, then 15 percent of their allotments from one type of services to another.) Where block grants were enacted, program funding and federal staff, regulations, reporting requirements, and programmatic leadership were reduced.

The WIC nutrition program and the Family Planning program were excluded from the block grants. The primary care block grant was approved as an option that only one state has exercised. Congress rejected amendments to the Older Americans Act that would have consolidated all Administration on Aging social services and nutrition programs into a single appropriation, but adopted an amendment that allows the states the flexibility to shift up to 20 percent of program funds between allotments.

While Congress struggled to deal with the administration's far-reaching budget and legislative proposals, the administration achieved significant reductions in federal staffing through hiring freezes and reductions in force (RIFs). The five agencies examined were affected to different degrees by hiring freezes, RIFs, and staff reassignments resulting from the RIFs. Staffing reductions ranged from 11 percent in the Food and Nutrition Service (which suffered only one small RIF from 1981 through 1983) to 18 percent in the Administration on Aging and 26 percent or more in each of the other agencies (see table 12).

Positive Outcomes for Programs of Demonstrated Effectiveness

In the face of pressures to reduce spending, analysts might have predicted that programs that enjoyed broad political support would withstand retrenchment pressures better than programs with weak political bases. And analysts might have hoped—but never dared predict—that programs of demonstrated effectiveness would fare better than programs generally recognized as ineffective or inappropriate.

Our research confirms that broad political supports helps. In a time of recession, for example, the Unemployment Insurance program was treated more gently than the Food Stamp program (see table 1). Political support helped Administration on Aging in two arenas: The administration proposed relatively modest cuts in AoA's nutrition and social services programs; Congress made even more modest cuts and then expanded AoA's Title III nutrition program (see table 8). (AoA's Title IV training, research, and discretionary programs, which enjoyed much less support, fared less well with both the administration and Congress.)

Unexpectedly, our data show that programs whose effectiveness had been demonstrated also fared relatively well. Although Congress agreed to substantial reductions in food and nutrition programs, employment and training programs, and health and mental health programs (making especially deep cuts in programs generally recognized as ineffective or inappropriate), Congress maintained several programs whose effectiveness had been well established (see table 10). Funding for the Job Corps was maintained in the face

TABLE 10

CHANGES IN FUNDING FOR "EFFECTIVE" AND "INEFFECTIVE" PROGRAMS,
FY 1983 vs. FY 1980

Agency/Program	Percentage Decreases for Programs Generally Considered to be Inappropriate or Ineffective[a]	Percentage Increases for Programs for which Program Effectiveness Has Been Demonstrated[a]
Food and Nutrition Service		
WIC Nutrition Program		WIC: +53[c]
Employment and Training Administration		
Job Corps		Job Corps: +54
Public Service Employment	PSE: −100[b]	
Trade Adjustment Assistance	TRA: −100[b]	
Health Resources and Services Administration		
PHS Hospitals	PHS Hosp.: −100[b]	
Community Health Centers		CHC: +13[c]
Health Professions		
Institutional Assistance	In. Assist.: −90[b]	
Student Assistance	St. Assist.: −100[b]	
Nurse Training	Nurse Tr.: −55[b]	
Health Planning	Health Pl.: −65[b]	
National Institute of Mental Health		
Community Support Program		CSP: −25[c]
Clinical Training	Clin. Tr.: −71[b]	

a. Percentage changes are changes in total obligations, FY 1983 vs. FY 1980, from tables 4–7.

b. Reduction or elimination of each of these programs has often been proposed. Most of these reductions are consistent with the U.S. General Accounting Office *Comments on the President's February 18, 1981, Budget Proposals and Additional Cost-Saving Measures*, OPP-81-2 (Washington, D.C.: 1981).

c. The Reagan administration proposed that such services be funded through one of the block grants, but Congress maintained each of these programs as a categorical federal program.

of administration proposals for sharp reductions. The WIC nutrition program, the Community Health Centers (CHC) program, and the Community Support Program (CSP) for the chronically mentally ill all escaped from administration pressures to fund their services through block grants. Instead, Congress maintained each of these programs as a categorical federal program.

Arguments of program effectiveness were used in congressional decisions to keep the WIC nutrition program separate from the maternal and child health block grant program, to minimize WIC program cuts in FY 1982, and to expand the WIC program in subsequent years. After making a 5 percent reduction in the WIC nutrition program in FY 1982, Congress expanded the WIC program by $200 million in FY 1983 and expanded the program again in FY 1984. As a result, for FY 1982 through 1985, WIC program expenditures are projected to be higher than the expenditures that would have occurred under the legislation as it existed in January 1981. Because the WIC legislation authorizes ongoing evaluation research, there have been many evaluations of the impact of the WIC program. In many congressional hearings on legislation and appropriations, principal investigators on evaluation studies have been asked to testify. There is evidence that the WIC program improves nutrition, increases infants' birth weight, produces healthier babies, improves children's growth and development, and saves health care dollars in the long run. In addition, longer periods of WIC participation are associated with greater increases in birth weight.[1]

Arguments of program effectiveness were also used in congressional decisions to maintain the Job Corps at the FY 1981 enrollment level. Evaluation had shown that, under many different assumptions as to how to project future benefits, Job Corps benefits outweigh the program's high costs.[2] More of the Job Corps trainees than people in an appropriate comparison group move into jobs, further education, or the military, and go on to better careers. Senator Orrin Hatch, chairman of the Senate Committee on Labor and Human Resources, had been impressed by a Job Corps Center that he had visited but was concerned that the center might not be typical. When the evaluation just mentioned was called to his attention, he concluded that, although the program costs a lot, it produces a good return.[3] Joined by other Senate conservatives, he helped persuade the Senate not to agree to the substantial cuts that the

1. See, for example, "Medical Evaluation of the Special Supplemental Food Program for Women, Infants, and Children (WIC),"Report prepared for the Department of Agriculture (Chapel Hill: University of North Carolina, School of Public Health, 1976); "An Evaluation of a Supplementary Feeding Program for Women, Infants, and Children" (New Haven: Yale University, School of Medicine, 1978); Eileen T. Kennedy, James E. Austin, and C. Peter Timmer, "Cost/Benefit and Cost/Effectiveness of WIC" and Eileen T. Kennedy, Stanley Gershoff, Robert Reed, and James Austin, "Effect of WIC Supplemental Feeding on Birth Weight" (1979); "Evaluation of the Effectiveness of WIC" (Washington, D.C.: Department of Agriculture, Food and Nutrition Service, Office of Policy, Planning, and Evaluation, January 1981); "Massachusetts Special Supplemental Food Program for Women, Infants, and Children (WIC) Follow-up Study," Report prepared for the U.S. Department of Agriculture (Boston: Massachusetts Department of Public Health, Division of Family Health Services, 1982).

2. See Charles Mallar et al., "Evaluation of the Economic Impact of the Job Corps Program: Second Follow-up Report," Report prepared for the Department of Labor, Employment and Training Administration, Office of Policy Evaluation and Research (Princeton, N.J.: Mathematica Policy Research, 1980)

3. See "The Job Corps," *Congressional Record*, February 26, 1981, pp. S 1600-S 1601.

administration had proposed. As the Congressional Budget Office reported, "This program—which has proven effective for those who complete it—has not undergone the more substantial reductions in real funding that have been made in most other employment programs for the disadvantaged."[4]

In the Department of Health and Human Services, the Bureau of Community Health Services (now the Bureau of Health Care Delivery and Assistance) has long stood out as one of the department's best-managed programs:

> Using program objectives, performance indicators, and performance targets that had been developed with the participation of regional offices and grantees over a four-year period, the bureau allocated staff and grant funds in ways that stimulated efficient, effective performance. The bureau allocated additional staff and grant funds to high-performing regions; regional offices allocated additional grant funds to high-performing projects.[5]

On the basis of information provided through the bureau's reporting system and evaluations that had been completed,[6] the bureau's Community Health Centers program was generally regarded as well-managed and effective in providing primary health care to underserved areas.

In the Omnibus Budget Reconciliation Act of 1981, when Congress consolidated twenty-one health care programs into four block grants, Congress enacted the primary care block grant in a form that allowed the states the option of accepting the block grant or of continuing federal funding of community health centers. At the insistence of the House, states could receive the primary care block grant only if they were prepared to continue funding community health centers at the 1981 level, were willing to appropriate significant additional resources, and used none of the block grant for administrative overhead costs. From 1981 through 1983, only one state opted for the primary care block grant. Congress reduced funding for the Community Health Centers program in FY 1982, but increased funding for the program in subsequent years (see table 6).

Arguments of program effectiveness played a part in congressional decisions to continue the Community Support Program (CSP) for the chronically mentally ill. There was evidence from federal, state, and local evaluations

---

4. See "Major Legislative Changes in Human Resources Programs Since January 1981: Staff Memorandum," Report prepared for Speaker Thomas P. O'Neill (Washington, D.C.: Congressional Budget Office, August 1983), p. 67.

5. See Joseph S. Wholey, *Evaluation and Effective Public Management* (Boston: Little, Brown, 1983), p. 21.

6. See, for example, "Final Report 1968–1976: Review of Federally Supported Neighborhood Health Centers," Report prepared for the Department of Health, Education, and Welfare, Health Services Administration, Bureau of Community Health Services (Albert Einstein College of Medicine, 1977); and "Final Report for Community Health Center Cost-Effectiveness Evaluation," Report prepared for the Department of Health and Human Services, Office of the Assistant Secretary for Planning and Evaluation (McLean, Va.: JRB Associates, 1981).

that participating states had redirected their service delivery systems to focus on the needs of chronically mentally ill adults, that CSP funds had helped to mobilize state and local funding for the chronically mentally ill,[7] and that CSP clients had less need for hospitalization as a result of the program.[8] Since the program was originally funded under the Public Health Service research and demonstration authority, the program was not included in the alcohol, drug abuse, and mental health block grant enacted as part of the Omnibus Budget Reconciliation Act of 1981. Although the Reagan administration made no effort to get an appropriation for the program (on the ground that states could fund such activities through the ADAMH block grant), Congress decided to maintain the program at approximately $6 million per year under the continuing resolutions for 1982 and 1983. After several years of funding as part of the mental health research appropriation, CSP now has its own appropriation.

Between 1981 and 1983, administration pressures and congressional responses produced a combination of reductions in service and improvements in efficiency that neither would have produced alone. Although the press tended to treat all of the administration's proposed program and staff cuts as equally good or equally bad, Congress was able to make reasonable distinctions—saving programs in which high performance had been demonstrated and making reductions in inappropriate and ineffective programs. The WIC nutrition program, the Job Corps, the Community Health Centers program, and the Community Support Program all had demonstrated effective performance. In every case, Congress maintained the program in the face of administration pressures to fold the program into a block grant or to reduce funding dramatically.

Changes in Agency Operations and Program Activities

Although administration and congressional decisions harmed the careers of civil servants and disrupted and delayed agency operations, most of the agencies survived and are functioning reasonably well. A number of the agencies used retrenchment "opportunities" to refocus agency activities on realistic sets of objectives, strengthen program performance, and better communicate the value of program activities to their publics.

---

7. See Jack Katz, "Report on the NIMH Community Support Program (CSP)" (Rockville, Md.: U.S. Department of Health and Human Services, Alcohol, Drug Abuse, and Mental Health Administration, December 1981).

8. See U.S. Congress, House, Committee on Appropriations, *Departments of Labor, Health and Human Services, Education, and Related Agencies Appropriations for 1984, Part 3: Health.* Hearings; 98th Cong., 1st sess., 1983, pp. 725–726.

This section traces changes in agency operations and program activities that accompanied the budget cuts between 1981 and 1983. Ultimate effects on clients are outside the scope of this inquiry.

Changes in Agency Operations

All the agencies examined were affected by one or more hiring freezes beginning in January 1981 (see table 11), and all were forced to cut staff training and travel. Three of the agencies experienced major reductions in force, reassignments, and downgradings, with resulting disruption, loss of staff expertise, low morale, and reduced staff productivity in 1981 and 1982. Except for the Food and Nutrition Service, where changes in program budgets had to be made through changes in authorizing legislation, agency planning and management were complicated by congressional delays in appropriations.

Faced with program and staff changes and uncertainties over appropriations, agencies transferred program responsibilities to other levels, reorganized, redirected agency activities toward narrower sets of objectives, and worked to educate their publics about agency mission and accomplishments (see table 11). Three of the agencies now provide less programmatic leadership, programmatic oversight, and technical assistance to grantees. Much federal staff effort has been redirected into financial management activities, such as efforts to improve cash management and debt collection, increase nonfederal program income, improve state and local procurement practices, and reduce fraud, waste, and abuse.

Most of the agencies have emerged with realistic sets of objectives, and program and staff activities likely to achieve progress toward those objectives. In three of the five agencies, however, reductions in discretionary programs, grantee reporting, and federal monitoring and evaluation will limit agency ability to sense changing needs and to test ways to meet those needs.

Food and Nutrition Service. From 1981 through 1983, FNS experienced hiring freezes and an 11 percent reduction in permanent staff (see table 12). In 1982, FNS reorganized to improve agency performance. As the General Accounting Office reported:

Effective April 1982 the Service transferred day-to-day financial management operations . . . to its regional offices and reorganized its headquarters financial management organization. These changes were in line with recommendations of a joint Service, USDA, and Office of Management and Budget study started in 1976. Headquarters and regional personnel in both the financial management and program management areas said that, although its impact on overall agency operations has not yet been measured, the decentralization should streamline and improve agency operations.[9]

9. U.S. General Accounting Office, *Organizational, Personnel, and Office Location Changes Made by the Food and Nutrition Service,* RCED-83-138 (Washington, D.C.: 1983), pp. 4 and 12.

TABLE 11

CHANGES IN AGENCY OPERATIONS

Agency	Constraints C1 C2 C3 C4				Changes to Adapt to Constraints 1 2 3 4 5 6						Changes to Strengthen Performance S1 S2 S3 S4			
Food and Nutrition Service	Y	X	Y	X			?	X					X	X	X
Employment and Training Administration	X	X	X	X	X	X	X	X	X	X			X		
Health Resources and Services Administration	X	X	X	Y	X	X	X	X			X	X	X		
Health Care Del.	X	X	X		X		?	?							
Indian Health Svc.	Y	X		X		X	X	X							
Health Prof. Education	X	X	X		X		X	X			X				
HMO & Resources Development	X	X	X		X		?	?							
National Inst. of Mental Health	X	X	X	X	X		?	X	X	X	X	X		X	
Administration on Aging	X	X	Y	X			X	X	X	X		X			

NOTE: C1 = Reduced agency staffing—and salaries and expenses.
　　　　 C2 = Hiring freeze.
　　　　 C3 = Reduction in force (RIF).
　　　　 C4 = Low morale.

　　　　　1 = Cut staff where programs are cut.
　　　　　2 = Minimize capital expenditures; defer maintenance and repair.
　　　　　3 = Cut training and staff development.
　　　　　4 = Cut travel.
　　　　　5 = Transfer program leadership to states.
　　　　　6 = Reduce technical assistance to states and localities.

　　　　 S1 = Refocus on narrower set of objectives; redirect agency activities to achieve
　　　　　　　　 the objectives.
　　　　 S2 = Reorganize to improve agency performance.
　　　　 S3 = Move overhead staff to operating levels.
　　　　 S4 = Educate relevant publics about agency mission and accomplishments.

　　　　　X = Major change in agency.
　　　　　Y = Some change in agency.

TABLE 12

STAFFING TRENDS IN FIVE FEDERAL AGENCIES

Agency	1980 Actual	1981 Actual	1982 Actual	1983 Actual	Percentage Change, FY 1983 vs. FY 1980
Food and Nutrition Service					
Full-Time Permanent Positions	2,446	2,382	2,410	2,183	−11
Full-Time Equivalent Employment	2,751	2,672	2,497	2,369	−14
Employment and Training Administration					
Full-Time Permanent Positions	3,185	3,126	2,557	2,308	−28
Full-Time Equivalent Employment	3,223	3,071	2,586	2,255	−30
Health Resources and Services Administration					−26
Full-Time Permanent Positions					
HSA	9,340	9,359	4,821	4,679	−56
HRA	1,208	1,120			
IHS	10,700	10,710	10,819	10,958	+2
Full-Time Equivalent Employment					−32
HSA	9,664	9,566	5,012	4,647	−58
HRA	1,302	1,294			
IHS	10,807	10,973	10,269	10,262	−5
National Institute of Mental Health					
Full-Time Permanent Positions	1,121	1,120	735[a]	738[a]	−34
Headquarters					
Intramural Research	432	432	432	435	+1
Program Support	528	527	303	303	−43
Regional Offices	161	161	0[a]	0[a]	−100
Administration on Aging Headquarters					
Full-Time Permanent Positions	146	146	119	119	−18

SOURCE: *Budget of the United States Government*, Fiscal Years 1982, 1983, 1984, and 1985; Health Resources and Services Administration budget memoranda; National Institute of Mental Health Position History; Administration on Aging Position History.

a. In FY 1982, sixty transitional positions were retained in the regional offices to close out service programs. In FY 1983, thirty transitional positions were retained.

The reorganization of financial management at FNS headquarters and the decentralization of day-to-day financial management resulted in a reduction of thirty-five FNS positions. There were no RIFs in FNS except in connection with this reorganization, in which five discontinued service retirements and nineteen early retirements were permitted to help ensure that openings would be available for all whose positions were abolished.

Although the staff reductions were less in FNS than in the other four agencies examined, the 1981–1983 period was reported to have been the first in which the agency was under such great stress. Although morale was low, one FNS staff member reported, "Operating with fewer personnel, the staff is pushed more, but minimum requirements are met and often exceeded."

There was a change in management orientation in FNS in this time period. More work has focused on increasing program efficiency and reducing fraud, waste, abuse, and error—in particular, on reducing payments to ineligibles and overpayment errors. There were major efforts to stabilize nutrition program spending. For example, computers are now being used to check food stamp recipients' wage statements against state employment data files. FNS initiated Operation Awareness, a joint federal-state-local effort to document and communicate promising and successful efforts to combat fraud, waste, and abuse in the Food Stamp program, to coordinate efforts to strengthen program administration, and to change public perceptions about the program.

Employment and Training Administration. From 1981 through 1983, ETA experienced a series of hiring freezes, reductions in salaries and expenses, and reductions in force that produced a 28 percent reduction in staff (see table 12). The hiring freezes, RIFs, reassignments, and reductions in other S&E accounts reduced ETA staff morale, efficiency, and effectiveness. Given the requirement to operate with fewer staff members and less overhead resources, ETA reduced staff in areas where programs had been cut and took other staff cuts across the board. To minimize the number of RIFs required, ETA reduced costs such as printing and overtime.

ETA staff were reallocated from policy analysis and program leadership, monitoring, and evaluation to financial management and audit activities. Reorganization reduced the number of ETA units and clarified accountability. ETA improved its cash flow management and debt collection and eliminated the backlog of unresolved ETA audits. A decision to open Job Corps Center contracts to competitive bidding reduced Job Corps unit costs from $18,000 to $15,000. Capital expenditures at Job Corps Centers were restricted to those needed to meet safety and health requirements.

Changes in legislation, reductions in ETA staff and discretionary funds, reductions in the frequency and level of detail of grantee reporting, and reductions in ETA monitoring and program evaluation have reduced ETA's ability to give direction to employment and training activities. Leadership responsibilities for training programs have been transferred to state and local levels. ETA has provided little guidance on how to implement the Job Training Partnership Act. At this point, the future role of ETA in employment and training program activities is far from clear.

Health Resources and Services Administration. Between 1981 and 1982, health resources and health services programs were dramatically restructured. Program changes were accompanied by significant staffing reductions, except in the Indian Health Service (IHS) (see table 12). Threats of RIFs led many young and talented people and many senior people to leave government service. Public Health Service RIFs were associated with the closing of the PHS hospitals and ripple effects stemming from the right of senior employees to "bump" more junior employees. Throughout the Public Health Service, 6,131 funded positions were abolished: 4,780 in connection with the closing of the PHS hospitals, 412 in the regions, and 939 in headquarters. As a result, 2,921 staff were involuntarily separated (2,794 from the PHS hospitals), 413 were downgraded, 713 were reassigned within HHS, 749 retired (722 from PHS hospitals), and 240 were transferred to other federal agencies.[10]

The large number of personnel changes had a negative effect on Health Resources Administration (HRA) and Health Services Administration (HSA) operations. With many positions eliminated and many staff members reassigned, operations suffered. Morale fell in 1981 and 1982 but appears to have recovered in many program areas.

After the separate RIFs in HRA and HSA late in 1981, leaders of the two agencies decided to seek a merger that would put services and resources in the same organization. This reorganization, which was not part of the administration's political agenda, is reported to have improved morale, efficiency, and coordination of services and educational programs related to medically underserved areas. As a result of the reorganization, HRSA was able to reallocate seventy positions from program support to direct program delivery.[11]

In the opinion of staff at department level, HRSA has functioned effectively. The secretary of HHS had tried to ensure that good managers would stay even though major changes were occurring in the programs they managed. One HHS staff member commented, "The agencies did a good job of man-

---

10. President's Private Sector Survey on Cost Control, *Task Force Report on the Department of Health and Human Services: Public Health Service, Health Care Financing Administration, Working Appendix,* vol. 3 (Washington, D.C.: U.S. Government Printing Office, 1983), Exhibit S.
    11. Ibid., exhibit D.

aging the double transition. The best people were put in key positions. This was good management of what were relatively massive changes." An HRSA manager agreed, adding, "The transition [to a merged HRA/HSA] was eased by the way the outplacements were handled. For example, RIF planning was widely perceived as a fair and open process, and direct job search services were given to employees jeopardized by the possibilities of a RIF."

For maternal and child health, the one set of HRSA programs that actually made the transition to block grant status, regional office staff shifted their role to that of consultants who await requests for assistance. Federal reporting requirements were eliminated under the maternal and child health block grant. Some states chose to continue requesting similar data, however.

The Bureau of Health Professions lost staff and travel funds as its activities were refocused from increasing the supply of health professionals to more narrowly targeted programs. One HRSA manager reported:

> There are no longer resources available for regular field monitoring, nor are there enough resources for technical assistance. . . . Instead of regular field visits, we visit only those grantees that are experiencing a major difficulty. We substitute for field visits by checking documents received in the central office: budgets, progress reports, etc.

Especially during 1982, funding limitations and restrictions on reprogramming authority for the Indian Health Service forced IHS to reduce training and travel for its staff, maintenance of facilities, and services to clients while the demand for services was increasing. For FY 1982 Congress appropriated $600 million for IHS, approximately 1 percent less than the 1981 appropriation and 4 percent less than the $625 million on which the conference committee had agreed. HSA rejected an IHS proposal to resolve its budget problem through a reduction in force. In the fourth quarter of the fiscal year, Congress approved an IHS reprogramming request and enacted a supplemental pay act that increased the IHS appropriation. Before these actions by Congress, IHS implemented a hiring freeze that left 3 percent of IHS positions unfilled, closed 400 beds in IHS hospitals, discontinued distribution of over-the-counter drugs, deferred purchase of supplies, curtailed overtime, and canceled travel and training in efforts to solve its budget problems.[12]

One IHS manager noted that the closing of the PHS hospitals had hampered IHS ability to upgrade operations while containing costs. He reported:

> The closing of PHS hospitals meant that we were required to absorb [PHS commissioned] officers. The IHS had to dismiss forty to fifty pharmacists and dentists, who were bumped by Corps officers formerly assigned to PHS hospitals. . . . We were forced to take senior people in slots that could have been filled by less expensive staff.

---

12. National Academy of Public Administration working paper, "Indian Health Service: FY 1982 Budget Formulation and Execution," (mimeographed), 1983.

By curtailing maintenance and training, IHS damaged its potential. As one IHS staff member commented:

> This chipping away at the IHS infrastructure is a false economy that will create greater costs in the not-too-distant future: five to ten years. Something like training may sound superfluous, but it is not when you are running a health care delivery operation that is constantly being upgraded with new procedures and technology. . . . In essence, IHS is mortgaging the future for the sake of achieving economy today. . . . Overall, IHS has suffered. Morale is low.

National Institute of Mental Health.   From 1981 through 1983, NIMH experienced major changes in program and staff activities and a 34 percent reduction in staff (see table 12). As NIMH relinquished responsibility for categorical funding of community mental health centers, services-related staff units were eliminated in headquarters and regional offices. Mental health services, services research, and technical assistance staff were reduced from approximately 290 in headquarters and regional offices to 35 "knowledge transfer" staff in headquarters and none in the regions. A limitation on staff travel reduced the ability of staff to provide the technical assistance still being requested by states and other grantees. NIMH responded by convening periodic meetings to which state representatives are invited.

The December 1981 RIFs in NIMH and other parts of the Alcohol, Drug Abuse, and Mental Health Administration (ADAMHA) had the following effects: a large number of support staff and younger professionals quit "voluntarily"; many staff members were reassigned to inappropriate positions; many staff members were bumped to positions of lesser responsibility (in some cases, down several grades from professional to support staff); a number of staff moved from one institute to another within ADAMHA; some workers took early retirement; and a number of staff members moved to part-time status. Intramural research was excluded from the RIF. In the end, only a few people in NIMH headquarters had to be separated, but many who remained were not well suited to the positions in which they found themselves. An NIMH manager commented that, "[The RIF] was done by the rules, but the rules aren't very good." Throughout 1982 and 1983, NIMH exceeded its ceiling and was under a virtual hiring freeze. NIMH continued to suffer from shortages of secretarial staff and was unable to hire young professionals.

Morale at the working level was dramatically reduced at times of threatened and actual RIFs. In an effort to let staff members know where they stood, NIMH ran a number of mock RIFs and posted the results. The uncertainty reduced staff productivity throughout 1981. Since the lows of 1981 and early 1982, many voluntary reassignments have taken place, and NIMH morale has improved somewhat.

The work of NIMH, the states, and other grantees was complicated by congressional inability to make timely decisions on appropriations. The Department of Health and Human Services had to live under three continuing resolutions in FY 1981, four in FY 1982, and two in FY 1983. In an unpublished study of HHS budget development and budget execution, the General Accounting Office noted:

> This creates problems for program managers who find it difficult to manage their programs efficiently since funding levels are uncertain and subject to substantial change with succeeding continuing resolutions. At times they hold up grant and contract awards until the funding level is certain. As a result, those receiving or expecting Federal grants, contracts, loans, or services cannot always proceed efficiently with their operations. Further, the funding uncertainty creates a serious constraint on their flexibility to manage the programs and it is difficult to hold the program managers accountable for program results.[13]

One NIMH staff member commented, "When you have clinical training funds . . . and the CSP appropriations [restored], we are not [staffed] for those activities. . . . A substantial management operations problem [results]. What we're prepared to do is create work teams detailing people to carry out the program development site visits and the review of those activities."

States have relatively little accountability or reporting responsibility under the block grants. States are, however, continuing to provide data to NIMH on a voluntary basis. Funds available for NIMH program evaluation have been sharply reduced, because none of the block grant funds can be used for federal evaluation activities. The NIMH Biometry and Epidemiology Division is gathering and analyzing data on the mental health service system and service needs, having taken over some of the functions previously performed by the services research staff.

OMB's ban on social research led NIMH to eliminate funding for social science research; instead NIMH is focusing on basic research related to mental illness. By refocusing NIMH activities on a narrower set of objectives, policymakers at ADAMHA and NIMH believe that they have enhanced the effectiveness of the institute. One ADAMHA manager commented:

> We're developing a reputation of accountability now. . . . We're funding the best research, good research, good priority scores. We're getting a lot of applications. . . . We probably have one of the most active fields in terms of the explosion in sciences. . . . People from other fields are coming into our field. . . . I don't know if this would have happened if we had just continued business as usual.

An NIMH manager commented along the same lines:

---

13. U.S. General Accounting Office working paper on the Department of Health and Human Services budget process during fiscal year 1982 (mimeographed), 1983, pp. H31-H33.

There was a soul-searching look at our mission. Especially in the research arena: What at NIMH is different from other institutions?. . . . So the issues were to move toward research that relates to mental illness specifically. . . . In mental health research, because of methodology and the state of our science, we've had an absolute mushrooming of excellent neuroscience research, basic research. We've won the Nobel Prize and several other awards in our field lately. Our intramural center and some of our extramural programs are really world leaders in this understanding of brain functioning. Ten years ago, that wasn't true.

Administration on Aging.   From 1981 through 1983 AoA experienced hiring freezes and 18 percent reduction in headquarters staff (see table 12). Although the Office of Human Development Services (HDS) made some effort to protect AoA when HDS issued 160 RIF notices in January 1982, AoA lost both experienced staff and promising younger staff members. By February 1982, 44 HDS staff had been separated and another 350 downgraded or reassigned. In some cased reassignment within HDS left specialists in aging working on children's programs, and vice versa. AoA lost forty positions that were vacant: eight AoA staff members were separated. By the end of FY 1983, AoA was still under a hiring freeze (except for secretarial positions), there were few if any opportunities for promotions, and morale remained low.

In December 1982 AoA's staff was reorganized into fewer offices. Managers were made more accountable through the reorganization and through the HDS Operational Planning System (a computerized management-by-objectives system). Although AoA had attempted to do two- to five-year planning, by the end of FY 1983 most AoA planning was for the current year.

From 1981 through 1983 AoA managers and staff worked to improve financial management and productivity. An HDS manager commented that the immediate effect of the budget process was "to shift the whole focus to economic efficiency and doing things more effectively. . . . Performance contracting defined units of service [and] increased efficiency in service delivery, certainly in meal delivery." AoA's financial management initiatives included the Program Income initiative (which encouraged states to seek higher nonfederal contributions to AoA-supported activities), efforts to encourage centralized buying in the congregate meals and home-delivered meals programs, and an initiative to promote performance-based procurement by area agencies (for example, through contracts for specific numbers of rides, rather than grants for provision of "transportation services"). AoA developed technical assistance manuals on financial management procedures and trained area agencies in the use of the manuals. Such initiatives were consistent with those recommended by the General Accounting Office in its November 1981 report on AoA's social services programs.[14]

---

14. U.S. General Accounting Office, *More Specific Guidance and Closer Monitoring Needed to Get More from Funds Spent on Social Services for the Elderly*, HRD-82-14 (Washington, D.C.: 1981).

Except in its financial management initiatives, by the end of FY 1983 AoA was providing less program leadership to state and local levels. HDS policy changes and reductions in AoA staff size, staff capacity, and funds for staff travel resulted in diminished AoA programmatic oversight. AoA has attempted to supplement state reporting with a National Data Base on Aging compiled by the National Association of State Units on Aging and the National Association of Area Agencies on Aging on the basis of voluntary data collection from state and area agencies.

Changes in Program Activities

Although services were reduced in every agency examined, the agencies achieved a number of changes designed to strengthen program performance. In each of the agencies, programs were simplified from the points of view of grantees. Faced with reductions in agency staff and in program budgets, four of the agencies allowed grantees greater flexibility in the use of funds and three of the agencies targeted resources on individuals or areas in greatest need. Three of the agencies were able to increase program support from nonfederal sources; four of the agencies made changes designed to increase program efficiency or productivity (see table 13). In the next several paragraphs, we review a number of the more significant of these changes in program activities.

Food and Nutrition Service. From 1981 through 1983, changes in the authorizing legislation reduced nutrition program resources and tightened eligibility requirements, reducing participation by those above the poverty line. Approximately 1 million people lost eligibility for food stamps.[15] Participation in the school lunch program dropped by more than 2 million children, with most of the reduction occurring among middle-class children who had been asked to pay an amount closer to the full cost of school lunches.[16] In the eyes of Department of Agriculture and FNS staff, the requirement to operate with reduced funds has contributed to improvements in program efficiency; for example, through simplified fund disbursement, elimination of complex formulas for reimbursing schools, elimination of requirements that schools keep detailed records of the costs of their meal programs, simplification of the definition of ''household,'' and greater use of surplus commodities available through the department. Faced with reductions

---

15. Linda E. Demkovich, ''Feeding the Young—Will the Reagan 'Safety Net' Catch the 'Truly Needy'?'' *National Journal*, April 10, 1982, pp. 624–629.

16. See, for example, U.S. Department of Agriculture, Food and Nutrition Service, ''Food Program Update for June 1983,'' September 1983.

TABLE 13

CHANGES IN PROGRAM ACTIVITIES

Agency	Constraints		Changes to Adapt to Constraints						Changes to Strengthen Performance	
	C1	C5	7	8	9	10	11	12	S5	S6
Food and Nutrition Service	Y	X	Y		X	X		Y	X	X
Employment and Training Administration	X	X	X		Y		X	X		X
Health Resources and Services Administration	X	X	X	X	X		Y	Y	Y	X
Health Care Del.	X	X	X	X	X			Y	Y	X
Indian Health Svc.	Y	Y	X						Y	
Health Prof. Education	X	X	X		X					
HMO & Resources Development	X	X	X	X			Y	X		
National Inst. of Mental Health	X	X	X				X	X		
Administration on Aging	X	Y	Y				Y	Y	X	X

NOTE:
C1 = Reduced agency staffing—and salaries and expenses.
C5 = Reduced federal spending.

7 = Reduce or eliminate services.
8 = Eliminate low-performing grantees.
9 = Tighten eligibility; target on greatest needs.
10 = Require greater cost-sharing.
11 = Allow grantees greater flexibility in use of funds.
12 = Reduce federal regulations and reporting requirements.

S5 = Increase program support from other sources.
S6 = Increase program efficiency/productivity.

X = Major change in program activities.
Y = Some change in program activities.

in federal support for school lunches, localities are joining in cooperative buying and thus achieving savings in their school lunch programs.[17]

    Employment and Training Administration.   From 1981 through 1983, changes in budgets and authorizing legislation reduced ETA employment and training activities, unemployment insurance benefits, and services for people seeking jobs. The Job Training Partnership Act included several changes

---

17. See Child Nutrition Forum, "Doing More with Less" (Washington, D.C.: Food Research and Action Center, 1983).

designed to improve employment and training program efficiency; examples include the elimination of stipends for trainees and the reduction of allowable state and local overhead costs.

Health Resources and Services Administration. In FY 1982, faced with reductions in the funds for community health centers, the Bureau of Health Care Delivery and the regional offices eliminated funding for 250 of the 800 community health centers. The centers affected were those in communities with less severe needs and those known to be poorly managed. Some clients lost services as thirty-five of the centers closed.[18] One HRSA manager, however, reported:

> The number of individuals served in 1982 was essentially the same as in calendar years 1981 and 1980. In part, that is because of a significant augmentation of community health center productivity, increased collections, and better management. . . . While we were able to serve the same numbers of people, two other phenomena did occur. There were a number of supplemental services, like health education and outreach, which were cut back in most health centers. In addition, there have been . . . a number of centers which continue to operate but no longer receive federal support.[19]

An administration initiative to increase Indian Health Service income from third-party reimbursements has helped IHS to overcome deficiencies. The third-party reimbursement income is especially helpful because it can be carried over for up to two years.

Administration on Aging. From 1981 through 1983, AoA was able to maintain service levels despite inflation. One AoA staff member commented:

> Technical assistance materials in financial management have generated more program income, in the nutrition program in particular. . . . One can argue that the federal investment has produced more for less money. For example, the number of meals has increased while federal dollars have remained the same or decreased. . . .

Title III program income from nonfederal sources increased from $67 million in FY 1980 to $79 million in 1981 and $101 million in 1982, with contributions likely to exceed the $120 million goal established for 1983.

Another AoA staff member said, "Contracting procedures have been changed at state, area agency, and local levels. Performance-based procurement is now more common. We now obtain past levels of service at the same or lower cost."

---

18. Linda E. Demkovich, "The Public Health Service—Suffering Budget Cuts in Relative Obscurity," *National Journal*, May 21, 1983, pp. 1063–1068.

19. U.S. Congress, House, Committee on Appropriations, *Department of Labor, Health and Human Services, Education, and Related Agencies Appropriations for 1984, Part 3: Health.* Hearings, 98th Cong., 1st sess., 1983, p. 318.

Conclusions

As we anticipate new rounds of budget cuts for federal agencies and programs, our research suggests that prospects at the federal level are more encouraging than might have been expected. (Further investigation is needed to clarify the picture at state, local, and client levels.) Given a public mandate and a clear set of objectives, a determined chief executive, a talented budget director, and like-minded agency appointees can achieve substantial savings through budget, legislative, and staffing changes. Legislative committees have proved capable of sorting through proposed cuts and saving programs that have demonstrated their effectiveness. Moreover, even under severe budget pressures, agencies have proved capable of reorganizing themselves to perform necessary staff functions and improve service delivery in the programs for which they retain responsibility.

In the future, however, personnel practices should be changed to allow managers to minimize the negative consequences of reductions in force. Selective hiring freezes can achieve substantial savings. Workers can be retrained for new responsibilities.[20] When RIFs are required, they can be made less disruptive if they are confined to the functions being reduced or eliminated. As the Health Services Administration has shown, agencies can take more aggressive steps to help employees find other positions in their own agency or in other agencies. And, as the administration has proposed, agencies could give greater weight to sustained superior performance in deciding which employees should be retained during RIFs.

Finally, agencies should routinely produce credible evidence on the extent to which important program objectives are being achieved. In the agencies examined, it proved worthwhile for agencies to agree on realistic objectives, to systematically assess performance and results, and to use this information to demonstrate accomplishments. To define program objectives and produce information on program outcomes, agencies can use outcome-oriented management systems or management-oriented evaluation systems. When decisions are being made on budget levels, credible program performance information can influence those decisions. When reductions have to be made, agencies can save higher-performing programs and projects—eliminating activities that contribute relatively little.

---

20. In her comments on a draft of this paper, Elsa Porter noted that, in the face of extraordinary changes in staff needs, the Internal Revenue Service has not resorted to RIFs but has instead made major efforts to retrain employees for new positions.

COMMENTS

Laurence E. Lynn, Jr.

Dramatic changes in the Reagan administration's approach to preparing the executive budget (described by Hugh Heclo in this volume) could be expected to alter substantially the role of the bureaucracy in the allocation of budgetary resources. Budgetary retrenchment, together with the adoption by the Office of Management and Budget of a proactive role in shaping programmatic choices, raises interesting questions:

- How have changes in the bureaucracy's role in budget making affected the issues and choices considered by the president and his senior advisers?

- Have changes in agency roles produced associated changes in the behavior of career officials and in the role of presidential appointees in superintending agency activity?

- How has the new budgetary environment affected the purposes, designs, costs, and effectiveness of agency programs?

- Have there been changes in the internal distribution of power among competitors for scarce resources? For example, have innovative, high-risk, or "soft" programs suffered relative to entrenched programs backed by powerful professional or economic groups?

- Were there characteristics of agency structures, processes, or political relationships that affected the extent to which agencies were either defensive or accommodating with respect to OMB-proposed changes?

- What lessons for the White House staff and OMB can be inferred from agency behavior in the new environment?

Joseph Wholey's study of responses to changes in the budgetary environment in five federal domestic agencies contains useful information concerning some of these questions. The agencies he investigated were the Food and Nutrition Service of the U.S. Department of Agriculture; the Employment and Training Administration of the U.S. Department of Labor; and the Health Resources and Services Administration, the National Institute of Mental Health, and the Administration on Aging of the U.S. Department of Health and Human Services. Wholey's primary objective was to describe changes in agency budgetary policies and practices. He based his report on interviews that he and several associates conducted with nearly seventy persons, most of them agency officials, and on agency and other government documents that were winnowed for evidence of changes in decision criteria used in budgetary choices, agency operations and program activities, and agency funding and staffing. Wholey regards his conclusions as "more encouraging than might have been expected": "In each of the agencies examined, the administration achieved substantial progress toward most of its retrenchment objectives. . . . [Yet] most of the agencies survived and functioned reasonably well [and] . . . . achieved a number of changes designed to strengthen agency and program performance."

Wholey is particularly impressed with what he believes is the rationality of the budgetary outcomes in these five agencies. Retrenchment made it possible for administration officials to achieve reductions in programs, such as Public Service Employment, Public Health Service Hospitals, and Health Professions Student Assistance, "known to be weak or inappropriate and already on a downward trend" and to restructure other programs in an effort to improve their performance and efficiency. Yet "when programs had demonstrated high performance"—his examples include Job Corps, NIMH's Community Support Programs, the Special Supplemental Food Program for Women, Infants, and Children, and Community Health Services—"Congress resisted administration pressures."

Wholey is less than convincing in presenting these conclusions, however. His evidence consists of observations that legislators made claims of program effectiveness in successfully resisting particular Reagan-proposed reductions. In contrast, programs for which Congress approved reductions had been on budget examiners' "hit lists" for years. But Wholey does not say whether the latter programs' reputations were founded on actual demonstrations of ineffectiveness. Nor does Wholey say whether any "effective" programs were nonetheless cut or "ineffective" programs supported. Without examining actual evaluation results for the significant programs in these agencies and determining the extent to which program reputations and support are in fact based on competent evaluation findings, he is justified in concluding no more than that OMB and Congress did not mete out budget cuts evenhandedly. All other things equal, a program's political reputation appeared to play a role in determining its fate, but the case that "legislative committees have proved capable of sorting through proposed cuts and saving programs that have demonstrated their effectiveness'' has not been made.

Of greater value is Wholey's evidence concerning changes in agency operations and program activities. A nicely textured picture emerges of the effects of Reagan's budgetary policies on daily operations in these agencies. ''Computers are now being used to check food stamp recipients' wage statements against state employment data files. . . . ETA reduced costs such as printing and overtime to minimize the number of RIFs required. . . . As a result of . . . reorganization, HRSA was able to reallocate seventy positions from program support to direct program delivery. . . . We substituted for field visits by checking documents received in the central office. . . . In an effort to let staff members know where they stood, NIMH ran a number of mock RIFs and posted the results.'' These are interesting observations that might be pieced together to produce new insights into the management of scarcity. Retrenchment produced turbulence and gloom in the ranks but also numerous opportunities for administration officials to revamp agency activities, and many of their actions no doubt led to improvements in program administration.

Here, too, however, Wholey's conclusions extend well beyond the reach of his data. ''Most of the agencies,'' he says, ''have emerged with realistic sets of objectives, and program and staff activities likely to achieve progress toward those objectives.'' Maybe so, maybe not. Wholey exhibits a propensity to accept at face value assertions and claims by interviewees that might well prove on close examination to be dubious, overly optimistic (or pessimistic), exaggerated, or wrong. We are not sure how he distinguished realistic objectives from unrealistic ones. Wholey did not gather the evidence necessary to support claims of significant actual gains in the effectiveness of administrative management.

Nor has Wholey taken advantage of the opportunity to outline the respective roles played by Reagan's political appointees, career budget officers, and program officials in these agencies. Surely the quality of leadership, adaptability of career officials, strength of legislative and interest group support, and degree of professionalism in program administration varied from agency to agency, and surely all these factors affected the results achieved by the administration. Wholey subordinates any interest he might have had in exploring the consequences of such variations to a determination to produce sweeping reductionist generalizations.

The flaws in his arguments notwithstanding, Wholey is surely on to something. He appears to have discovered a substantial degree of resilience and a significant capacity for constructive adaptation to change in agencies under siege by a hostile president and budget director. Although he advises people who would seek similar changes to minimize their negative consequences, his evidence supports, albeit indirectly, the view that aggressive, one might say fearless, efforts to use the budget to overcome bureaucratic inertia are both necessary and desirable in promoting increased efficiency and reordered priorities. He is clearly encouraged—and others will be emboldened—by what he believes he has found.

But has he really found what he says he has? The important lessons of Reagan's approach to the administrative management of the federal bureaucracy—lessons that might be drawn on the basis of answers to the questions posed at the beginning of this comment—are more elusive and difficult to substantiate than Wholey admits. Evidence gathered over the next few years may vindicate the view that scarcity and relentless pressure breed both effectiveness and efficiency in social welfare administration, but the story that will emerge from the future record—indeed from a more thorough analysis of the existing record—is likely to be more ambiguous.

To give Wholey his due, however, the contrast between Jimmy Carter's timidity and Reagan's bravado in promoting bureaucratic change has to be evaluated in Reagan's favor. Change in agency operations is costly but achievable, and the cost may well be bearable. The consequences of those changes constitute another subject, however, one that Wholey has not seriously addressed.

COMMENTS

Robert D. Behn

Joseph S. Wholey draws from his research an interesting, startling, unprecedented, and potentially significant conclusion: Public programs with "demonstrated effectiveness" fared better, when the Reagan administration attempted to cut their budgets, than did programs "generally recognized as ineffective or inappropriate." Specifically, Wholey concludes, "Congress was able to make reasonable distinctions—saving programs in which high performance had been demonstrated and making reductions in ineffective programs." And Wholey found that one agency was able to target its own cuts on subunits "with less severe needs" and those "known to be poorly managed."

Wholey's conclusion is truly path-breaking: Effectiveness counts! If he is correct, much of the conventional wisdom about the Reagan budget cuts will have to be rethought.

Wholey divided the twelve programs that he examined into two categories depending on their effectiveness. Four of the twelve are "programs for which program effectiveness has been demonstrated." They are (with the percentage change in their budgets between FY 1980 and FY 1983 in parentheses):

1. Women, Infants, and Children (WIC) Nutrition Program (+46%)

2. Job Corps (+47%)

3. Community Health Centers (+13%)

4. Community Support Programs for the Chronically Mentally Ill (-25%).

The other eight are "programs generally considered to be inappropriate or ineffective":

5. Public Service Employment (-100%)

6. Trade Adjustment Assistance (-97%)

7. Public Health Service Hospitals (-100%)

8. Health Professions Institutional Assistance (-90%)

9. Health Professions Student Assistance (-100%)

10. Health Professions Nurse Training (-55%)

11. Health Planning (-66%)

12. Clinical Training of the National Institute of Mental Health (-71%).

The largest cut sustained by any program in the first category was 25 percent; indeed, for three of the four programs in this category the budgets were actually increased. By contrast, the smallest reduction in the second category was 55 percent, with three of the eight programs being completely eliminated. Clearly, the first four programs fared much better than the second eight.

But how can you determine, a priori, which programs belong in the first category and which belong in the second? How can you tell a program with "demonstrated effectiveness" from one "generally considered to be inappropriate or ineffective"?

For the four programs in the first category, Wholey provides evidence that they have, indeed, demonstrated their effectiveness. He cites six studies to document the effectiveness of WIC and observes (without quotation or reference), "Program effectiveness arguments were used in congressional decisions." For the Community Health Centers program, Wholey cites two analyses prepared for the Department of Health and Human Services, plus his own work. For the Community Support Program for the Chronically Mentally Ill, he cites one HHS study plus congressional testimony.

For the Job Corps, he provides the best evidence. He quotes the Congressional Budget Office ("has proven effective"), cites a study by Mathematica, and again observes, "Program effectiveness arguments were also used in congressional decisions." And this time he is specific: Effectiveness arguments influenced Senator Orrin Hatch, the chairman of the Senate Committee on Labor and Human Resources, and he used these arguments to rally support for the Job Corps. Indeed, after touring a Job Corps center with the program's national director, Hatch reported in the *Congressional Record* (as cited but not quoted by Wholey):

> As I walked through classrooms and dormitory areas at the Clearfield [Job Corps] Center . . . and spoke spontaneously with individual students and staff members alike, I learned first-hand how the Job Corps works and why. How could a program not succeed that gives dignity to kids heretofore locked into the slavery of America's rural and urban poverty? . . . The Job Corps has been a leader in synthesizing methods and materials to educate and train the most hardcore disadvantaged. . . . Undoubtedly, a visit to the Job Corps Center has been one of

the most impressive experiences of my career and provides some of the impetus for insuring these opportunities are continued for young people throughout the country who otherwise would not have had a chance.[1]

Any program that can convert Orrin Hatch into a conventional liberal has clearly demonstrated its effectiveness at something.

Wholey does not offer a program-by-program analysis of the eight programs that he lists as "generally considered to be inappropriate or ineffective." Rather, he writes, "Reduction or elimination of each of these programs has often been proposed." (Indeed, a few weeks before President Reagan released his budget proposals in February 1981, the Congressional Budget Office issued a report on "possible strategies" for reducing the federal budget. Included in CBO's ninety-four "possible budget reductions" were public service employment, Public Health Service hospitals, and trade adjustment assistance.[2]) Also, Wholey quotes a staff member of the Health Resources and Services Administration about (among other programs) federal assistance to the Health Professions Education program: "It's important to note that reductions in many areas were sought by prior administrations." Indeed, both the Ford and Carter administrations had attempted to eliminate aid for health professions education.

Finally, Wholey states: "Most of these [eight] reductions are consistent with the U.S. General Accounting Office *Comments on the President's February 18, 1981, Budget Proposals and Additional Cost-Saving Measures.*"

This GAO report specifically discusses three of these eight programs plus the health professions education programs in general: For the Public Service Employment program, GAO had clearly concluded that the program was ineffective: "CETA programs had a limited success in moving participants from public service employment jobs into unsubsidized employment."[3]

For the Public Health Service Hospitals, GAO's evaluation suggested that the program was having a diminishing impact: "During fiscal years 1972 through 1975 the eight PHS hospitals experienced a decline in the numbers of hospital admissions, the average daily patient load, and outpatient visits provided to all of its beneficiaries."[4]

---

1. "The Job Corps," *Congressional Record*, February 26, 1981, p. S 1600.

2. Congressional Budget Office, *Reducing the Federal Budget Strategies and Examples: Fiscal Years 1982-1986* (Washington, D.C.: Government Printing Office, 1981).

3. General Accounting Office, *Comments on the President's February 18, 1981, Budget Proposals and Additional Cost-Saving Measures* (Washington, D.C.: Government Printing Office, 1981), pp. 2–78.

4. Ibid., pp. 2–105.

Regarding the support for the Health Professions Education program, GAO found that "the loan repayment program . . . had not induced substantial numbers of physicians to enter shortage areas, and it seems that many physicians participating in the programs received windfall repayment of their education loans by the Federal Government since they would have established their practice in those shortage areas anyway." Indeed, GAO concluded that "the broad objective of this budget reduction proposal is reasonable and warranted."[5]

In assessing the Trade Adjustment Assistance program, GAO found that it "helped few import-affected workers adjust to the changed economic conditions during the layoff." But rather than eliminate the program, GAO suggested that "adjustment assistance should be targeted on the workers who remained unemployed after exhausting their unemployment benefits."[6]

It may well be that the distribution of Wholey's twelve programs along the effectiveness dimension is bi-model—with four programs at the "effective" end and eight at the other. It may also be that these twelve programs are similarly distributed along the scale labeled "reputation for effectiveness." But, Wholey has not convinced me. For his four "effective" programs, he cites evaluations to document their effectiveness, but he provides little evidence that these evaluations have affected the programs' political or public reputations. For the other eight, he provides some evidence about their reputations for ineffectiveness, but hardly enough to distinguish these from many other "ineffective" public programs (such as maritime industry subsidies) that continue to be funded. Indeed, he has offered no evidence that either health planning or clinical training were "generally recognized as ineffective or inappropriate."

Neither does Wholey make a convincing case that "Legislative committees have proved capable of sorting through proposed cuts and saving programs that have demonstrated their effectiveness." He cites no examples of congressional committees sorting through programs in terms of their effectiveness. Indeed, with the exception of Senator Hatch's support for the Job Corps, Wholey offers no evidence that a program's effectiveness—or reputation for effectiveness—influenced any congressional votes. In fact, many programs with reputations for ineffectiveness (as measured by inclusion in the GAO and CBO reports) were not marked for reduction by the Reagan administration or by Congress.

Does a program's effectiveness—or reputation for such—influence Congress's decision (if only at the margin) about whether to go along with an

---

5. Ibid., pp. 2–107.
6. Ibid., pp. 2–78.

executive branch proposal to cut the program's budget? To answer that question requires more detailed analysis than is contained in this paper. It requires the drawing of a representative sample of programs. It requires analysis, based on uniform standards, of the effectiveness of each program, so that it is clear why programs are classified as they are. It requires an examination of the relationship between the program's effectiveness (as somehow measured objectively) with its reputation for effectiveness. It requires comparative analysis of the impact of various factors influencing budget cutback choices: interest group pressures; politics within both the executive and the legislative branches that affect choices about priorities; outside events; the strategies used by various parties; and the effectiveness—and reputation for effectiveness—of the programs.

Such an analysis would indeed be interesting—perhaps revealing. It might even conclude that "effectiveness counts." Unfortunately, Wholey's report does not contain that analysis.

LEGISLATIVE POLITICS AND BUDGET OUTCOMES

Kenneth A. Shepsle and Barry R. Weingast

Dissatisfaction with the policy performance of the federal government is widespread. People who oppose a strong federal presence denounce over-regulation, massive deficits, "out-of-control" bureaucracies, and exploding entitlement expenditures. People who favor a strong government presence find fault with public laws, programs, and regulatory decisions that are typically rigid, bureaucratic, mistargeted, and lacking in coordination or rationality. Still others indict the government for its tendency to serve special-interest groups with generous subsidies, tax preferences, and anticompetitive privileges, and for its concomitant failure to provide for the more general interest.[1]

Disagreements over what constitutes the problem extend to differences in the diagnosis of the causes as well as to potential cures. From our perspective, this lack of consensus on why the government does what it does—independent of one's values concerning what is good or bad—reflects serious disagreements over and misunderstandings of how the system works. Regulatory decisions, spending on particular entitlement programs, and revenue-raising activities do not just happen; the pattern of policy decisions follows a profound and subtle logic. Improving policy, no matter what the goal, must

Some of these ideas were discussed in "Public Policy Excesses: Government by Congressional Subcommittee," Formal Publication No. 50 (St. Louis: Center for the Study of American Business, 1982), written by the two authors and Clifford M. Hardin. We are grateful to Dr. Hardin and the staff of the Center for the Study of American Business at Washington University for their encouragement and criticism. We are also grateful to Professor John Ellwood of Tufts University for thoughtful comments on an earlier draft.

1. See Charles Schultze, *The Public Use of Private Interest* (Washington, D.C.: The Brookings Institution, 1977).

be based on a thorough understanding of why the government does what it does.

Controversies surrounding the federal budget exhibit this same lack of consensus. There is little agreement on how and why today's budgetary problems arise or even on what constitutes the problem. In order to make sense of these problems, we need three analytical and empirical tools: (1) a normative model that specifies the desirable role of the public sector in our economy; (2) an empirical assessment of actual public-sector performance measured against the derived normative ideal; and (3) a positive model explaining why the actual performance diverges from the normative ideal.

Analysts often begin with the question, "Is our budget too big (too small)?" In our opinion this is simply the wrong question. Indeed, answers to this question are likely to resemble those of the blind men touching the various parts of the proverbial elephant, since assessments typically are based on specific programmatic performances. There simply is no basis for inferring much about *aggregate* performance unless there are universal and pervasive biases to report at the programmatic level.

Even then, the answer to an optimal budget total may be elusive. Roger Noll has pointed out that there simultaneously may be areas in which the government underproduces (e.g., not enough correction of market failure) and other areas in which it overproduces (e.g., too many private goods to politically relevant special interests). Even if each individual case is clear, little can be said about the appropriate size of the public sector. It does too little in some areas and too much in others, a condition which in no way translates into a judgment about the aggregate.[2]

Our analysis, following Noll's suggestion, focuses on programmatic performance. The forces driving defense policy differ from those driving entitlements or regulation, and we must therefore study these separately. In doing so, we approach public-sector performance from the vantage point of Congress. Today's key budgetary problems can be understood only as an integral part of the congressional system. The roots of our fiscal problems—budgetary growth, deficit financing, inexplicable programmatic forms, attention to special interests—are anchored in Congress; unless this fact is understood, reforms are unlikely to be effective.

Members of Congress, at least since the turn of the century, have been motivated by two strong desires: to secure reelection by serving their con-

---

2. See Roger Noll, "The Case Against the Balanced Budget Amendment," in Laurence H. Meyer, ed., *The Economic Consequences of Government Deficits* (Boston: Kluwer-Nijhoff, 1983), pp. 201–210.

stituents and to develop a personal power base in Congress. That is the system. Moreover, to strengthen their power bases and to provide for constituents, members have, with considerable success, altered the very ways Congress conducts business. In so doing, they have produced a policymaking machinery that often serves more general public purposes only as an incidental by-product of these political objectives. As the political scientist, David Mayhew, noted a decade ago:

> The organization of Congress meets remarkably well the electoral needs of its members. To put it another way, if a group of planners sat down and tried to design a pair of American national assemblies with the goal of serving members' electoral needs year in and year out, they would be hard pressed to improve on what exists.[3]

The main purpose of this paper is to highlight the legislative contribution to public policy and apply this logic to today's fiscal concerns. In arguing that policies are the by-product of the legislator's pursuit of election and power, we shall give special prominence to the way legislators have organized the Congress. Some important elements of our story are the division of labor of the committee system, the self-selection to committees of what we call "preference outliers" by the committee assignment process, the institutional bargains that constitute reciprocity among committees and universal distributive tendencies, and the relative weakness of institutional regulators like parties and leaders.

In the first section, we discuss congressional institutions and decision making. We focus on the decline of centralized leadership and strong parties as well as on the rise first of independent committees and then of subcommittees. We also examine the subcommittee system and emphasize its policy consequences. The second section extracts some general principles of policymaking that derive from legislative structure and politics. The principles provide some insight about the features characteristic of legislatively produced policies. Throughout this section, we demonstrate the applicability of these principles to existing fiscal policies. The final section is a discussion of political ingenuity in which we tie together our emphasis on legislative structure and governmental performance by focusing on the adaptability of legislative politicians. Throughout we paint with rather bold strokes, not because we are unaware of exceptions and other details, but rather because we believe it is the central tendencies that leave their imprint on public policies.

---

3. David Mayhew, *Congress: The Electoral Connection* (New Haven: Yale University Press, 1974), pp. 81–82.

Congress: The Root of the Problem

According to traditional wisdom,[4] the twentieth century has witnessed the decline of the Congress and the strengthening of the presidency. Congress enjoyed something of a resurgence during the 1970s—consider the Budget Act, the War Powers Resolution, the growth of legislative oversight, the legislative veto, and miscellaneous fallout from Watergate. But over the longer run, academics, popular commentators, and members of Congress themselves have viewed Congress as a much weakened branch of government. This common view, if not erroneous, is an extreme and unbalanced one.

Let us briefly sketch our revisionist interpretation before making the more detailed case. Observers of national politics, focusing on grand issues like inflation, deficits, and "out-of-control" spending, often forget that these are simply labels given to the effects of an accumulation of many smaller, seemingly unrelated, policy decisions. To address these broad effects and to ameliorate their consequences, it is necessary to understand the underlying mechanisms that operate at the level of actual policy decisions. In short, it is necessary to appreciate the division of labor that characterizes policymaking.

We argue that the so-called decline of Congress has not meant an ascendant executive branch. Instead, both Congress, the collective entity, and the presidency have been eclipsed by the now-autonomous committees and subcommittees of Congress. Over the past fifty years these units have developed a much freer hand in policymaking within their own narrow jurisdictions. Each is positioned in its own issue bailiwick to protect relevant constituencies from adverse changes. Although no one of them can plausibly be saddled with responsibility for any of the "grand problems," each contributes its own small part.

The consequent problems of our federal government may appear out of control and unresolvable, but this situation is not attributable to imperial presidents or evil bureaucratic spirits dominating a supposedly powerless legislative branch. Rather it exists because key institutional figures—subcommittee members—are biased against remedies that harm their constituents, and these members have the power to block ameliorative initiatives. People with the incentive to advocate and pursue remedial courses of action—the president and major party leaders—lack the institutional power to effect these changes. The problem, then, is not one of uncontrollable policies. It is

---

4. A comprehensive recent statement is found in James L. Sundquist, *The Decline and Resurgence of Congress* (Washington, D.C.: The Brookings Institution, 1981).

one of mismatched capabilities and incentives—people who can change policies, will not; people who want to, cannot.[5]

Broadly speaking, our interpretation of events focuses on the evolution of committee and subcommittee autonomy in the Congress. Accompanying this evolution—indeed elevating it to decisive status—is the concomitant decline of institutional constraints inside the legislature. Congress can no longer check the narrow, provincial impulses of its subunits as it once could. Indeed, we argue that a major flaw in the way policy is now made is the unwillingness or inability of Congress to counteract and neutralize this central fact. Before entertaining this proposition, however, let us provide some substantive meat for our interpretive skeleton.

Some Historical Details

Table 1 displays some of the major landmarks on the twentieth-century historical landscape of Congress. Space precludes a detailed discussion, but several observations are offered.[6] First, there has been a remarkable trend toward decentralization of control in Congress; power has been transferred from strong institutional and party leaders initially to committees and later to subcommittees. This process began in the second decade of this century with the revolt against the imperious Speaker of the House, "Boss" Cannon; his enormous powers ultimately gravitated to the chairmen of the standing committees. By the mid-1930s, partly in response to Roosevelt's New Deal, cross-party ideological coalitions in both the House and the Senate (the so-called conservative coalition) further weakened central party control. In the 1960s, the power of institutional-regulator committees like Rules and Appropriations was weakened. By the end of the 1970s, several additional events served to consolidate the fifty-year trend toward decentralization. The Legislative Reorganization Act (1970), the Subcommittee Bill of Rights (1973), and the Committee Reform Amendments (1974) constrained full committees, and strengthened the hand of and provided independence for the now numerous subcommittees. On the surface, these events gave the appearance of weakening the influence of Congress over policymaking, because they diminished

---

5. Morris P. Fiorina, "Congressional Control of the Bureaucracy: A Mismatch of Incentives and Capabilities," in Dodd, Lawrence, and Bruce Oppenheimer, eds., *Congress Reconsidered*, 2nd ed. (Washington, D.C.: Congressional Quarterly, 1981). See also his masterful study, *Congress: Keystone of the Washington Establishment* (New Haven: Yale University Press, 1977).

6. For a popular historical account, see Alvin H. Josephy, *On the Hill: A History of the American Congress* (New York: Simon and Schuster, 1979). See also Kenneth A. Shepsle, "Geography, Jurisdiction, and the Congressional Budget Process," Working Paper No. 73, Center for the Study of American Business, Washington University, St. Louis, 1982.

TABLE 1

CALENDAR OF SOME TWENTIETH-CENTURY LEGISLATIVE DEVELOPMENTS

1911	Revolt against the Speaker of the House: independence of commitees and committee chairmen; strengthening of minority party
1911–1920	Growth of the seniority system: separation of party and committee leaders
1921–1922	Budget and Accounting Act: re-creation of separate House and Senate Appropriations Committees
1934	Reciprocal Trade Agreements Act: transfer of responsibility for tariff making from Congress to the president
1938	Origins of Republican/Southern Democratic "Conservative Coalition"
1946	Legislative Reorganization Act creating the "modern" committee system in House and Senate
1946	Employment Act of 1946
1961	Attack on the ability of the House Rules Committee to control and restrain legislative flow
1964–1966	Growth of incumbency effect: reelection of congressional incumbents becomes more regularized
1970	Legislative Reorganization Act (greatly accelerating the growth of professional legislative staff)
1973	Subcommittee Bill of Rights: fixed subcommittee jurisdictions, automatic referral of bills to subcommittees, guaranteed budgets for subcommittees, guaranteed staff for subcommittees, seniority criterion for subcommittee chairs, bidding process for subcommittee assignments
1974	Committee Reform Amendments in House: the removal of some powerful committee chairmen; rise of the Democratic Caucus
1974	Congressional Budget and Impoundment Control Act

the capacities of the old power centers (the speaker, party leaders, and committee chairmen). Below the surface, however, new power centers were developing inside Congress.[7]

---

7. Most of the details in table 1 trace shifts in power to the executive branch from the legislative branch (House and Senate, collectively) or internal trends of decentralization inside the House. This is not meant to imply that the Senate has been immune to these trends. We choose to feature the House more prominently only because the developments there have been more dramatic and because the Senate has been highly decentralized for many years. Many of the features of policymaking that have come to characterize the House have been part of the Senate's standard operating procedure for most of this century. The House, as a legislative institution, has drifted toward the Senate so that, although some of the specifics we give later are tailored to the situation in the House, the general conditions that these specifics add up to apply to the Senate as well.

Second, there has been a trend toward giving powers to the president, seemingly at the expense of Congress. The Budget and Accounting Act of 1921 gave the president responsibility for proposing an executive budget each fiscal year. The Reciprocal Trade Act of 1934 gave the executive branch the power to set tariff levels. The Employment Act of 1946 declared the government to be responsible for full employment in the economy, and the president has been embroiled in the economy's macroperformance ever since.

An odd feature of this story—the weakening of Congress and the strengthening of the president—is the implicit belief that redistribution of power between the two branches of government has been a one-way street. This impression is erroneous for it gives little weight to the adaptations and adjustments within Congress that followed these major developments. Reforms of the past half-century have indeed weakened Congress, the institution. But the institutionalized presidency has not been the only, or even the most important, beneficiary. These reforms, especially those of the early 1970s, have produced significant effects and adaptations *inside the legislature*. First, they have emancipated individual representatives and senators from the restraints of their parties, and, second, they have liberated congressional committees and subcommittees from the preferences of chamber majorities.

Each house of Congress, more than at any time in history, now consists of members free to pursue their own electoral ambitions through service to constituencies, geographic or otherwise.[8] Members sit on committees and subcommittees that are capable of operating with relative independence in well-defined policy jurisdictions. Thus, the destruction of institutional and party power centers during the past half-century of reform and decentralization in the Congress must be seen alongside the creation of new power centers (committees and subcommittees). In the same light, the nominal shift of the policymaking initiative to the president must be interpreted alongside (and qualified by) the veto power and "continuous watchfulness" (in the words of the Legislative Reorganization Act of 1946) of decentralized committees and subcommittees.

Even if policymaking appears to come at the initiative and insistence of the executive branch, even if implementation and administration appear to be at the behest of an enormous executive bureaucracy, and even if Congress, the collective body, appears unable to respond decisively or expeditiously, the jurisdictional subunits of the legislature—committees and subcommittees—are increasingly vital in the policymaking process. Members of these subunits, because they have been freed from party control and the bullyboy

---

8. See Shepsle, "Geography and Jurisdiction," and Richard F. Fenno, *Home Style* (Boston: Little, Brown, 1978).

tactics of institutional leaders, are at liberty to pursue their own narrow interests. Even majorities in the full chambers are placed at a disadvantage, because their initiatives may be vetoed or blocked by committees and sub-committees if those actions would harm or otherwise jeopardize benefits currently being enjoyed by committee and subcommittee constituents. Poli-cies, as a consequence, are victimized by two territorial imperatives emanating from the legislative branch—geography and jurisdiction, constituencies and committees—which help explain the past decade's growth in federal bud-getary commitments.

Geographic Constituencies: The Electoral Connection

With the decline of political parties in the post-World War II Congress, legislators have learned that they have but one master to serve—their con-stituencies. During the 1950s, Speaker Sam Rayburn could tell freshmen Democrats, "To get along, go along," but even then that appeal to party loyalty was quite weak. It was weakened further during the 1960s and 1970s as legislators began amassing the taxpayer-supported private perks—franking privileges, personal staff, district offices, trips to the home district—that enabled them to forge independent electoral support in their districts, by-passing legislative party leaders altogether.

In sum, legislators are bound to the tugs of geography, since it is the geographic constituency that looms largest in each legislators' career calcu-lations. For most legislators most of the time, it is the political contract that must be renegotiated every second or sixth year with their electoral consti-tuencies that is the final consideration.

There is a second important consequence of the electoral connection. Committees and subcommittees are instrumental to legislators grappling with the tugs of geography.[9] When legislators arrive in Washington, they find in Congress a complex division of labor consisting, in each chamber, of 15 or 20 standing committees and upwards of 150 subcommittees. Each of these units has a well-defined policy jurisdiction in which it occupies a commanding position in originating new legislation, and in monitoring and overseeing existing statutes implemented by executive branch agencies. If legislators expect to have some impact on new and existing policies that are of special importance to their constituents, they must seek an appropriate niche in the division of labor. And the evidence on committee assignments is quite con-clusive: they do! Most legislators gravitate to the committees and subcom-

---

9. See Richard F. Fenno, *Congressmen in Committees* (Boston: *Little, Brown*, 1973); Mayhew, *Congress: The Electoral Connection*; and Fiorina, *Congress: Keystone*.

mittees whose jurisdictions are more important to their geographic constituencies.[10]

As a consequence, committees and subcommittees are not collections of legislators representing diverse views from across the nation or collections of disinterested members who develop objective policy expertise. Rather, committees and subcommittees are populated by legislators who have the highest stake in a given policy jurisdiction, what we have termed "preference outliers." Hence, farm-state members of Congress dominate the agriculture committees; urban legislators predominate on the banking, housing, and social welfare committees; members with military bases and defense industries in their districts are found on the armed services committees; and westerners are disproportionately represented on the public works, natural resources, and environmental committees. In short, the geographic link, forged in the electoral arena, is institutionalized in the committee system of the legislature.

Committee and Subcommittee Jurisdictions

Legislators seek particular committees and subcommittees because they occupy key locations in policymaking. Three distinct reasons underpin their importance. First, committees and their subcommittees originate legislation. Although there is some built-in overlap in committee and subcommittee jurisdictions, these units typically have jurisdictional monopoly over specific public policies. As a result, changes in statutory policy require the assent of relevant committee and subcommittee majorities. In other words, changes in policy may be vetoed by committees and subcommittees if their preferences are not reflected in the new policy.

Second, committees and subcommittees are oversight agents. According to traditional wisdom on the ascendancy of the executive branch, the infrequency of official, public, oversight hearings and investigations represent evidence that Congress has abdicated its job of overseeing executive activities. Oversight, however, does not require legislative intervention in day-to-day executive administration. As congressional committee staffs have grown, a good deal more oversight goes on, often surreptitiously, than is acknowledged by people who believe that the executive branch is unchecked. Moreover, the traditional interpretation is based on the premise that, in order to know whether an agency is pursuing the right course, intensive study, in-depth hearings, and investigations are necessary. This premise is false. Rather, members of particular subcommittees know whether an agency is making "appropriate"

---

10. The evidence is presented in Kenneth A. Shepsle, *The Giant Jigsaw Puzzle: Democratic Committee Assignments in the Modern House* (Chicago: University of Chicago Press, 1978).

decisions by the decibel meter: something is amiss when they hear relevant constituents clamoring. Thus, the infrequency of resource-intensive activities like hearings and investigations is as consistent with a system of high bureaucratic responsiveness to the wishes of an oversight committee as with the more common view that Congress is unable and unwilling to engage in much oversight. Finally, a subcommittee wields a "club behind the door." It may impose a variety of sanctions on errant agencies. During 1980, for example, the Federal Trade Commission (FTC) was forced to close its doors for a day when Congress failed to approve its budget for the fiscal year.[11] Like a warning shot across the bow, that action was intended to have a sobering effect.

These mechanisms restrain executive agencies in their implementation of current policies. Wise bureau chiefs appreciate that, in exercising whatever policy discretion they have, they had best attend to the concerns of relevant committee and subcommittee members who can embarrass or otherwise complicate the bureau chiefs' lives through the adverse publicity of oversight, and who can directly affect the bureaus' authority and budget through the annual authorization and appropriations process.[12]

The origination of legislation and the monitoring of its implementation explain not only why committees and subcommittees are important in policymaking, but also how policies will be tailored in particular ways. Given the unrepresentativeness of committee composition ("preference outliers"),

---

11. For additional details, see Barry R. Weingast and Mark J. Moran, "Bureaucratic Discretion or Congressional Control: Regulatory Policymaking by the Federal Trade Commission," *Journal of Political Economy* 91 (1983), pp. 765–800. See also idem, "The Myth of the Runaway Bureaucracy: The Case of the FTC," *Regulation*, vol. 6, no. 3 (1982), pp. 33–38.

12. The recent events at the FTC illustrate this view. From 1979 through early 1982, the FTC was vigorously criticized by its oversight subcommittee for "regulating all kinds of business activities that should not be the concern of the government." The legislators participating in this assault, as well as much of the popular press, viewed the furor over the FTC as an instance of Congress's finally catching a "runaway, uncontrollable bureaucracy." Indeed, in this three-year period, nearly every program initiated by the FTC during the 1970s was substantially altered or halted outright. But this rendering of the traditional wisdom had little to do with the realities of recent policy reversals and sanctions at the FTC. The major FTC initiatives of the 1970s are more accurately interpreted as a partnership between an activist FTC and an activist Senate subcommittee. Members of the Senate Commerce Committee's oversight subcommittee sought to establish themselves as advocates of the new consumerism (the most visible members were Senators Magnuson, Moss, and Hart). In 1977 these activist members all had left the subcommittee—Magnuson moved to the chairmanship of Appropriations, Hart died, and Moss was defeated for reelection. Opponents of the consumerism their predecessors had fostered took their places. Prior to 1977, activists in the FTC worked hand in hand with activists on the subcommittee. The sanctions that followed in 1979 were the result of a newly composed subcommittee's reversing the policies of its predecessor, not the harnessing of a runaway, uncontrollable bureaucracy. The point here is that ties between agencies and subcommittees are subtle, behind the scenes, and easily missed by outsiders.

agencies in the executive branch respond to biased interests. In terms of budgets, there is a predisposition to increase spending. Thus, it is not surprising that observers have reflected on the decline of Congress since, from all outward appearances, any given executive branch agency may not be responding to legislative majorities. In reality, these agencies are responding to the dominant coalition on the subcommittee overseeing it, whose members are rarely representative of the larger legislature.

There is a third element in our argument for the decisiveness of legislative committees and subcommittees. There is no question that these units control the policy agenda in their respective jurisdictions. Nor is there any question about their capacity to influence executive agencies. But in order for them to maintain this control and influence, as well as to take even more affirmative steps in representing the interests of the policy constituencies, it must be the case that legislative majorities or other power centers in the legislature cannot or will not frustrate their designs. We maintain that this circumstance is achieved by the honoring of subcommittee veto power and other forms of reciprocity. Each subcommittee has its own turf, both to protect and to cultivate. The current arrangement among the committees of Congress embodies the bargain, "You can retain veto power and influence in your area if I can retain it in mine."[13] The important consequence of this bargain among subcommittees is that people on the relevant subcommittees hold the power to protect and enhance the flow of public benefits to their constituents.

To summarize, committee and subcommittee jurisdiction and veto power have an enormous, but largely unappreciated, impact on policymaking. While committees and subcommittees may not have a completely free rein in formulating new policy, they are given a long leash and, once a program or agency is in place, subcommittees can protect it against policy change they deem undesirable. The obvious consequence of this power is what some people call the uncontrollability of government operations. Reform proposals and policy initiatives to alter bad programs regularly fall upon deaf ears or have little effect when put in operation. The reason is that subcommittees veto all proposals that make their constituents worse off. And they may do so in an innocuous manner—by simply taking no action. Their monopoly jurisdiction—protected by congressional majorities composed of representatives all who have something to protect—ensures that there are rarely penalties for

---

13. This is an unappreciated part of the reciprocity system in Congress. It is described, and its implications traced, in Donald Matthews, *U.S. Senators and Their World* (Chapel Hill, N.C.: University of North Carolina Press, 1960). Also see Mayhew, *Congress*; and Morris P. Fiorina, "Legislative Facilitation of Governmental Growth: Universalism and Reciprocity Practices in Majority Rule Institutions," Social Science Working Paper No. 226, California Institute of Technology, August 1978.

inaction. Attempts to improve even some of the most egregious features of programs are fended off because such reforms typically make current beneficiaries worse off. The result is that programs are difficult to reform not because the executive branch is too powerful, but because the programs are protected by subcommittees consisting of the most (and perhaps the only) enthusiastic supporters. Only a serious crisis (as in the recent experience with Social Security) or the creative blitz of a new administration (as in reconciliation, 1981-style) is capable of penetrating the facade of the congressional committee system. In more normal times, members find the system electorally rewarding because it gives them a decisive voice in policy areas dearest to their constituents' hearts.

"Decline of Congress" Equals Government by (Sub)Committee

Having examined the dominant factors of geography and jurisdiction in Congress, we examine briefly the only remaining possibility for moderating committee and subcommittee decisiveness: other institutional sources of power. Congress once had powerful Speakers, strong party leaders, and dominant Appropriations and Rules Committees that, to some extent, thwarted overly ambitious schemes hatched by authorizing committees and subcommittees. These "institutional regulators" have been constrained and compromised (often in the name of reform). By the middle of the 1970s, Congress had dramatically modified its two most important institutional regulators—the House Committee on Rules and the Committee on Appropriations. It had also restructured itself—through the Legislative Reorganization Act of 1970, the Subcommittee Bill of Rights of 1973, and the Committee Reform Amendments of 1974—into an organization dominated in each chamber by its subcommittees. Even the full committees and their chairmen were generally reduced to "holding companies" and "traffic cops," respectively. The destruction of internal regulators for short-term advantage has meant that Congress has been eclipsed not by the executive branch, but by its own subunits. The decline of Congress is, in fact, the rise of government by (sub)committee.

Congress and Modern Budgetary Problems

Having provided a broad-brushed picture of legislators and the legislature, we now seek to derive some fiscal policy consequences of a legislative system with strong subunit autonomy, unrepresentative subunit composition, and weak centripetal forces. We do so by detailing four principles and exploring their applicability to existing policies. In showing how current budgetary problems directly result from the congressional system, we consider specific budgetary issues in defense policy (and the size of the defense budget), the matter of "out-of-control" entitlements and other fiscal end runs like off-budget expenditures, and one proposed "solution" to budgetary excesses, the balanced-budget amendment.

Two Principles of Expenditure Policies

Expenditure policies are those public programs that entail dollar outlays in order to purchase, build, or produce some good or service. This category includes many programs in defense, urban renewal, mass transit, and environmental cleanup, as well as the traditional pork barrel of rivers and harbors. Various transfer payments are excluded from this category, as are most regulatory programs.

Two related but distinct principles follow from our model of the congressional system. Each reveals a systematic bias that distorts public spending. As our illustrations indicate, these have important implications for budgetary policy.

Principle 1. Productive Inefficiency. The omnipresent electoral imperative induces members of Congress to target expenditures to their electoral constituents or to those who can provide electorally relevant resources. This implies that legislators invent programs, seek funding, and are especially attentive to policy areas that create or maintain jobs within their electoral constituency. More generally, members of Congress favor owners of economic factors (land, labor, and capital), especially if they are organized in their district and possess electorally relevant resources. Expenditure programs are, as a consequence, biased away from least-cost methods of production so as to favor those methods that yield greater electoral support. To understand how this system works, consider the components associated with any given expenditure program:

a. Programmatic benefits: This component consists of the benefits consumed by individuals as a result of achieving programmatic objectives, for example, national defense or a mass transit system.
b. Expenditures on inputs: These are the dollar outlays for project inputs that flow from the public purse to factor owners.
c. Taxes: Revenue is extracted from citizens to cover the expenditures on inputs.

In a purely economic respect, the second category—expenditures on inputs—is simply the funds raised as taxes to finance a program's benefits. In a political sense, however, an important distinction affects every expenditure program. Although the program's benefits may be spread across many geographic constituencies and taxes may be derived from general revenue devices, the distribution of dollar outlays may be quite concentrated. That is to say, the method of producing some public good or service, and consequently the incidence of spending, is endogenous—it may be selected for its political consequences. Because public expenditures often have a significant impact on a local economy and on the wealth of factor owners, the purchase of program inputs is politically valuable wholly apart from the objectives sought by the program. Put simply, economic costs become political benefits when they are appropriately targeted.

The transformation of economic costs into political benefits, as revenues are transformed into expenditures, changes the political cost-benefit calculus into something different from its underlying economic counterpart. Economically, expenditures on inputs are costs, but politically, they are opportunities. Hence, legislators with the ability to target program expenditures judiciously see more benefits than are economically warranted.

This peculiar political transformation has two effects, one concerning the scope or scale of the project, the other concerning the input mix of production. Regarding the first effect, it is apparent that the transformation of economic costs into political benefits implies that the politically optimal scale is systematically larger than its economic counterpart.[14] Expenditure policies are therefore biased so as to be larger than the economically efficient scale. The very label "pork barrel," deriving from the first major congressional expenditure program in the nineteenth century, the improvement of rivers and harbors, connotes economically unwarranted projects. This same tendency to overspend is present to some extent in all expenditure programs.

Regarding the second effect, this calculus distorts the choice of means of production. Legislators value locally targeted expenditures and thus are not disposed to choose the most efficient—that is, least-cost—method of production. For any given level of output, there are many possible combinations of inputs. It is well known in standard production theory in economics that for any given level of production and any level of input prices there is a least-cost method of production. When expenditures become political ends in themselves, however, this purely economic calculus is no longer appropriate. Legislators seek to secure those input combinations that produce electoral rewards. Unless coincidentally the input mix that maximizes political

14. This argument is developed formally in Barry R. Weingast, Kenneth A. Shepsle, and Christopher Johnsen, "The Political Economy of Benefits and Costs: A Neoclassical Approach to Distributive Politics," *Journal of Political Economy* (August 1981), pp. 642–665.

rewards and the one that is economically most efficient are identical, this bias will distort the input mix of production.

Perhaps the most obvious illustration of this principle is found in the method with which we handle water pollution. Politicians have turned a deaf ear to the consensus articulated by professional economists that some scheme of taxes, subsidies, or marketable pollution entitlements be employed to control pollutants at their sources. Instead, politicians prefer cleaning pollution ex post with a capital-intensive technology that entails massive public expenditure. Sewage treatment plants mean contracts for local factor owners and bright, shiny objects for public consumption.

The siting of military bases, and the unwillingness to shut down even the most transparently useless of them, provides another example of productive efficiency yielding to political calculation. The same holds for the production of military hardware: it is no accident that shipyards in Mississippi and aerospace industries in Washington have prospered by virtue of the presence of John Stennis and Henry Jackson in the senior leadership of the Senate Armed Services Committee. As a final example, Linda Cohen and Roger Noll have convincingly argued that even in research and development, government programs seeking to develop and commercialize new technologies are distorted by calculations of political opportunity and advantage. They argue that government development programs move much too rapidly to the demonstration project and commercialization phases because these phases promise political visibility and targeted expenditures.[15]

Despite the lore of traditional welfare economics about a government role in the provision of public goods not otherwise provided in the marketplace, it must be appreciated that goods that are *public* in consumption are normally *private* in production.[16] Hence, although the benefits of many public goods may be widely enjoyed, their production can be targeted to suit political purposes. This is the content, and importance, of Principle 1.

Principle 2. The Distributive Tendency. Public programs do not materialize out of the blue. Rather the congressional system puts its particular stamp on them. One clearly necessary condition for the success of new programs is that they must gain majority support in both houses of Congress. As a result, Congress is biased against programs that are narrowly defined

---

15. Linda Cohen and Roger Noll, "The Political Economy of Government Programs to Promote New Technology," paper delivered at the annual meeting of the American Political Science Association, Chicago, 1983.

16. The view was first brought to our attention by Peter H. Aranson and Peter C. Ordeshook, "The Political Bases of Public Sector Growth in a Representative Democracy," paper delivered at the Conference on the Causes and Consequences of Public Sector Growth, Dorado Beach, Puerto Rico, November 1978.

so as to benefit only a few select states or districts. The need to gain majority support means that politically successful programs are formulated so as to spread the benefits widely across many districts. David Stockman refers to this phenomenon as the distributive tendency, and cites the Model Cities program and the Economic Development Administration as policy initiatives quintessentially affected by pressure to distribute goodies broadly in order to survive politically.[17]

The necessity to spread program expenditures broadly often radically redefines the objectives of a program and thus transforms its impact. This, in turn, breaks the linkage between the program's objectives and the distribution of funds. Some districts in which the particular problem to be solved is acute end up getting fewer resources in comparison with the magnitude of the problem, while other districts obtain substantially more funds than are objectively required. The distributive tendency to spread the dollars across many districts means that too little of the program's goal is achieved relative to the amount of resources spent. In some cases (such as model cities), this transformation may be so complete that it is not clear whether the program's objectives are achieved at all!

The Two Principles Applied: Defense Policy

Defense is by far the largest expenditure category in the federal budget; its size and rate of growth play a prominent role in any discussion of deficits. The consequence of the congressional system discussed earlier plays a major role in tailoring defense policy to suit the needs of legislators.

Goal Distortion.   The logic concerning inefficient production applies with a vengeance here. Coalitions of factor owners—producers, their employees, and members of the local economy whose incomes depend on serving these factor owners—generate political rewards for legislators responsible for local defense expenditures. To the local economy—and therefore to the electoral ambitions of their political representatives—these expenditures represent constituency benefits that accrue to local residents regardless of the level of national defense actually produced. These same citizens will share in the economic burdens of inflation, government borrowing, and higher taxes to accommodate these expenditures, but the local spending effect is far more important.

---

17. David A. Stockman, "The Social Pork Barrel," *The Public Interest* (Spring, 1975), pp. 3–30. Also see Fiorina, "Congressional Control of the Bureaucracy."

The political transformation of economic costs into political benefits has several distinct consequences for defense policy. First, because the distribution of funds becomes an end in itself, committee members with significant concentrations of defense producers in their districts are willing to make tradeoffs between the total amount of defense produced, on the one hand, and the size of the flow of funds to their districts on the other. Since a major source of political support for defense expenditures (and for increases in defense expenditures) comes from current factor owners, production of defense is biased in favor of current producers. As a result, political emphasis is placed on large capital acquisitions, because these are what defense producers manufacture. Moreover, when faced with a choice between additional weapon systems produced by existing manufacturers and a more efficacious defense strategy not targeted to existing producers, legislators facing local constituency pressures are biased in favor of the former.

Similar problems occur in the location of military facilities. As defense needs and capabilities change over time, the optimal location and mix of facilities (bases, hospitals) also change. Because current locations receive economic benefits, however, the representatives of those locations regularly seek to veto base closings.

Cost overruns and other forms of waste are particular manifestations of productive inefficiency in the defense sector. Although this inefficiency is generally characterized as part of some inherent bureaucratic tendency, or rationalized in some ad hoc fashion, we note that it is perfectly consistent with, if not sought and sustained by, the congressional system. Because local expenditures representing economic costs are transformed into political benefits, the political liabilities of waste or cost overruns for members of the relevant committees are substantially mitigated—if present at all. When local expenditures are ends in themselves, independent of the level of defense actually produced, advantaged members of Congress have no problem with cost overruns. This is especially true if this form of productive inefficiency represents a transfer of cost uncertainties from their constituents onto the general taxpayer. We should not be surprised, therefore, if this preference persists despite the fact that it has the perverse economic effect of increasing the ultimate costs of production.

These tendencies are commonly observed by defense analysts. For example, according to Stubbings (in his paper in this volume),

> The status quo is also clearly evident in the strong reluctance by Defense leaders to terminate marginal programs or to shut down unneeded facilities. Once a weapons program commences, its in-house supporters and its outside political constituencies (members of Congress, contractors, local interest groups) band together to guarantee survival.

Similarly, Jacque S. Gansler argues in *The Defense Industry* that "far less military equipment (with lower overall military performance) has been produced than could have been produced at the same level of expenditures."[18]

In sum, the congressional policy process builds in a tremendous bias in favor of existing factor owners and distorts expenditures to benefit them. Electoral concerns about the distribution of expenditures swamp the larger issue of the efficient production of defense.

The Distributive Tendency.   Principle 2 has its effects here, too. Major defense projects nearly always involve many geographically diffuse subcontractors. Programs spread the political benefits—that is, expenditures—across many districts so as to increase their political support. Hence, inefficient producers become politically valuable. A subcontractor may be included not because his firm is the cheapest or best producer, but because his inclusion changes the political calculus of a particular legislator.

The point we want to emphasize is that to understand the political production of national defense, one needs to appreciate the logic of congressional policymaking. And herein lies a paradox: we can have too little production of defense and, at the same time, have defense budgets too high!

Two More Principles of Political Public Finance: End Runs Around the Appropriations Process

As noted earlier, Congress once had powerful institutional regulators. The Appropriations Committees, dominated by fiscally conservative legislators were, until very recently, protectors of the public purse. The growing demand for federal programs, however, led entrepreneurial presidents, legislative committees, and their supporting chamber majorities to make "end runs" on the Appropriations Committees. Political entrepreneurs invented ways around fiscal constraints imposed by these guardians of the Treasury. Our next principle expresses this as follows.

Principle 3. Fiscal Constraints Invite Political Ingenuity.   Legislative committees responsible for authorizing programs have been jealous of the power of the purse controlled by the Appropriations Committees almost from the time of their creation in 1865. Indeed, in the 1880s, authorizing committees recaptured much of this power, stripping the Appropriations Committees of their authority until the Budget and Accounting Act of 1921 restored the separation between authorization and appropriation.[19] In the modern era, legislators on authorizing committees (in alliance with activist presidents)

---

18. Jacque S. Gansler, *The Defense Industry* (Cambridge: MIT Press, 1982), p. 2.
19. See Richard F. Fenno, *The Power of the Purse* (Boston: Little-Brown, 1966).

have resorted to more sophisticated methods of bypassing the fiscal constraints of conservative Appropriations Committees.

Entitlements, obligating federal payment to "entitled" categories of citizens, are the most impressive products of this political ingenuity. This mechanism allowed legislative committees to mandate payments from the federal Treasury without prior consent from the Appropriations Committees. Authorizing committees devised criteria of eligibility and payment schedules linked to these criteria, so that any citizen who qualified held a claim against the government for payment. The Appropriations Committees were obligated to provide the necessary monies; they were faced with *faits accomplis.*

Entitlements are often, but not always, the products of authorizing committee ingenuity. A powerful president, in cahoots with an unusually large legislative majority, may engineer end runs around the appropriations process. It is no accident that the two largest and fiscally problematic entitlement programs, Social Security and Medicare, were proposed and passed by activist presidents possessing unprecedented majority support in Congress. In each case, a means around the Appropriations Committees was found— through Ways and Means—that insulated these programs from the fate of future (shifting) majorities. These programs are not solely the product of legislative ingenuity—powerful presidents surely play central roles. But once the unusual circumstances generating their inception are gone, the mechanisms put in place to protect the programs from future changes are *congressional* mechanisms.

In the 1982 fiscal year, entitlement/uncontrollable expenditures constituted nearly 60 percent of all federal outlays. As a result, the Appropriations Committees, once the institutional holders of the power of the purse, have been reduced essentially to a monitor of the "change purse." Today, the Appropriations Committees' role is but a cheap imitation of their past significance.

Although entitlements are often referred to as "uncontrollable" expenditures—indeed, as "out-of-control" expenditures—this label is both inaccurate and misleading. To outsiders, entitlements may appear out of control, but it would be more accurate to say not that entitlements are uncontrollable, but that they are *not controlled by the appropriations process.* This phenomenon is a direct product of congressional politics. In order to make an end run around Appropriations, it was necessary, *by design*, to preclude annual scrutiny and adjustment by the Appropriations Committees. The proof of the pudding is found in the resilience of entitlements to budget cutting. The entitlement mechanism makes it harder to cut a dollar of expenditure than it is to cut a dollar from those programs that go through the appropriations process. It is no accident that the largest cuts by Reagan have come from the discretionary domestic budget, not from the entitlement areas. This is surely not because Reagan and Stockman desired less reduction in entitlements than in the discretionary domestic budget, but rather because the congressional-financial mechanism made the entitlements significantly harder to cut.

A second sense in which entitlements remained uncontrolled by design can be discovered by a close reading of the 1974 Budget Act. In what seems a significant move, the act put an end to any new entitlement program unless consented to by the Appropriations Committees. But much of the damage had already been done. Pre-1974 entitlement programs were given protection through a "grandfather clause" in the 1974 Budget Act—a strong indication of the ability of subcommittees to protect and entrench previous programs from efforts to contain or gut them. Existing entitlements remain outside the scrutiny of the new system—that is, uncontrolled—because legislators chose to write the law that way. Had the law been written to include existing entitlements, its enactment would have been jeopardized. A coalition of people opposed to a strong centralized congressional budget process vetoed this prospect, thereby underscoring the fact that so-called uncontrollability is endogenous to the politics of Congress.

It has been argued that the logic of subcommittee veto power is obviated by the reconciliation mechanism that permits chamber majorities to alter entitlements. In principle, this is true, but in practice, the reconciliation mechanism is hard to use and has been implemented with significant results in only one year of the past ten, 1981. The atypicality of the 1981 reconciliation effort, in comparison with more modest (or unimplemented) efforts in other years, further underscores the relative protection afforded programs enacted as entitlements.

Finally, there is a third sense in which these programs have remained uncontrolled. It follows from our fourth principle.

Principle 4. Subcommittee Veto. As already noted, subcommittee jurisdiction conveys veto power. Subcommittee members, who invariably develop strong ties to the current beneficiaries of the programs within their jurisdictions, veto reforms that make their constituents worse off. This veto is exercised not by explicit, public rejection of plans but rather by simply failing to act on them. Subcommittee veto in the hands of legislators representing a program's beneficiaries poses a formidable barrier to fiscal reform. Unless a crisis threatens the entire program, why should beneficiaries sacrifice current advantages for the benefit of the general taxpayer and the larger public? Existing "uncontrollable" entitlements were invented as a means around the then current "controllers." They now remain uncontrolled because the Budget Act explicitly grandfathered them into the system and because the subcommittee veto protects them from reform under nearly all but crisis circumstances.

A crisis in the Social Security system was anticipated years in advance. Although a variety of proposals emerged to deal with the problem, efforts to reform the system were stymied until the solvency of the system was jeopardized. And even then, protectors of current beneficiaries (like Claude Pepper, chairman of the House Rules Committee) exerted considerable influence. Similarly, problems with existing financing mechanisms for Medicare are predicted to reach crisis proportions by the end of the decade. Moves to avert this crisis are likely to run up against the same barriers.

Other Applications. Although the Budget Act controls the creation of additional entitlement programs, political ingenuity prospers as new policy instruments and practices have been honed to neutralize the Appropriations Committees in the post-Budget Act environment. Two of special significance are regulatory controls and credit programs. The former bypass the Appropriations Committees largely by shifting financial responsibility to the private sector or to other levels of government. The latter are "off the budget" and, much like the entitlement programs of the 1960s, present the Appropriations Committees with spending obligations over which they have no discretion. This little-known but potent process works as follows: The Federal Financing Bank (FFB) handles loans granted by federal agencies. When an agency reaches its appropriated limit on direct loans, it simply turns its notes over to the FFB for cash. FFB has limited discretion over whether to purchase the notes. Because an agency may repeat this process, the limits imposed by the Appropriations Committees on an agency's ability to lend money are virtually without effect. Moreover, FFB's budgetary authority and outlays are by law excluded from the unified budget totals of the government. By 1981 FFB activity had reached nearly $30 billion.

Still another application of the principle of political ingenuity concerns the use of creative accounting. The extreme focus on current outlays has produced new financing techniques that reduce current-dollar obligations— that is, items in the current fiscal-year budget—by increasing future obligations. Even if there is no change in the total real obligation incurred, these techniques reduce current outlays and hence current *deficits*. For example, even though it might increase costs in the long run, agencies have increasingly turned to leasing space for their operations, rather than purchasing space outright, because this practice reduces current-year outlays. This means that, in comparison with the way budget deficits were counted in previous years, current methods understate the size of the deficit. (See Hartman's paper in this volume.)

A final application of these principles concerns the balanced-budget amendment. This popular fiscal constraint is touted by its advocates as a solution to our current budgetary problems. Yet Principle 3 strongly suggests that constituency-minded legislators will invent ways around this constraint. For example, regulation is a substitute mechanism that shifts the financial burden of federal goals onto private parties.[20] Fiscal constraints will lead legislators to invent and substitute mechanisms like this for actual federal spending. Second, even if currently popular off-budget categories are brought within the definition of federal outlays, it is highly unlikely that a balanced-budget amendment can exclude all possible future "innovations." Hence, in the face of a balanced-budget constraint, we will see the rise of newly devised "off-off-budget" categories. Finally, fiscally constrained legislators can always mandate private spending to finance public goals.

It is unlikely that any of these adjustments, innovations, and adaptations by legislators committed to serve their constituencies will be recognized or well understood in advance. Just as the long-term fiscal consequences of many early entitlement programs were not well appreciated in the 1960s, newer forms of legislative ingenuity will probably not be appreciated (until after they are well entrenched and protected by veto groups) for what they are— namely the dressing up of a current fiscal problem in new clothes.

To summarize, we have argued in this section that many of today's looming fiscal problems have their roots in Congress. The large sums going to defense probably will not purchase the maximum amount of defense to be had from such sums. Out-of-control entitlements remain uncontrolled because they were engineered that way to begin with and are a logical consequence of the system. Indeed, the very label—uncontrollable—suggests a misplaced emphasis and a misunderstood source. So, too, with waste, cost overruns, and inefficient input mixes in the defense sector. Entitlements are uncontrollable and defense inefficiency ingrained only if you consider the congressional system exogenous.

Discussion and Conclusions

This paper has focused mainly on the effects of legislative structure and politics on the character of federal programs. Although we do not argue that

---

20. See Murray L. Weidenbaum, "The Impacts of Government Regulation," Working Paper No. 32, Center for the Study of American Business, Washington University, St. Louis, 1978.

Congress is the only relevant political actor, we believe that Congress plays a central but unappreciated role in policymaking. We have restricted ourselves to the programmatic level, and therefore have not addressed the larger issues concerning the appropriate scope and scale for federal activities. However, in characterizing the imprints in policies left by legislative motivations, we are providing a more general picture.

First, as to matters of scale, we describe a bias toward the wishes of "preference outliers" at the programmatic level. This bias follows from the central role played by legislative committees in policy formation, the self-selection of committee assignments, and consequently the overrepresentation on committees of legislators whose constituencies bear disproportionate costs or enjoy disproportionate benefits from programs in each committee's jurisdiction. Will government programs be too large or too small? We cannot say. We can say that whether a program will be too large or too small will depend on the decisive majority on the committee.

Second, we have emphasized a legislative predilection in favor of expenditure programs. Legislators like money to be targeted to their constituencies almost independent of program purposes. While nuclear plants, waste disposal sites, and chemical warfare laboratories stand as exceptional cases, the norm is for legislators to seek dollars and to claim credit for the economic stimulus it provides. Moreover, our logic implies that the congressional system biases expenditure programs toward projects that are too large.

Third, we have underscored the necessity, in many spending programs, of distributing expenditures widely. The distributive tendency is necessitated by the requirement to obtain majorities in both houses in order to secure authorization and appropriations. This fact is appreciated both by wise legislative supporters of a program and by wise bureau chiefs whose welfare depends on continued legislative support.

The distributive tendency, along with the legislative disposition to service organized interests, produces a fourth effect—a political bias in the mix of program inputs and concomitant productive inefficiencies.

Fifth, we have described a distinct bias against self-correction. Because representatives of current beneficiaries hold positions on relevant subcommittees, the effect is that of the fox guarding the henhouse. Subcommittees have substantial veto power over program changes, so it is extremely difficult to implement ameliorative changes, by statute or by bureaucratic discretion.

Our general principles, we should add, are not restricted to expenditure programs. Traces of geography and jurisdiction may be detected in many of our regulatory and revenue policies as well.

All these principles derive from the fact that professional politicians possess ingenuity, an entrepreneurial spirit, and adaptability. Legislative institutions and the policies they foster reflect this central fact. Legislators, motivated to secure reelection and legislative influence, devise institutions to further these objectives. The resulting policies possess the features we have described.

Our theory of congressional intervention in the policy process has implications for a number of new ideas percolating in Congress and should serve as a flag of caution. Ideas proposed to ameliorate some social problem or market failure become vehicles for political ambitions. We see the mark of the congressional distributive tendency in each of the examples that follow. The original goal of the program or reform is diluted so that the benefits can be more widely or specifically targeted to relevant constituents. This transformation of objectives into politically viable programs is a regular feature of the congressional system and therefore a significant factor hindering efficient public performance.

Thus, funny things have happened to enterprise zones, to take one currently fashionable idea, in its trip from the think tank to the committee rooms of Congress. As suggested by the distributive tendency, the criteria of eligibility are being weakened, producing two noticeable effects: the number of eligible districts is being expanded and the original purposes of the legislation are being distorted. Indian reservations, for example, have appeared in the Kemp-Garcia bill as eligible for enterprise zone designation (Jack Kemp's upstate New York district contains several tribal areas). In the Senate, the idea sounds so good that several legislators have proposed expanding the program to take in rural enterprise zones. And, if the Model Cities program is a reliable guide, the secretary of commerce will come under intense pressure to reduce the criteria of eligibility so that areas in nearly every state and congressional district qualify for designation.

Surely the same story can be told about industrial policy—another hot item on the political agenda. What begins, whether for good reasons or bad, as an effort to target sectors of the economy for government support and stimulation, will end up being dissipated (at substantial cost to the Treasury) as distributive forces take hold in Congress. Objective criteria of need—for example, those industries most likely to be successful competitors in a new high-tech environment—will be sacrificed to alternative criteria that allow benefits to flow more widely. Almost assuredly the program's criteria will be rewritten to allow funds to flow to existing and declining industries in the districts of prominent members of Congress. Funds that save existing jobs are politically valuable regardless of whether they contribute to the program's objectives. In the face of the congressional distributive tendency, it is therefore unlikely that any plan of this type will meet its objectives.

Ditto the flat tax. The DeConcini bill, the legislative version of the Hall-Rabushka plan, is a relatively pure flat tax scheme. No plan of this type is likely to be politically viable in the congressional system. A flat tax treats all groups of constituents equally, regardless of their political power. Hence, legislators can gain electorally by making some groups better off at the expense of others. Notably, signs of this tendency have appeared already as substitute bills make finer gradations. A major competitor to the DeConcini bill is the Bradley-Gephardt bill, which, although called a flat tax, looks like our current tax schedule with fewer brackets. Moreover, politically popular "loopholes," like the mortgage interest deduction, have been included to spice it up.

Summary

The basic message of our paper is that expenditure, regulatory, and revenue programs take on the particular cast that they do because they are the products of legislative politics. The admixture of legislator motivations (especially the tugs of geography) and institutional practices (especially the tugs of committee jurisdictions) produce systematic biases in policy products. We cannot say that government is too big (or small), but we can say that individual programs are distorted toward the preferences of "outliers." We cannot always say that too much (or too little) is spent by government, but we can say that there is little incentive to employ an efficient mix of program inputs and that the scale of expenditure projects is too large. We cannot say that committees and subcommittees are absolutely decisive in creating new programs (chamber majorities count for something), but we can say that those same subunits are extremely effective in protecting beneficiaries of current programs. And we cannot say the executive agencies are without influence, but we can say that agency discretion is often harnessed to the interests of legislative overseers.

The logic of our approach implies a pessimistic moral. So long as the ties that bind legislators to their electoral constituencies remain strong, and so long as legislative institutions like the committee system enable legislators to serve parochial interests, simple solutions aimed at ameliorating the biases in policy we have reported are likely to be superficial. Add to this the adaptability and ingenuity of legislators in dealing with constraints imposed on them and one is almost prepared to accept John Adams's aphorism (in the play *1776*) that "the opposite of *pro*gress is *Con*gress."

COMMENTS

John W. Ellwood

Much of the Shepsle and Weingast argument is clearly correct. Legislators do respond to the electoral imperative by seeking to grant benefits to their geographic constituencies. Their ability to gravitate to those committees and subcommittees with jurisdiction over these benefits clearly provides them with added power over the nature and outcome of the political debate of these benefits. For those programs whose benefits are geographically concentrated, the calculus of concentrated benefits and dispersed costs does result in the inefficient provision of these public goods. And the weakening of aggregating forces such as the party leadership in Congress has created a logrolling pattern in which minimum winning coalitions are created by spreading the benefits of programs to districts and states to such an extent that the program's objectives cannot be achieved (i.e., Model Cities). Finally, the chief barrier to true "reform" is indeed the desire of legislators to build personal power bases in the Congress.

Although these arguments are true, I believe that the thrust of Shepsle's and Weingast's basic contention—that when it comes to public dissatisfaction with federal budget policy the problem is Congress—is overdrawn, shows a misunderstanding of the forces currently driving federal budget policy, and underestimates the ability of the system to correct the excesses of the pull of geography and the power of subcommittees.

The Changing Congressional System

I assume that Shepsle and Weingast are not simply saying that the provision of public goods by Congress is bound to be less efficient than an equivalent provision through efficient markets. Although they are not explicit on this point, they appear to contend that changes in the relative power of congressional units have created a new system and that this new system is

368

more likely to produce an oversupply of inefficiently targeted benefits. They spend a good deal of time describing the decline in the power of party leaders in Congress, the seniority system, and those committees, such as the Rules Committee and the Appropriations Committees, that performed the institutional maintenance function of restraining the upward bias caused by the pull of geography.

One has to assume, therefore, that Shepsle and Weingast are claiming that as these forces for "good" decline in power, the growth of inefficient benefits accelerated.[1] But just the opposite has occurred. The best empirical work on the geographic pull on congressional decision making has been undertaken by R. Douglas Arnold.[2] In contrast to Shepsle's and Weingast's argument, Arnold points out that "Congressmen are not single-minded seekers of local benefits, struggling feverishly to win every last dollar for their districts. However important the quest for local benefits may be, it is always tempered by other, competing concerns."[3] Arnold also notes, "Adherents of the distributive theory would have one believe that a single set of simple hypotheses can adequately explain allocation decisions for these diverse programs. In fact, congressional politics and bureaucratic decision making are far more complex than that."[4] In addition to being interested in the costs and benefits of a program for their district, legislators are interested in the program's general costs and benefits and the costs and benefits for groups. Finally, the geographic pull on congressional decision making will vary with the scope of the benefits, eligibility criteria, and program administration.

---

1. It is hard to determine from the Shepsle and Weingast discussion the date at which the old congressional system (in which the pull of geography was restrained by party leaders, committee chairmen, and powerful Rules and Appropriations Committees) was replaced by the new system in which power lies in subcommittees and legislators are free to seek maximum benefits for their districts. It is generally agreed that strong party leadership ended with Lyndon Johnson's rise to the vice presidency and Speaker Rayburn's death in the early 1960s. Committee membership tended to reflect the entire membership of the House and the Senate until the mid-1960s. The seniority system was effectively undermined with the enactment of the Subcommittee Bill of Rights in 1973 and the removal of several powerful committee chairmen in the House in 1974. For our purposes I will take 1970 as a turning-point year. In addition, if Shepsle and Weingast are correct, one would expect an increase in the growth of the programs providing local benefits after 1974, all things being equal, rather than before that date.

2. R. Douglas Arnold, *Congress and the Bureaucracy* (New Haven: Yale University Press, 1979); "Legislatures, Overspending and Government Growth," paper presented at the conference on the causes and consequences of public sector growth, Dorado Beach, Puerto Rico, November 1978; and idem, "The Local Roots of Domestic Policy," in Thomas E. Mann and Norman J. Ornstein, ed., *The New Congress* (Washington, D.C.: The American Enterprise Institute, 1981). The following discussion relies heavily on Arnold's work. One interesting question is why those who follow Shepsle's and Weingast's logic have refused to modify their conclusions to take into account Arnold's empirical results.

3. Arnold, "Local Roots of Domestic Policy," p. 252.

4. Arnold, *Congress and the Bureaucracy*, p. 210.

Arnold points out that Congress has kept for itself the privilege of allocating federal programs with exceptional local payoffs. Into this category one would put federal water projects. But as one moves away from the classic pork barrel, legislators have to share with bureaucrats (federal, state, and local) the power over the allocation of federal dollars. In what seems to be a useful rank ordering, Arnold lists water projects as being the most affected by the congressional geographic pull. But, as one goes from intergovernmental grant to federal facilities construction, to personnel and federal operations, to procurement contracts, and to research and development, the impact of the geographic pull declines. The two types of federal spending that appear to be least affected by the needs of local interests are (1) entitlements providing benefit payments to individuals and (2) interest on the public debt.

In figure 1, Arnold shows the division of the federal budget according to the categories listed in 1950, 1960, 1970, and 1980. The clear message is that (with the exception of intergovernmental grants) those budget accounts funding programs with the greatest geographic pull have accounted for a smaller and smaller proportion of the federal budget since 1950. This trend has been most evident during the 1970s—the period of the rise of the subcommittee and the decline of the party leadership and the power of the Rules and Appropriations Committees. Moreover, the trend has accelerated since 1978. Specifically:

- *Water Projects.* Combined appropriations (budget authority) for water project construction by the Army Corps of Engineers, Bureau of Reclamation, Soil Conservation Service, and Tennessee Valley Authority declined from $2.2 billion in fiscal year (FY) 1978 to $1.9 billion in FY 1983. When measured in 1982 constant dollars the decline was more rapid; from $3.1 billion in FY 1978 to $1.8 billion in FY 1983—a 42 percent decline.

- *Intergovernmental Grants.* Measured in constant dollars, outlays for grants to state and local governments (excluding grants for payments to individuals) declined 37 percent between FY 1978 and FY 1983. Of these grant outlays, those associated with programs for major physical investments declined by 26 percent during this period.

- *Other Federal Operations.* When measured in constant dollars, outlays for the Office of Management and Budget (OMB) category "Other Federal Operations," which includes Arnold's categories of federal facilities construction and personnel and federal operations, declined by 14 percent between FY 1978 and FY 1983. The growth in federal spending continues to be driven by entitlements providing benefit

FIGURE 1

COMPOSITION OF FEDERAL EXPENDITURES

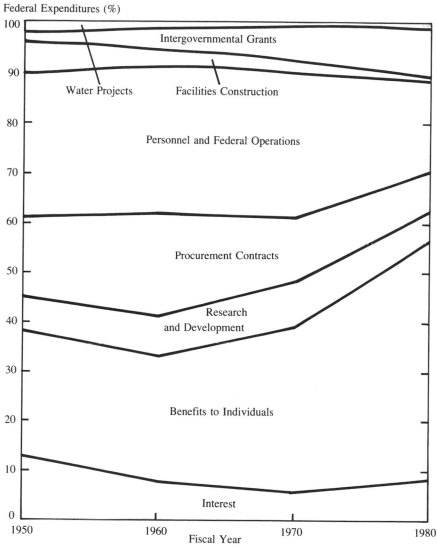

Federal Expenditures (%)

NOTE: The eight categories of expenditure are listed in order of the degree to which the quest
         for local benefits leaves its mark on public policy. Water projects are the most sharply
         affected, research and development least so; interest and benefits to individuals are
         unaffected.
SOURCE: U.S. Office of Management and Budget, *The Budget of the United States*, Special
         Analyses and Appendix, fiscal years 1950, 1960, 1970, and 1980.
SOURCE: R. Douglas Arnold, ''The Local Roots of Domestic Policy,'' in Thomas E. Mann
         and Norman J. Ornstein, eds., *The New Congress* (Washington, D.C.: The American
         Enterprise Institute, 1981), p. 282.

payments to individuals; constant-dollar outlays rose by 30 percent between FY 1978 and FY 1983. In addition, recent growth in outlays has been spurred by a rapid increase in the amount of outlays necessary to cover interest on the public debt—up 72 percent between FY 1978 and FY 1983 when measured in constant dollars. Only the increase in defense spending, up 31 percent between FY 1978 and FY 1983 when measured in constant-dollar outlays, can be said to support Shepsle and Weingast's thesis. But this increase appears to be driven by the perceived Soviet threat rather than by a desire for more local benefits.

It could be argued that although Congress has provided fewer outlays for those programs with the greatest concentrated benefits, those funds that were provided were spent in a less efficient manner than they would have been before the decline in the power of party leaders and the rise of subcommittee and member autonomy. Unfortunately, we do not have any information to indicate that this is the case. Thus Shepsle and Weingast's argument can be supported only by anecdotal evidence; and for every Model Cities program and unsuccessful attempt to close a base one can think of a counter example of the tightening of CETA (Comprehensive Employment and Training Act) eligibility or successful base closing.

Models of Control

I have held for some time that we have a "two cultures" problem when it comes to analysis and prescriptions of the problems associated with the federal budget process. Most of the participants at this conference would hold that budgeting, in the words of Allen Schick, is a war between the parts and the whole. In this model, the budget's totals act as a "budget line" that is used to constrain decisions on individual accounts. Although it is clear that an interactive process occurs, John Crecine has shown that for accounts other than defense, the OMB target numbers that are sent to federal agencies are associated with OMB's aggregate outlay targets that, in turn, are associated with the administration's economic forecast and desired fiscal policy. Crecine has also shown that in the case of nondefense accounts, the agencies eventually modify their position until they come into line with the OMB target. Thus, at least in the nondefense area, the budget aggregates act as a "budget line" constraint on the parts.[5]

---

5. John P. Crecine, "Coordination of Federal Fiscal and Budgetary Processes: Research Strategies for Complex Decision Systems," paper delivered at the 1977 annual meeting of the American Political Science Association, Washington, D.C.

Shepsle and Weingast reflect the second—and older—school of budgeting. In this model, budget control is achieved by controlling the funding levels of individual programs.[6] Shepsle and Weingast believe that:

> There simply is no basis for inferring much about aggregate performance unless there are universal and pervasive biases to report at the programmatic level. . . .
>
> Observers outside Congress focusing on grand issues like inflation, deficits, and "out-of-control" spending, often forget that these are simply labels given to the effects of an accumulation of many smaller, seemingly unrelated, policy decisions.

An insight into Shepsle and Weingast's model of budget control can be gained by reviewing how the congressional budget process worked before subcommittees and their members became autonomous in the 1970s. As Shepsle and Weingast point out, "Congress once had powerful speakers, strong party leaders, and dominant Appropriations and Rules Committees that, to some extent, thwarted overly ambitious schemes hatched by authorizing committees and subcommittees." Although it is true that the existence of strong Speakers and party leaders can lead to forms of coalition building (logrolling) that constrain the effects of the pull of geography (as will be discussed later), the roles of the Rules and Appropriations Committees were not to strive for the "public" of "general interest" but to balance the expansionist desires of the authorizing committees by blocking the enactment of new programs and slowing down the growth of existing accounts.

Control was achieved, to the extent it occurred, through conflict among types of committees. Judge Smith and Chairman Cannon were not disinterested representatives. They believed in fewer, rather than more, public services and used their power to thwart the popular majorities of their day. One could argue—most strongly in the case of the decline of the power of the Rules Committee—that the old control system fell apart because its leaders were so out of touch with the popular majority as reflected by the members of the House.

Although Shepsle and Weingast do not formally suggest what should be done to reestablish control over autonomous subcommittees and legislators, I infer from their statements in this paper and their previous writings on the budget process that they would be in favor of reforms that (1) reestablished the power of the Speaker and the party leadership of Congress and (2) re-

---

6. This older school of budgeting defines budgeting narrowly. Thus, Shepsle and Weingast believe that the congressional system creates a "legislative predilection in favor of expenditure programs." But the newer school of budgeting would point out that the same logic that Shepsle and Weingast use to explain an upward bias in the provision of expenditures can be used to explain the rapid growth of tax expenditures. Finally, the older school of budgeting tends to focus on short-term control (by fiscal year), whereas the newer school stresses multiyear control.

established the power of the Rules and Appropriations Committees to constrain the expansionist plans of subcommittees.[7]

I agree with the notion of expanding the power of the Speaker and the party leadership and will suggest later that Congress is already moving in this direction. Expanding the power of the Appropriations Committees, however, would have little effect on controlling expenditure growth.

The most frequently mentioned change to reestablish the old norms and power of the Appropriations Committees is the reimposition of what Richard Fenno referred to as the *Cannon-Taber norm*. Under this committee rule, the two ranking members of the full committee assigned committee members to those subcommittees whose jurisdiction would not benefit their districts. Thus, when George Mahon joined the House Appropriations Committee in the 1920s he was put on the Navy Subcommittee; when he inquired why this was done, Chairman Cannon supposedly said, "There's no water in west Texas."

The reimposition of the Cannon-Taber norm would probably reduce spending levels on those budget accounts, particularly defense accounts, that require an annual appropriation. But the Cannon-Taber norm would have only a small effect on the overall growth in federal expenditures. Although 77 percent of the federal budget's accounts are funded through an annual appropriation, most of the growth in federal outlays since 1970 resulted from the remaining accounts. For example, when interest on the public debt and defense expenditures are excluded, those budget accounts requiring an annual appropriation (70 percent of all FY 1983 accounts) were responsible for only 25.1 percent of the growth in federal outlays between FY 1970 and FY 1983.

Budget systems are routinized struggles among guardians and advocates. The problem with the Appropriations Committees is that they lack the jurisdiction to become effective guardians. They lack this jurisdiction because although they control most budget accounts, the accounts that they do not

---

7. On other occasions Shepsle has suggested that the Appropriations Committees use the Holman Rule to control the funding levels of entitlements. The Holman Rule, formulated in the 1870s, allowed the Appropriations Committees to include authorization language in appropriations bills if that language led to lower levels of spending. There is some question whether, under the current rules of the House and Senate, the Holman Rule could be used to modify the substantive rules of entitlements or whether it could be used only to modify the authorization of appropriations limit of the entitlement (which is the position of the House parliamentarian). If the latter position holds, all that the Holman Rule would do is to change pure entitlements into appropriated entitlements—a step that, on the basis of experience, would have little if any effect on expenditure levels. See Kenneth A. Shepsle, "Geography, Jurisdiction, and the Congressional Budget Process: A Memo to the Chairman of the House Budget Committee," paper delivered at the conference on the congressional budget process, The Carl Albert Center, Norman, Oklahoma, 1982.

control—the entitlement and appropriated entitlement accounts—are the ones that are causing current expenditure problems.[8]

Reconciliation and Leadership Power

Shepsle and Weingast correctly imply that we need to increase the power of the Speaker and the party leadership of Congress if we are to increase control over the federal budget. What is remarkable, however, is that the authors never mention the procedure—reconciliation—that has the potential to be the tool that the Speaker and the other party leaders can use to build their power over budgetary questions.

The Need

An increase in the power of the congressional leadership is required for two reasons. First, as Shepsle and Weingast correctly point out, one effect of the entitlement structure is that the committees with jurisdiction over entitlements have a veto over the control of expenditures. Unless Congress has a mechanism to force these committees to change the provisions of entitlement authorizations, the programs' expenditure pattern cannot be modified.

One alternative to achieve this end would be to require an annual appropriation for entitlements—that is, to reinstate Appropriations Committee control. The experience with appropriated entitlements, such as Medicaid and AFDC (Aid to Families with Dependent Children), however, suggests that appropriations limits are not an effective means of controlling entitlement growth. In addition, entitlement status is a policy decision that should not necessarily be waived to achieve short-term budget control. Finally, the traditional norms of the Appropriations Committees—that waste exists in the budget and that it is the duty of the members of the committee to find that fat and eliminate it—are not very useful in achieving the reforms that would be needed to limit entitlement growth.

A better alternative is to switch from Shepsle and Weingast's notion of controlling the budget's totals by controlling the growth of each program, to a model under which the leadership (through the Budget Committees) develops a consensus of the proper size of the budget's aggregates and then uses those aggregates to expand programs, limit program growth, or achieve program reductions. For such a strategy to work, a mechanism is required that will

---

8. The mismatch between the number of budget accounts under the jurisdiction of the Appropriations Committees and the percentage of federal expenditures under their jurisdiction is another reason that the old system of bottom-up budgeting will not control expenditures.

break the veto power of committees. The reconciliation process has evolved into such a mechanism.

A second basic advantage of strong party leadership in Congress is that it can build coalitions through logrolling across programs rather than from the provisions of a single program.[9] Shepsle and Weingast correctly describe the effects of trying to build a coalition within a single program: the benefits of the program are extended to more and more districts until a minimum winning coalition is achieved. The result is that the program becomes larger than it need be, ends up by failing to provide enough benefits in any one district to achieve its stated goals, or both. I have the feeling that several of the participants in this conference have built program simulation models that allowed congressional staff to engage in this type of coalition building.

The alternative form of coalition building, which appears to have occurred during the Rayburn and Johnson eras, is to engage in logrolling across programs. For example, the leadership seeks the support of farmers for a bill that would benefit inner cities in return for a promise that the representatives of inner-city districts will support the next farm bill. Although this form of coalition building will not necessarily slow the growth in the scope of the public sector, it will increase the targeting of individual efforts. By grouping a series of program changes into a single bill, the reconciliation process provides the party leadership with a tool to engage in cross-program logrolling.

The Nature of Reconciliation

Reconciliation is a process and a bill. Under the process, instructions are sent by the House and the Senate to one or more of their committees to report out by a certain date legislation that will reduce or raise expenditures or revenues or both by a certain amount. The reconciliation process is neutral between raising or lowering expenditures and revenues. Although during the current period the process has been viewed as a mechanism for achieving reductions in expenditures and increases in revenues, it could be used to raise expenditures. Once the various committees have reported their legislative changes, the Budget Committees group them into a single bill—a reconciliation bill.

The advantages of the reconciliation process for budget control and leadership control should be obvious:

1. The reconciliation process breaks the veto power of committees and subcommittees. Reconciliation should be viewed as a giant discharge

---

9. This idea was first suggested by R. Douglas Arnold in *Congress and the Bureaucracy*, pp. 210–214.

petition that forces committees and subcommittees to act by a certain date. In this regard, it is particularly effective as a mechanism to bring about changes in entitlements and permanent provisions of the tax code.

2. The reconciliation process changes the calculus of concentrated benefits and dispersed costs. By grouping a series of reductions into a single bill, it gives greater power to the aggregates (the "budget line"). The political debate can be shifted from the merits of the individual parts to the virtues of the whole, particularly when the party leadership (at least in the House) obtains a limited or closed rule for the bill.

3. By grouping many program changes into a single bill, the reconciliation process can be used to facilitate cross-program logrolling at the expense of single-program logrolling.

4. Because Congress has implemented the process in connection with the passage of the first budget resolution, the reconciliation process gives committees enough time to make reflective changes in programs.

5. Because the reconciliation process has been implemented with multiyear instructions (requiring committees to make program changes that will achieve dollar targets for the upcoming fiscal year and several years into the future), the process can be used to bring about real change.

6. Finally, as stated, because the reconciliation process is neutral with respect to expansion or contraction of the budget, the party leadership can use the mechanism routinely to achieve the party's legislative program.

Conclusion

When the Congressional Budget Office (CBO) was first formed, its director, Alice Rivlin, arranged for a series of speakers to introduce the organization's staff to the ways of Capitol Hill. The first speaker was Walter Kravitz, then staff director of the newly formed House Budget Committee. The new CBO staff, who were highly qualified in terms of their analytical skills but had little if any experience working for Congress, immediately asked Kravitz when he expected the new budget process to lead to dramatic changes in policy through the application of their analytical techniques. Kravitz replied that he did not care about their techniques and did not expect them to have a policy impact in the near future. His goal, he said, was "to make the passage of budget resolutions just as routine as the passage of appropriations bills." In short, he wanted to make the new process routine.

The most important event of the past five years was not the enactment of the Omnibus Reconciliation Act of 1981 that brought about changes that reduced FY 1982 outlays by $35 billion below current policy levels. Rather, the most important event was a series of events—the enactment of reconciliation bills for three years in a row.

The press has been interested in reconciliation only when it achieves large dollar savings. But of greater significance are the facts that the process has been used by Democrats and Republicans, that it has been used to achieve savings and to increase expenditures, and that it has been used routinely.

The Democratic leadership of the House is only beginning to realize the power of the tool in its possession. The danger now is that because of the events of 1981, the process will forever be associated with the specific policies of the Reagan administration. It would be a tragic mistake if the next administration and future leaders of the Congress fail to grasp that the reconciliation process is neutral on its face.

COMMENTS

Charles L. Schultze

The authors identify—although they are not the first to do so—some important characteristics of the legislative political process which, they suggest, strongly bias legislative outcomes in a particular way and, in the terms of reference of this conference, exert an upward tilt to budgetary outcomes.

Their paper attributes the budgetary behavior of Congress in recent times to a combination of two major systemic elements: the decentralization of power in Congress and some long-standing congressional political characteristics. Power has derogated from political parties and from the congressional leadership to individual committees and subcommittees and indeed from committees themselves to their subcommittees. This development has combined with a long-existing set of congressional political characteristics including the tendency of Congress to view inputs (particularly job inputs) as outputs and its propensity to spread benefits around widely, rather than concentrating them where they are needed—to produce major budgetary problems.

The authors have contributed some important insights, but I have a number of problems with their thesis. First, I have difficulty understanding the timing of developments as they describe them. Are the authors contrasting current behavior with the 1920s or with the 1960s? In some places they talk of developments that have occurred over a half-century and give examples, but in other places they emphasize how current behavior differs from that of the 1960s: For example, ''Reforms of the last half-century have indeed weakened Congress, the institution. But the institutionalized presidency has not been the only, or even the most important, beneficiary. These reforms, especially those of the 1970s, have produced significant effects and adaptations *inside the legislature.*''

I think we can fairly interpret the authors as saying that although the developments they speak of have antecedents that go well back in the past, most of the characteristic budgetary behavior they are describing has developed more recently.

A much more important criticism is that although the authors have correctly identified some interesting and important characteristics of the congressional political process as it has recently developed, what they analyze has little to do with today's budgetary problems. Here I share much of John Ellwood's criticism but have some additional evidence and a slightly different point of view.

The characteristics that Shepsle and Weingast describe—the distributive tendency, the tugs of geography, and the tendency to maximize inputs rather than outputs—are simply not applicable to the design or funding of *entitlement* programs. Geographic pulls and input-output confusion are all irrelevant in the case of most entitlement programs. Neither the basic structure of those programs nor the obstacles to reforming them, nor the difficulties of cutting back the size of benefits stem principally from the veto power of committees or subcommittees or from the various congressional characteristics cited by Shepsle and Weingast. Ronald Reagan, Tip O'Neill, and the ordinary member of Congress were no more anxious to get out ahead on this issue than were the chairmen of the relevant committees—Robert Dole and Dan Rostenkowski. And Claude Pepper's influence arose not because of his subcommittee chairmanship but because of his leadership of the "old folks" lobby. And remember that the person who gave us indexing, Medicare, and Medicaid was no representative of the modern postreform congressmen, but one of the traditional barons of fiscal prudence, Wilbur Mills. Nor was the invention of either Social Security or its indexing an end run around the House Appropriations Committee. A large fraction of the government's entitlement programs have been lodged in the Ways and Means Committee for more than forty years.

The Shepsle and Weingast characteristics do seem to apply to the design of the discretionary programs of the federal government. But insofar as the nondefense part of the budget is concerned, the evidence is quite strong that in recent years the discretionary programs were not the real cause of the upward trend in federal spending (relative to the gross national product— GNP). If one breaks the budget down into four major parts—defense, transfer payments to persons (basically entitlements), net interest, and "all other" programs—and calculates the "all other" category as a percentage of GNP,[1] the results emerge as described in the next paragraph.

---

1. OMB publishes an "all other" category that is a residual, and as a consequence nets out the large negative "offsetting receipts" item. In order to arrive at a true measure of "all other" (discretionary) programs, I added back the offsetting receipts item to the OMB "all other" category.

As table 1 makes clear, the share of GNP taken by federal discretionary programs rose rather sharply between fiscal year (FY) 1957 and FY 1962 but by FY 1967 had stabilized and remained on a plateau through 1981. (In a few intervening years, FY 1976 and FY 1980, the share did move up a bit above that in the other years but then fell back to the plateau.) By FY 1982 the discretionary programs had already been cut significantly and by FY 1986, even with no further major cuts, they will drop quite a bit further as a share of GNP. Whatever the budget malpractices of Congress, they did not result—at least in the past fifteen years—in an explosive growth of discretionary programs. Yet these are the areas to which the Shepsle and Weingast characteristics apply.

Moreover, whatever the reasons for the recent growth of entitlement programs, they do not stem from the lack of an effective control mechanism over such programs by Congress as a whole nor from the power of committees and subcommittees. Shepsle and Weingast are clearly incorrect when they say that entitlements remain outside the scrutiny of the congressional budget process. As Ellwood has pointed out, for three straight years Congress as a whole has used the reconciliation process to force the authorizing committee to cut at least some of the entitlements.

Still, Shepsle and Weingast have identified some aspects of the congressional legislative process that are quite important in determining the kind of legislation that Congress enacts. But they have been insufficiently precise and too all-encompassing in describing the kind of situation to which their analyses apply. Let me therefore try my hand at supplying more precision and at setting

TABLE 1

FEDERAL SPENDING ON "DISCRETIONARY PROGRAMS FOR SELECTED FISCAL YEARS, 1957–1986

Year	Percentage of Gross National Product
1957	2.6
1962	4.3
1967	4.6
1972	4.5
1977	4.7
1981	4.5
1982	4.0
1986[a]	3.3

NOTE: See the footnote in the text for definition of discretionary programs.

a. Author's estimate based on OMB and CBO projections; assumes no further cuts in programs.

forth, in a more circumscribed way, the effects of the congressional characteristics that Shepsle and Weingast have identified.

First, while the committee and subcommittee veto powers described by the authors do exist, those veto powers do not tend in any positive sense to generate large increases in expenditures, as the evidence in table 1 indicates. The derogation of power within Congress, and the resulting committee and subcommittee veto powers, probably do tend to increase the difficulty Congress has in cutting spending below prior levels. But that obstructive power itself is limited in various ways. When, for example, Congress and the president are operating under what they perceive to be a strong public mandate to cut spending, they can in fact cut spending and the veto power is not effective. Moreover, as both Ellwood and I have indicated, the reconciliation process provides a new mechanism to force the will of Congress as a whole on authorizing committees with respect to budget matters.

In short, as far as the overall budget is concerned, the devolution of power within Congress *does* make it somewhat more difficult to achieve absolute reductions in budget outlays. But the power to obstruct is far from absolute. A mechanism is available for overcoming the difficulty, although to be truly effective it does seem to require a major sense of public mandate.

Indeed, as far as aggregate spending is concerned, one might—with at least some plausibility—argue that the decentralization of power within Congress works in the direction of *less* rather than *more* spending. The United States has by far the most decentralized and fragmented system of budgetary decision making and least party control of any major industrial country. This is surely true at the central governmental level. Parliamentary systems as a rule have a much more centralized mechanism for budgetary decision making. And yet, if defense spending is excluded, the United States has the smallest ratio of total government expenditures to GNP of any major country, and the increase in the ratio over the past several decades has been less than in most of those countries.

The characteristics of the current congressional political process described by Shepsle and Weingast do have important applications for policy of a different sort, not primarily in the area of budgeting. In the first place, power has devolved not simply to committees and subcommittees. The further weakening of the already tenuous political party influence in Congress has pushed veto power down to small groups of legislators within committees and subcommittees. That power is a negative power; it is a veto power, not a positive power to get things done or even to spend money. As a consequence, except in response to what is perceived as a massive public mandate or in the presence of a crisis, putting together the coalitions and consensus needed to enact significant complex legislation has become increasingly difficult. On any single issue, however important, a majority can often be put together. But if the new program or the reform of an old program involves five or six or seven major components, it is exceedingly difficult to secure the necessary votes even within a single subcommittee, given the substantially increased independence of individual members of Congress. Because more than ever before these legislators will not subject themselves to the will of the congressional leadership or the political party, the difficulty of achieving a majority vote on a program with different components increases exponentially with the number of components. These problems are exemplified by the current difficulty of securing any major changes in the Clean Air and Clean Water Acts; enacting energy legislation; pushing major tax reforms through Congress, when those reforms include closing major loopholes; and devising structural reforms for Social Security (as opposed to making relatively simple across-the-board cuts).

The authors are exactly right about the consequences of what they call the "distributive tendency." Perhaps a better way to describe the phenomenon is to label it the American political system's Hippocratic oath: "Never be seen to do direct harm." Congress and the executive branch can do all sorts of things that *indirectly* impose costs on groups of citizens. But the formal and informal rules of our political system render it virtually impossible for Congress and the executive branch to make hard-nosed, efficiency-oriented choices among firms, individuals, and regions, rewarding some and penalizing others. As a consequence, the United States cannot have an effective regional economic policy or, assuming it was otherwise warranted, an industrial policy. When, as often happens, it becomes absolutely necessary for the government to make choices among specific individuals or firms, we tend to hand these kinds of decisions over to the judicial system or, as in the case of environmental regulations, to quasi-judicial administrative procedures with the right of appeal to the courts. In France, in contrast, a few bureaucrats in Paris can, apparently without political retribution, make very difficult decisions as to which firm shall live and which firm shall die. The upshot, by the way, appears to be that France has many bureaucrats and few private lawyers while the United States has relatively few bureaucrats but hundreds of thousands of private lawyers. The moral is that any proposal that requires government officials to make efficiency-oriented and necessarily invidious choices among individual firms and regions ought to be subjected to a critical and skeptical review before adoption. It most likely will not work.

Finally, I think we tend to make two mistakes in discussing current budgetary problems. First, there is too much searching for systemic structural causes of the budgetary difficulties in which the country now finds itself. Some systemic problems with respect to the growth of entitlement programs may indeed exist, but if so, they are far less than the problems faced by almost all the other major countries of the world. Growth in entitlement programs, in any event, explains only a modest part of the nation's budgetary difficulties. The large structural budget deficits that now face us stem from the big mistake we made in 1981, when we decided to launch a large defense buildup and simultaneously to enact a massive tax cut. The mistake was encouraged, but not fundamentally caused by, an excessively optimistic economic forecast. It is important to note that there is no structural obstacle to correcting that mistake. But correction does require fundamental agreement between the executive branch and Congress that a substantial increase in taxes will be necessary. So far that agreement has been lacking. While the possibility of an impasse between the executive and congressional branches on a matter of major public importance may be labeled a systemic problem, it is one that originated in 1789.

Much of the discussion about the consequences of the deficit is too apocalyptic. The large and growing structural deficits probably will not abort the recovery. But they will give us a recovery characterized by high consumption and defense spending and low investment and exports. This problem is a serious and long-term one, but not an imminent or catastrophic one. Rather, as Edward Gramlich pointed out in his paper elsewhere in this volume, the problem must be viewed in terms of a long-term and gradual decline in the rate of economic growth. Better outcomes are not likely to be obtained by analyses which suggest that there is some inherent structural problem in our budgetary and congressional system or that we are in danger of an imminent catastrophe. Neither analysis is true. What is true is that action needs to be taken on the budget deficit to prevent a serious but gradual long-term slowdown in the nation's economic growth.

THE CONGRESSIONAL BUDGET PROCESS

Robert D. Reischauer

During the first three years of the Reagan administration, unprecedented shifts occurred in federal budget priorities.[1] Resources devoted to national defense expanded sharply, while the growth in spending for domestic programs was reduced. Individual and corporate income taxes were slashed, while gasoline excise taxes and payroll taxes were raised. Yet these shifts represent only a beginning. Unacceptably large structural deficits lie ahead because the size of the tax cuts, the increase in defense spending, and the added cost of servicing the growing federal debt far exceed the reductions that have been enacted in domestic program spending. Further wrenching budget adjustments will be required during the next few years if these deficits are to be reduced.

Recent budget shifts and the necessity for equally large adjustments in the near future suggest that this is an appropriate time to examine the major institution through which the nation deals with federal budgetary dilemmas, namely, the congressional budget process. In particular, it is worth analyzing the extent to which the budget process facilitated the economic and budgetary policy shifts of the past few years, in order to determine the degree to which this process will be capable of handling the difficult budgetary trade-offs ahead.

Both the nation's budget problems and the congressional budget process have changed since the start of the Reagan administration. Therefore, the first

---

1. For a review of these shifts see Gregory B. Mills and John L. Palmer, *The Deficit Dilemma: Budget Policy in the Reagan Era* (Washington, D.C.: The Urban Institute Press, 1983); and *Baseline Budget Projections for Fiscal Years 1985–1989*, A Report to the Senate and House Committees on the Budget, Part II, Appendix D, Congressional Budget Office, Washington, D.C., February 1984.

section of this paper sketches the budgetary history of the past few years. The second section analyzes the ways in which the congressional budget process changed to cope with the demands placed on it by the Reagan administration's radical proposals and by the prolonged deterioration of the economy. The third section examines the extent to which the process facilitated the early legislative successes of the administration, and isolates the key ingredients of those victories with an eye to their future replicability.

The budget dilemmas of the future look more intractable than those of the past. As a result, some members of Congress advocate strengthening the budget process. The successes of the first years of the Reagan administration, however, generated tensions that have reinforced a movement toward weakening the process. The final section of this paper reviews these countercurrents in an effort to discover how the budget process may be able to facilitate the difficult adjustments that must be made over the next few years.

The major conclusions from this examination of the congressional budget process are as follows:

- Although the budget process was an essential tool in the recent large budget shifts, a number of other peculiar factors were probably more important to the Reagan administration's budget triumphs.

- Although it is congressional, the process is incapable of producing major shifts in priorities or dealing with the difficult issues of retrenchment and deficit reduction without the cooperation and leadership of the president. The presidential role is more important when the two houses of Congress are not under the control of the same party.

- The process can produce major budget retrenchments only when there is agreement on policy within Congress and between Congress and the executive branch. Split party control of Congress or between Congress and the executive branch is likely to reveal the weaknesses of the budget process.

- Although the budget process was stronger by 1983 than it was at the beginning of the Reagan administration, it remains a fragile institution threatened by forces both within Congress and external to Capitol Hill.

- In and of itself, the current process, or even a much strengthened rendition of it, will not be able to compel Congress or the executive branch to act on the deficit. Only a more fundamental shift of power between the legislative and executive branches, a major internal restructuring of congressional power, or the perception of some immediate crisis could significantly increase the probability that the large deficits facing the nation will be reduced significantly.

The Reagan Years

By the time President Reagan was inaugurated in January 1981, the congressional budget process had been tested in six budget cycles with varying degrees of success. In some years the process operated fairly smoothly; in others it seemed on the verge of collapse, threatened by the inability of the House to agree on a budget resolution or by the defiance of a powerful authorizing or appropriations committee. Despite these perilous episodes, the overall impact of the process could not be judged highly constraining or revolutionary. The process had marginal, not significant, impacts on the levels of aggregate spending and taxing. In the early years the process probably generated deficits higher than those that would have occurred under the pre-Budget Act procedures, whereas in the last years of the decade a case could be made for the reverse.[2] Similarly, the process led to some modest, but not radical, shifts in spending priorities.

The process was not a strong instrument of fiscal discipline or change. The budget resolutions were forged to reflect consensus, business-as-usual positions. The process got under way when the consensus policy advocated stimulating a depressed economy back to health with countercyclical spending programs and tax cuts; Congress undertook these policies with enthusiasm. During these early years it was the spending shortfall, not the size of the deficit, that worried congressional leaders. (During the first four budget cycles—fiscal years [FY] 1976 through 1979—actual outlays and the deficit fell below the levels approved in the budget resolutions.) When the budget resolutions did threaten to curtail Congress's distributive activities, either because of unexpected weaknesses in the economy or evolving congressional

---

2. For discussion of whether the Budget Act of 1974 has affected spending levels, see Louis Fisher, "The Budget Act of 1974: Its Impact on Spending," paper presented to the Conference on the Congressional Budget Process, Carl Albert Congressional Research and Studies Center, University of Oklahoma, February 12–13, 1982 (revised November 23, 1982); Lance T. LeLoup, *The Fiscal Congress* (Westport, Conn.: Greenwood Press, 1980); Dennis S. Ippolito, *Congressional Spending* (Ithaca: Cornell University Press, 1981); and Mark S. Kamlet and David C. Mowery, "An Analysis of Congressional Macrobudgetary Priorities and the Impact of the Congressional Budget Act," paper presented at the Fifth Annual Research Conference of the Association for Public Policy Analysis and Management, Philadelphia, Pa, October 21–22, 1983.

priorities, little effort was made to invoke the disciplinary features of the process. Rather, the second budget resolution was replaced by a third or even fourth resolution, or waivers were granted to offending pieces of legislation.

Although the process did not impose the sharp changes in the level of budgetary aggregates or priorities that some people had hoped for, the Budget Act did lead to some significant improvements. It organized and rationalized congressional debate and action on economic and budgetary matters. It heightened Congress's relative role and sense of budgetary responsibility. It increased budgetary and economic literacy and understanding on Capitol Hill. It provided the opportunity for many more members to participate in budget decisions. It focused attention on neglected dimensions of federal activity such as the long-run implications of current decisions, entitlement programs, credit policies, tax expenditures, and off-budget spending.

By and large the president or executive branch did not play a major role in the early functioning of the budget process. Both President Ford and President Carter voiced their encouragement of the new process, but the actions of their administrations often suggested a lack of concern or even an unawareness of the restrictions and timetables of the process. With both houses of Congress controlled by the Democrats and Congress eager to make the new process "congressional," President Ford's inattention was understandable. The Carter administration's failure to exploit or embrace the process is less explicable, especially considering the willingness of the Budget Committees to accommodate the new Democratic administration's policies and the key role that the chairman of the Council of Economic Advisers had played in shaping the Budget Act.

The Year of the President

On March 10, 1981, President Reagan provided Congress with his detailed budget plan—a plan that called for major reductions in taxes and domestic spending, and increases in defense expenditures. For the first time the budget process was faced with a presidential request for sharply altered priorities. The newly Republican Senate responded first by approving a reconciliation resolution that, closely adhering to the president's budget reduction request, called for $36.9 billion in savings for FY 1982. The House Budget Committee, under the new and more conservative leadership of Representative Jim Jones, approved a budget resolution that endorsed the administration's defense buildup, a one-year $38 billion tax cut, and a number of the domestic program cuts proposed by the administration. This resolution, which included reconciliation instructions saving $15.8 billion in FY 1982, was denounced as "business as usual" and "unacceptable" by the administration. A substitute resolution (Gramm-Latta I), which mirrored the president's request, was approved on the House floor by a coalition of Republicans and conservative Democrats.

In the Senate Budget Committee, the Democrats, aided by three conservative Republicans who were concerned about future deficits, defeated a resolution embodying the president's plan. After making some "smoke and mirrors" changes (such as increasing the assumed savings from reduced waste, fraud, and abuse, and from unspecified future-year program reductions) to produce a balanced budget by 1984, the committee and then the full Senate approved a budget resolution. The conference committee quickly fashioned a final first budget resolution for FY 1982 that closely followed the president's spending and tax plans; this measure, which included reconciliation instruction to save $36 billion, was based on the administration's highly optimistic economic assumptions with a revised interest rate forecast.

With the budget resolution passed by mid-May, Congress's attention turned to reconciliation. This element of the budget process had been invoked only once before, in 1980, when it had been used to save $8.3 billion. The task before Congress now involved more than four times these savings and the participation of fourteen Senate and fifteen House committees. "Meeting with a gun pointed at (their) heads"[3] and only a month to act, the House committees reported back to the Budget Committee reconciliation legislation that incorporated many of the administration's proposed cuts. However, the reductions fell several billion dollars short of the total specified in the resolution and reduced domestic programs less sharply than the president desired. The administration labeled the work of the House committees "unacceptable" and Representatives Phil Gramm and Delbert Latta, with the director of the Office of Management and Budget (OMB), David Stockman, fashioned a substitute reconciliation bill that reflected the administration's policies. A coalition of Republicans and conservative Democrats passed this Gramm-Latta II reconciliation substitute.

In the Senate, where it was never questioned that the president's program would be embodied in the reconciliation bill, the committees ran amok, stuffing their reconciliation legislation with authorizations, reauthorizations, new regulations, and all sorts of "extraneous" legislation. Following Senate passage of its reconciliation bill, fifty-eight subconferences involving some 250 members hammered out the final omnibus reconciliation bill, a bill that had twenty-seven titles and more than six hundred pages of legislative language and was fully understood by few, if any, of those voting on it. When

---

3. Representative Carl D. Perkins, quoted in *Congressional Quarterly Almanac for 1981*, p. 258.

passed on July 31, it significantly changed many long-standing domestic spending programs.

On August 4, Congress gave final approval to equally large changes in the tax code when it sent to the president the Economic Recovery Tax Act of 1981 (ERTA). The president had argued that tax reductions, if provided in a supply-side form, would allow the economy to deflate while experiencing a vigorous economic expansion. The budget resolution had provided room for large multiyear tax reductions.

The tax bill represented another defeat for the House Democrats. After a bidding war between Democrats and Republicans and lobbying by the White House, which offered "sweeteners" for numerous special interests, the House rejected the bill reported by the Ways and Means Committee in favor of a substitute offered by Republican Representatives Conable and Hance. In its major provisions, this substitute incorporated the administration's revised tax initiative. The Senate passed a similar measure. The conference had to address few major differences, both bills having provided a cornucopia of tax relief.

Having enacted the most significant reordering of budget priorities since the New Deal, Congress departed for summer recess. By the time Congress returned it was clear that the hoped-for economic miracle was not under way, that the economy was slipping into a recession, and that the economic projections contained in the budget resolution were highly unrealistic. The president responded to the spectre of a deepening deficit in late September with a call to cut an additional $16 billion from the FY 1982 budget. Rather than holding out the prospect for instant nirvana, as he had during the lobbying for the budget resolution, the tax bill, and the reconciliation bill, he described an "economic swamp" that would require many rounds of cuts to drain.

The president's call for further budget belt-tightening met with little congressional enthusiasm. In this environment, neither house of Congress was eager to formulate a second budget resolution. The House Budget Committee, without recommendation, sent the first budget resolution to the floor as a second resolution. The Senate reaffirmed the first budget resolution. All agreed that the outlay, revenue, and deficit figures in these "second resolutions" were totally unrealistic. In contrast to the debate on the first resolution, when the Congress was grappling with the second resolution the president and his administration aides were nowhere to be seen.

When FY 1982 started on October 1, none of the thirteen regular appropriation bills had been passed, in part because of the administration's attempt to cut the FY 1982 budget in late September and the related threats of presidential vetoes. Three continuing resolutions had to be enacted to fund the government. The first continuing resolution got caught in the issue of members' pay and hence was not passed until the government had gone the better part of a day without funding. The second continuing resolution was vetoed by the president, who denounced it as "budget busting" because it had not reduced social programs sufficiently or conformed to his foreign aid requests. In a mood of frustration and fatigue, Congress voted to extend the termination date of the first continuing resolution by three weeks, but not before much of the government had gone without spending authority for three days and thousands of federal workers had been sent home. These appropriation battles began to unravel the tight unity that existed between congressional Republicans and the administration.

The Reemergence of Congress

The gradual withdrawal of the administration from the congressional budget process in the fall of 1981 turned out to be more than a temporary, tactical retreat. In early February 1982, the president submitted his FY 1983 budget proposal to Congress. To everyone's horror, this budget predicted a $98.6 billion deficit for FY 1982, up from the $37.6 billion deficit included in the budget resolution and more than double OMB's previous estimate, released seven months earlier. For FY 1983 the president predicted a $91.5 billion deficit—which the Congressional Budget Office (CBO) reestimated to be $120.6 billion. In an election-year frenzy, members from both sides of the aisle quickly denounced this budget proposal because the deficits were too high, the economic assumptions were daily being proved too optimistic, and the proposed "Deficit Reduction Plan" was unpalatable. This plan included further major reductions in domestic programs, virtually no cuts in the huge defense buildup, and only a modest increase in taxes.

Once the president's proposal had been rejected as a starting point for compromise, a stalemate quickly developed. Democrats in the House, still shell-shocked from their 1981 defeats, were reluctant to put together a budget plan. Senate Republicans were wary of moving until the president indicated the direction in which he was willing to compromise. The White House, led by James Baker III because OMB Director Stockman was in disfavor after his revelations in *The Atlantic Monthly*,[4] began negotiating a compromise with congressional leaders ("the Gang of Seventeen").

This was not the first White House-Congress summit to negotiate the outlines of a budget resolution. Much the same thing had happened in 1980 when President Carter's staff developed a revised FY 1981 budget plan with Democratic leaders. But unlike the earlier version, both political parties were

---

4. William Greider, "The Education of David Stockman," *The Atlantic Monthly*, December 1981.

involved in this round of summitry. Although meetings between the White House and Congress narrowed the range of the debate, settled on a common baseline, and chose a less optimistic set of economic assumptions, they collapsed in a final session when neither Speaker Tip O'Neill nor the president would compromise their most cherished policies, namely Social Security and personal tax cuts.

In despair, the Senate Budget Committee began to draft a resolution without White House participation. Realizing that his budget proposals might be ignored, the president quickly worked out a compromise budget resolution with committee Republicans that called for substantial revenue increases ($95 billion over the FY 1983–FY 1985 period) while freezing indexed benefits (except those for Social Security, Supplemental Security Income, and food stamps) and instituting pay freezes and various other unpopular reductions. On the floor some of these reductions were modified or deleted before the Senate passed the first resolution.

The House committee resolution included deeper cuts in defense, a more substantial tax increase ($147 billion over the FY 1983–FY 1985 period), and smaller cuts in domestic programs. On the House floor the committee's resolution and several alternatives were defeated by wide margins. After regrouping, the House Budget Committee presented a revised resolution to the House, but this was defeated by a Republican substitute. Thus for the second consecutive year the minority party, with the help of conservative Democrats, was able to define the House budget resolution. The conference agreement on the budget resolution was crafted largely by Senate and House Republicans caucusing alone. In contrast to the previous year, the heavy hand of the administration was not defining the compromises and cutting the deals.

With the budget resolution battle over, Congress's attention turned to reconciliation. By August 19, Congress had sent to the president the Omnibus Reconciliation Act of 1982, which cut spending for FY 1983 through FY 1985 by some $13.3 billion, and the Tax Equity and Fiscal Responsibility Act of 1982 (TEFRA), which raised revenues by $98.3 billion and cut entitlement program spending by $17.5 billion over the FYs 1983–1985. Large as these adjustments were, they encompassed far less of the budget resolution's anticipated savings than did the 1981 reconciliation exercise. Smarting from criticism of the "overpowering" reconciliation bill of 1981, the reconciliation effort in 1982 was scaled back to cover less than 40 percent of the deficit reduction steps called for by the budget resolution. Some of the remainder, such as management savings, were in the hands of the executive branch, while others, such as assumed reductions in interest costs, were left to fate.

Exhausted from its budget process demands, faced with an economy that once again had failed to follow the recovery path laid out in the budget resolution, and confronted with an election, Congress avoided the job of putting together a second budget resolution. Anticipating this situation, the Budget Committees had inserted language into the first resolution that made it binding if a second resolution were not passed by October 1.

The appropriations process provided further indications that the administration's ability to single-handedly define the terms and pace of the budget debate was slipping. In June, Congress passed a supplemental appropriations bill for FY 1982 which the president vetoed because it provided more than he requested for certain domestic programs and provided only three-quarters of his requested rescissions. After an override attempt failed in the House, Congress passed a scaled-down supplemental bill, which was also vetoed. Finally, the president accepted an even further scaled-down supplemental bill, but only after further erosion of the White House relations with Congress.

In the late summer Congress passed a second supplemental bill for FY 1982. Although this supplemental bill included funds for the president's Caribbean Basin Initiative and money needed by the Defense Department, the president vetoed it. The president once again characterized the bill as a "budget buster," but the real issue lay not in its size, which was less than the administration's alternative, but in its allocation of spending. The bill contained more for social programs and less for defense than the president had wanted. On September 10, first the House and then the Senate overrode the president's veto.

Thus ended a twenty-month period during which the president's budget wishes had turned into legislation with few compromises. During Reagan's first year, the administration had defined the budget process and congressional Republicans were compliant. During his second year, the administration still had shaped the overall budget policy, but congressional Republicans were at least equal partners in the definition of that policy. The tax bill (TEFRA) was a congressional initiative to which the White House reluctantly acquiesced. The passage of TEFRA in the House, which depended on Democratic votes, and the override of the president's veto of the second supplemental bill, showed that by mid-1982 the Democrats once again were becoming a force to be reckoned with on budgetary matters.

The Year of Inaction

In certain respects, 1983 began as did 1982 with the president submitting a budget proposal with deficits that awed even the most jaded on Capitol Hill. Using economic assumptions that were close to the most pessimistic then available, the administration proposed a budget with a deficit of $189 billion for FY 1984 and deficits remaining above $125 billion through

FY 1988. As in the past, the administration's budget imposed significant restraint on domestic spending, but proposed no significant tax increase or defense spending cutbacks. The president's budget proposal included a contingency tax plan that would go into effect in FY 1986 only if the administration's deficit reduction program was accepted in total, the economy was growing, and the deficit was expected to exceed 2.5 percent of GNP.

As in 1982, both Democrats and Republicans quickly rejected the president's proposal as a starting point for the budget debate. Bolstered by the twenty-six new Democrats in the House, the House Budget Committee shed its hesitancy of the previous two years and crafted a Democratic first budget resolution that was passed easily by the House. Considerable ground work, including extensive consultations with the Democratic leadership, a major role for the Democratic Caucus, and feedback from a fourteen-page budget questionnaire (appropriately labeled "An Exercise in Hard Choices") preceded action on the House floor. The House resolution called for major tax increases ($120 billion over the FY 1984–1986 period), a reduction in the growth of real defense spending from the president's 10 percent figure to 4 percent, (the Congressional Budget Office estimated that the House resolution would provide only 2.3 to 2.9 percent real spending growth for defense) increased money for programs designed to help the poor and unemployed, and minuscule ($2.2 billion for FY 1984) outlay savings from reconciliation. Although the Republicans had written the successful resolutions in the two previous years, they refrained from even offering a substitute resolution in 1983.

In contrast to the situation in the past, chaos reigned in the Senate. The Senate Budget Committee's first attempt to forge a resolution was stalled by the president's plea that the committee delay while the administration explored the grounds for compromise. In particular the president wanted to avoid an embarrassing defeat on his defense request by the Budget Committee Republicans. After a three-week delay during which the president exhibited little of his promised "flexibility," the Senate Budget Committee overwhelmingly approved growth figures for defense that were half those requested by the administration. The committee then bogged down, unable to agree on revenue increases. After weeks of failure to agree on a budget acceptable to the White House, the committee approved a plan drafted by its Democratic minority which included revenue increases similar to those passed by the House but increases in domestic spending that were more moderate.

The lack of Republican cohesion characterizing the committee's markup carried over to the floor, where the Senate rejected the committee's resolution and a number of alternatives. The White House took the position that no budget resolution would be better than a resolution that failed to adhere to the administration's tax and defense policies. After a second effort resulted in the defeat of a handful of plans, the Senate finally approved, by one vote, a resolution crafted by Senator Slade Gorton. Democrats supplied twenty-nine of the fifty votes for the successful Gorton plan.

Aided by an improved economic forecast that cut the deficit by $14 billion, House and Senate conferees reached agreement on a first budget resolution in late June. This resolution allowed for a 5 percent rate of real growth in defense, provided for substantial tax increases, and finessed the domestic spending differences through the creation of a "reserve fund." (The Senate used a similar device in 1976 to cover countercyclical assistance to combat the recession.) Various elements of the Democrat's "Phase II Economic Recovery Plan" were put in this reserve fund, which could be used only if the necessary authorizing legislation were enacted, a doubtful prospect given the threat of presidential vetoes. Nevertheless, it fulfilled the Democrats' partisan need of not appearing to abandon social program goals. The president quickly denounced the budget resolution as "irresponsible" and "a step backward," and he promised to "oppose it vigorously."

As was the case in the previous three years, the final budget resolution included reconciliation instructions requiring outlay reductions of $12.3 billion and revenue increases of $73 billion from FY 1984 through FY 1986. Although the outlay savings were small and relatively noncontroversial, the revenue figures were greeted less than enthusiastically not only by the president but also by the chairmen of the two tax-writing committees. Senator Robert Dole, reflecting a widely shared view, labeled the resolution "unbalanced and unworkable" and the tax increases "a dead cat." Work on the reconciliation bills moved ahead at a snail's pace. The deadline for reporting reconciliation legislation back to the Budget Committees was extended twice. Finally Congress adjourned for the year without passing even a significantly scaled-back tax increase proposal or the spending reductions.

Following the agreement on the budget resolution and its denunciation by the president, the White House threatened a "siege" of presidential vetoes affecting the appropriation bills that exceeded the administration's budget requests. Nevertheless, congressional action on appropriations bills moved faster than in the previous two years. Rather than confront the president and "create a media extravaganza" in which the president could be pictured "standing up to the big spenders,"[5] Congress scaled back its bills and reached compromises with the administration, which exhibited some flexibility motivated in part by a need to gain congressional support for its Central American,

---

5. Representative Les Au Coin (Democrat-Oregon), quoted in *Congressional Quarterly*, June 18, 1983, pp. 1209–10.

Lebanese, and MX policies. By the start of FY 1984, four appropriations bills had been enacted; by the time Congress adjourned, nine appropriations bills had been passed.

Although the first resolution automatically became a binding second resolution on October 1, the search for solutions went forward on the Hill with various members of Congress pressing plans that would balance spending cuts more evenly with tax increases. While some chose to freeze social spending, others suggested reducing the degree of indexation of both the tax system and benefit programs.

With the existing process seemingly unable to force movement toward the widely accepted objective of deficit reduction, new institutions and processes were proposed. These included creating a blue-ribbon Presidential Deficit Reduction Commission fashioned after the successful Social Security Commission; convening a White House-Congress summit meeting on the deficit; and providing the president with line-item veto power on appropriations bills, expanded rescission authority, or temporary authority to adjust the rate by which taxes and benefit programs were indexed.

By the end of 1983 a clear stalemate had developed. The president was adamant in his rejection of tax increases to close the deficit gap. The Democrats were not eager to lead a deficit reduction effort that could get embroiled in election-year politics. The Republicans were reluctant to openly defy their president, although Senators Pete Domenici and Dole continued to provide leadership in the fight to reduce the deficit. With the economy recovering strongly, the harm of huge deficits was not apparent to the public, which seemed content with a rhetorical assault on the problem. On Capitol Hill many hoped that some external crisis—a collapse of domestic or international financial markets or a spike in interest rates—would force the administration to compromise and accept a significant deficit reduction plan.

Changes in the Budget Process and Its Roles

The pressures generated by the president's request for a sharp redirection of budget priorities and by the prolonged deterioration of the economy led to a number of changes in the budget process. Some of these changes accelerated developments that were already under way; others were haphazard inventions needed to surmount particular impasses. There were changes both in budget procedures and in the roles the process was expected to play. Overall, these developments tended to strengthen the process.

New Procedures

Foremost among the evolutionary changes that gathered steam during the Reagan administration was an expansion of the scope of the budget process. A major dimension of this expansion was the multiyear focus, which became firmly entrenched during this period. Realizing that the process would have to have a multiyear focus if spending were to be controlled, the House Budget Committee began to include discussions of the future (out-year) implications of its budget resolutions in its reports in 1977; the Senate followed suit in 1978. Another factor encouraging the multiyear focus was the desire by the Budget Committees to show that the budgetary outlook (deficit) would improve (decline) under their proposed policies. This would occur because the weak economy, which characterized the 1970s, was always projected to strengthen.

The FY 1980 budget resolutions were the first to incorporate multiyear figures; these covered the fiscal year of the resolution and the two following fiscal years. However, little serious consideration was given to these out-year numbers. The Senate wanted policy changes incorporated in the out-year targets, whereas the House wanted them to be projections of current House policies reflecting no change in priorities. The 1980 resolutions thus included two separate sets of aggregate out-year numbers. Even if agreement had been reached, no mechanism existed to enforce future fiscal year limits. For FY 1981, the resolutions included out-year estimates incorporating policy changes. Functional as well as aggregate numbers were specified. However, the House and Senate could not agree on the desirable out-year policies, and so the resolutions once again contained two sets of numbers.

The Reagan administration's economic and budget policy was multiyear in scope and thus served to strengthen the nascent multiyear focus of the budget process. The president proposed a policy that in the long run promised reduced tax burdens, a vigorous and low-inflation economy, and a balanced budget, but in the short run involved the sacrifice of reduced domestic spending. The skepticism many budget and economic experts expressed over the long-term impact of the president's program also helped to focus attention on the future. Thus, it was never really an issue that the budget resolution for FY 1982 would be a multiyear resolution incorporating multiyear policy changes.

Not only were the aggregate spending and revenue limits multiyear, but so too were the reconciliation instructions. Both OMB Director Stockman and the Budget Committees had learned a lesson from Congress's initial experiment with reconciliation for FY 1981. In this experiment the tax-writing committees had circumvented the spirit of the one-year reconciliation instructions and had obtained some of their required savings by pushing year-end Medicare payments into the next fiscal year; other committees had reported legislation that provided only temporary savings. Multiyear reconciliation instructions were essential in order to avoid such game playing, especially in what was thought to be a Democratic-controlled House.

The multiyear focus of the FY 1982 resolution was maintained in FY 1983 and 1984 but with considerable difficulty. By early 1982 the economic picture had deteriorated. Rather than revealing paradise, the out-year focus disclosed what the president called an "economic quagmire" and "horrendous" deficits. The pressure presented by the bleak budgetary outlook and the difficulty of crafting a resolution acceptable to the Republicans caused Senator Domenici's multiyear fervor to waiver during the preparation of the FY 1984 resolution. After dissociating himself from the "Democratic" resolution reported out by his committee, Senator Domenici, with Senator Baker, fashioned a "two-year" Republican resolution that was designed to avoid the question of whether large tax increases would be required in FY 1986. The defeat of this resolution on the floor ensured continuation of the three-year budget focus.

The reconciliation efforts of the Reagan years constitute a second important extension of the budget process.[6] During the early years of the process, legislated savings had been assumed in virtually all the first budget resolutions. But the fragility of the process and the tentative position of the Budget Committees precluded use of the potent reconciliation tool. For the most part, the assumed savings never materialized, as powerful committees chose to ignore the pleadings of the process. The Senate included reconciliation instructions in its second resolution for FY 1980, but the provision was dropped by a skittish conference. The following year, with both President Carter and Congress striving for an election year resolution showing a balanced budget, reconciliation instructions were included in the first budget resolution. These instructions to reduce the FY 1981 deficit by $10.6 billion affected eight Senate and seven House authorizing committees and the appropriations committees. With much praise from President Carter and considerable self-congratulation, Congress approved a reconciliation bill in December 1980 that reduced the deficit by $8.3 billion.

The FY 1981 achievement was dwarfed both in size and comprehensiveness by the reconciliation efforts of the first three years of the Reagan administration. As many as fifteen House committees and fourteen Senate

---

6. For a thorough analysis of reconciliation, see Allen Schick, *Reconciliation and the Congressional Budget Process* (Washington, D.C.: American Enterprise Institute for Public Policy Research, 1981).

committees were touched by the heavy hand of reconciliation and the savings each year exceeded those of the 1981 exercise. (The 1981 reconciliation experience had also generated much criticism from the authorizing committee chairmen; the opposition had been muted only by the fact that Democrats controlled the process.) But the use of reconciliation, particularly for FY 1982, generated a wave of resentment on Capitol Hill that threatened the continued operation of the budget process. Democrats described this reconciliation exercise in such terms as "draconian," "a brutal and blunt instrument," a process "out of control," and an "abuse of procedure." Some of their frustration no doubt was attributable to the victory of the Gramm-Latta II substitute reconciliation bill, which effectively excluded them from having a voice in determining where the cuts were to be made; but some represented legitimate objections to the unorthodox way in which reconciliation had been implemented.

One target of criticism was the tying of reconciliation to the first resolution rather than to the second resolution, as the Budget Act had clearly envisaged. (The FY 1981 reconciliation instructions were contained in the first budget resolution, but this deviation had been viewed as deviation needed to pass a balanced budget before the election.) This shift of timing implied a shift of focus away from adjustments in tax laws and in newly passed appropriations.

Friction also stemmed from the fact that the reconciliation process was directed at authorizations. (The resolutions reported by the House Budget Committee did not call for changes in discretionary program authorizations but this resolution was defeated on the House floor by the Gramm-Latta II substitute, which, like the Senate's reconciliation resolution, did call for changes in authorizing legislation.) As a result there were major changes in program structure, such as the creation of nine block grants and modification of the benefit levels and eligibility standards of many entitlement programs.

A third source of discomfort was the use of the reconciliation bill to enact substantial amounts of non-budget-related legislation ranging from revised safety standards for power lawnmowers to new Federal Communications Commission procedures for allocating radio and TV licenses.

A fourth irritant was the feeling among the old-line authorizing committees that the Budget Committees and budget process were expropriating their power. Reconciliation instructions can specify only the aggregate amount of savings a committee must report out, not the particular form of such savings. Nevertheless, the debates within the Budget Committees and on the floor, the specification of both budget authority and outlay amounts, and the magnitude of the required cuts can greatly restrict the savings options that a committee has. Finally, the short time period during which the reconciliation bills were marked up, debated, and passed was a source of resentment. (The time allowed committees to report back reconciliation legislation to the budget committees was twenty-two days for FY 1982, thirty days in the Senate and forty-one days in the House for 1983, and twenty-nine days for 1984.) The hastily assembled bills covered hundreds of pages and dozens of programs and included numerous inconsistencies and drafting errors. No one voting on these bills could claim to have even a modest grasp of their contents, let alone understand their possible impacts.

The hostility generated by the FY 1982 reconciliation effort led to a concerted effort to scale back the scope of reconciliation for FY 1983 and 1984. More of the assumed savings in these resolutions were left to the appropriations process than to reconciliation, the required program cuts were kept small relative to the revenue increases, and modifications in authorizing legislation were concentrated on entitlement or quasi-entitlement programs.

There can be no doubt that reconciliation was the tool that led, in Chairman Jones's view, to "the most monumental and historic turnaround in fiscal policy that has ever occurred."[7] While haste and executive dominance of the exercise for FY 1982 led to abuses and mistakes that later had to be corrected, the reconciliation tool was crucial for the achievement of major reduction in spending. The abbreviated time period, aggregation of unpalatable legislation into single omnibus bills, and the rule providing for limited floor amendments circumvented the normal congressional processes that have proved so successful at protecting special interests. Reconciliation raised the visibility of the decisions, denied interest groups their normal channels of influence, and prevented powerful committee chairmen from stalling and defining the dimensions of debate. By acting collectively and for a presumed greater good, members of Congress could share the blame for the bloodletting. The Budget Committees, the budget process, the president, the OMB director, and the hoped-for new economic order could be saddled with the responsibility for specific unpopular actions.

A third area in which the scope of the budget process expanded during the Reagan years was credit controls. During the late 1970s the explosive expansion in government lending spurred concern over the growth of federal credit activity. This prompted the president to expand the description of federal credit activities in his budget proposals, and the Budget Committees to focus more of their attention on credit programs. The FY 1981 budget resolutions were the first to incorporate credit budget targets. These nonbinding targets were directed at new, direct loan obligations and new government commitments for loan guarantees.

---

7. Representative Jim Jones, quoted in *Congressional Quarterly Almanac for 1981*, p. 256.

During the FY 1982 budget battles, controls over government lending activity were clearly less vital than tax cuts or reconciliation. Nevertheless, with the president's encouragement, the resolution included credit limits similar to those in the previous year's resolutions. The following year, the conference accepted the House language on credit which provided an enforcement procedure similar to that existing for spending programs. Aggregate ceilings were set for new direct loan obligations, new primary loan guarantee commitments, and new secondary loan guarantee commitments. These aggregates were broken down both by function and by committee. In addition, the resolution required that authorizations for new direct loans or loan guarantee commitments be subject to limits established in appropriation legislation. Although these enforcement mechanisms were significant steps forward along the road to credit limitations, political and technical realities precluded them from being comprehensive; they gave escape hatches to the lending activities of the Commodity Credit Corporation and Veterans Administration. Sensing that they had gone too far too fast and that the "overreaching" budget process was in some jeopardy, both committees reverted to nonbinding credit targets in the FY 1984 resolutions.

The first years of the Reagan administration also saw budget process changes designed to strengthen the discipline of congressional budgeting. Reconciliation and constraints on government lending activity were two developments in this direction. The disappearance of the second budget resolution represented another. The framers of the Budget Act had presumed that the first, nonbinding, resolution would be less important than the second, binding, resolution, but early experience proved that the major policy battles would be fought over the first resolution and simply reestimated in the second resolution. A natural deemphasis of the second resolution took place. This trend reached an embarrassing culmination in the fall of 1981 when the battle-weary Congress would not craft a second budget resolution for 1982 and reaffirmed the unrealistic figures of the first resolution.

During committee markup of the budget resolution the following year, both committee chairmen attempted to formalize the previous year's procedure by including language that would make the limits of the first budget resolution binding if a second resolution had not been approved by the beginning of the fiscal year. This would ensure that congressional inaction did not create a hiatus in budgetary discipline. These proposals encountered opposition from Democrats in the Senate and from the Appropriations Committee in the House and were dropped from the committee resolutions. The substitute Republican resolution approved by the House gave this enforcement device new life, and the conference agreed to language transforming the first resolution into a binding second resolution on October 1 if Congress did not act on a second resolution. The same provision was included in the FY 1984 resolution. (The House-passed resolution would have allowed an automatic update of the limits in the resolution to take account of changed economic and technical circumstances, but this was rejected by the Senate.) Neither house made a serious effort to craft second budget resolutions for FY 1983 or 1984. It is safe to assume that a shift to a single budget resolution has occurred without reducing the enforceability of the budget process.

Another procedure strengthening budget process enforcement that appeared during the turbulence of the first Reagan years was deferred enrollment. The primary enforcement mechanism of the budget process, the point of order provided in Section 311(a) of the Budget Act, suffered the weakness of being available only when the second budget resolution's aggregate limits on budget authority, outlays, or revenues were threatened by a piece of legislation. While these aggregates were broken down among spending committees and appropriation subcommittees by the Section 302 allocation process, there was no binding means of ensuring that each committee or subcommittee stayed within the limits established by the resolution. Despite elaborate scorekeeping reports and early-warning advisories prepared by the Budget Committees and much jawboning by the Budget Committee chairmen, committees that acted early could avoid the discipline of the process.

In an effort to put teeth into the process, the resolution for FY 1981 called for deferred enrollment, a procedural innovation requiring that bills exceeding the spending limits contained in the Section 302 allocations could not be enrolled or sent to the president until after the second budget resolution had been passed and any associated reconciliation effort completed. Similar restrictions were placed on legislation that would reduce aggregate federal revenues by more than $100 million. This deferred-enrollment mechanism for spending authority was included in the FY 1982 resolution as well.

With resentment against the power of the budget process running high on Capitol Hill, the chairman of the House Appropriations Committee attempted to "de-fang" the budget resolution for FY 1983. An amendment deleting deferred enrollment was approved by the House but the conference agreement inserted deferred-enrollment provisions in both the final resolutions for FY 1983 and 1984.

Deferred enrollment has not directly affected any legislation in the four years it has been practiced.[8] The major reason for this is that Congress

---

8. Through 1983, deferred enrollment had not directly affected any bills in the Senate and had temporarily affected only two bills in the House. The first, H.R. 3765, a walnut marketing order, was held up from November 17 through November 20 because of a technicality. The second, H.R. 3499, a bill to extend and improve programs for veterans, was held up for several days in 1981 because of a misfiled Section 302(b) allocation report.

approved few appropriations bills before the start of the fiscal year or by the time the second budget resolutions came into force. This does not mean that deferred enrollment has not had an effect. Appropriations subcommittees, committees, and conferences have trimmed bills to stay within the Section 302(b) limits out of concern that the spotlight of fiscal irresponsibility would shine on them if their legislation were held at the desk. Deferred enrollment also has delayed action on some bills. Realizing that their bills exceeded their allocations, some subcommittees have slowed their pace of action until the turn of the fiscal year when the deferred-enrollment provision loses its force.

While much that strengthened the congressional budget process occurred between 1981 and 1983, the process did not eschew what Chairman Jones called "mirrors and magic" to make its impossible dreams come true. The most obvious resort to fantasy was the acceptance of the administration's economic assumptions for the FY 1982 resolution. Even the members voting to accept these assumptions acknowledged that they were absurd. In addition, the budget resolution placed heavy reliance on unspecified future-year savings, reductions in waste, fraud, and abuse, and management efficiencies that few members of Congress thought could be realized. Unsophisticated gimmicks also were used to reduce the size of the deficit, the most glaring being the decision to put the Strategic Petroleum Reserve off-budget. When several billion dollars in savings were needed to grease the conference agreement for FY 1983, an arbitrary assumption was made that interest rates, and hence federal borrowing costs, would miraculously fall once credit markets saw the responsible job Congress was doing on the budget. All told, the performance on the "truth in budgeting" front suffered during the early Reagan years.

New Roles

The heightened concern surrounding budgetary matters, the split party control of the two houses of Congress, and the deterioration of relations between the White House and Congress encouraged new roles for the budget process during the first three years of the Reagan administration. The budget process became a serious game in which strategy, tactics, and timing were increasingly important. Players took positions not on policies they ultimately desired but rather on ones that afforded a good bargaining situation.

It is unlikely that the administration thought this way when formulating its first two budgets. The initial Reagan proposal was an ideological and philosophical statement. Fresh from a complete triumph in his first foray into congressional budgeting, the president was probably not affected by such considerations in drafting his FY 1983 proposals. However, by the time the administration's FY 1984 and 1985 budgets were being crafted, it was clear to the White House and to OMB that the game was at least a two-party game. Statements of administration officials indicated that they were thinking this way. The foremost example of this was the debate on defense associated with the FY 1984 budget. In the negotiations with Senate Budget Committee Republicans, the secretary of defense refused to reduce the president's 10 percent real growth request below 7.5 percent because the House resolution contained only 4 percent real growth. As it turned out, the administration overplayed its hand, staking out an initial position that proved to be off the playing board. Thus, the conference compromise was between the 6 percent real growth provided by the Senate's Gorton resolution and the 4 percent growth offered in the House resolution.

With the House and Senate controlled by different parties, the budget process has become a congressional, as well as a legislative-executive, game. The wrangling in the Senate over levels of real growth for defense in FY 1984 had as much to do with the starting position needed to counter the low figure in the House resolution as with the desire for a rapidly increasing defense budget. This was expressed most bluntly by Senator James Abdnor who argued, "While this figure (the 7.5 percent figure for real growth in defense spending) is entirely responsible and defensible in its own right, the truth of the matter, as we all realize, is that whatever number we settle on will be our starting point when we go to conference with the House. The House approved only a 2.3 percent increase."[9]

Congressional budgeting also became an intramural game. The Budget Committees increasingly have fashioned resolutions that they expect to be amended on the floor. To preserve the process and their power, they do not want to appear to be defining the nation's budget priorities alone. To succeed, they must show some flexibility by accepting floor amendments that will engender support for the resolution by key groups of legislators. During a discussion of the lack of enthusiasm the Ways and Means Committee showed for the great tax increases included in the Budget Committees' resolution for FY 1984, Richard Gephardt, a member of both committees, reminded his colleagues that the initial resolution was merely a "bargaining point" to start a dialogue with other committees. The fact that the congressional budget process is being played like a serious game on all three levels is a testament to the growing importance and power of its decisions within each house, between the two houses, and between the legislative and executive branches.

During the Reagan administration's first three years, the budget process also assumed an important symbolic role. Adherence to the procedures of the

---

9. Senator James Abdnor, quoted in *Congressional Record*, May 12, 1982, p. S.6565. The 2.3 percent figure for the House reflects the CBO reestimates of the House resolution.

process became an immensely important measure of congressional fiscal responsibility. Failure to approve a budget resolution or to enact a reconciliation bill took on tremendous significance to many members. The spectres of the "chaos," "confrontation," and "fiscal anarchy" that would prevail without a budget were frequently raised during debates. Some members clearly felt any budget resolution was better than none. As Senator Gorton put it, "It is more important that this process continue than it is to come up with any particular figures."[10] The final approval of an FY 1984 resolution in the Senate was due, in no small part, to Senator Baker's similar statement, "It is essential in my view that we pass a budget."[11]

Adherence to the budget process took on symbolic importance for two reasons. First, Congress was fearful that failure to approve a budget would result in a never-ending barrage of presidential criticism that Congress was unable to live up to its own budget procedures. Economic problems, the deficit, or appropriation impasses could then be blamed on Congress. Second, with the two houses controlled by different parties, neither chamber wanted to appear to be the cause of deadlock. Members of Congress perceived that the budget process had symbolic value extending beyond Washington. Wall Street, they thought, looked to the budget process to "send a message that deficits (were) coming down" and that the economic recovery would not be "aborted."[12]

All did not share the belief in the symbolic importance of maintaining the budget process. Members who were dissatisfied with the policy outcomes of the process expressed displeasure over their colleagues' voting in favor of resolutions more to preserve the process than to support the policies implied by the resolutions. Conservatives outside Congress argued that the process was not worth saving, that "budget process groupies . . . are more interested in the process than the product and in the political power of budget committee members than the control of aggregate federal spending growth."[13]

Accomplishments of the Congressional Budget Process

The congressional budget process was clearly vital to the successful enactment of the major policy shifts of the first three years of the Reagan

---

10. Senator Gorton, quoted in *Congressional Quarterly*, April 23, 1983, pp. 767–68.

11. Senator Baker, quoted in *ibid.*, May 21, 1983, p. 986.

12. Senator Domenici, quoted in *ibid.*, April 16, 1983, p. 731.

13. Letter to the *Washington Post*, May 24, 1983, by James A. Clifton, Chamber of Commerce of the United States.

administration. The president presented Congress with a coherent, multiyear program that would have been fragmented, stalled, and substantially modified had it not been for the budget process. Through use of the process, the president's policy packages were kept bundled together. The purity of the program's elements was preserved, the benefits were integrated with the sacrifices, and decisions were expedited to the point that opposition had difficulty organizing. Reconciliation provided the mechanism for bypassing normal congressional methods of operation.

The budget process also reduced the tendency Congress has to reverse the painful decisions that it makes. The FY 1982 and 1983 budget resolutions served as proof of congressional agreement with the policy changes. Using these resolutions, the president could force Congress to live up to its own promises.

The process led to the fiscalization of the public policy debate.[14] The measure of all arguments became dollars. What would the policy do to the deficit? Would it cost more or less than the amount included in the president's budget or the budget resolution? Relegated to secondary status were discussions of the number of public service jobs provided, the number of housing units supported by the program, the number of acres added to the national park system, or the number of college students receiving Pell grants. In part, this was the natural result of retrenchment. Looking at and measuring the harm done by one's actions does not promote reelection.

But even in the defense area, where spending increases have been the norm, fiscalization was the rule. The administration was able to couch the debate in terms of how large a real increase the military should be provided or what fraction of gross national product (GNP) should be devoted to defense. Relying on such measures was a way to gather support for the administration's defense buildup from a public that had no ability to judge whether twelve deployable aircraft carriers were too few but fifteen were sufficient to meet the Soviet threat. What the public could understand was that defense spending had declined from 9.1 percent of GNP in 1960 to 5.0 percent at the end of the 1970s, and that inflation-adjusted defense spending was lower in 1980 than it had been in 1960.

The budget process was essential for achievement of the budgetary shifts between 1981 and 1983. But other circumstances were equally vital, if not more so. Foremost among these was the political climate that existed in the first years of the Reagan administration. The election of 1980 was overly

---

14. This point was made by Allen Schick in *Reconciliation and the Congressional Budget Process.*

interpreted as a pro-Reagan mandate, not as a rejection of Carter.[15] This interpretation arose chiefly from the unexpected victory of the Republicans in the Senate. Eager to please their president and to share in the "mandate," congressional Republicans exhibited an unusual degree of unity on budget votes during the first two years. In fact, on each of the key votes in 1981 on the first budget resolution, the reconciliation bill, and the tax bill, only one Republican in the House and no more than two in the Senate did not support the president's position.

One-party dominance was facilitated by the disarray and demoralization of the defeated Democrats. With a loss of thirty-three seats and the emergence of the conservative "Boll Weevils," the fractionalized Democratic party did not have a working majority in the House. Early defeats on the budget resolution, the reconciliation bill, and the tax bill left many dejected House Democrats willing to give the president his whole program, hoping that when it failed they could escape being blamed.

The knowledge and mode of operation of Budget Director Stockman also were crucial to the administration's budget success. For the first time a president had an OMB director who knew not only the budget but also the members, procedures, and weaknesses of Capitol Hill. With this knowledge, Stockman explicitly set out an "orchestration of the congressional machinery to implement 'our' policy through the framework of 'their' budget."[16] His success was not only a tribute to his grasp of budget detail and boundless energy but also to the centralization of executive budget making in his hands. The meekness of the cabinet secretaries and the deference shown by the White House staff meant that there were no competing centers of budgetary power, no one else in the administration to turn to for an appeal, and no uncertainty that when Stockman cut a deal it would stick. With his "black book" in hand, Stockman dominated the budget resolution and reconciliation processes in the House. As Representative Jones described it, "The Democratic cloak room had all the earmarks of a tobacco auction"[17] where votes were bought and rented for considerations ranging from solar energy projects to reexamination of the administration's sugar subsidy policy.

The effectiveness of the budget director was surpassed only by that of the president. Unlike his predecessors, President Reagan did not remain aloof from the congressional budget process. His personal lobbying of members

15. Thomas E. Mann and Norman J. Ornstein, "Sending a Message: Voters and Congress in 1982," in *The American Elections of 1982* edited by Mann and Ornstein (Washington, D.C.: American Enterprise Institute for Public Policy Research, 1983).

16. David Stockman, quoted in *Congressional Quarterly*, May 14, 1983, p. 929.

17. Representative Jim Jones, quoted in *Congressional Quarterly Almanac 1981*, p. 263.

for votes on budget resolutions, rules, reconciliation bills, tax bills, and appropriation bills was unprecedented in scale. To ensure passage of the Gramm-Latta II substitute reconciliation bill for FY 1982, he contacted each of the sixty-three House Democrats that had supported the Gramm-Latta I substitute resolution. The "great communicator" used every opportunity— press conferences, speeches, meeting with members, state of union messages, and his weekly radio address—to generate congressional support for his budget policies. To spur passage of the Gramm-Latta I resolution, he even dictated letters from the hospital bed where he was recovering from an assassination attempt.

Moreover, he communicated in strong language. Frustrated over the pace at which his program was moving through Congress, he attacked the process as "the most Mickey Mouse arrangement that any governmental body has ever practiced."[18] Displeased with the tax increase in the Democratic House resolution for FY 1984, he attacked it: "Yes, the deficit doctors have their scalpels out all right but they're not poised over the budget. . . . What they're ready to operate on is your wallet."[19] The fear of being labeled by the president a "big spender," a "budget buster," or the party that sabotaged the economic recovery restrained many members of Congress. By 1983, however, it was clear that close presidential involvement in the budget process had stirred up considerable resentment, not only among Democrats but also within the Republican leadership.

The president's effectiveness was due to his personal popularity and his ability to characterize his program as arising from a popular mandate. The prevalent interpretation of the 1970s was that Democratic budget and economic policies had failed. The president promised a new and different policy, one that was cohesive, philosophically distinctive, and radical. Decisions were successfully framed in black and white. As a member of Congress, you were for the president or against him, you would support the will of the people or defy it, you were in favor of the economic recovery or willing to abort it, you heard the tax payers revolt or you didn't. Compromises, negotiations, and flexibility were not considered necessary or desirable in such an environment.

Thus, although the budget process was an essential ingredient of the policy shifts between 1981 and 1983, other factors were at least as important. These other factors will be difficult to replicate in the future.

---

18. *Congressional Quarterly*, August 7, 1982, p. 1890.
19. Remarks of the president to the National Association of Home Builders, May 16, 1983.

The Challenges for the Future

Projections of current budget policy show deficits of close to $200 billion extending "as far as (the) eye can see."[20] Elimination of these deficits will require tax increases and spending cuts exceeding 4 percent of GNP. This represents a huge budgetary adjustment; the recent tax cuts (ERTA and TEFRA) amounted to some 2 percent of GNP, the domestic spending reductions totaled 1.5 percent of GNP, and the defense increases amounted to 1.6 percent of GNP. Whether the current budget process can facilitate such a large adjustment is far from clear.

One reason for pessimism is that the process is threatened from a number of sources. Foremost among these is the growing tendency for people who have lost budget battles to blame their defeat on the process. After using the process so effectively for the FY 1982 and 1983 budgets, the administration lost the budget resolution battle for FY 1984 and let it be known that it regarded the process as expendable. In Senator Dan Quayle's words, "They're like a little kid playing with marbles. If they don't win they pick up their marbles and go home."[21] Secretary of Defense Weinberger, who did "not worship with the faithful at the altar of the Congressional Budget Process,"[22] advised the president to abandon the process because defense spending would be higher if there were no budget resolution and the administration had to deal only with the appropriations process. In an impassioned defense of the process, David Stockman reminded the president that his previous victories could not have occurred without the process and warned that an aborted recovery and huge deficits would result from failure to pass a resolution.[23] Nevertheless, the president opted to oppose the resolution reported out of the conference.

Having failed to dictate the dimensions of the budget, numerous other Republicans accepted Representative Bill Frenzel's judgment that "the process is not worth more than the product."[24] Some simply dropped out of the game, others proposed plans that would seriously weaken or even repeal the Budget Act. Among the prominent Republicans who made proposals that would weaken or scrap the budget process are Senators Howard Baker, William V. Roth, and Barry Goldwater and Representative Silvio Conte.

On the Democratic side, support for the process grew in 1983 only because the Democrats were able to define the budget resolution and to see

---

20. Office of Management and Budget "Budget Outlook," April 18, 1983.
21. Senator Quayle quoted in *Washington Post*, April 20, 1983.
22. *Washington Post*, Letter to the Editor, June 29, 1983.
23. "Budget Outlook," April 18, 1983, Office of Management and Budget.
24. Representative Frenzel, quoted in *Congressional Quarterly*, June 25, 1983, p. 1270.

the process as a mechanism for differentiating their policies from those of the administration. Nevertheless, the traditional sources of opposition to the process, namely the authorizing and appropriations committee chairmen, are as strong as ever. Their authority and power were seriously eroded by the reconciliation exercises for FY 1981 and 1982. As a result they have waged a continual battle through "Dear Colleague" letters, amendments to the resolutions, and pressures on the Rules Committee and House leadership to undermine the reconciliation powers of the process. One major effort in this direction occurred in April 1983, when eight authorizing committee chairmen led by Representative John Dingell proposed major revamping of the Budget Act.[25]

Support within the Democratic leadership for the budget process has grown stronger largely for partisan reasons. With the White House abandoning the process and then being criticized for this "irresponsibility" in many newspaper editorials, the Democrats assumed the role of the party of fiscal responsibility and the defenders of the process. The Democratic leadership thus denounced the advice the secretary of defense gave to the president and decried the White House's "cavalier attitude toward the budget process."[26]

In the election-year environment of 1984, the budget process and its preservation could become partisan issues. Party differences are likely to be defined along budgetary dimensions. Both parties will find it difficult to compromise on budget issues because such compromising will be seen as threatening party identity. In this environment the budget process could grind to a halt or even collapse if a subsequent economic downturn is blamed on congressional budgetary inaction.

Although the pressures that weaken the ability of the budget process to deal with future deficits are clear, there are also movements afoot that are intended to strengthen the way in which the Congress handles budget matters. Numerous suggestions have been made to improve the process,[27] and changes have been made. From year to year the process has evolved to reflect political and budget realities. These ad hoc changes have been possible because of the act's elastic clauses that permit the committees to follow "any other procedure

---

25. See H.R. 2777 and supporting materials.

26. *Washington Post*, April 21, 1983.

27. For a summary of these changes, see "Summarization of Current Budget Reform Prospects: Preliminary Draft Listings of Key Proposals Set Forth in 1981 in Bills, Statements, and Reports to the Congress," General Accounting Office, Janaury 1982, in *The Congressional Budget Act and Process: How Can They Be Improved?* Compendium and Proceedings of a Symposium Convened by the Committee for a Responsible Federal Budget and the Joint Educational Consortium, De Gray State Park, Arkadelphia, Arkansas, January 11–12, 1982.

which is considered appropriate to carry out the purposes of the Act."[28] With such a blank check, the balance of informed opinion has generally concluded that opening the Budget Act to amendment would be a mistake as long as the process is under pressure.

The second budget resolution for FY 1981 called for a review of the Budget Act and the budget process. This provision was intended to defuse some of the objections of the authorizing and appropriations committee chairmen to the first uses of reconciliation and deferred enrollment. In the Senate, with the president's party in control of the process, the enthusiasm for major restructuring of the budget process was minimal through 1982 and the review has not proceeded rapidly. On the House side, where opposition was far stronger, a task force (the Beilenson Task Force) with representation from the authorizing committees was established to recommend changes to the process. During the first year of its existence the task force appeared openly hostile to the process. In early 1982 the task force recommended eight procedural changes that would have shifted the responsibility for the enforcement provisions of the budget resolution from the Budget Committee to the Rules Committee and would have excluded alterations in authorizations from reconciliation. After an acrimonious battle between the Budget Committee chairman and the task force, the Democratic leadership let the proposal die. By late 1983 with the budget process back in the control of the Democrats and concern rising over huge future deficits, the Beilenson Task Force appeared convinced of the importance of preserving and strengthening the process.[29]

A number of proposals have been advanced to strengthen and streamline the congressional budget process. Some call for a codification of the ad hoc prededural changes, such as deferred enrollment and elimination of the second budget resolution, that have been made during the past few years. Other proposals, such as those requiring passage of biennial budgets and limiting the debate on budget resolutions, are aimed at the growing tendency for the budget process to absorb the entire calendar. Still other proposals are attempts to reduce the amount of gimmickry that now occurs in the process. Among such proposals are those that would require that the economic and technical assumptions of the budget resolutions be determined by outside experts, not by committee votes. Finally, some suggestions are directed at improving coordination on budget matters between the executive and legislative branches.

---

28. P.L. 93-344, Section 301(b) (2). Section 301 (a) (b) permits the budget resolutions to contain "such other matters relating to the budget as may be appropriate to carry out the purpose of this Act."

29. See Richard E. Cohen, "House Task Force May Propose Radical Changes to Toughen the Budget Process," *National Journal*, August 20, 1983.

Although many of these reforms have considerable merit, it is unlikely that singly or together they would significantly enhance the ability of the budget process to handle the difficult problems that lie ahead. They could ease tensions between the Budget Committees and other committees, but they won't make retrenchment more palatable or increase the incentives to act.

More fundamental shifts of power would be required to significantly increase the probability that Congress will act expeditiously to reduce future deficits. Such shifts might involve only Congress. Steps that would increase the authority of the leadership and strengthen party discipline would be constructive. Alternatively, radical changes could be made in the manner in which budget decisions are made. These might involve major increases or decreases in power for the Budget Committees. Under one such plan presented by Representative David Obey, the Budget Committees would prepare a resolution but would not send it to the floor.[30] Working from the allocations implied by that budget resolution, the spending and taxing committees would craft their budget legislation, which would then be rolled into one giant omnibus budget bill for floor consideration. The Budget Committees could propose floor amendments in areas in which the omnibus bill exceeded their budget resolution. If the Budget Committee amendments were defeated, the budget resolution would be automatically revised. Thus, Congress would act on its budget goals (the resolutions) and its substantive action (the omnibus budget bill) at one time, creating a valuable linkage that does not now exist between objectives and reality. The difficult retrenchment decisions would have to be voted on only once rather than twice as now occurs with votes on the resolutions and the appropriations bills. Whether this omnibus bill approach would be unwieldy, confusing, susceptible to abuse and deadlock, or uncontrollable, as the critics have claimed, is open to question.

Shifts of power might also extend beyond Capitol Hill. The various proposed constitutional amendments to balance the budget or limit the growth of outlays represent one such thrust. Another approach would be to increase the budgetary power of the executive relative to the legislative branch by providing the president with a line-item veto on spending bills, enhanced ability to rescind appropriations, authority to limit tax and benefit indexing, or power to impose standby taxes.

Whether such radical changes in current practice are desirable depends on whether one believes that the nation's current budgetary problems are endemic to the existing system or are the product of a rather peculiar con-

---

30. See "Additional Views of The Honorable David R. Obey" in Committee on the Budget, House of Representatives, *Report on the First Concurrent Resolution on the Budget-Fiscal Year 1983*, Report No. 97-521, May 17, 1983, and H. Con. Res. 602, 97th Congress.

fluence of recent events. If the latter is the case, some ad hoc mechanism for muddling through the next few years would be preferable to any permanent shift in budgetary power.

Conclusion

The paramount domestic problem facing the nation is its huge structural budget deficits. Whether the United States has the political leadership, institutional mechanisms, or public will needed to handle this problem is an open question. Although some people may take heart from the fact that significant budgetary adjustments were made during the past three years, the deficit dilemma facing the nation today represents a profoundly different challenge. The policy shifts advocated by the Reagan administration and implemented through the congressional budget process tied the immediate sacrifice of domestic program reductions to the promise of future benefits arising from a secure defense, low taxes, and a robust, low-inflation economy. These proposals were put forward after a prolonged period of poor economic performance. The solutions to the structural deficits of the future offer no such opportunity for real or imagined trade-offs. Higher taxes and reduced program levels are required to keep an economy that has improved but not yet reached an acceptable level from faltering.

Meeting this challenge will call for leadership, institutional flexibility, and a willingness to compromise deeply held goals. Leadership will be required if disruptive partisan political advantage is to be eschewed and if unity is to be provided during the inherently disintegrating retrenchment process. Institutional flexibility will be required because the congressional system and the budget process are not designed to facilitate prolonged periods of decremental budgeting. Compromise will be required because there is no strong consensus regarding what should be done to reduce the deficits. The congressional budget process can facilitate but not force action, leadership, and compromise.

COMMENTS

Louis Fisher

Reischauer argues that enormous future deficits appear to be inevitable because of the Reagan administration tax cuts and defense spending increases, combined with additional costs of servicing the federal debt. He implies that economic growth will not generate enough revenues to materially reduce those deficits. "The budget dilemmas of the future," he says, "look more intractable than those of the past." He further notes that these dramatic shifts in the federal budget were facilitated by the congressional budget process inaugurated in 1974.

Reischauer concludes that without the active cooperation, participation, and leadership of the president, Congress cannot change priorities sufficiently to control the deficits. That is particularly the case when different parties control the two houses of Congress or the two political branches. Only a fundamental shift of power between the branches or a major internal restructuring of congressional power will create the conditions necessary for reducing future deficits.

According to Reischauer, the Budget Act had only marginal impact on budget outcomes prior to Reagan. Little evidence exists that the congressional budget process constrained spending. Neither the Ford nor the Carter administration took much interest in the process, even though Carter depended on it for his economic stimulus program in 1977. It took the Reagan administration, combined with a newly Republican Senate and a coalition of Republicans and conservative Democrats in the House, to use the congressional budget process for presidential objectives. The Gramm-Latta budget resolution and reconciliation bill led to deep cuts in domestic programs, major tax reductions, and a huge defense buildup. The result, in Reischauer's words, was "the most significant reordering of budget priorities since the New Deal."

Reagan's initiatives produced profound changes in the congressional budget process (some of them already under way). Budget resolutions reflected a multiyear focus, especially for entitlement changes and tax cuts. Reconciliation became firmly entrenched as a spring exercise associated with the

414

first resolution, rather than the autumn operation anticipated by the Budget Act. The 1981 reconciliation also dwarfed in size and comprehensiveness the effort made the previous year by President Carter and Congress. Moreover, reconciliation by Reagan was directed at authorizations and spawned a number of extraneous, non-budget-related legislation. Finally, budget resolutions exercised new controls over federal credit activity; Congress used deferred enrollment to control spending bills; and Congress for all intents and purposes dispensed with the second budget resolution. As a result, budget targets in the spring became the binding totals for subsequent spending bills.

Throughout this period, passage of a budget resolution assumed more significance than the substance of the resolution itself. Process triumphed over content, in large part because Congress feared presidential criticism and public condemnation if it failed to adopt a budget resolution.

Reischauer further notes that Reagan was able to exploit the congressional budget process to achieve a coherent, multiyear program that would have been impossible to enact under the prior, fragmented legislative process. Reagan's accomplishment also reflected conditions unrelated to procedure: his "mandate" in 1980, Republican control of the Senate, the remarkable unity and loyalty among congressional Republicans, Reagan's rhetorical skills and personal lobbying, Stockman's knowledge, and the disarray among Democrats who calculated that a failure of supply-side economics could damage Reagan and the GOP.

By 1982, many of these forces had either disappeared or subsided. What can we expect of the future? Can the political process yield the necessary tax increases and spending cuts that are necessary to reduce out-year deficits? Reischauer sees the budget process threatened. The Reagan administration has withdrawn much of its support for the congressional budget process. Prominent Republicans in Congress now advocate the repeal or weakening of the Budget Act of 1974. Authorizing and appropriating committees continue to have deep misgivings about the process. Democrats, perhaps to pose as the party of fiscal responsibility, voice support for the congressional budget process. Nevertheless, according to Reischauer, the process "could grind to a halt or even explode if a subsequent economic downturn is blamed on congressional budgetary inaction."

While alluding to a number of reform ideas considered by the Beilenson Task Force and others, Reischauer does not endorse any particular proposal or believe that singly or together they would permit the process to handle current problems. He sees the need for "fundamental shifts of power" to increase the authority of the leadership and to strengthen party discipline. How this is to be achieved in the present climate of decentralization in Congress and subcommittee independence he does not say, but I would agree with Reischauer that if the process is to work well it needs far greater interest and direction from party leaders. He also suggests, without much enthusiasm, that Congress might strengthen the Budget Committees or experiment with the Obey omnibus budget bill.

Constitutional amendments to balance the budget or to give the president line-item veto authority are other proposals identified by Reischauer, but he discourages such permanent shifts in power in favor of ad hoc mechanisms to deal with what he regards as the "rather peculiar confluence of recent events." He sees more hope in broad spending freezes, reduced indexation of taxes and entitlements, or across-the-board cuts that will appear to the public as fairly distributed.

I have no basic disagreement with Reischauer's account of the congressional budget process during the three Reagan years. What I find peculiar is that in the final pages of the paper the process drifts into the background, gradually fading from view. I have said some unkind things in the past about the Budget Act. Reischauer, I think, delivers the ultimate insult by ignoring the congressional budget process as a vehicle for effective control, pushing it to the side as an irrelevance not worth fixing.

Why do we have such difficulty focusing on the congressional budget process? It has been *described* in many studies, but rarely does anyone bother to ask fundamental questions about the *purpose* of the process. Why is it there? What do we expect of it? How has it performed?

If we are unclear, or uncaring, about its objectives, how can we decide if the process is worthwhile or worthless? Surely after eight years we should be in a position to ask basic questions and come up at least with some tentative assessments.

Why does Congress go through this agonizing process? Is it to restrain spending? I think the history of the 1974 statute makes restraint a key objective. The notion that the Budget Act was meant to be "neutral" toward spending seems to me wholly unsupportable. Yet I find very little evidence that the act has operated with restraint. In fact, because of the incentives (and we should identify them as clearly as possible), I believe that the process generates more spending than would otherwise have occurred. There are many reasons for this situation, but in part it results from the ability of authorizing and appropriations committees to rationalize their actions by pointing to the higher levels allowed by budget resolutions. (Other incentives are discussed in a paper I delivered at the University of Oklahoma in early 1982, to be published by the Johns Hopkins University Press in a book entitled *Congressional Budgeting: Power, Process, and Policy.*)

Was the purpose of the 1974 act to accelerate the authorization-appropriation process, permitting Congress to complete action by the start of the fiscal year and avoid continuing resolutions? Yes, that was indeed a purpose, and for the first few years the record looked promising. But the last four to five years have taken a turn for the worse, so that the timetable is now far behind what it was prior to 1974—even with the additional three months gained by moving the fiscal year from July 1 to October 1.

The Budget Act was supposed to provide a mechanism by which members of Congress could decide budget priorities by voting on functional categories in the budget resolution. The record here has not been good. Transfer amendments—taking money from one functional category and placing it in another—inevitably fail. Members of Congress seem to follow the principle cited by Charles Schultze: never openly do harm. Under the old system, without explicit floor votes, budget priorities could be altered by reporting an appropriations bill with less than the administration wanted, whereas in a separate appropriations bill Congress could add more.

What were the other goals in 1974? To make members of Congress more accountable and responsible by forcing them to vote on aggregate and deficits? Especially in recent years, members have used a number of ingenious strategems to avoid a vote on deficits: adopting a second resolution that "reaffirms" the totals in the first resolution (when everyone knows that the earlier figures were wholly unrealistic); relying on an automatic triggering device for the second resolution, thereby dispensing with the need to vote; and tucking in the higher deficits the following year when Congress adopts a revised second resolution (but without a separate vote or debate because attention is then turned to the upcoming year).

In 1983 the House advocated an "adjustment resolution" that would raise the totals to take into account "technical and economic adjustments." The resolution would be facilitated by fast-track procedures and limited time for debate. The Senate refused to go along, partly because political mistakes and miscalculations can be hidden behind "technical and economic adjustments."

I might also point to the procedure adopted by the House in 1979 to handle increases in the public debt limit. Instead of taking a separate vote on this bill, the new procedure lifts the public debt limit from the spring budget resolution and places it in a joint resolution, which is then "deemed" to have passed the House. In effect, the vote on the budget resolution counts also as a vote on the joint resolution raising the debt limit. This may seem an efficient approach, but the public debt limit rarely commands much attention during debate on the budget resolution, and budget resolutions in recent years have been notoriously unrealistic about budget deficits. This appears to be another step away from accountability.

One final question. Should Congress try to be president? Should an inherently decentralized institution pretend that it can act in a comprehensive, systematic, coordinated manner? If the process called for in the 1974 act is good, wouldn't the Obey omnibus budget bill be even better, bringing all appropriations, entitlements, and revenues together for action at a single stroke? To me the answer in every case is no, but it is time to begin asking basic questions about what we want from Congress.

COMMENTS

Douglas J. Bennet

Robert Reischauer's excellent paper is elegantly instructive. We see a relatively young institution maturing in a time of writhing partisan and philosophical change as the Reagan administration takes over, the Senate changes hands, and large numbers of Democrats scramble to adjust. Reischauer estimates the effects of this turbulence on the budget process: the development of a multiyear focus as policymakers stretched out toward the warmth of promised economic recovery, only to recoil in the cold prospect of large structural deficits "as far as the eye can see"; the draconian use of reconciliation; the atrophy of the second resolution; budgetary gamesmanship coming out of the closet; and the very preservation of the budget process becoming a measure of achievement. He quite correctly deemphasizes magical procedural fixes that might somehow save us from our current budgetary paralysis.

Looking ahead, Reischauer concludes that the budget process may be able to sustain *either* the political pressures necessary to handle out-year deficits, *or* fights over special interest issues, but not both. I differ with Reischauer only in believing, forlornly, that we must do both.

To appreciate fully the stresses of the past three years, we need only think back to the deliberative environment at the beginning of the budget process about a decade ago: Congress, after careful consideration and political compromise, acted to create what everyone knew could be a sweeping innovation in the way America did its public business. In the Senate, at least, the Muskie-Bellmon team gave forceful bipartisan leadership from the outset.

The acknowledged purpose of the reform was to *enhance deliberation* while preserving the organic pluralism of the political process. The first resolution was for making broad priority decisions; the second was for cleanup; and reconciliation was available only if the political process failed. The idea of a single spasm of binding "reconciliation" at the outset of a budget year would have seemed irresponsible and politically unachievable in those far-off times.

419

Of course life was easier then. Those were the days of double-digit deficits. The Budget Committees had a tactical advantage because they knew a little about how the system was supposed to work, whereas other committees, individual members, and the White House, in that order, only later learned how to play the game. As Reischauer points out, the Reagan White House was the first for which the budget process was a familiar and usable instrument.

Back then, the primary objective was setting spending priorities. Fiscal policy was an important but secondary concern. Tax expenditure priorities came third. Reischauer demonstrates how, with the "fiscalization" of the policy debate, this pattern has been partially reversed; now revenue, expenditure, deficits, and defense numbers drive out consideration of all other substantive priorities.

To comprehend the difference in mood and behavior between 1974 and the early 1980s, we need to recall one series of dismal events that Reischauer was perhaps too polite to include—those surrounding the constitutional amendment to require a balanced budget. This was to be the ultimate structural weapon to guarantee what political deliberation and economic reality denied.

By 1981, proponents were only four states short of the two-thirds necessary for a constitutional convention to take up the balanced budget amendment. It became a litmus test issue in the 1982 election year. The Senate passed it comfortably on August 4.

One year ago today President Reagan led a street demonstration beneath the windows of the Capitol in support of House action. The next day a majority in the House voted for the amendment but missed the magic two-thirds, and the amendment evaporated like the mirage it always was.

Where are we on this anniversary of what has to count as an historic low point in deliberate fiscal and budgetary management? The budget process itself has clearly survived, and Reischauer believes it is strong, on balance. The voice of responsible leadership can once again be heard among both parties in Congress. Political processes short-circuited in the blitz of 1981 have begun to reassert themselves. Perhaps we are relearning the differences between demonstrations and deliberation, form and substance, and escapism and leadership.

Perhaps the spasms of the early 1980s will prove to have marked America's adolescent passage from an era of plenty and pork-barrel decisionmaking to an era of constraints requiring deliberate allocation. On the spending side, this process began before the Budget Act and may have completed itself with the blockbuster reconciliation of 1981. On the revenue side, this process may have occurred somewhere between the profligate tax reductions of 1981 and the morning-after reforms of 1982. Perhaps we are approaching a time when we can face up to the fiscal and budgetary decisionmaking that reality requires of us.

For the moment, however, we are paralyzed. We are numbed into inaction by the out-year structural deficits. All eyes are focused on those macro numbers, and no one sees a way to act upon them. There appears to be agreement that there will be no significant tax increase before 1985, by which time the need for general revenues will be compounded by the prospect of a more or less imminent Medicare default. Only through crisis, one hears, will the logjam be broken.

Meanwhile, challenges far beyond reducing the size of the deficit lie untended. We should be making choices today about improving the capabilities of our people, renewing our infrastructure, enhancing and deploying our savings for greater productivity, and constraining global military expenditures.

Somehow we have to mobilize the political will to deal with these choices as we deal with the deficits. We really do not have the luxury of tending just one or the other, and certainly not the luxury of ignoring both. Nor is tinkering with budget procedures likely to do more than momentarily distract us from our real work. Unless we are to abandon our collective destinies to the stresses of accelerating social inequities here at home and to the leadership of other nations in the world, we must begin now to act on the choices before us.

ISSUES IN BUDGET ACCOUNTING

Robert W. Hartman

In the early 1980s, interest has revived in the issues concerning federal budget concepts, coverage, and accounting that had been discussed—and resolved or buried—in the past. Some problems that were "solved" in the past—such as inclusion of Social Security in the unified budget—have recently come unstuck. The fast growth of tax preferences and federal credit activities and the slow growth of spending for public works have all spurred new interest in revising budgetary accounting rules and procedures to attain greater control and balance in federal fiscal policy. Although budgetary accounting rules, as such, have no peer in the roster of dull subjects, the debate over such rules has become quite heated.

One reason for the heat is that accounting rules are often a smoke screen for obtaining a desired political outcome. Advocates of a particular treatment of tax preferences in the budget process, for example, may invoke public finance principles, but each advocate almost always has in mind some specific outcome that supplies the motivating force for the procedural reform.

Second, many of the proposals for changes in budget concepts or accounting reflect a reaction in Congress to the budget reforms of the past decade. Because the new procedures realigned power within Congress, many members whose turf was constrained would like to restore the good old days— or to prevent budget reform from going even further—and accounting changes can often provide the vehicle for power shifts.

Finally, budget concepts and accounting rules generate strong feelings because attainment of the ideal set of rules is, ultimately, a frustrating quest for the impossible. People expect too much from the federal budget. It should be a document that steers Congress toward the appropriate fiscal policy, encourages comparison of all relevant alternatives, helps federal managers keep track of what is going on, and remains simple enough so that meaningful public debate can be based upon it. As this paper illustrates, these goals cannot be fully achieved by one set of accounting rules and definitions, and pursuit of this Holy Grail is probably counterproductive. (On the other hand, some changes in federal accounts are probably warranted and as long as these are not oversold, their adoption could help decision making.)

This paper reviews the thinking on these issues. The next section summarizes the recent controversies over old issues relating to budget concepts. Then comes a discussion of newer issues that have received less attention. These issues relate to the timing and definition of budget outlays.

Traditional Issues of Coverage and Concept

The budget's treatment of trust funds and of credit programs and taxes was last comprehensively revised in 1969, following (for the most part) the recommendations of a national commission.[1] Recent challenges to current budget practices have been so ably reviewed by the Committee for Economic Development (CED) that in this section I will frequently refer the reader to its report for further details.[2]

Social Security.   Far and away the most important change made by the unified budget, first introduced in 1969, was to consolidate federal trust funds with other federal accounts. Previously the administrative budget (which excluded trust funds) had vied for attention with the consolidated cash budget (which included them). In making the case for inclusion of trust funds, the President's Commission on Budget Concepts argued that the financial activity of any government-owned entity should be included in the budget. Such comprehensiveness was needed to ensure that the impact of the government on income and employment and on Treasury cash borrowing needs would be properly measured. In addition, the commission stressed the need to have one budget rather than the several budgets that are inevitable if a major part of government is left out of the central budget. The aim was to gain simplicity and to avoid confusing the public and Congress. The commission did not stress the idea that including the trust funds in the budget would facilitate trade-offs between trust fund programs and other government activities. In fact the commission endorsed the continuation of earmarking specific revenue

---

1. Report of the President's Commission on Budget Concepts (Washington, D.C.: U.S. Government Printing Office, October 1967).

2. Committee for Economic Development (CED), *Strengthening the Federal Budget Process: A Requirement for Effective Fiscal Control* (Washington, D.C.: August 1983).

sources for "well-defined programs of a long-run character" despite the "partial isolation from the budget and appropriations process that results."[3] Since 1969, trust funds have been included in the budget.

The Social Security amendments enacted in March 1983 require that Social Security—including the Medicare Hospital Insurance (HI) Trust Fund as well as the Old Age, Survivors, and Disability Insurance (OASDI) Trust Funds—be removed from the budget in fiscal year (FY) 1993. As a transitional step the amendments require that these programs be isolated as functionally distinct lines but remain in the budget from 1985 to 1993. The Budget Committees have already implemented the latter requirement by splitting out function 570 (Medical Insurance, which includes all of Medicare) and function 650 (Old Age, Survivors, and Disability Insurance). Receipts of the OASDHI payroll tax have not been "paired" with these functions, however.

The decision to eventually remove Social Security from the budget, which emerged as a compromise from the conference committee on the amendments,[4] did not turn at all on the key issues stressed by the president's budget commission. By now everyone agrees, as a matter of principle, that the budget should be comprehensive and simple. Most of the members supporting exclusion regard it as an important exception to the rule of comprehensiveness, and they would, I surmise, believe that since we already have two budget deficits to contend with (on-budget and off-budget, see below), adding a third component ought not be too complicated for a computerized world.

Exclusion was favored by an unusual assortment of bedfellows. Because severe budget deficits appear likely for years, some members of Congress viewed Social Security as vulnerable. They feared "balancing the budget on the backs of the elderly" through such measures as raising the retirement age and cutting cost-of-living adjustments.[5] Getting Social Security out of the budget seemed to be a remedy. On the other side was a group who believed that political pressures caused by skyrocketing medical costs and constant increases in the population receiving Social Security would make it all but inevitable that general revenues rather than a dedicated payroll tax would be used to finance Social Security. And then the lid on spending would really be off. Taking Social Security out of the budget would lessen the chances of that happening. Interestingly, neither people who feared Social Security spending cuts nor people who feared that resources would be drawn unceasingly to

---

3. Report of the President's Commission on Budget Concepts, pp. 6–7, 24–28.

4. The Senate bill had not endorsed removal from the budget; the House bill had called for immediate removal.

5. The 1983 amendments already were making some of these changes. Taking Social Security off the budget represents a "never again" kind of gesture.

Social Security from other sectors admitted that these considerations were germane: Everybody argued exclusively for the fiscal integrity of Social Security. (It's a bad time when the only way to get fiscal integrity is off the budget.)

The recent CED report put this issue into perspective. It called for Congress to rescind the provision in the 1983 amendments that takes Social Security out of the federal budget. The report repeated the budget commission's call for comprehensiveness and simplicity, but it stressed the precedent-setting nature of taking Social Security off-budget. If Social Security should be off-budget because it represents "major long-term concerns...that should not be thrown into the same hopper with ordinary budget items and become subject to year-to-year adjustments," CED asks whether the same case cannot be made for defense spending or human capital programs. If one program that relies on earmarked funds goes off the budget, "demands will grow that other similarly funded programs should be removed as well." Finally the CED report acknowledged that although Social Security is a very special program that should not be subject to frequent change from short-term considerations, but for the long run it endorses Alice Rivlin's view that:

> Inclusion of Social Security in the unified budget does force the Congress to ask the right question: how much can the nation's economy afford for social insurance given competing claims on the economy and given the willingness of taxpayers to pay? Making Social Security a separate entity would unnecessarily narrow this question into "how high a level of benefits can payroll taxes support?"—a question that ignores competing claims, alternative tax sources, and the burden of other taxes.[6]

The CED view seems about right to me. If Social Security *alone* were handled apart from the regular budget (as it indeed was in 1983—the amendments flowed from a special commission, not from a budget resolution), we could avoid confusion and get the total deficit right. But its exclusion from the budget threatens to be imitated in scores of other programs, and that outcome would destroy the simplicity and controllability of the budget. Moreover, if Congress decides that Social Security benefits must be pared or that general funds should become a major source of financing, it will be able to "find" Social Security whether it is on- or off-budget.[7]

---

6. CED, *Strengthening the Federal Budget Process*, p. 28.

7. The creation of separate functions for Social Security was supposed to draw the eye to this program. I always managed to find it by a simpler method: I looked for the biggest nondefense number.

The Federal Financing Bank and the Budget

The largest item now excluded from the unified budget is the activities of off-budget federal entities. In FY 1982 those entities spent $17 billion that was not recorded in the unified budget. About 20 percent of this spending was for the purchase of petroleum for the Strategic Petroleum Reserve (SPR), which was shifted off the budget in the Omnibus Budget Reconciliation Act of 1981. But for that, under current budgetary accounting rules, SPR would be on-budget. (The desirability of counting asset purchases and sales in the budget is discussed later.)

Virtually all of the remaining off-budget activity is attributable to the Federal Financing Bank (FFB). FFB was established in 1974 as an off-budget unit within the U.S. Treasury, with the intention of lowering government agencies' interest costs by having the Treasury borrow on their behalf.

For one segment of the FFB's activity, its off-budget status is appropriate, and this treatment enhances the meaning of the budget. For two other segments, the budget treatment is misleading and may have distorted program decisions.

About one-fifth of the $124 billion in assets that FFB had accumulated by the end of FY 1982 was in "agency debt" (see table 1). Such holdings arise when an agency like the Export-Import Bank issues its own debt to (that is, borrows from) FFB and lends the proceeds to a foreign importer. Since the loan to the foreigner is counted as a federal outlay in the Export-Import Bank account (after netting against repayments as is explained later), there is no need for the transaction with FFB to appear in the budget. (Counting it as an outlay of the FFB would be counting the same loan twice.) Thus such transactions properly show the spending to be emanating from the program agency and contributing to the unified budget deficit.

A quite different story holds for FFB's purchases of "loan assets"—nearly one-half of its holdings. For these transactions, the Farmers Home Administration (FmHA) and the Rural Electrification Administration (REA), after making direct loans to their clients, use the loans as collateral for issuing Certificates of Beneficial Ownership to FFB. Under the statutes establishing FmHA and REA, the sale of certificates is to be treated in those agencies' budget lines as negative outlays.[8] As a result, if FmHA lends $1 billion for rural housing and borrows $1 billion from FFB by selling it certificates, FmHA's net outlays as reported in the budget will be zero. Since the government nonetheless disburses $1 billion,

---

8. This situation is further complicated by the fact that the REA itself is an off-budget federal entity.

TABLE 1

FFB OUTSTANDING HOLDINGS BY TYPE OF ACTIVITY
FY 1980–FY 1982
(In $ billions)

Type of Activity	1980	1981	1982
Loan Assets			
Agricultural Credit Insurance (FmHA)	37.9[a]	22.4	23.4
Rural Housing Insurance (FmHA)	—	21.1	23.9
Rural Development Insurance (FmHA)	—	5.3	6.4
Rural Electrification Administration	1.9	2.6	3.1
Other	0.6	0.4	0.4
Subtotal	40.4	51.8	57.2
Direct Loans to Guaranteed Borrowers			
Foreign Military Sales	7.2	9.1	11.4
Rural Electrification Administration	8.4	12.3	16.3
Student Loan Marketing Association	2.3	4.3	5.0
Low-Rent Public Housing	0.1	0.9	1.6
Rail Programs	1.1	1.5	1.1
Small Business Administration	0.5	0.6	0.7
Seven States Energy Corporation	0.7	0.9	1.3
Other	1.2	1.5	1.9
Subtotal	21.5	31.1	39.3
Agency Debt			
Export-Import Bank	10.1	12.4	14.0
Tennessee Valley Authority	8.9	10.9	12.3
Postal Service	1.5	1.3	1.2
Other	0.6	0.3	0.3
Subtotal	21.1	24.9	27.8
Total ($ billions)	$83.0	$107.8	$124.3

SOURCE: *Budget of the U.S. Government, Fiscal Years 1982, 1983, and 1984*, Special Analyses.
   a.   Includes activities of the Rural Development Insurance Fund and Rural Housing Insurance Fund.

an outlay entry of $1 billion is needed somewhere. If FFB were on the budget, the outlay would be shown in its accounts. Since FFB is not on the budget, the budget documents show the purchase of loan assets by the FFB as outlays of "off-budget federal entities," which, when added to the unified budget deficit, yield the "total deficit."[9]

9. Both OMB and CBO have settled on a common terminology for *budget deficit* and *total deficit. Budget of the United States Government, Fiscal Year 1984* (Washington, D.C.: U.S. Government Printing Office, January 1983), table 22; and *Baseline Budget Projections for Fiscal Years 1984–1988* (Washington, D.C.: Congressional Budget Office, February 1983), summary table 5.

What is the problem here? It is that the budget understates the activity in the originating agency—FmHA, in our example—and the activity of the budget functions that can take advantage of loan asset sales to the FFB. (The energy function would have been 111 percent greater in FY 1982 if all FFB activity related to it had been attributed to that function.) The solution to this problem has nothing to do with FFB's being off the budget, but has to do with the treatment of loan asset sales as a negative outlay. If loan asset sales were treated as a means of finance, as in the case of agency debt, then the activity would be properly attributed to the originating agency.[10]

A somewhat different problem is caused by a third facet of FFB activity. Loans guaranteed by federal agencies are excluded from the budget, and such guarantees (until recently, as described in the next section) have not required enacting an appropriation. (Funds to make good on a default would require an appropriation, but at a later date.) FFB, however, is authorized to lend directly to borrowers whose loan notes carry a full guarantee of repayment by a federal agency. Thus, for example, in FY 1982 the Department of Defense (DoD) guaranteed loans of $4.4 billion to foreign governments for the purchase of military equipment, services, and training with the funds provided by FFB.[11] This transaction gave rise to no budget entry for DoD, since its role was solely as guarantor.[12] The disbursement of funds by FFB is a direct loan and in principle should enter the budget, but since FFB is an off-budget entity the $4.4 billion (after netting for repayments) enters the government's books under-the-line as a component of the off-budget deficit.

The problem here is threefold. First, these loans clearly are direct loans, with the capital provided directly by the government. To be consistent with the treatment of other direct loans, they should be in the budget despite the appearance of being only a guaranteed loan. Second, such FFB direct loans to guaranteed borrowers should be recorded under the agency that gives the guarantee, if the budget document is to accurately reflect how the government is channeling resources. Third, just as any other direct loan requires an appropriation, so should the agencies that originate these loans be required to receive budget authority. The solution is quite simply to treat FFB direct loans as on-budget outlays, attribute them to the originating agency, and make them subject to appropriations limits.

---

10. When the originating agency is also off-budget, as the REA is, simply correcting the accounting treatment of loan asset sales may not be enough to straighten out the budget documents.

11. When these loans are forgiven, outlays are recorded in the budget. Incidentally, these functions are classified under international affairs, not national defense, and under ''Funds Appropriated to the President,'' not the Department of Defense.

12. Interest rates are set by FFB on these (and all other transactions) at a slight margin above Treasury borrowing costs.

Although no one can prove that loan asset sales and FFB direct loans have caused Congress to allocate more to the agencies that are heavy users of these financing means than would have been the case with more sensible accounting rules, the tenacity with which such agencies oppose budgeting changes suggests they may have reaped some benefits. The Budget Committees have long been aware of these problems, and the FY 1984 budget resolution contains "sense of Congress" language calling upon the committees with jurisdiction over FFB to "consider expeditiously legislation" to correct the loan asset and FFB direct loan problems. At least one bill that would do just that (S. 1679, modestly titled the "Honest Budgeting Act of 1983") was considered in the Senate in 1983.

Credit Budget Issues.   Credit washed through the FFB is only part of the iceberg of federal lending activity. Most of the ice is excluded from the unified budget because it is in the form of guaranteed loans. Between 1972 and 1982 net guarantees outstanding rose by $172 billion, while net direct loans outstanding rose by $158 billion.

Under current budget practices the principal extended to a borrower under a federal guarantee is not counted in the budget because the transaction does not give rise to a cash flow from any federal entity to an outsider. Outlays are registered only when the government pays a lending institution for a defaulted loan. Some people see this practice as an accounting flaw. They argue that the omission of guaranteed loans from the budget understates federal activity or influence, and therefore the guarantee should be added to the budget. If this logic were accepted, it is hard to know where one stops. Federal safety and health regulations are not meaningfully counted in the budget, nor are financial regulations, monetary policies, or tax preferences. Yet all these are an exercise of federal influence, and potentially more important than federal credit programs (or even direct spending). There is no way to really add up federal credit guarantees, regulatory activities, tax preferences, and monetary policy into a single budget entity.[13]

---

13. The government does do some indiscriminate adding up in the federal credit area. Each year the Special Analyses of the Budget report a federal participation rate, which is the ratio of the sum of all federal direct and guaranteed loans and the lending activity of government-sponsored enterprises to the total volume of credit extended. If you think this is a meaningful measure, consider the following experiment: Suppose the federal tax laws were revised to eliminate the exclusion from taxable income of interest on state and local bonds. In its place would be a federal guarantee on these municipal bonds—a much weaker form of subsidy we'd all agree. The "federal participation rate" would go way up even as federal involvement went down. By the same token, in the 1970s and early 1980s when high interest rates, bracket creep, and federal spending restraints greatly increased the attractiveness of tax-exempt instruments, their expansion was probably pulling the federal participation rate down. In short, the classification of "loans extended under federal auspices" that defines federal participation is an incomplete measure of federal influence on credit markets.

The legitimate issue in the federal credit province is one of control. If the ordinary budget does not encompass loan guarantee activity except when a default occurs—much later than the point of decision on lending—how can the government limit such activity and prevent its substitution for the more tightly controlled on-budget programs?

The answer to this has been evolving in the years since 1980 under the rubric of "the credit budget." Recognizing that greater control over burgeoning credit required a vehicle outside the regular budget, the Carter administration in 1980 invented the credit budget, a free-standing accounting and (in principle) control mechanism. The credit budget covers direct lending and loan guarantees. Each of these is counted on a "gross" basis, without offset for repayment of past loans, on the grounds that such loan originations are a better basis for control.[14] Moreover, since 1980 most (but not all) direct loan obligations and guaranteed loan commitments have received prior approval in the pertinent appropriations law.[15]

The remaining problems of control in the credit area are twofold. First, the mechanism by which the credit budget is implemented in Congress has not been fully worked out. Under the regular budget the aggregate levels of spending and taxes specified in the budget resolution are allocated to committees and then enforced by various means. In addition, reconciliation (instructions to committees to report legislation achieving specified dollar savings) has been used to enforce the budget resolution. This process has never been used fully on the credit budget and, as a result, full control over federal credit has not been attained. Establishment of enforcement procedures for the credit budget ranks high on most budget reformers' agenda for the future.[16] Second, Congress has not seriously tackled the problem of how to compare programs controlled by the credit budget with kindred programs in the regular budget. Specifically, if the credit budget were fully implemented, each Appropriations Committee would be given three ceilings: one for budget authority (and outlays) of regularly budgeted items, one for direct loans, and one for guaranteed loans. A properly functioning budget process would allow the committee to trade an excess in one account for savings in another, but not

14. Direct loans, thus, appear in both the credit budget and the regular budget. If properly understood, there is nothing wrong with this arrangement. Gross direct loan volume is controlled under the credit budget, while net direct loan outlays appear in the unified budget as an entry that properly identifies cash flows between the government and the public.

15. The appropriations laws now contain language limiting direct loan obligations and new guarantee loan commitments. These place an upper limit on the amount of loan activity an agency can undertake in the same way that budget authority sets an upper bound on conventional program activity.

16. CED, *Strengthening the Federal Budget Process.*

necessarily on a dollar-for-dollar basis. One suggestion has been that for purposes of enforcing budget resolutions, loan dollars be weighted to reflect their interest subsidy content.[17] Other possibilities include the creation of a federal bank that would be the exclusive purveyor of federal credit. All federal agencies would have to receive appropriations sufficient to compensate the bank for loss arising from the issuance or guarantee of loans to the agencies' clients.[18]

Tax Expenditures

Tax expenditures are the budgetary consequences of special provisions of the tax code that provide for more lenient tax treatment of an item than would be the case under a normal tax structure.[19] How you count these things and what you do with the resulting list of numbers now numbering 105 items under the definition applied by the Congressional Budget Office (CBO), depend very much on what you think "the problem" is.

From one perspective, a tax expenditure is simply an alternative to a direct spending program. For example, instead of allowing individuals to deduct interest paid on home mortgages, the government could subsidize lenders to allow them to offer the equivalent benefits (in the form of lower interest rates) to homeowners. Indeed, this approach argues that Congress would be well advised to think about tax expenditures as if they were spending programs and ask, "Would we ever vote for that in comparison with other spending programs?"

From this perspective, the right accounting concept is what is called "outlay equivalents." This is the amount of money that the government would have to spend to replace a tax preference item and leave the recipients just as well off. Like regular spending programs, outlay equivalents should be measured on a before-tax basis. Thus if the exclusion of income from transfer payments (a tax expenditure) currently saved beneficiaries (i.e., caused a revenue loss of) $100, the outlay equivalent of this program would be $125

17. Alice M. Rivlin and Robert W. Hartman, "Control of Federal Credit Under the Congressional Budget Process," *Toward A Reconstruction of Federal Budgeting* (New York: The Conference Board, 1983), pp. 80–88.

18. In this case there would be no need for a separate credit budget, and it would be necessary for the federal bank to be off-budget. CED, *Strengthening the Federal Budget Process*, pp. 56–58.

19. This is the definition that has been in use since the 1960s, when the tax expenditure concept was invented; it is still used by Congress. The Reagan administration developed a new definition in 1982. For a discussion of the differences, see *Tax Expenditures: Five-Year Budget Projections for Fiscal Years 1984–1988* (Washington, D.C.: Congressional Budget Office, October 1983).

if the beneficiaries' marginal tax rate was 20 percent. (The grant of $125 would be taxed at 20 percent, leaving the recipient with $100, exactly the gain now received from the tax preference.) Although this approach seems simple, it is not always so clear what an outlay-equivalent program would look like. For example, the outlay equivalent of the exemption of state and local bond interest could be derived by asking how much it would cost to keep all current bondholders equally well off, or alternatively by calculating the amount needed in grants to state and local governments to leave them as well off. The results are not the same.

Advocates of outlay equivalents would introduce their numbers into congressional budget considerations by allowing committees to trade off outlay equivalents against regular outlays as part of the regular budget process. The Ways and Means Committee and Finance Committee, however, have jurisdiction over taxes, while other committees have jurisdiction over comparable spending programs. A recent CBO publication discussed a mechanism for joint committee review, but so far interest in this approach is slim.[20]

In an alternative approach, the problem is viewed in more aggregative terms: Growing tax expenditures are holding federal revenues down and keeping tax rates high, thereby worsening deficits and inhibiting economic growth. From this angle, where the objective is clearly to eliminate many of the tax preferences, the proper accounting concept is "revenue loss."[21] Thus eliminating the exclusion of transfer payment income in the previous example would bring in $100 to the Treasury—which is the objective. Most lists of tax expenditures (if not otherwise described) are on a revenue-loss basis.

The people who worry about tax expenditures because of their aggregative effect usually propose to include in budget resolutions some aggregate limit on the level or growth of these items.[22] As the Treasury, the Joint Committee on Taxation, and CBO have repeatedly pointed out, however, the individual revenue-loss measures cannot simply be added up to yield the revenue gain from repeal. In estimating revenue loss from each tax preference item, it is assumed that the remainder of the tax code stays the same and that economic choices are unaffected. The revenue loss from repealing several preferences may be greater or less than the sum of the individual estimates. For example, if the deduction of mortgage interest is disallowed, some taxpayers would switch to taking the standard deduction; the same applies to

---

20. *Tax Expenditures: Budget Control Options and Five-Year Budget Projections for Fiscal Years 1983–1987* (Washington, D.C.: Congressional Budget Office, 1982).

21. Both outlay-equivalent and revenue-loss concepts are reported in Special Analyses G of the Budget and in *Tax Expenditures: Five-Year Budget Projections for Fiscal Years 1984–1988* (Washington, D.C.: Congressional Budget Office, October 1983).

22. See H.R. 1879, 98th Congress.

repeal of consumer loan interest. But the revenue gain from repealing deductibility of consumer interest, given that mortgage interest deductibility has been eliminated, will be much less than the estimate based on current law. Thus the revenue gain from joint repeal is less than the sum of the parts. An opposite example would be if several exclusions from income (such as municipal bond interest and employer-provided insurance) were repealed. In that case, because of the progressive rate structure, the revenue gain from repeal would be greater than the sum of the individual estimates. Finally, economic behavior is virtually sure to change if some tax preferences are removed, (Would you buy as much medical insurance if you had to pay tax on your employer's contribution?), but the official estimates do not take this into account.

There are enough intractable problems in both the microeconomic trade-off and the aggregate revenue approaches to tax expenditures to warrant great caution before formally installing new procedures into the budget process. For these reasons the CED has recommended limited experiments with joint consideration of tax expenditure and spending programs in related areas.[23]

It is important to rethink how the revenue procedures in the budget process could be improved in the next few years. Currently budget resolutions set targets for aggregate revenues and may issue reconciliation instructions to the tax committees to raise revenues by X dollars in each of Y years. Since it is a near certainty that the X's are going to be very large in the near future, the question becomes whether Congress as a whole wishes to offer guidance to the tax committees beyond a specific dollar amount of revenue enhancement. According to one school of thought, it is the exclusive job of the tax committees to evaluate alternative revenue raisers against tax policy criteria and so budget resolutions should not go beyond specifying aggregate revenue changes. This argument is very strong for small revenue changes, but it weakens when we are talking about major tax increases. In that event, Congress as a whole may want to guide the tax committees further, and the tax committees should welcome nonintrusive guidance.

Current budget procedures are flexible enough to allow for the dollar amounts specified in reconciliation instructions to be supplemented by "sense of Congress" language that would guide tax committee deliberations. For example: "The sense of Congress is that at least one-quarter of the new revenue be derived by base broadening in the functional areas of commerce and housing credit and health and that no more than one-quarter of any proposed base broadening be in the function income security." This is the

---

23. CED, *Strengthening the Federal Budget Process*, p. 60.

kind of guidance that makes use of the tax expenditure concept, but does not push the numbers beyond their capability or tie the hands of the tax committees.

Capital Budgeting. Capital budgeting was Washington's favorite buzzword in the 1980s, before it was crowded out by industrial policy. The pleading for the institution of a capital budget for the federal government preceded any agreement over what such a change meant. Indeed, there are still many formulations of capital budgeting, although one version seems to have temporarily won out in the political arena.

Office of Management and Budget (OMB) Director David Stockman has provided a useful summary of the three major conceptions of capital budgeting.[24] At the weak end of the spectrum is simply providing more and better information about how the budget is divided among capital and operating programs. In the middle is the proposal that the existing budget be split into two parts with the "implied notion of general tax financing for (the) operating budget and debt financing or dedicated revenue sources for capital expenditures." Finally comes what Stockman terms the "Academic Version," in which a comprehensive balance sheet of the government showing all assets and liabilities (including contingent liabilities) would become a major supplement to a narrower operating budget.

To make a long story short, the better-information variant appears to be the victor. Under H.R. 1244 reported in 1983 by the House Public Works Committee, the current presentation of the budget found in Special Analysis D of the Budget would be broadened to include analysis of projected as well as past capital spending. Other information could be provided as well. It is hard to be against more information, although OMB has made a pretty persuasive case that aggregating by "bricks and mortar" versus everything else may obscure rather than illuminate real issues. For example, hospital capital needs are inextricably bound up with third-party payments, including Medicare and Medicaid. If the capital component of these programs were split off, needed reforms of the incentive system would be harder to make. Segmenting these programs distracts attention from the crucial reimbursement and pricing issues of health care.[25]

The main alternative to the better-information route in the debate over capital budgeting was various proposals to divide the unified budget itself

---

24. David A. Stockman, "Statement on Capital Budgeting and Public Infrastructure Policy" May 3, 1983, mimeographed. Also CED, *Strengthening the Federal Budget Process*, and Sidney Jones, "The Capital Budget Alternative" in *Toward a Reconstruction of Federal Budgeting*, pp. 71–79.

25. See Stockman, "Statement," p. 25.

into two parts: a capital budget and an operating budget. Although the advocates did not always freely admit it, the clear intent was to allow substantial deficit financing only of the capital budget. In the 1967 budget commission report, the principal argument against capital budgeting of this sort ran along Keynesian lines. Because the overall balance of government spending and taxation drives aggregate spending, it is improper to distinguish between road building and soldiers' pay from a fiscal policy perspective. Moreover, the commission argued that deficits or surpluses should be geared to the overall state of employment and inflation, not to the character of public spending.

Although these arguments are repeated today, others are emphasized more in our post-fine-tuning era. For example, the CED notes that trade-offs among capital and operating alternatives that have the same objective are readily made in a unified budget but would be biased toward capital in a two-part budget. (The example chosen by CED, dam building versus research and training in irrigation methods, is not a particularly apt example of the unified budget's assistance in rational policy making.)[26]

To my mind, the capping argument against a two-part capital budget is that it would lead to chaos as program after program tried to qualify for capital budget treatment to escape being measured against taxes. Because there is no objective criterion for public capital, the line to be drawn for the two-part budget would be arbitrary and subject to endless contention. As table 2 shows, alternative definitions of capital could leave the capital share of the budget anywhere between 1 percent and 22 percent.

Finally we have what Stockman labels the "Academic Version." Although Stockman's summary evaluation (*"Alice-in-Wonderland nonsense not remotely possible or useful"*)[27] is perhaps overstated, there are indeed many problems with this approach.

The basic case against a total restructuring of the federal accounts into a comprehensive balance-sheet framework (for capital) and a properly defined (accrual accounting, capital charges) income statement is that it can't be done, except arbitrarily. For example, Social Security assets (discounted present value of Social Security tax) and liabilities (discounted present value of the benefits promised) could vary enormously with small variations in assumed economic variables. Similarly, many assets have no markets by which to ascertain a value. (What is 90 percent of Alaskan land worth?) Other assets have prices that the government could easily manipulate. (Uncle Sam has a lot to do with secondhand sales of bombers.) Policymakers should have considerable interest in attempts

---

26. CED, *Strengthening the Federal Budget Process: A Requirement for Effective Fiscal Control*, pp. 62–63.

27. Stockman, "Statement." The emphasis is his.

TABLE 2

ALTERNATIVE CAPITAL BUDGETS

Criteria	Illustrative Description	Amount	Unified Budget Division		Percentage Capital
			Capital	Operating	
			($ Billions)		
1) Federal ownership of physical structures/equipment	Corps, TVA, FAA, Forest Service facilities, Veterans Hospitals	$ 7.5	$ 7.5	$765.8	1.0
2) (1) plus commodity inventories and public acquisitions	CCC, stockpiles forest service land, parkland	5.4	12.9	760.5	1.7
3) (2) plus non-federal ownership physical acquisitions (e.g., grant-in-aid)	Highway, mass transit, sewer grants	19.5	32.3	741.0	4.2
4) (3) plus defense investments	Procurement, construction, family housing	61.9	94.3	679.1	12.2
5) (4) plus research and development	Defense, NASA, NSF, NIH	41.3	135.6	637.8	17.5
6) (5) plus net investment	FFB, SBA, Ex-Im	15.2	150.8	622.5	19.5
7) (6) plus "human capital expenditures"	Higher education aid, vocational education, manpower training, agricultural extension	20.6	171.4	602.0	22.2

SOURCE: David R. Stockman, "Statement on Capital Budgeting and Public Infrastructure Policy," May 3, 1983, mimeographed, p. 8.

to estimate all these values—in the case of Social Security, we do it all the time—but basing the nation's major planning document on such squishy and manipulable numbers strikes most people as going too far.[28]

The Academic Version's treatment of sales of physical assets exposes a shortcoming of the unified budget. As I understand it, neither the nation's balance sheet nor its operating statement would be affected by a sale of physical assets. The balance sheet would record less physical assets but more money; or if the proceeds of the sale were used to retire debt, it would show an equal reduction in assets and liabilities. By contrast, the unified budget records the sale of physical assets as negative outlays; such a sale reduces the budget deficit. Given that the government owns, for example, 744 million acres of land in the United States, this leads to the frightening prospect that someone will conclude that the way to balance the budget is to sell all that land. In fact the sale of land would not, as far as I can determine, reduce the federal stimulus at all.[29]

This shortcoming of the unified budget has long been recognized by national income accountants who strip asset sales (or purchases) from the government accounts in deriving the National Income and Product Accounts (NIPA). This supplementary account provides perhaps the best compromise in that it preserves the cash flow character of the unified budget while providing an alternative budget more suited to macroeconomic analysis (the federal sector in NIPA accounts). All too often, however, popular macroeconomic debate focuses on the unified rather than the NIPA budget; the result will be mighty misleading if the government ever does try to dump a lot of assets on the market.[30]

Emerging Accounting Issues

Some new issues of budgetary accounting, coverage, and concepts have arisen in recent years. The discussion here is intended to whet your interest, not to solve the problems.

---

28. For some further discussion and criticism, see Howard W. Bordner, "Consolidated Financial Statements for the Federal Government" *The Government Accountants Journal*, vol. 26 (Spring, Summer 1977).

29. If the government used the proceeds of the land sale to retire debt, the main economic impacts would be a lower price of land and lower interest rates. I don't believe one can give an unambiguous answer to whether these changes would lower or raise GNP (because of complicated wealth effects) but if I had to pick one it would be to raise GNP.

30. Sale of products and property by the federal government in FY 1982 amounted to "only" about $15 billion. See the *Budget of the United States Government, Fiscal Year 1984* (U.S. Government Printing Office, January 1983), pp. 9-18 and 9-19.

Timing

As the congressional budget process has evolved (and deficits have grown), the highlighting of the bottom line has focused more attention on multiyear budget costs. One requirement of the budget reform act is that CBO report the costs over a five-year period for all bills reported from a committee. In addition, budget resolutions specify spending and revenue targets over a multiyear period. This attention to the "out-years" is clearly superior to prereform myopia, but the attention also has created some new problems in budgeting, including an incentive to push costs beyond five years and a conflict between multiyear costs and budget simplicity. In this section I will summarize several recent cases in which timing was a crucial issue, indicate some of the analytical problems raised—and then not solve the problems.

Financing the Clinch River Breeder Reactor Project. In 1970 Congress authorized an electric power generating project to test a new technology. Estimated cost of building the Clinch River Breeder Reactor Project was $699 million in 1972. By 1982 the cost had mounted to over $4 billion, and Congress directed the Department of Energy (DOE) to report on options to secure private participation in the project and to reduce federal budget requirements. DOE submitted a plan in mid-1983. The plan was rejected a few months later.

The essence of the proposal was that during the construction phase of the project (1984–1990) a private corporation would provide about one-third of the construction funds in exchange for certain federal guarantees with respect to tax advantages and a guaranteed minimum rate of return. The corporation would receive a substantial share of power revenues realized after 1990, which would otherwise accrue to the federal government. The federal deficit, thus, would be less in the short run and more after 1990.[31]

Leasing or Building Federal Office Space. The General Services Administration (GSA) manages office and other space used by about 880,000 federal civilian employees, 40 percent of the entire civilian work force. In the past twenty years the portion of these workers occupying government-owned facilities has dropped from 82 percent to 50 percent. The remaining workers use space leased by GSA from private property owners. A number of budgetary accounting and legislative factors impinge on the choice of leasing versus construction of office space, but a major factor has been the OMB stipulation of the appropriate discount rate to use in cost comparisons.

---

31. For a full description of this issue, see "Comparative Analysis of Alternative Financing Plans for the Clinch River Breeder Reactor Project" (Congressional Budget Office, September 1983).

Since 1972, real property leasing versus building choices have been guided by OMB Circular A-104, specifying a real rate of interest of 7 percent, which OMB claims is the rate of return on general property leased in the private sector. (For most other investment decisions, the OMB has specified a 10 percent real discount rate since 1972.) An alternative estimate by CBO came up with 3 percent as the appropriate rate. The General Accounting Office (GAO) used yet another rate. At 3 percent, a representative set of build-lease comparisons would have resulted in a decision to build 64 percent of the space, while a 7 percent discount rate would have resulted in a decision to build only 34 percent of the space rather than leasing it.[32]

What do these cases have to say about federal budgetary accounting? First, there is a lot less here than meets the eye. Whenever the government directly finances an activity, the budget costs are front-loaded; and when the government adopts measures that substitute private finance, the costs are strung out into the future. These alternative arrangements for timing cash flows can produce drastically different short-run budgetary effects, but they don't have much to do with the real economic questions. (Do we need a Clinch River Breeder Reactor, however financed? How do we control use of office space, no matter who owns the building?) Unfortunately, the big budgetary differences catch the eye, and dealing with them rather than the underlying issues has great attraction. There should be some way for budgetary accounting to flash a red light when differences don't matter, but I don't know how to generalize such a procedure.

The second issue, which I will resolve in an equally decisive fashion, is that if deficit flows with contrasting time shapes are going to be compared in making program decisions, there is no getting around the need for "the appropriate discount rate." Readers who are familiar with the history on this subject will remember that over the years it has engaged great minds who have written at length and at great inconclusivity. This is not the place to summarize the issue, especially since an excellent summary is readily available.[33] What is evident is that a mechanism for specifying the appropriate rate of time discount should be devised to replace OMB's unmodified 1972 edicts. (Such studies, I understand, are now under way.)

Military Retirement.   Military personnel who stay in the U.S. armed forces for twenty years are eligible for an immediate, substantial annuity

---

32. This case is discussed in detail in *The Federal Buildings Program: Authorization and Budgetary Alternatives* (Washington, D.C.: Congressional Budget Office, June 1983), especially chapter 4.

33. Edward M. Gramlich, *Benefit-Cost Analysis of Government Programs* (New York: Prentice-Hall, 1981), chapter 6.

called "military retired pay." Retired pay is a noncontributory system, so the costs show up in the budget only when the beneficiary begins to draw the annuity. Today's national defense decisions are based on a concept of personnel costs that greatly understates the full costs. It is estimated, for example, that if the government were to set aside at interest each year a sum sufficient to pay future military retirement benefits, the set-aside would be in excess of 50 percent of the military payroll. As a result, the FY 1984 Department of Defense Authorization Act changed the basis for budgeting military retired pay so that the defense budget is charged budget authority and outlays for the current accrual of military retired pay liabilities. In order to preserve the cash basis of the budget—the accruals are only paper entries— off-setting accounts will be created (and counted outside of the DoD accounts) to keep the budget's bottom line on a cash basis.[34]

Accrual accounting for military retired pay will be the first significant incursion of a "foreign" concept into cash flow airspace. It could be the forerunner of further such incursions. (Indeed, the inclusion of civilian re- tirement accruals would seem to follow automatically.) The need for off- setting accounts to offset the accrual flows certainly does not help to keep the budget simple. On the basis of everything said in this paper, I should be opposed to including accruing military retired pay liabilities in the budget. Yet I favor it because avoiding the distortions in assessing full costs of military personnel seems to outweigh the possibly unfortunate precedents set by this accounting treatment. Nonetheless, the enunciation of some principles to guide the choice between simplicity and accurate measures is sorely needed.

Outlays That Aren't

In early 1983, as part of the Social Security Amendments package, Congress voted to include newly hired federal civilian employees in Social Security beginning in January 1984. Because the current civil service retire- ment system was designed to provide a major portion of employees' retirement needs, it is clear to all concerned that civil service retirement will have to be modified to be a suitable supplement to the Social Security coverage for newly hired workers.

Surprisingly enough, at the time the Social Security Amendments were enacted, only one comprehensive redesign of civil service retirement had

---

34. This case is discussed in *Accrual Accounting for Military Retirement: Alternative Ap- proaches, July 1983* (CBO). Outlays for current retirees will be removed from the defense budget.

received much legislative attention.[35] The Civil Service Pension Reform Act, which the Senate considered in 1982, provides for the supplementary pension program to have the character of a defined-contribution plan—that is, one in which the rate of contribution, rather than the rate of ultimate benefit, is fixed by law.[36] The plan combines employer contributions and voluntary employee savings (with a partial match by the government) in a fund to be invested in equities, bonds, and other prudent investments. The employer contribution would belong irrevocably to the employees in a few years, so that if the employees quit working for the government, the retirement accumulation would still be theirs.

By now everyone should be familiar with these arrangements. They are similar to the Teachers Insurance and Annuity Association/College Retirement Equities Fund (TIAA/CREF) retirement plan available to employees of educational institutions since 1950 and to the individual retirement accounts (IRAs) whose growth was encouraged by the Economic Recovery and Tax Act of 1981. But the legislation fails to simply carry over these familiar arrangements to the proposed pension program.

Instead, the Civil Service Pension Reform Act establishes a government fund to hold the employer and employee contributions. Moreover, it prohibits the government fund in its earliest years from investing in anything but government securities. To ensure that employees suffer no losses from having their contributions locked into Treasury securities during this transition, the legislation guarantees them a minimum real rate of return. In other words, a considerable amount of the complexity in the legislation is devoted to creating and defining a role for a government bureau that will ultimately do what a private industry already does.

At least part of the reason for this arrangement is its effects on federal outlays as currently defined. If the legislation called for a straight employer payment into a private IRA, the annual employer contribution would be treated as a budgetary outlay. (The employee voluntary contribution would be ignored by the budget, as it would be a transaction between two private parties.) But under the Civil Service Pension Reform's government fund, the employer

---

35. Since then another comprehensive plan—the Federal Annuity and Investment Reform (FAIR) proposal—has been introduced in the House of Representatives. See *The Congressional Record*, August 3, 1983, P.E. 3994-E4009.

36. See U.S. Congress, Senate, Committee on Governmental Affairs, *Civil Service Pension Reform Act*, 97th Cong. 2nd Sess., 1982. A full discussion of the broader issues of retirement policy appears in Robert W. Hartman, *Federal Pay and Pensions* (Washington, D.C.: The Brookings Institution, 1983).

contribution would not constitute a budgetary outlay at all.[37] Moreover, the employee contribution would enter the budget as a receipt! Finally, by prohibiting the fund from investing in private-sector securities (which would constitute an outlay) and forcing it for a period to buy only U.S. Treasury obligations (an intragovernmental transaction with no impact on the deficit) the arrangement would appear to provide a pension at less short-term budgetary cost than providing no pension at all.

The frightening thing about this example is that it shows how accounting procedures and concern about deficits could drive policy in a direction that no one, sans accounting, would want it to go. The Civil Service Pension Reform Act's sponsors are in fact vigorous supporters of converting pension reserve assets into private investment, and it would be a shame if accounting rules made that course appear too costly.

The remedy for the possibility that budgetary accounting will force the creation of an unneeded government retirement fund is to establish rules determining that federal payments will not count as outlays if they are made to the private sector under accompanying rules that the funds cannot be spent until a later time (as would be the case with a supplementary pension). Unfortunately, I suspect that if one wrote down such a set of accounting rules, someone would invent a way to finance the Clinch River Breeder Reactor by using disbursed federal "non-outlays" as collateral. More generally, it could lead to schemes by which the government obtained current resources that would escape the budget because the financing would be arranged as a delayed payment.

Real Growth in Defense

Inflation makes comparison of budget numbers over time very difficult. Although everyone by now is accustomed to talking about spending and taxes in real (after inflation) terms, the specifics of the corrections are by no means straightforward.

The debate in Congress and the media over national defense has been conducted in terms of real growth rates. The FY 1984 budget President Reagan proposed was for 10 percent real growth, the House budget resolution was for 4 percent (or maybe less), and the Senate budget resolution for 5 percent. That there may be something unhealthy about this debate is attested to by a

---

37. An agency's payment on behalf of its employee would be an outlay for the agency. But the receipt of the payment by the government retirement fund would be treated as a negative outlay of the same amount in another budget account. This is the same as current budget treatment of civil service retirement contributions by agencies. *Civil Service Retirement: Financing and Costs* (CBO, May 1981).

radio broadcast I heard which reported that the Senate had cut President Reagan's defense budget in half.

Why are the nation's political leaders using single numbers to define such a huge and complex enterprise? Should defense decisions be based on such summary measures? In the best of worlds the answer is no, but given the congressional budget process I'm afraid the answer is that some summary measure is needed. The role of the first budget resolution is to set targets for budget authority and outlays by function (and by committee, in the conference report). No "defense policy" is being made in the budget resolution; that happens when the Armed Services Committees and Defense Appropriations Subcommittees meet. So the budget resolution's role is to decide aggregative budget shares; in this context, numbers like real growth rates for various sectors are relevant—and unavoidable.[38]

Given that we need a simple number that captures defense growth, are the ones used in last year's debate the right ones? All the growth rate numbers bandied about in the defense debate were for the growth of budget authority, not outlays, which is the concept used for most of the rest of the budget. Most national defense experts contend that budget authority is the only mean- ingful planning concept for defense, because of the great variation in the rate at which different parts of defense budget authority are expended and because of the long-term nature of much of the defense budget. Thus if a major component of budget authority is a $10 billion shipbuilding program, to be expended over ten years, with only $100 million in outlays in the first year, it would be absurd to focus on outlays rather than budget authority for al- locative decisions.[39] So the focus on budget authority in the defense debate seems right. It's all downhill after that.

To calculate real growth of defense budget authority, CBO first derives a single price deflator for the defense budget by weighting price changes in each defense subsector by its share of base-year budget authority. The three primary subsectors used are personnel (26 percent of budget authority in 1983); military retired pay (7 percent of budget authority) and investment and related accounts (the remaining 67 percent of budget authority).

The inflation rate used for the personnel sector is based on the *pay increase proposal* in the budget plan being evaluated. Thus when President Reagan early in the year proposed a pay freeze for FY 1984, the personnel

---

38. Alice Rivlin has suggested that, in certain areas, setting aggregates may be as far as Congress should go. See Alice M. Rivlin, "An Intelligent Politician's Guide to Dealing with Experts" (Rand Paper P-6884-RGI, Rand Graduate Institute) April 29, 1983.

39. For macroeconomic analysis, a third budget concept—obligations—is probably the most relevant.

component of the price index used to evaluate his defense budget contributed nothing. Had Congress accepted Reagan's total for the national defense budget authority but then supported a pay increase, real growth in defense under the congressional budget would have been recorded as less than the administration's. Congress did support a pay raise in FY 1984 budget, and it was the cause of endless confusion. Everyone knew that pay rates were not the issue in defense, these rates were moving real-growth numbers around. My recommendation would be to separate personnel accounts from the rest of defense for purposes of putting together the budget resolution so as to isolate investment and related accounts. (I am not recommending a separate ceiling on personnel spending for defense, but an analytical and decision-making separation.) This action would avoid manipulation of the proposed pay raise to influence hardware decisions.

Inflation in military retired pay presents the same problems as personnel accounts. In assessing a budget plan's real growth, CBO uses the plan advocate's cost-of-living adjustment as the inflation factor. The case for removing military retired pay from the overall debate about real growth in the past was strengthened by the fact that because it was based on pay to retirees, it had absolutely nothing to do with national defense. Now that the budget is shifting to an accrual basis for retired military pay, this objection is weakened. But military retired pay still suffers from the same problems as the personnel accounts.

Finally, for those investment accounts whose budget authority represents the summation of outlays projected over many years, inflation adjustments are based on projected price levels over the period during which the budget authority will be spent. Base-year spend-out rates are assumed to hold in the future. At best, real growth in such a complex account is hard to interpret. Moreover, if the composition of investment accounts changes radically from the base year, the real-growth projections begin to lose meaning.

To summarize, the real-growth numbers at the heart of the defense budget debate were based on one part that was irrelevant to defense, another whose manipulability is confusing, and a third part that is highly relevant but tough to interpret. I wonder whether we would not do better to deflate defense numbers by the price deflator for the gross national product (the price trend for goods and services taxpayers are being asked to give up for defense) than to try to define real growth in defense.[40]

---

40. Some interesting dialogue among senators debating an armed services bill in the summer of 1983 is reported in *The Congressional Record*, (July 13, 1983), pp. S9863–S9874. See particularly the remarks of Senator Gorton on the importance of the real-growth numbers in the Senate's deliberations and his comments on OMB's eleventh-hour attempt to change the pricing assumptions made in the budget resolution.

Net Interest Outlays in the Budget

Because the growth of federal spending is so much in the public eye, it would be convenient if there were an agreed-upon, inflation-free measure of federal outlays. For some years now OMB has published a series on budget outlays in constant dollars for four major categories of spending (national defense, payments for individuals, net interest, and all other). The most intractable part of this exercise has been the choice of a deflator for net interest outlays.[41]

OMB made a significant shift in the conceptual basis for deflating interest in 1982. Under the old concept of interest outlays in constant dollars, these payments rose very little in the 1970s, but under the revised and now official estimates they accelerated sharply, more than doubling between 1972 and 1982.

Before 1982 OMB corrected interest outlays for inflation as follows: First, OMB deflated the debt held by the public using the GNP deflator to restate it in terms of base-year dollars. OMB then applied the percentage increase in this real debt to net interest in the base year to determine net interest in constant dollars. This approach assumed that the only source of growth in real interest outlays was growth of real debt (not real interest rates).

Because this procedure appears to have overcorrected for changes in the price level, OMB, in January 1982, began treating net interest outlays like any other transfer payment. Payments for individuals (encompassing Social Security, Food Stamps, etc.) are deflated by the personal consumption expenditure deflator in the OMB constant-dollar series, while net interest outlays are deflated by the implicit price deflator for GNP.

At a more fundamental level, the counting of all the federal government's net interest outlays as expenditures—and therefore income to bondholders—in inflationary times has been called into question. To the extent that part of these interest payments represents depreciation of the real debt of the government and thus a return of capital to the bondholders, a good case can be made to adjust net interest outlays and the budget deficit downward. (The federal budget does not count payments made on maturing debt as outlays, so if some of the debt is paid back each year as a return of capital, shouldn't those repayments be treated the same way?) In a study of five West European countries, Cukierman and Mortensen found that making adjustments for inflation-induced distortions in public debt (and in other nominally denominated assets) significantly changed the analysis of fiscal policy in those

---

41. Net interest is gross interest on the public debt less interest received by trust funds and agencies.

countries in the past twenty years.[42] In the United States in FY 1980, reducing net interest by the inflation erosion of the public debt would have converted the federal deficit into a small surplus. Unfortunately, deficit projections for the 1980s show unprecedented growth even when corrected for inflation erosion. But perhaps that sorry circumstance should lead us to reexamine what is the conceptually correct measure of interest on the public debt when the general price level rises.

Conclusion

Maybe the 1967 Commission on Budget Concepts had it right after all. It is important that the government's fiscal activities be recorded and planned in a comprehensive statement, and that a summary of the government's activity be represented by a single unambiguous measure (the deficit) that Congress and the public can understand. It is quite another thing to say that budget entries and their backup accounting conventions represent the only concepts that should be considered when policies are made. Although the budget should probably be kept simple and the current measure of the total deficit be kept in the forefront, it is important to avoid being simple-minded about cutting deficits. Analysts and policymakers perhaps need to start and end with budget numbers, but good decisions make use of more information than can ever be crammed into one set of accounts.

---

42. Alex Cukierman and Jorgen Mortensen, "Monetary Assets and Inflation-Induced Distortions of the National Accounts—Conceptual Issues and Correction of Sectoral Income Flows in 5 EEC Countries," *Economic Papers* (No. 15, June 1983), Commission of the European Communities, Brussels. For an extended discussion of these issues, see Robert Eisner and Paul J. Pieper "A New View of the Federal Debt and Budget Deficits" 1983, mimeographed. An earlier application to federal budget trends is given by Robert W. Hartman, "The Budget Outlook," in Joseph A. Pechman (ed.) *Setting National Priorities: The 1982 Budget* (Washington, D.C.: The Brookings Institution, 1981).

COMMENTS

Darwin G. Johnson

In her opening remarks, Alice Rivlin said that a good paper addresses issues that are important and about which something can be done. Bob Hartman's paper, "Issues in Budget Accounting," has both characteristics. Budget concept and accounting issues are highly important and can greatly influence the allocation of billions of dollars of federal budget resources; and they are subject to change, as evidenced by major changes that have been made over the last fifteen years. Unfortunately, the discussion of such issues tends to be highly technical. Hartman deserves to be commended for his efforts to discuss a number of concept and accounting issues with a minimum of highly technical description.

Hartman's paper is divided into two parts. The first part discusses what he calls "Traditional Issues of Coverage and Concept," which is an apt title for a discussion of the comprehensiveness of budget coverage, the credit budget, capital budgeting, and tax expenditures. The second part discusses what he refers to as "Emerging Accounting Issues." This part might be more appropriately titled "A Potpourri of Narrower Accounting and Concept Issues." I agree that some of the issues in this part are emerging but several emerged long ago.

Before discussing the specific issues Hartman addresses, I want to emphasize one point that I believe underlies much of Hartman's paper and all of what I have to say: No single budget concept can meet all the potential needs. It cannot simultaneously be:

—the best measure of the economic impact of the budget on the economy;
—the best tool for making programmatic decisions;
—the best guide for budgetary control and auditing; and

The author acknowledges the assistance of Tom Cuny and Bob Kilpatrick in preparing these comments.

—the best measure for making a clear and simple presentation of the government's priorities to the Congress and the public.

As Hartman's concluding sentence notes: "Analysts and policymakers perhaps need to start and end with budget numbers, but good decisions make use of more information than can ever be crammed into one set of accounts."

This point is not new, but it seems to be easily forgotten by people who perceive a deficiency in the current budget and accounting measures and leap to the conclusion that an entirely different budgetary concept—such as capital budgeting—is needed. Their time would be better spent developing appendages to the current budget—such as the high employment budget and the credit budget—rather than trying to overhaul the current budget.

Traditional Coverage and Concept Issues

Social Security

The first issue Hartman addresses is Social Security. The inclusion of Social Security (and other trust funds) was an issue in the 1960s when the old administrative budget, which excluded trust funds, was in use. In response to recommendations in 1967 by the President's Commission on Budget Concepts, Social Security and other trust funds were included in the budget totals beginning with the 1969 budget. The chief aim was to make the budget comprehensive.

The issue of Social Security is with us again because the Social Security Amendments enacted in March 1983 removed Old Age, Survivors, and Disability Insurance (OASDI) and Medicare from the budget beginning with fiscal year (FY) 1993. As Hartman notes, this action will add another, far larger, off-budget pot to the one that already exists. If this law is unchanged, an additional 25 to 30 percent of both taxes and spending will be removed from the budget ten years hence—and, the five-year projections of the Congressional Budget Office (CBO) and the Office of Management and Budget (OMB) could begin to be affected only five years hence.

Hartman refers to the recent report of the Committee for Economic Development, "Strengthening the Federal Budget Process: A Requirement for Effective Fiscal Control," and notes its recommendation that this provision of the Social Security Amendments be rescinded, both to maintain comprehensiveness of the budget and to avoid setting a precedent for removing other programs from the budget. Hartman seems sympathetic with only the second of the two arguments, as evidenced by the following quotation:

If Social Security *alone* were handled apart from the regular budget . . . we could avoid confusion and get the total deficit right. But its exclusion from the budget threatens to be imitated in scores of other programs, and that outcome would destroy the simplicity and controllability of the budget.

Why Hartman is so cavalier about removing 25 to 30 percent from the budget for its own sake is perplexing to me.

The Federal Financing Bank and the Budget

The issue that Hartman addresses in this section is, in principle, the same as the issue in the previous section: the comprehensiveness of the budget. Unfortunately, when we move into the world of the existing off-budget entities, and particularly the Federal Financing Bank (FFB), the budget accounting becomes more difficult to follow.

As Hartman notes, of the $17 billion of off-budget outlays in FY 1982, $14 billion were for the Federal Financing Bank. Hartman divides the activities of the FFB into three areas:

- First, FFB purchases agency debt, largely from the Export-Import Bank and the Tennessee Valley Authority (TVA). Hartman refers to the alleged off-budget status for this segment of FFB activity as being "appropriate" and claims it "enhances the meaning of the budget." In fact, the spending of the proceeds of this agency borrowing would be counted exactly as it is now if FFB were on the budget or did not even exist—that is, as outlays of the agencies that borrow from the FFB at the time they disburse the proceeds. So one need not defend the off-budget status of FFB on this account.

- Second, FFB purchases loan assets. Almost all these purchases are for certificates of beneficial ownership (CBOs), which are securities backed by loans that the issuing agency continues to hold and service. As Hartman says, the real solution is that the sale of CBOs should be considered borrowing rather than offsets to outlays, but legal provisions prevent this.

- Finally, FFB makes direct loans to the public that are fully guaranteed by the issuing agency, thus converting guarantees into direct federal loans.

Hartman correctly concludes that the solution is to "treat FFB direct loans as on-budget outlays, attribute them to the originating agency, and make them subject to appropriations limits," and he notes that S. 1679, the "Honest

Budgeting Act of 1983,'' would do just this. The administration has supported this bill.

Political and technical difficulties abound nonetheless. Cries for exemptions are already appearing. For example, in testimony presented earlier this month the president of the National Rural Electric Cooperatives, when asked why the Rural Electrification Administration (REA) should be exempt from provisions of this bill, stated, ''Right now we deal with Congress and FFB to finance our programs. If we are put on-budget, we will also have to deal with OMB.''

Senator Pete Domenici, in testimony the same day, indicated that the political prospects for this bill were not good unless REA is exempted. TVA too, supports S. 1679 but argues for an exemption for TVA.

The major *technical* problem associated with putting FFB on-budget is in deciding what securities must be channeled through it. Currently, FFB has accepted only 100 percent guarantees. If FFB were shifted on-budget, one could imagine the temptation to shift 100 percent guarantees to 99 percent guarantees (with subordination of the one percent of private risk, of course) to reduce reported budget outlays.

Credit Budget Concepts

Hartman also discusses the broader subject of controlling federal credit. At issue is how to control federal credit, and particularly guaranteed loans, since the latter show up in the unified budget only in case of default.

Hartman observes that the answer has been the ''credit budget,'' which was established in 1980. This ''budget'' covers direct loan obligations and guaranteed loan commitments. These measures are on a gross basis (i.e., excluding repayments) to facilitate control of new activity. Hartman notes that most credit activity is controlled by appropriations limitations, but that the reconciliation provisions ''have never been fully used'' in the credit area. I would say that is a big understatement. Hartman's response to this problem, to establish greater enforcement mechanisms in the Congress, is well taken.

Hartman raises another important issue in this area, namely, how to measure credit programs on some comparable basis. He suggests, as others have, that the interest subsidy content be the common denominator. And he cites the recent CED suggestions that a federal bank be created—again as an adjunct to the current budget structure. The bank would receive reimbursements from government agencies equivalent to the cost of providing subsidized loans or guarantees. This idea deserves careful consideration, but measuring the subsidy element of federal credit programs is difficult. OMB has never attempted to estimate the subsidies for guaranteed loans, and we consider our published estimates for direct loans to be very shaky, even for display purposes.

The Concept of Tax Expenditures

At issue here are (1) how do you measure tax expenditures and (2) how do you integrate the review of tax expenditures into the budgetary process. Hartman reviews some of the difficulties associated with tax expenditures and discusses the two alternative measures that are now regularly published by the Congressional Budget Office (CBO) and OMB: (1) outlay equivalence and (2) revenue loss. Hartman correctly argues that the outlay equivalence measure, which is estimated on a pretax basis, is best suited to comparative analysis with individual spending programs, whereas the revenue loss measure is best suited to aggregative analyses of the effects on receipts and the deficit.

With regard to integrating tax expenditures into the budgetary process, Hartman notes that recent CBO and CED reports suggest the possibility of joint reviews by tax committees and the relevant spending committees to consider trade-offs between ordinary expenditures and tax expenditures. Hartman says that interest has been "slim" in this recommendation and adds, "There are enough intractable problems in both the microeconomic trade-off and the aggregate revenue approaches to tax expenditures to warrant great caution before formally installing new procedures into the budget process."

I agree. Expenditures are an objective measure of what the government does; tax expenditures are a subjective measure (with countless alternatives) of what the government does *not* do. There are widely varying views on what the "normal" or "reference" tax structure is; one need only look at the changes in definition between Carter and Reagan for an example.

Tax expenditure estimates provide useful supplementary information and they should continue to be provided in congressional and executive branch reports. The budget currently presents them in a single special analysis, with a discussion of the concept and estimating methods, and in Part 5 of the budget where they are mentioned by function along with their spending counterparts.

Capital Budgeting

"Washington's favorite buzzword in the 1980s . . . ," says Hartman. "Not the favorite of everyone in Washington," I respond.

Hartman lists three major conceptions of a capital budget currently being debated: (1) better information; (2) a split of the existing budget between capital and operating expenditures; and (3) a comprehensive balance sheet of the government showing all assets and liabilities.

Hartman argues that the two-part division of operating and capital expenditures would "lead to chaos as program after program tried to qualify for capital budget treatment to escape being measured against taxes. Because there is no objective criterion for public capital, the line to be drawn for the two-part budget would be arbitrary and subject to endless contention." I couldn't agree more!

Hartman dismisses the comprehensive balance sheet for similar reasons, arguing that we should not base the "nation's major planning document on such squishy and manipulable numbers. . . ." Again, I wholeheartedly concur.

That leaves the "better information" variant, which Hartman sees as the likely outcome on Capitol Hill. I have trouble thinking of this as a variant of a capital budget in a substantive sense, although it clearly is an alternative to a capital budget in a legislative sense. With regard to the issue of information on federal capital spending, let me mention first what has already been done and then comment on legislation currently being considered in Congress.

In the past year, OMB tried to expand the understanding of federal capital spending by discussing the general subject of capital budgeting and by creating a data base on federal investment spending covering the past three decades. Some of the new data were published in the Special Analysis D section of the 1984 budget. The complete new data base is available upon request from OMB, along with other historical budget data that we routinely make available to people who are interested. In addition to the historical data that OMB recently developed, agencies are already required by law to prepare periodic major reports on certain aspects of federal capital investment needs, such as for highways and sewer systems.

With regard to the bill that Hartman mentions, the Federal Capital Investment Program Information Act (H.R. 1244 and S. 1432), let me just note a few of the requirements of the bill as it now stands:

- Ten-year projections of federal capital investment spending in the major areas specified in the bill on (1) a current services basis; (2) a high and low basis; and (3) a "needs" basis; and

- State-by-state and metropolitan area projections for ten years for those programs allocated by formula.

As Hartman says, it is hard to be against more information. But at what cost? And are data necessarily information? The requirements of this bill remind me of the quotation, "We are drowning in irrelevant data, inappropriately collected, using old models based on confused goals."[1]

Emerging Accounting Issues

As I noted at the outset, I believe the title for this section of the paper is a misnomer. Some of the issues are not new, and others, in my view, are not emerging. The first general "emerging" issue discussed by Hartman relates to the incentives in cash budgeting to shift reported outlays (but not the related economic activity) beyond the planning horizon, which for most budget exercises is now three to five years.

One example Hartman cites is lease versus purchase decisions related to federal office space, and here the capital budget enthusiasts clearly have the better of the cash budgeters. His second example is related to an alternative plan to finance the Clinch River Breeder Reactor Project that would substitute future tax and regulatory preferences for direct spending. This is a poor example, because the substitution is not from one year to another, but rather from one type of federal activity to another.

Hartman also discusses the imminent shift to accrual accounting for military retired pay that is required by this year's defense authorization bill. Hartman sees this shift as "the first significant incursion of a 'foreign' concept into cash-flow airspace." In fact, there are already numerous intragovernmental flows on an accrual basis, of which this would be but another. Also, interest on the public debt is on an accrual basis. Hartman supports the change, but I fear that he will be secretly disappointed if the change turns out to *reduce*, rather than *increase* reported defense outlays. And what it will do to the simplicity of the budget presentation remains to be seen.

Hartman then turns his attention to the fact that, beginning next year, new federal employees will be covered by Social Security and need a private pension equivalent. The only existing bill that addresses this need is offered by Senator Ted Stevens. The feature that Hartman addresses under the subject of "Outlays that Aren't" is one that would establish a government fund to administer these funds and would require that it initially invest only in Treasury securities. Why only Treasury securities? Hartman guesses that it is because payments to purchase private sector securities would be counted as outlays. I am not sure of the motives; Hartman may be right. But my concern here is

---

1. Statement by Hazel Henderson, co-director of the Princeton Center for Alternative Futures, before the Joint Economic Committee, November 18, 1976.

the reverse of Hartman's. I am bothered by the federal government's administering a fund that invests in private sector securities, regardless of the budget accounting. Do we really want the government to purchase a "piece of the rock?"

Real Growth in Defense.   This is both an interesting conceptual issue and an important political one. It has been important since Carter announced in 1979 that his defense policy was to provide real growth of 3 percent (and later 5 percent). Once a policy of real growth has been determined, of course, the only thing left in determining the total for defense is projecting the deflator.

Hartman highlights the importance of real growth calculations in the current legislative process, but bemoans the complexities involved in making the calculations, especially because personnel and other defense expenditures are not separated. His first recommendation is to separate these two segments of defense spending, so that one can focus better on the "investment" accounts ("investment" is a misnomer because Hartman is also including operations, maintenance, and other "current" expenditures). This is a reasonable suggestion, and the data are readily available. Barring that disaggregation, Hartman wonders if we should not throw up our hands and use an overall deflator like the deflator for the gross national product (GNP) (much as OMB did for net interest, as discussed later). To that I answer no. I believe that taking account of the specific prices for defense goods and services will more accurately measure what policymakers need.

Hartman also says that "All national defense experts contend that budget authority is the only meaningful planning concept for defense." I disagree, but maybe my disagreement just highlights the fact that I am no defense expert. Outlays and budget authority are both important, they just have different time dimensions.

Net Interest Outlays in Constant Dollars

Much has been written about the economic impact of net interest outlays and the best way to measure these outlays for economic analysis. It is presumably for this reason that Hartman has included the issue of how best to deflate net interest outlays. I believe that the two issues are different and that the method of deflation is less important.

Hartman offers two alternatives: (1) deflating net interest by a general price deflator such as the GNP deflator, which is what OMB now does (Hartman correctly notes that before 1982 OMB had a quite different approach); and (2) subtracting the erosion of capital from current-dollar net interest outlays and expressing the remainder in constant dollars.

Both approaches have merit. OMB argues that, through its current treatment, it is deflating outlays as measured in the unified budget. However, adjusting for erosion of the value of the debt is a conceptual change that would apply to current-dollar outlays as well as to constant-dollar outlays. (Also, if adjustment is to be made for erosion of the public debt, what about the erosion of federal loans owed to the government?) For purposes other than deflating budget outlays, such as in Edward Gramlich's paper presented elsewhere in this volume, the second approach may well be better.

Conclusion

Hartman has discussed a large number of concept and accounting issues that have, or could have, a significant impact on the way the government conducts its business. I can summarize my response to his paper with two points:

1. No matter what budget concept is chosen, there will always be program advocates—in Congress, the administration, and special-interest groups—working to devise ways to increase program activity without reflecting that activity in the budget.

2. To end where I started, no single budget concept can meet all the needs that are asked of it.

COMMENTS

Michael J. Boskin

I am sympathetic with much of what Robert Hartman and Darwin Johnson have had to say. Like them, I favor simplicity and comprehensiveness—I just sometimes find them mutually exclusive. I also believe in comprehensibility. Therefore I think it important that the budget document be kept as simple and as commonsensical as possible; there is much to the notion that extra information should be developed in appendices and special analyses. There are many barriers to comprehensiveness and comprehension, which I plan to discuss. First, however, let me acknowledge that there have been many improvements in the budget—for example, the credit budget. Nor do I suggest that trying to get balance sheets for the federal government would be easy.

I wonder how many people are aware of the way deposit insurance is treated in the federal budget. We heard this morning that the major threat to the recovery was an international financial collapse. The lending of major U.S. banks to just four or five Latin American countries exceeds the capital and subordinated debt of those banks. How many people are aware that, in 1982, spending by the Federal Deposit Insurance Corporation on deposit insurance was reported in the budget as minus $1.5 billion (and that a smaller negative amount was reported for the Federal Savings and Loan Insurance Corporation)? Clearly we were accruing large future liabilities, but our budget accounting had us netting the premium income and the interest received against the *contemporaneous* payouts. I do not believe there is any debate about the fact that expected future payouts are a large positive number. We are reporting in our budget that we spent a negative number and that spending and the deficit were reduced by a corresponding amount!

In answer to the question, What was *real* accrued government spending or revenue, or the real deficit? There are literally dozens of adjustments we have to make in any particular year. Hartman goes into some of them— adjustments that would bring things into the budget—changing the treatment of credit activities and dealing with Social Security and its unfunded liabilities. I just want to raise a couple of important issues.

First, recall that a balance sheet for the federal government has assets as well as liabilities. We have heard about the erosion of the real value of the previously issued national debt because of inflation. The federal government also owns gold, land, oil, other mineral rights, and so on, and during the 1970s the government enjoyed enormous capital gains on these assets. We have the same sorts of problems in the national income accounts. We ignore capital gains and losses in the private sector, but they can be so large that ignoring them is ludicrous in any commonsense evaluation of what we as a society can afford or not afford. For example, should Norway not count the expected revenues from its North Sea oil in making public-sector spending and tax decisions? Or Alaska ignore oil revenue in fiscal management?

In addition to taking account of capital gains and losses, it is crucial to maintain a separate capital account and a current services budget, to separate public investment from consumption, and to measure *economic*, not just physical, depreciation. If we had had a plausible separate capital account, we would have noticed the deterioration of our infrastructure. I am not in favor of rebuilding every bridge and road in the upper Midwest. Proper cost-benefit analyses would probably have us divert public investment in infrastructure to the Sun Belt. In any event, at least we would have known the investment was far short of depreciation, and we could have had some part in making those decisions as opposed to the huge increases in Social Security benefits that occured in the 1970s. The trade-off would have been made much more explicit.

Not only have items been omitted from the budget, but also ridiculous accounting conventions have been adopted inside the budget—conventions that distort the measures of the size and growth of government as a whole or of different components of government. For example, our view about the importance of housing and agriculture clearly must be affected by how we value the interest subsidies that Johnson talked about. Housing and agriculture constitute the overwhelming bulk of loans and loan guarantees. Direct expenditures on housing and agriculture at times are less than implicit expenditures through credit programs.

The problems of omission, accounting, and conceptual issues get to the heart of intelligent decision making. I did not see anything in Hartman's paper about government-sponsored enterprises. I suppose that is because these enterprises are supposedly 100 percent private, but some of them have statutory authority to borrow from the Treasury. If one looks at the rates these enterprises pay when they go into the market to borrow, it is clear that private investors are treating these enterprises basically as an adjunct to the government and assuming that in an emergency the government would step in and bail them out. Hence it is important to try to provide the supplemental information, primarily to give us an idea of what is happening in our society. Hartman refers correctly to the history of budget concept reviews, but in the 1960s the government accounted for a much smaller share of our economy and was not even involved in some of the activities it is now involved in. For example, the government was much less active in credit markets.

Many of the problems associated with developing a separate capital account in the public sector also exist in the private sector. The same kinds of artificial conventions have to be adopted. For instance, three years is the distinction between current and capital expenditures; if we make that distinction two or four, we change all our data. Advertising is included for the research and development tax credits. Of course, there are problems concerning where to draw the line and how to deal with things conceptually. The two major conceptual issues in a separate capital account are two major, but potentially abused, assets—the power to tax and the power to print money. I can only figure out a way to get an *upper bound* on the *potential value of these assets, not their actual utilized value.*[1] These assets are far more difficult to evaluate than the share of some particular spending program we are going to count as capital expenditures versus current expenditures. Except for public goods, most of these issues are not greatly different from those we encounter in the private sector.

I want to echo Johnson's concern about the general lack of concern about the removal of Social Security from the budget in 1993, which is probably the single most reprehensible thing I have witnessed in the budget process. It dominates a lot of foolish programmatic spending decisions. We face the following scenario: The projection is that Old Age Survivors and Disability Insurance (OASDI), after riding out the 1980s with the recent compromise "solution," is going to start running a surplus. I predict that by about 2017 or 2018 the accumulated value of that surplus, if it is not used for other purposes, will exceed the national debt. Social Security, off the budget, may wind up owning all government bonds, and then may move into the private capital market. We may even have to change the laws governing what the Social Security program can invest in. We are likely to be spared that prospect, however, by the fact that the Hospital Insurance (HI) program will start running deficits around the time OASDI starts running a surplus. Eventually, the HI deficit, under current law and projections, will become much larger than the OASDI surplus. We may just wind up borrowing from OASDI to

---

1. See Boskin, M., *The Real Federal Budget*, in process.

finance HI; therefore the "long-term solution" to the retirement fund's insolvency will prove not to have been a solution at all.

I share everyone's concern about the potential prostitution of capital budgeting by the political process. But I believe that a common set of principles can be worked out—however difficult they will be to implement and however much pressure there will be on the Office of Management and Budget and the agencies to misuse them—principles that will provide information to enable us to compare alternatives that we cannot possibly compare now. Developing such principles would be the single most useful step we could take to improve government budgeting. That does not mean that people will not try to spend more than they are willing to pay for, so long as somebody else finances it. Improved budget measures and concepts are no substitute for good decisions or good cost-benefit analyses, but cost-benefit analyses simply cannot be performed properly without that information. Providing that information is no guarantee of better cost-benefit analyses, but there is just no hope of improving these analyses without the information.

ABOUT THE AUTHORS

William J. Beeman is an assistant director of the Congressional Budget Office. He directs the CBO's Fiscal Analysis Division, which is responsible for economic projections and macroeconomic analysis.

Robert D. Behn is the director of Duke University's Institute of Policy Science and Public Affairs. He is the coauthor of *Quick Analysis for Busy Decision Makers* and has written numerous articles on policy termination and cutback management.

Douglas J. Bennet is the president of National Public Radio. He was the first staff director of the Senate Budget Committee when the budget process was established in 1974, and subsequently served as assistant secretary of state for congressional relations and administrator of the Agency for International Development.

Michael J. Boskin is professor of economics at Stanford University and a research associate at the National Bureau of Economic Research, Inc. He is the author of over forty articles and editor of five volumes of essays on the subjects of taxation, fiscal policy, government budgeting, capital formation, labor markets, and Social Security.

Hale Champion is executive dean of the John F. Kennedy School of Government at Harvard University. He specializes in public management and intergovernmental program delivery systems. Mr. Champion has been undersecretary of Health, Education and Welfare, director of finance of the state

461

of California, director of the Boston Redevelopment Authority, and financial vice-president of Harvard University and the University of Minnesota.

John W. Ellwood is associate professor of public policy and management at the Amos Tuck School of Business Administration at Dartmouth College. He has written numerous articles on federal budget procedures. He is also the editor of *Reductions in U.S. Domestic Spending*.

Louis Fisher is a specialist in American national government at the Congressional Research Service of the Library of Congress. Author of *President and Congress*; *Presidential Spending Power*; *The Constitution Between Friends*; and *The Politics of Shared Power*, he is currently at work on *American Constitutional Law: A Political Framework*.

Edward M. Gramlich is a professor of economics and public policy at the University of Michigan, presently serving as chairman of the economics department. He is the author of numerous books and articles in the fields of both public finance and macroeconomics. His most recent book, *Benefit Cost Analysis of Government Programs*, raises many of the issues discussed in the paper from a different perspective.

Robert F. Hale is currently the assistant director for national security and international affairs at the Congressional Budget Office. During eight years at CBO, he has also been the deputy assistant director for national security and international affairs, and has worked as the principal analyst of defense manpower issues. Before coming to the Congressional Budget Office, Mr. Hale was with the Center for Naval Analysis. He has also served three years as an officer with the U.S. Naval Security Group.

William G. Hamm is California's legislative analyst. In this capacity, Mr. Hamm and his staff of ninety people provide analysis and recommendations to the California legislature on every aspect of state government. Previously, he held a variety of positions with the U.S. Office of Management and Budget.

Robert W. Hartman is senior analyst for budget process at the Congressional Budget Office, advising the director on budget concept, process, and accounting issues. He also was responsible for part III (*Reducing the Deficit: Spending and Revenue Options*) of CBO's annual report issued in February 1984. Prior to working at CBO, Dr. Hartman was a senior fellow at the Brookings Institution for over a decade, contributing to the *Setting National Priorities* series. His most recent book is *Federal Pay and Pensions*.

Robert H. Haveman is Bascom professor of economics at the University of Wisconsin-Madison, and a staff member of the Institute for Research on Poverty. Professor Haveman specializes in public finance, the economics of human resources, and poverty income distribution. He has written numerous articles and monographs on these and related topics, including *Earnings Capacity, Poverty, and Inequality* (with Irwin Garfinkel), and *Disability and Work: The Economics of U.S. Policy* (with Richard Bunkhauser).

Hugh Heclo is a professor of government at Harvard University and permanent visiting professor at the University of Konstanz, West Germany. His published works are concerned with American executive institutions and comparative social policy. He is author of *A Government of Strangers: Executive Politics in Washington*, as well as "OMB and the Presidency–The Problem of Neutral Competence."

Darwin G. Johnson is chief of the fiscal analysis branch of the U.S. Office of Management and Budget. Dr. Johnson specializes in fiscal policy and budget issues and is the author of several journal articles and papers on the sensitivity of the budget to economic conditions.

Helen F. Ladd, associate professor of city and regional planning at Harvard's John F. Kennedy School of Government, specializes in state and local public finance. She has written extensively about state and local tax issues, tax and expenditure limitations, and intergovernmental fiscal relations. She is coeditor of *Tax and Expenditure Limitations* (Urban Institute Press, 1981).

Laurence E. Lynn, Jr., is dean and professor at the University of Chicago's School of Social Service Administration and a member of the university's Committee on Public Policy Studies. He has served in policy and management positions in the U.S. Department of Defense, the National Security Council, the U.S. Department of Health, Education and Welfare, and the U.S. Department of the Interior. He has taught at the Graduate School of Business at Stanford University and the John F. Kennedy School of Government at Harvard University.

Jack A. Meyer is currently a resident fellow in economics and director of the Center for Health Policy Research at the American Enterprise Institute in Washington, D.C. He is the editor of two recently published volumes: *Market Reforms in Health Care: Current Issues, New Directions, Strategic Decisions*; and *Meeting Human Needs: Towards a New Public Philosophy*.

Prior to joining AEI in 1979, Mr. Meyer worked with the U.S. Council on Wage and Price Stability. In 1977 and 1978 he served as the Council's assistant director for wage and price monitoring. He has held positions at the U.S. Department of Labor and the U.S. Department of Housing and Urban Development and has worked as a consultant for the Organization for Economic Cooperation and Development (OECD) in Paris.

Gregory B. Mills is a research associate on the staff of The Urban Institute's Changing Domestic Priorities project. His prior research has focused on federal policies to improve welfare administration, especially in the Aid to Families with Dependent Children program. Before joining the Institute, Dr. Mills served as an economist in the U.S. Department of Health and Human Services. He is a coauthor of *The Deficit Dilemma* and a contributing author of *The Reagan Experiment* and *The Reagan Record*.

Joseph J. Minarik has divided his career between economic research and public service. As an academic researcher, he has investigated topics such as the distribution of income, poverty, income security policy, the consequences of inflation, fiscal policy, and taxation. Before joining The Urban Institute in January of 1984 as a senior research associate, Dr. Minarik served as deputy assistant director in the Tax Analysis Division of the Congressional Budget Office.

Richard A. Musgrave is H.H. Burbank professor of political economy emeritus, Harvard University, and adjunct professor of economics at the University of California at Santa Cruz. He is the author of *The Theory of Public Finance* (1959), *Public Finance in Theory and Practice* (with Peggy Musgrave, 1973), as well as numerous other contributions to the economics of the public sector.

John L. Palmer is codirector of The Urban Institute's Changing Domestic Priorities project of which this volume is part. His current research interests include economic, social, and budget policy. Dr. Palmer has been an assistant professor of economics at Stanford University, a senior fellow in the Economic Studies Program of the Brookings Institution, and an assistant secretary for the U.S. Department of Health and Human Services. His publications include *The Deficit Dilemma*; *The Reagan Experiment*; *Inflation*; *Unemployment and Poverty*; *Creating Jobs*; *Toward an Effective Income Support System*; and several chapters in the Brookings Institution's annual *Setting National Priorities* volumes.

Robert B. Pirie is the assistant vice-president of the Institute for Defense Analyses for Program Development and Review. His varied background has included twenty years' service as an officer in the U.S. Navy, command of a nuclear submarine, service on the staffs of the National Security Council and the Congressional Budget Office, and three tours of duty on the staff of the secretary of defense. He was assistant secretary of defense (Manpower, Reserve Affairs and Logistics) in the Carter administration.

Robert D. Reischauer is the senior vice-president of The Urban Institute. Before joining The Urban Institute in 1981, he served as the deputy director of the Congressional Budget Office (CBO). He left the Economic Studies Program of the Brookings Institution to help establish CBO at its inception in 1975. Mr. Reischauer is the author of many publications dealing with the federal budget, social welfare policy, and intergovernmental fiscal relations.

Alice M. Rivlin is director of the Economic Studies Program at the Brookings Institution. She was the first director of the Congressional Budget Office.

Charles L. Schultze is a senior fellow at the Brookings Institution. Mr. Schultze specializes in macroeconomic analysis and budgetary policy. He is the author or coauthor of numerous books and articles on these subjects.

Kenneth A. Shepsle is professor of political science and research associate of the Center for the Study of American Business at Washington University in St. Louis. His specialties include American political institutions and political economy. He has written extensively about the U.S. Congress and has been published in leading political science and economics journals. He is also the author of several books, including *The Giant Jigsaw Puzzle: Democratic Committee Assignments in the Modern House* (University of Chicago Press, 1978).

Richard A. Stubbing is assistant provost at Duke University. From 1962–1981 he worked at the Bureau of the Budget Office of Management and Budget reviewing the defense program. From 1974–1981 he was deputy chief of the national security division with responsibility for the defense and intelligence programs. He is currently working on a book evaluating performance of the defense establishment over the last twenty years.

Barbara Boyle Torrey is an economist in the fiscal analysis branch of the Office of Management and Budget. Her areas of research include the fiscal implications of aging, income security, and health policy analysis.

James M. Verdier is a lecturer in public policy at the John F. Kennedy School of Government at Harvard. He served from 1975–1983 in the Tax Analysis Division of the Congressional Budget Office, most recently as assistant director for tax analysis. He served for a number of years in staff positions in the United States Senate and House of Representatives.

Barry R. Weingast is associate professor of economics and business and research associate of the Center for the Study of American Business at Washington University in St. Louis. His latest publication is "Bureaucratic Discretion or Congressional Control? Regulatory Policy at the FTC" in the *Journal of Political Economy.*

Joseph S. Wholey is a professor of public administration in the University of Southern California's School of Public Administration. He teaches at the school's Washington Public Affairs Center and at the school's centers in Los Angeles and Sacramento. Dr. Wholey is a member of the Virginia Board of Social Services and is president of the Evaluation Research Society. He is the author of *Evaluation and Effective Public Management.*

PARTICIPANTS

Henry J. Aaron
The Brookings Institution

William J. Beeman
Congressional Budget Office

Robert D. Behn
Duke University

Douglas J. Bennet
National Public Radio

Michael J. Boskin
Stanford University

Hale Champion
Harvard University

Frank de Leeuw
Department of Commerce

John W. Ellwood
Dartmouth College

Louis Fisher
Library of Congress

Edward M. Gramlich
University of Michigan

Robert F. Hale
Congressional Budget Office

William G. Hamm
California State Legislature

Robert W. Hartman
Congressional Budget Office

Robert H. Haveman
University of Wisconsin

Hugh Heclo
Harvard University

Darwin G. Johnson
*Office of Management and
Budget*

Helen F. Ladd
Harvard University

Laurence E. Lynn, Jr.
The University of Chicago

Jack A. Meyer
*American Enterprise Institute for
Public Policy Research*

Gregory B. Mills
The Urban Institute

Joseph J. Minarik
The Urban Institute

467

Richard A. Musgrave
University of California, Santa Cruz

Van D. Ooms
House Budget Committee

John L. Palmer
The Urban Institute

George Peterson
The Urban Institute

Robert B. Pirie

Perry D. Quick
Private Consultant

Robert D. Reischauer
The Urban Institute

Alice M. Rivlin
The Brookings Institution

Lester Salamon
The Urban Institute

Isabel V. Sawhill
The Urban Institute

Charles L. Schultze
The Brookings Institution

Kenneth A. Shepsle
Washington University

Charles F. Stone
The Urban Institute

Richard A. Stubbing
Duke University

Barbara Boyle Torrey
Office of Management and Budget

James M. Verdier
Harvard University

Barry R. Weingast
Washington University

Joseph S. Wholey
University of Southern California